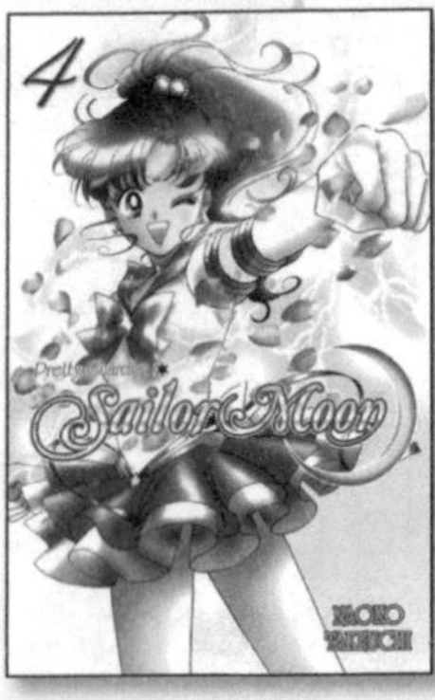
4
Pretty Guardian
Sailor Moon
NAOKO TAKEUCHI

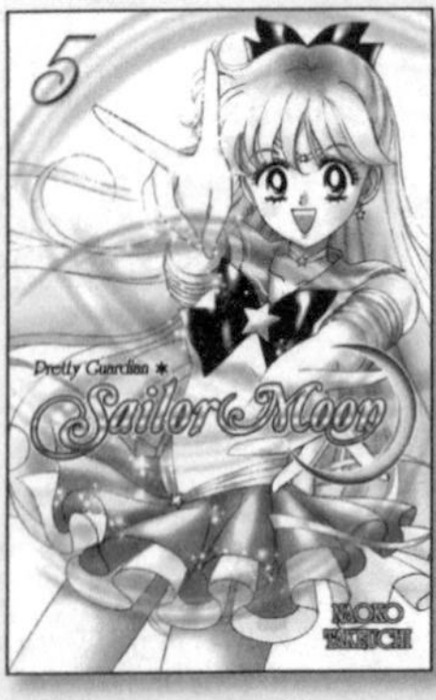
5
Pretty Guardian
Sailor Moon
NAOKO TAKEUCHI

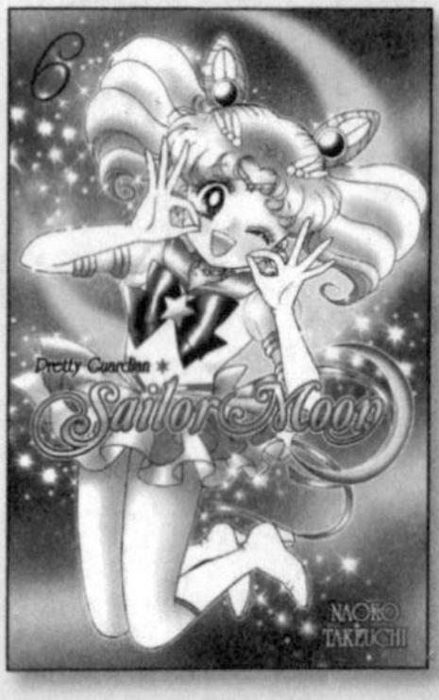
6
Pretty Guardian
Sailor Moon
NAOKO TAKEUCHI

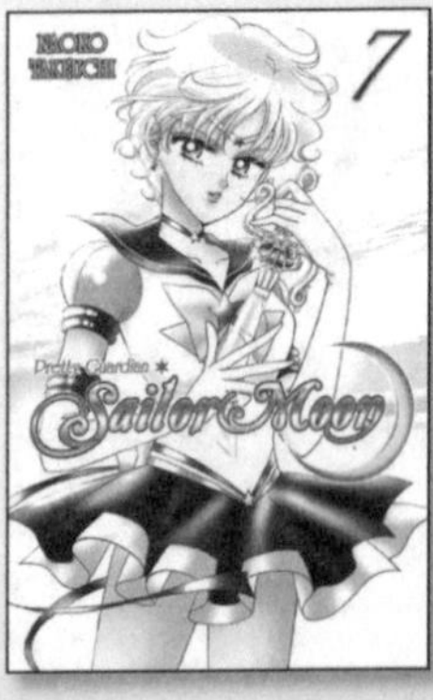
NAOKO TAKEUCHI
7
Pretty Guardian
Sailor Moon

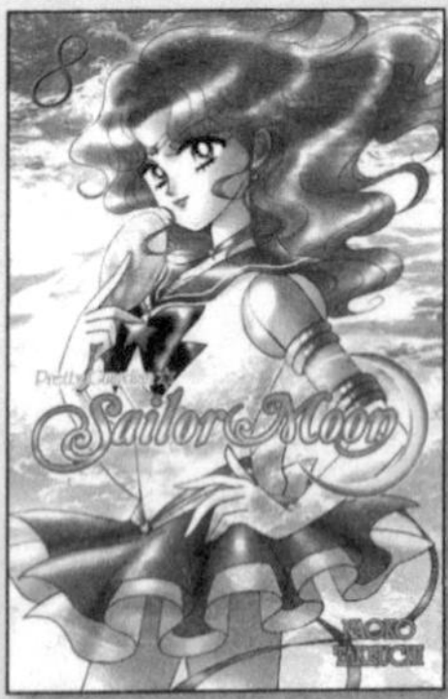
8
Sailor Moon
NAOKO TAKEUCHI

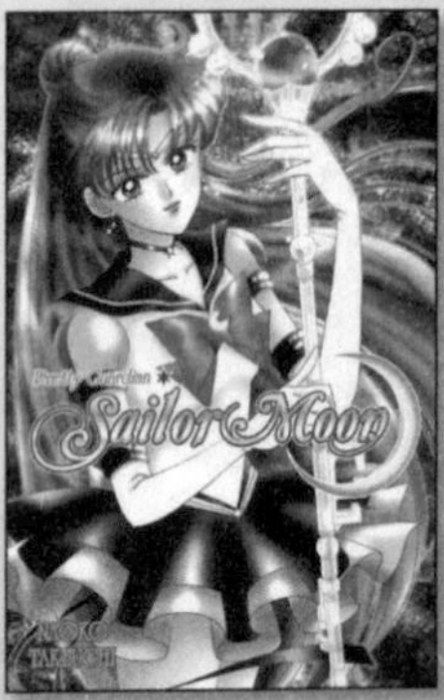
Pretty Guardian
Sailor Moon
NAOKO TAKEUCHI

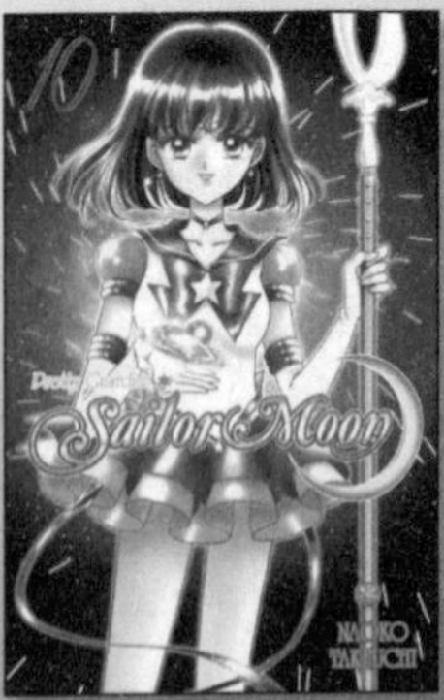
10
Sailor Moon
NAOKO TAKEUCHI

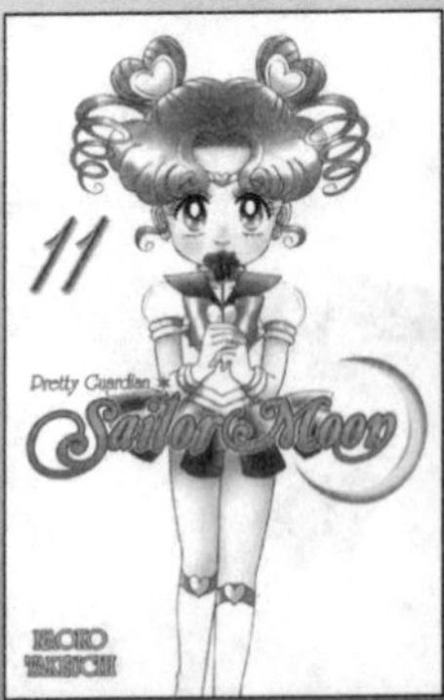
11
Pretty Guardian
Sailor Moon
NAOKO TAKEUCHI

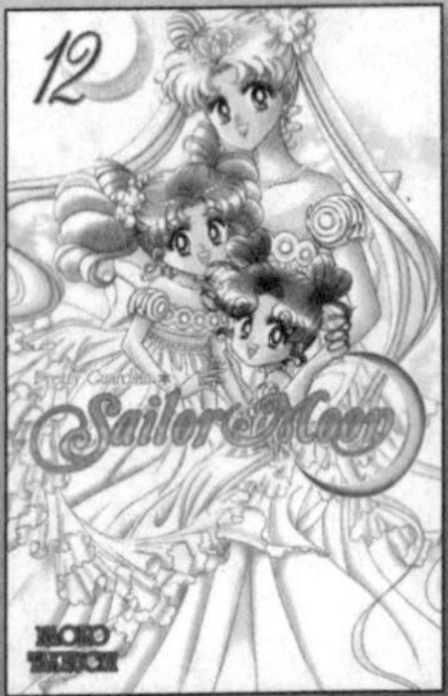
12
Pretty Guardian
Sailor Moon
NAOKO TAKEUCHI

KC
KODANSHA COMICS

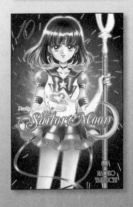

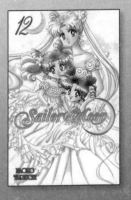

The Pretty Guardians are back!

Kodansha Comics is proud to present ***Sailor Moon*** with all new translations.

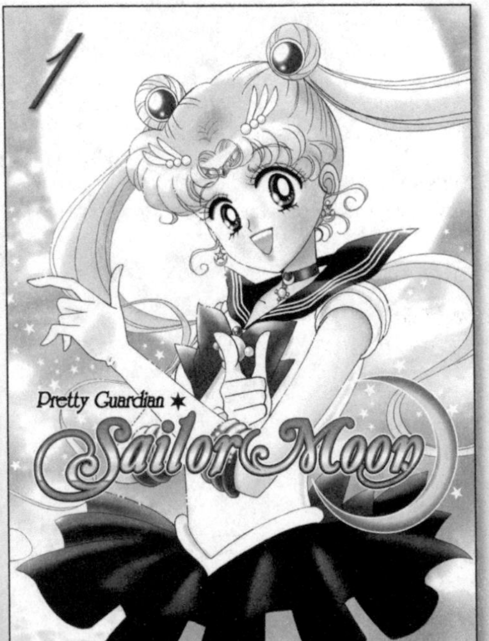
1
Pretty Guardian
Sailor Moon
NAOKO TAKEUCHI

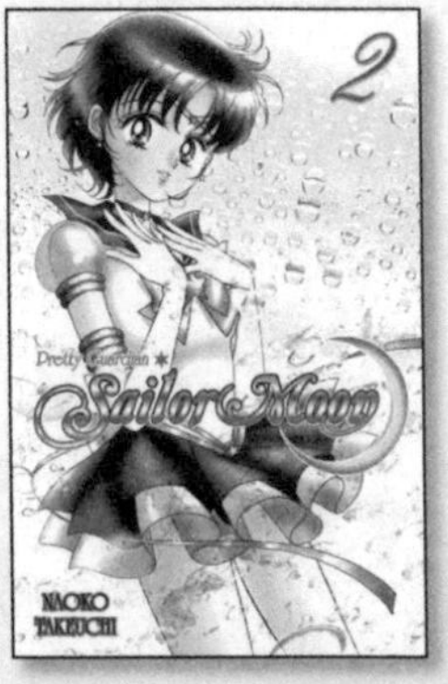
2
Pretty Guardian
Sailor Moon
NAOKO TAKEUCHI

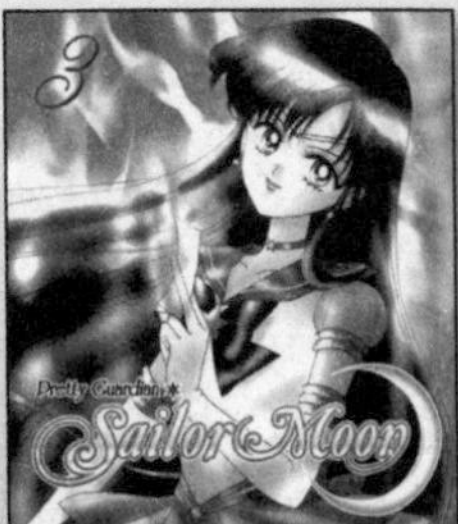
3
Pretty Guardian
Sailor Moon

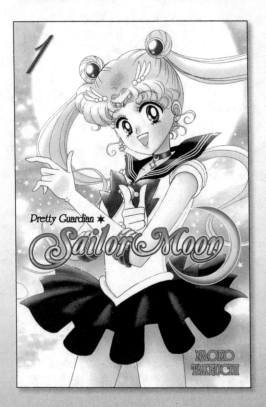

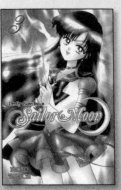

For more information, go to **www.kodanshacomics.com**

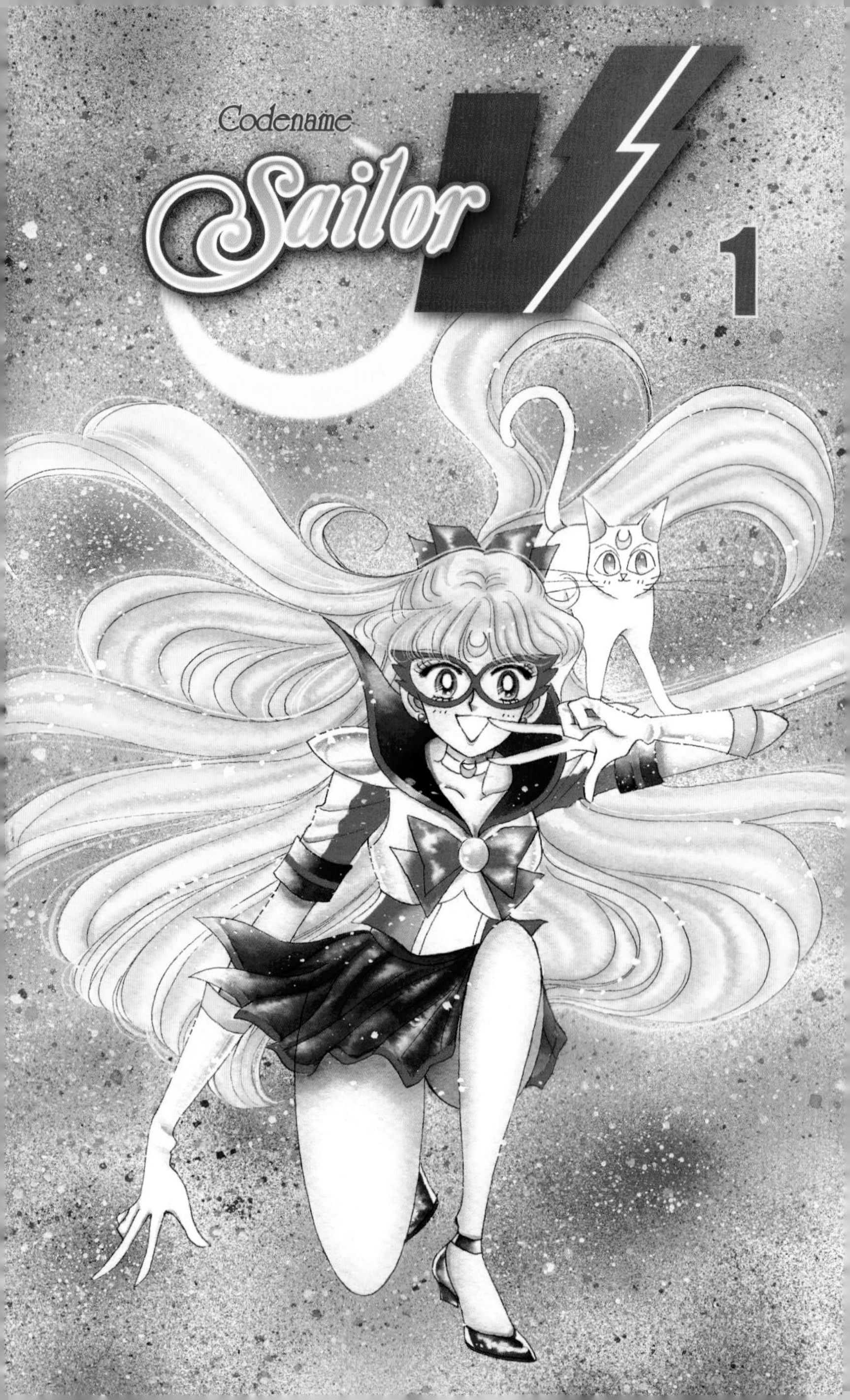
Codename
Sailor
V
1

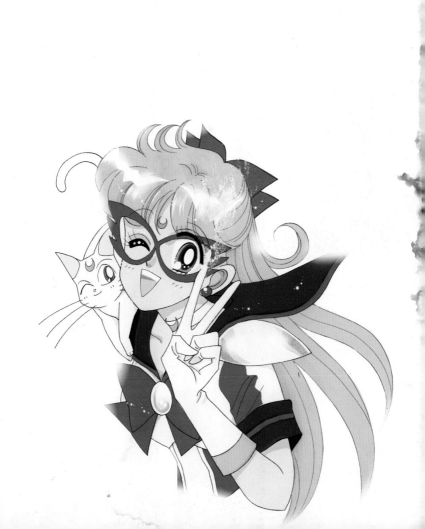

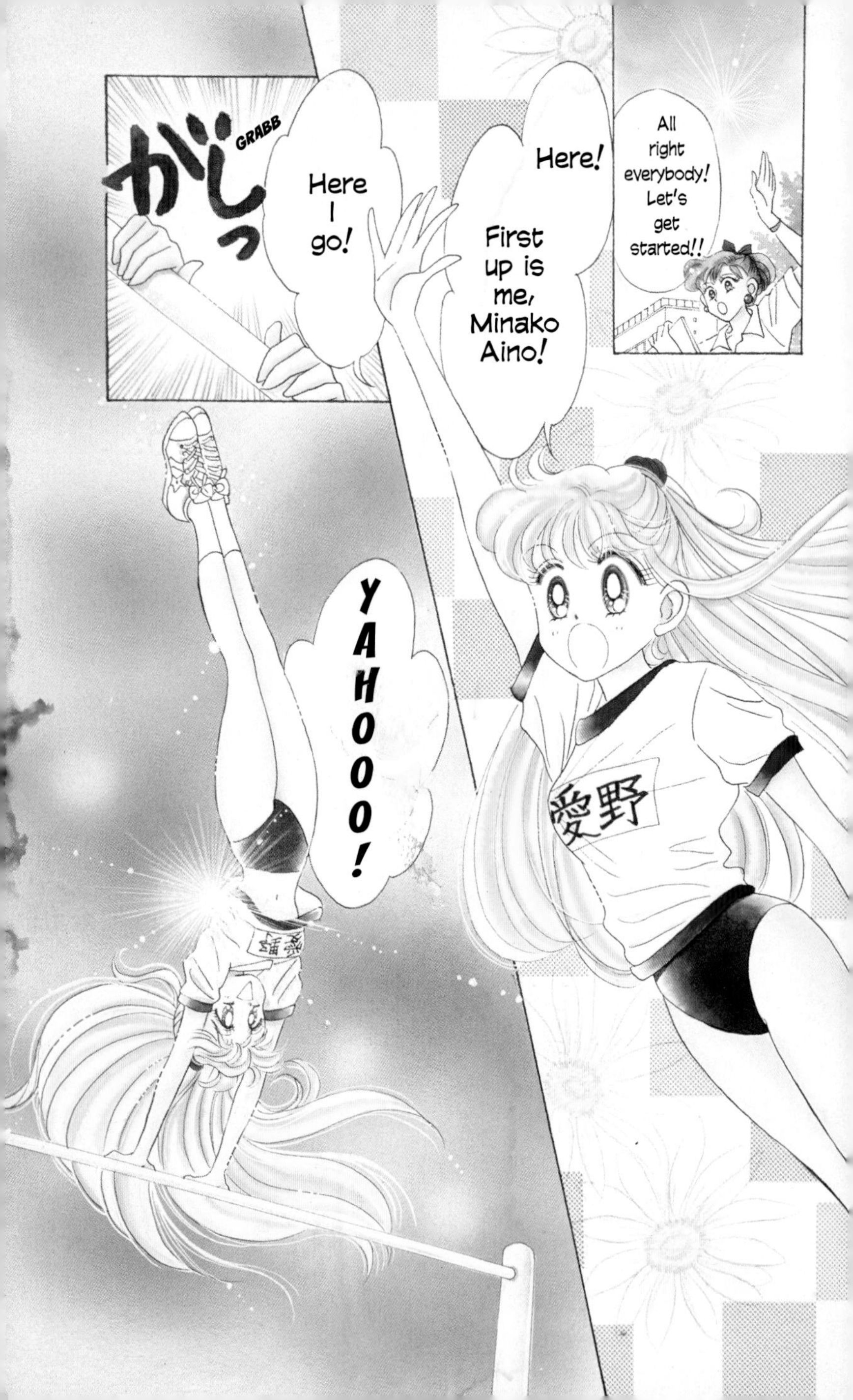
All right everybody! Let's get started!!
Here!
First up is me, Minako Aino!
がしっ
GRABB
Here I go!
愛野
YAHOOOO!

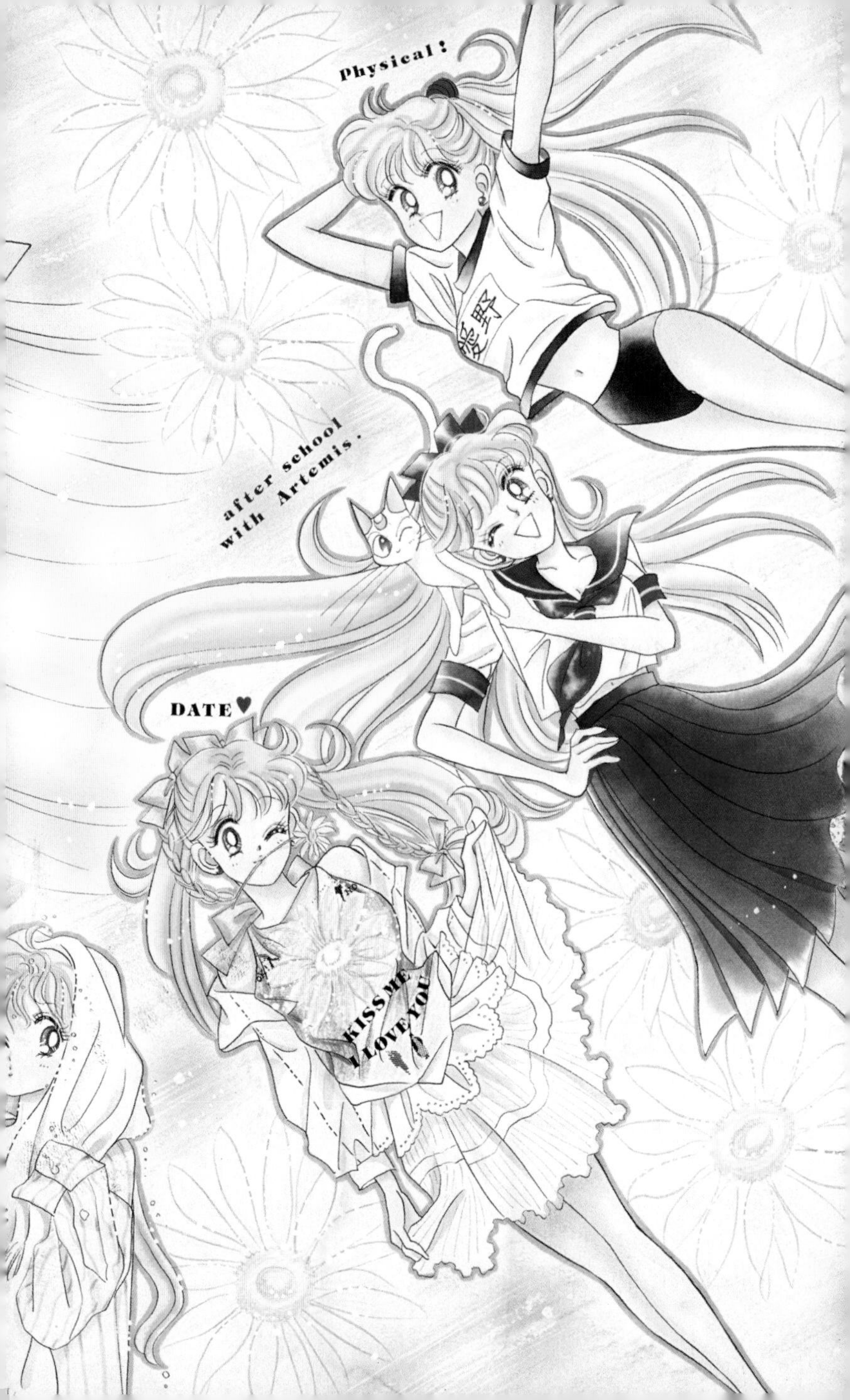
Physical!
after school
with Artemis.
DATE♥
KISS ME
I LOVE YOU

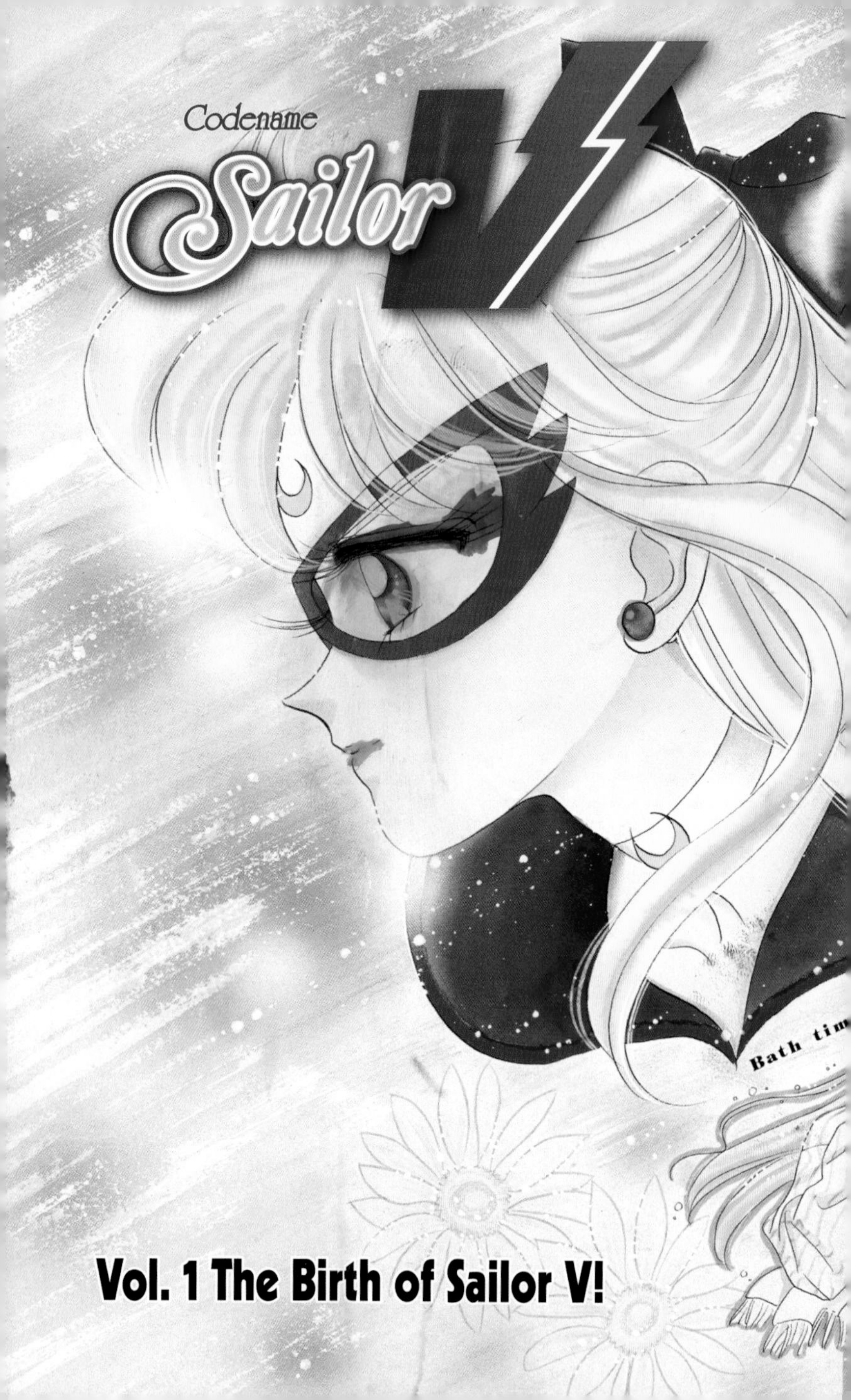
Codename
Sailor V
Bath tim
Vol. 1 The Birth of Sailor V!

CONTENTS

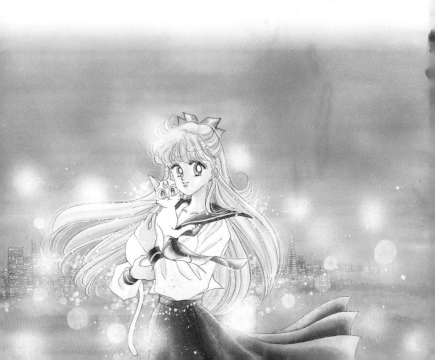

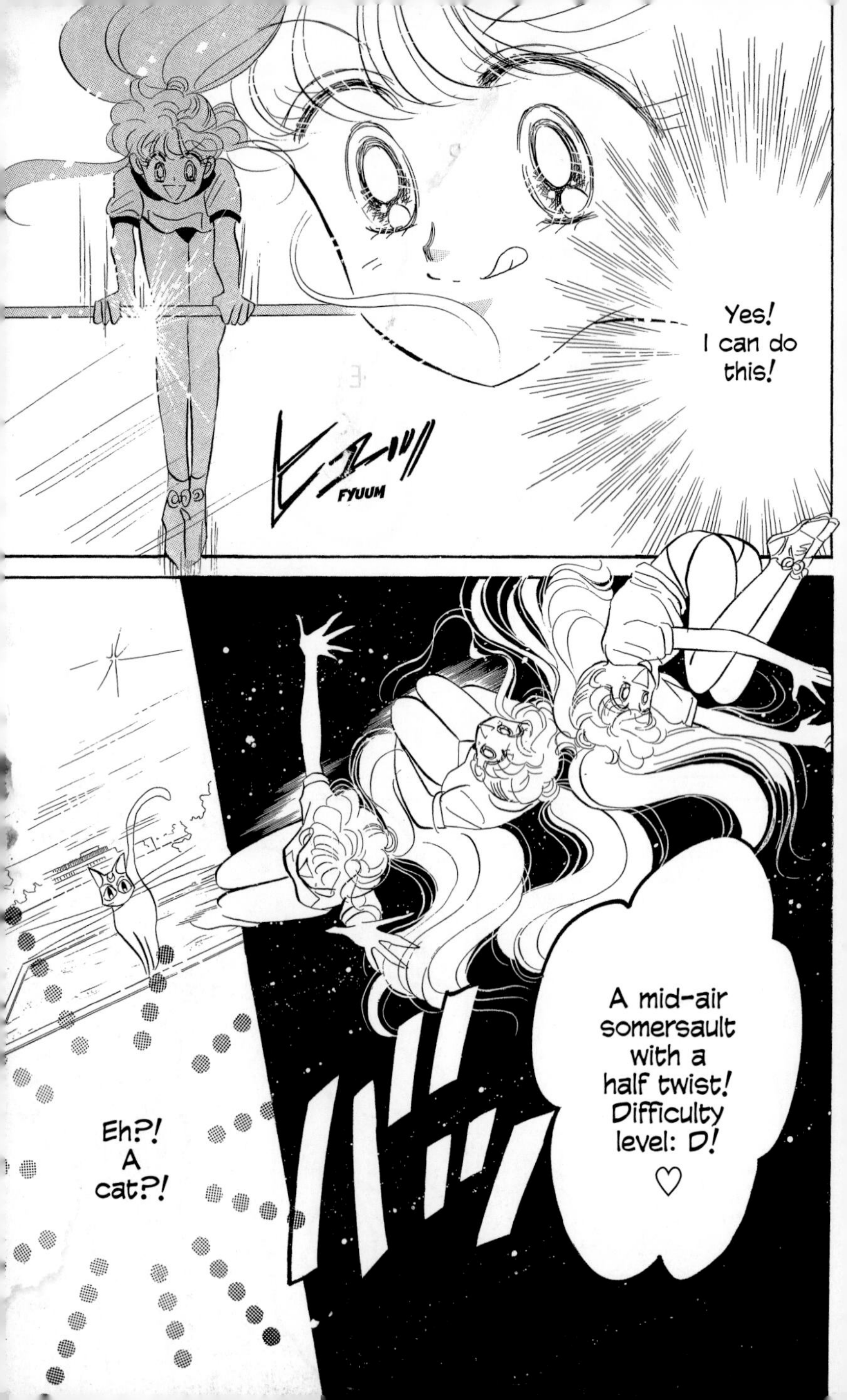
Yes! I can do this!
FYUUM
A mid-air somersault with a half twist! Difficulty level: D! ♡
Eh?! A cat?!

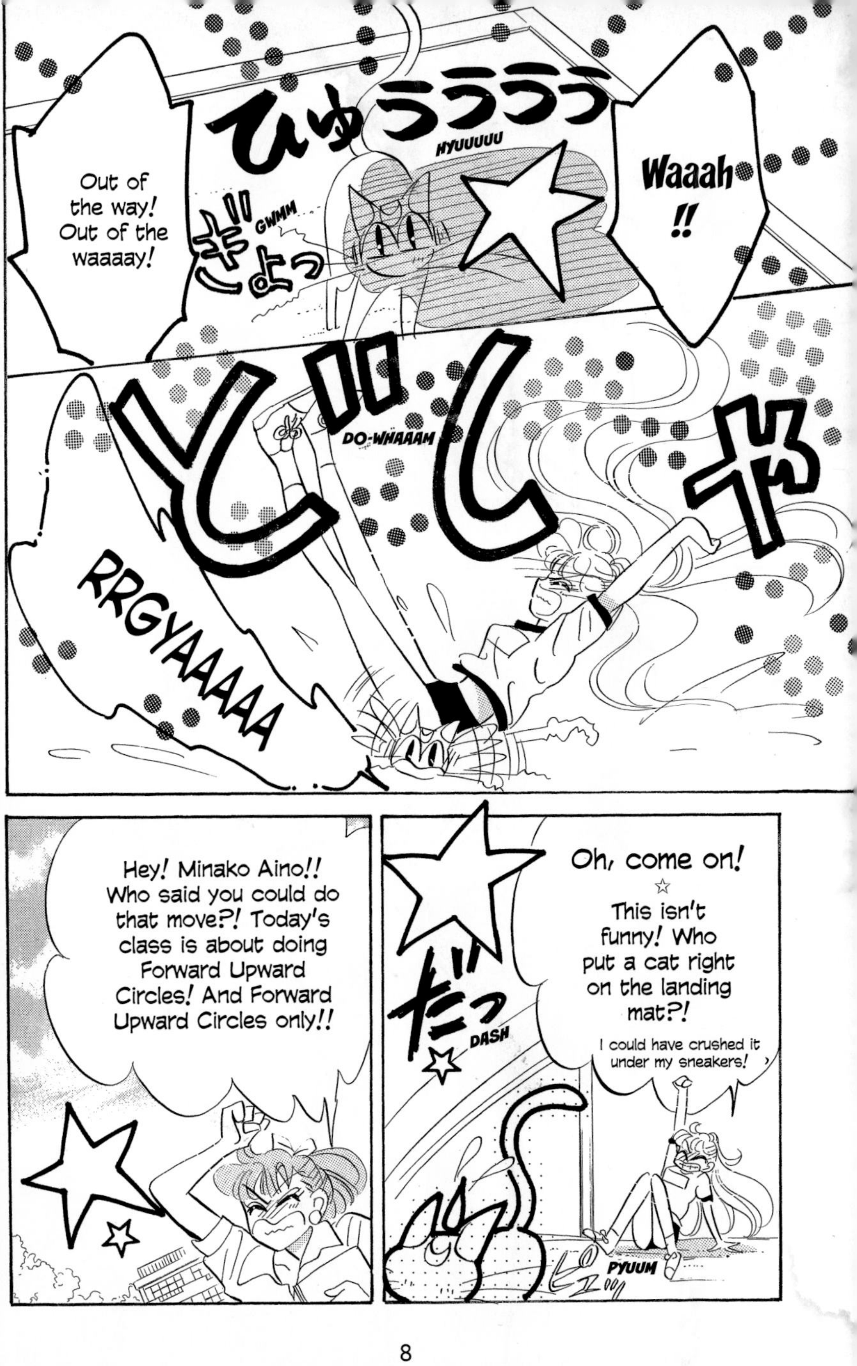
Waaah!!
ひゅうううう
HYUUUUU
ぎょっ
GWMM
Out of the way! Out of the waaaay!
どしゃ
DO-WHAAAM
RRGYAAAAAA
Oh, come on! ☆ This isn't funny! Who put a cat right on the landing mat?!
I could have crushed it under my sneakers!
だっ
DASH
PYUUM
Hey! Minako Aino!! Who said you could do that move?! Today's class is about doing Forward Upward Circles! And Forward Upward Circles only!!

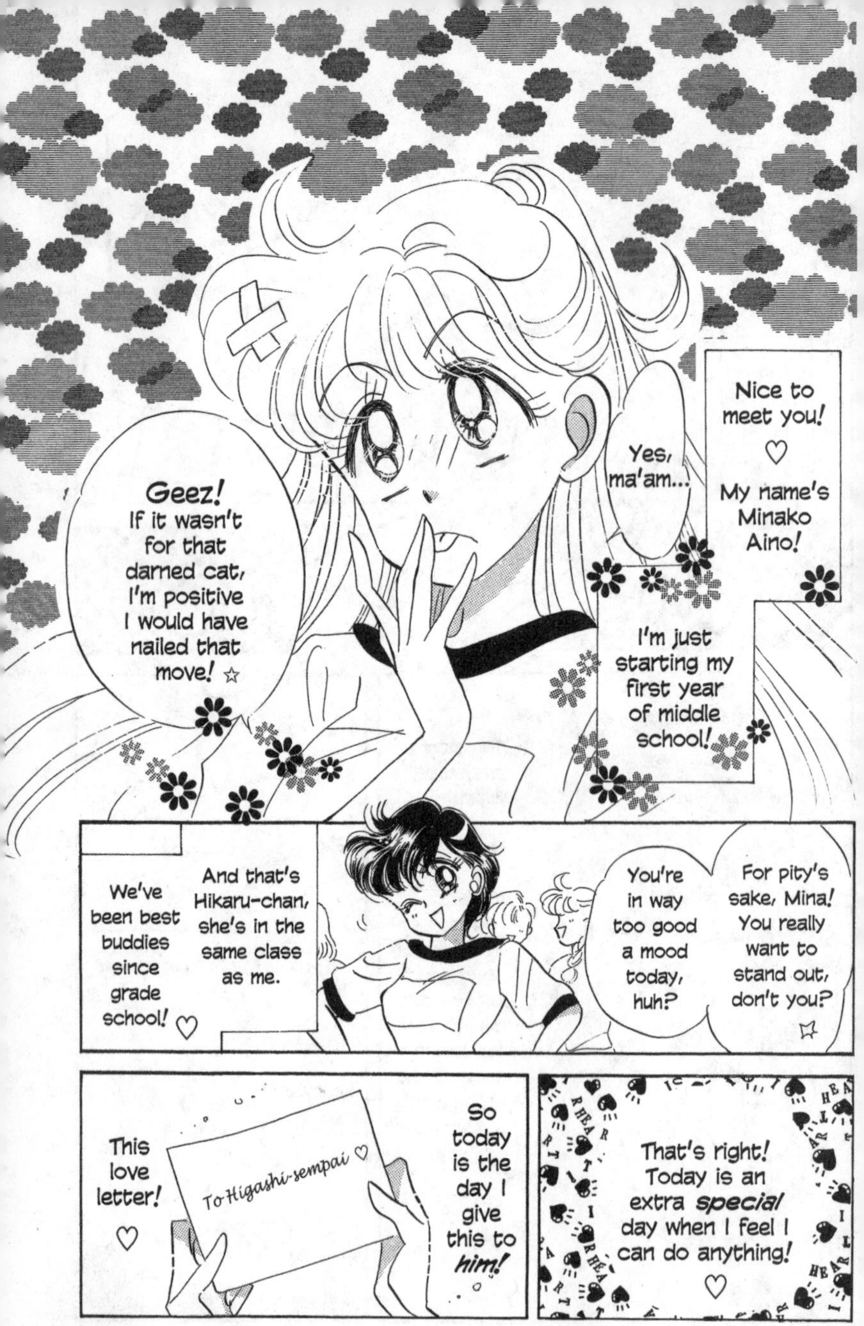
Nice to meet you! ♡ My name's Minako Aino!
Yes, ma'am...
I'm just starting my first year of middle school!
Geez! If it wasn't for that darned cat, I'm positive I would have nailed that move! ☆
For pity's sake, Mina! You really want to stand out, don't you?
You're in way too good a mood today, huh?
And that's Hikaru-chan, she's in the same class as me.
We've been best buddies since grade school! ♡
That's right! Today is an extra *special* day when I feel I can do anything! ♡
So today is the day I give this to *him*!
To Higashi-sempai ♡
This love letter! ♡

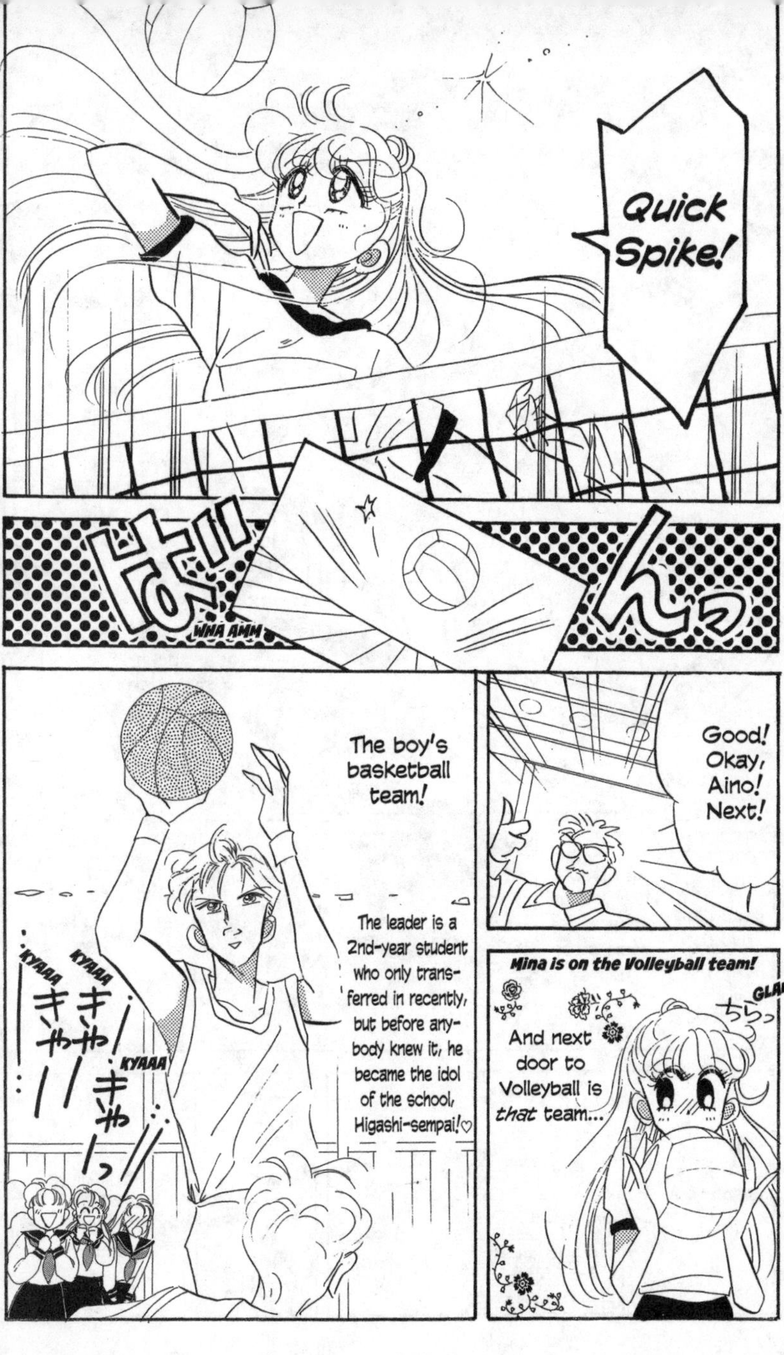
Quick Spike!
ば!!
んっ
WHA AMM
Good! Okay, Aino! Next!
Mina is on the Volleyball team!
ちらっ
GLANCE
And next door to Volleyball is *that* team...
The boy's basketball team!
The leader is a 2nd-year student who only transferred in recently, but before anybody knew it, he became the idol of the school, Higashi-sempai!♡
KYAAA
KYAAA
KYAAA

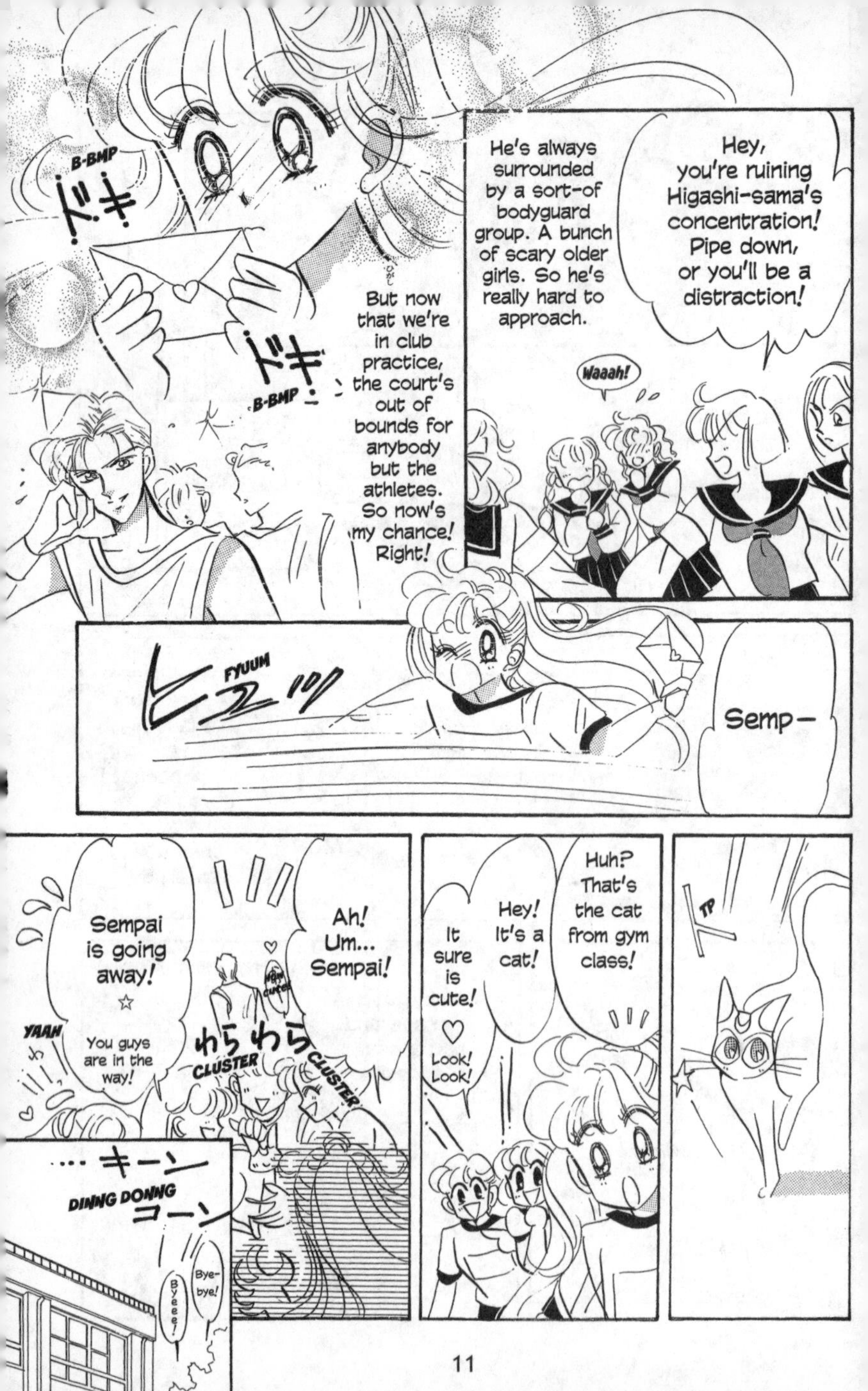
Hey, you're ruining Higashi-sama's concentration! Pipe down, or you'll be a distraction!
He's always surrounded by a sort-of bodyguard group. A bunch of scary older girls. So he's really hard to approach.
Waaah!
B-BMP
ドキ
ドキ
B-BMP
But now that we're in club practice, the court's out of bounds for anybody but the athletes. So now's my chance! Right!
Semp—
FYUUM
TP
Huh? That's the cat from gym class!
Hey! It's a cat!
It sure is cute!
Look! Look!
Ah! Um... Sempai!
Sempai is going away! ☆
You guys are in the way!
YAAH
わらわら
CLUSTER
CLUSTER
…キーン
DINNG DONNG
コーン
Bye-bye!
Byeee!

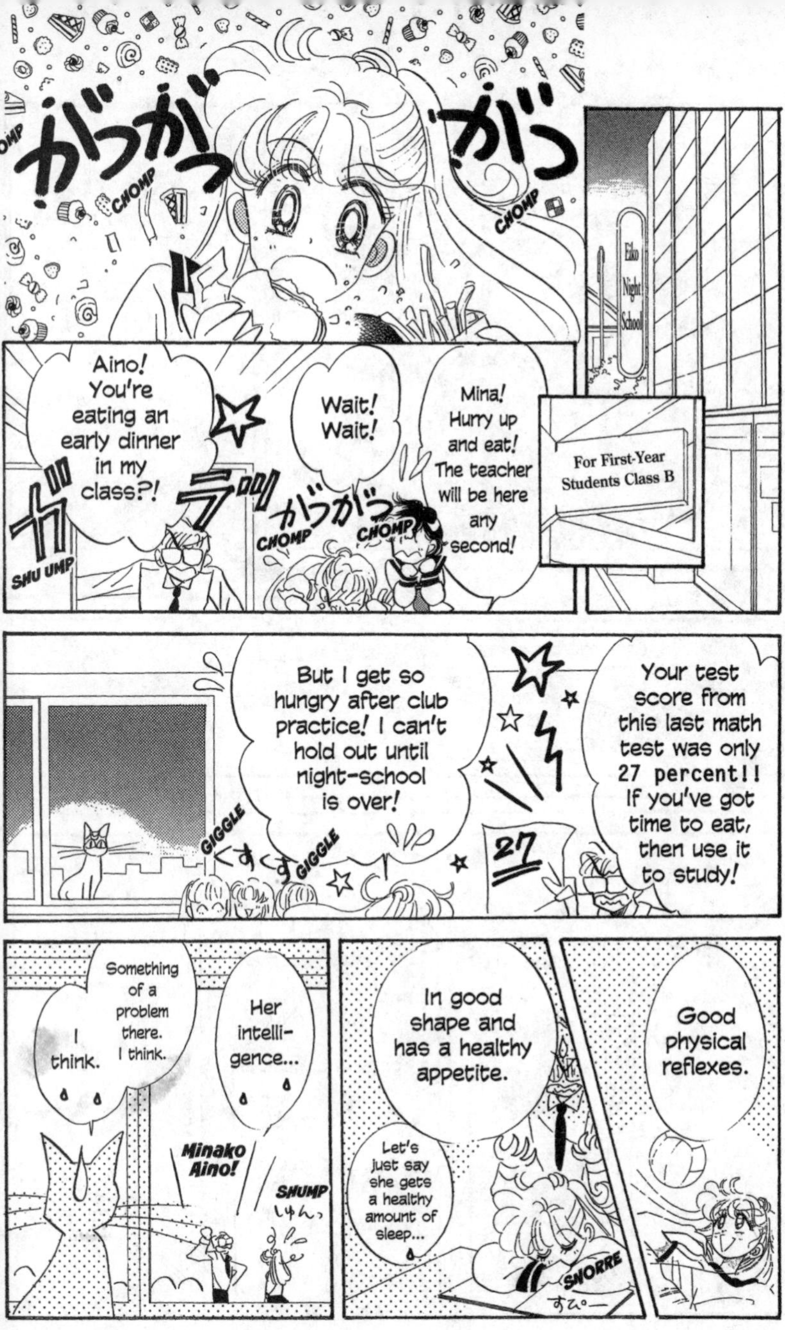

Eiko Night School
For First-Year Students Class B
がつがつ
CHOMP
CHOMP
がつ
CHOMP
Mina! Hurry up and eat! The teacher will be here any second!
Wait! Wait!
がつがつ
CHOMP
CHOMP
Aino! You're eating an early dinner in my class?!
ガラ
SHU UMP
Your test score from this last math test was only 27 percent!! If you've got time to eat, then use it to study!
27
But I get so hungry after club practice! I can't hold out until night-school is over!
くすくす
GIGGLE
GIGGLE
Good physical reflexes.
In good shape and has a healthy appetite.
Let's just say she gets a healthy amount of sleep...
SNORRE
すぴー
Her intelli-gence...
Something of a problem there. I think.
I think.
Minako Aino!
SHUMP
しゅんっ

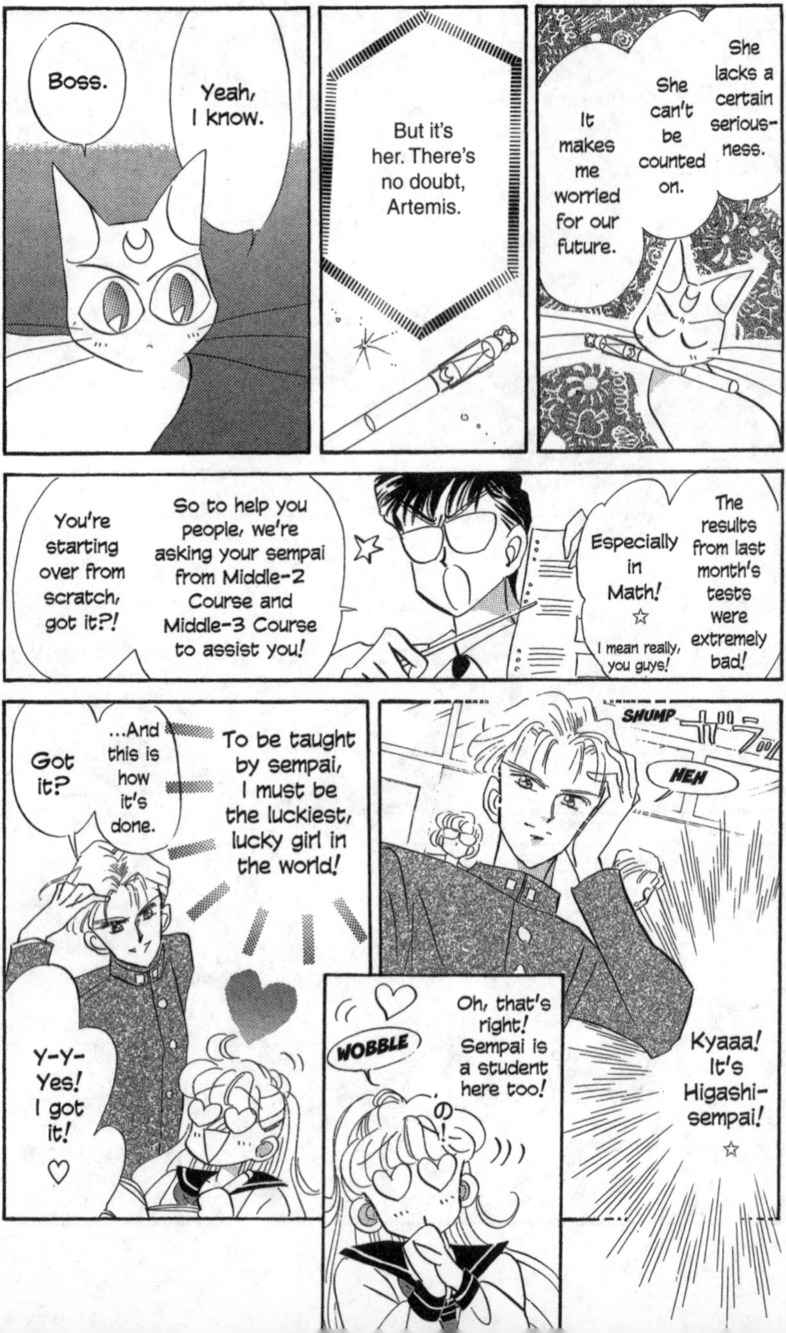

She lacks a certain seriousness.
She can't be counted on.
It makes me worried for our future.
But it's her. There's no doubt, Artemis.
Yeah, I know.
Boss.
The results from last month's tests were extremely bad!
Especially in Math! ☆
I mean really, you guys!
So to help you people, we're asking your sempai from Middle-2 Course and Middle-3 Course to assist you!
You're starting over from scratch, got it?!
SHUMP
HEN
Kyaaa! It's Higashi-sempai! ☆
Oh, that's right! Sempai is a student here too!
WOBBLE
To be taught by sempai, I must be the luckiest, lucky girl in the world!
...And this is how it's done.
Got it?
Y-Y-Yes! I got it! ♡

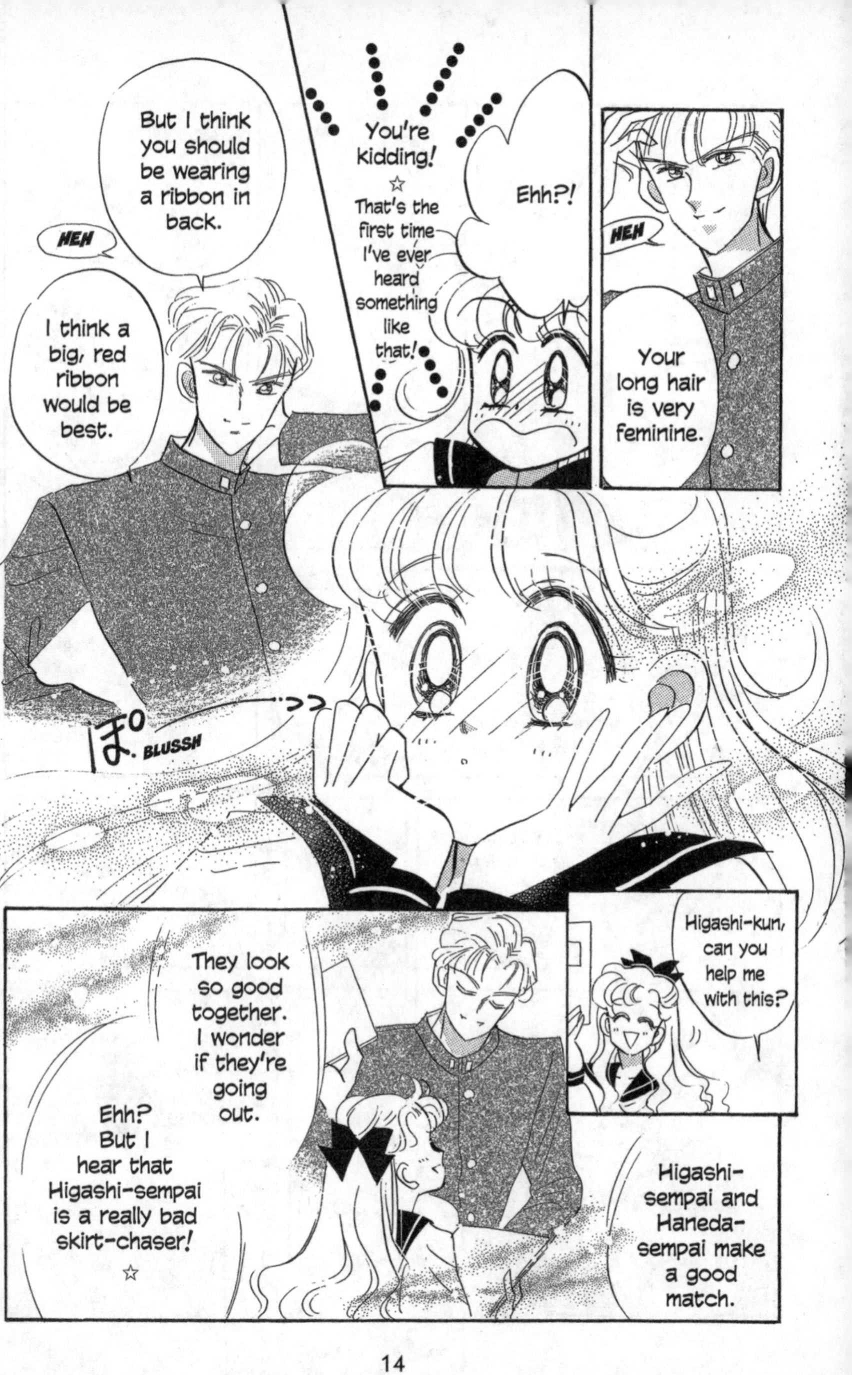
HEH
Your long hair is very feminine.
Ehh?!
You're kidding! ☆ That's the first time I've ever heard something like that!
HEH
But I think you should be wearing a ribbon in back.
I think a big, red ribbon would be best.
ぽ。 BLUSSH
Higashi-kun, can you help me with this?
Higashi-sempai and Haneda-sempai make a good match.
They look so good together. I wonder if they're going out.
Ehh? But I hear that Higashi-sempai is a really bad skirt-chaser! ☆

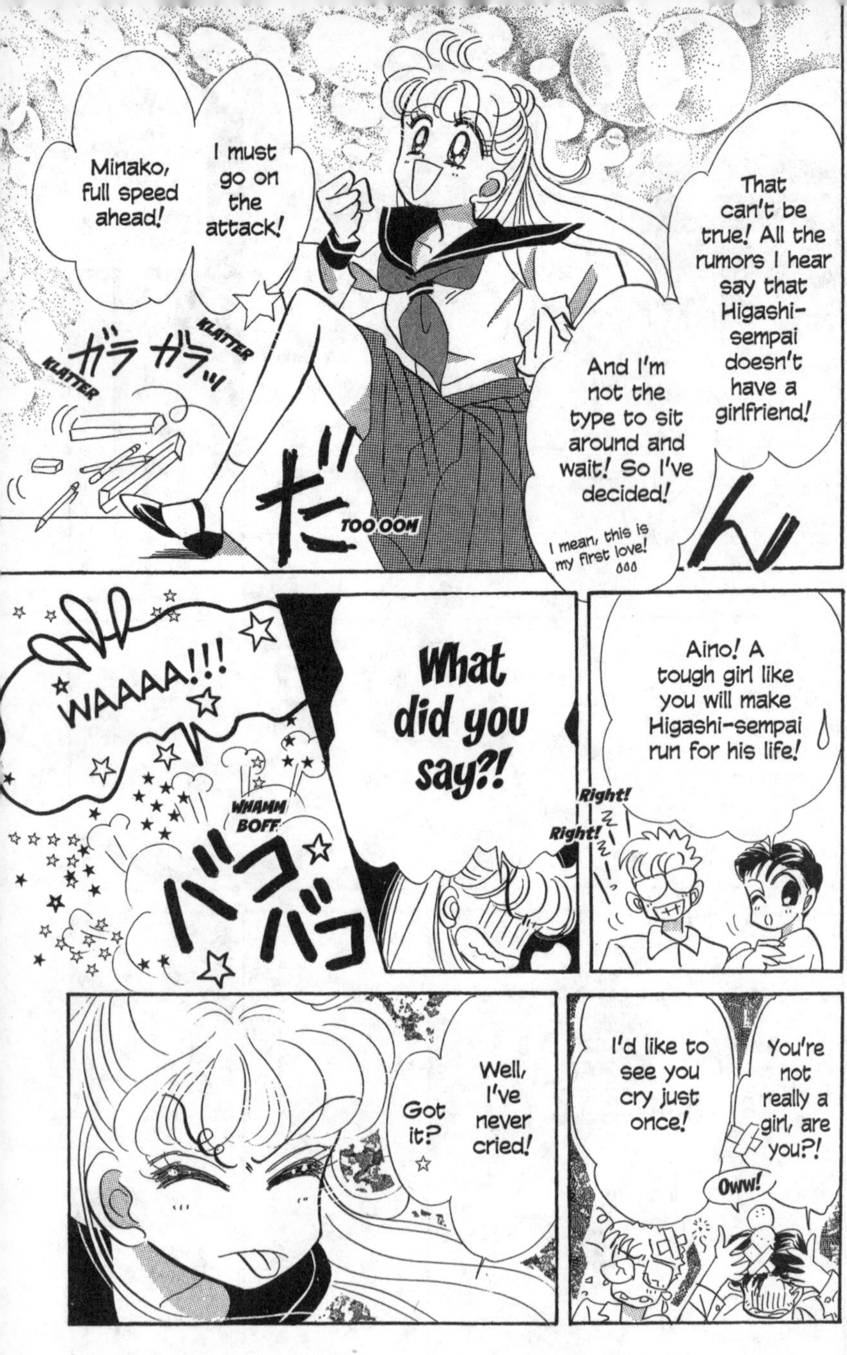

That can't be true! All the rumors I hear say that Higashi-sempai doesn't have a girlfriend!
And I'm not the type to sit around and wait! So I've decided!
I mean, this is my first love!
I must go on the attack!
Minako, full speed ahead!
KLATTER
KLATTER
TOO OOM
Aino! A tough girl like you will make Higashi-sempai run for his life!
Right!
Right!
What did you say?!
WAAAA!!!
WHAMM
BOFF
You're not really a girl, are you?!
I'd like to see you cry just once!
Oww!
Well, I've never cried!
Got it?

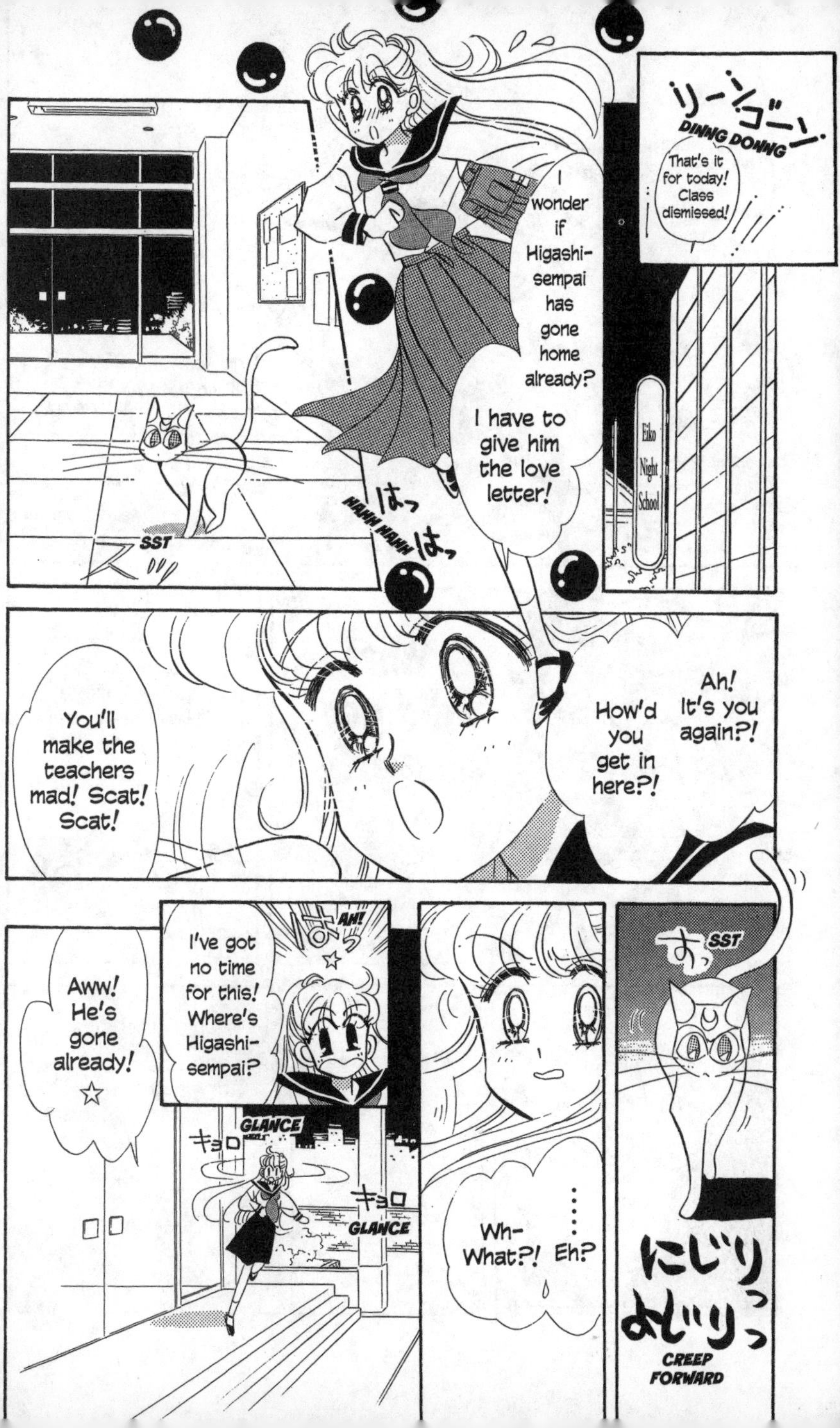
リーンゴーン
DINNG DONNG
That's it for today! Class dismissed!
Eiko Night School
I wonder if Higashi-sempai has gone home already?
I have to give him the love letter!
はっ はっ
HAHH HAHH
SST
Ah! It's you again?!
How'd you get in here?!
You'll make the teachers mad! Scat! Scat!
すっ
SST
にじりっ よじりっ
CREEP FORWARD
......Eh?
Wh-What?!
はっ
AH!
I've got no time for this! Where's Higashi-sempai?
キョロ
GLANCE
キョロ
GLANCE
Aww! He's gone already! ☆

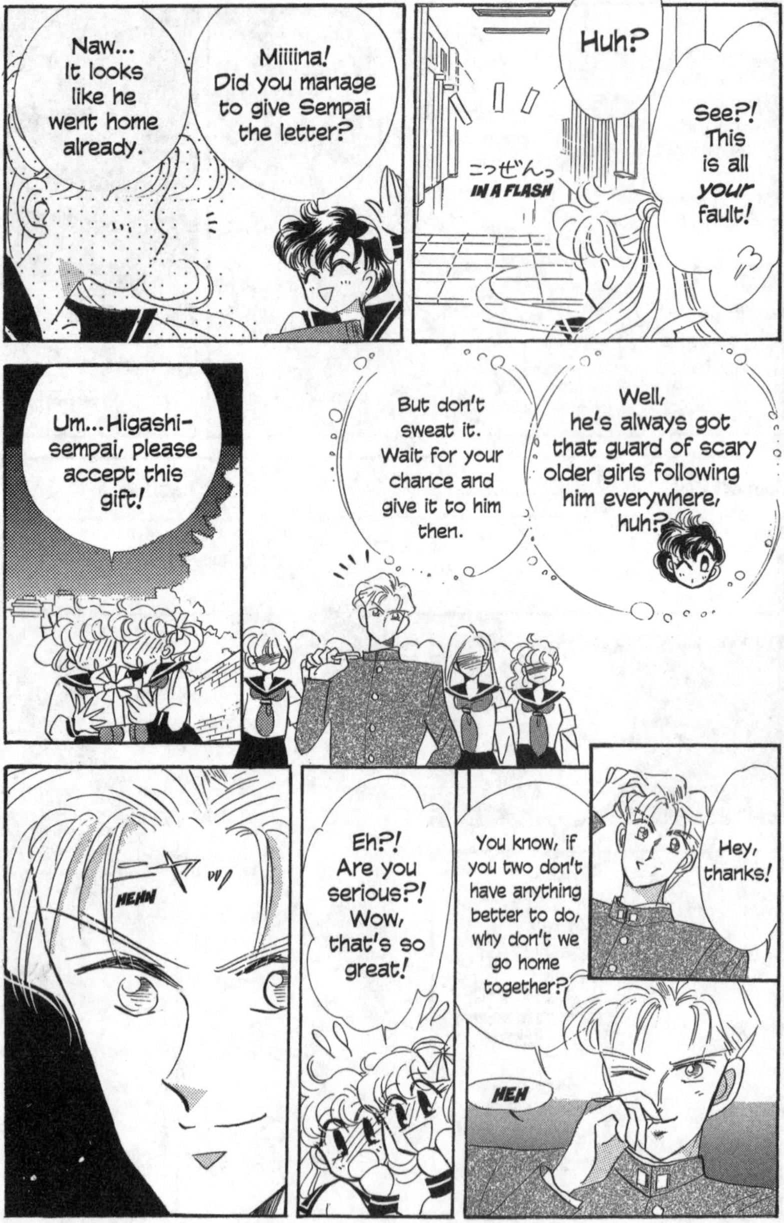
Huh?
See?! This is all *your* fault!
こっぜんっ
IN A FLASH
Miiiina! Did you manage to give Sempai the letter?
Naw... It looks like he went home already.
Well, he's always got that guard of scary older girls following him everywhere, huh?
But don't sweat it. Wait for your chance and give it to him then.
Um...Higashi-sempai, please accept this gift!
Hey, thanks!
You know, if you two don't have anything better to do, why don't we go home together?
HEH
Eh?! Are you serious?! Wow, that's so great!
HEHN

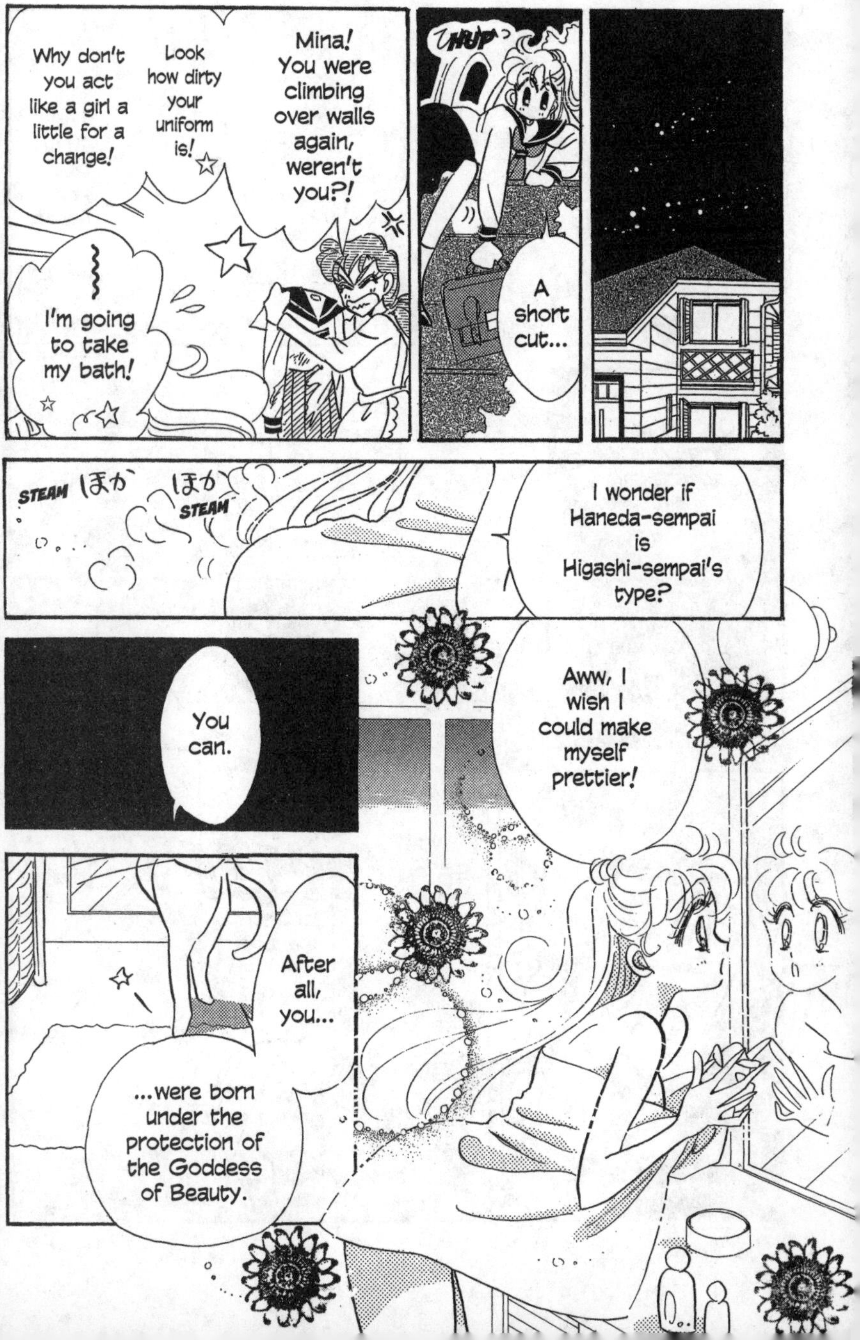
HUP
A short cut...
Mina! You were climbing over walls again, weren't you?!
Look how dirty your uniform is!
Why don't you act like a girl a little for a change!
I'm going to take my bath!
I wonder if Haneda-sempai is Higashi-sempai's type?
ほか STEAM
STEAM ほか
Aww, I wish I could make myself prettier!
You can.
After all, you...
...were born under the protection of the Goddess of Beauty.

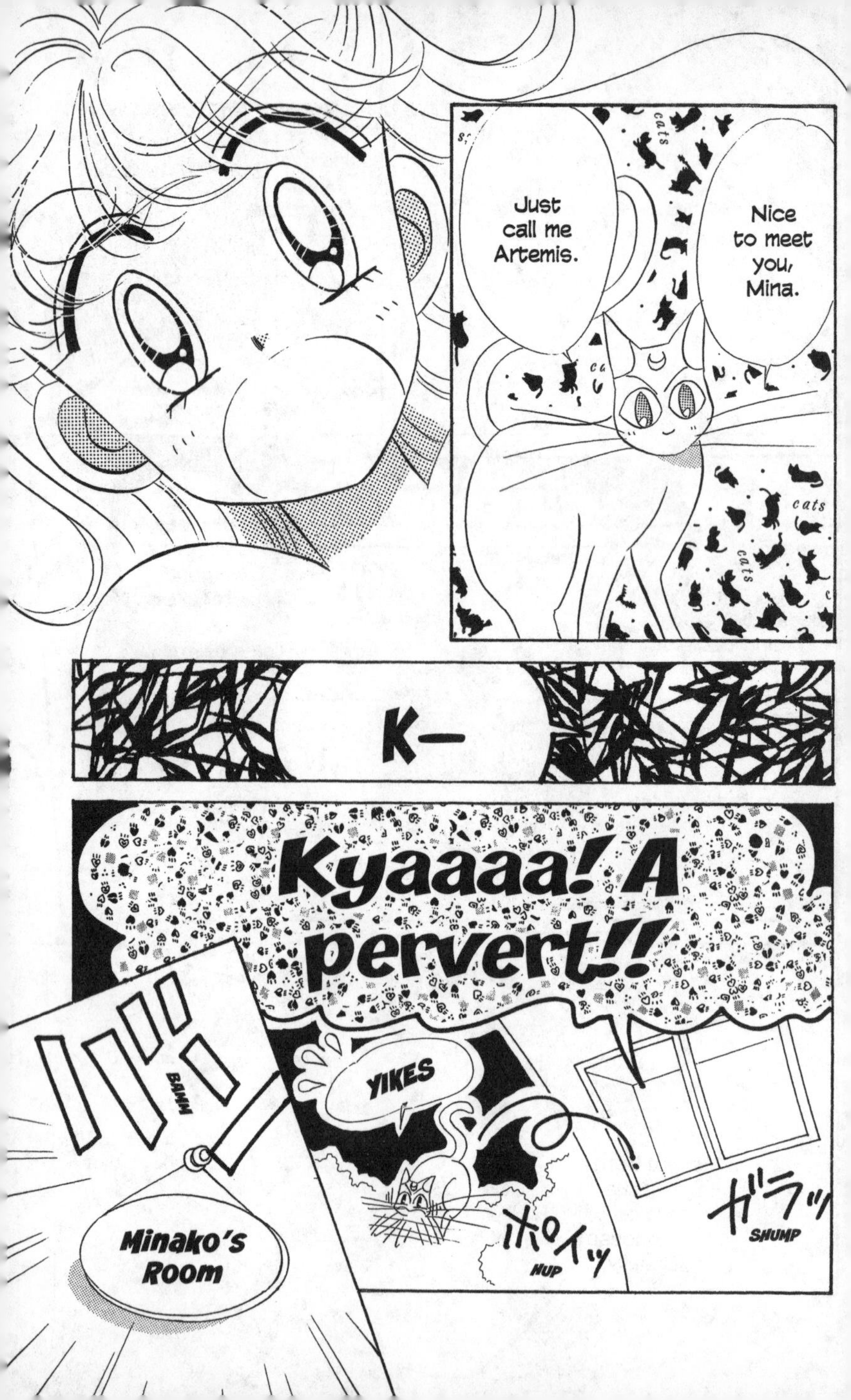
Nice to meet you, Mina.
Just call me Artemis.
K—
Kyaaaa! A pervert!!
ガラッ
SHUMP
YIKES
ポイッ
NUP
BAMM
Minako's Room

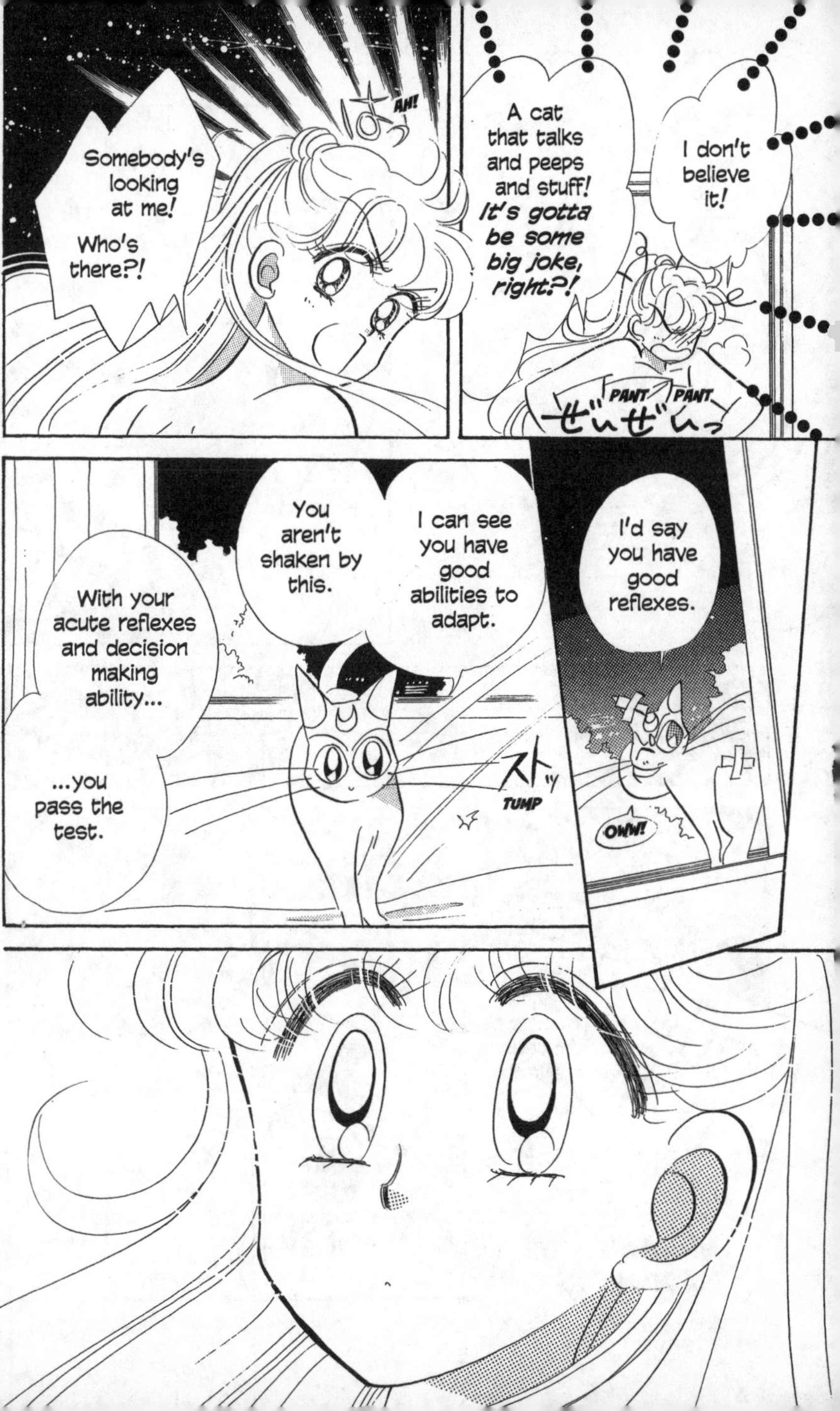
I don't believe it!
A cat that talks and peeps and stuff! *It's gotta be some big joke, right?!*
PANT PANT
ぜいぜいっ
はっ
AH!
Somebody's looking at me!
Who's there?!
I'd say you have good reflexes.
OWW!
I can see you have good abilities to adapt.
You aren't shaken by this.
ストッ
TUMP
With your acute reflexes and decision making ability...
...you pass the test.

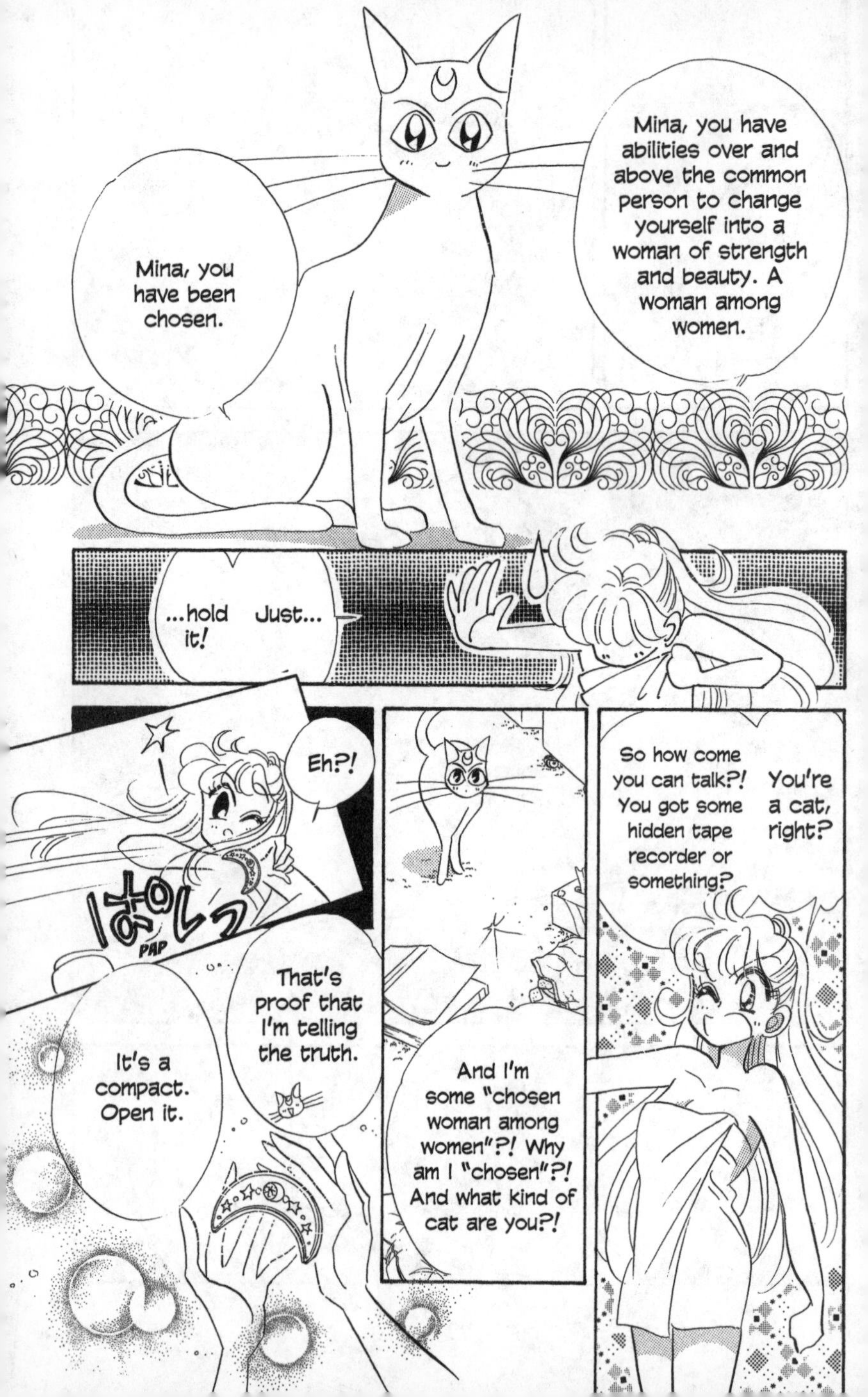

Mina, you have abilities over and above the common person to change yourself into a woman of strength and beauty. A woman among women.
Mina, you have been chosen.
Just...
...hold it!
You're a cat, right?
So how come you can talk?! You got some hidden tape recorder or something?
And I'm some "chosen woman among women"?! Why am I "chosen"?! And what kind of cat are you?!
Eh?!
PAP
That's proof that I'm telling the truth.
It's a compact. Open it.

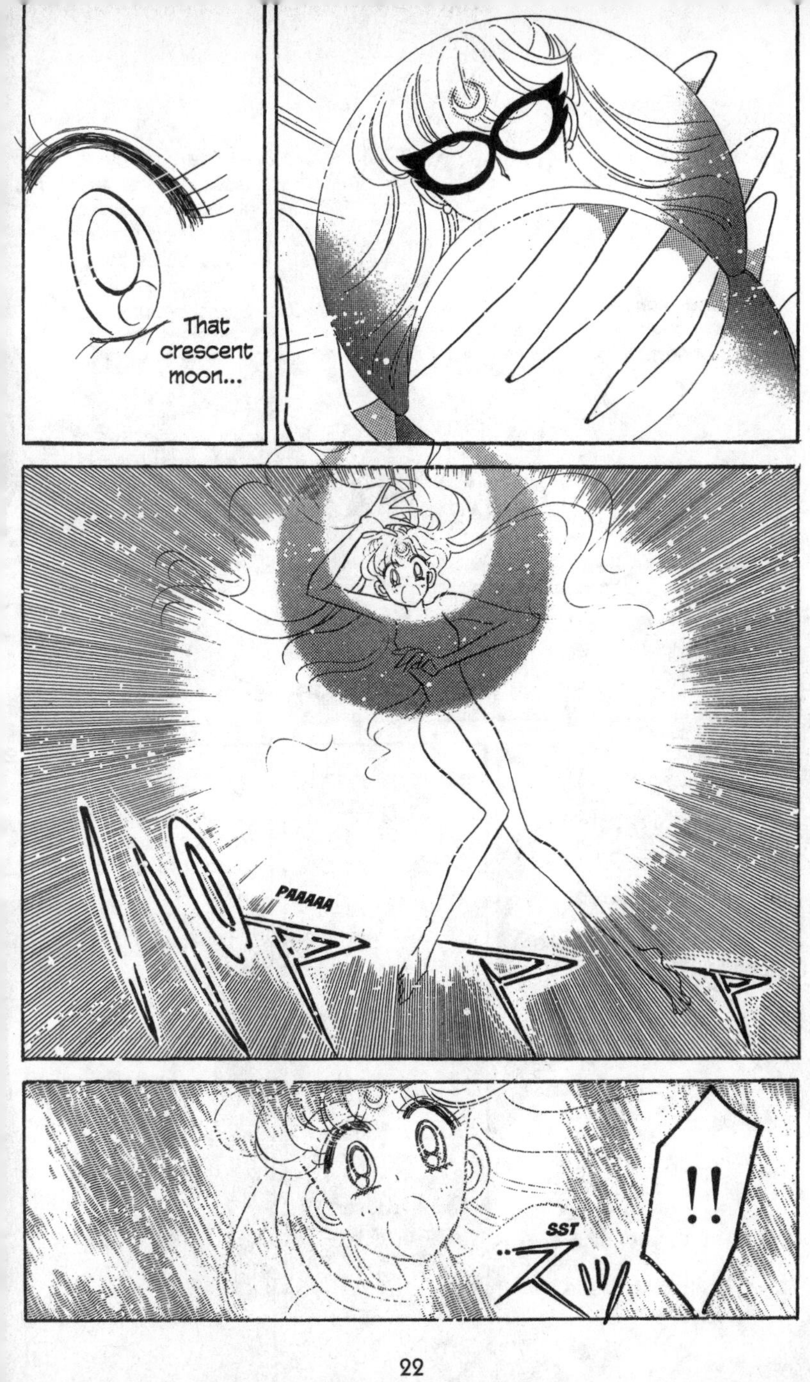
That crescent moon...
PAAAAA
SST
!!

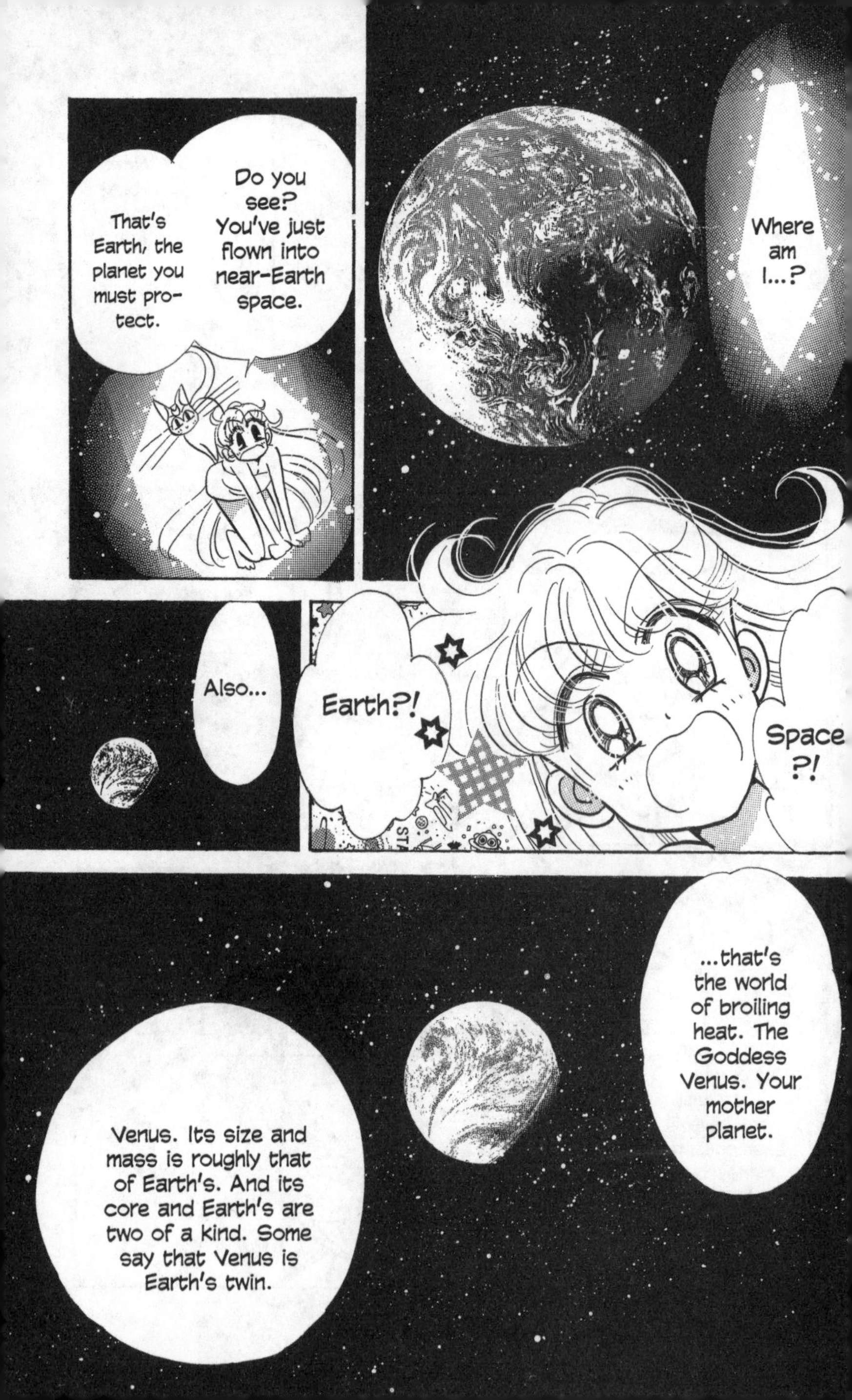
Where am I...?
Do you see? You've just flown into near-Earth space.
That's Earth, the planet you must protect.
Space ?!
Earth?!
Also...
...that's the world of broiling heat. The Goddess Venus. Your mother planet.
Venus. Its size and mass is roughly that of Earth's. And its core and Earth's are two of a kind. Some say that Venus is Earth's twin.

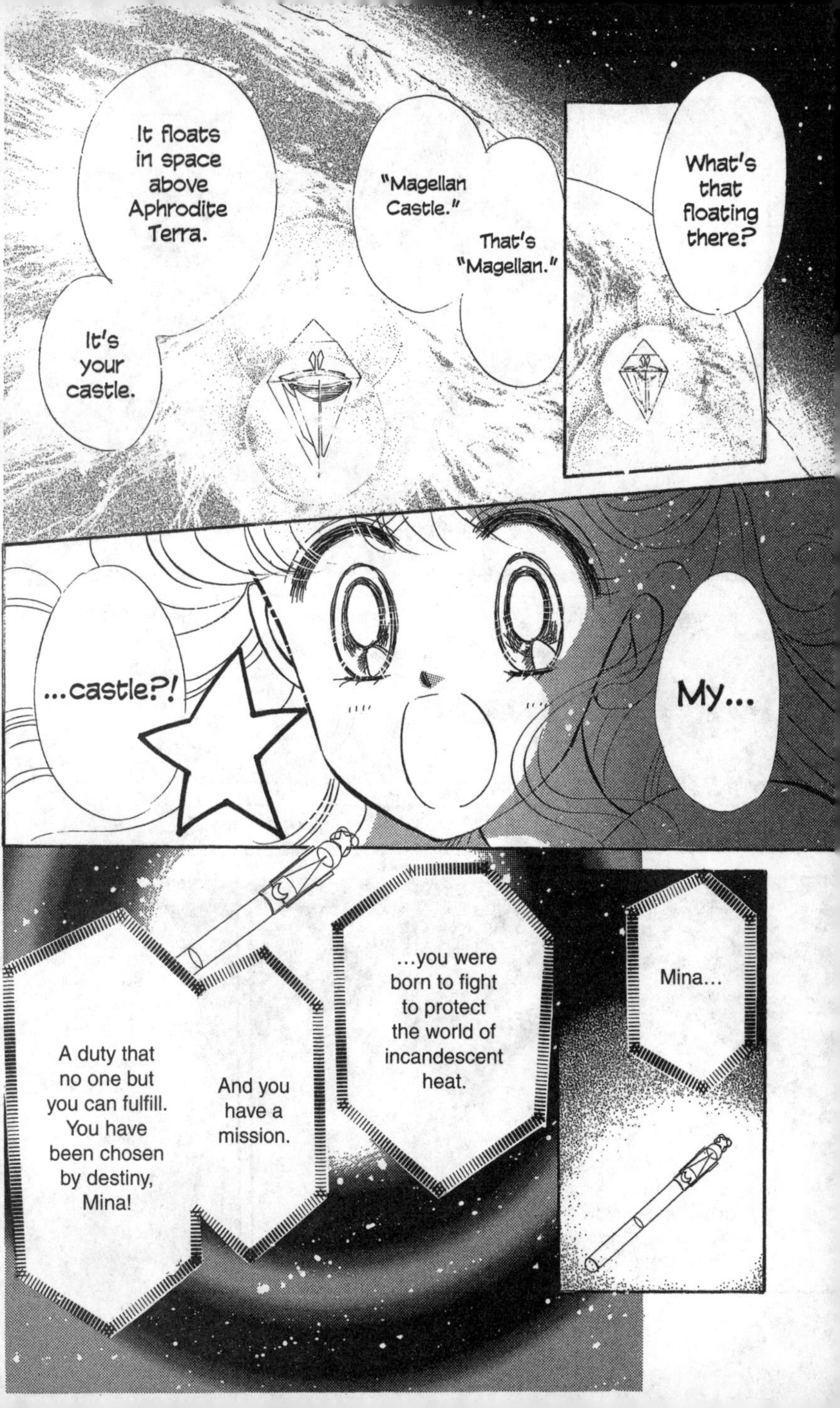
What's that floating there?
That's "Magellan."
"Magellan Castle."
It floats in space above Aphrodite Terra.
It's your castle.
My...
...castle?!
Mina...
...you were born to fight to protect the world of incandescent heat.
And you have a mission.
A duty that no one but you can fulfill. You have been chosen by destiny, Mina!

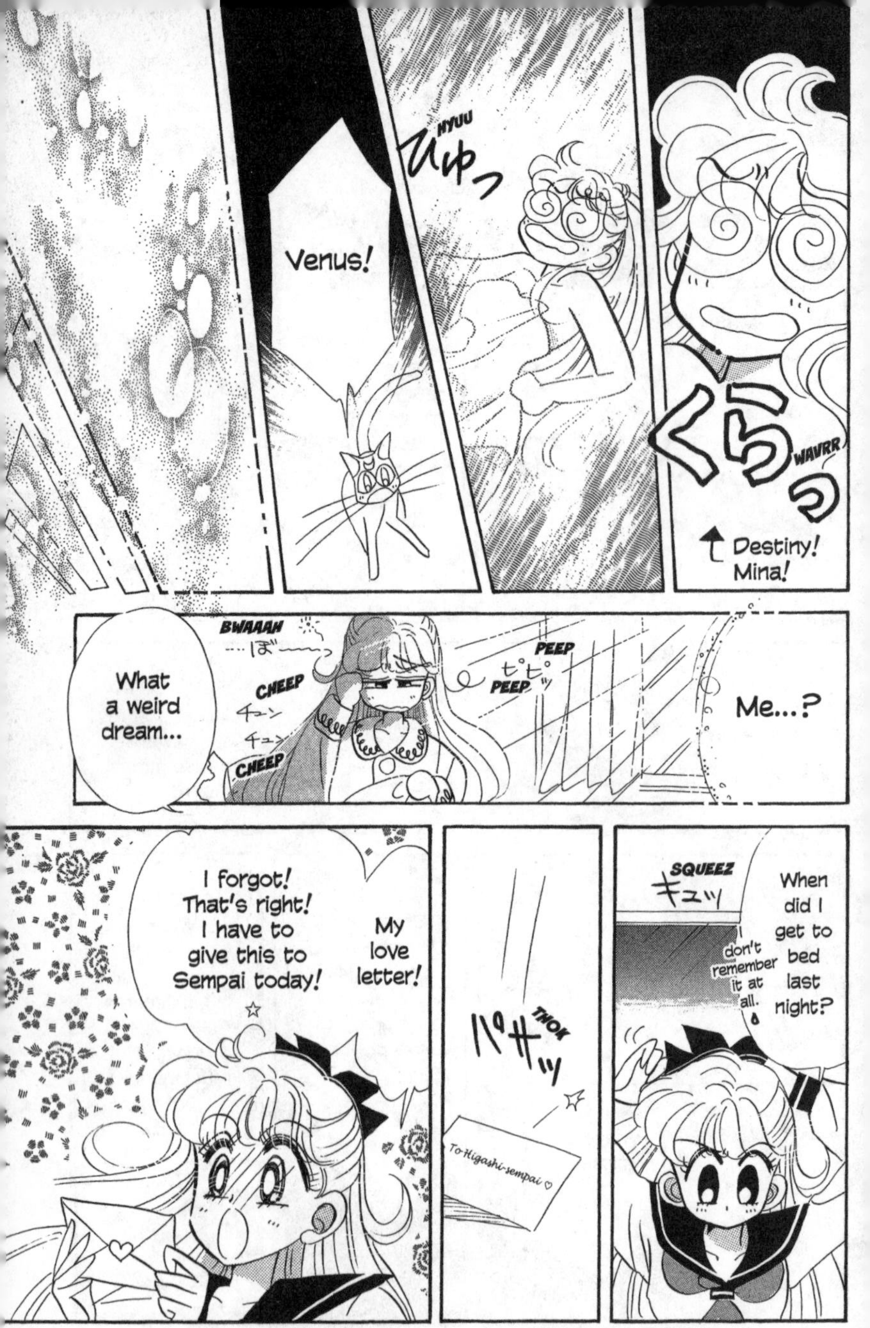
くらっ
WAVRR
Destiny! Mina!
ひゅっ
HYUU
Venus!
Me...?
PEEP
ピピッ
PEEP
CHEEP
チュン
チュン
CHEEP
BWAAAH
ぼー
What a weird dream...
SQUEEZ
キュッ
When did I get to bed last night?
I don't remember it at all.
THOK
パサッ
To Higashi-sempai ♡
My love letter!
I forgot! That's right! I have to give this to Sempai today!

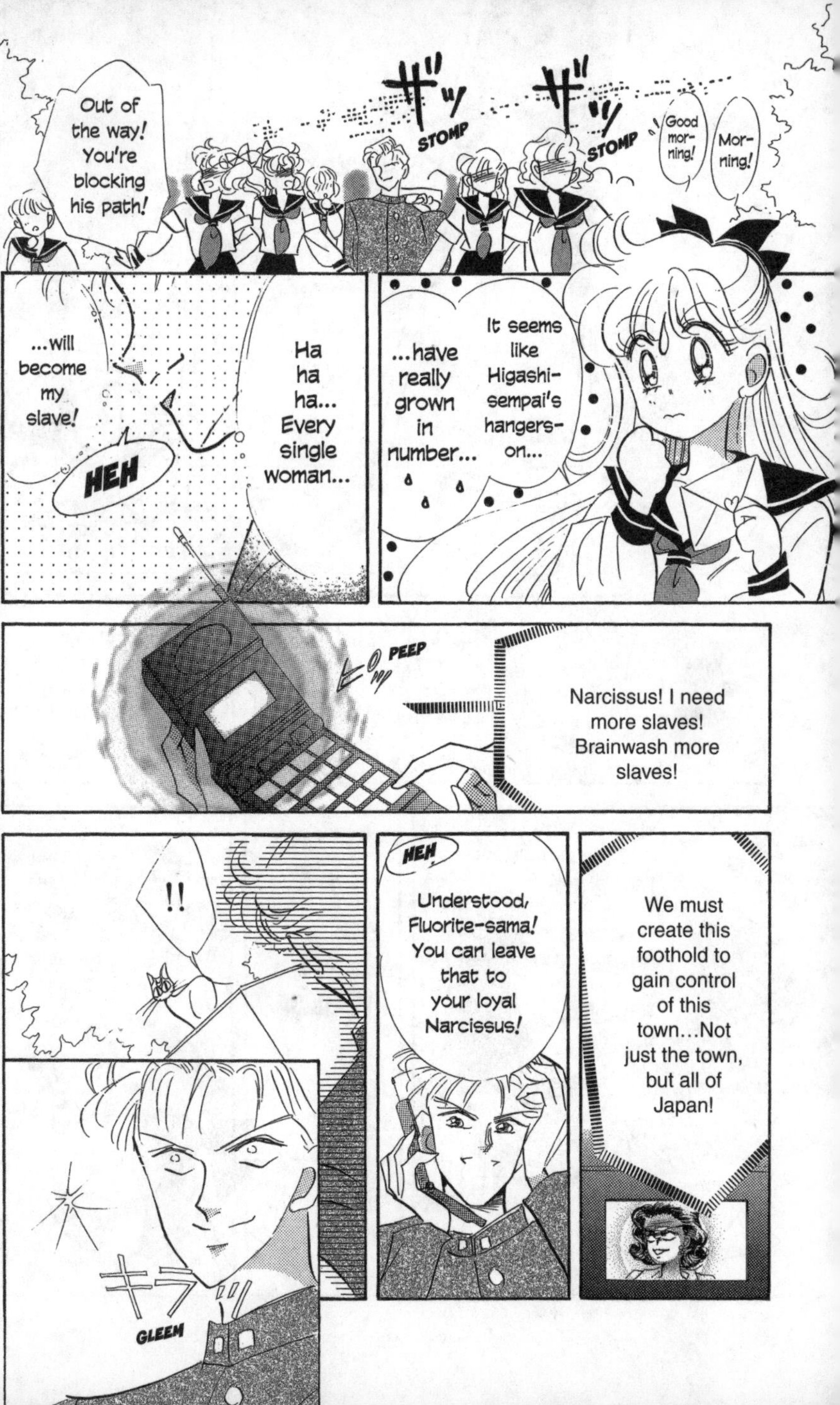
Morning!
Good morning!
ザッ
STOMP
ザッ
STOMP
Out of the way! You're blocking his path!
It seems like Higashi-sempai's hangers-on...
...have really grown in number...
Ha ha ha... Every single woman...
...will become my slave!
HEH
Narcissus! I need more slaves! Brainwash more slaves!
PEEP
We must create this foothold to gain control of this town...Not just the town, but all of Japan!
HEH
Understood, Fluorite-sama! You can leave that to your loyal Narcissus!
!!
キラッ
GLEEM

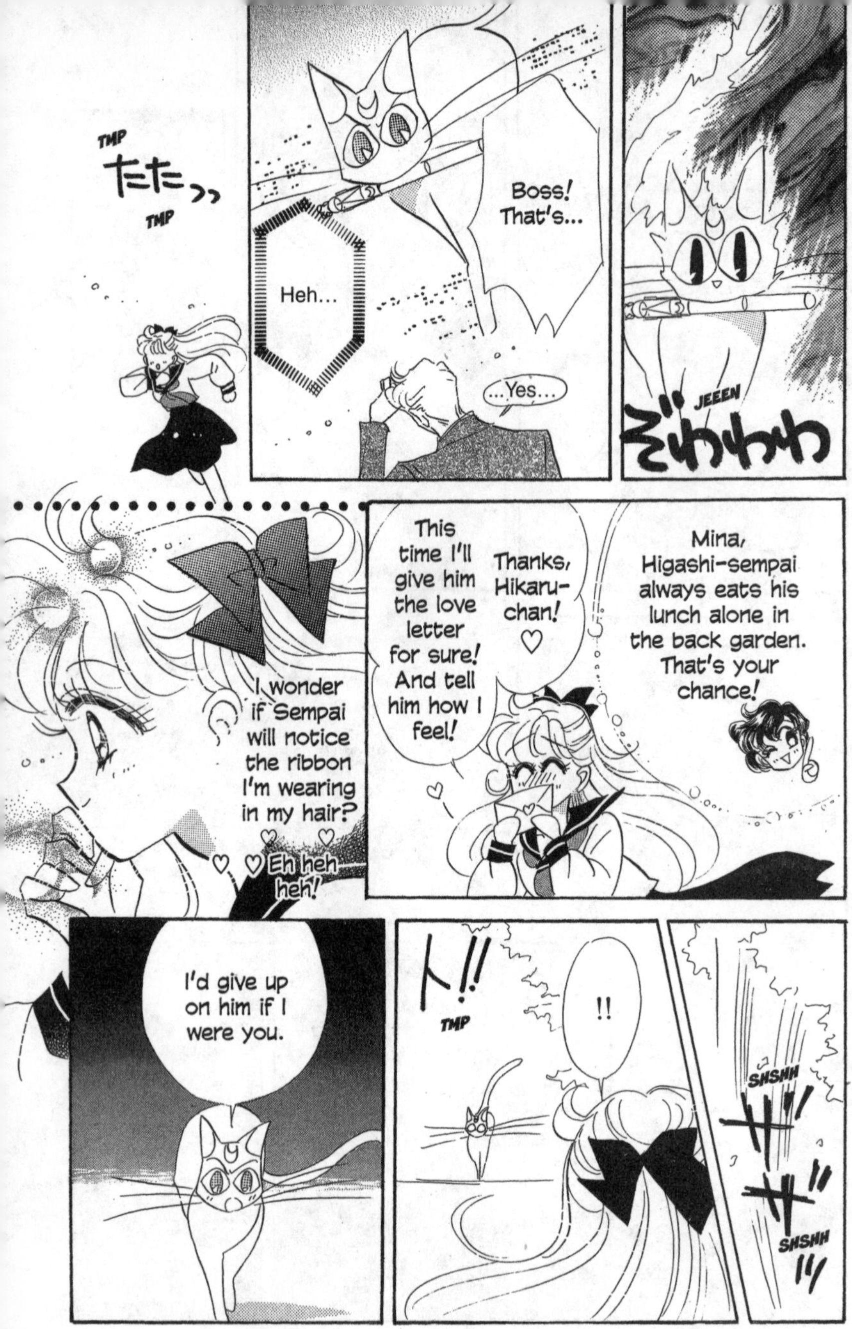
JEEEN
ざわわわ
Boss! That's...
Heh...
...Yes...
TMP
たたたっっ
TMP
Mina, Higashi-sempai always eats his lunch alone in the back garden. That's your chance!
Thanks, Hikaru-chan! ♡
This time I'll give him the love letter for sure! And tell him how I feel!
I wonder if Sempai will notice the ribbon I'm wearing in my hair? ♡ ♡
♡ ♡ Eh heh heh!
SHSHH
ザッ
ザッ
SHSHH
ト!!
TMP
!!
I'd give up on him if I were you.

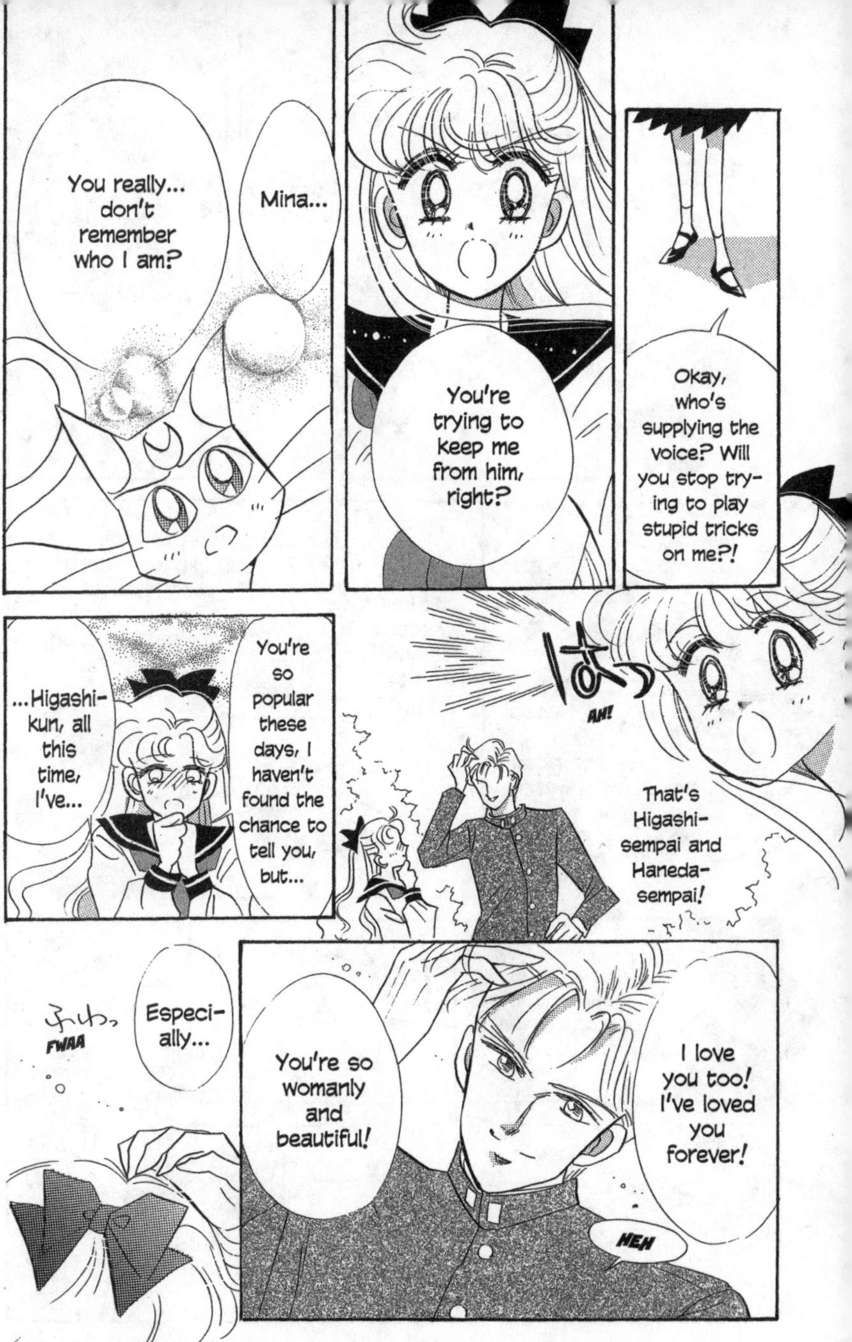
Okay, who's supplying the voice? Will you stop try-ing to play stupid tricks on me?!
You're trying to keep me from him, right?
Mina...
You really... don't remember who I am?
はっ
AH!
That's Higashi-sempai and Haneda-sempai!
You're so popular these days, I haven't found the chance to tell you, but...
...Higashi-kun, all this time, I've...
I love you too! I've loved you forever!
HEH
You're so womanly and beautiful!
Especi-ally...
ふわっ
FWAA

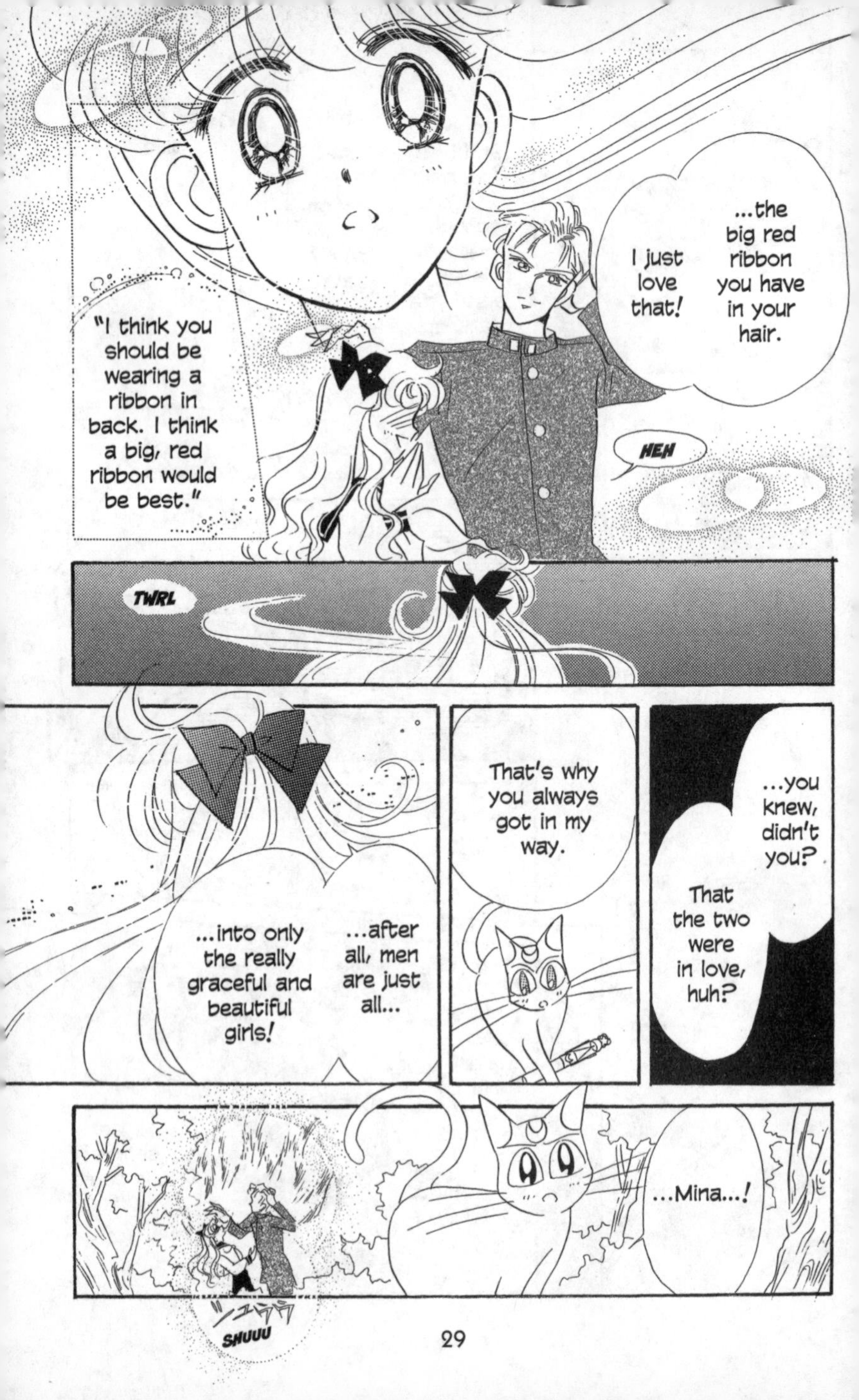
...the big red ribbon you have in your hair.
I just love that!
HEH
"I think you should be wearing a ribbon in back. I think a big, red ribbon would be best."
TWRL
...you knew, didn't you?
That the two were in love, huh?
That's why you always got in my way.
...after all, men are just all...
...into only the really graceful and beautiful girls!
...Mina...!
SHUUU

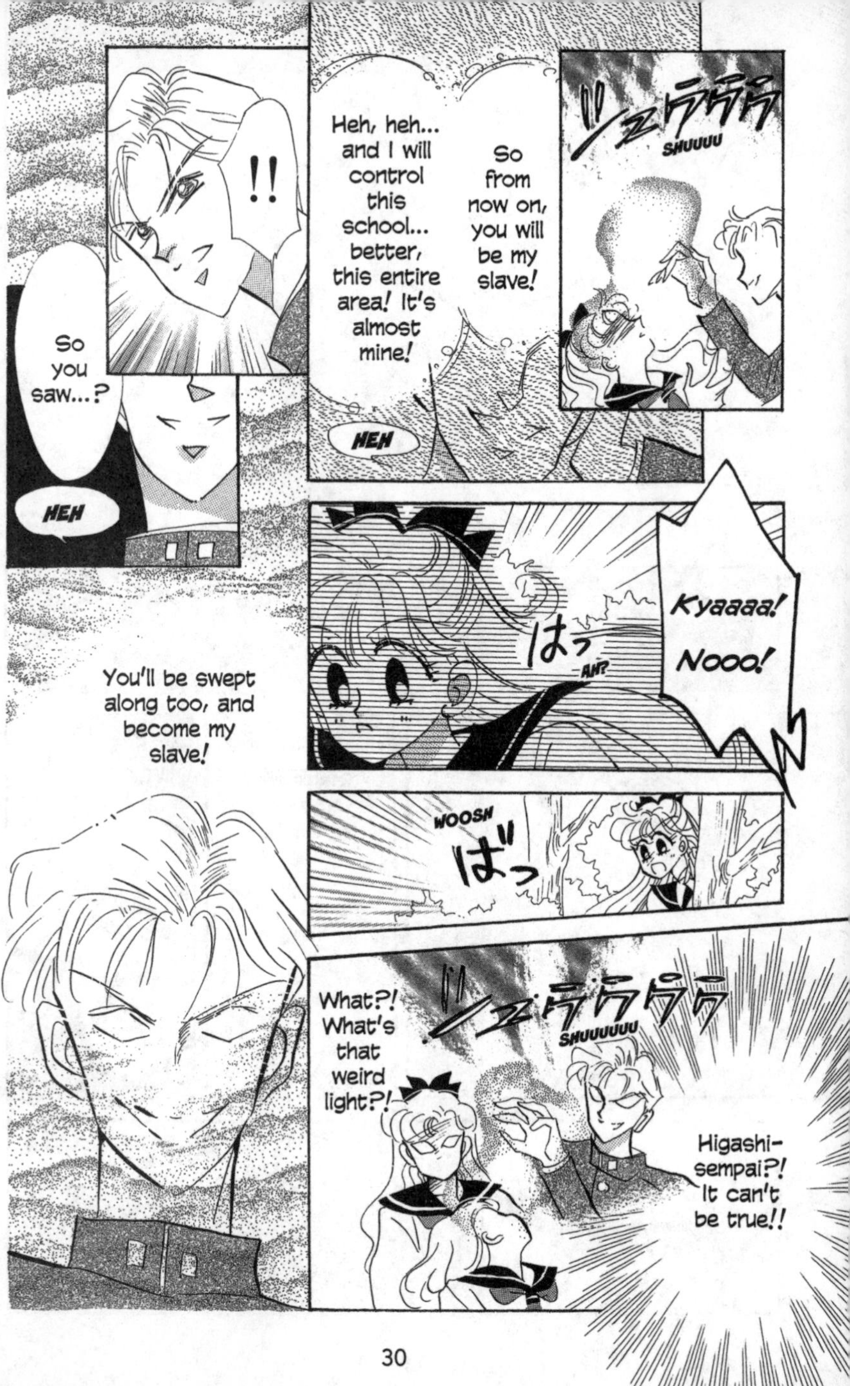

シュラララ
SHUUUU
So from now on, you will be my slave!
Heh, heh... and I will control this school... better, this entire area! It's almost mine!
HEH
!!
So you saw...?
HEH
Kyaaaa! Nooo!
はっ
AH?
WOOSH
ばっ
You'll be swept along too, and become my slave!
シュラララ
SHUUUUUU
Higashi-sempai?! It can't be true!!
What?! What's that weird light?!

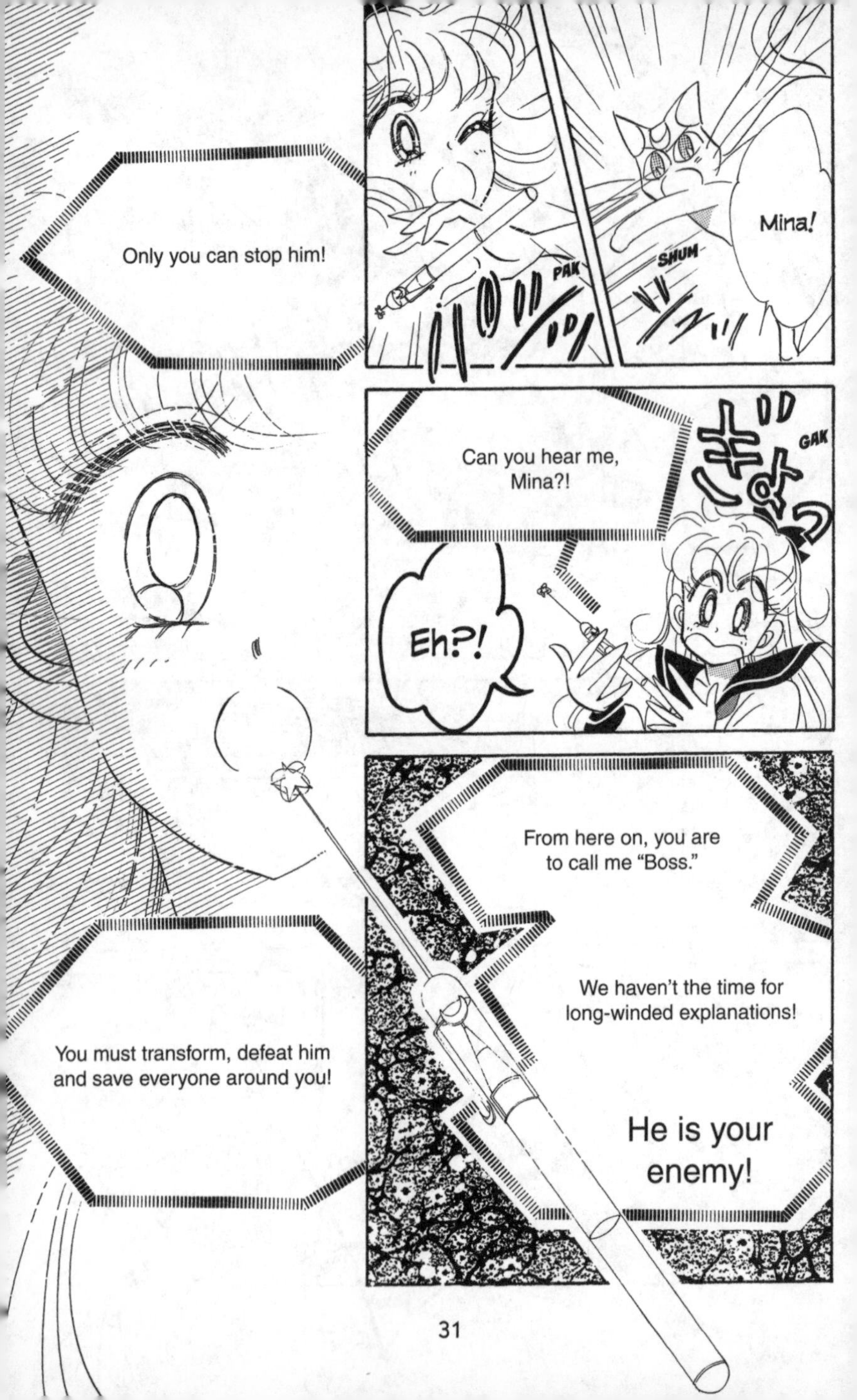
Mina!
SHUM
PAK
Can you hear me, Mina?!
GAK
Eh?!
From here on, you are to call me "Boss."
We haven't the time for long-winded explanations!
He is your enemy!
Only you can stop him!
You must transform, defeat him and save everyone around you!

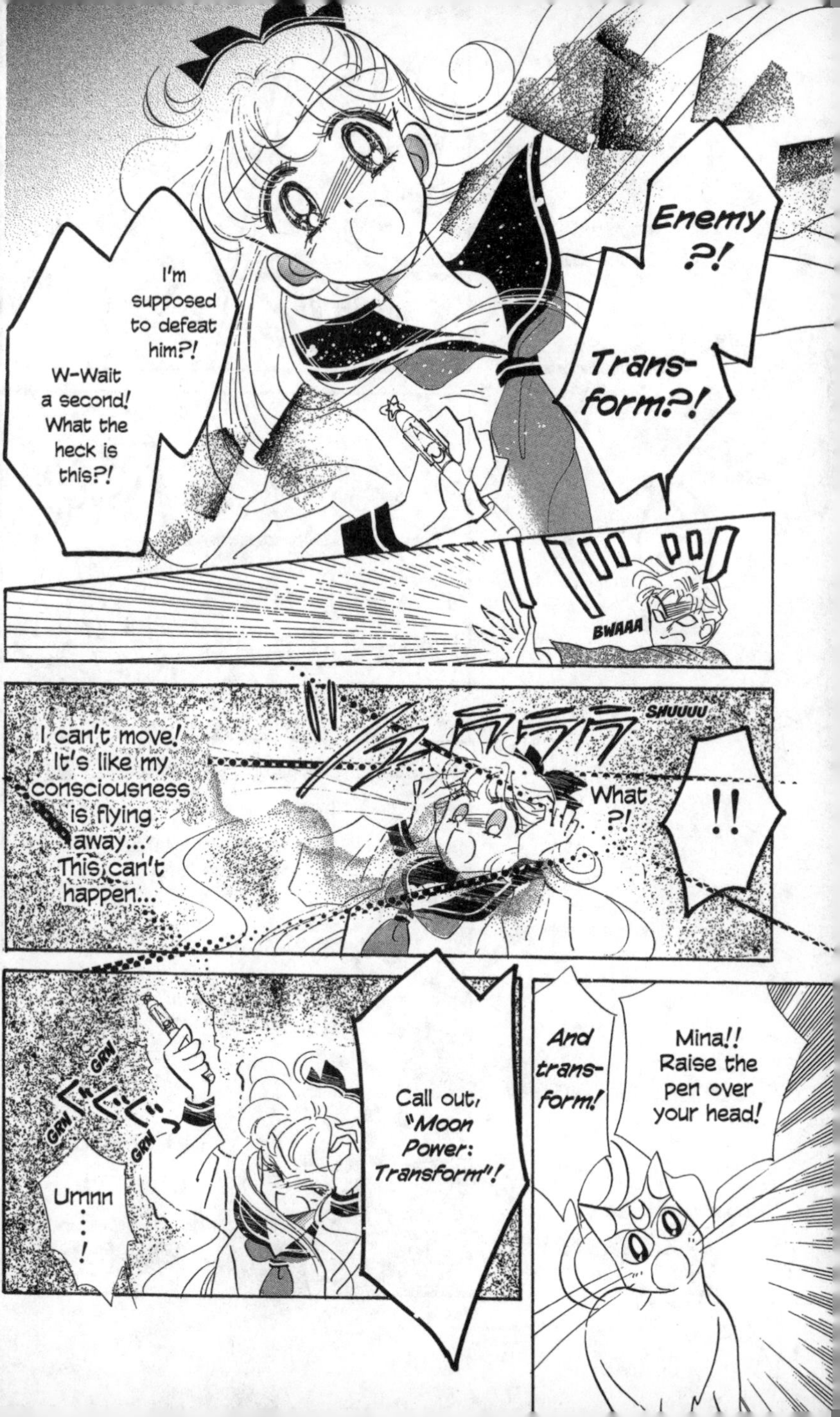
Enemy?!
Transform?!
I'm supposed to defeat him?!
W-Wait a second! What the heck is this?!
BWAAA
SHUUUU
!!
What?!
I can't move! It's like my consciousness is flying away... This can't happen...
Mina!! Raise the pen over your head!
And transform!
Call out, "Moon Power: Transform"!
GRN
GRN
GRN
GRN
Umnn...!

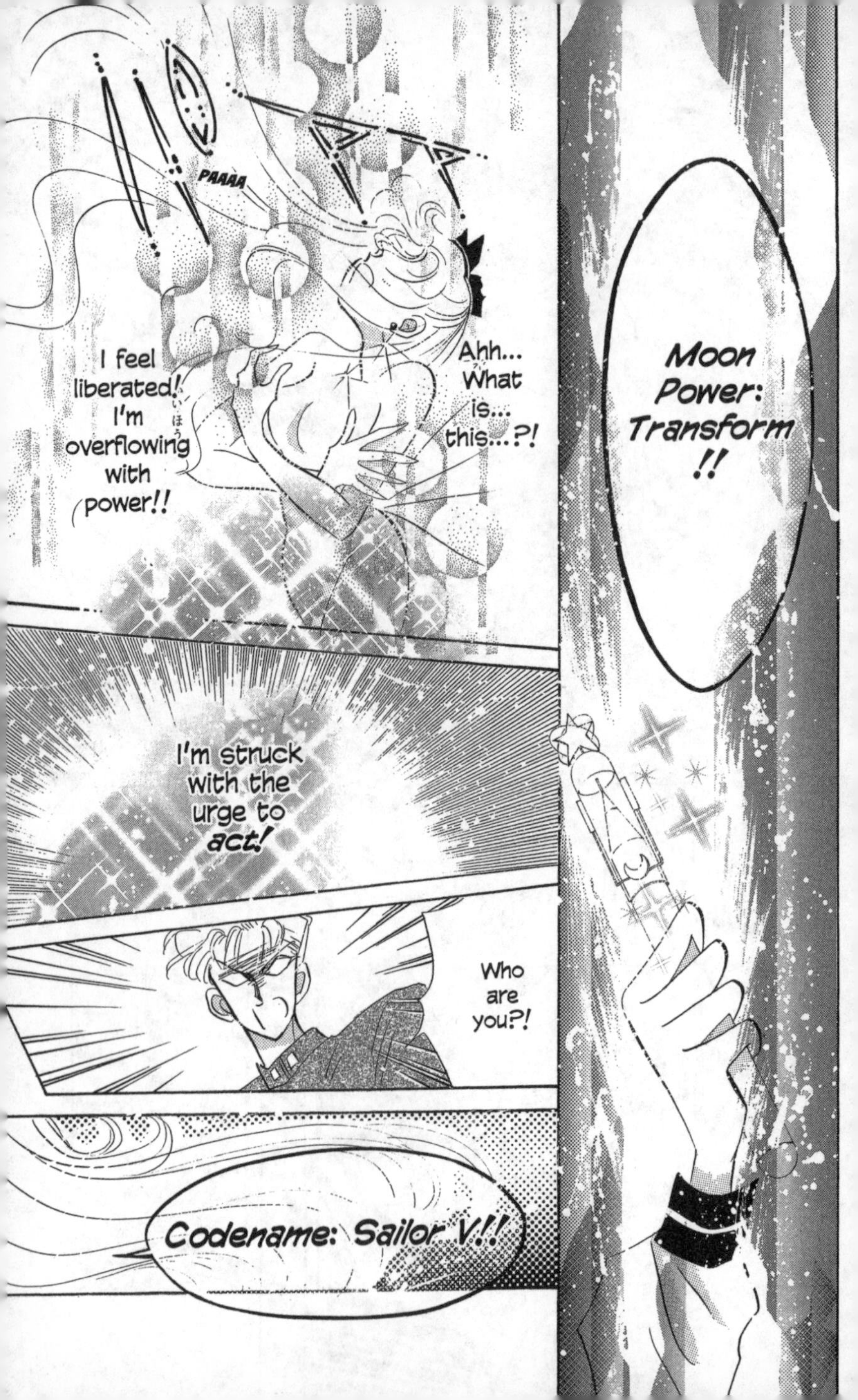
Moon Power: Transform!!
PAAAA
Ahh... What is... this...?!
I feel liberated! I'm overflowing with power!!
I'm struck with the urge to act!
Who are you?!
Codename: Sailor V!!

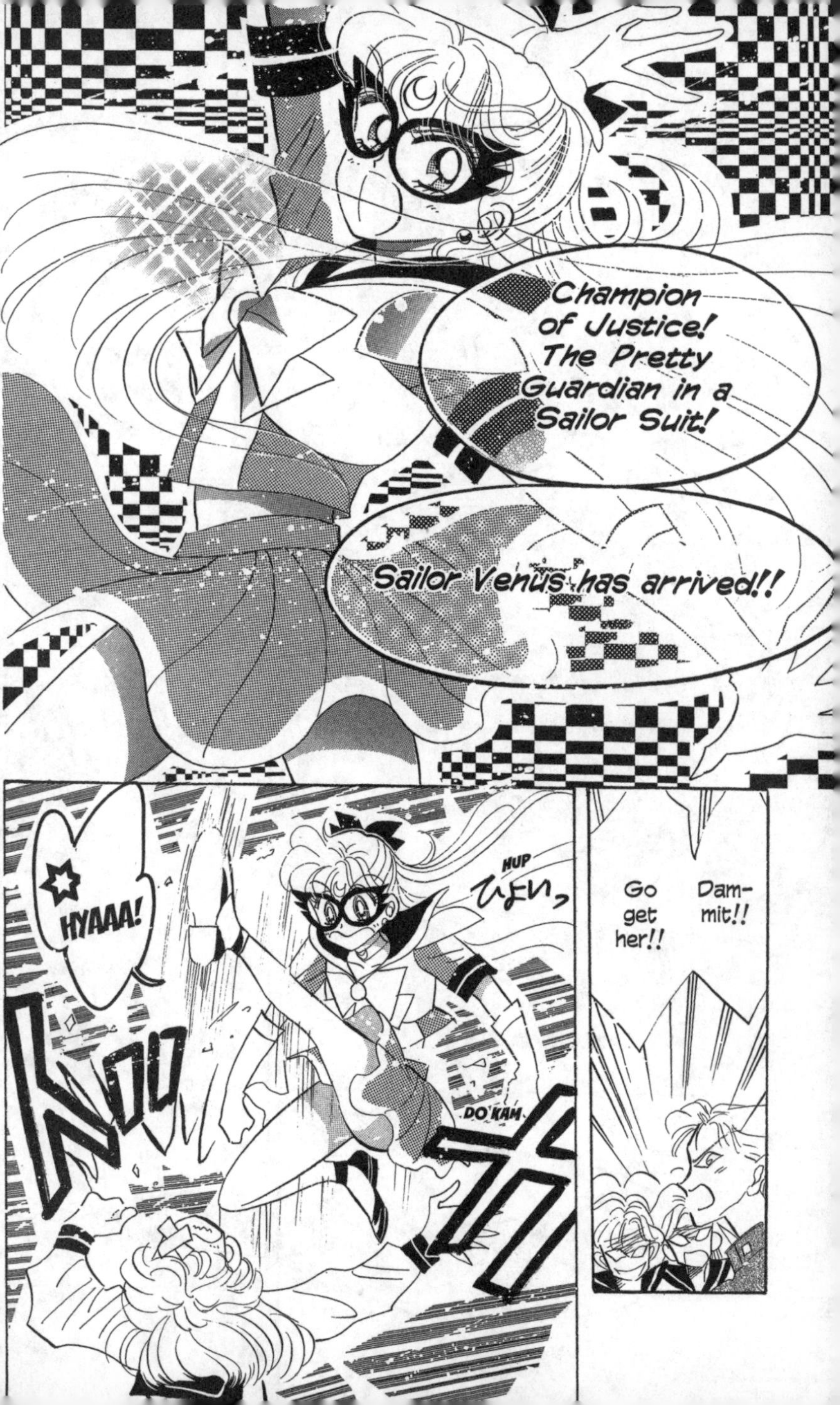
Champion of Justice! The Pretty Guardian in a Sailor Suit!
Sailor Venus has arrived!!
Dam-mit!!
Go get her!!
HUP
ひょいっ
HYAAA!
DO KAM

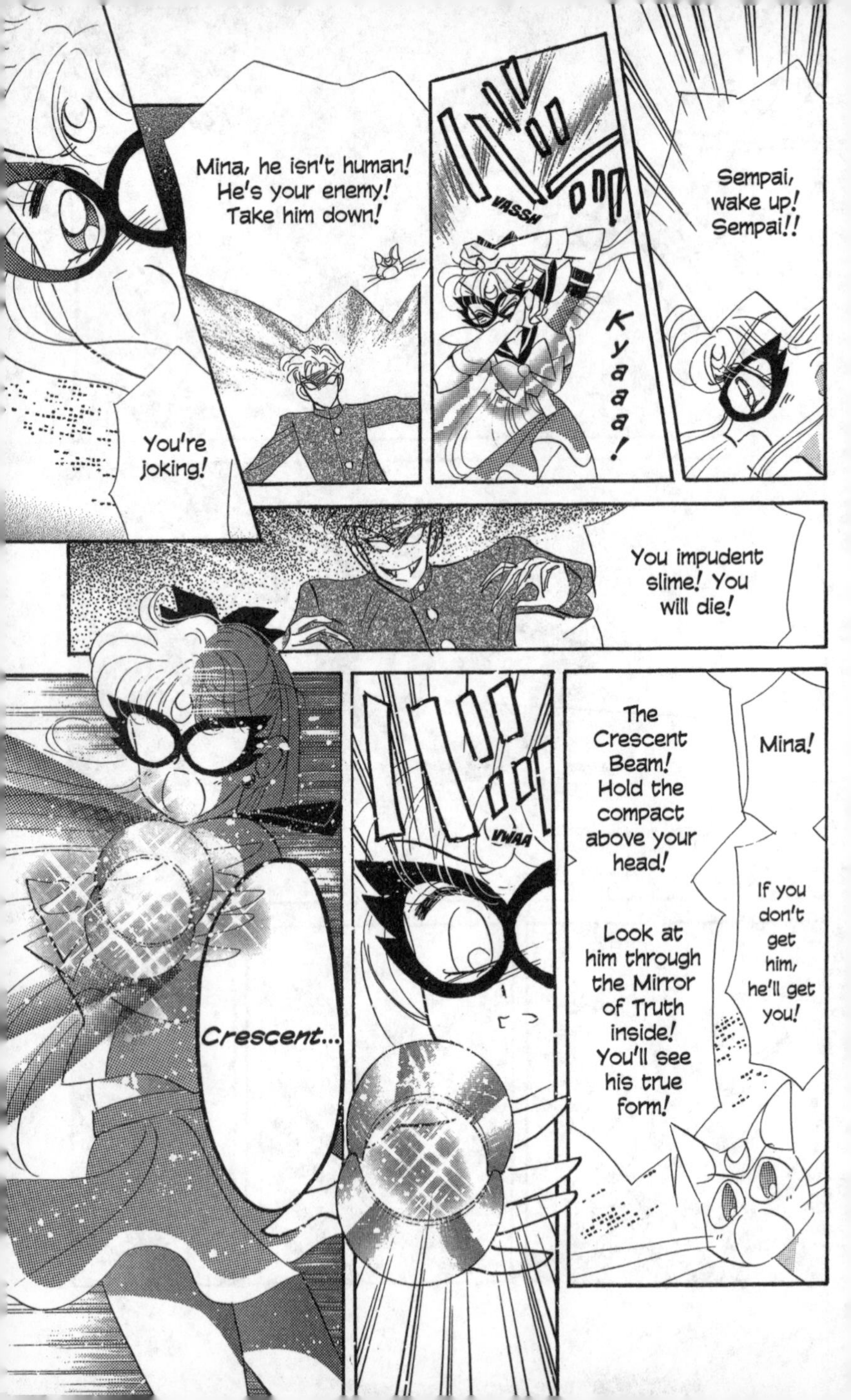
Sempai, wake up! Sempai!!
VASSH
Kyaaa!
Mina, he isn't human! He's your enemy! Take him down!
You're joking!
You impudent slime! You will die!
Mina!
If you don't get him, he'll get you!
The Crescent Beam! Hold the compact above your head!
Look at him through the Mirror of Truth inside! You'll see his true form!
VWAA
Crescent...

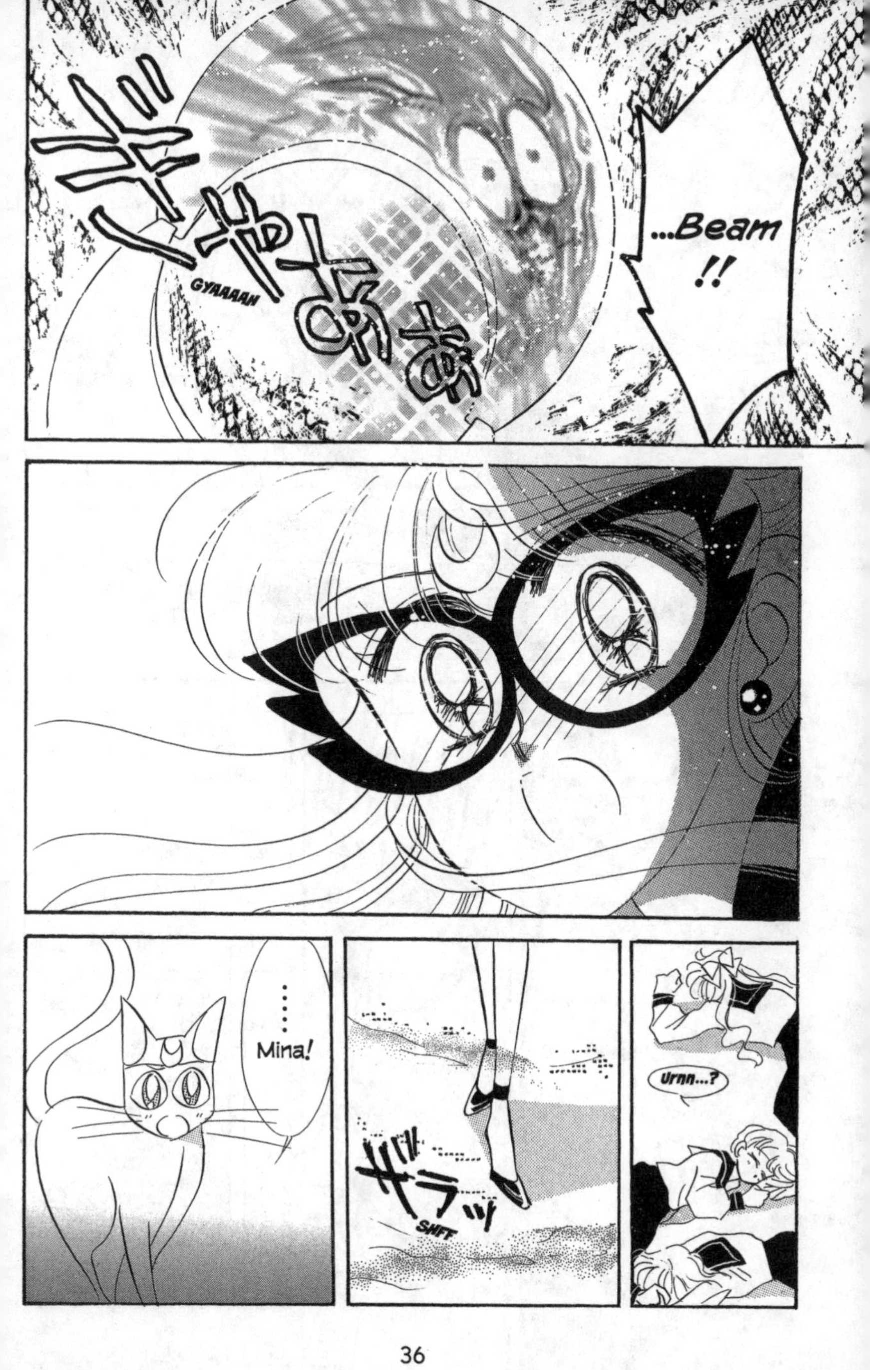
...Beam !!
GYAAAAN
Urnn...?
SHFF
......Mina!

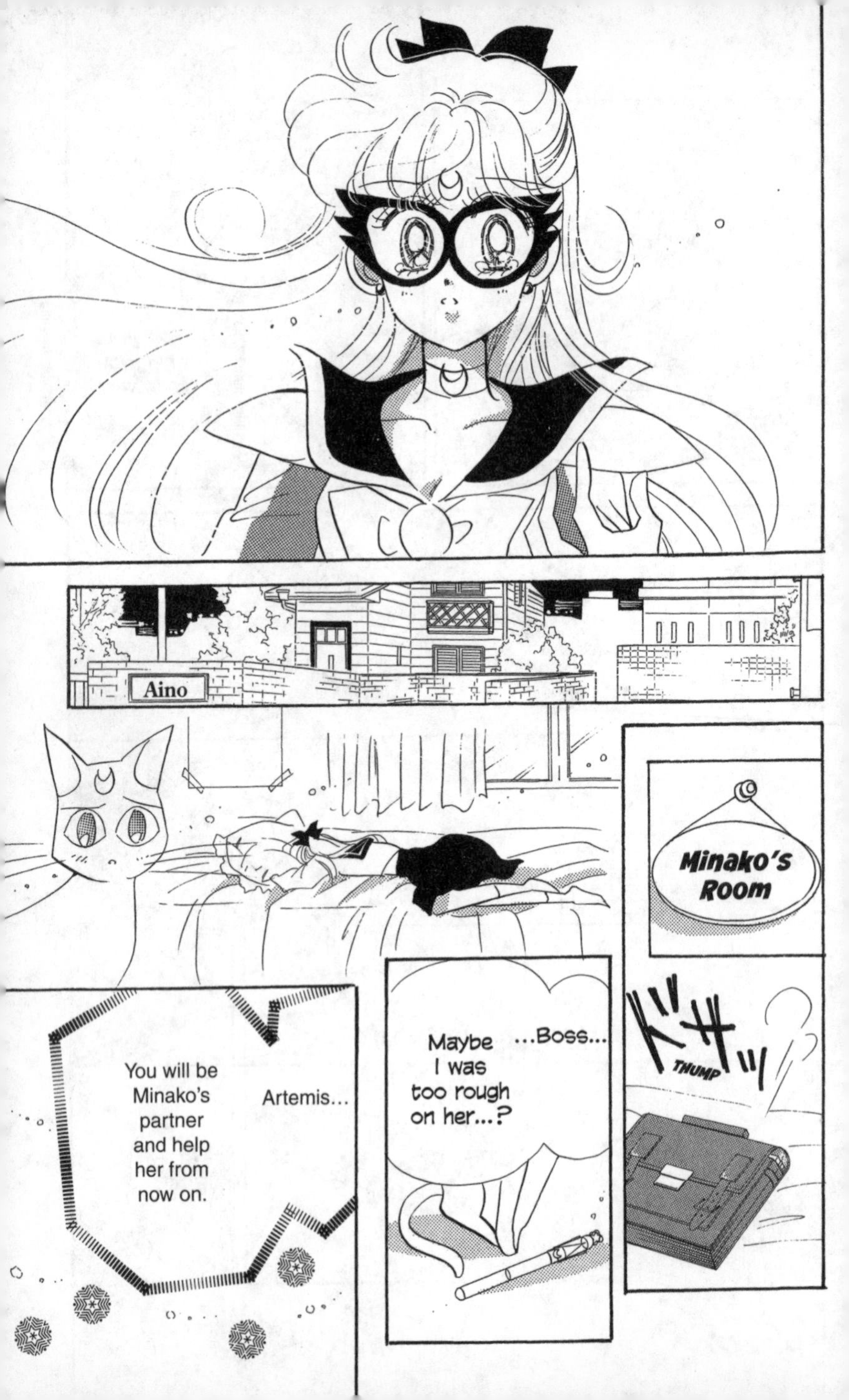
Aino
Minako's Room
ドサッ
THUMP
...Boss...
Maybe I was too rough on her...?
Artemis...
You will be Minako's partner and help her from now on.

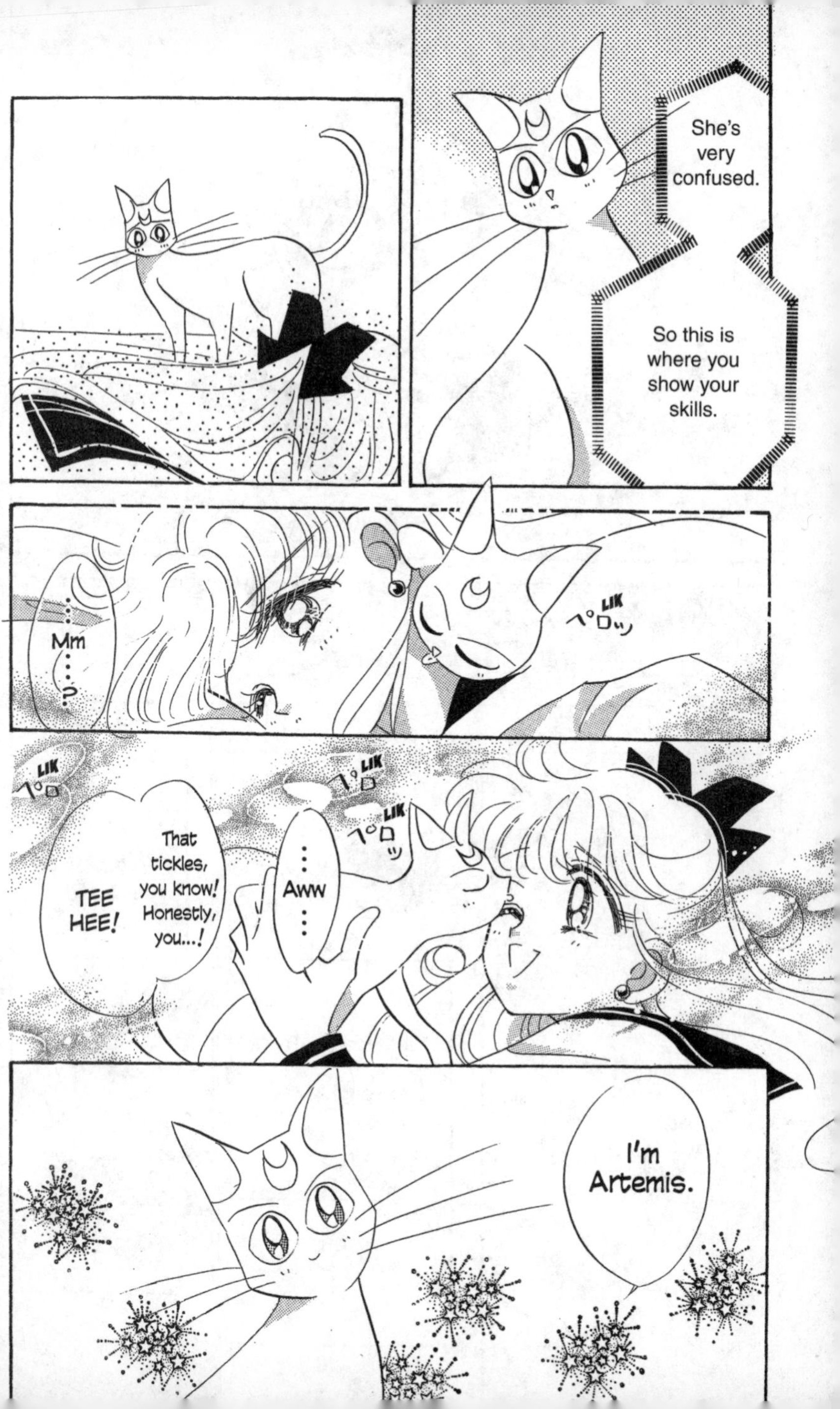
She's very confused.
So this is where you show your skills.
LIK
ペロッ
...Mm...?
LIK
ペロッ
LIK
ペロ
LIK
ペロ
...Aww...
That tickles, you know! Honestly, you...!
TEE HEE!
I'm Artemis.

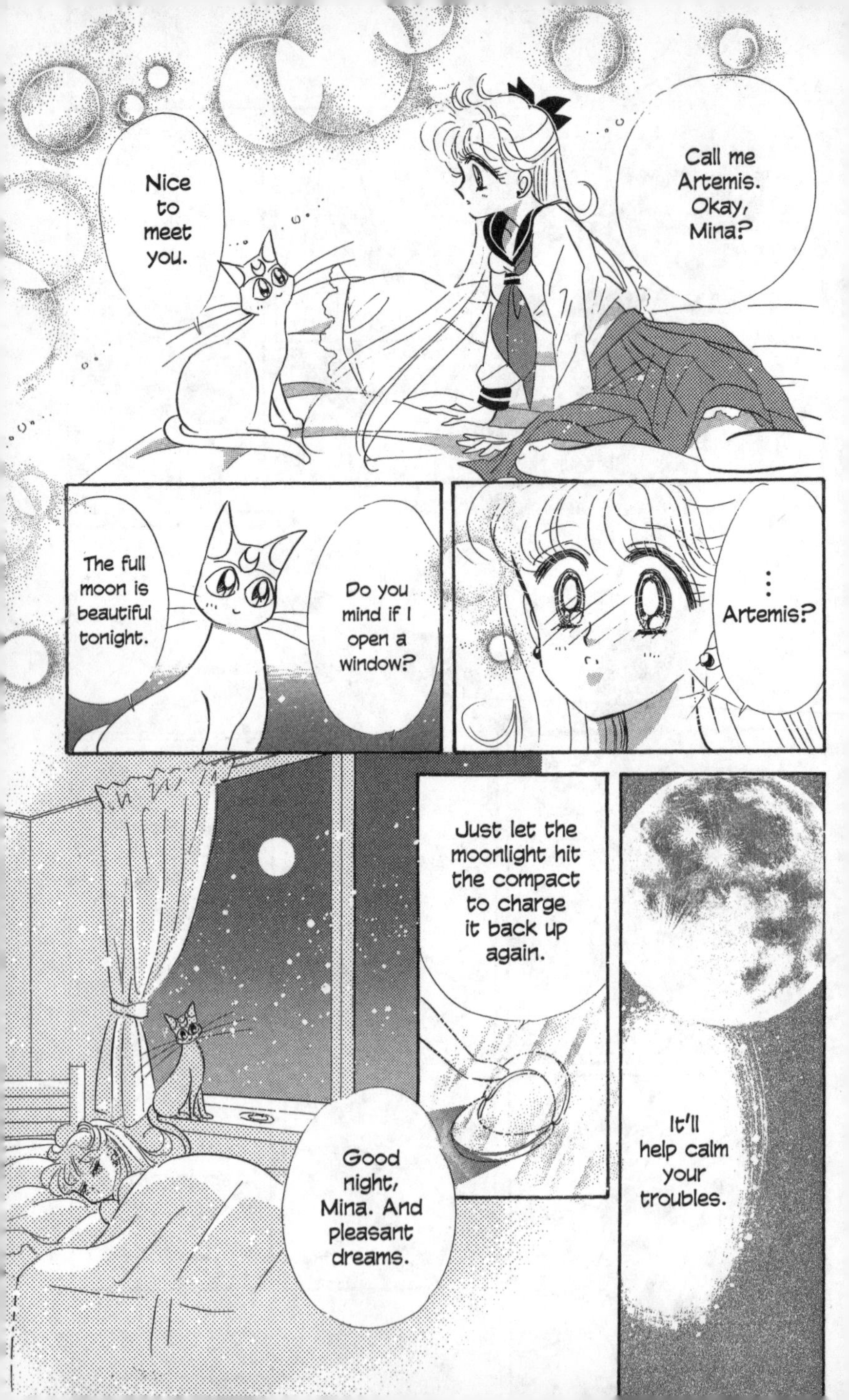
Call me Artemis. Okay, Mina?
Nice to meet you.
... Artemis?
Do you mind if I open a window?
The full moon is beautiful tonight.
It'll help calm your troubles.
Just let the moonlight hit the compact to charge it back up again.
Good night, Mina. And pleasant dreams.

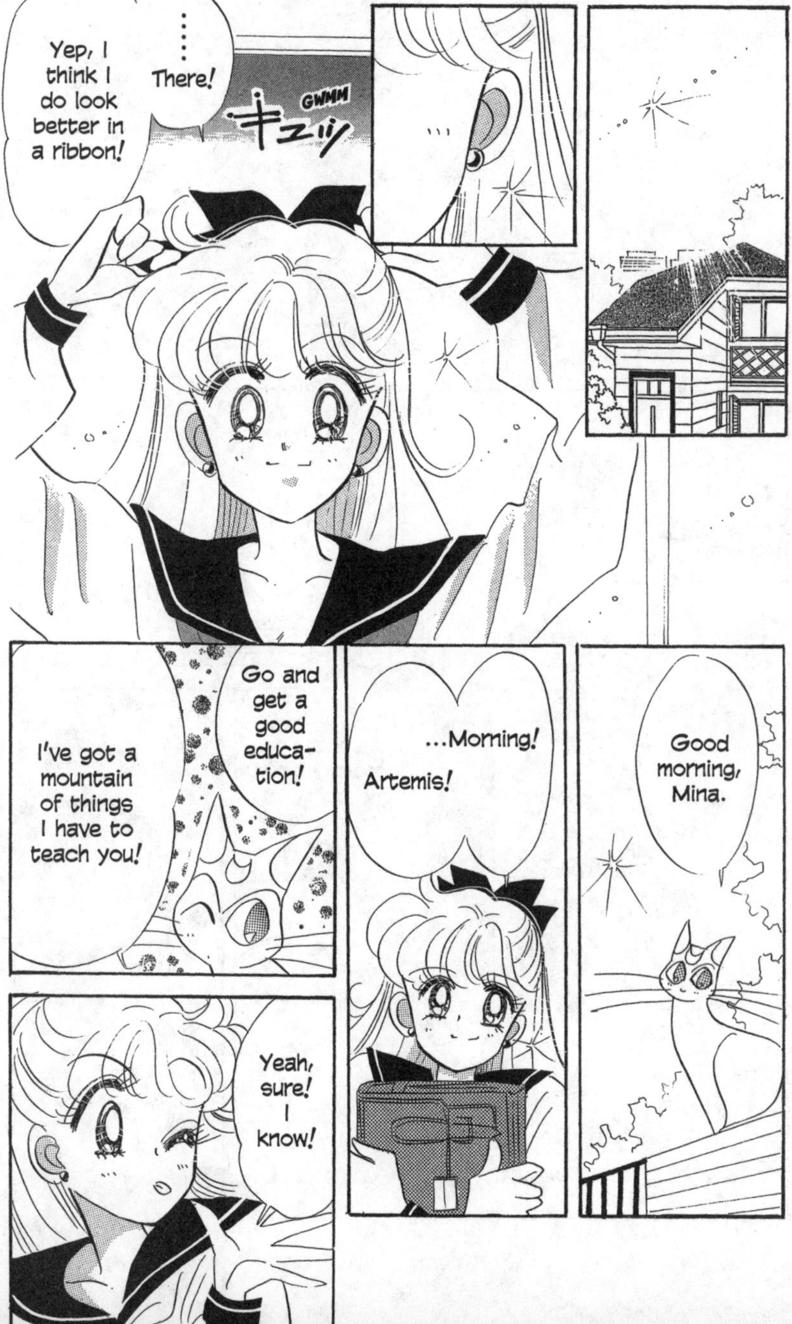

......There!
GWMM
キュッ
Yep, I think I do look better in a ribbon!
Good morning, Mina.
...Morning! Artemis!
Go and get a good education!
I've got a mountain of things I have to teach you!
Yeah, sure! I know!

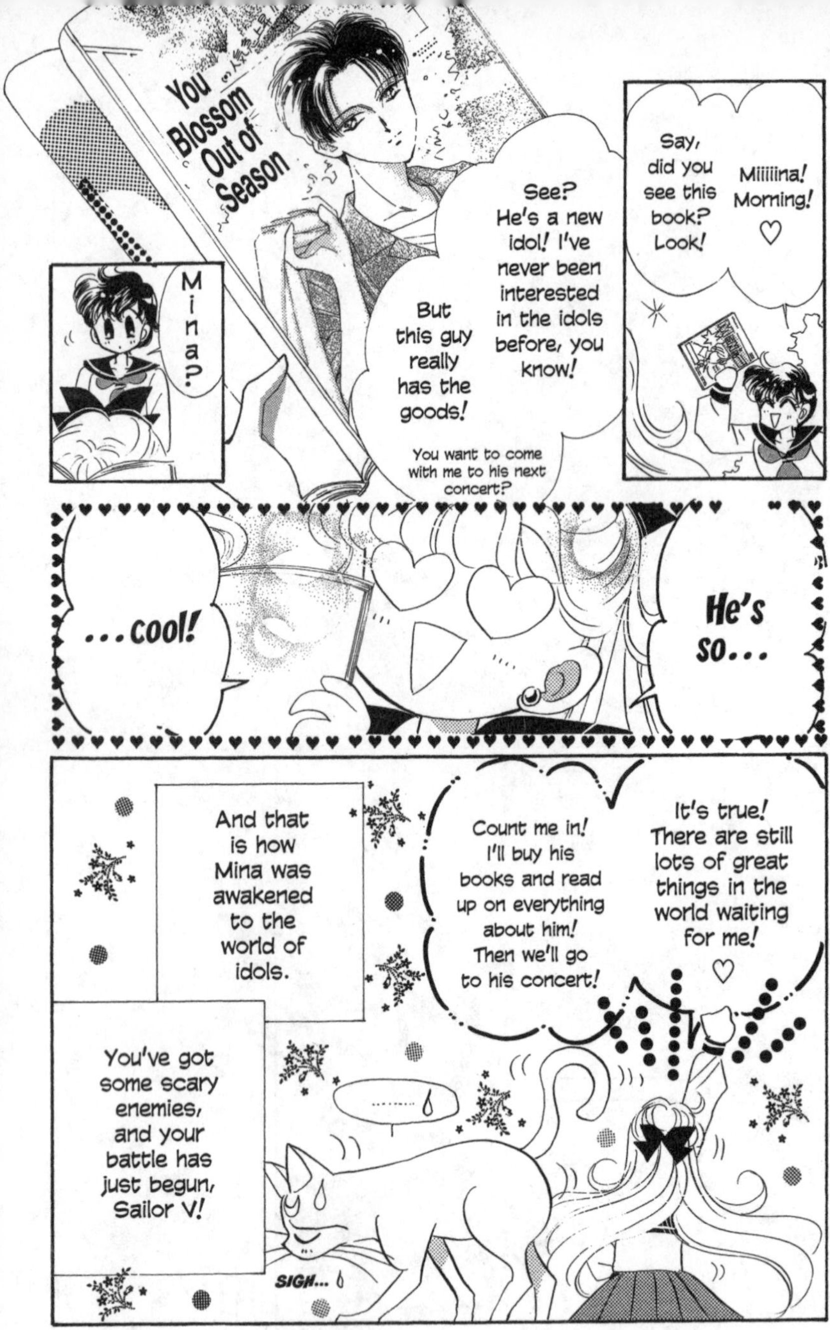
Miiiiina! Morning! ♡
Say, did you see this book? Look!
You Blossom Out of Season
See? He's a new idol! I've never been interested in the idols before, you know!
But this guy really has the goods!
You want to come with me to his next concert?
Mina?
He's so...
...cool!
It's true! There are still lots of great things in the world waiting for me! ♡
Count me in! I'll buy his books and read up on everything about him! Then we'll go to his concert!
And that is how Mina was awakened to the world of idols.
....
You've got some scary enemies, and your battle has just begun, Sailor V!
SIGH...

•The End•

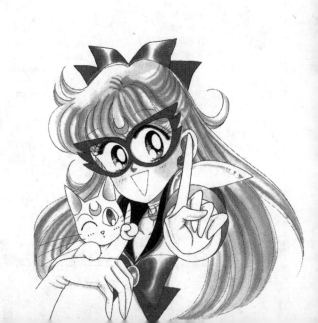

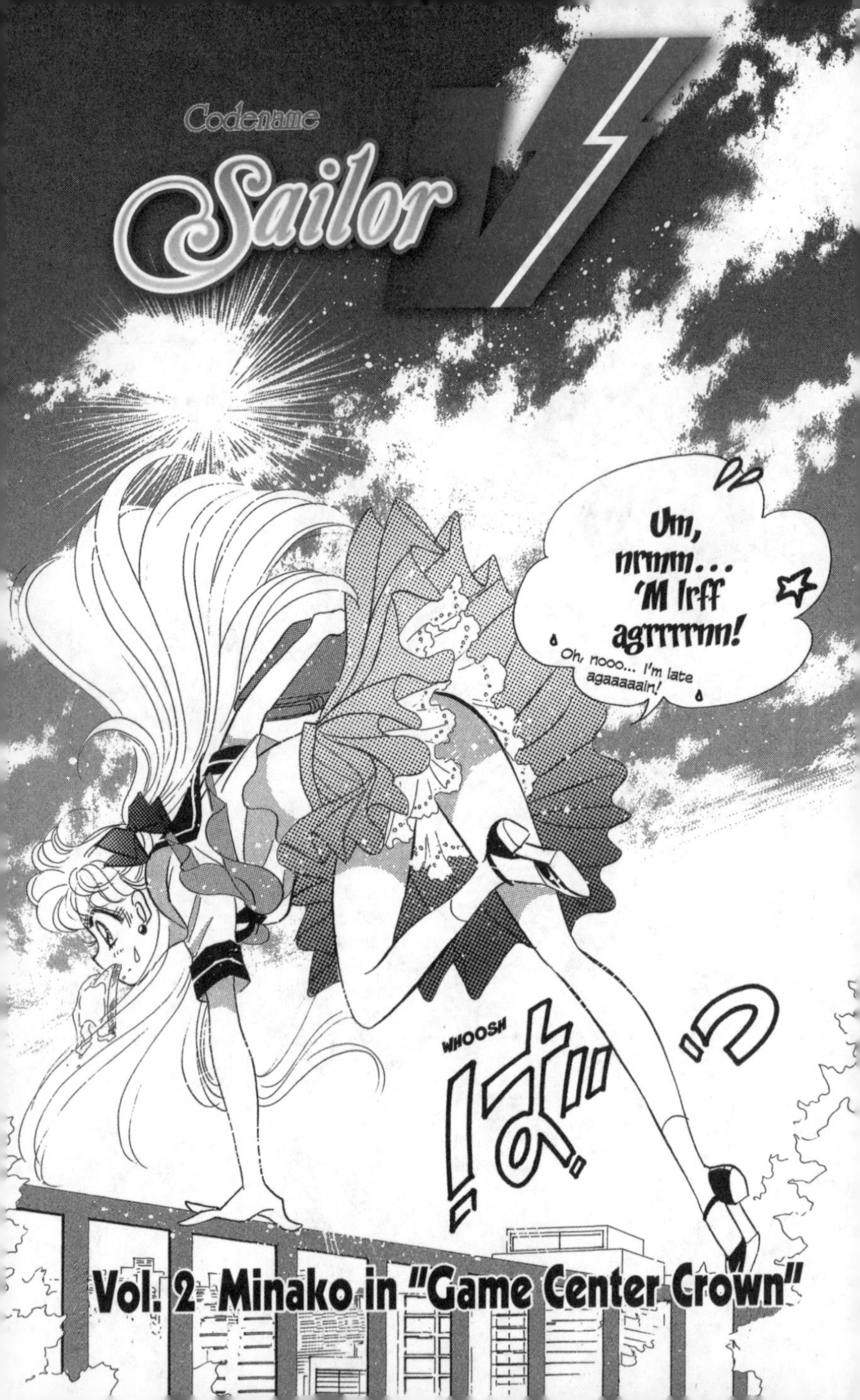
Codename Sailor V
Um, nrmm... 'M lrff agrrrrnn!
Oh, nooo... I'm late agaaaaain!
WHOOSH
ばっ
Vol. 2 Minako in "Game Center Crown"

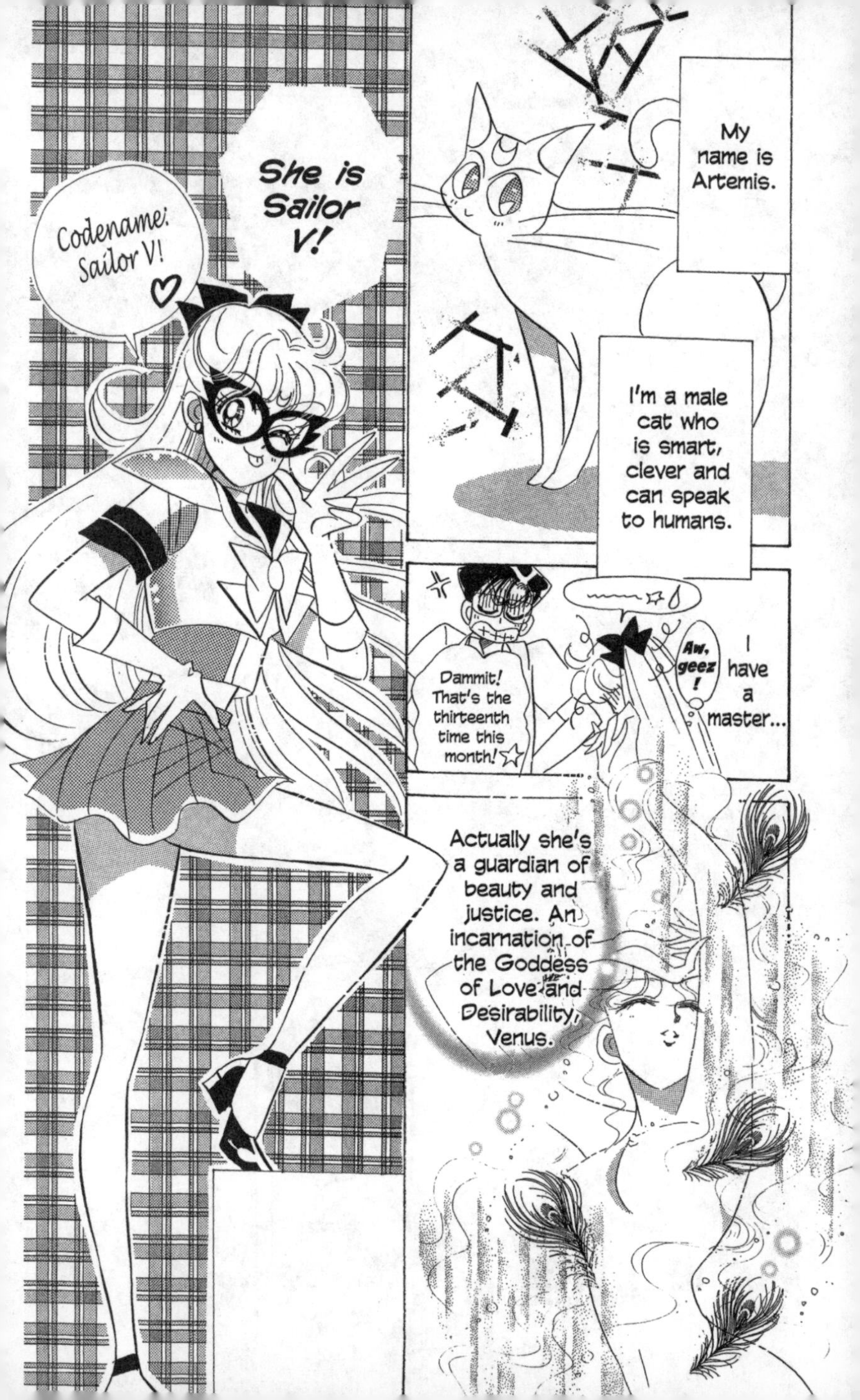
My name is Artemis.
I'm a male cat who is smart, clever and can speak to humans.
I have a master...
Aw, geez!
Dammit! That's the thirteenth time this month! ☆
Actually she's a guardian of beauty and justice. An incarnation of the Goddess of Love and Desirability, Venus.
She is Sailor V!
Codename: Sailor V! ♡

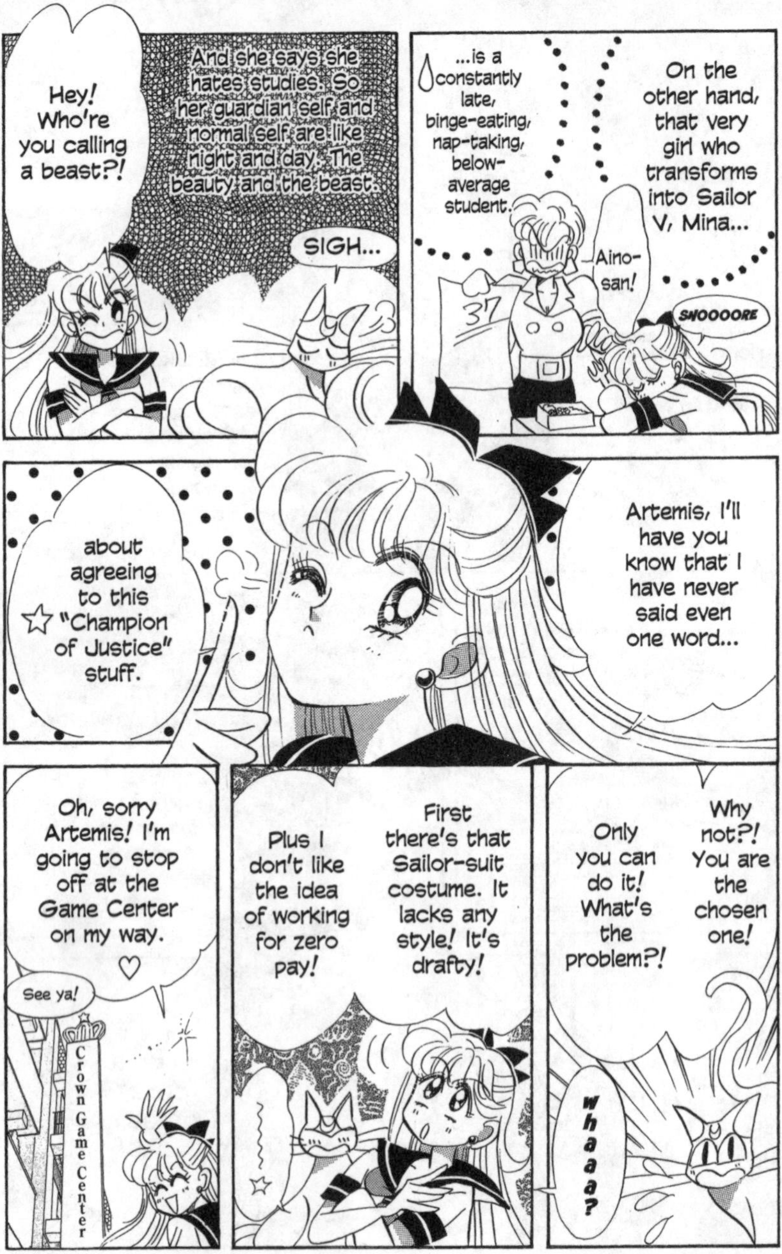

On the other hand, that very girl who transforms into Sailor V, Mina...
...is a constantly late, binge-eating, nap-taking, below-average student.
Aino-san!
SNOOOORE
And she says she hates studies. So her guardian self and normal self are like night and day. The beauty and the beast.
SIGH...
Hey! Who're you calling a beast?!
Artemis, I'll have you know that I have never said even one word...
about agreeing to this ☆ "Champion of Justice" stuff.
Why not?! You are the chosen one!
Only you can do it! What's the problem?!
Whaaa?
First there's that Sailor-suit costume. It lacks any style! It's drafty!
Plus I don't like the idea of working for zero pay!
Oh, sorry Artemis! I'm going to stop off at the Game Center on my way. ♡
See ya!
Crown Game Center

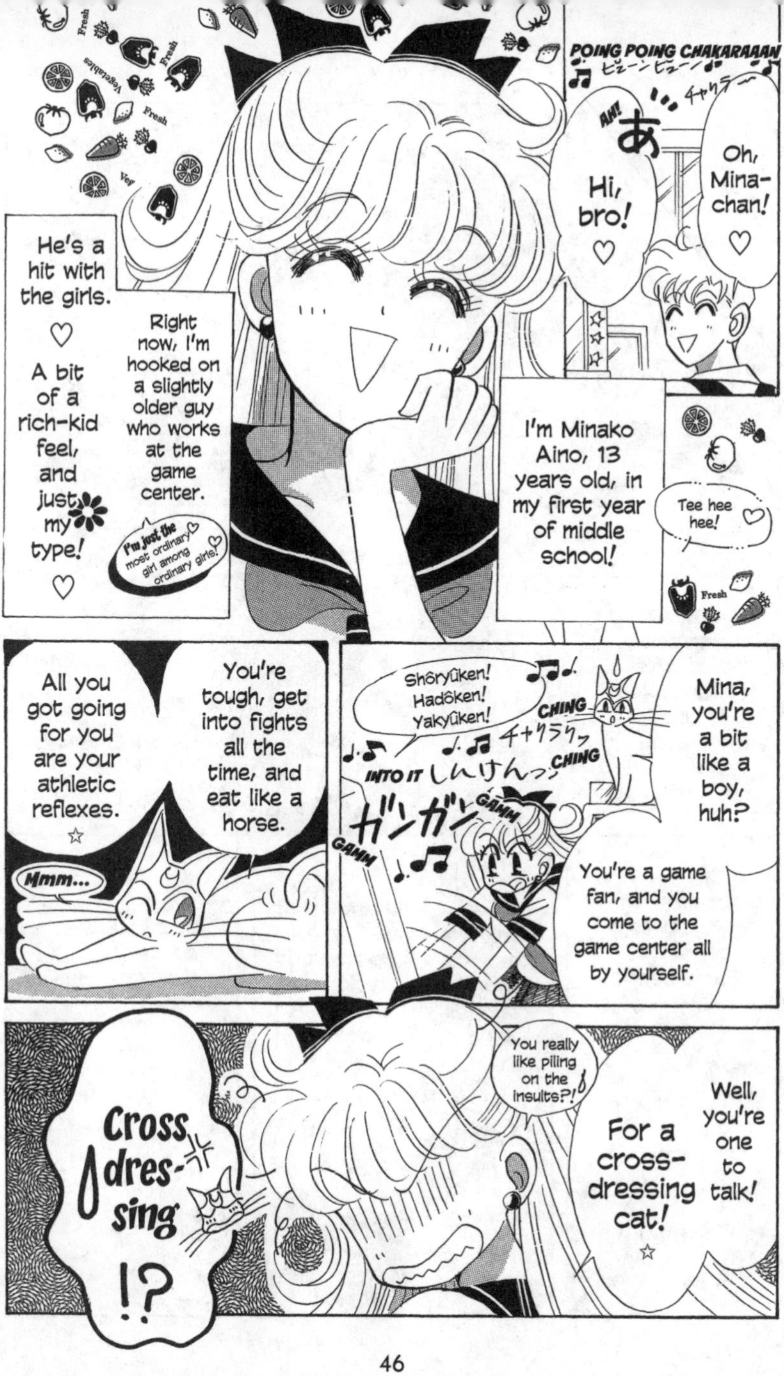
POING POING CHAKARAAAN
AH!
Oh, Mina-chan!
Hi, bro!
I'm Minako Aino, 13 years old, in my first year of middle school!
Tee hee hee!
Right now, I'm hooked on a slightly older guy who works at the game center.
He's a hit with the girls. A bit of a rich-kid feel, and just my type!
I'm just the most ordinary girl among ordinary girls
Mina, you're a bit like a boy, huh?
You're a game fan, and you come to the game center all by yourself.
CHING
CHING
Shôryûken! Hadôken! Yakyûken!
INTO IT
GAMM
GAMM
You're tough, get into fights all the time, and eat like a horse.
All you got going for you are your athletic reflexes.
Mmm...
Well, you're one to talk!
For a cross-dressing cat!
You really like piling on the insults?!
Cross dres-sing !?

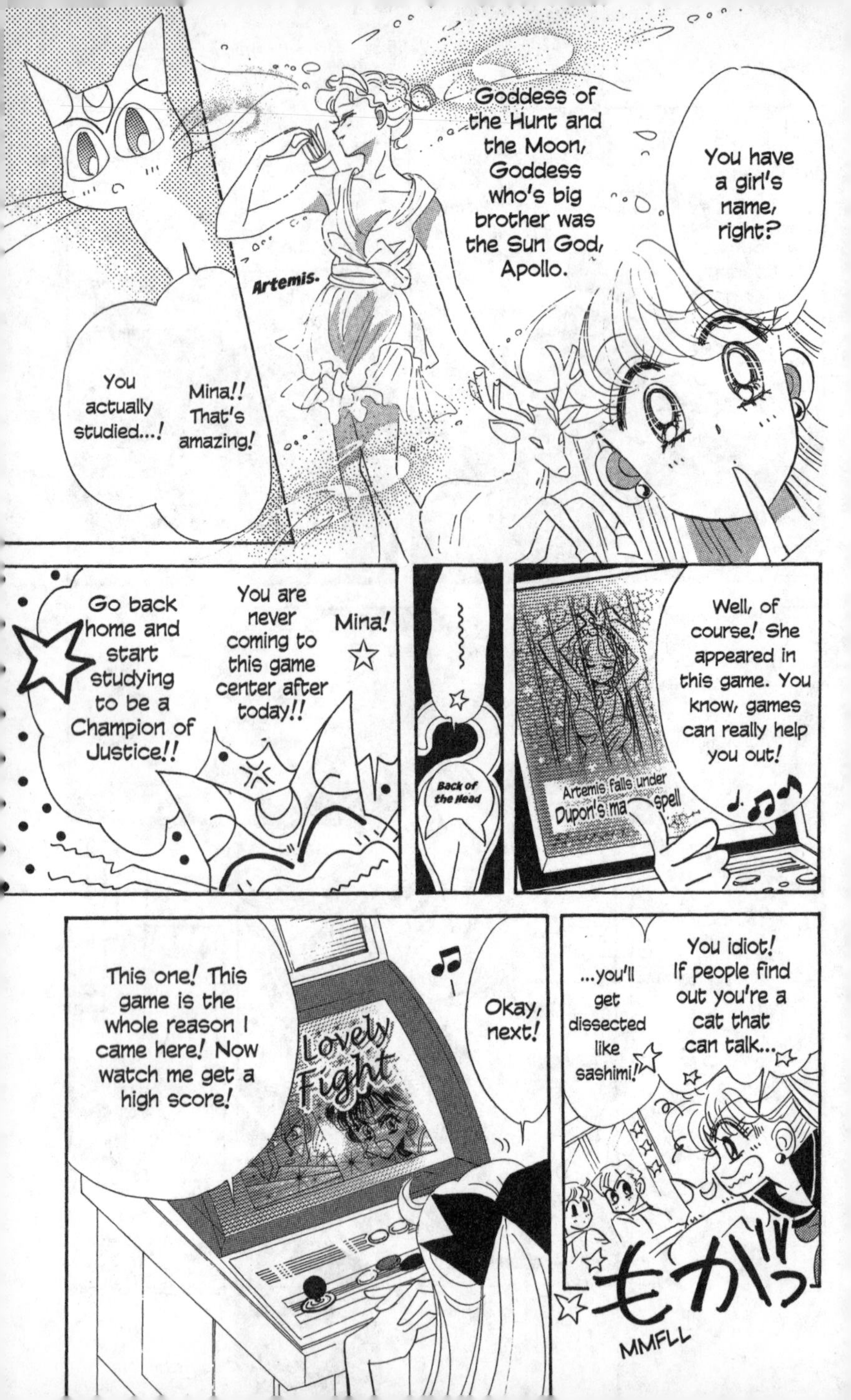
You have a girl's name, right?
Goddess of the Hunt and the Moon, Goddess who's big brother was the Sun God, Apollo.
Artemis.
Mina!! That's amazing!
You actually studied...!
Well, of course! She appeared in this game. You know, games can really help you out!
Artemis falls under
Dupon's ma
spell
Back of the Head
Mina!
You are never coming to this game center after today!!
Go back home and start studying to be a Champion of Justice!!
You idiot! If people find out you're a cat that can talk...
...you'll get dissected like sashimi!
もがっ
MMFLL
Okay, next!
Lovely Fight
This one! This game is the whole reason I came here! Now watch me get a high score!

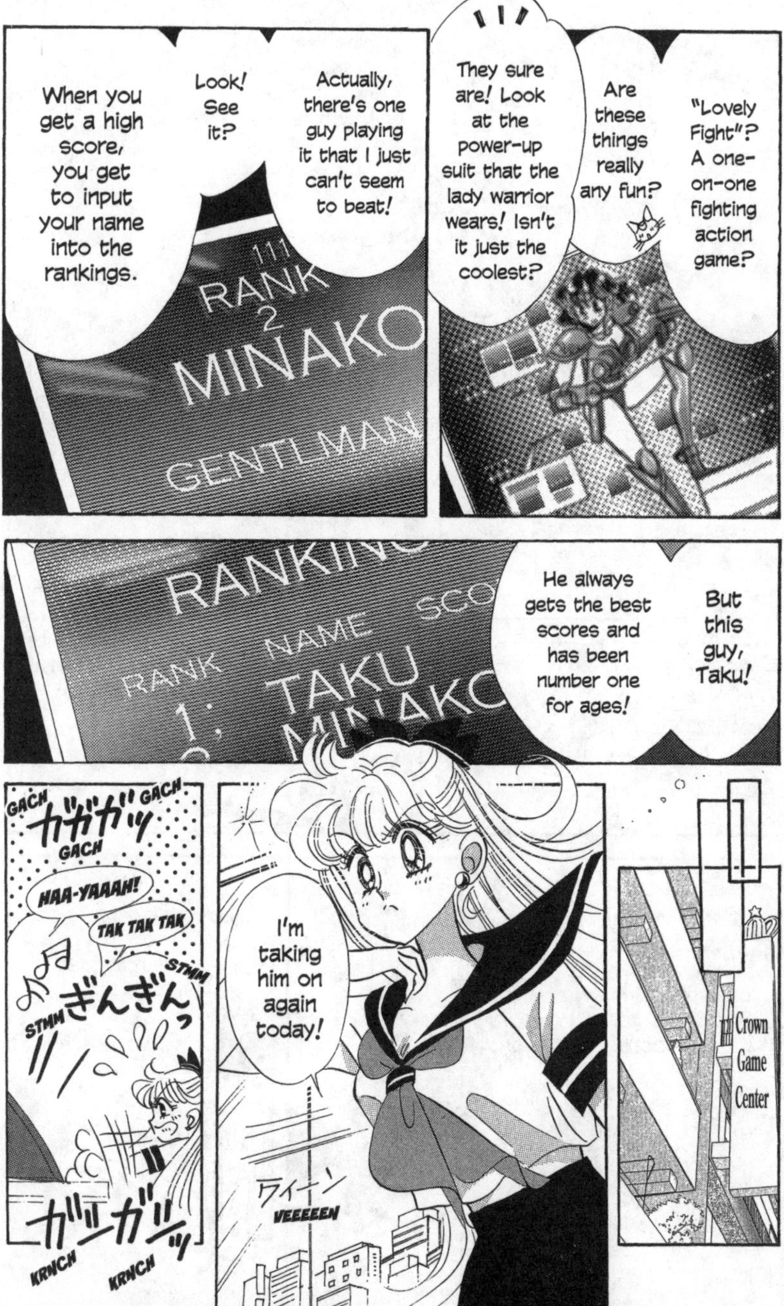
"Lovely Fight"? A one-on-one fighting action game?
Are these things really any fun?
!!!
They sure are! Look at the power-up suit that the lady warrior wears! Isn't it just the coolest?
Actually, there's one guy playing it that I just can't seem to beat!
Look! See it?
When you get a high score, you get to input your name into the rankings.
RANK 2
MINAKO
GENTLMAN
But this guy, Taku!
He always gets the best scores and has been number one for ages!
RANKING
RANK NAME SCO
1: TAKU
MINAKO
Crown Game Center
I'm taking him on again today!
ワイーン
VEEEEEN
ガガガッ
GACH GACH GACH
HAA-YAAAH!
TAK TAK TAK
ぎんぎん
STMM STMM
ガッガッ
KRNCH KRNCH

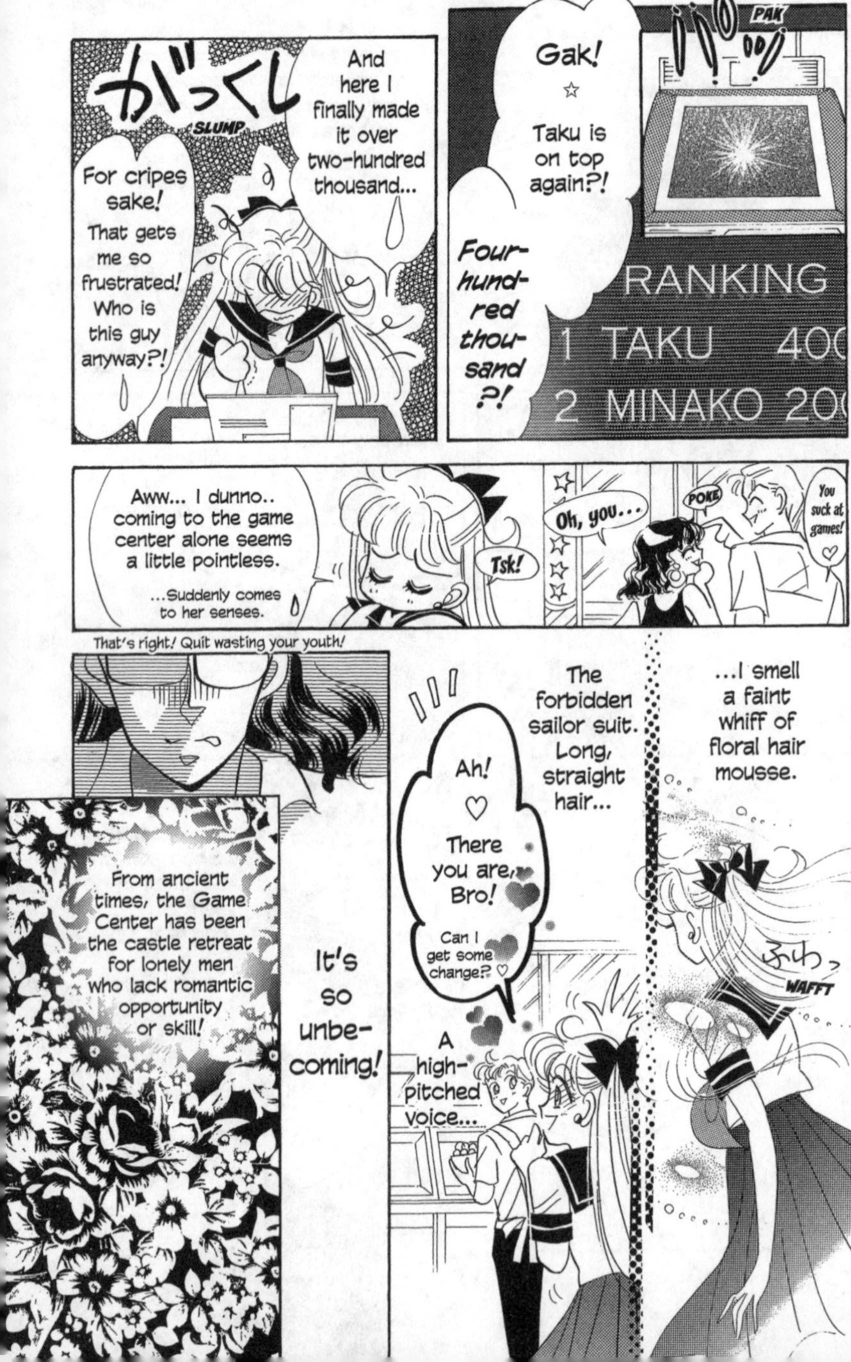
PAK
Gak! ☆ Taku is on top again?!
Four-hundred thousand?!
RANKING
1 TAKU 40
2 MINAKO 20
がっくし
SLUMP
And here I finally made it over two-hundred thousand...
For cripes sake! That gets me so frustrated! Who is this guy anyway?!
You suck at games! ♡
POKE
Oh, you...
Tsk!
Aww... I dunno.. coming to the game center alone seems a little pointless.
...Suddenly comes to her senses.
That's right! Quit wasting your youth!
...I smell a faint whiff of floral hair mousse.
ふわっ
WAFFT
The forbidden sailor suit. Long, straight hair...
Ah! ♡ There you are, Bro!
Can I get some change? ♡
A high-pitched voice...
From ancient times, the Game Center has been the castle retreat for lonely men who lack romantic opportunity or skill!
It's so unbecoming!

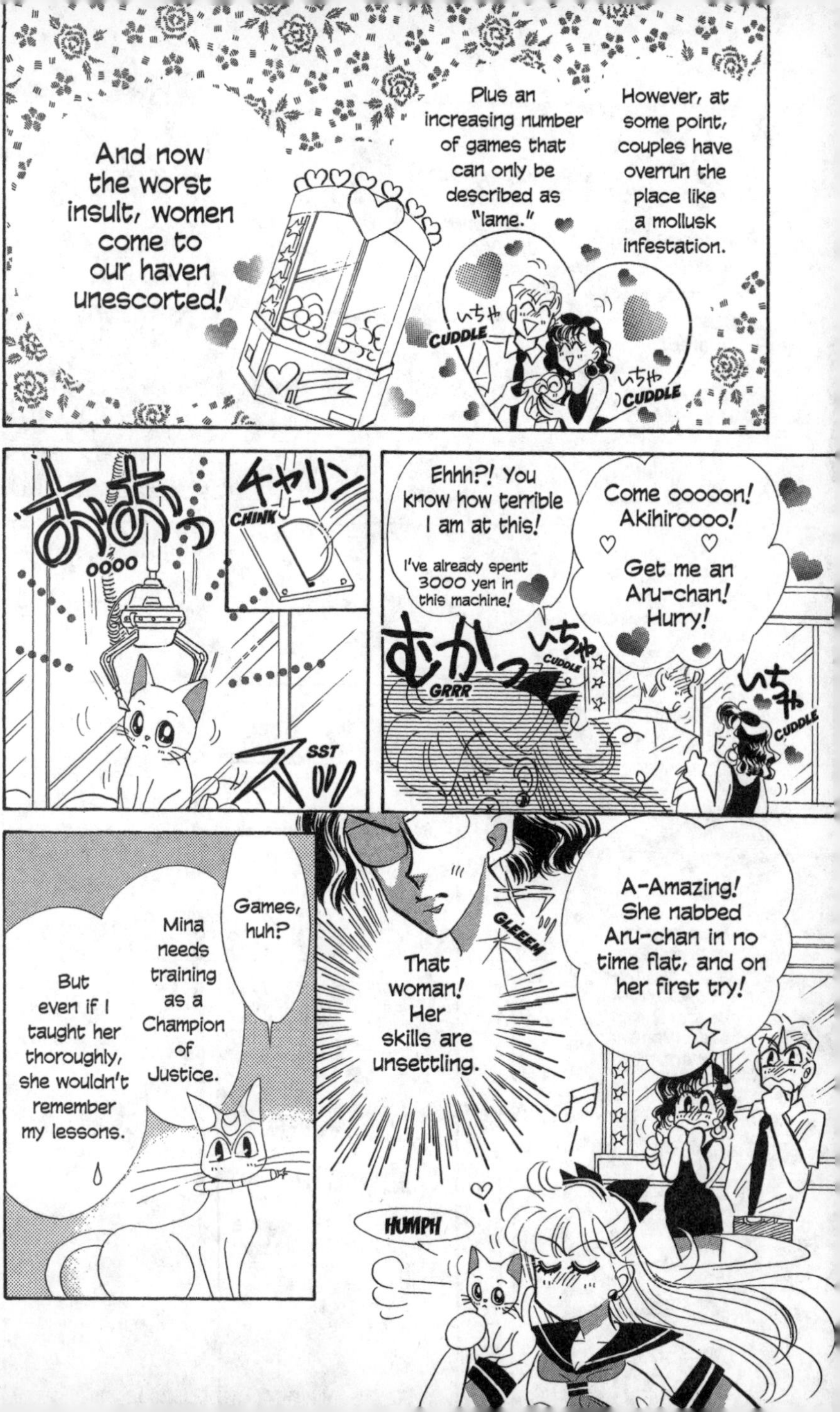

However, at some point, couples have overrun the place like a mollusk infestation.
Plus an increasing number of games that can only be described as "lame."
And now the worst insult, women come to our haven unescorted!
いちゃ CUDDLE
いちゃ CUDDLE
Come oooooon! Akihiroooo!
Get me an Aru-chan! Hurry!
Ehhh?! You know how terrible I am at this!
I've already spent 3000 yen in this machine!
いちゃ CUDDLE
いちゃ CUDDLE
むかっ GRRR
チャリン CHINK
おおっ OOOO
ス SST
A-Amazing! She nabbed Aru-chan in no time flat, and on her first try!
GLEEEM
That woman! Her skills are unsettling.
HUMPH
Games, huh?
Mina needs training as a Champion of Justice.
But even if I taught her thoroughly, she wouldn't remember my lessons.

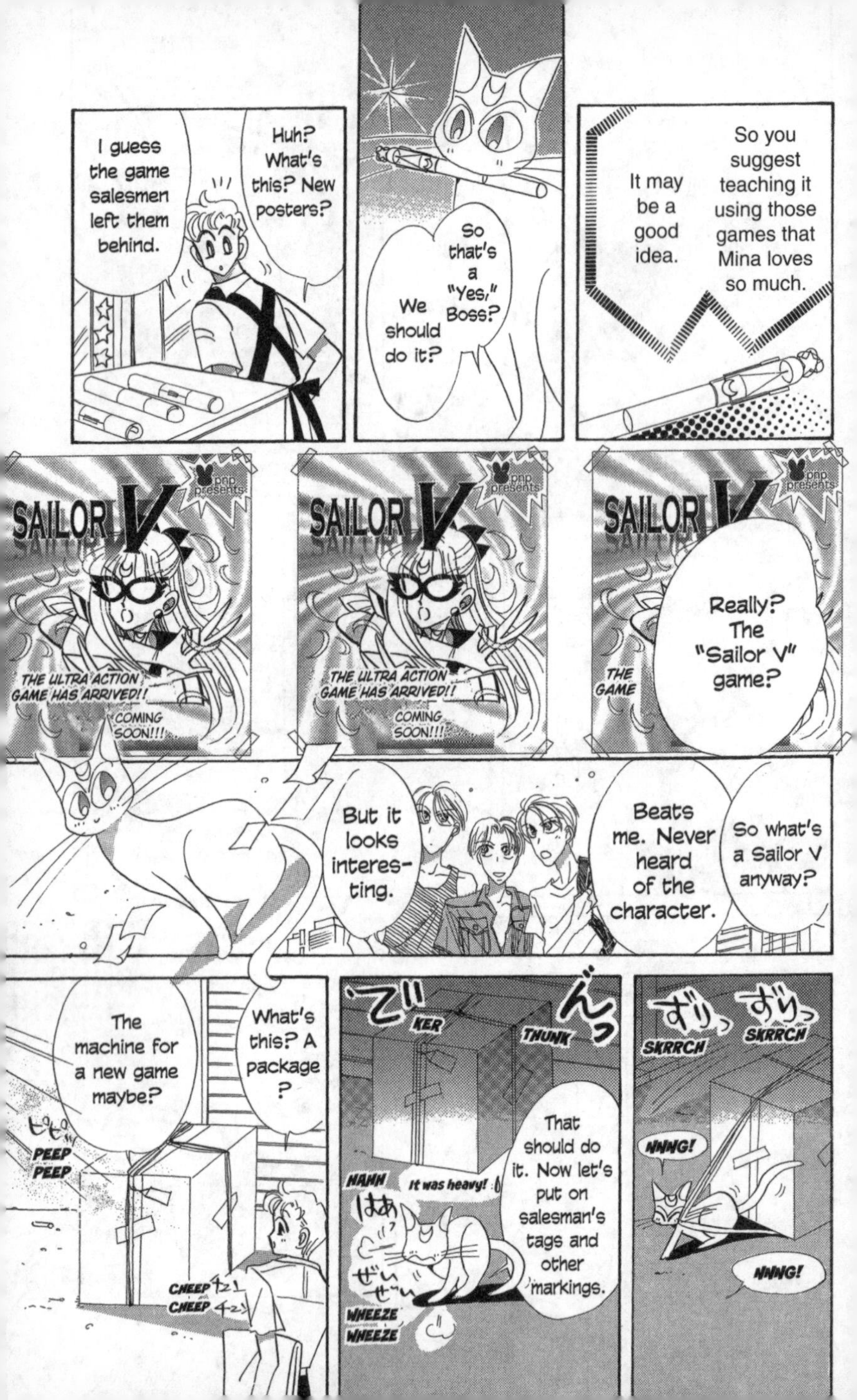
So you suggest teaching it using those games that Mina loves so much.
It may be a good idea.
So that's a "Yes," Boss?
We should do it?
Huh? What's this? New posters?
I guess the game salesmen left them behind.
pnp presents
SAILOR V
THE GAME
Really? The "Sailor V" game?
pnp presents
SAILOR V
THE ULTRA ACTION GAME HAS ARRIVED!!
COMING SOON!!!
pnp presents
SAILOR V
THE ULTRA ACTION GAME HAS ARRIVED!!
COMING SOON!!!
So what's a Sailor V anyway?
Beats me. Never heard of the character.
But it looks interesting.
ずりっ SKRRCH
ずりっ SKRRCH
NNNG!
NNNG!
んっ THUNK
KER
That should do it. Now let's put on salesman's tags and other markings.
It was heavy!
HAHH はあ
ぜいぜい WHEEZE WHEEZE
What's this? A package?
The machine for a new game maybe?
PEEP PEEP
CHEEP CHEEP

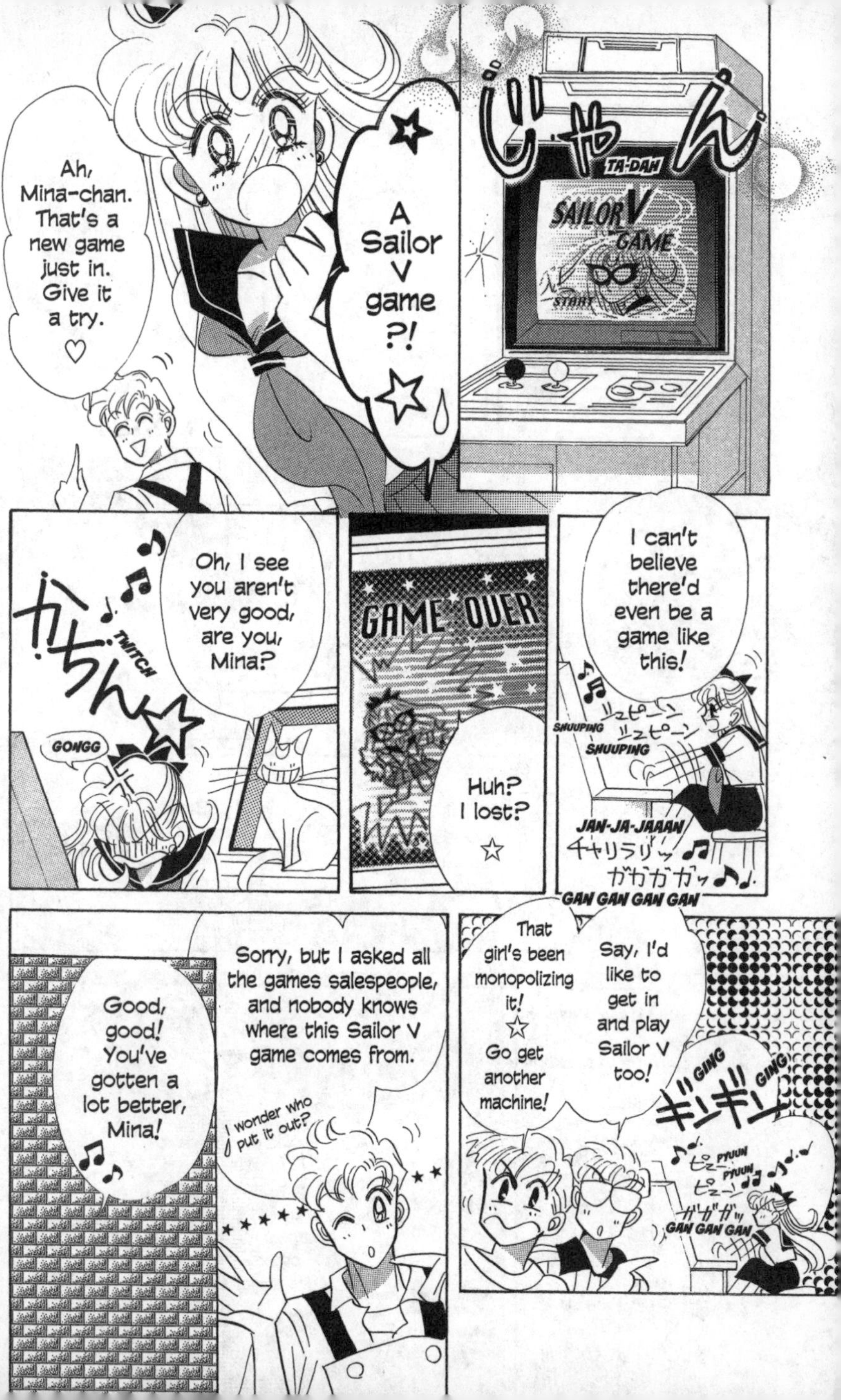

じゃん
TA-DAH
SAILOR V GAME
START
A Sailor V game?!
Ah, Mina-chan. That's a new game just in. Give it a try. ♡
I can't believe there'd even be a game like this!
シュピーン シュピーン
SHUUPING SHUUPING
チャリラリッ
JAN-JA-JAAAN
ガガガガッ
GAN GAN GAN GAN
GAME OVER
Huh? I lost? ☆
Oh, I see you aren't very good, are you, Mina?
かちん
TWITCH
GONGG
Say, I'd like to get in and play Sailor V too!
That girl's been monopolizing it! ☆ Go get another machine!
ギンギン
GING GING
ピュー ピュー
PYUUN PYUUN
ガガガッ
GAN GAN GAN
Sorry, but I asked all the games salespeople, and nobody knows where this Sailor V game comes from.
I wonder who put it out?
Good, good! You've gotten a lot better, Mina!

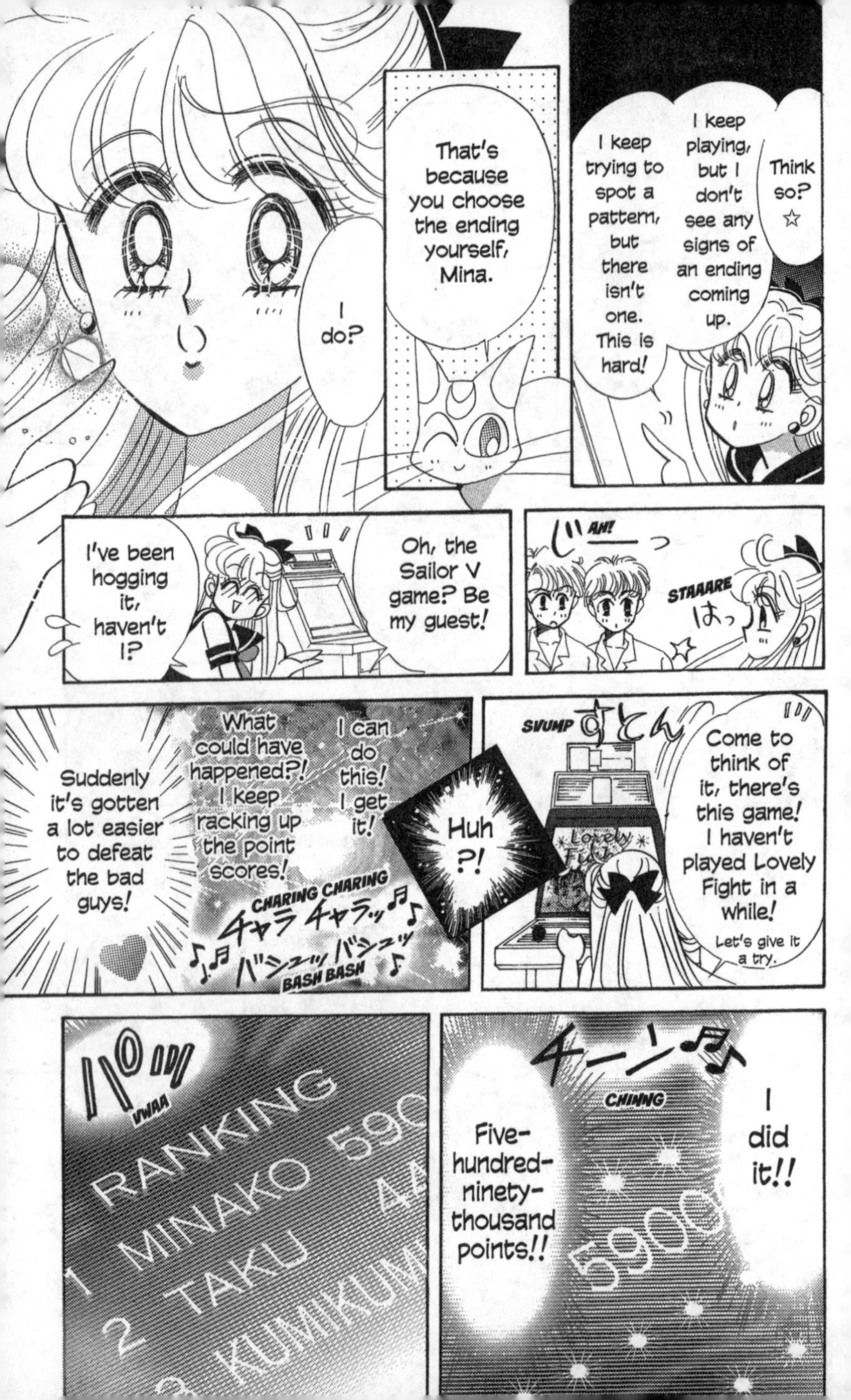

Think so? ☆
I keep playing, but I don't see any signs of an ending coming up.
I keep trying to spot a pattern, but there isn't one. This is hard!
That's because you choose the ending yourself, Mina.
I do?
じーっ
AH!
はっ
STAAARE
Oh, the Sailor V game? Be my guest!
I've been hogging it, haven't I?
すとん
SVUMP
Come to think of it, there's this game! I haven't played Lovely Fight in a while!
Let's give it a try.
Huh?!
I can do this! I get it!
What could have happened?! I keep racking up the point scores!
Suddenly it's gotten a lot easier to defeat the bad guys!
チャラチャラッ
CHARING CHARING
バシュッバシュッ
BASH BASH
チーン
CHINNG
I did it!!
Five-hundred-ninety-thousand points!!
パァ
VWAA
RANKING
1 MINAKO
2 TAKU

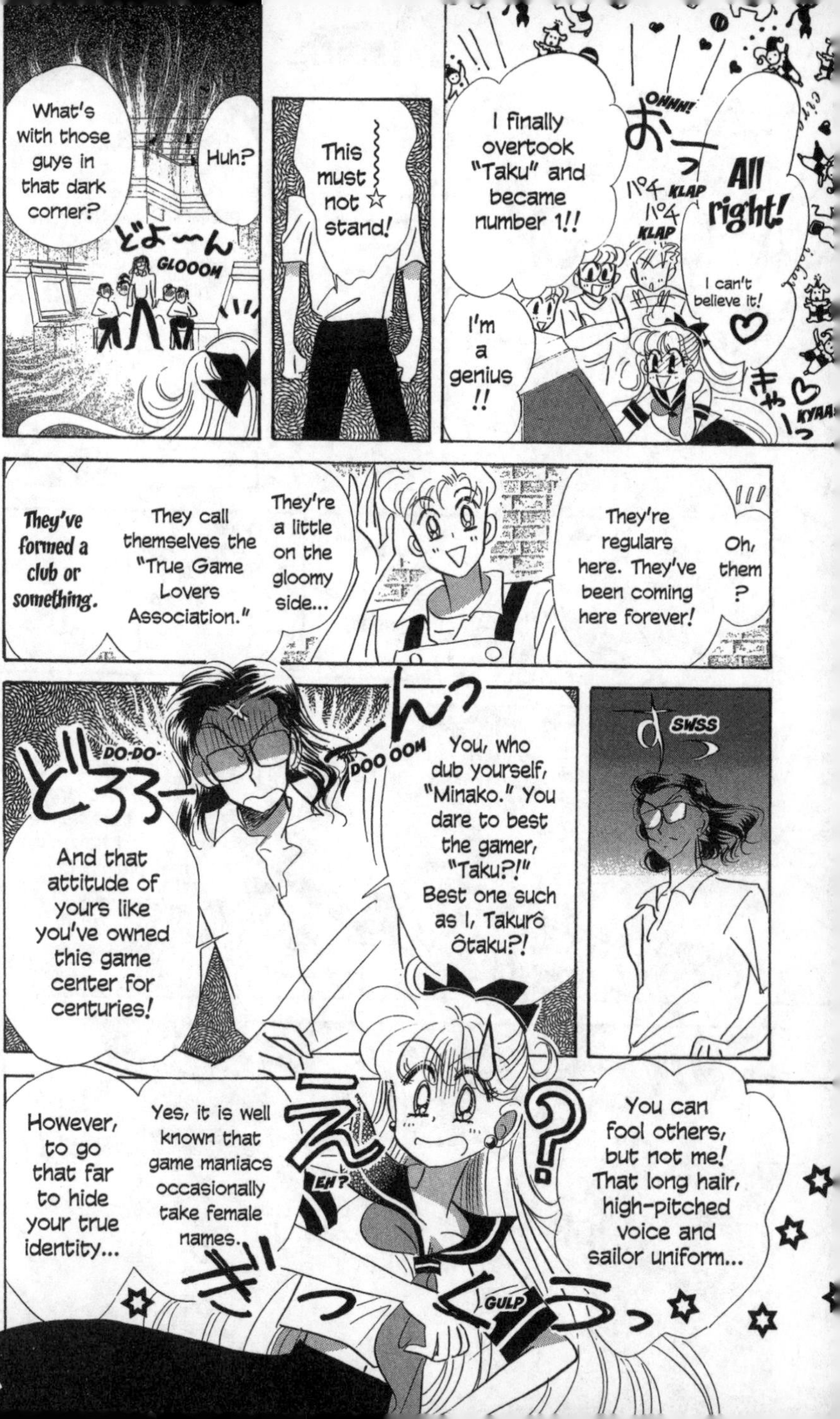
おーっ
ONHHH!
All right!
I finally overtook "Taku" and became number 1!!
パ4パ4
KLAP KLAP
I can't believe it! ♡
I'm a genius!!
きゃーっ
KYAA
This must not stand! ☆
Huh?
What's with those guys in that dark corner?
どよ～ん
GLOOOM
Oh, them?
They're regulars here. They've been coming here forever!
They're a little on the gloomy side...
They call themselves the "True Game Lovers Association."
They've formed a club or something.
すっ
SWSS
どろろーーんっ
DO-DO-DOO OOM
You, who dub yourself, "Minako." You dare to best the gamer, "Taku?!" Best one such as I, Takurô Ôtaku?!
And that attitude of yours like you've owned this game center for centuries!
You can fool others, but not me! That long hair, high-pitched voice and sailor uniform...
え？
EH?
Yes, it is well known that game maniacs occasionally take female names.
However, to go that far to hide your true identity...
ぎっくうっ
GULP

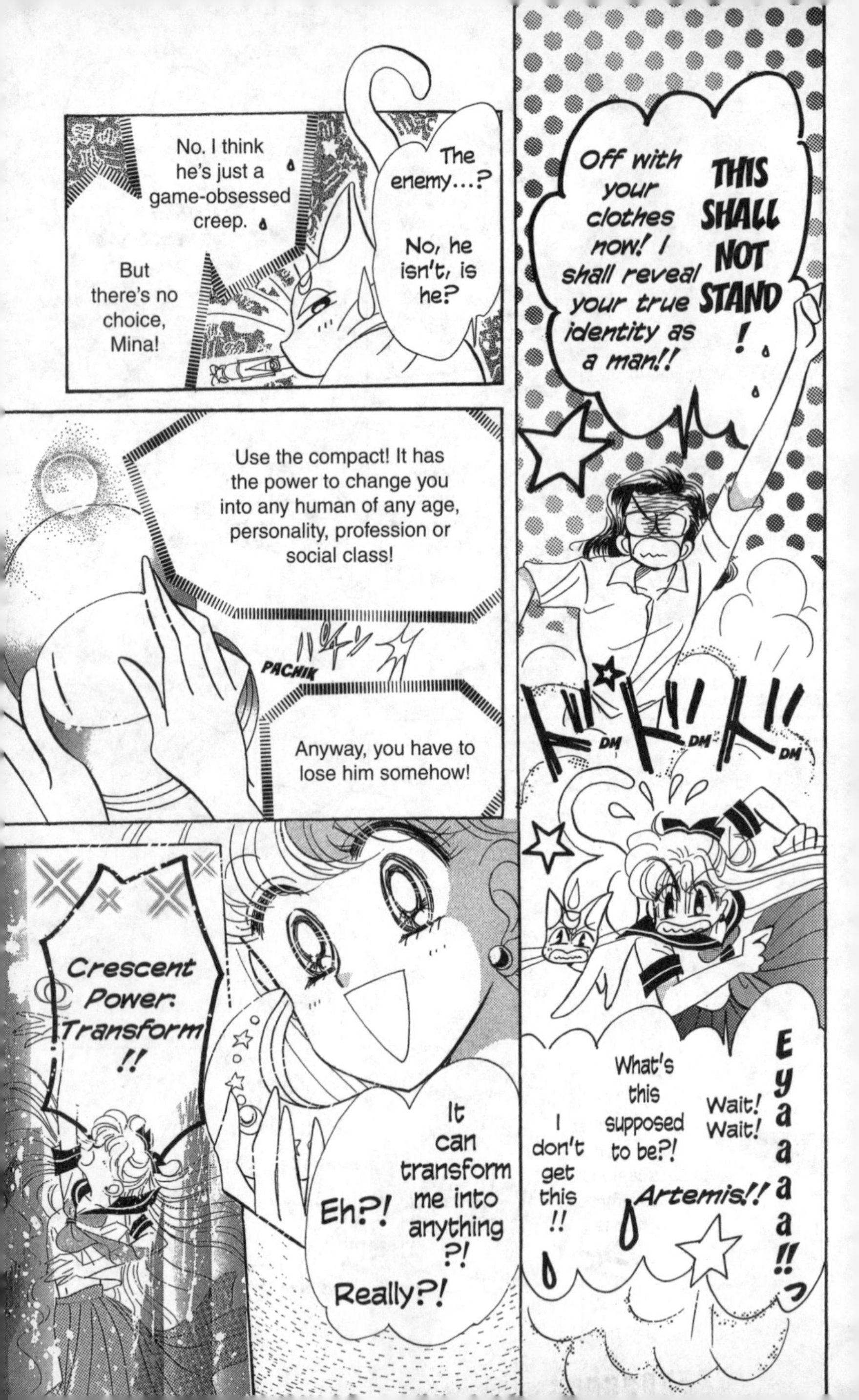
THIS SHALL NOT STAND!
Off with your clothes now! I shall reveal your true identity as a man!!
DM
DM
DM
Eyaaaaa!!
Wait! Wait!
Artemis!!
What's this supposed to be?!
I don't get this!!
The enemy...?
No, he isn't, is he?
No. I think he's just a game-obsessed creep.
But there's no choice, Mina!
Use the compact! It has the power to change you into any human of any age, personality, profession or social class!
PACHIK
Anyway, you have to lose him somehow!
It can transform me into anything?!
Eh?!
Really?!
Crescent Power: Transform!!

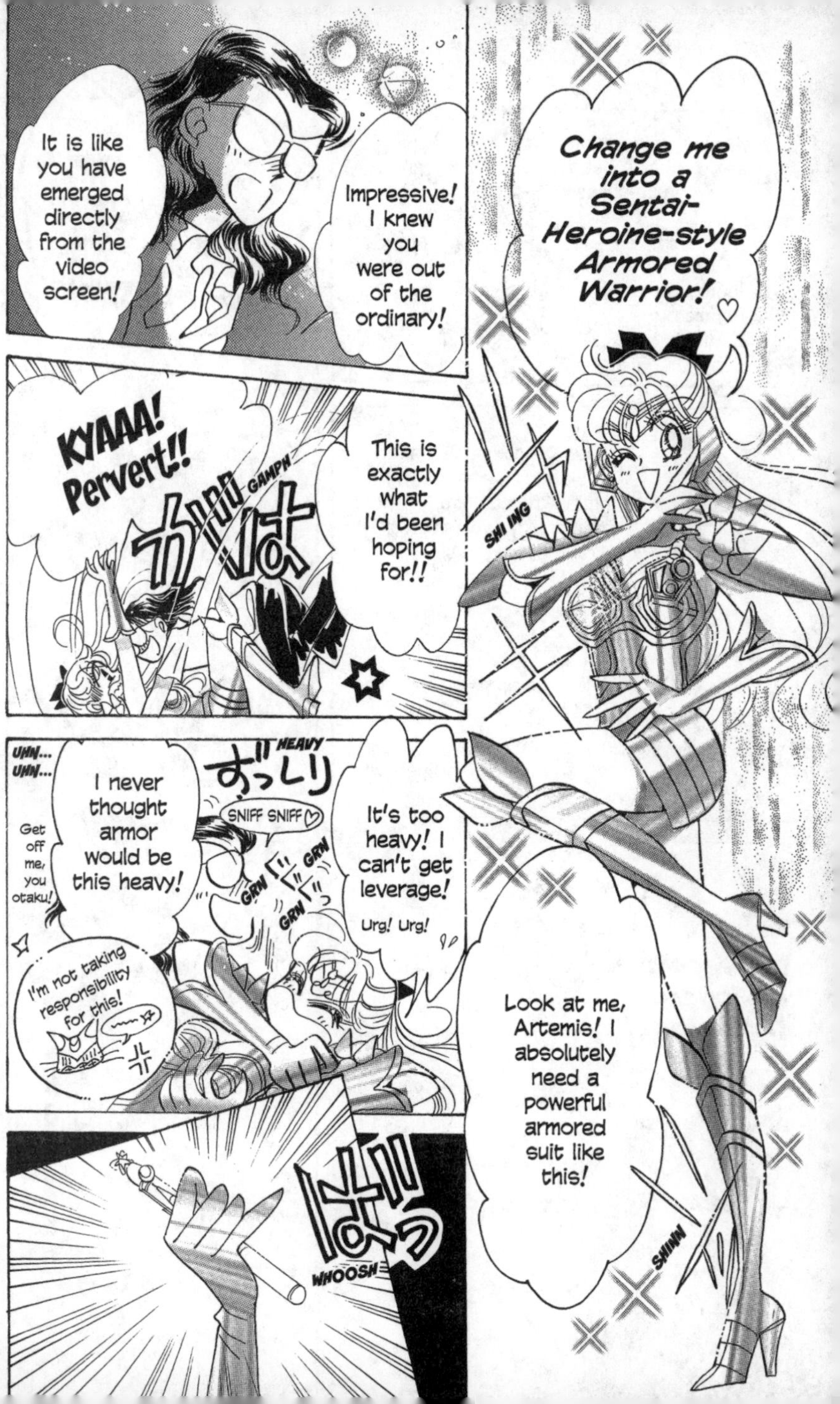
Change me into a Sentai-Heroine-style Armored Warrior! ♡
SHI ING
Look at me, Artemis! I absolutely need a powerful armored suit like this!
SHINN
Impressive! I knew you were out of the ordinary!
It is like you have emerged directly from the video screen!
This is exactly what I'd been hoping for!!
GAMPH
KYAAA! Pervert!!
HEAVY
ずっしり
It's too heavy! I can't get leverage!
Urg! Urg!
SNIFF SNIFF ♡
GRN GRN GRN GRN
I never thought armor would be this heavy!
UNN... UNN...
Get off me, you otaku!
I'm not taking responsibility for this!
WHOOSH

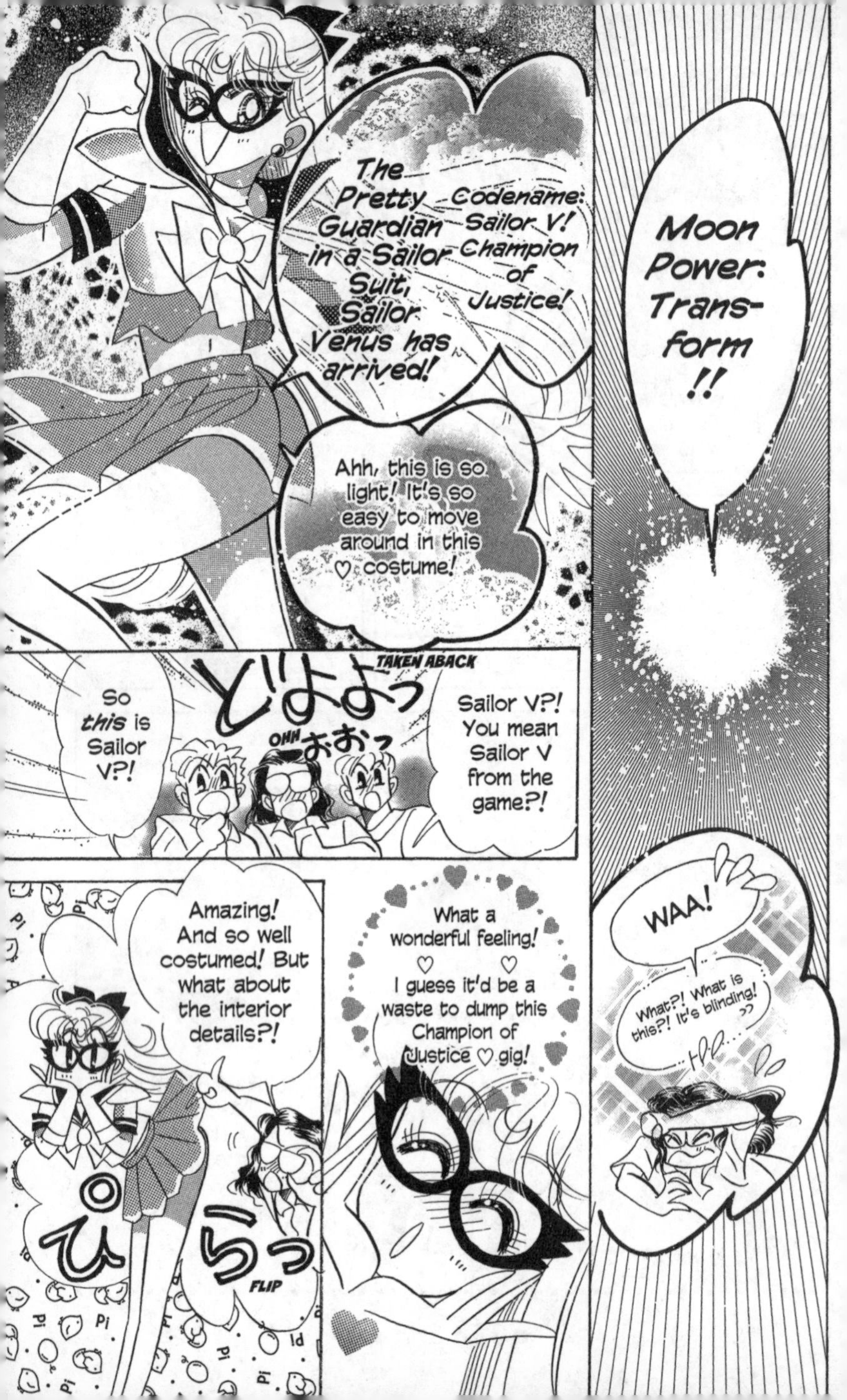
Moon Power: Trans-form!!
WAA!
What?! What is this?! It's blinding!
Codename: Sailor V! Champion of Justice!
The Pretty Guardian in a Sailor Suit, Sailor Venus has arrived!
Ahh, this is so light! It's so easy to move around in this ♡ costume!
TAKEN ABACK
どよよっ
Sailor V?! You mean Sailor V from the game?!
OHH
おおっ
So *this* is Sailor V?!
What a wonderful feeling! ♡ ♡ I guess it'd be a waste to dump this Champion of Justice ♡ gig!
Amazing! And so well costumed! But what about the interior details?!
ぴらっ
FLIP
Pi

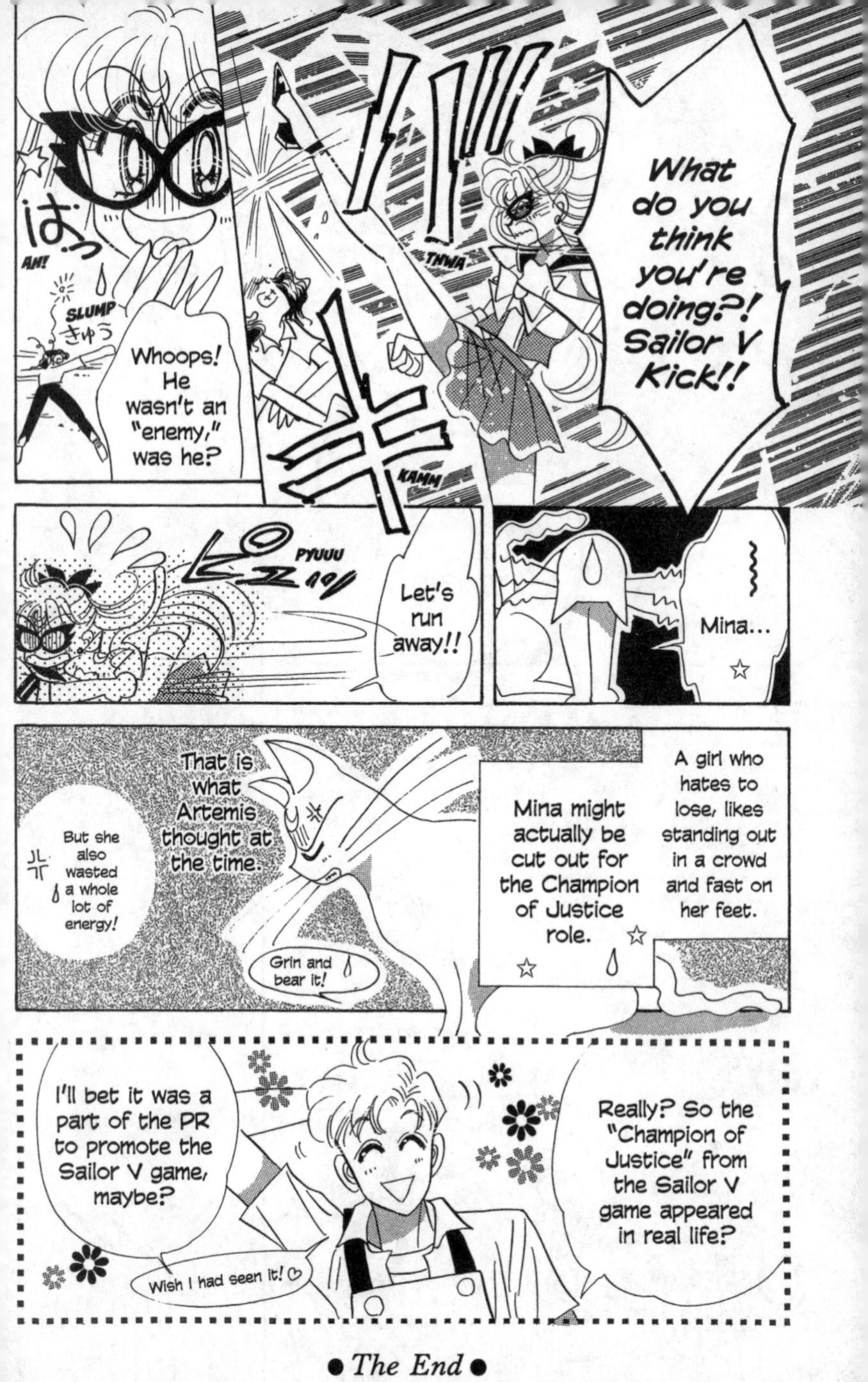

What do you think you're doing?! Sailor V Kick!!
THWA
KAMM
はっ
AH!
SLUMP
きゅう
Whoops! He wasn't an "enemy," was he?
Mina...
PYUUU
Let's run away!!
A girl who hates to lose, likes standing out in a crowd and fast on her feet.
Mina might actually be cut out for the Champion of Justice role.
That is what Artemis thought at the time.
But she also wasted a whole lot of energy!
Grin and bear it!
Really? So the "Champion of Justice" from the Sailor V game appeared in real life?
I'll bet it was a part of the PR to promote the Sailor V game, maybe?
Wish I had seen it! ♡

• *The End* •

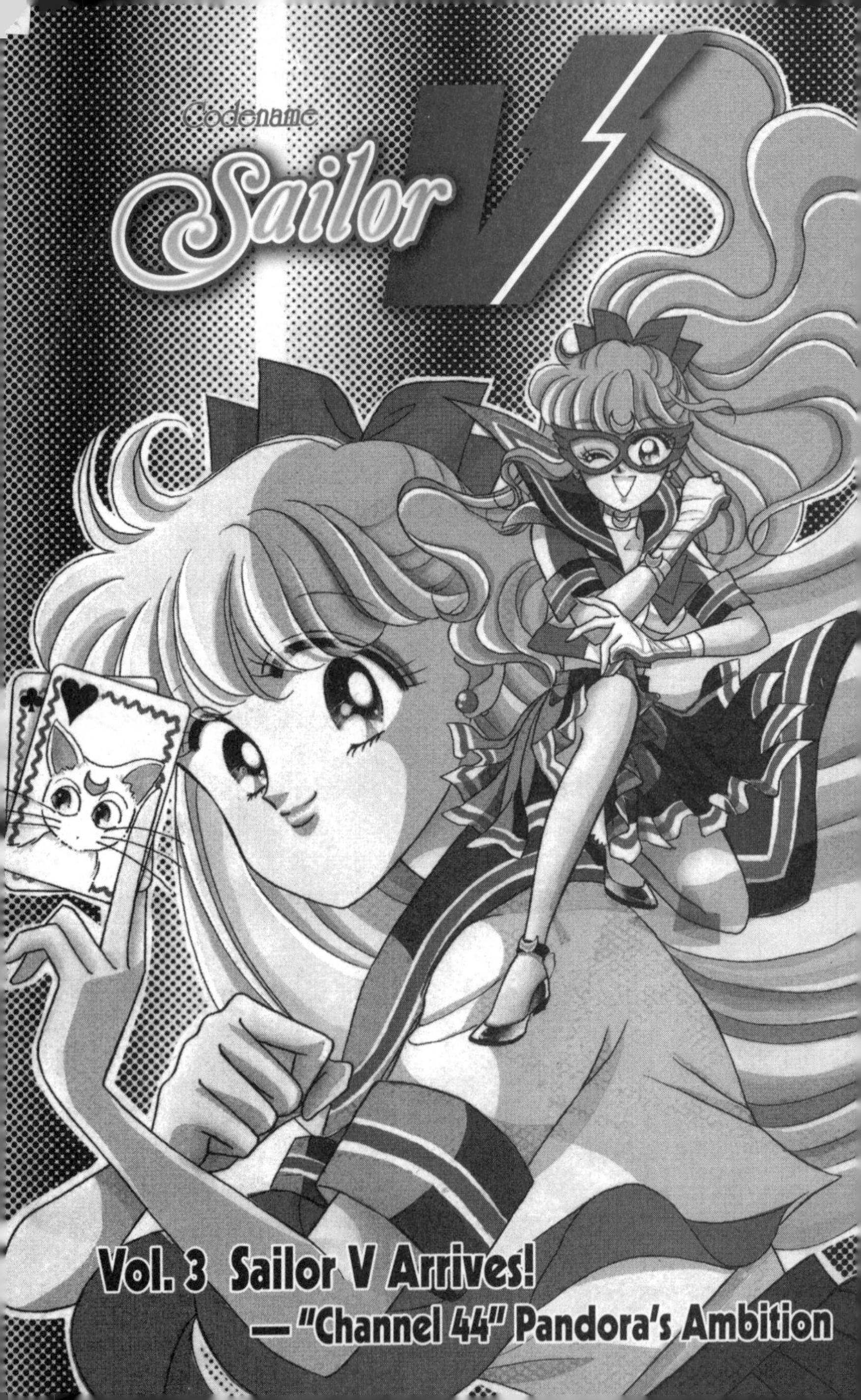
Codename
Sailor V
Vol. 3 Sailor V Arrives!
— "Channel 44" Pandora's Ambition

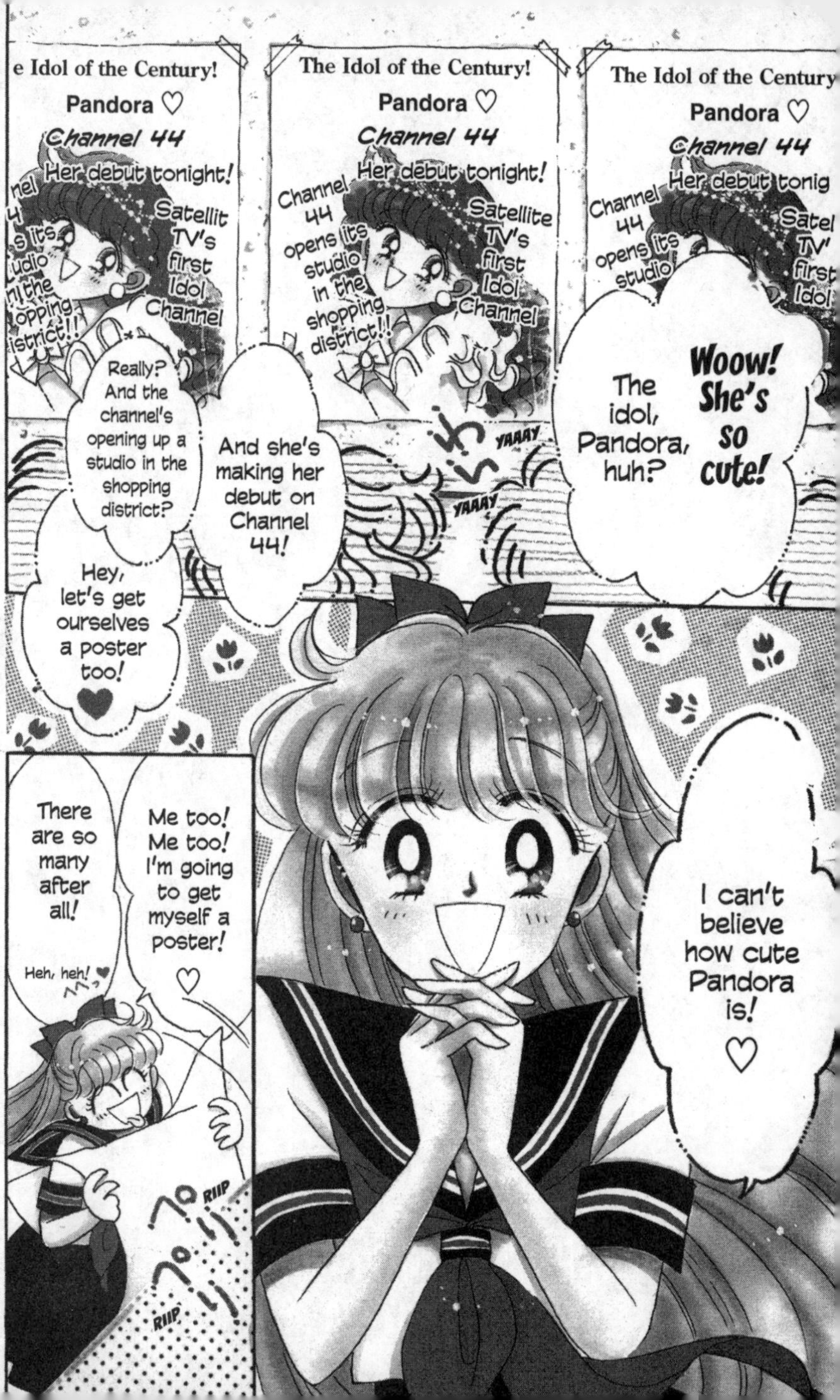

The Idol of the Century!
Pandora ♡
Channel 44
Her debut tonight!
Satellite TV's first Idol Channel
Channel 44 opens its studio in the shopping district!!
Woow! She's so cute!
The idol, Pandora, huh?
YAAAY
YAAAY
And she's making her debut on Channel 44!
Really? And the channel's opening up a studio in the shopping district?
Hey, let's get ourselves a poster too! ♥
I can't believe how cute Pandora is! ♡
Me too! Me too! I'm going to get myself a poster! ♡
There are so many after all!
Heh, heh! ♥
RIIP
RIIP

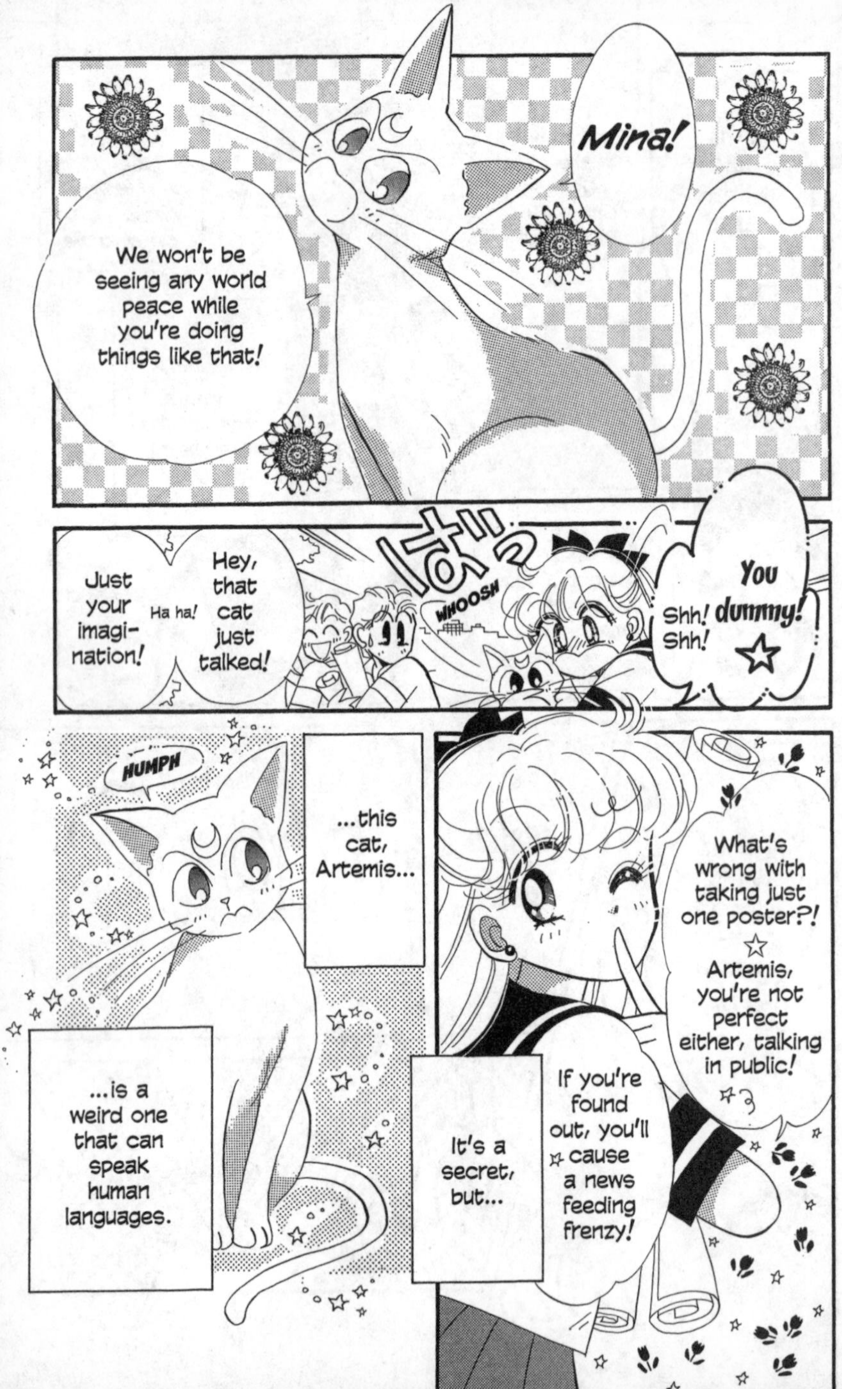
Mina!
We won't be seeing any world peace while you're doing things like that!
You dummy! ☆
Shh! Shh!
WHOOSH
Hey, that cat just talked!
Ha ha!
Just your imagination!
What's wrong with taking just one poster?! ☆ Artemis, you're not perfect either, talking in public!
If you're found out, you'll cause a news feeding frenzy!
It's a secret, but...
...this cat, Artemis...
HUMPH
...is a weird one that can speak human languages.

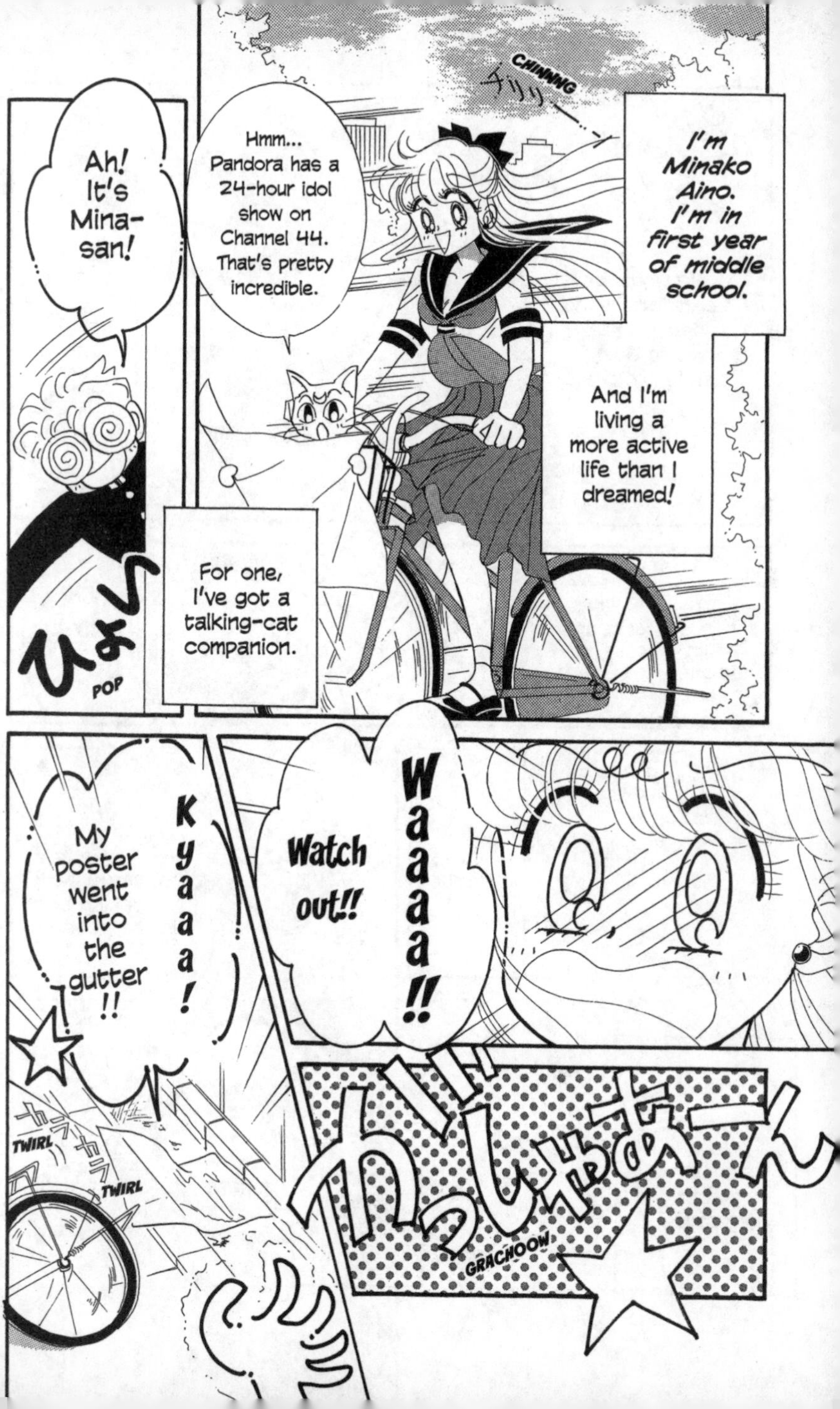

CHINNNG
I'm Minako Aino. I'm in first year of middle school.
Hmm... Pandora has a 24-hour idol show on Channel 44. That's pretty incredible.
And I'm living a more active life than I dreamed!
For one, I've got a talking-cat companion.
Ah! It's Mina-san!
POP
Waaaaa!!
Watch out!!
GRACHOOW
Kyaaaa!
My poster went into the gutter!!
TWIRL
TWIRL

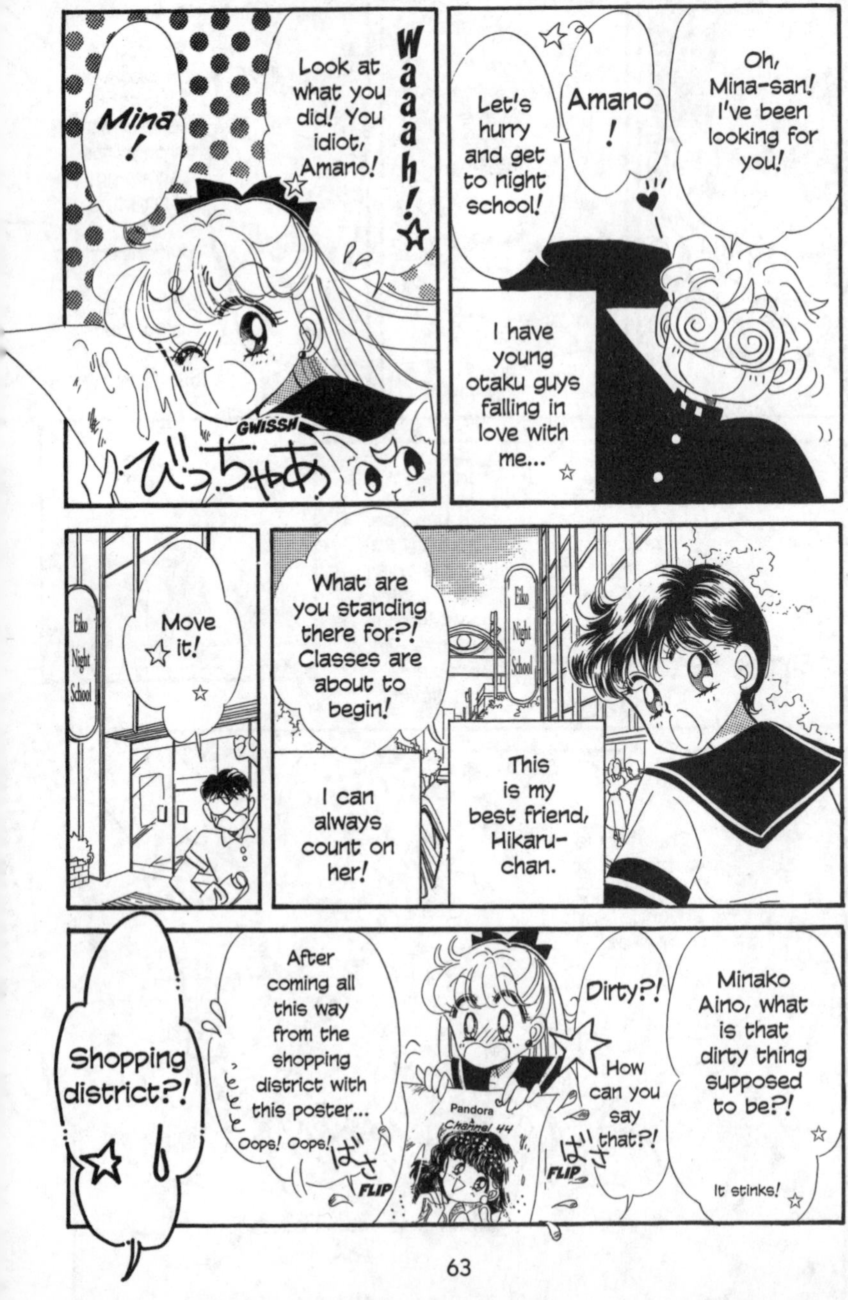

Oh, Mina-san! I've been looking for you!
Amano!
Let's hurry and get to night school!
I have young otaku guys falling in love with me...
Waaah!
Look at what you did! You idiot, Amano!
Mina!
GWISSH
びっちゃあ
Eiko Night School
What are you standing there for?! Classes are about to begin!
This is my best friend, Hikaru-chan.
I can always count on her!
Eiko Night School
Move it!
Minako Aino, what is that dirty thing supposed to be?!
It stinks!
Dirty?!
How can you say that?!
ばさ
FLIP
Pandora
Channel 44
After coming all this way from the shopping district with this poster...
とととと
Oops! Oops!
ばさ
FLIP
Shopping district?!

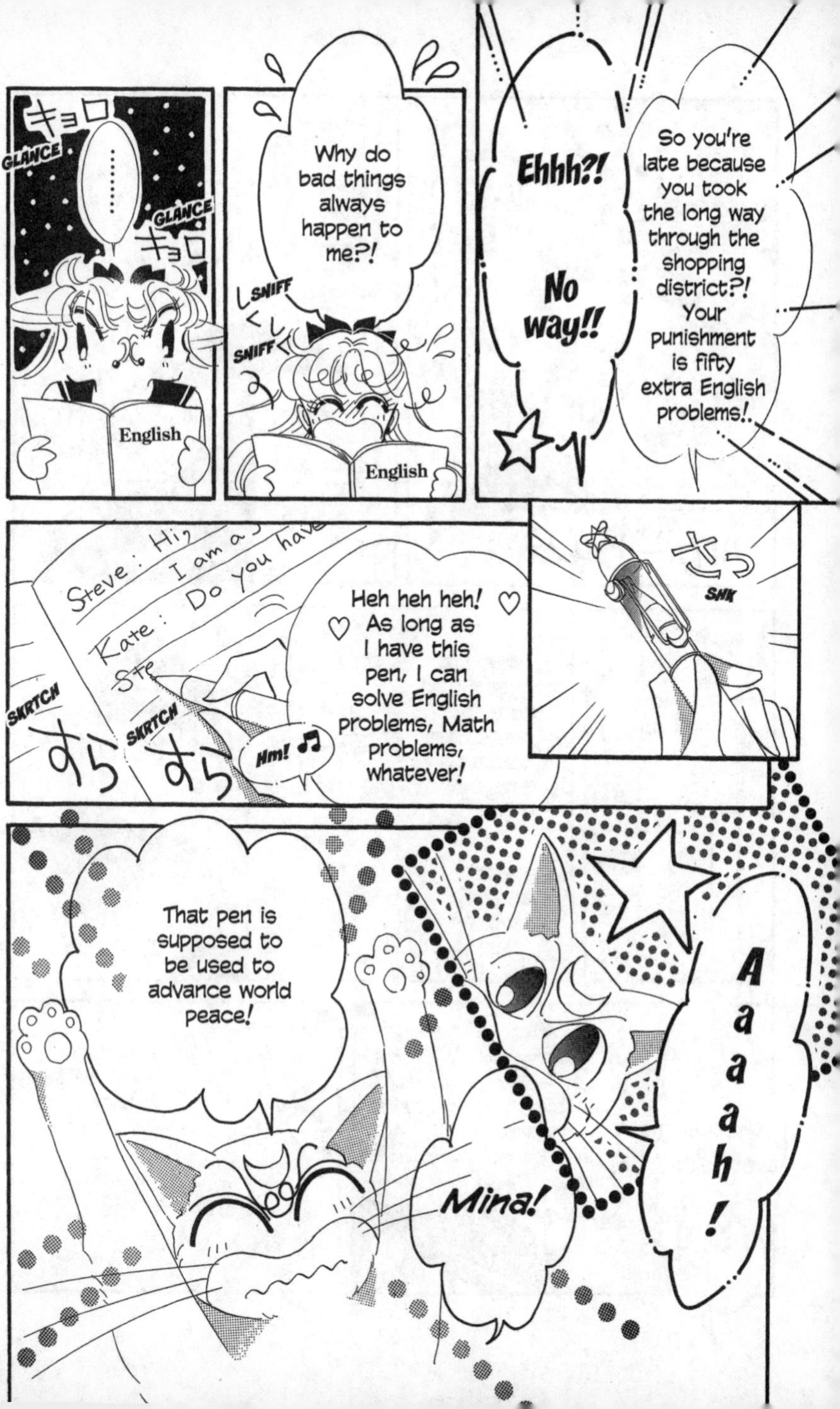
So you're late because you took the long way through the shopping district?! Your punishment is fifty extra English problems!
Ehhh?! No way!!
Why do bad things always happen to me?!
SNIFF
SNIFF
English
キョロ
GLANCE
......
キョロ
GLANCE
English
さっ
SNK
Heh heh heh! ♡ As long as I have this pen, I can solve English problems, Math problems, whatever! ♡
Hm! ♫
すら
SKRTCH
すら
SKRTCH
Steve: Hi,
I am a
Kate: Do you have
Ste
Aaaaah!
Mina!
That pen is supposed to be used to advance world peace!

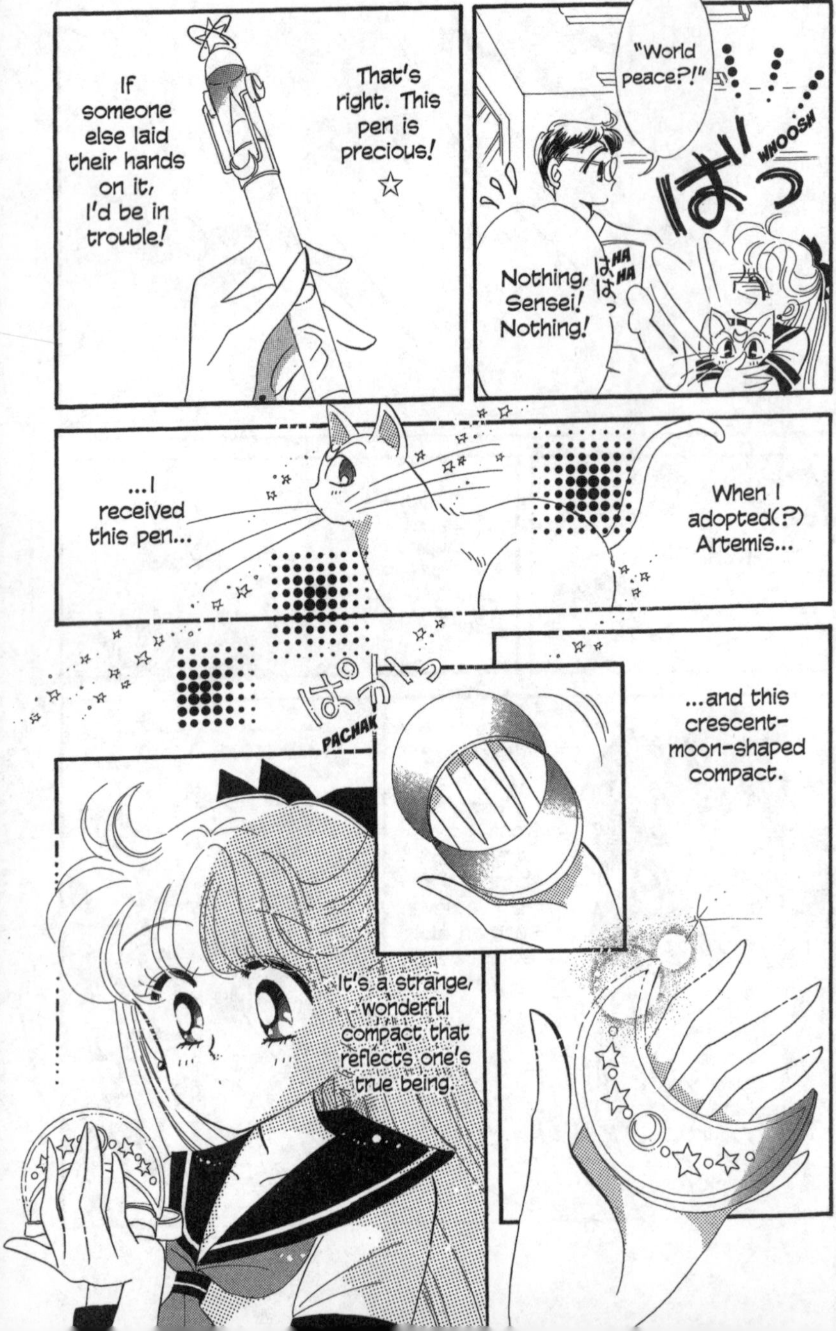

"World peace?!"
ばっ
WHOOSH
ははっ
HA HA
Nothing, Sensei! Nothing!
That's right. This pen is precious! ☆
If someone else laid their hands on it, I'd be in trouble!
When I adopted(?) Artemis...
...I received this pen...
...and this crescent-moon-shaped compact.
ぱかっ
PACHAK
It's a strange, wonderful compact that reflects one's true being.

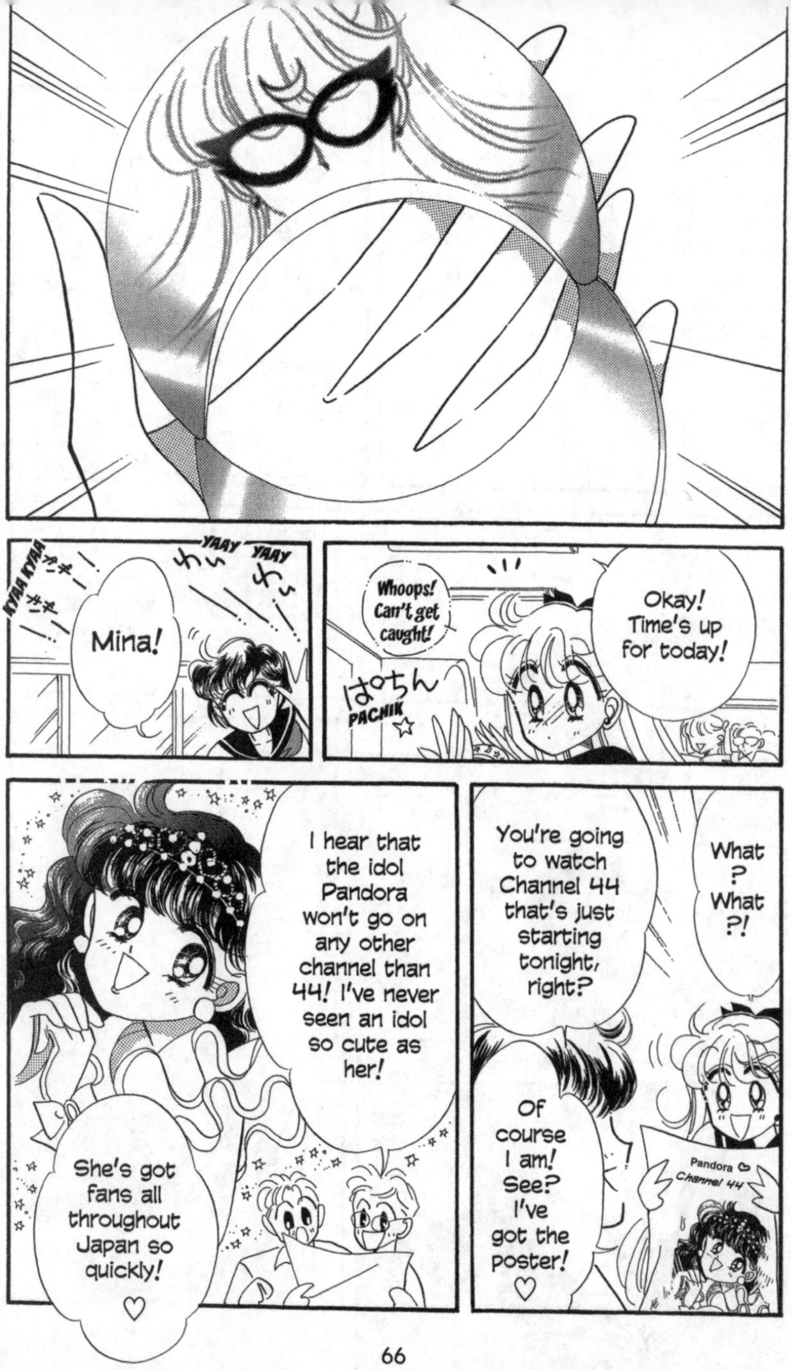

Okay! Time's up for today!
Whoops! Can't get caught!
ぱちん
PACHIK
YAAY
YAAY
Mina!
KYAA KYAA
What? What?!
You're going to watch Channel 44 that's just starting tonight, right?
Of course I am! See? I've got the poster!
Pandora Channel 44
I hear that the idol Pandora won't go on any other channel than 44! I've never seen an idol so cute as her!
She's got fans all throughout Japan so quickly!

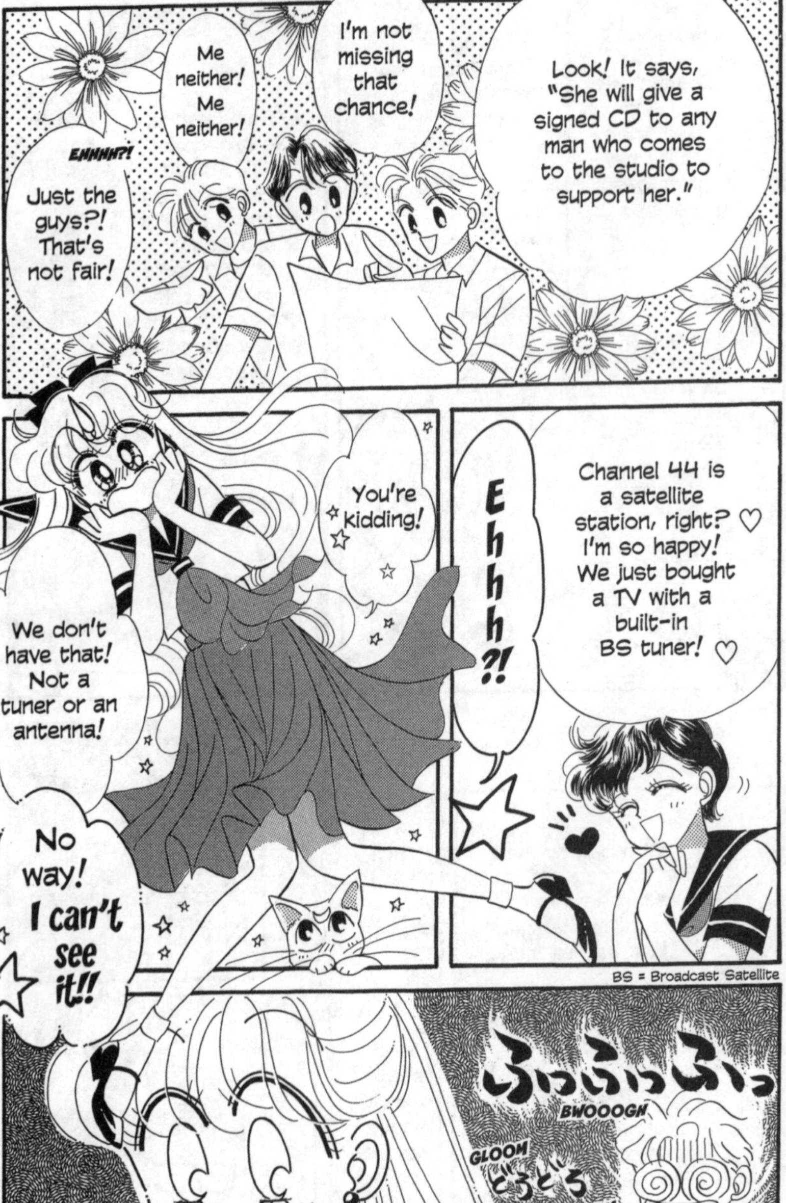
Look! It says, "She will give a signed CD to any man who comes to the studio to support her."
I'm not missing that chance!
Me neither! Me neither!
EHHHH?!
Just the guys?! That's not fair!
Channel 44 is a satellite station, right? ♡ I'm so happy! We just bought a TV with a built-in BS tuner! ♡
Ehhh?!
You're kidding!
We don't have that! Not a tuner or an antenna!
No way! I can't see it!!
BS = Broadcast Satellite
ふっふっふっ
BWOOOGH
GLOOM
どろどろ
GLOOM

☞ BS = Broadcast Satellite
CS = Communication Satellite

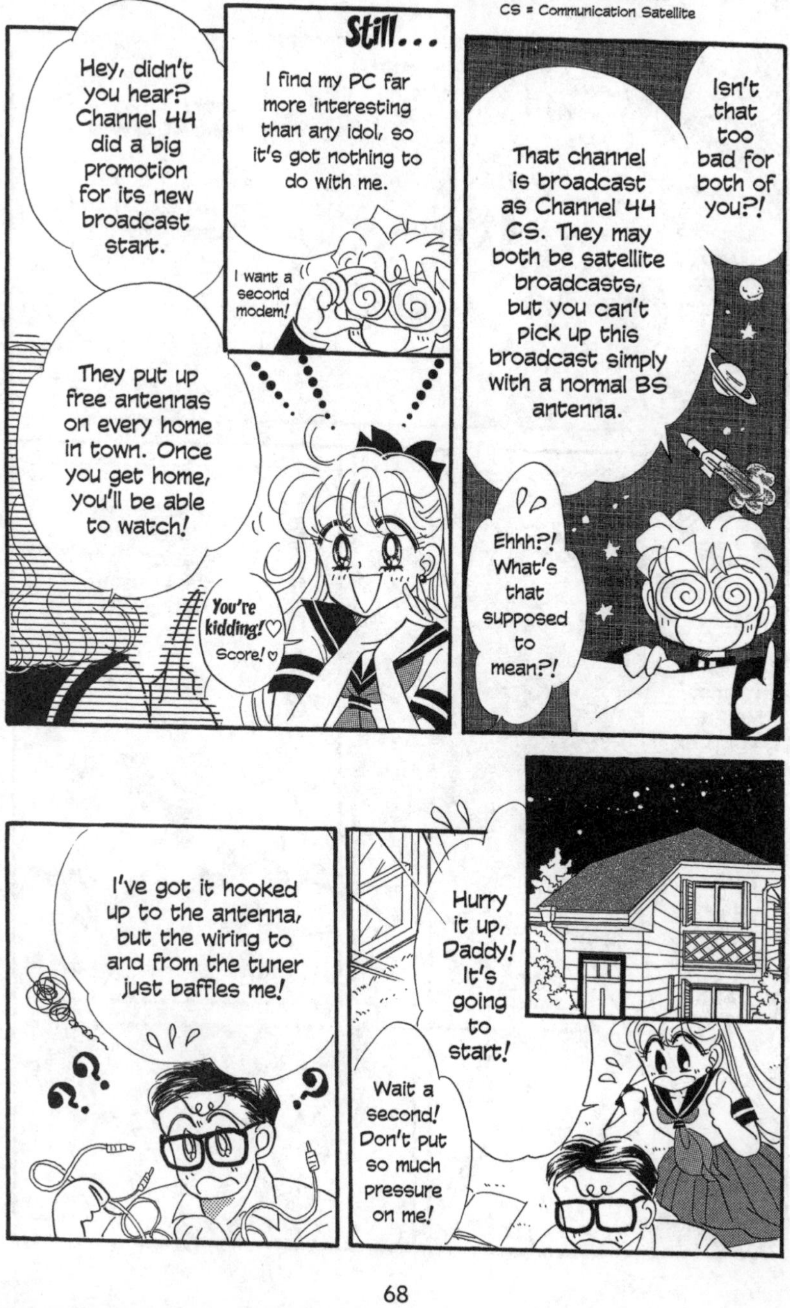
Isn't that too bad for both of you?!
That channel is broadcast as Channel 44 CS. They may both be satellite broadcasts, but you can't pick up this broadcast simply with a normal BS antenna.
Ehhh?! What's that supposed to mean?!
Still...
I find my PC far more interesting than any idol, so it's got nothing to do with me.
I want a second modem!
You're kidding!♡
Score!♡
Hey, didn't you hear? Channel 44 did a big promotion for its new broadcast start.
They put up free antennas on every home in town. Once you get home, you'll be able to watch!
Hurry it up, Daddy! It's going to start!
Wait a second! Don't put so much pressure on me!
I've got it hooked up to the antenna, but the wiring to and from the tuner just baffles me!

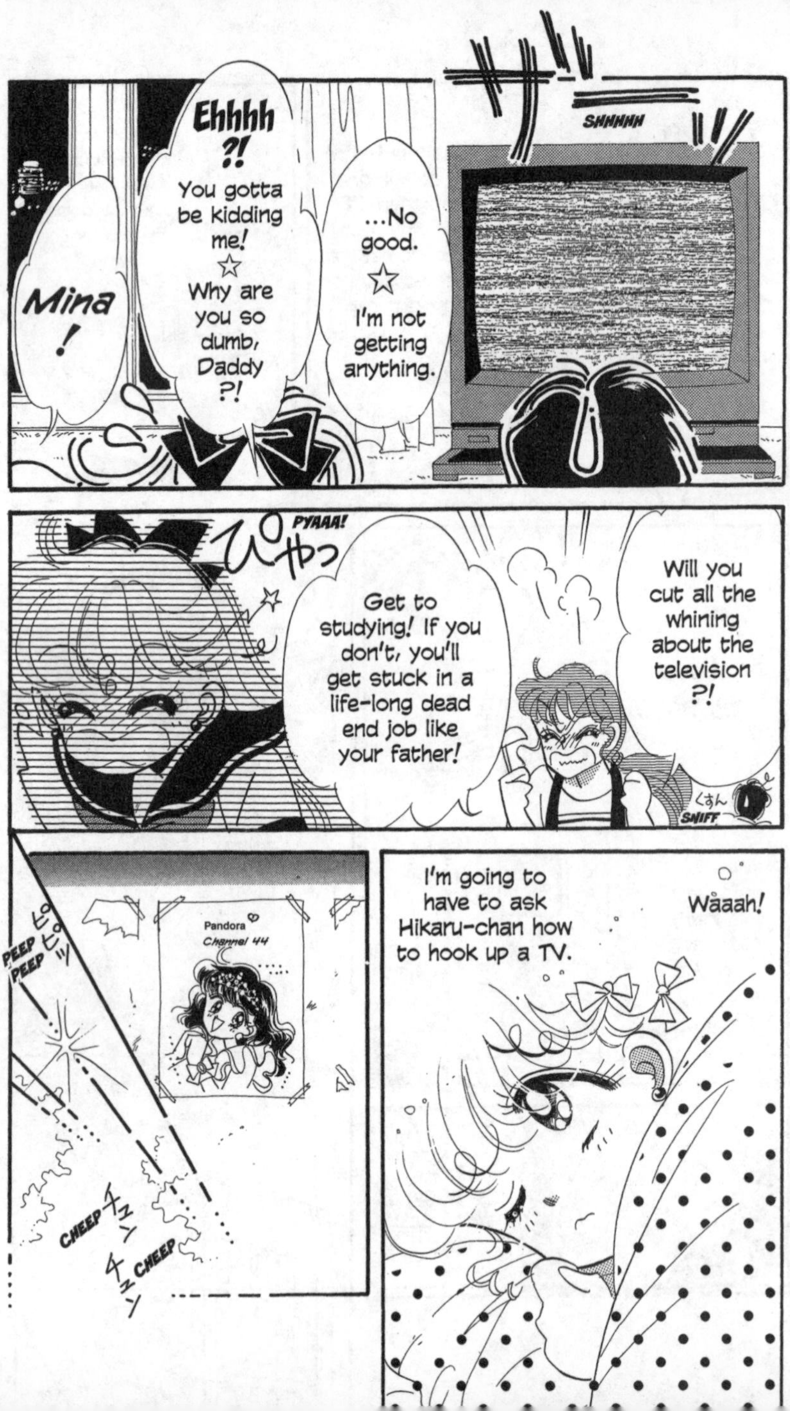
SHHHHH
...No good. ☆ I'm not getting anything.
Ehhhh?! You gotta be kidding me! ☆ Why are you so dumb, Daddy?!
Mina!
Will you cut all the whining about the television?!
ぴやっ PYAAA!
Get to studying! If you don't, you'll get stuck in a life-long dead end job like your father!
くすん SNIFF
Waaah!
I'm going to have to ask Hikaru-chan how to hook up a TV.
Pandora
Channel 44
ピピッ PEEP PEEP
チュン CHEEP
チュン CHEEP

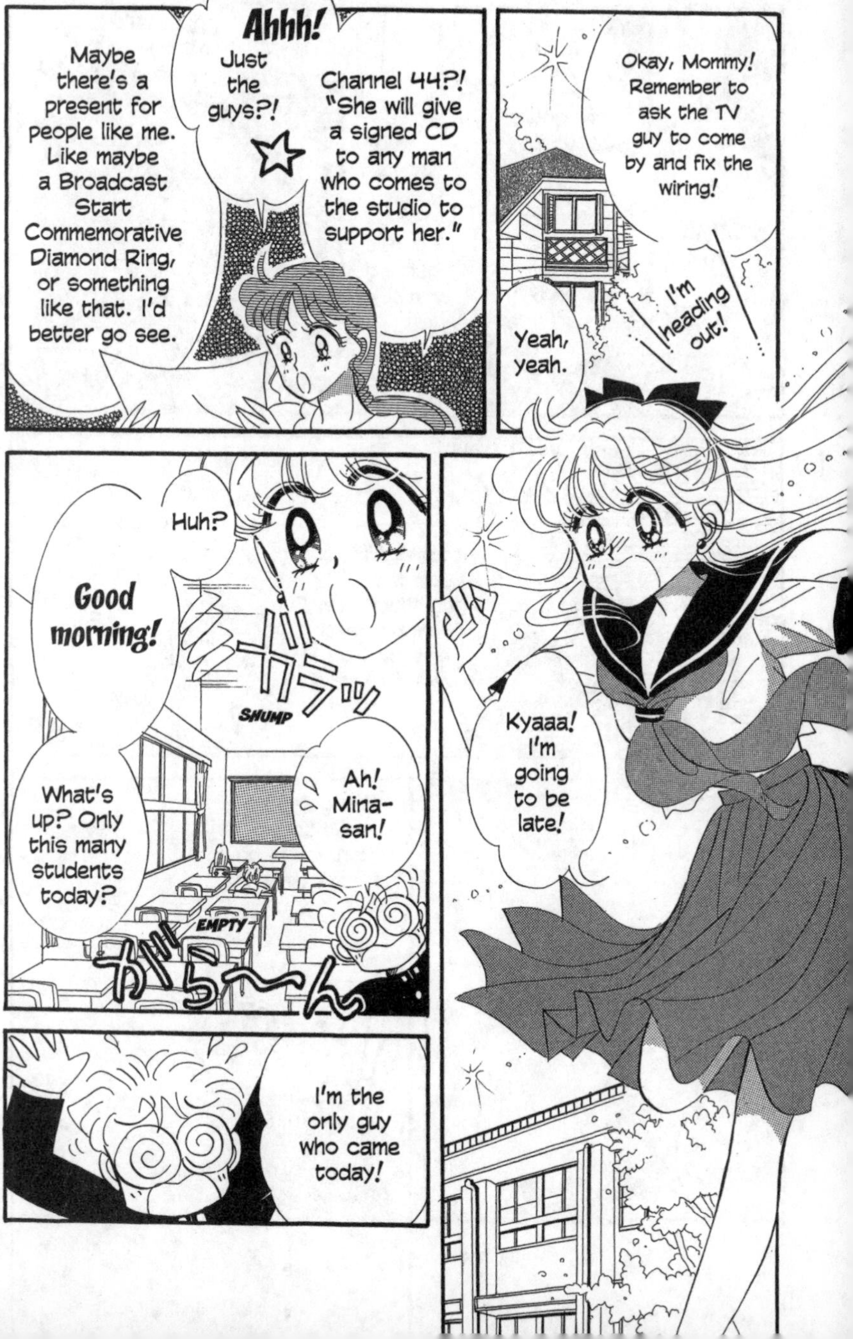
Okay, Mommy! Remember to ask the TV guy to come by and fix the wiring!
I'm heading out!
Yeah, yeah.
Channel 44?! "She will give a signed CD to any man who comes to the studio to support her."
Ahhh! Just the guys?!
Maybe there's a present for people like me. Like maybe a Broadcast Start Commemorative Diamond Ring, or something like that. I'd better go see.
Kyaaa! I'm going to be late!
Huh?
Good morning!
ガラッ
SHUMP
Ah! Mina-san!
What's up? Only this many students today?
EMPTY
がら～ん
I'm the only guy who came today!

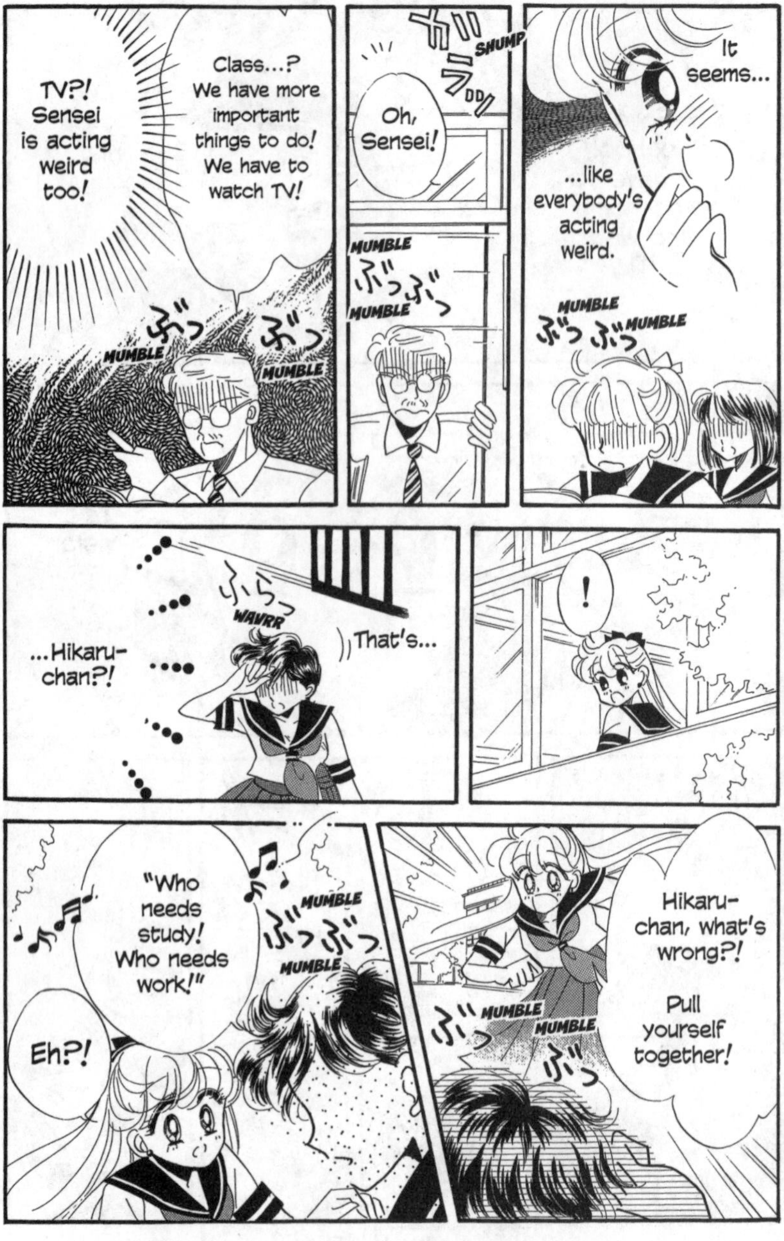
It seems...
...like everybody's acting weird.
MUMBLE
MUMBLE
SHUMP
Oh, Sensei!
MUMBLE
MUMBLE
Class...? We have more important things to do! We have to watch TV!
TV?! Sensei is acting weird too!
MUMBLE
MUMBLE
!
That's...
WAVRR
...Hikaru-chan?!
Hikaru-chan, what's wrong?!
Pull yourself together!
MUMBLE
MUMBLE
"Who needs study! Who needs work!"
MUMBLE
MUMBLE
Eh?!

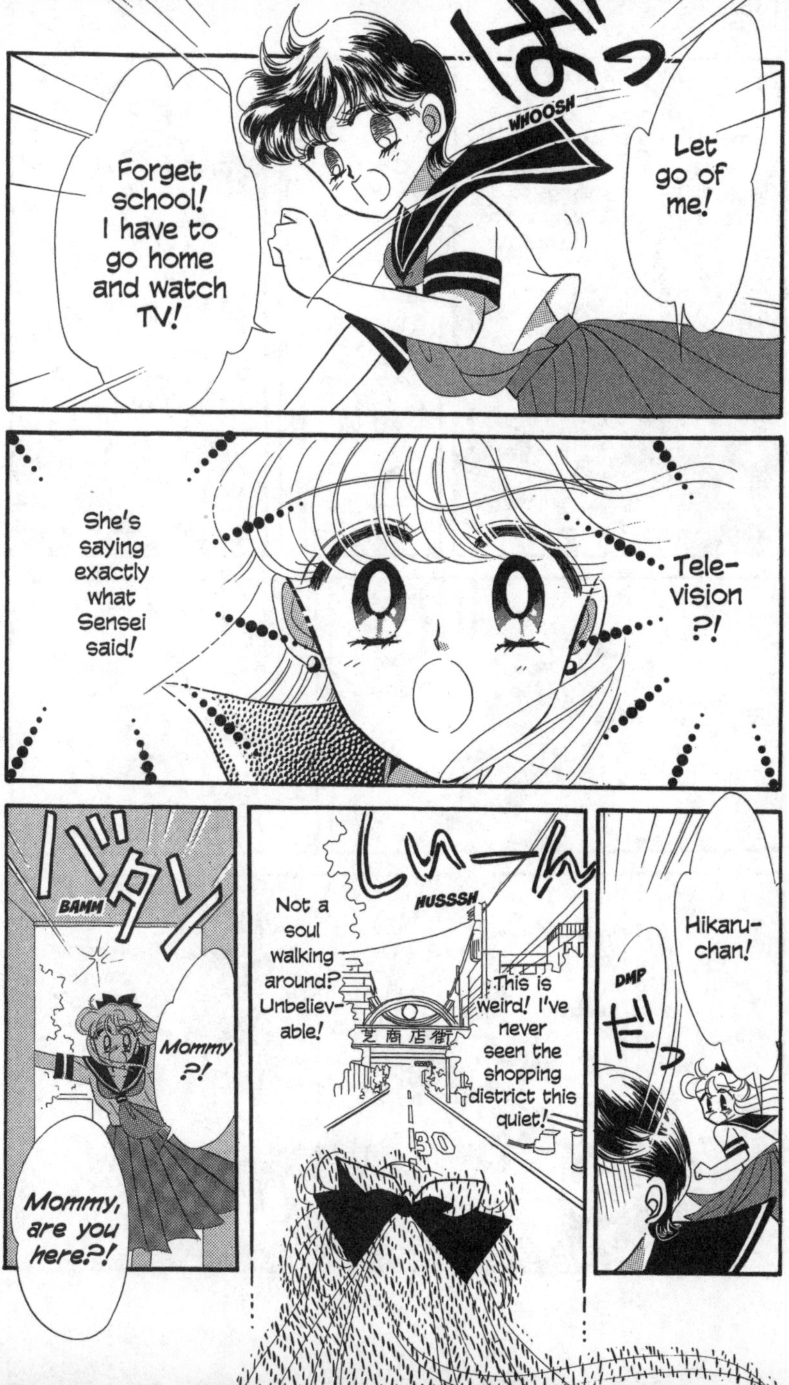
ばっ
WHOOSH
Let go of me!
Forget school! I have to go home and watch TV!
Tele-vision?!
She's saying exactly what Sensei said!
Hikaru-chan!
だっ
DMP
しーん
HUSSSH
This is weird! I've never seen the shopping district this quiet!
芝商店街
Not a soul walking around? Unbeliev-able!
バタン
BAMM
Mommy?!
Mommy, are you here?!

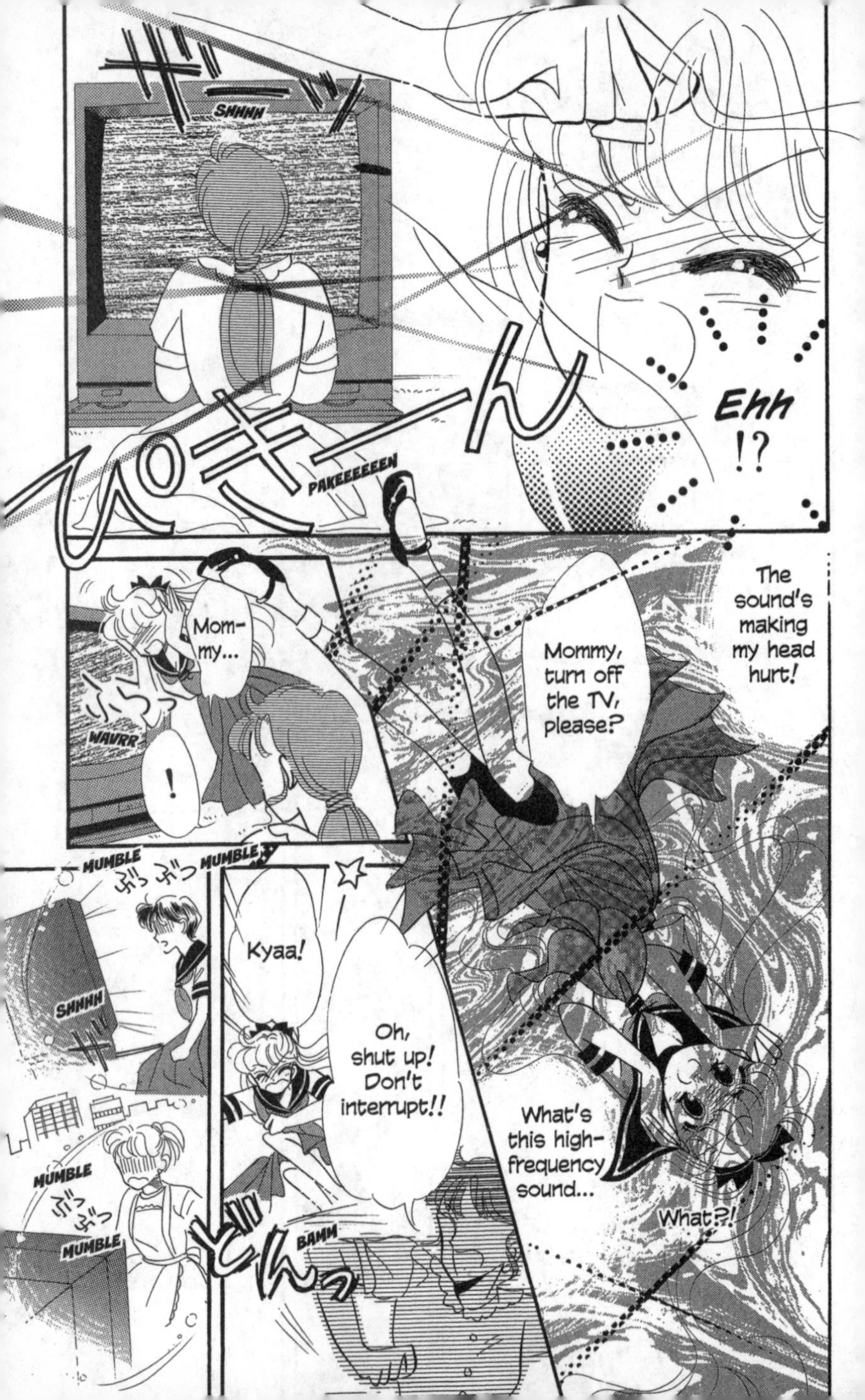
Ehh !?
SHHHH
PAKEEEEEEN
The sound's making my head hurt!
Mommy, turn off the TV, please?
What's this high-frequency sound...
What?!
Mom-my...
WAVRR
!
Kyaa!
Oh, shut up! Don't interrupt!!
BAMM
MUMBLE
MUMBLE
SHHHH
MUMBLE
MUMBLE

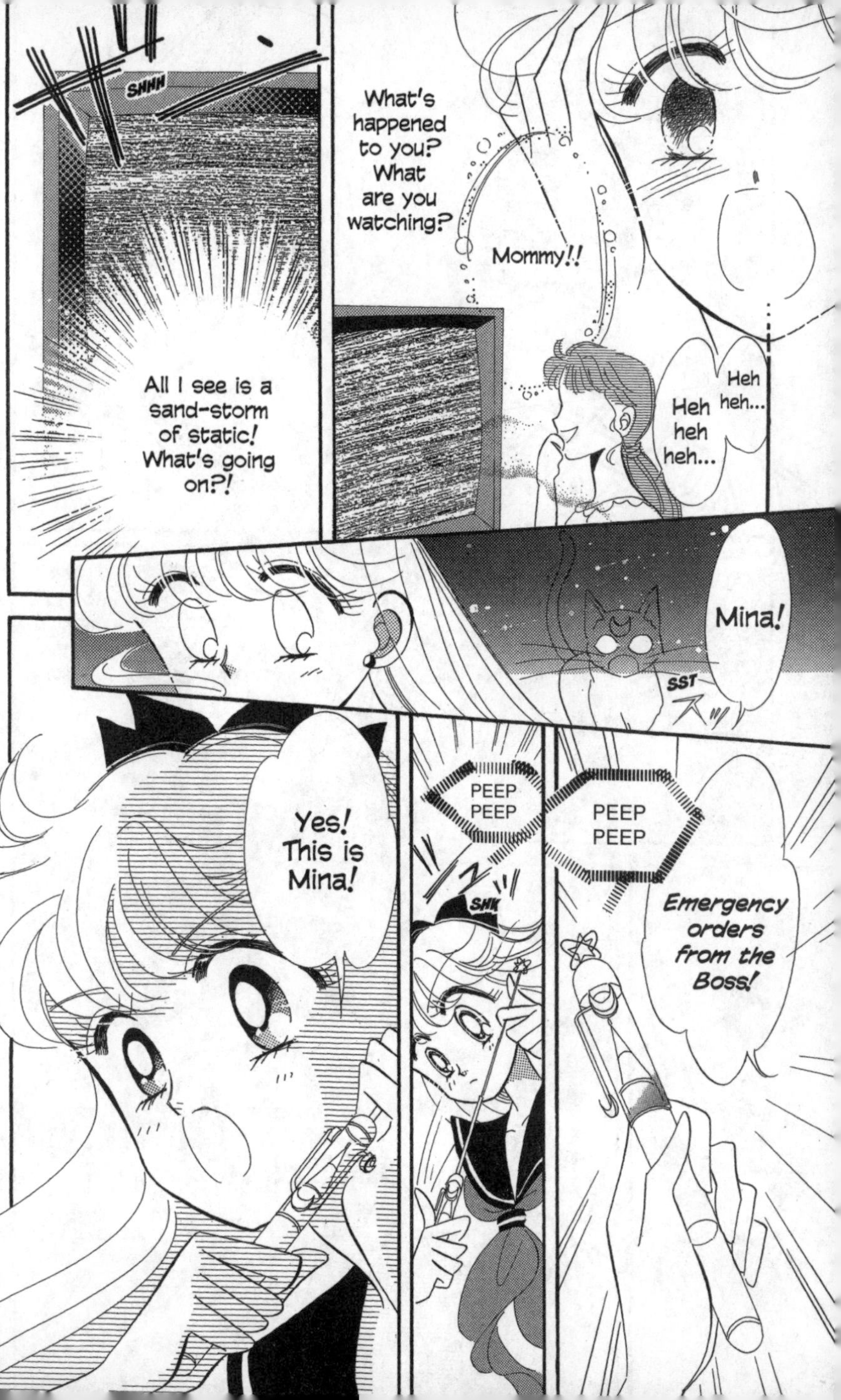

What's happened to you? What are you watching?
Mommy!!
Heh heh...
Heh heh heh...
SHHH
All I see is a sand-storm of static! What's going on?!
Mina!
SST
PEEP PEEP
Emergency orders from the Boss!
PEEP PEEP
SHK
Yes! This is Mina!

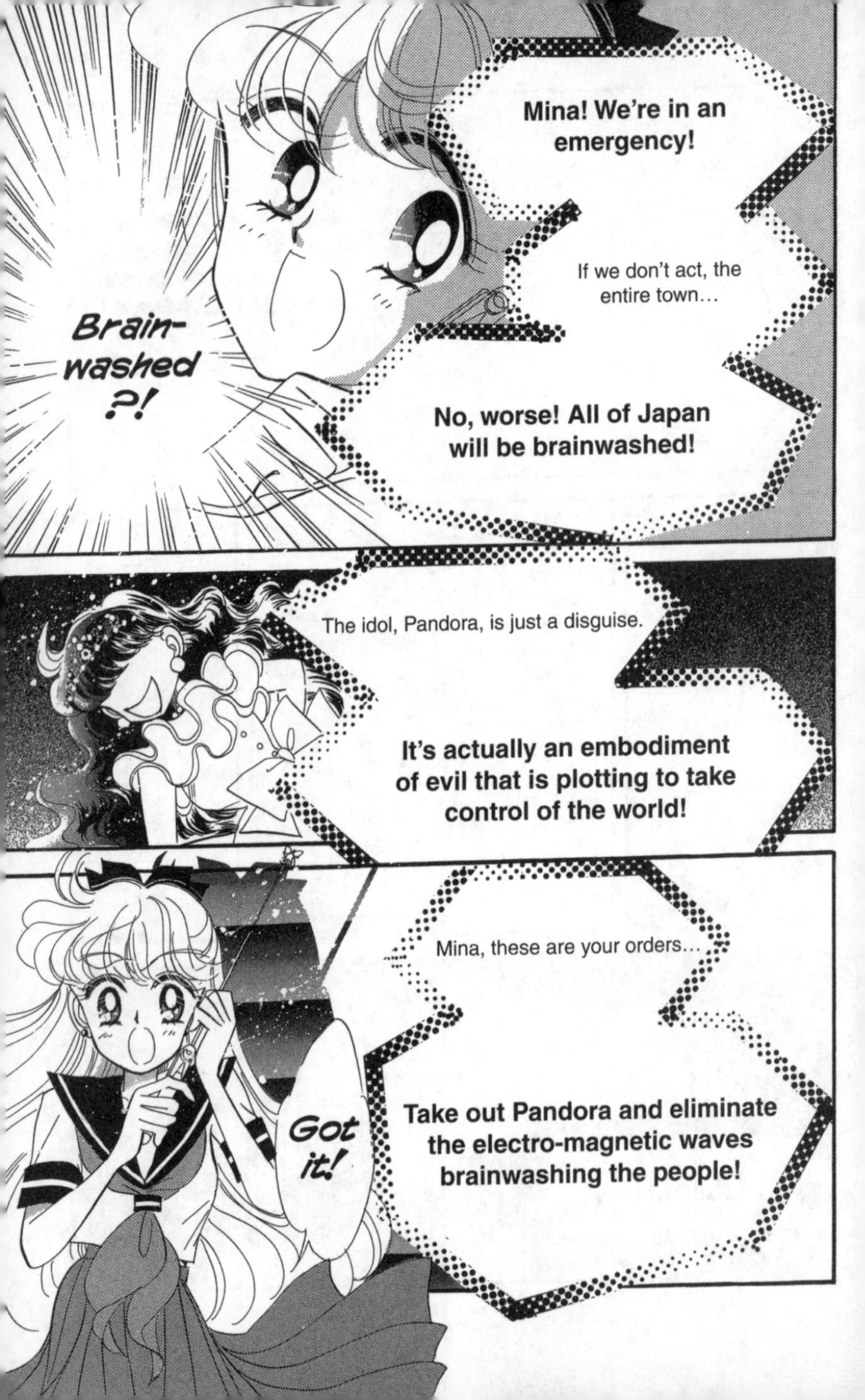
Mina! We're in an emergency!
If we don't act, the entire town…
Brain-washed ?!
No, worse! All of Japan will be brainwashed!
The idol, Pandora, is just a disguise.
It's actually an embodiment of evil that is plotting to take control of the world!
Mina, these are your orders…
Take out Pandora and eliminate the electro-magnetic waves brainwashing the people!
Got it!

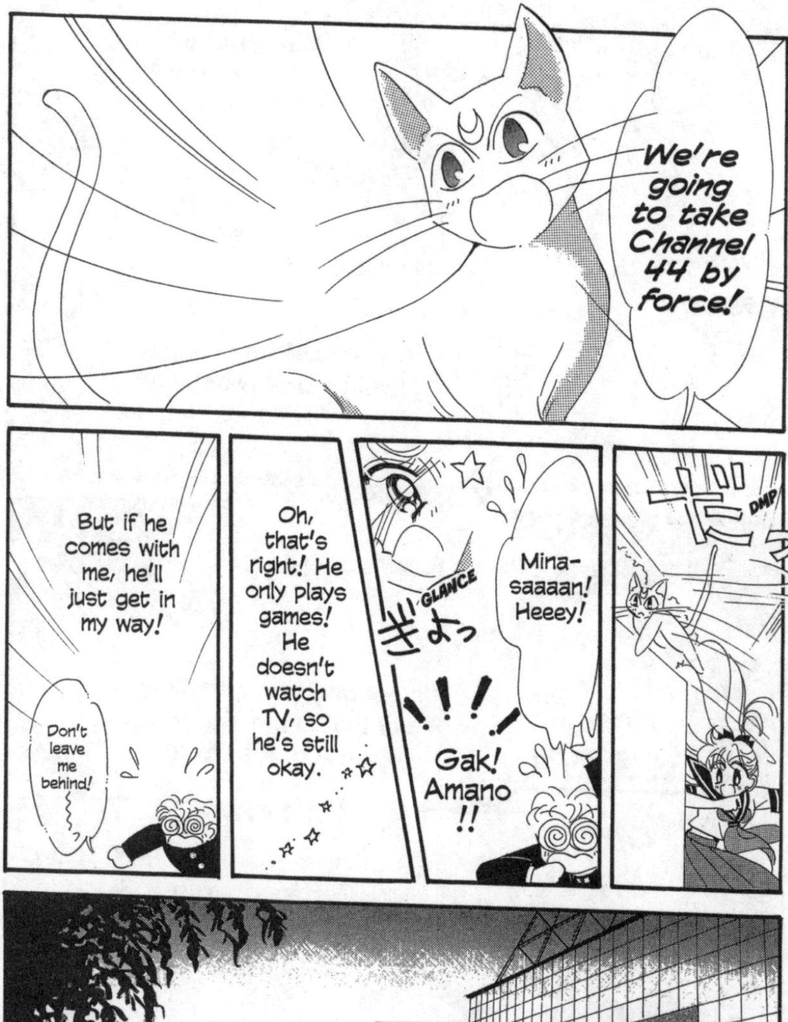
We're going to take Channel 44 by force!
だっ
DMP
Mina-saaaan! Heeey!
ぎょっ
GLANCE
Gak! Amano!!
Oh, that's right! He only plays games! He doesn't watch TV, so he's still okay.
But if he comes with me, he'll just get in my way!
Don't leave me behind!
Channel 44

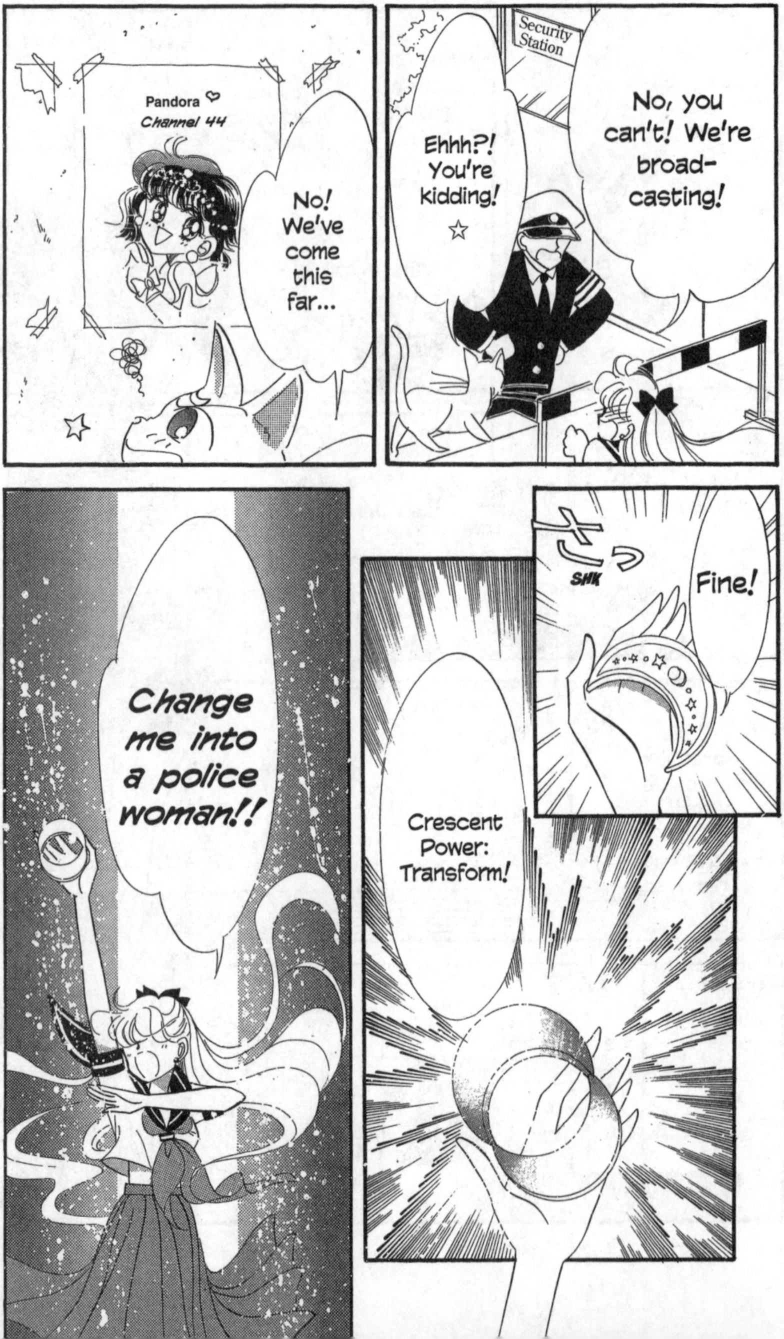
Security Station
No, you can't! We're broad-casting!
Ehhh?! You're kidding!
Pandora
Channel 44
No! We've come this far...
さっ
SHK
Fine!
Crescent Power: Transform!
Change me into a police woman!!

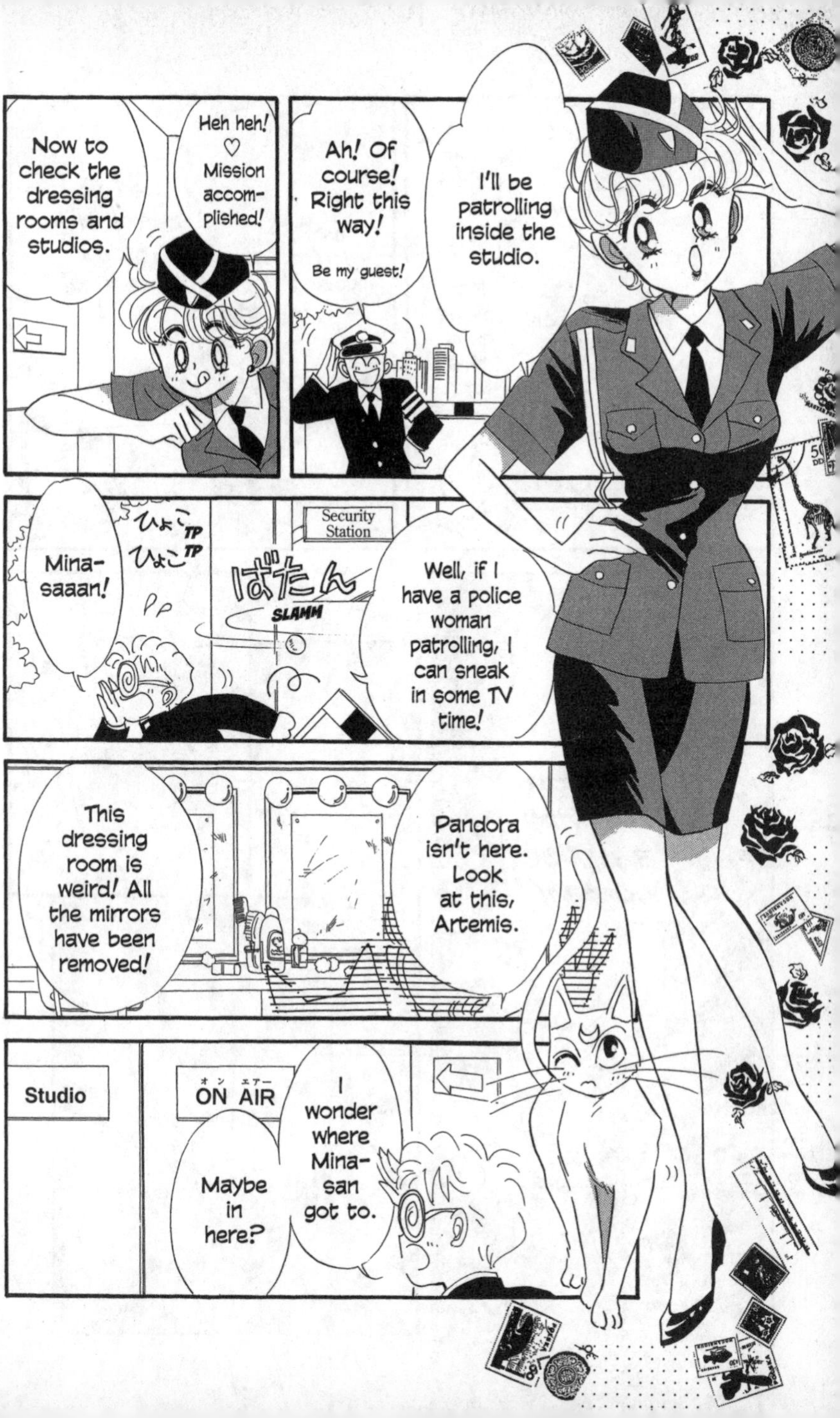
I'll be patrolling inside the studio.
Ah! Of course! Right this way!
Be my guest!
Heh heh! ♡ Mission accomplished!
Now to check the dressing rooms and studios.
Security Station
Well, if I have a police woman patrolling, I can sneak in some TV time!
ばたん
SLAMM
ひょこ TP
ひょこ TP
Mina-saaan!
Pandora isn't here. Look at this, Artemis.
This dressing room is weird! All the mirrors have been removed!
I wonder where Mina-san got to.
オンエアー
ON AIR
Studio
Maybe in here?

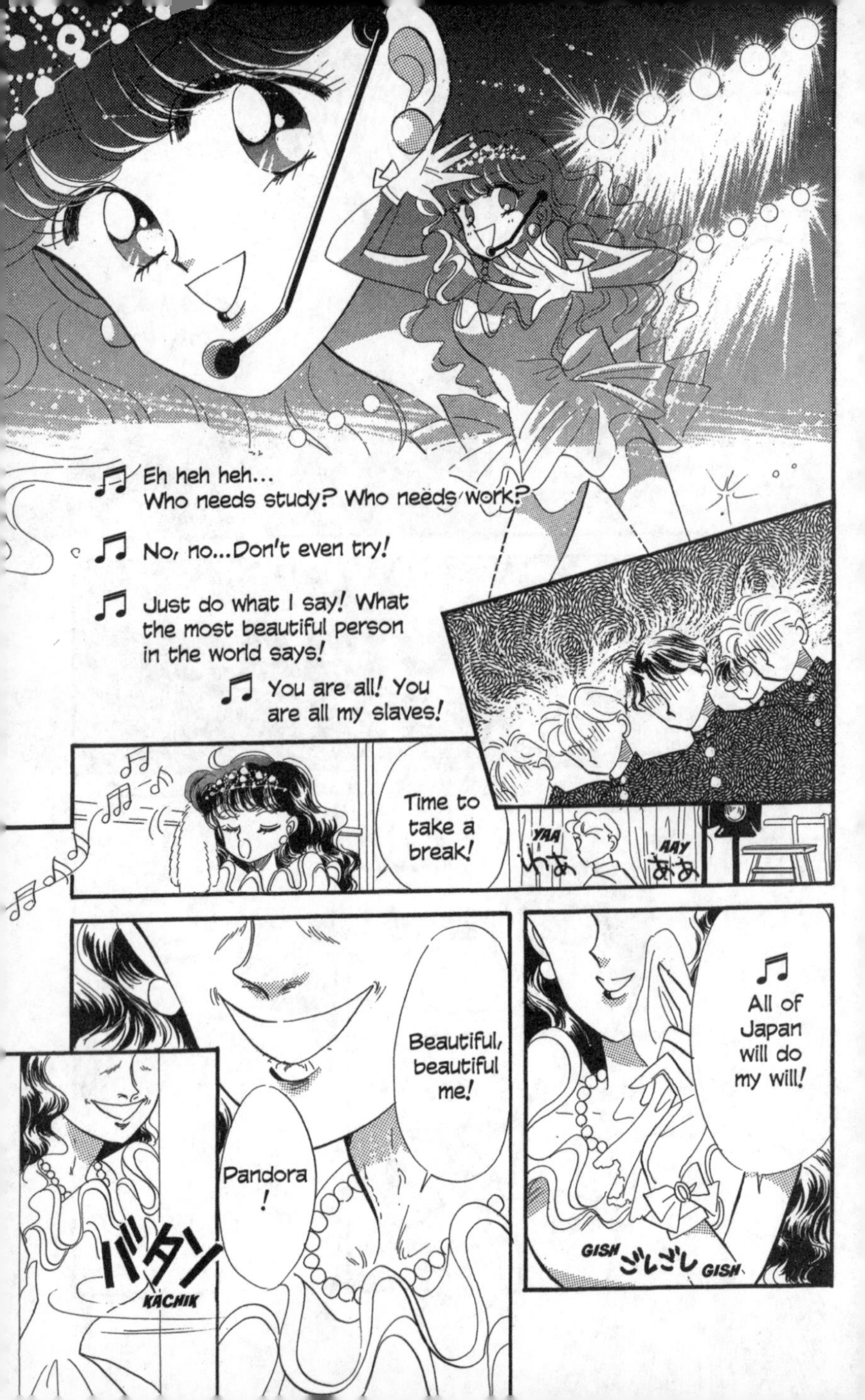

♫ Eh heh heh... Who needs study? Who needs work?
♫ No, no...Don't even try!
♫ Just do what I say! What the most beautiful person in the world says!
♫ You are all! You are all my slaves!
YAA ゆあ
AAY ああ
Time to take a break!
♫ All of Japan will do my will!
GISH ごしごし GISH
Beautiful, beautiful me!
Pandora!
バタン
KACHIK

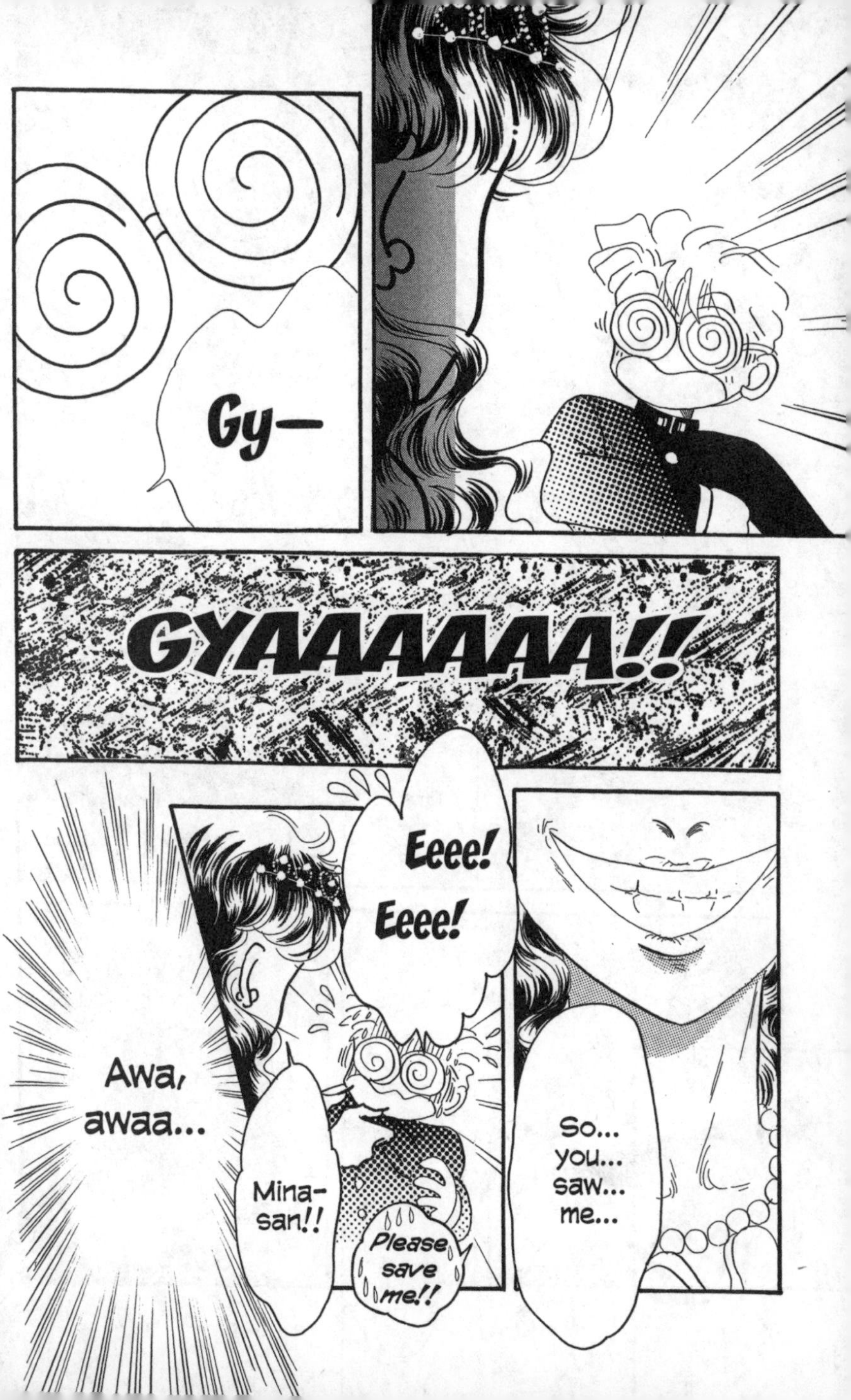
Gy—
GYAAAAAA!!
So... you... saw... me...
Eeee! Eeee!
Mina-san!!
Please save me!!
Awa, awaa...

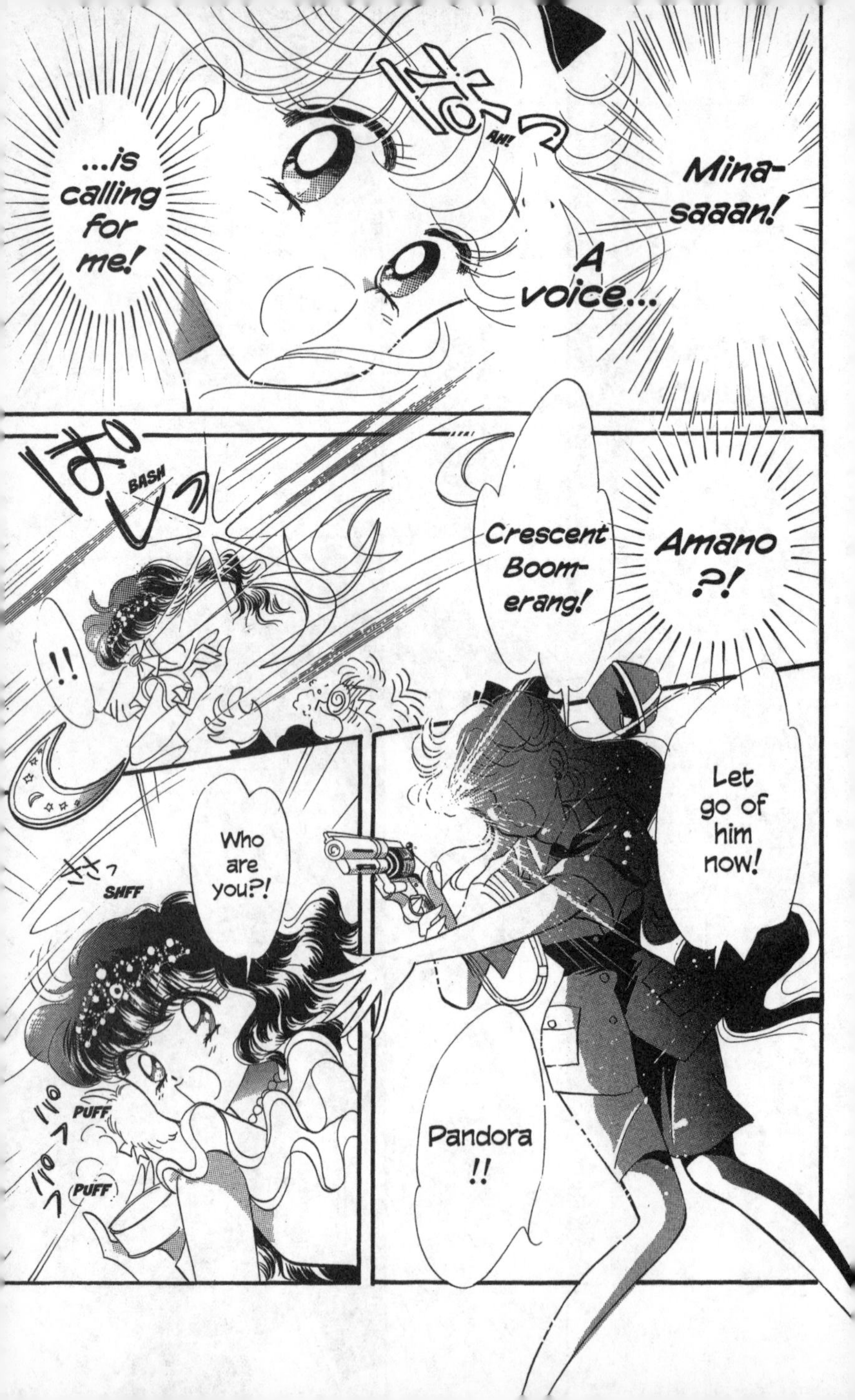
Mina-saaan!
AH!
A voice...
...is calling for me!
Amano ?!
Crescent Boomerang!
BASH
!!
Let go of him now!
Pandora !!
Who are you?!
SHFF
PUFF
PUFF

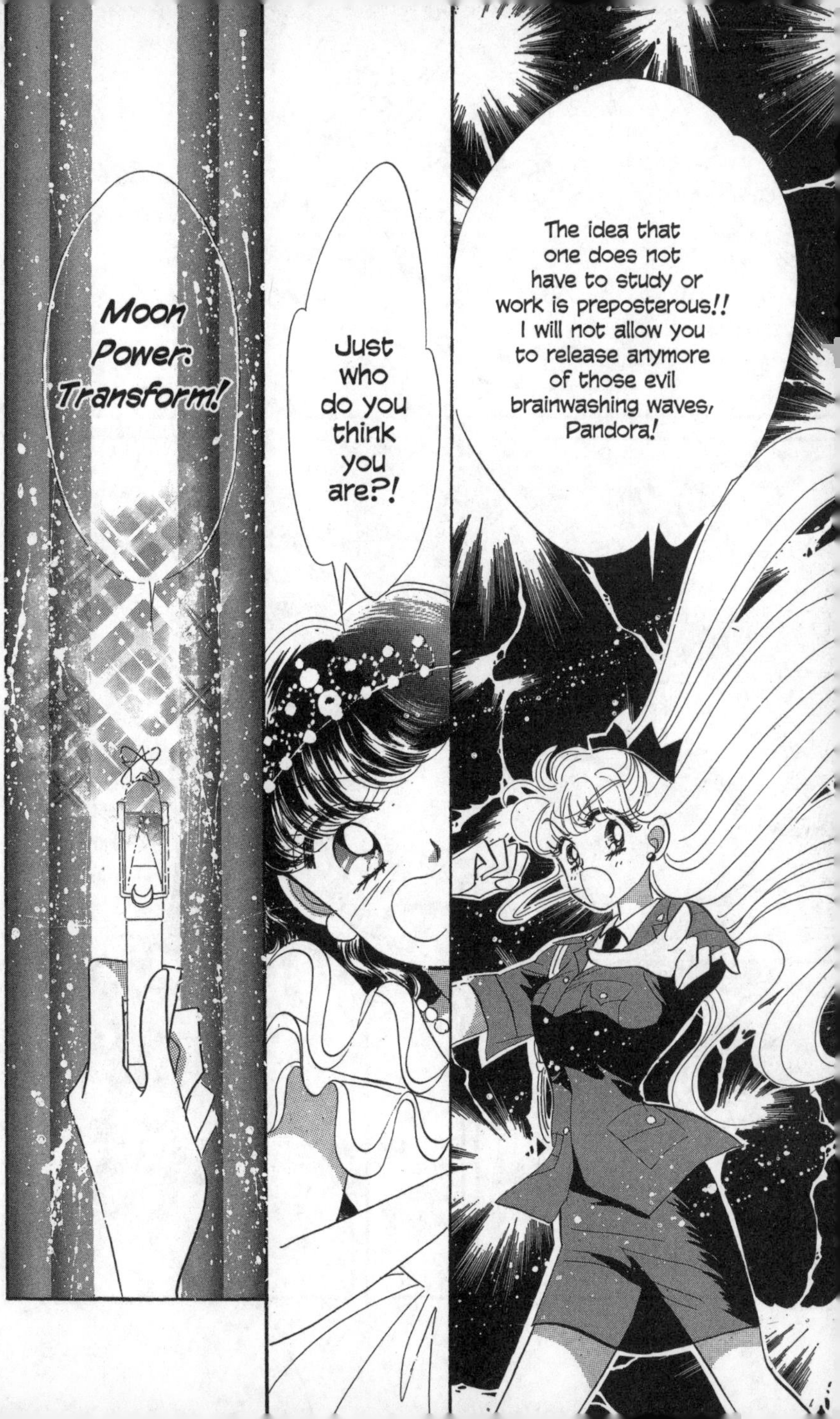
The idea that one does not have to study or work is preposterous!! I will not allow you to release anymore of those evil brainwashing waves, Pandora!
Just who do you think you are?!
Moon Power: Transform!

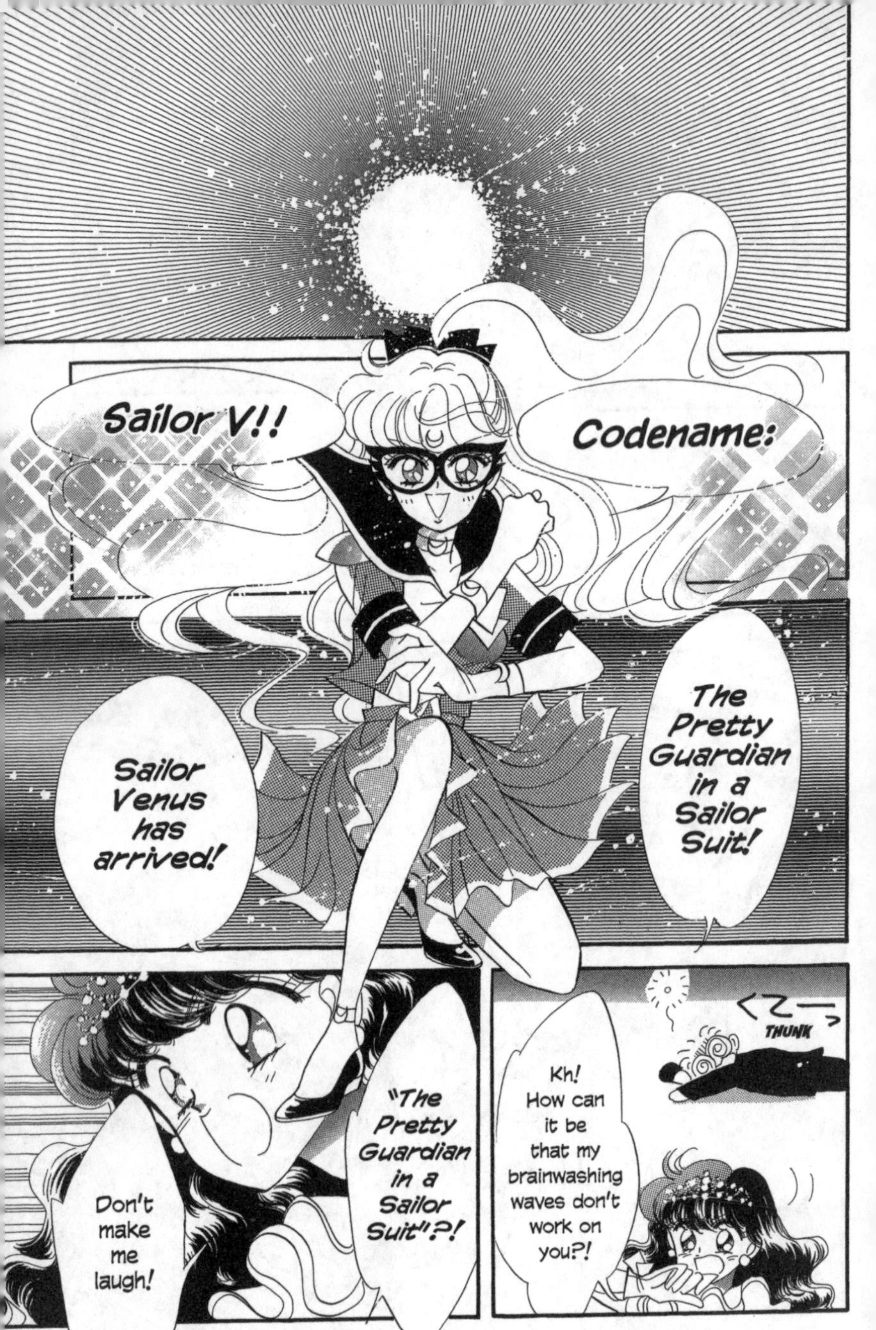
Codename:
Sailor V!!
The Pretty Guardian in a Sailor Suit!
Sailor Venus has arrived!
THUNK
Kh! How can it be that my brainwashing waves don't work on you?!
"The Pretty Guardian in a Sailor Suit"?!
Don't make me laugh!

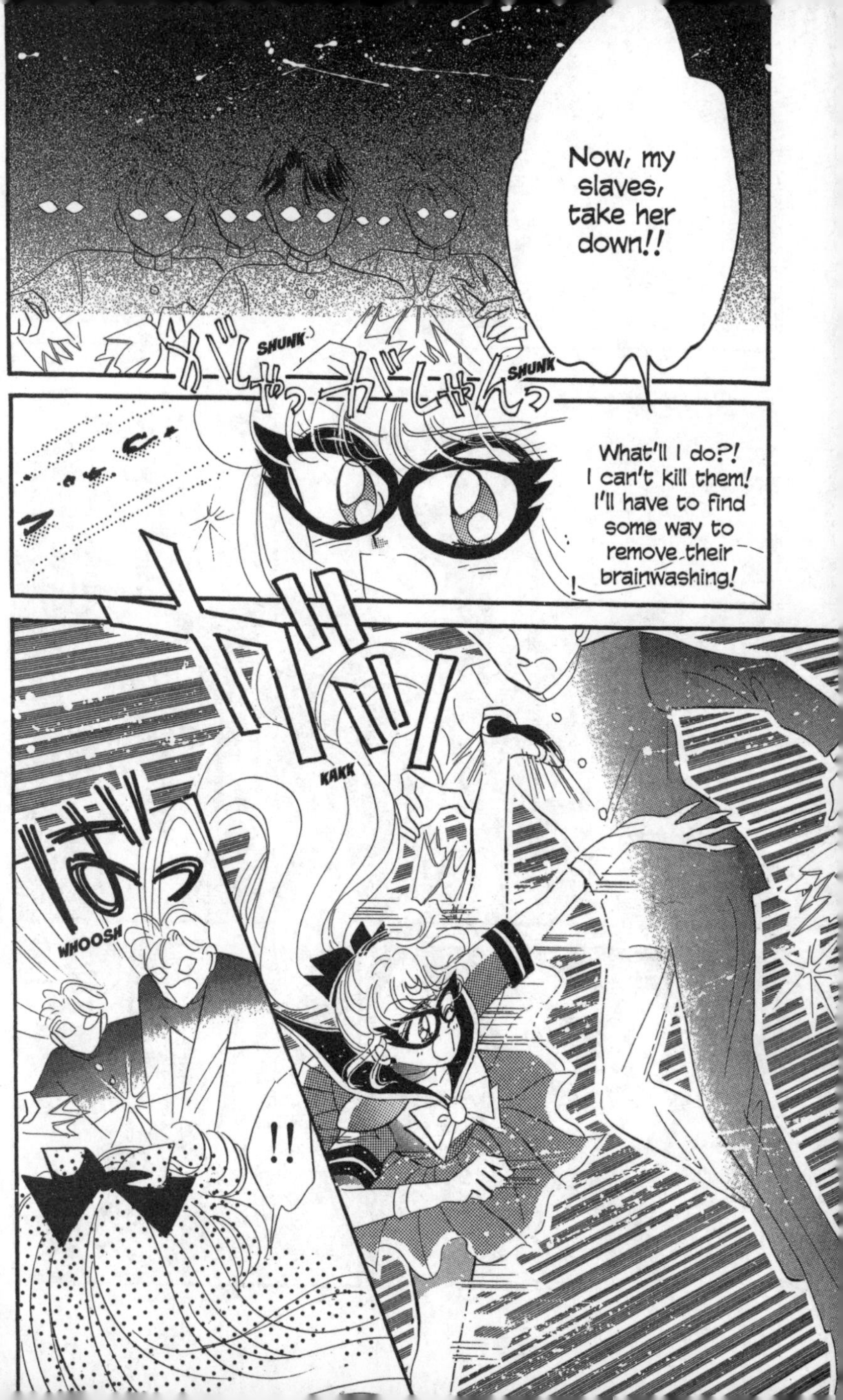
Now, my slaves, take her down!!
がしゃんっ
SHUNK
がしゃっ
SHUNK
What'll I do?! I can't kill them! I'll have to find some way to remove their brainwashing!
!
ガッ
KAKK
はっ
WHOOSH
!!

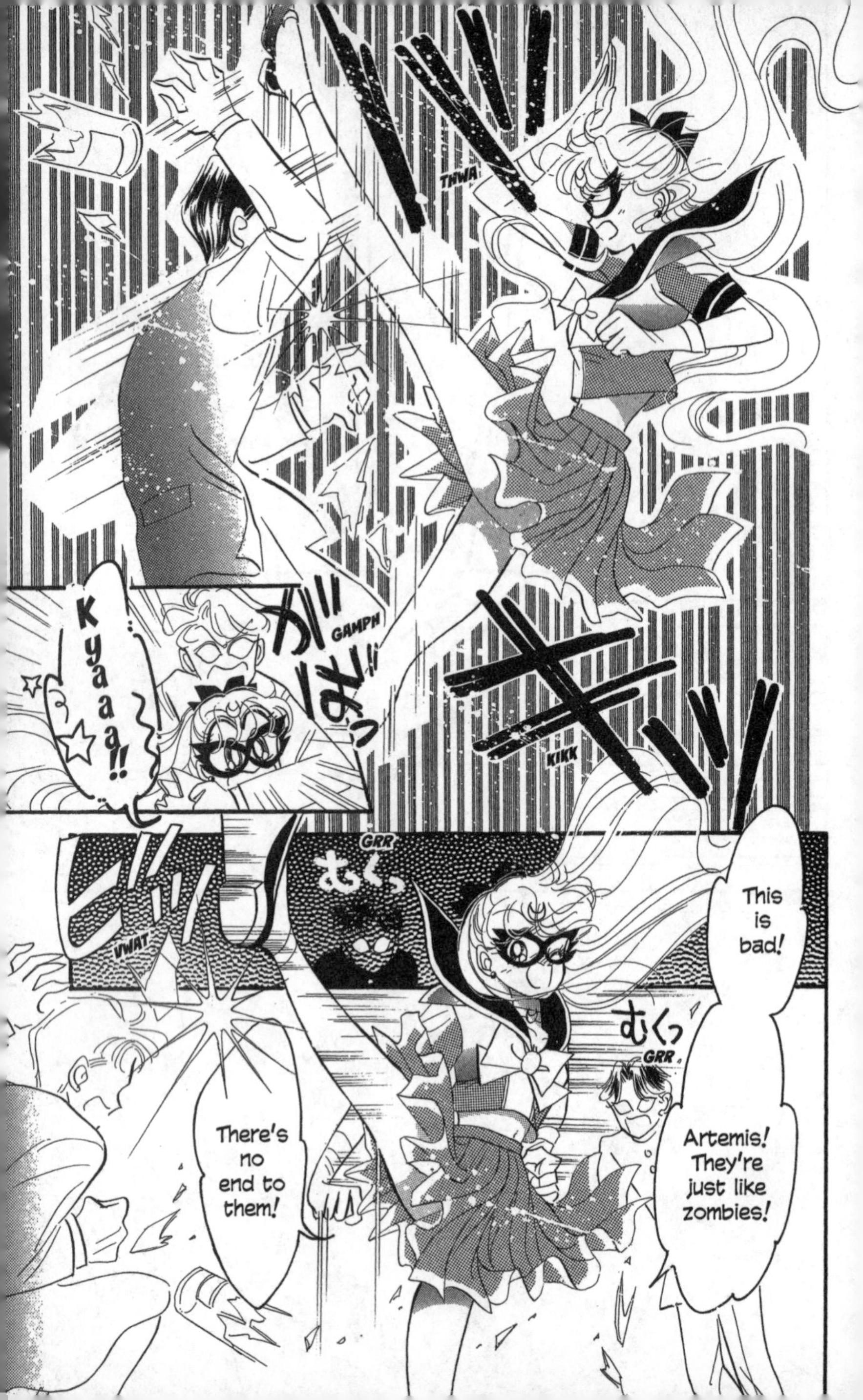
THWA
GAMPH
KIKK
Kyaaa!!
This is bad!
むくっ
GRR
Artemis! They're just like zombies!
むくっ
GRR
There's no end to them!
VWAT

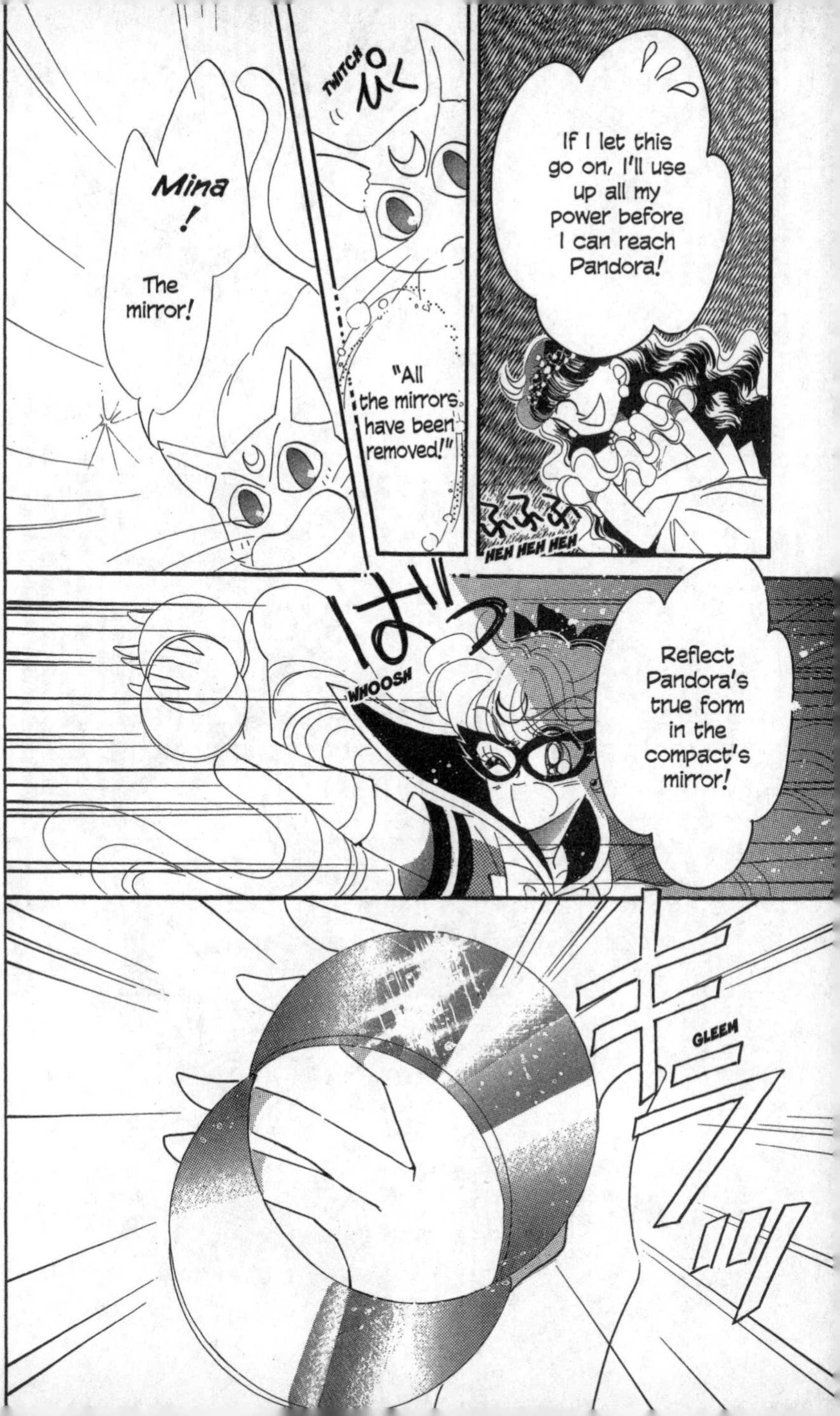
If I let this go on, I'll use up all my power before I can reach Pandora!
ふふふ
HEH HEH HEH
ぴく
TWITCH
"All the mirrors have been removed!"
Mina!
The mirror!
Reflect Pandora's true form in the compact's mirror!
はっ
WHOOSH
キラッ
GLEEM

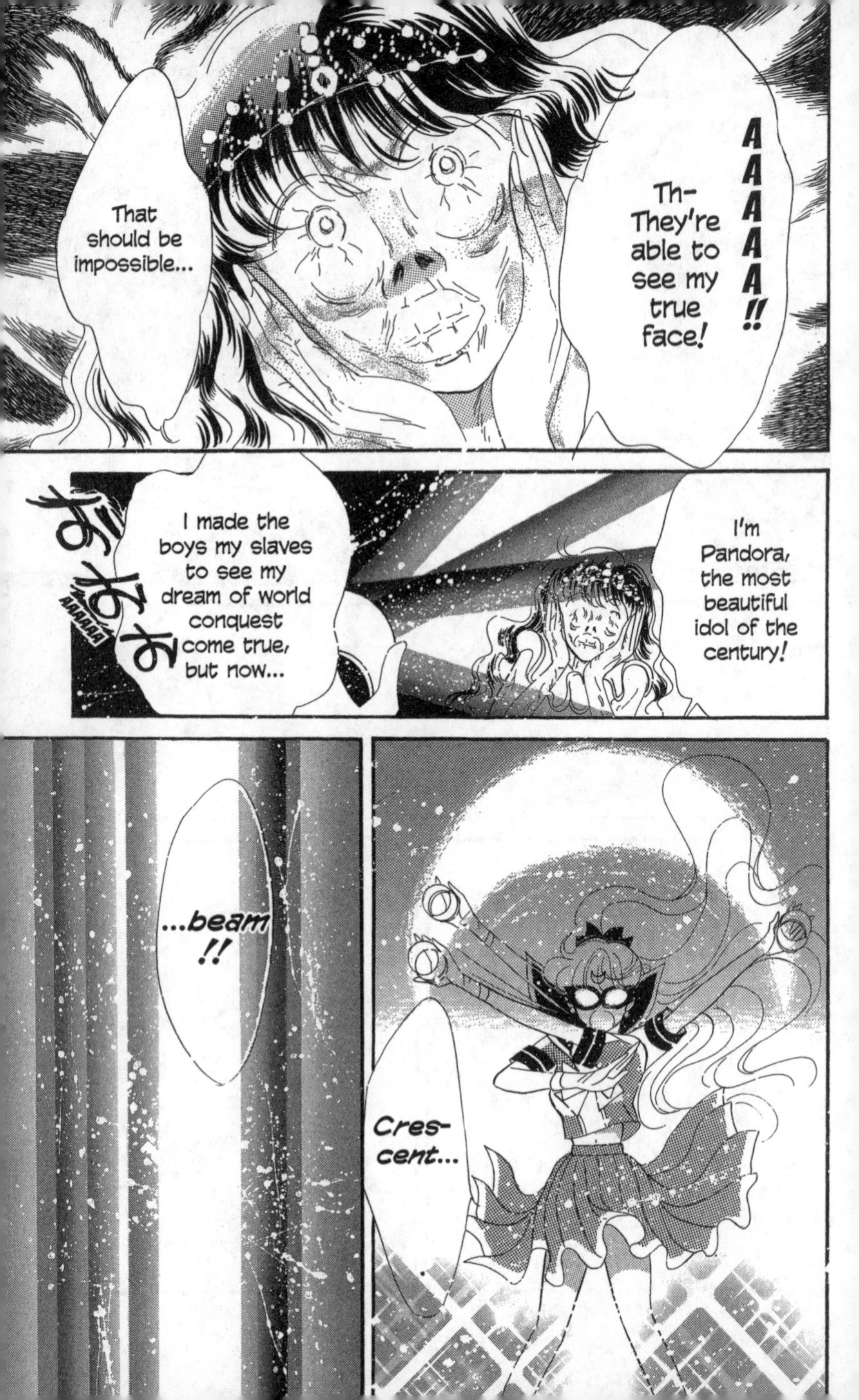
AAAAA!!
Th- They're able to see my true face!
That should be impossible...
I'm Pandora, the most beautiful idol of the century!
I made the boys my slaves to see my dream of world conquest come true, but now...
Cres- cent...
...beam !!

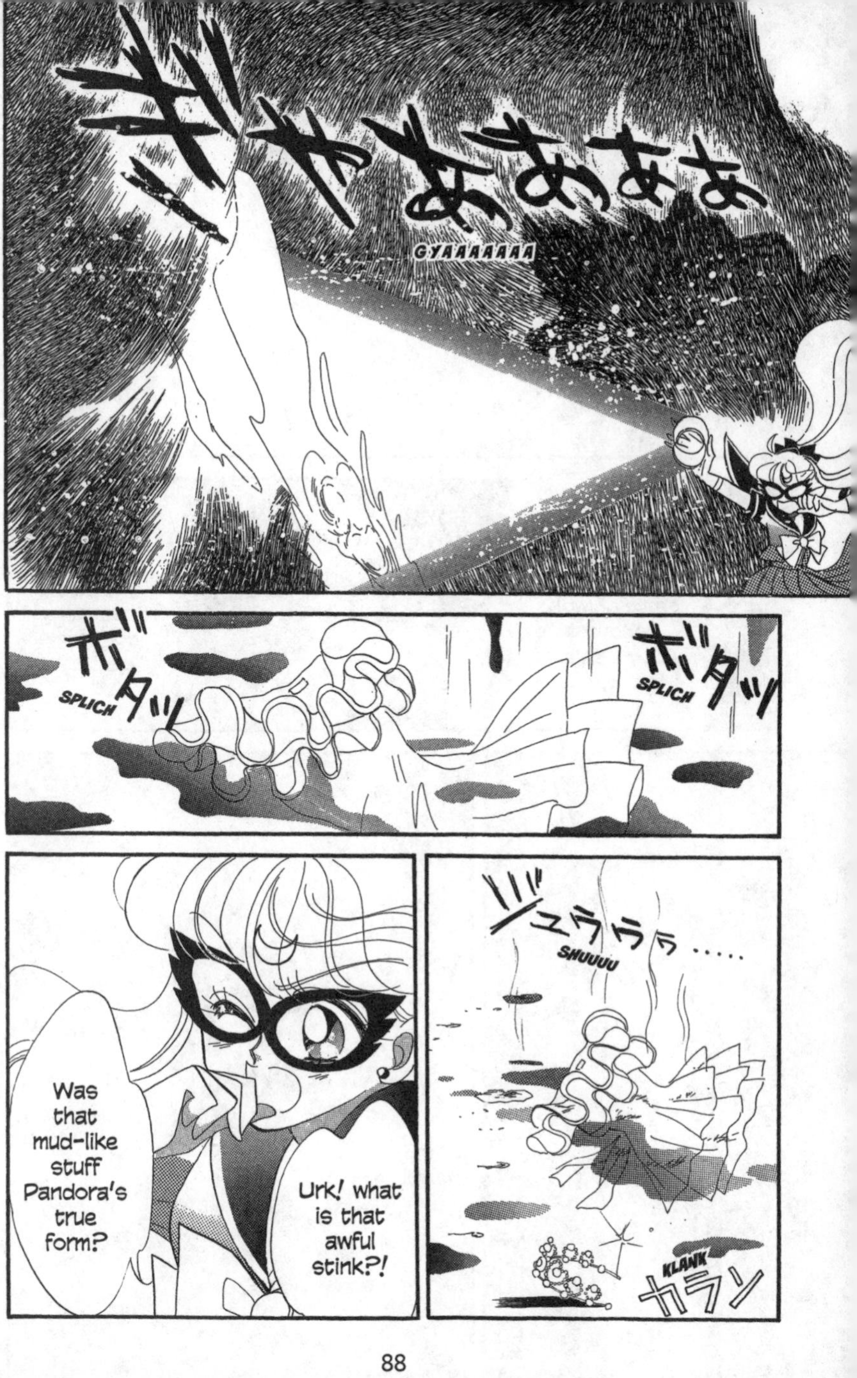
GYAAAAAAA
SPLICH
SPLICH
SHUUUU
KLANK
Urk! what is that awful stink?!
Was that mud-like stuff Pandora's true form?

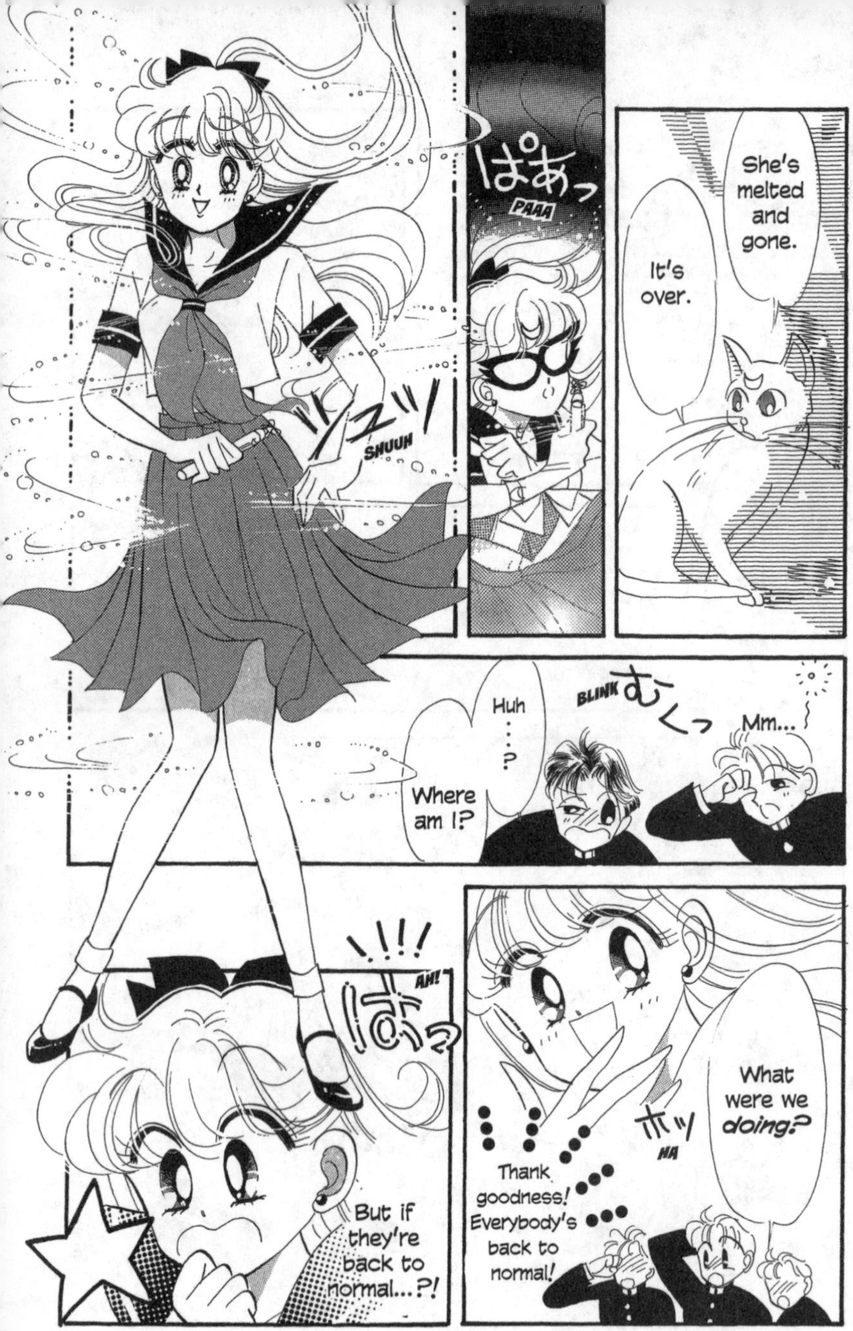
She's melted and gone.
It's over.
ぱあっ
PAAA
ズッ
SHUUH
Mm...
むくっ
BLINK
Huh...?
Where am I!?
What were we doing?
ホッ
HA
Thank goodness! Everybody's back to normal!
はっ
AH!
But if they're back to normal...?!

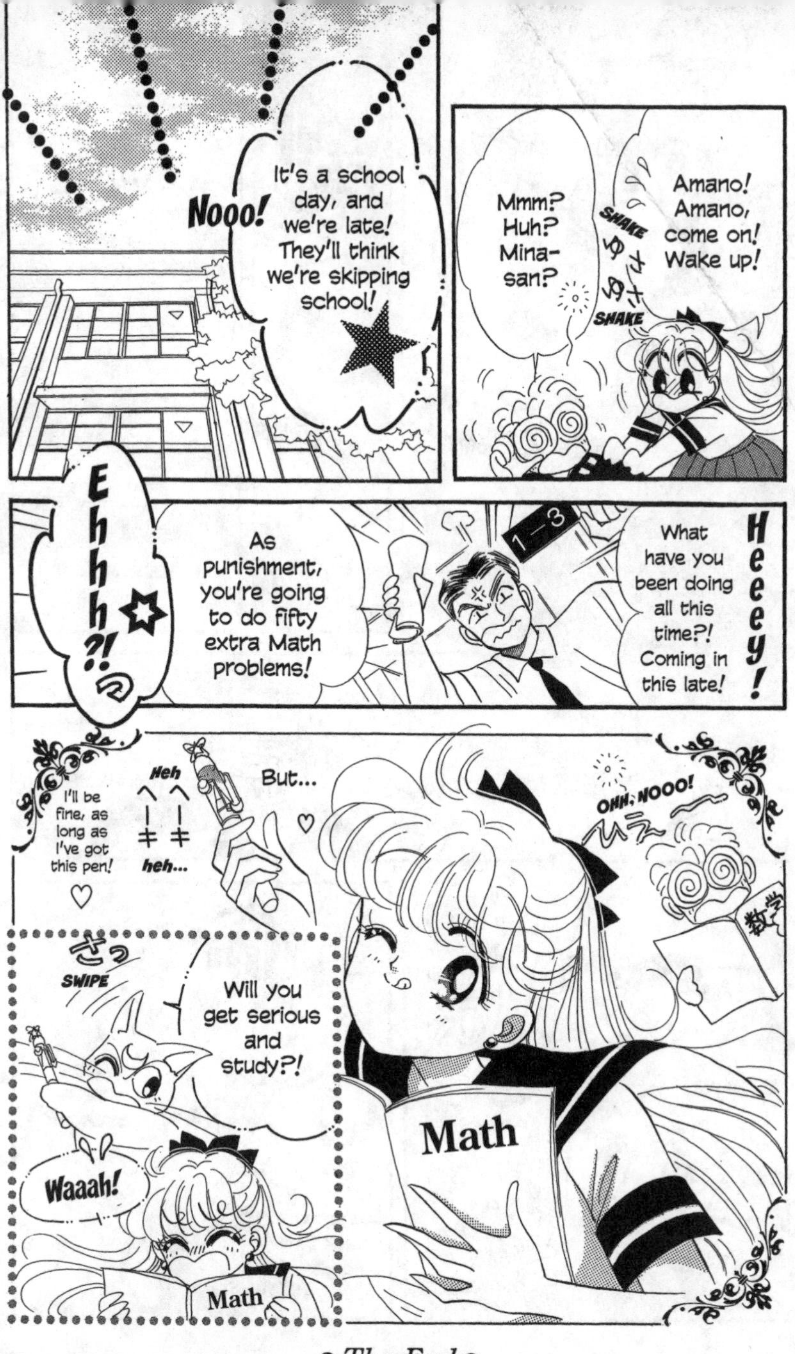
Amano! Amano, come on! Wake up!
SHAKE
SHAKE
Mmm? Huh? Mina-san?
Nooo!
It's a school day, and we're late! They'll think we're skipping school!
Heeey!
What have you been doing all this time?! Coming in this late!
1—3
As punishment, you're going to do fifty extra Math problems!
Ehhh?!
OHH, NOOO!
But...
Heh
heh...
I'll be fine, as long as I've got this pen!
Math
SWIPE
Will you get serious and study?!
Waaah!
Math

• *The End* •

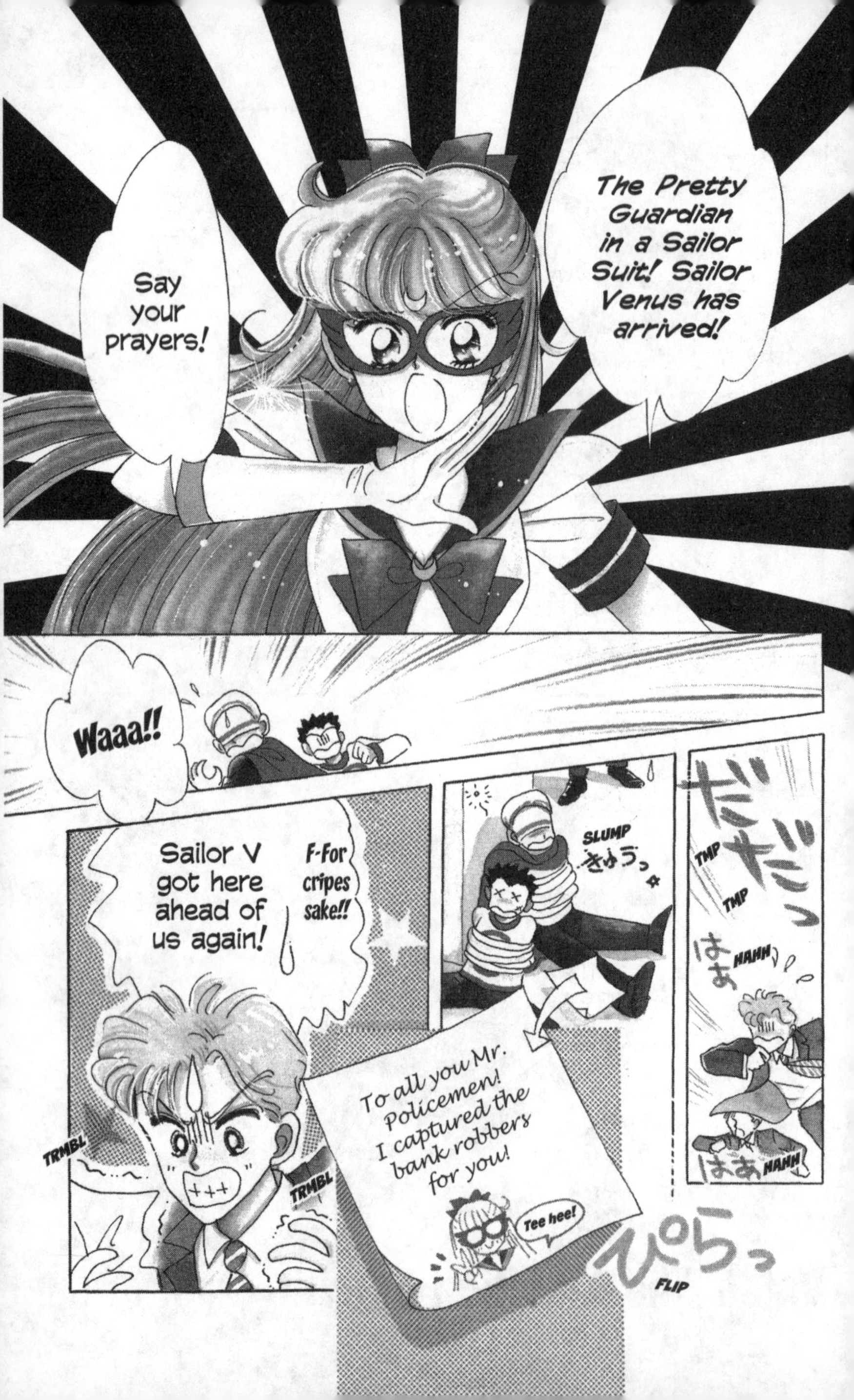
The Pretty Guardian in a Sailor Suit! Sailor Venus has arrived!
Say your prayers!
Waaa!!
だだっ
TMP
TMP
はぁ HAHH
はぁ HAHH
SLUMP
きゅうっ
F-For cripes sake!!
Sailor V got here ahead of us again!
TRMBL
TRMBL
To all you Mr. Policemen! I captured the bank robbers for you!
Tee hee!
ぴらっ
FLIP

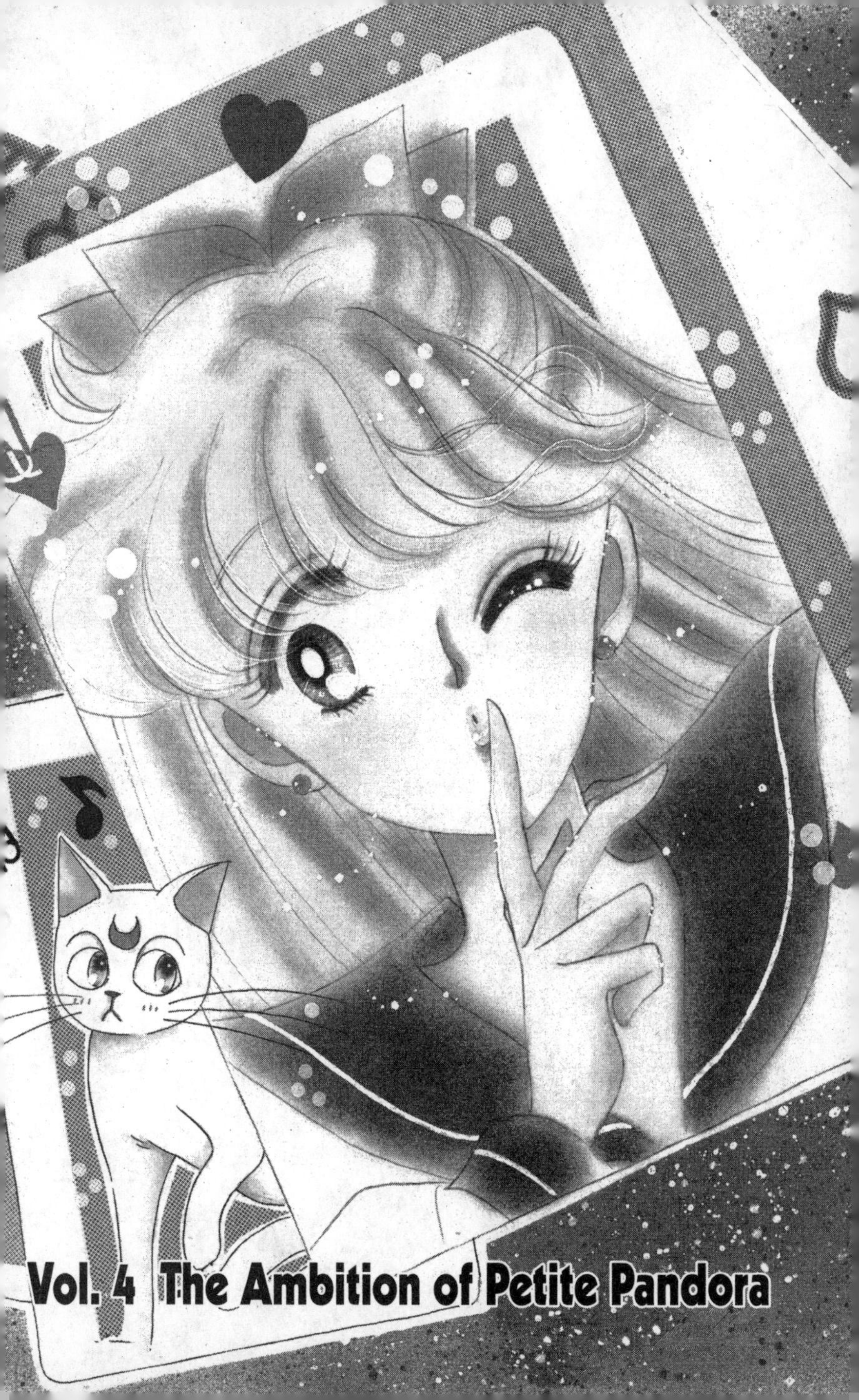

Vol. 4 The Ambition of Petite Pandora

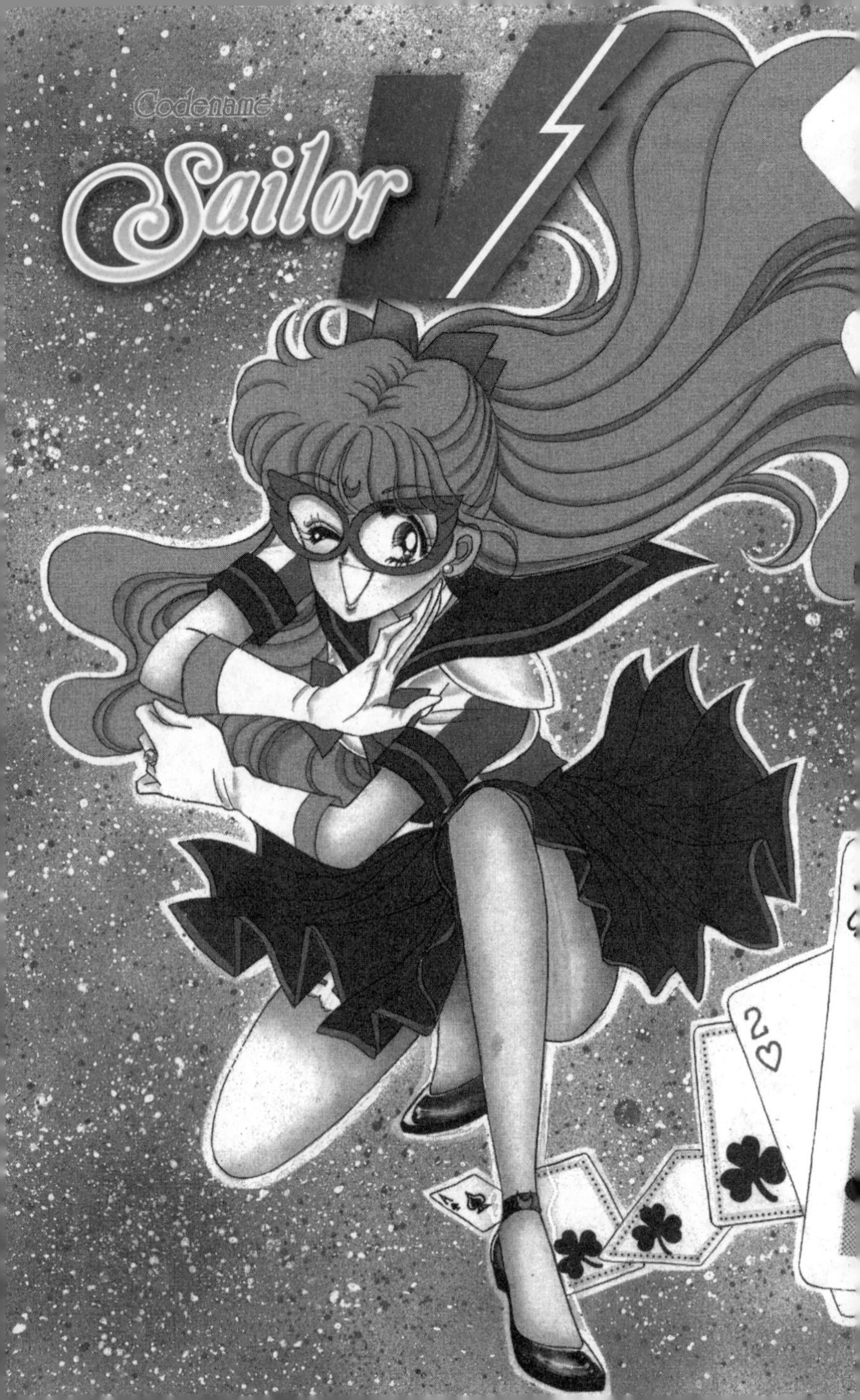
Codename
Sailor V

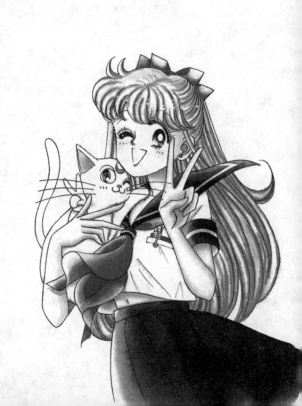

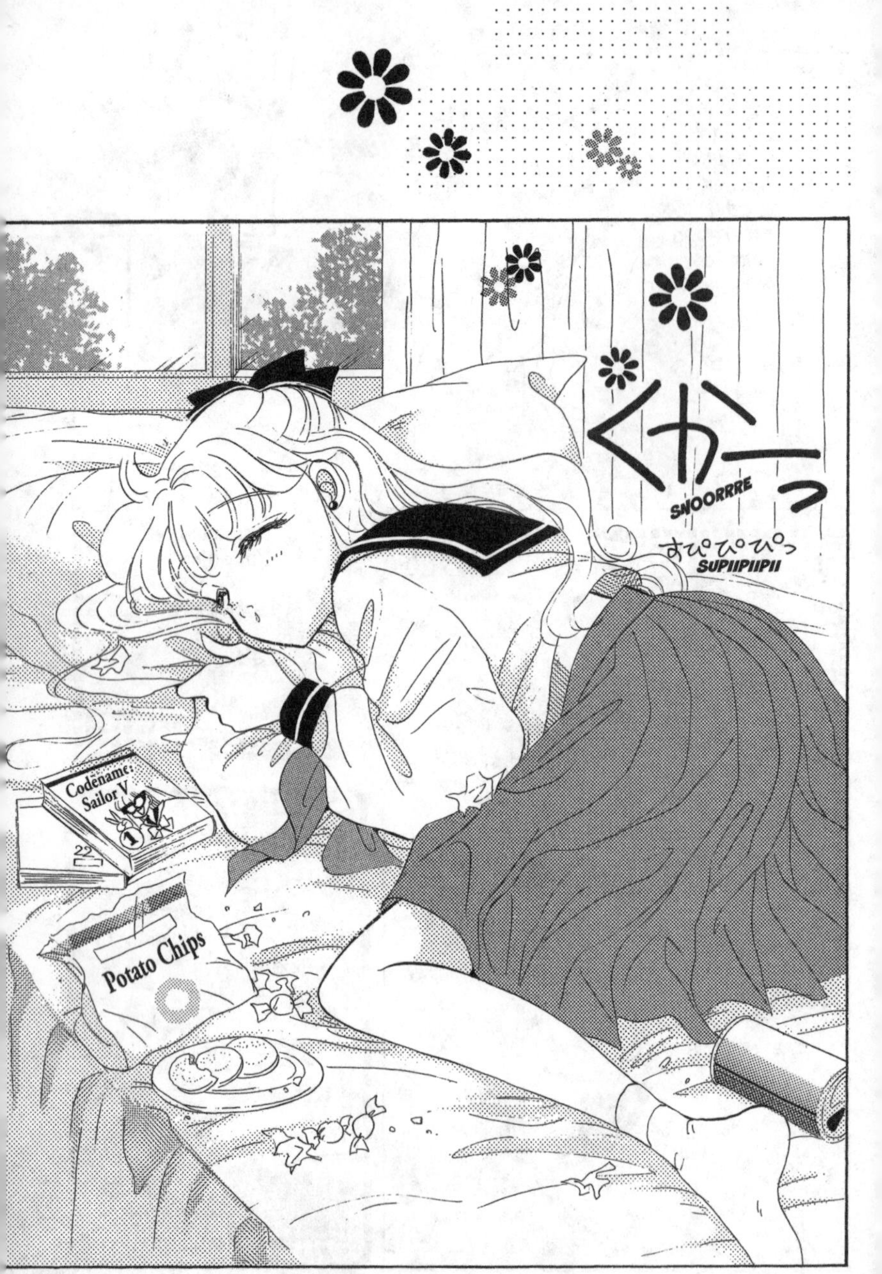
くかーっ
SNOORRRE
すぴぴぴっ
SUPIIPIIPII
Codename: Sailor V
1
22
Potato Chips

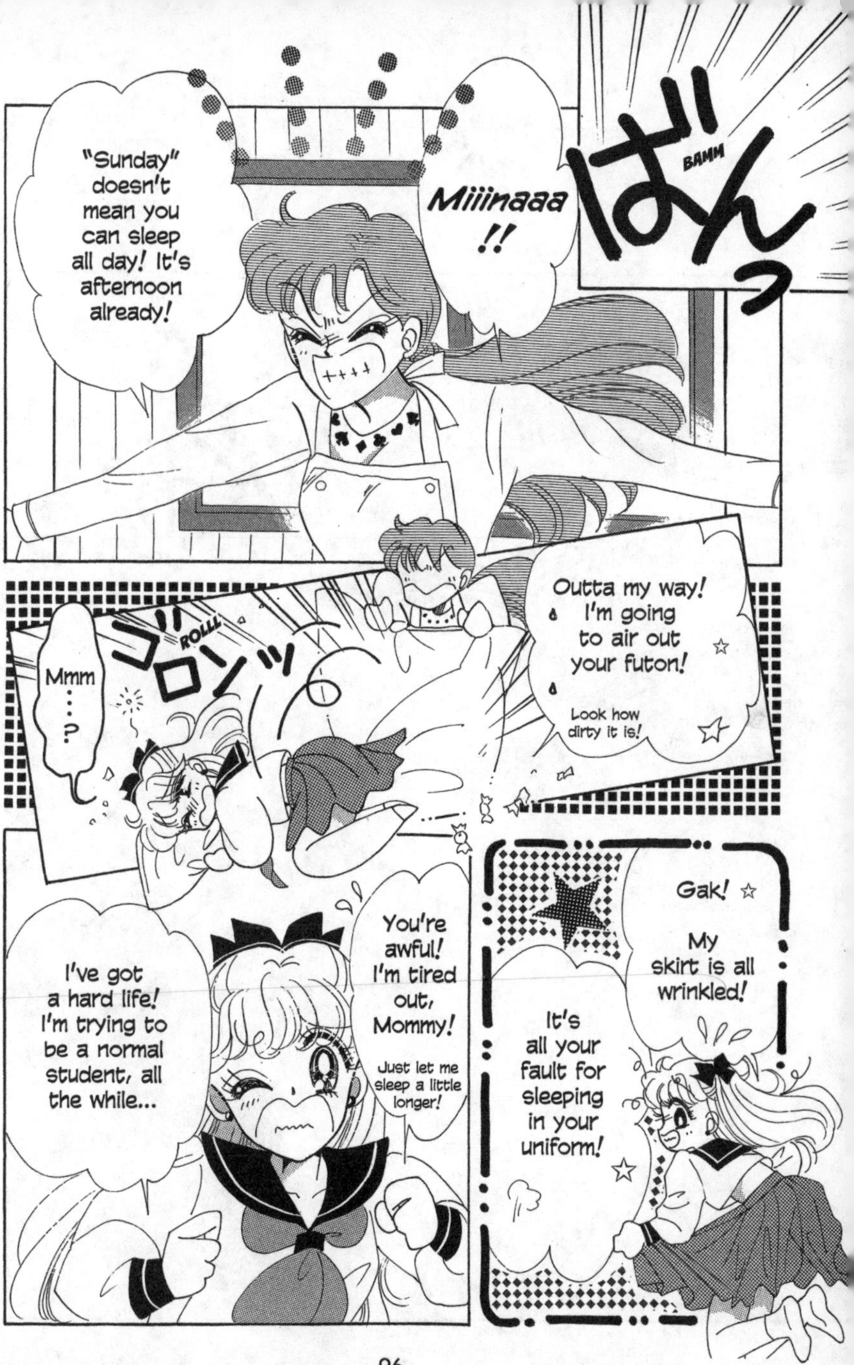

ばんっ
BAMM
Miiinaaa !!
"Sunday" doesn't mean you can sleep all day! It's afternoon already!
Outta my way! I'm going to air out your futon!
Look how dirty it is!
ゴロンッ
ROLLL
Mmm...?
Gak! ☆
My skirt is all wrinkled!
It's all your fault for sleeping in your uniform!
You're awful! I'm tired out, Mommy!
Just let me sleep a little longer!
I've got a hard life! I'm trying to be a normal student, all the while...

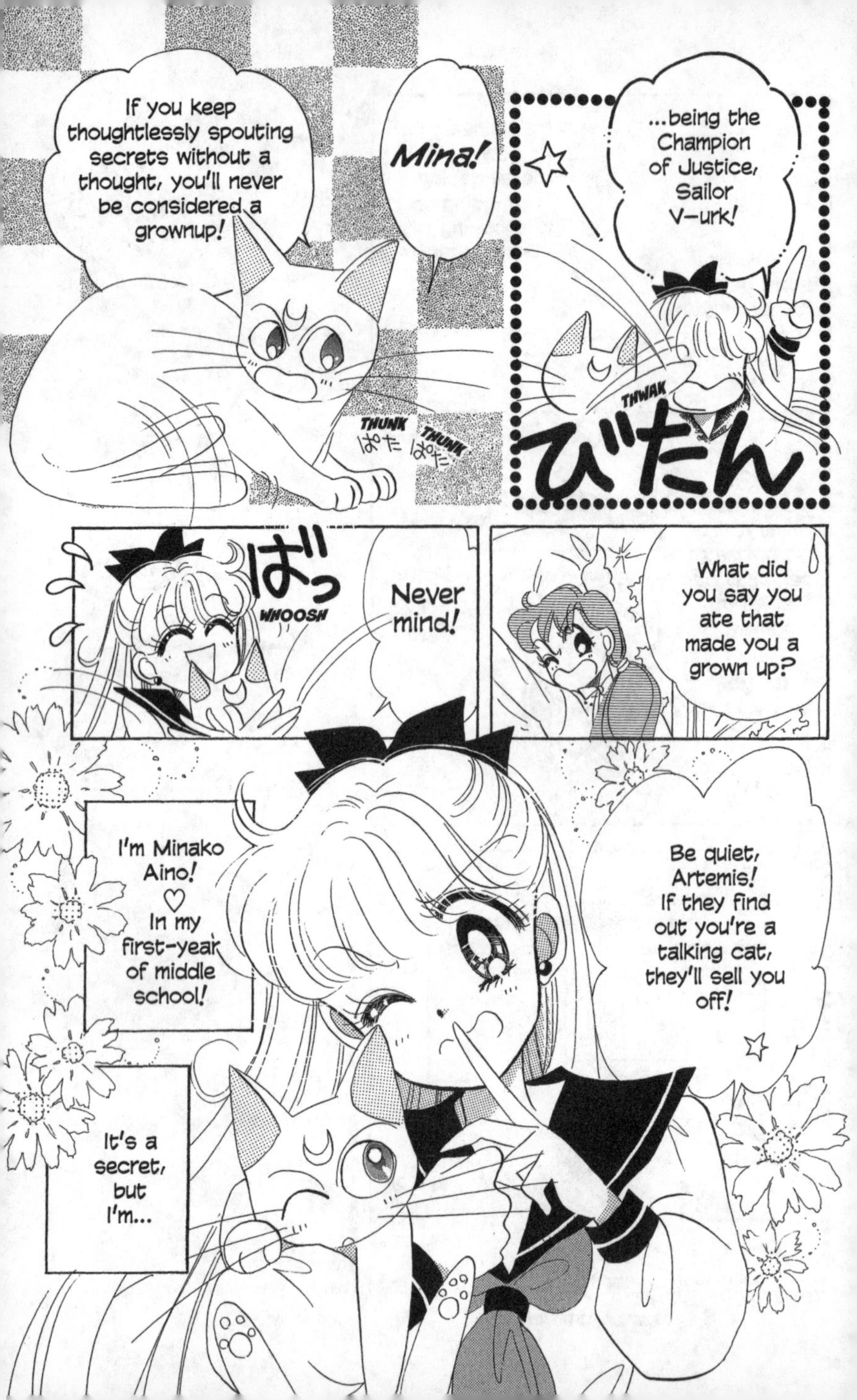
...being the Champion of Justice, Sailor V—urk!
THWAK
びたん
Mina!
If you keep thoughtlessly spouting secrets without a thought, you'll never be considered a grownup!
THUNK
ぱた
THUNK
ぱた
What did you say you ate that made you a grown up?
Never mind!
ばっ
WHOOSH
Be quiet, Artemis! If they find out you're a talking cat, they'll sell you off!
I'm Minako Aino! ♡ In my first-year of middle school!
It's a secret, but I'm...

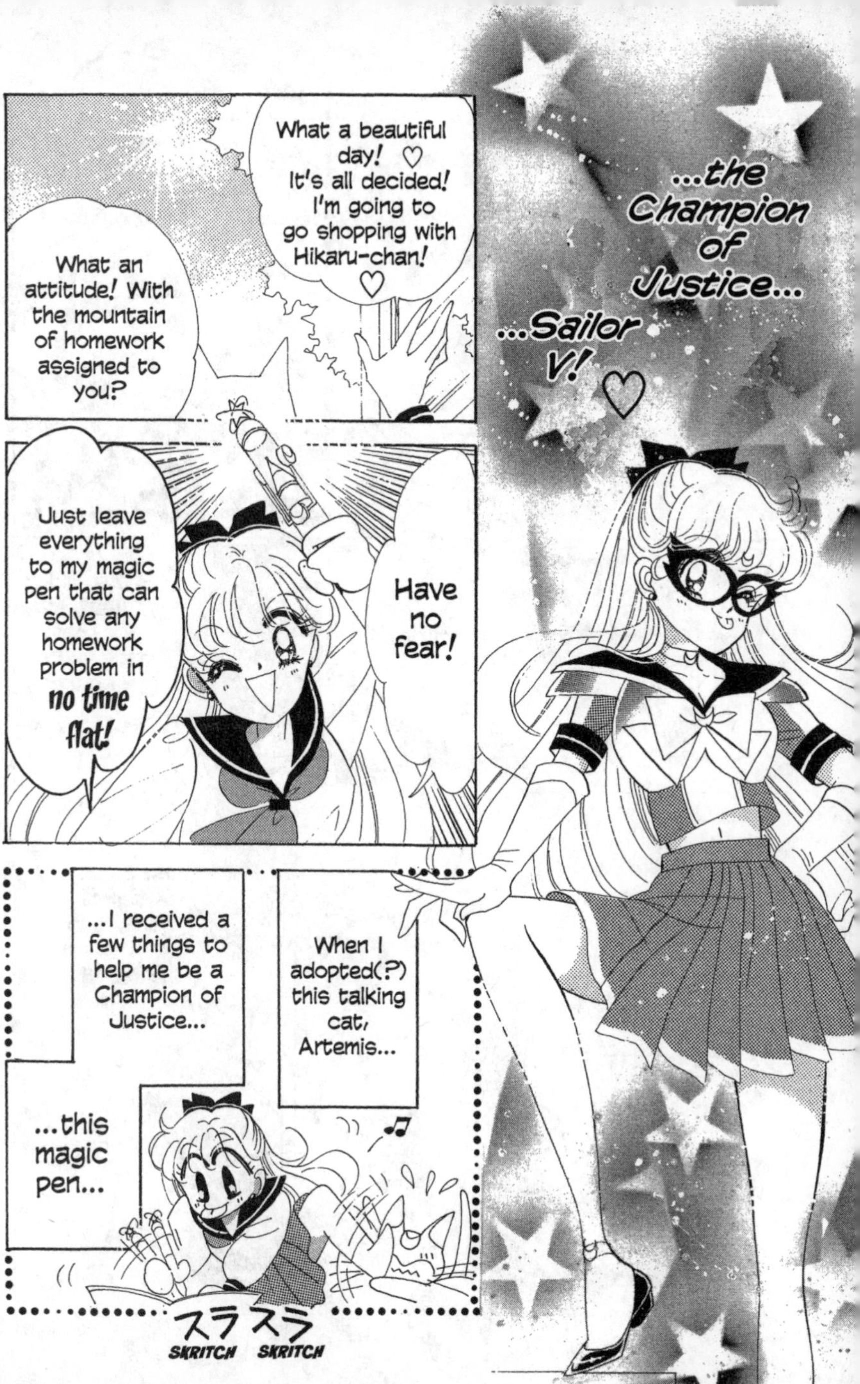
...the Champion of Justice...
...Sailor V! ♡
What a beautiful day! ♡ It's all decided! I'm going to go shopping with Hikaru-chan! ♡
What an attitude! With the mountain of homework assigned to you?
Have no fear!
Just leave everything to my magic pen that can solve any homework problem in no time flat!
When I adopted(?) this talking cat, Artemis...
...I received a few things to help me be a Champion of Justice...
...this magic pen...
スラ スラ
SKRITCH SKRITCH

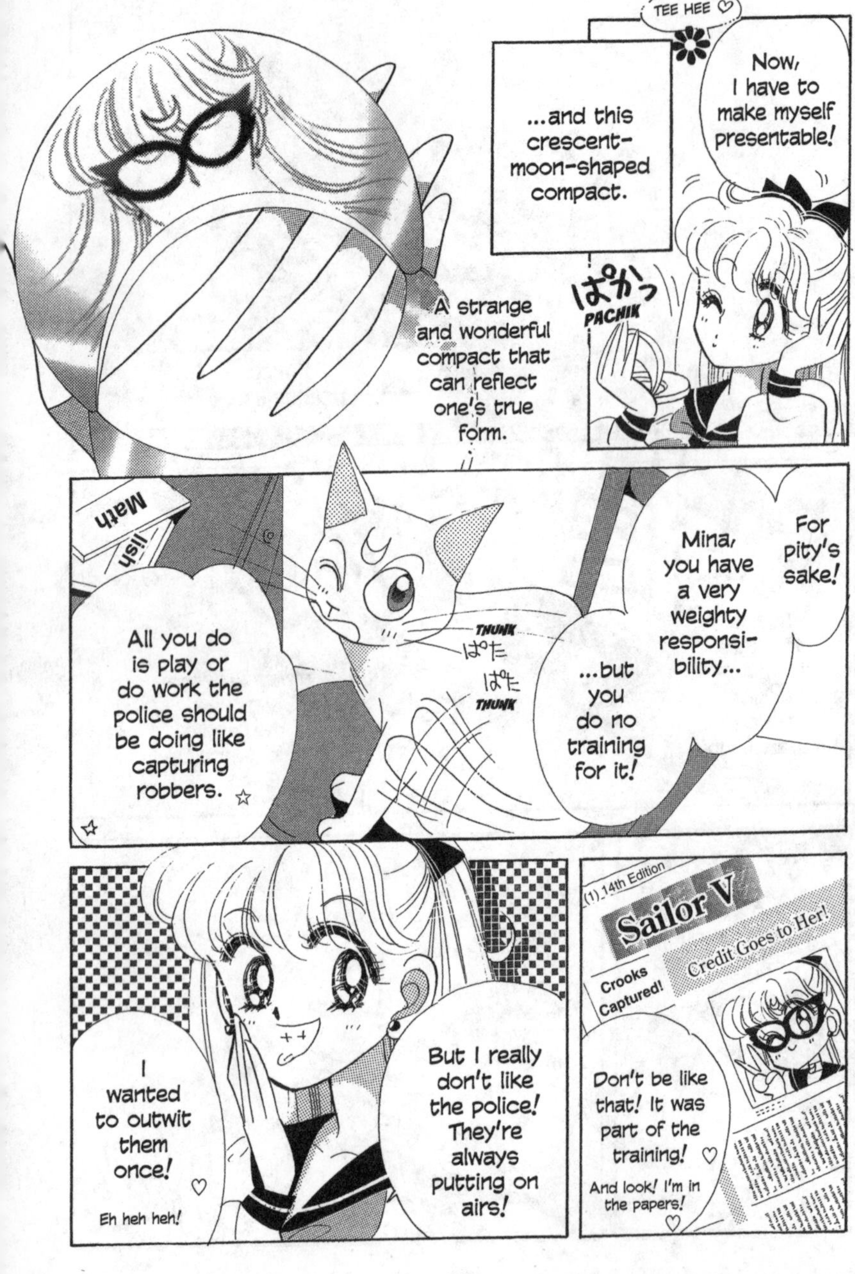
TEE HEE ♡
Now, I have to make myself presentable!
ぱかっ PACHIK
...and this crescent-moon-shaped compact.
A strange and wonderful compact that can reflect one's true form.
For pity's sake!
Mina, you have a very weighty responsibility...
...but you do no training for it!
THUNK ぱた
ぱた THUNK
Math
lish
All you do is play or do work the police should be doing like capturing robbers. ☆
(1) 14th Edition
Sailor V
Credit Goes to Her!
Crooks Captured!
Don't be like that! It was part of the training! ♡
And look! I'm in the papers! ♡
But I really don't like the police! They're always putting on airs!
I wanted to outwit them once! ♡
Eh heh heh!

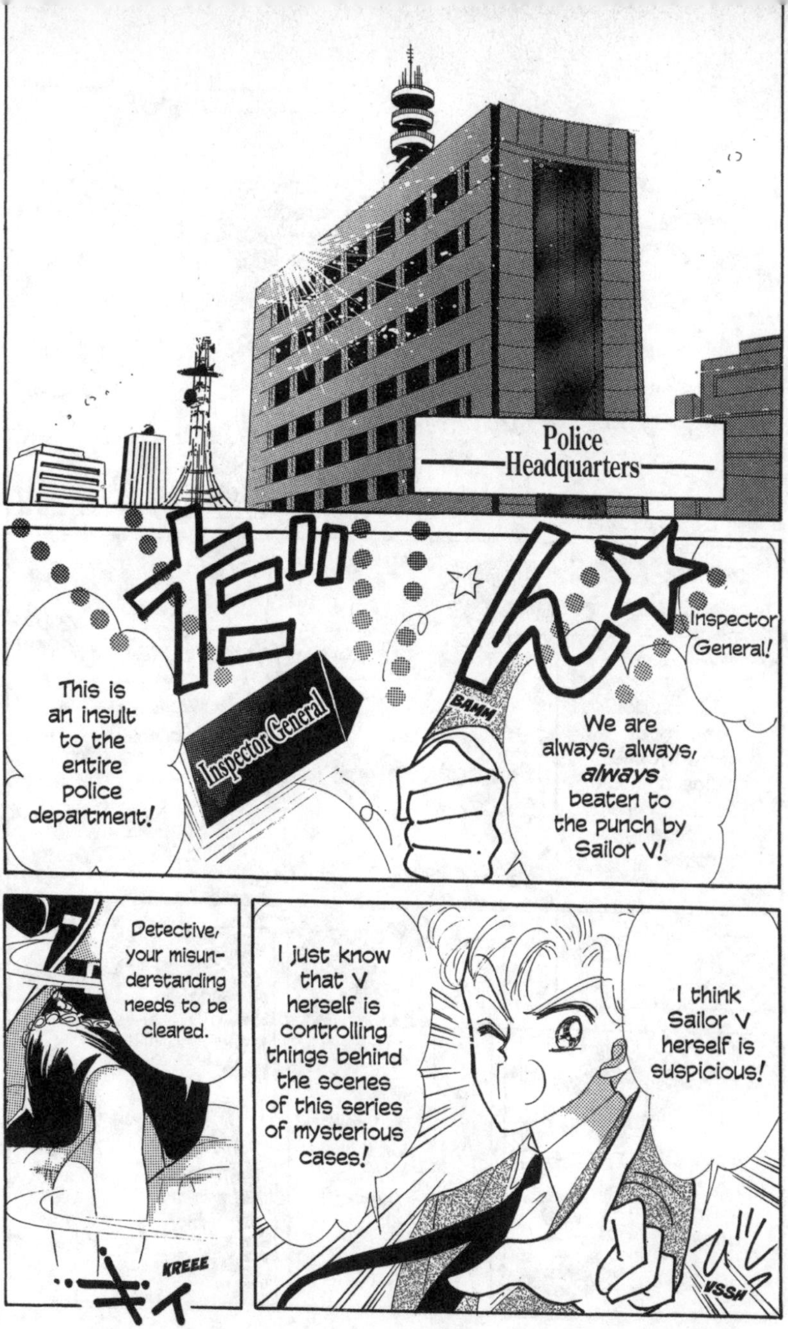
Police
Headquarters
Inspector General!
We are always, always, *always* beaten to the punch by Sailor V!
BAMM
Inspector General
だん☆
This is an insult to the entire police department!
I think Sailor V herself is suspicious!
VSSH
びし
I just know that V herself is controlling things behind the scenes of this series of mysterious cases!
Detective, your misunderstanding needs to be cleared.
KREEE
ギイ

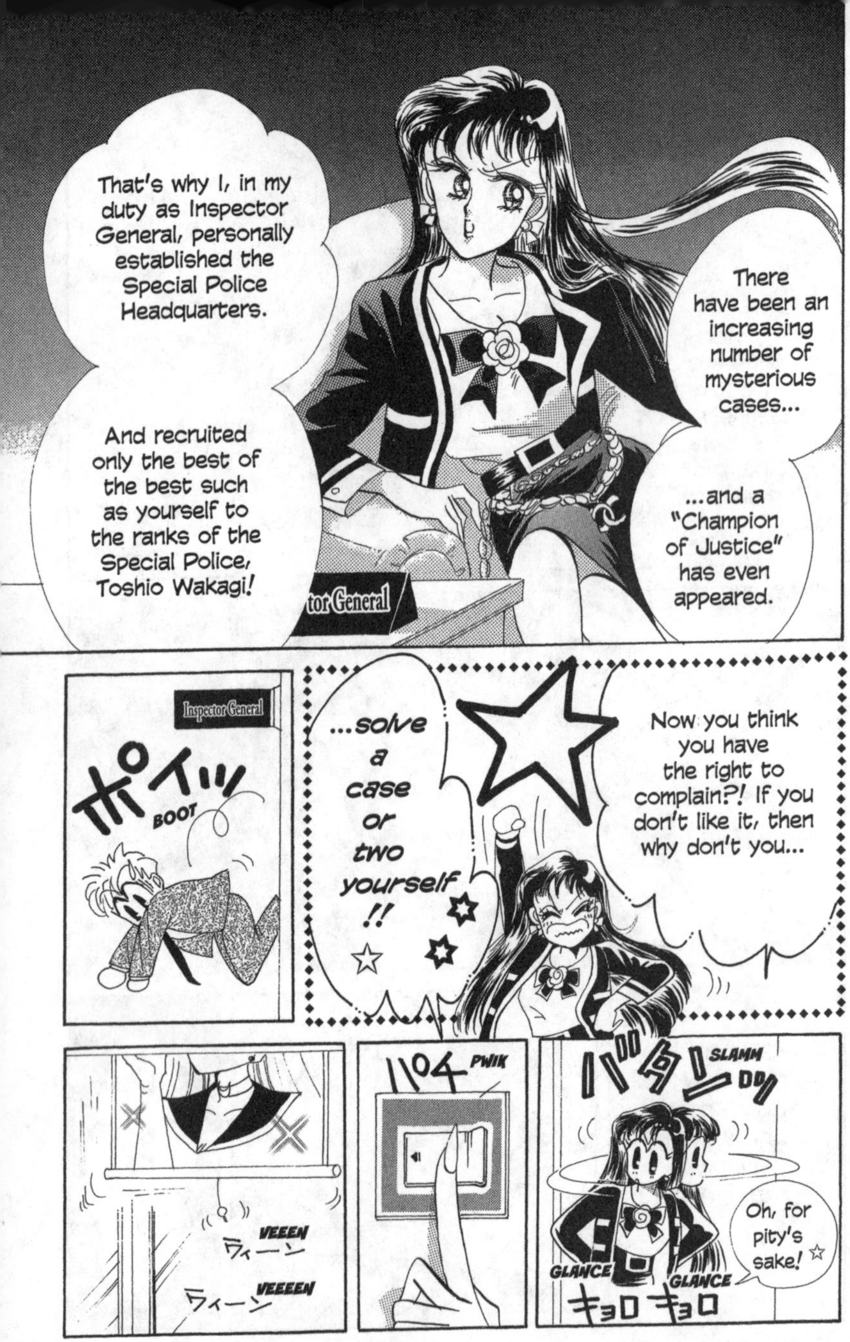

There have been an increasing number of mysterious cases...
...and a "Champion of Justice" has even appeared.
That's why I, in my duty as Inspector General, personally established the Special Police Headquarters.
And recruited only the best of the best such as yourself to the ranks of the Special Police, Toshio Wakagi!
tor General
Now you think you have the right to complain?! If you don't like it, then why don't you...
...solve a case or two yourself !!
Inspector General
ポイッ
BOOT
バタン
SLAMM
Oh, for pity's sake! ☆
GLANCE
GLANCE
キョロ キョロ
パチ
PWIK
VEEEN
ウィーン
VEEEEN
ウィーン

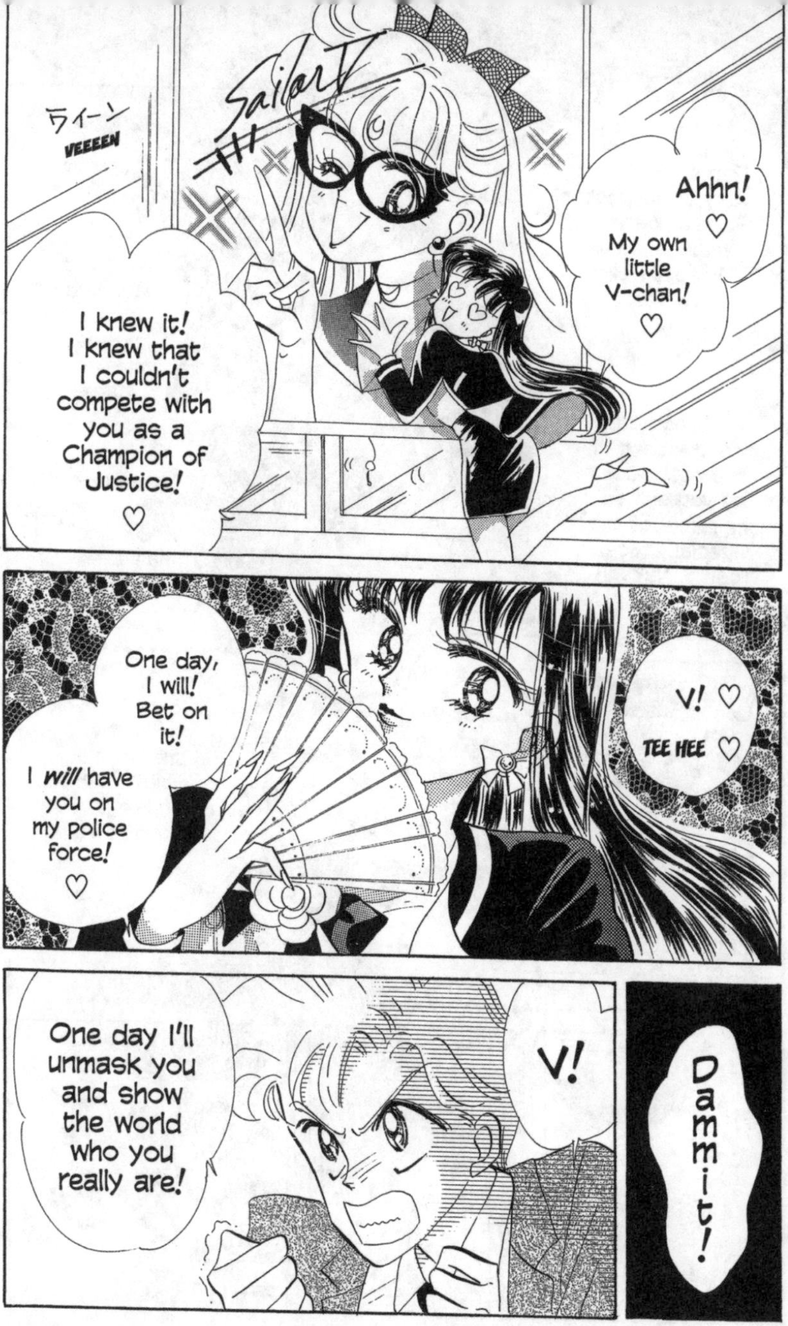
Sailor V
ワイーン
VEEEEN
Ahhn! ♡ My own little V-chan! ♡
I knew it! I knew that I couldn't compete with you as a Champion of Justice! ♡
V! ♡ TEE HEE ♡
One day, I will! Bet on it!
I *will* have you on my police force! ♡
Dammit!
V!
One day I'll unmask you and show the world who you really are!

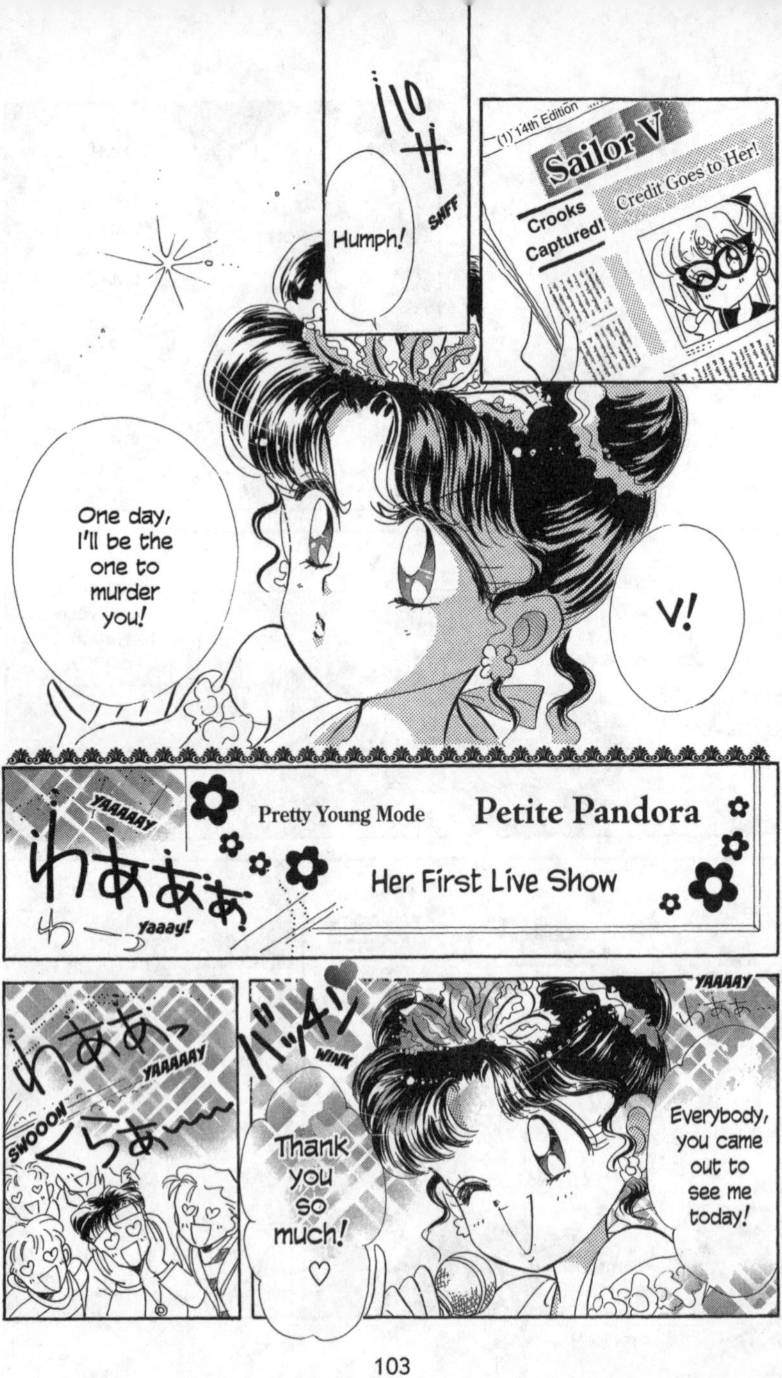
(1) 14th Edition
Sailor V
Credit Goes to Her!
Crooks Captured!
SNFF
Humph!
V!
One day, I'll be the one to murder you!
Pretty Young Mode
Petite Pandora
Her First Live Show
YAAAAAY
わあああ
わーっ
Yaaay!
YAAAAY
わあぁ…
Everybody, you came out to see me today!
Thank you so much! ♡
WINK
わあああっ
YAAAAAY
くらあ〜
SWOOON

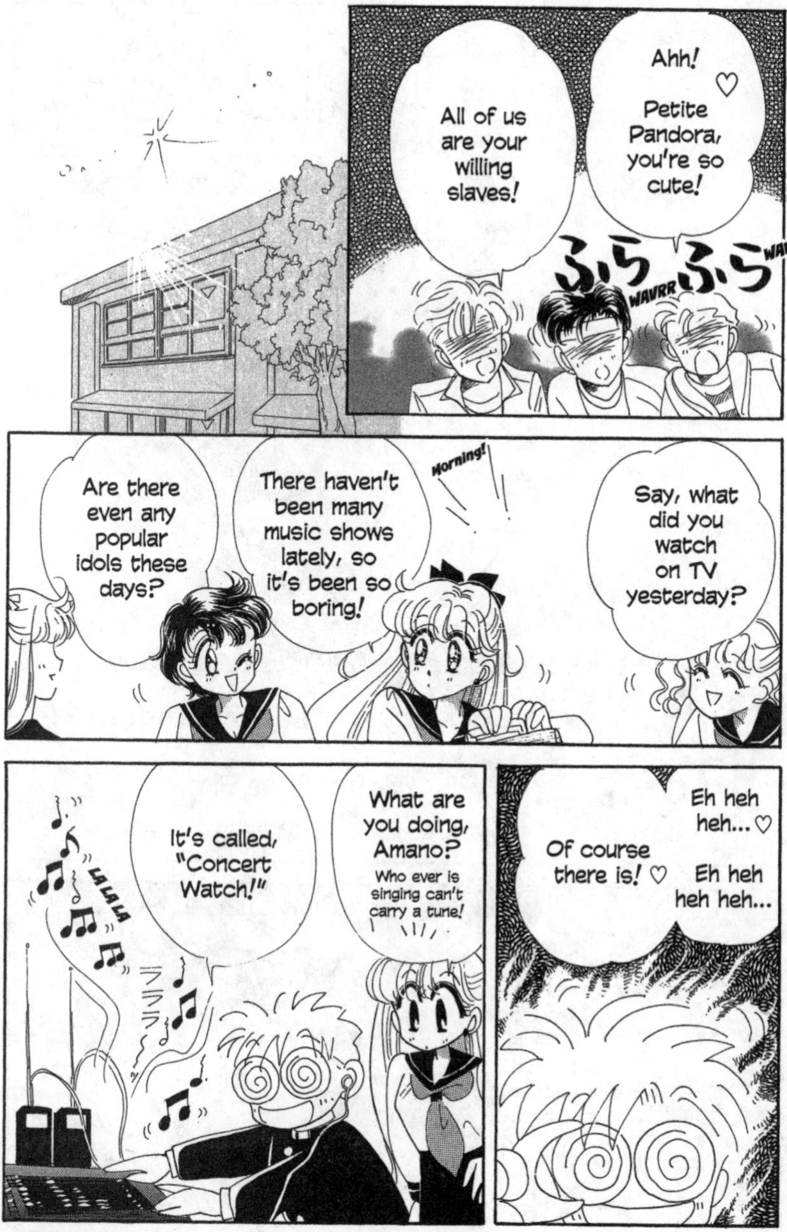
Ahh! ♡ Petite Pandora, you're so cute!
All of us are your willing slaves!
ふら WAVRR ふら WAVRR
Say, what did you watch on TV yesterday?
Morning!
There haven't been many music shows lately, so it's been so boring!
Are there even any popular idols these days?
Eh heh heh... ♡ Eh heh heh heh...
Of course there is! ♡
What are you doing, Amano? Who ever is singing can't carry a tune!
It's called, "Concert Watch!"
LA LA LA
ラララ
Th-This is incredible!

Apparently you need to be very close to the concert hall to do it. It's illegal too.

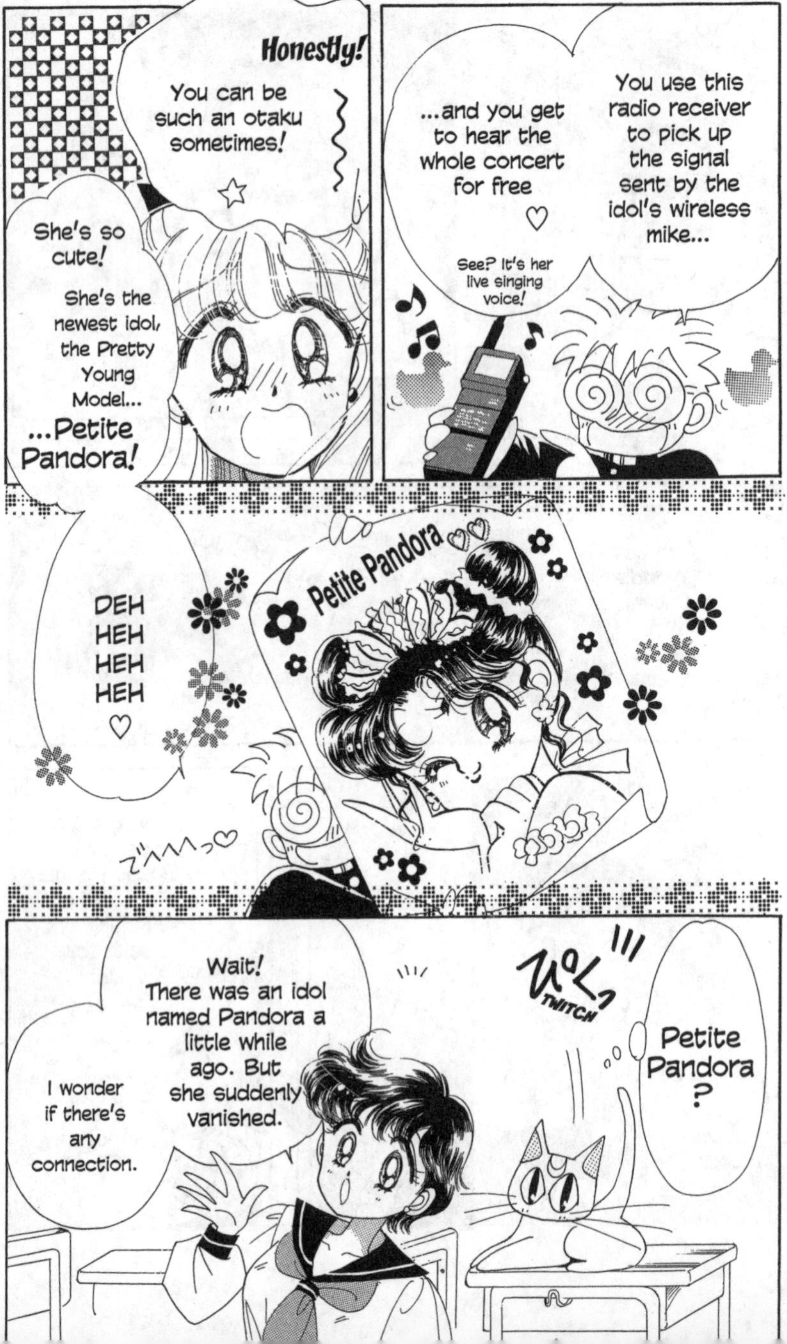
You use this radio receiver to pick up the signal sent by the idol's wireless mike...
...and you get to hear the whole concert for free ♡
See? It's her live singing voice!
Honestly!
You can be such an otaku sometimes!
She's so cute!
She's the newest idol, the Pretty Young Model...
...Petite Pandora!
Petite Pandora
DEH HEH HEH HEH ♡
Petite Pandora?
TWITCH
Wait! There was an idol named Pandora a little while ago. But she suddenly vanished.
I wonder if there's any connection.

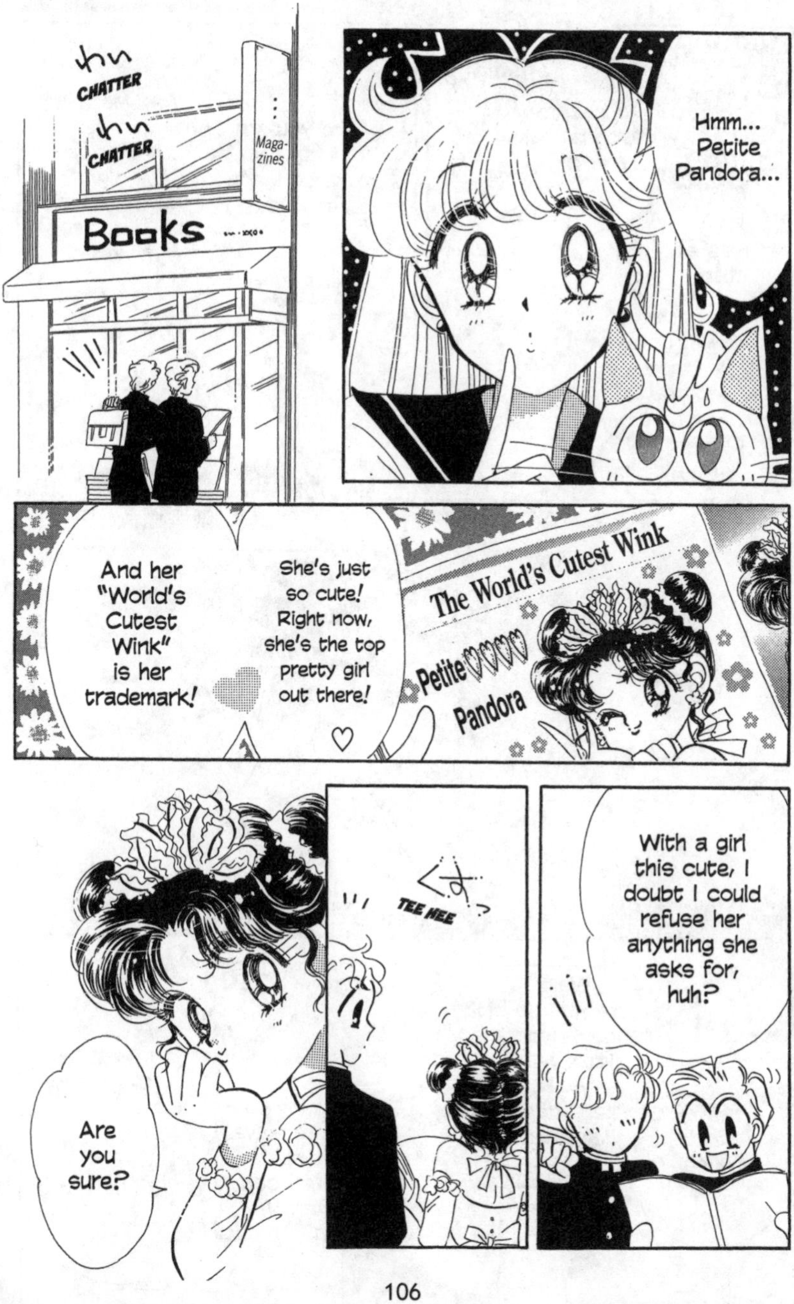
Hmm... Petite Pandora...
Books
Magazines
CHATTER
CHATTER
The World's Cutest Wink
Petite
Pandora
She's just so cute! Right now, she's the top pretty girl out there!
And her "World's Cutest Wink" is her trademark!
With a girl this cute, I doubt I could refuse her anything she asks for, huh?
TEE HEE
Are you sure?

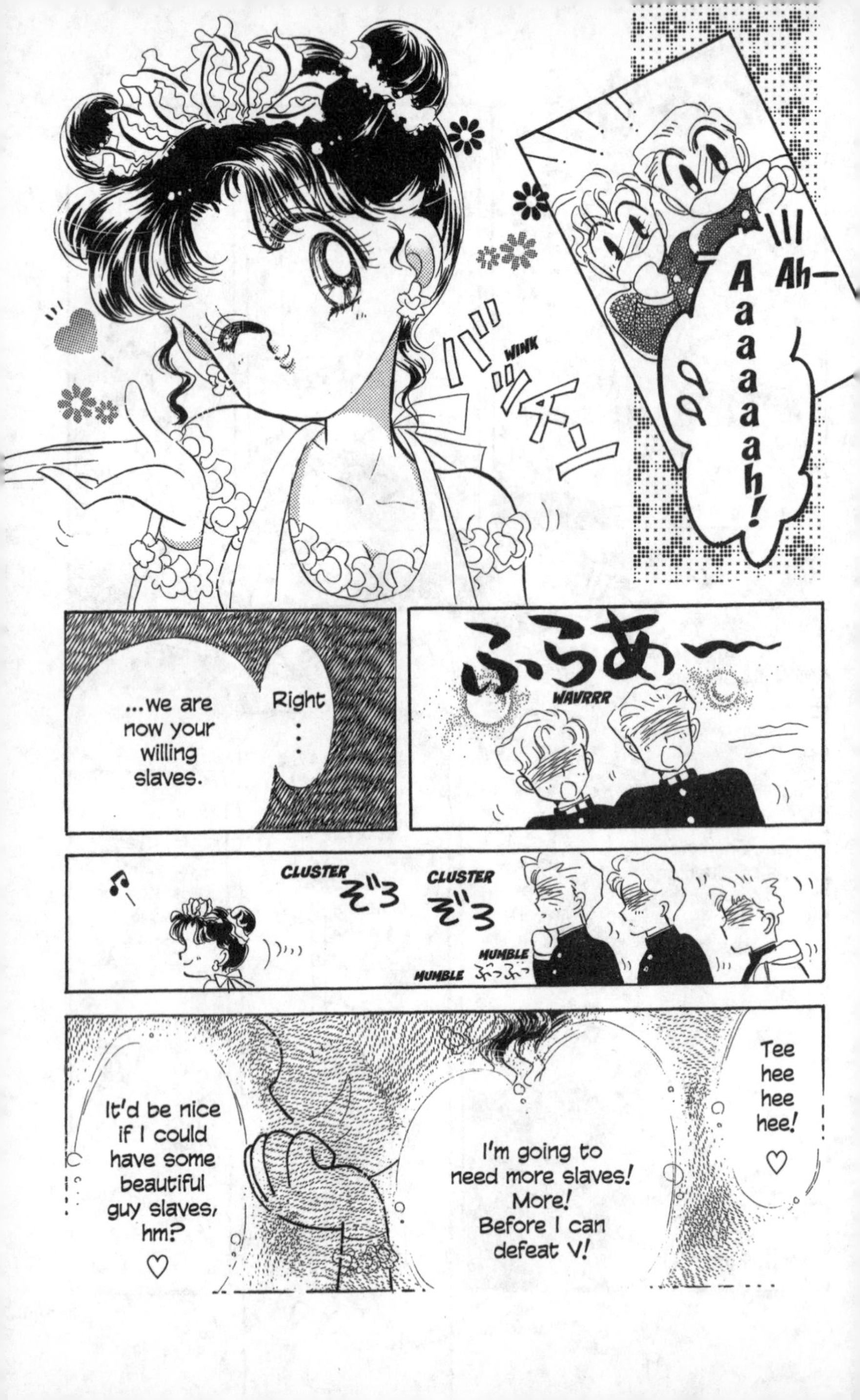
Ah— Aaaaaah!
WINK
ふらあ〜
WAVRRR
Right...
...we are now your willing slaves.
CLUSTER ぞろ
CLUSTER ぞろ
MUMBLE ぶつぶつ
MUMBLE
Tee hee hee hee! ♡
I'm going to need more slaves! More! Before I can defeat V!
It'd be nice if I could have some beautiful guy slaves, hm? ♡

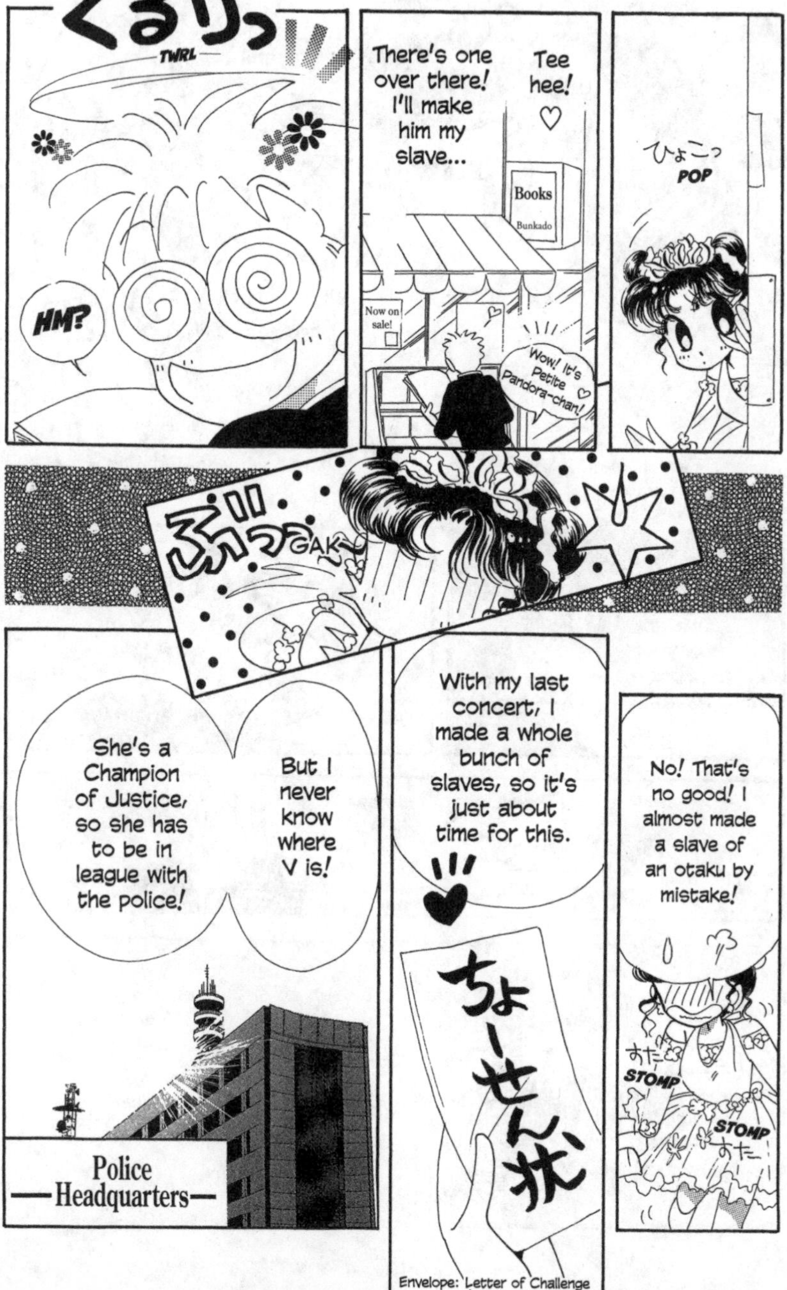
ひょこっ
POP
Tee hee! ♡
There's one over there! I'll make him my slave...
Books
Bunkado
Now on sale!
Wow! It's Petite Pandora-chan! ♡
くるりっ
TWRL
HM?
ぶつっ
GAK
No! That's no good! I almost made a slave of an otaku by mistake!
おた
STOMP
STOMP
おた
With my last concert, I made a whole bunch of slaves, so it's just about time for this.
ちょーせん状
Envelope: Letter of Challenge
But I never know where V is!
She's a Champion of Justice, so she has to be in league with the police!
Police
—Headquarters—

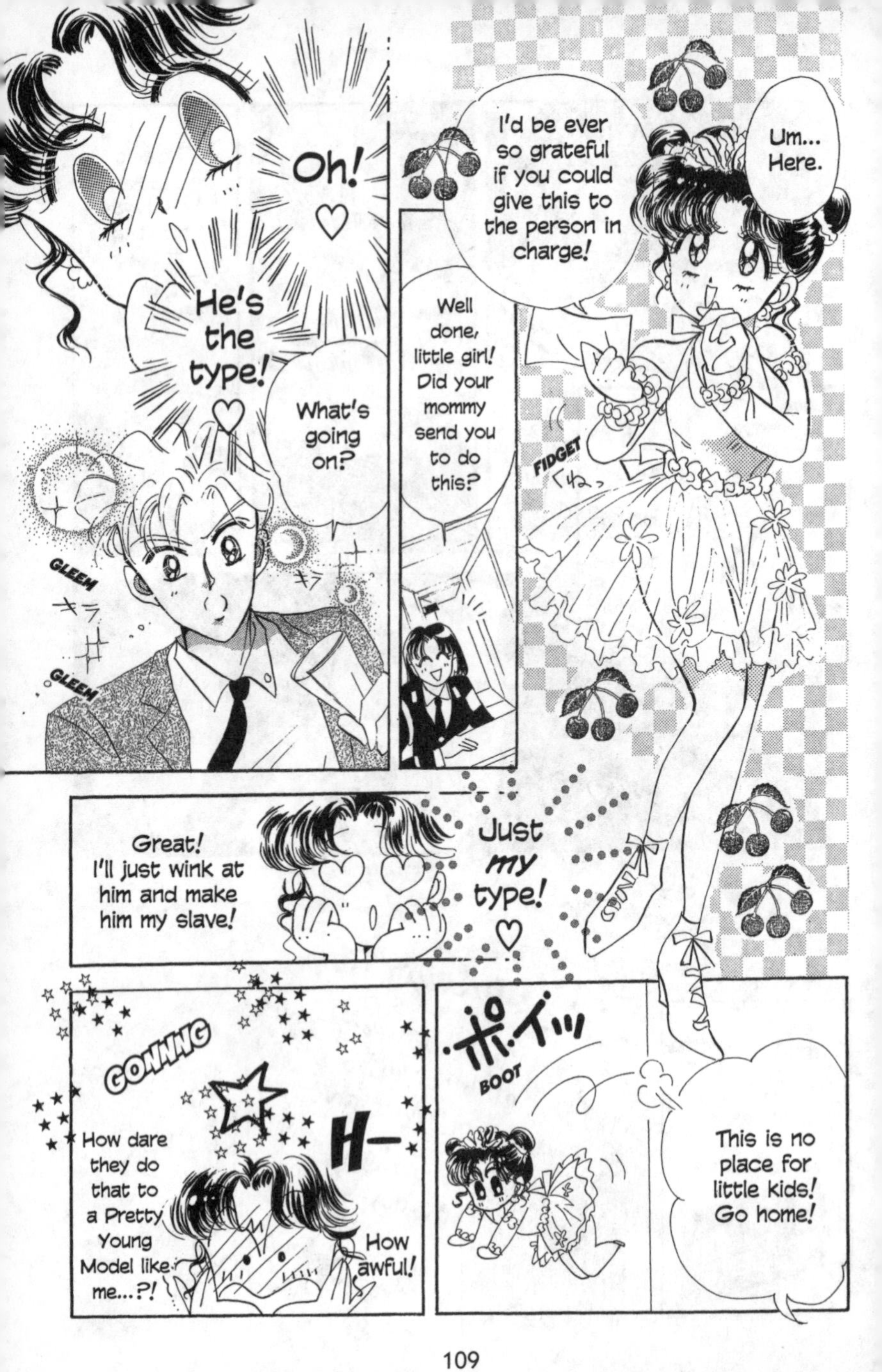
Um... Here.
I'd be ever so grateful if you could give this to the person in charge!
FIDGET
くねっ
Well done, little girl! Did your mommy send you to do this?
Oh! ♡
He's the type! ♡
What's going on?
GLEEM
キラ
GLEEM
Just my type! ♡
Great! I'll just wink at him and make him my slave!
This is no place for little kids! Go home!
ポイッ
BOOT
GONNNG
H—
How dare they do that to a Pretty Young Model like me...?!
How awful!

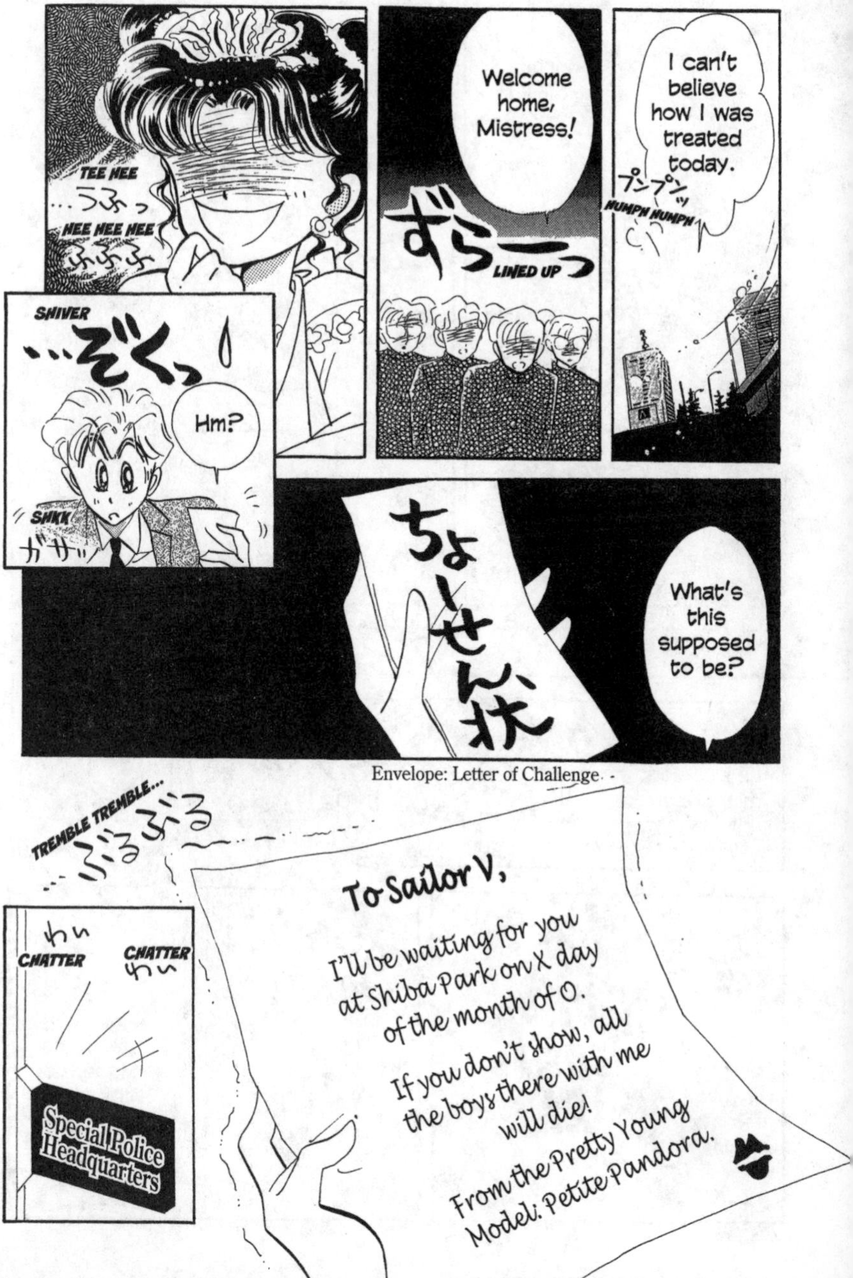
I can't believe how I was treated today.
HUMPH HUMPH
プンプンッ
Welcome home, Mistress!
ずらーっ
LINED UP
TEE HEE
…うふっ
HEE HEE HEE
ふふふ
SHIVER
…ぞくっ
Hm?
SHKK
ガサッ
What's this supposed to be?
ちょうせん状
Envelope: Letter of Challenge
TREMBLE TREMBLE…
…ぶるぶる
To Sailor V,
I'll be waiting for you at Shiba Park on X day of the month of O.
If you don't show, all the boys there with me will die!
From the Pretty Young Model: Petite Pandora.
わい
CHATTER
CHATTER
わい
Special Police Headquarters

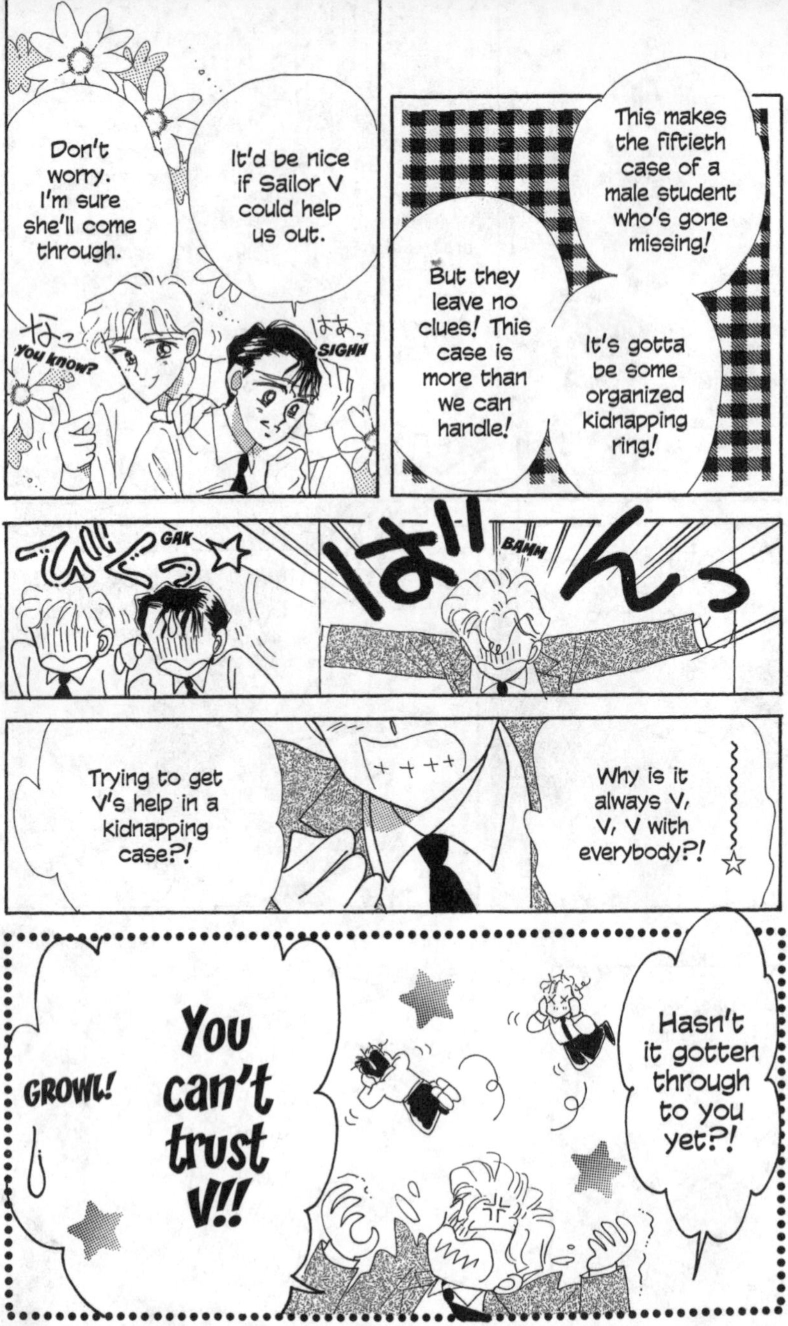
This makes the fiftieth case of a male student who's gone missing!
It's gotta be some organized kidnapping ring!
But they leave no clues! This case is more than we can handle!
It'd be nice if Sailor V could help us out.
はあっ
SIGHH
Don't worry. I'm sure she'll come through.
なっ
You know?
ばんっ
BAMM
びくっ
GAK
Why is it always V, V, V with everybody?!
Trying to get V's help in a kidnapping case?!
Hasn't it gotten through to you yet?!
You can't trust V!!
GROWL!

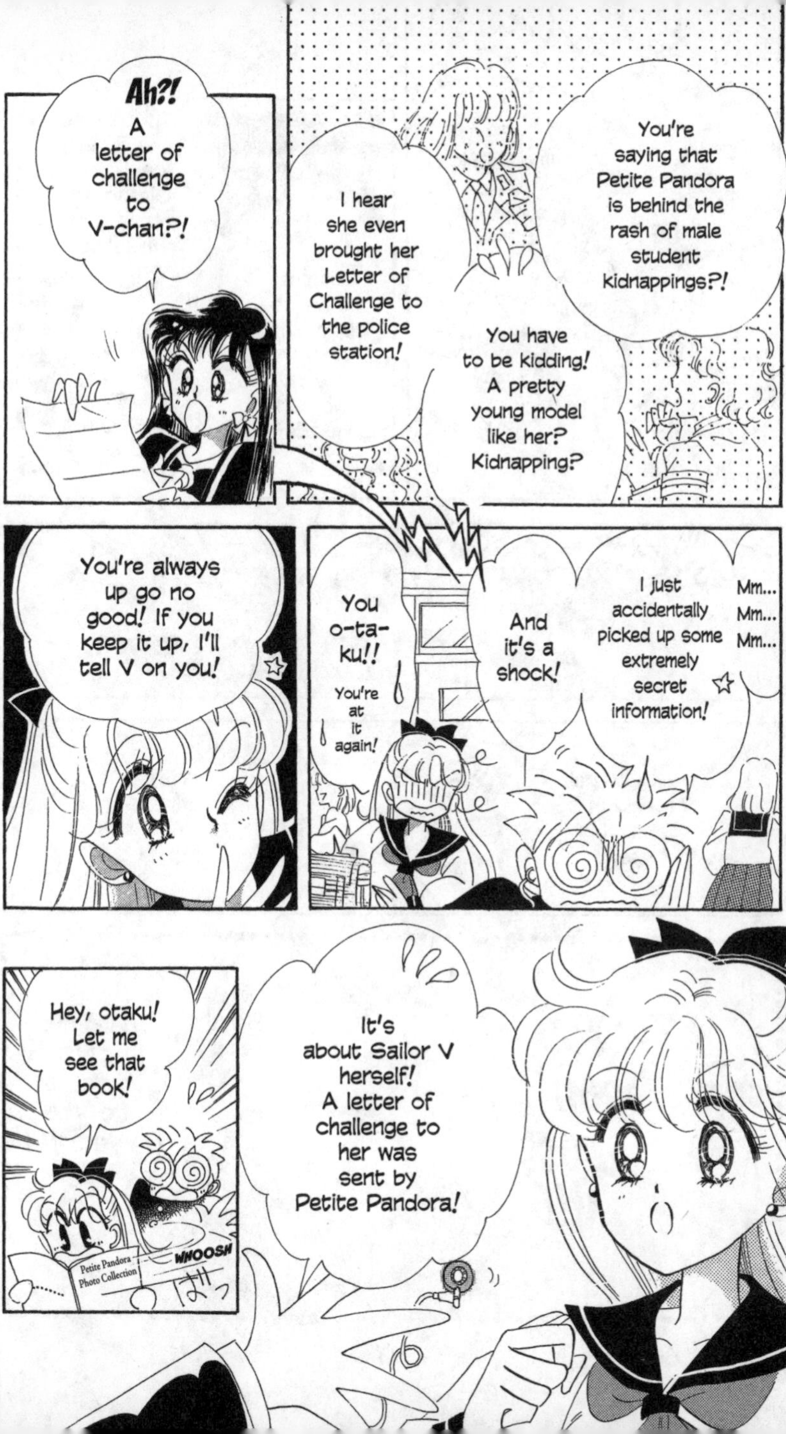
You're saying that Petite Pandora is behind the rash of male student kidnappings?!
I hear she even brought her Letter of Challenge to the police station!
You have to be kidding! A pretty young model like her? Kidnapping?
Ah?! A letter of challenge to V-chan?!
Mm... Mm... Mm...
I just accidentally picked up some extremely secret information!
And it's a shock!
You o-ta-ku!!
You're at it again!
You're always up go no good! If you keep it up, I'll tell V on you!
It's about Sailor V herself! A letter of challenge to her was sent by Petite Pandora!
Hey, otaku! Let me see that book!
Petite Pandora Photo Collection
WHOOSH
ばっ
......

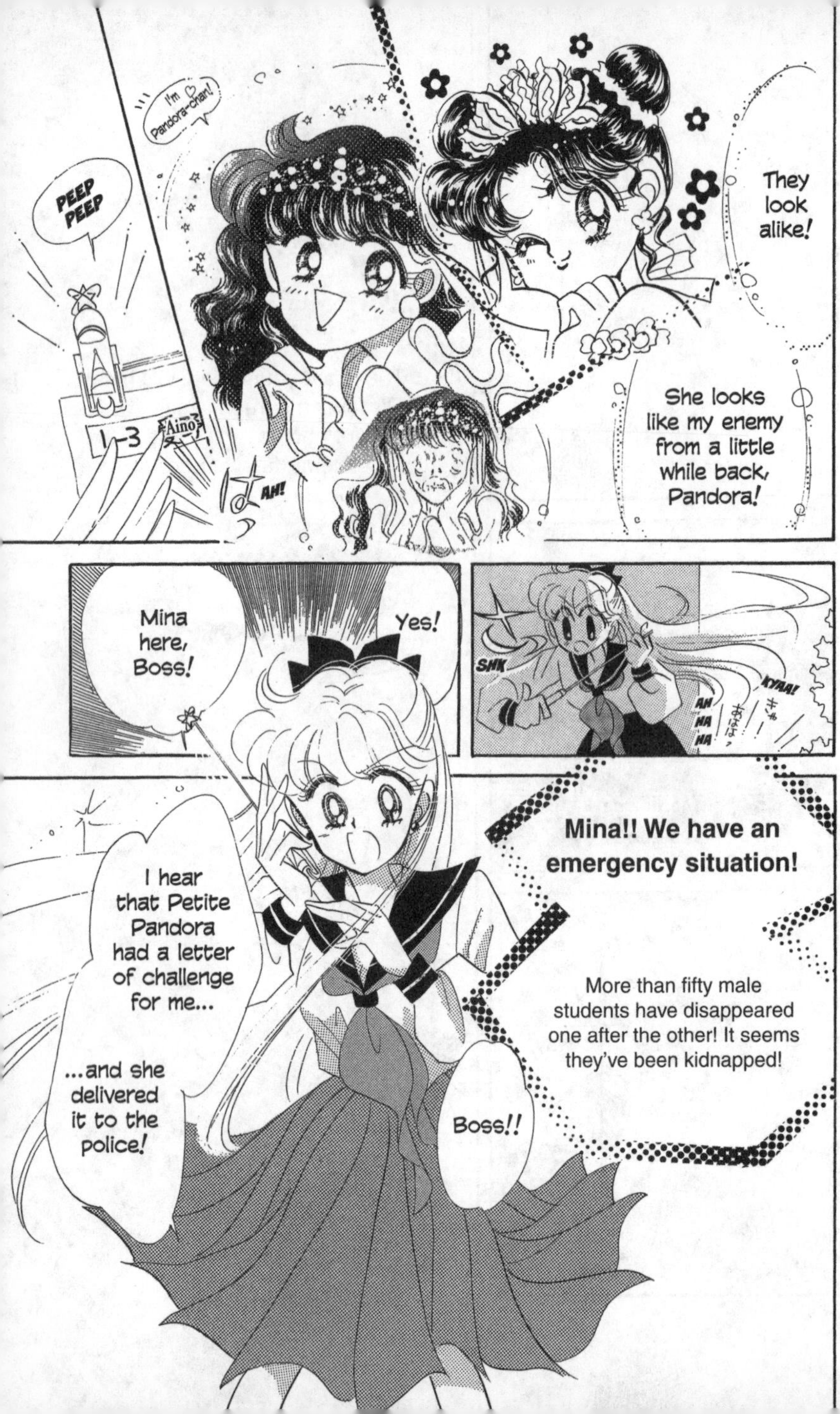

They look alike!
She looks like my enemy from a little while back, Pandora!
I'm ♡ Pandora-chan!
PEEP PEEP
1-3
Aino
AH!
SHK
KYAA!
AH HA HA HA
Yes!
Mina here, Boss!
Mina!! We have an emergency situation!
More than fifty male students have disappeared one after the other! It seems they've been kidnapped!
Boss!!
I hear that Petite Pandora had a letter of challenge for me...
...and she delivered it to the police!

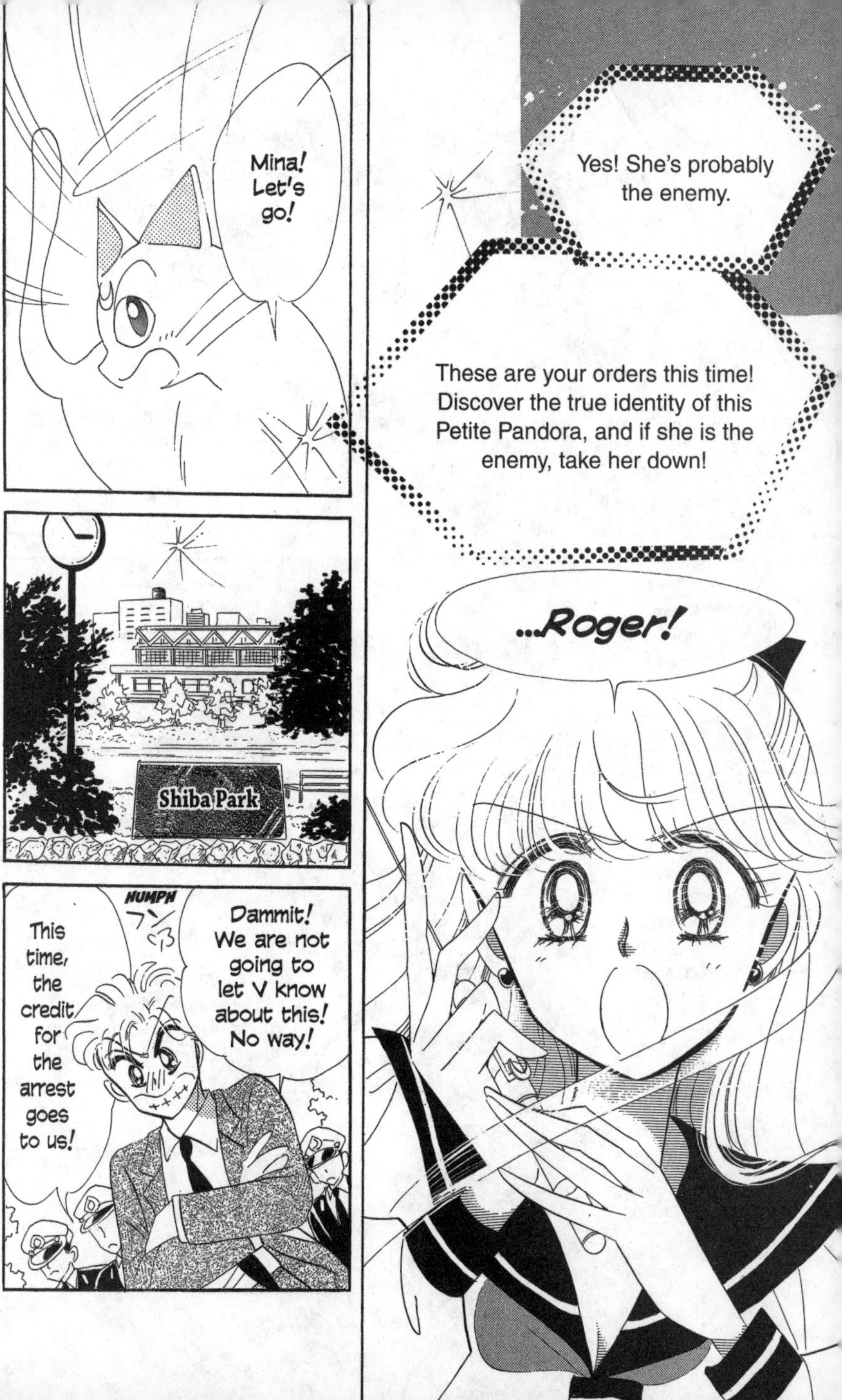

Yes! She's probably the enemy.
These are your orders this time! Discover the true identity of this Petite Pandora, and if she is the enemy, take her down!
...Roger!
Mina! Let's go!
Shiba Park
HUMPH
Dammit! We are not going to let V know about this! No way!
This time, the credit for the arrest goes to us!

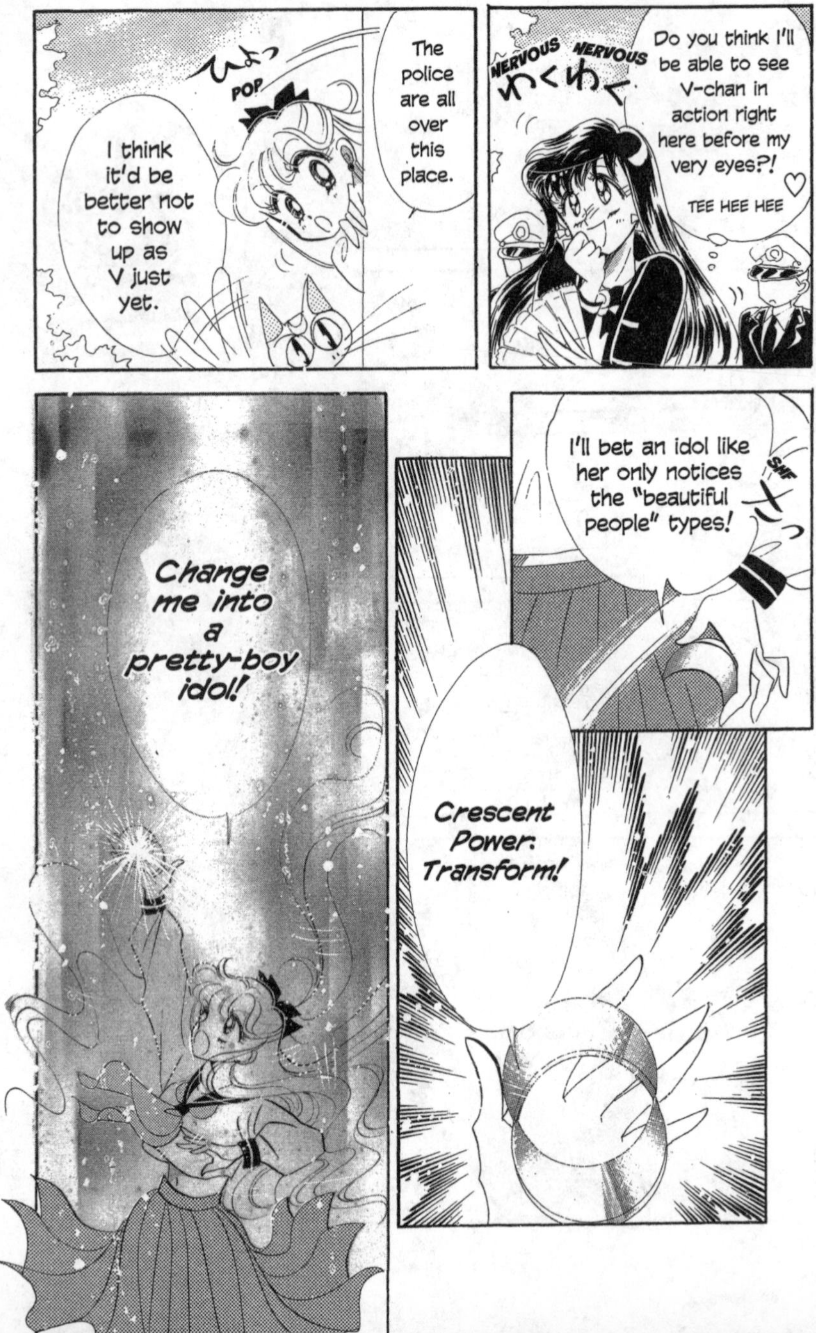
NERVOUS NERVOUS
わくわく
Do you think I'll be able to see V-chan in action right here before my very eyes?!
TEE HEE HEE
The police are all over this place.
ひょっ
POP
I think it'd be better not to show up as V just yet.
I'll bet an idol like her only notices the "beautiful people" types!
SHF
さっ
Crescent Power: Transform!
Change me into a pretty-boy idol!

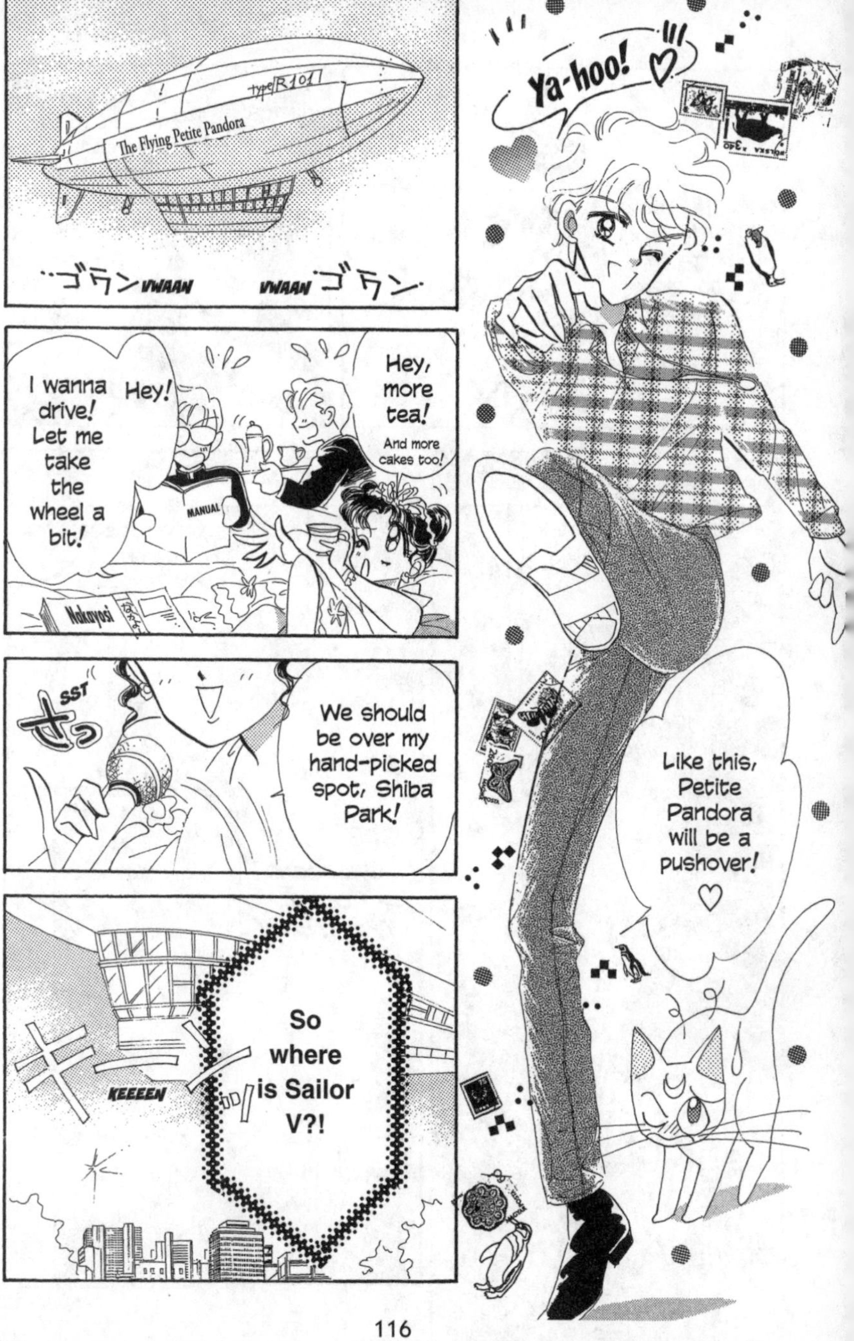
Ya-hoo!
Like this, Petite Pandora will be a pushover!
type R101
The Flying Petite Pandora
ゴワン VWAAN
VWAAN ゴワン
Hey, more tea!
And more cakes too!
Hey!
I wanna drive! Let me take the wheel a bit!
MANUAL
Nakayosi
SST
さっ
We should be over my hand-picked spot, Shiba Park!
So where is Sailor V?!
キーン
KEEEEN

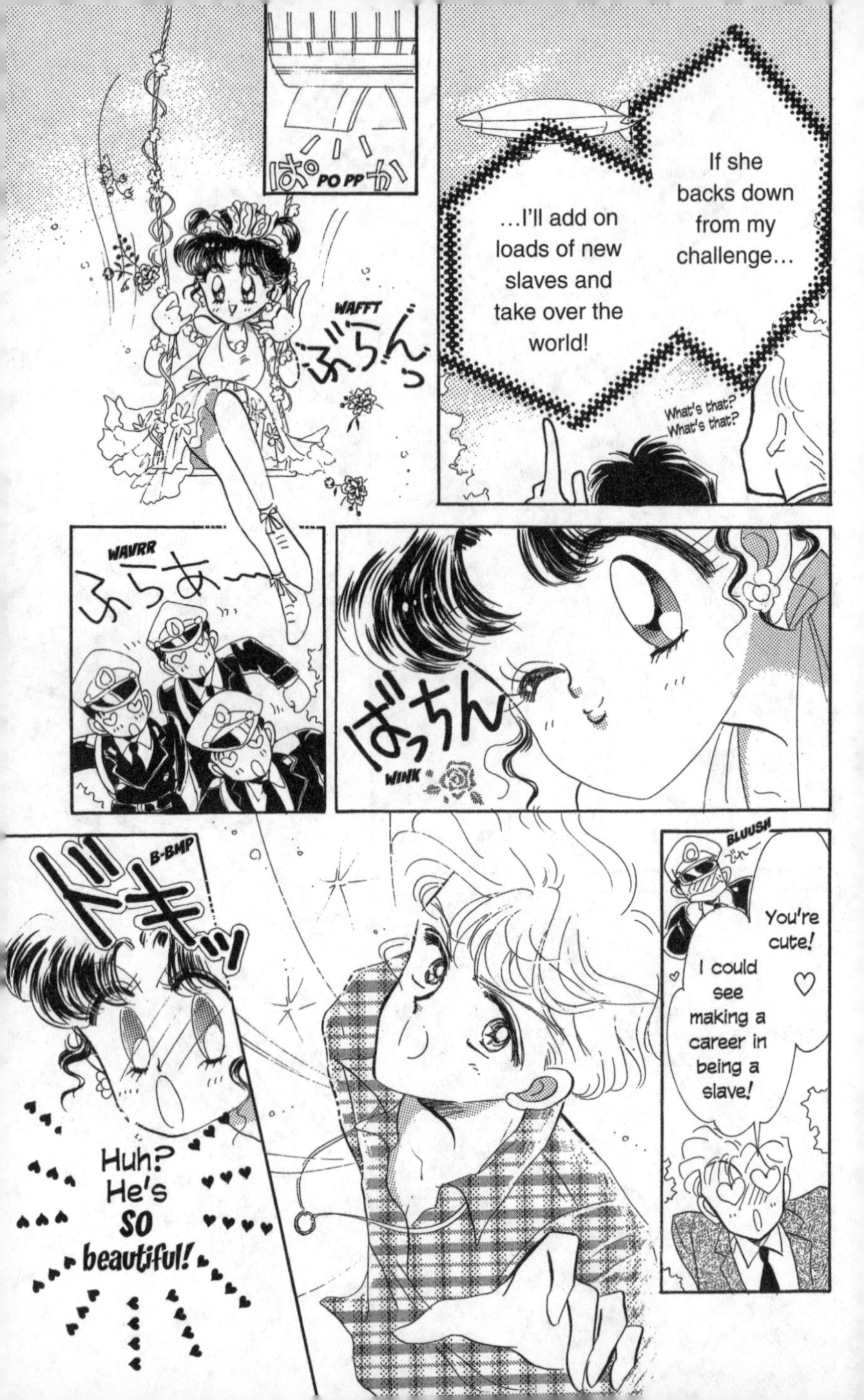
If she backs down from my challenge…
…I'll add on loads of new slaves and take over the world!
What's that? What's that?
ぱっか
PO PP
WAFFT
ぶらんっ
ばっちん
WINK
WAVRR
ふらあ〜
BLUUSH
でれ〜
You're cute! ♡
I could see making a career in being a slave!
B-BMP
ドキッ
Huh? He's SO beautiful!

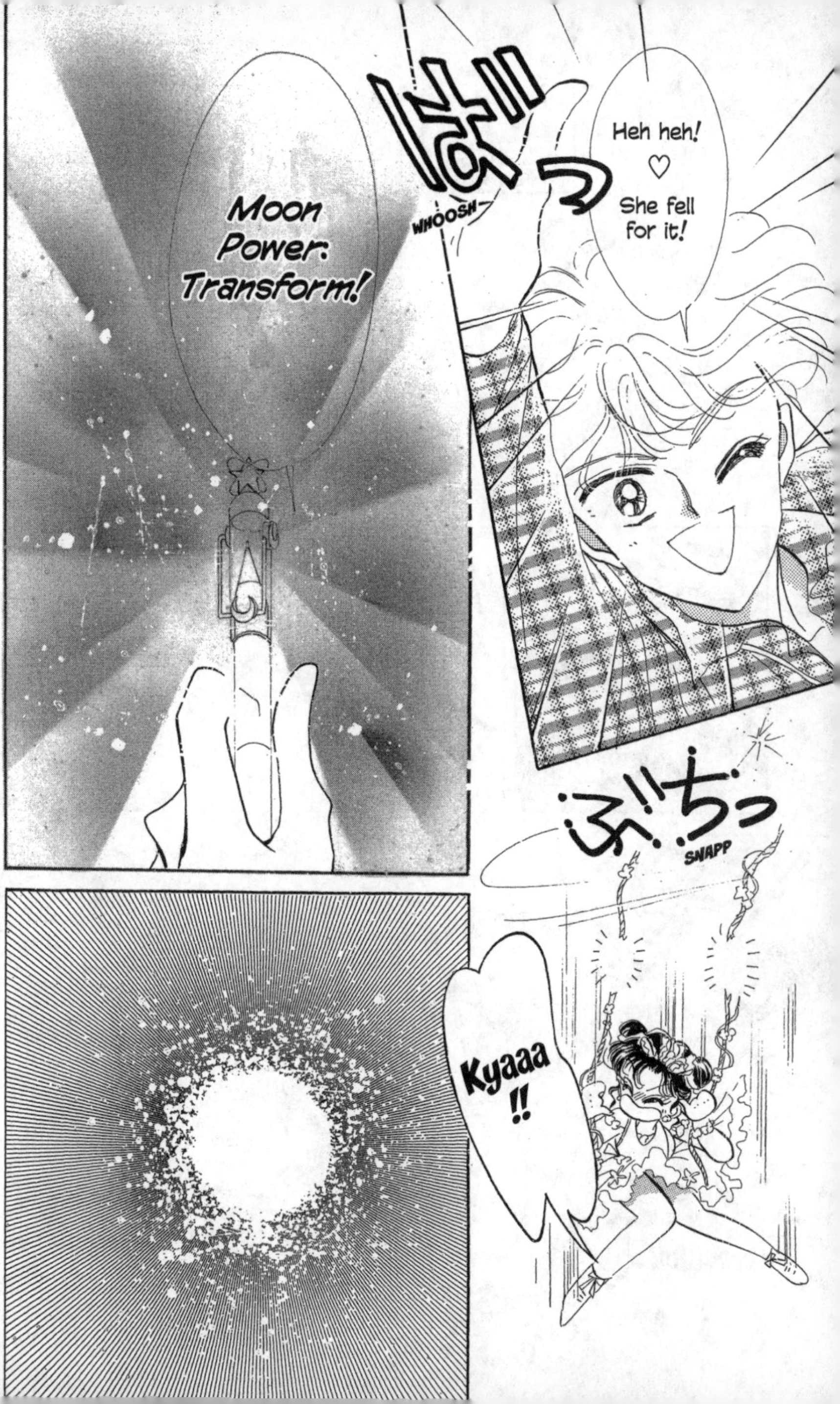
はっ
WHOOSH
Heh heh! ♡ She fell for it!
Moon Power: Transform!
ぷちっ
SNAPP
Kyaaa!!

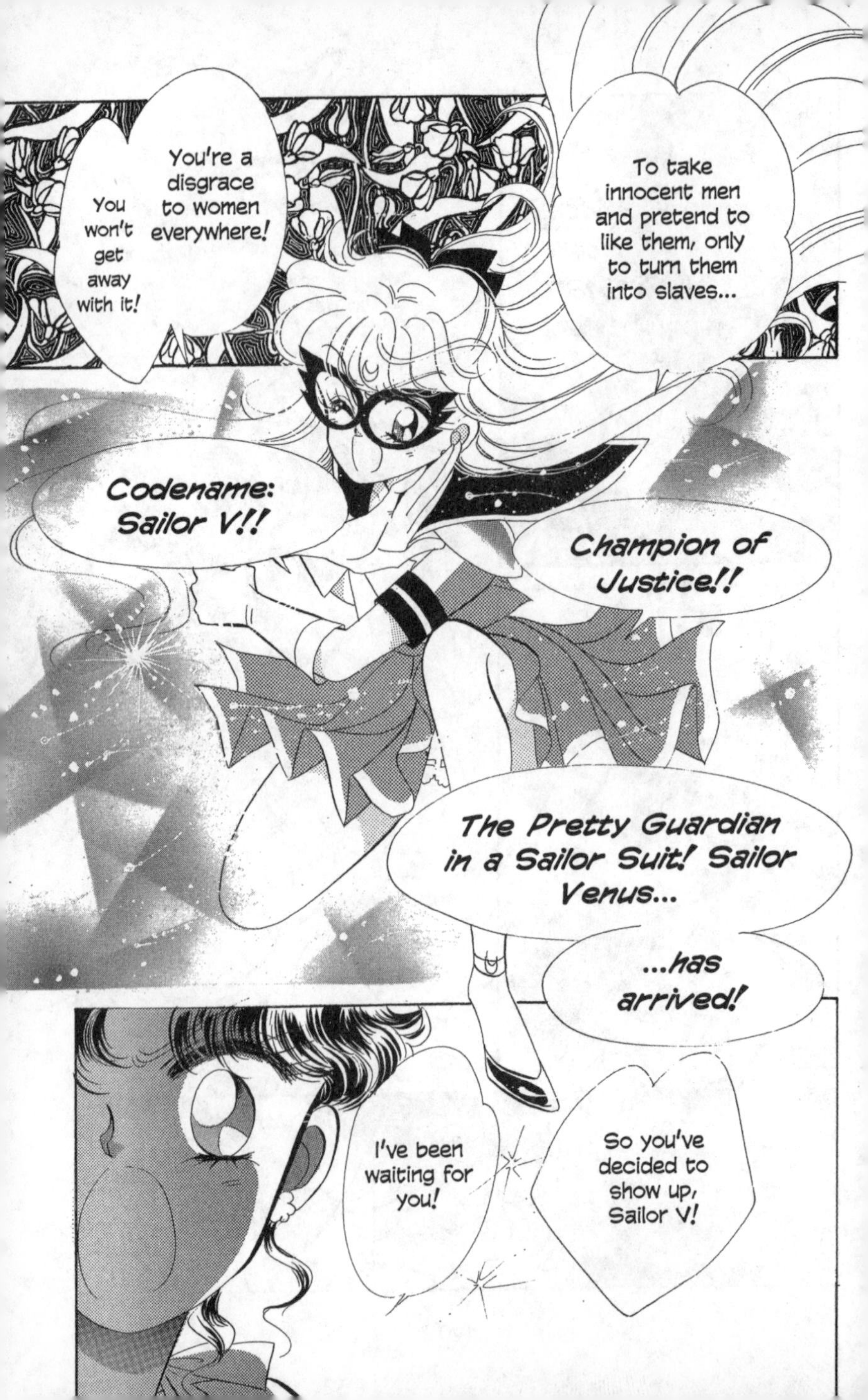
To take innocent men and pretend to like them, only to turn them into slaves...
You're a disgrace to women everywhere!
You won't get away with it!
Champion of Justice!!
Codename: Sailor V!!
The Pretty Guardian in a Sailor Suit! Sailor Venus...
...has arrived!
So you've decided to show up, Sailor V!
I've been waiting for you!

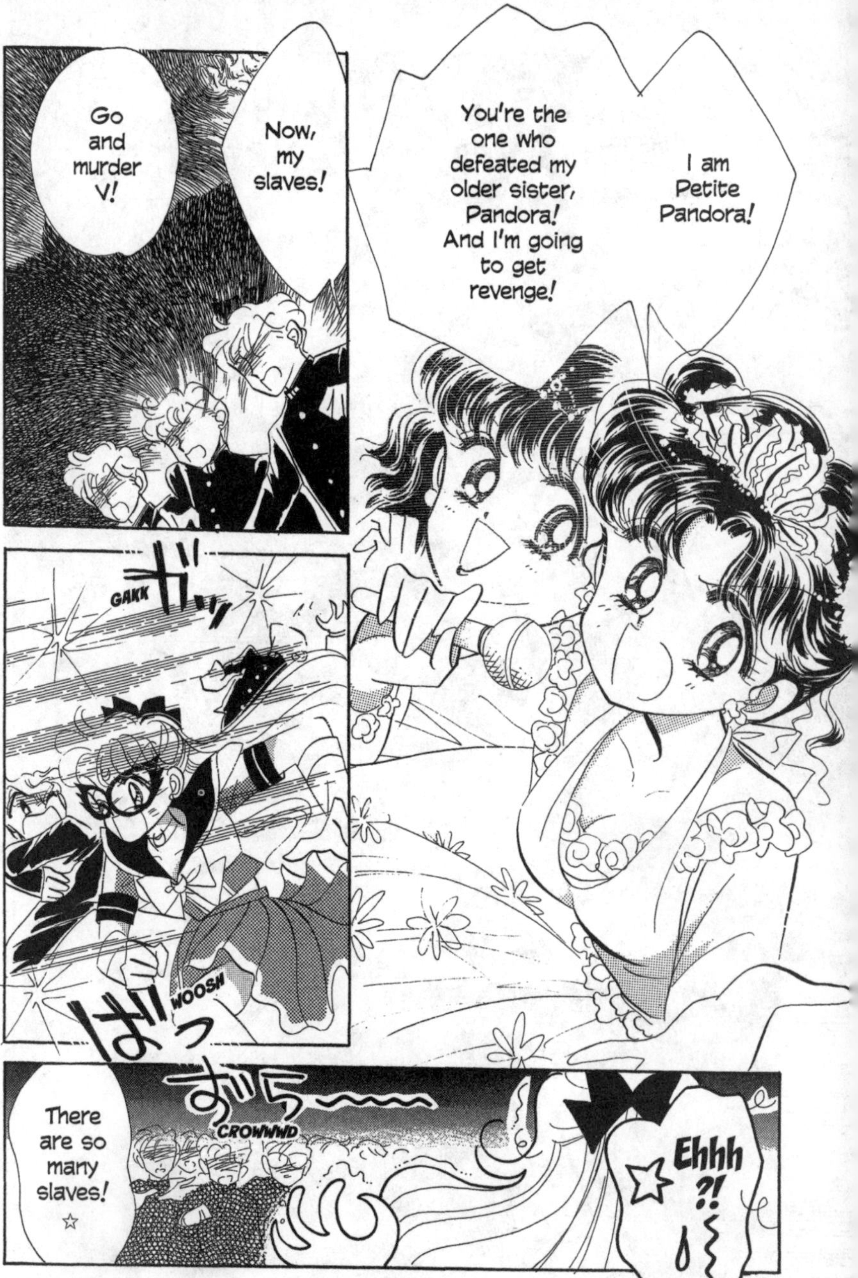
I am Petite Pandora!
You're the one who defeated my older sister, Pandora! And I'm going to get revenge!
Now, my slaves!
Go and murder V!
GAKK
WOOSH
Ehhh?!
CROWWWD
There are so many slaves! ☆

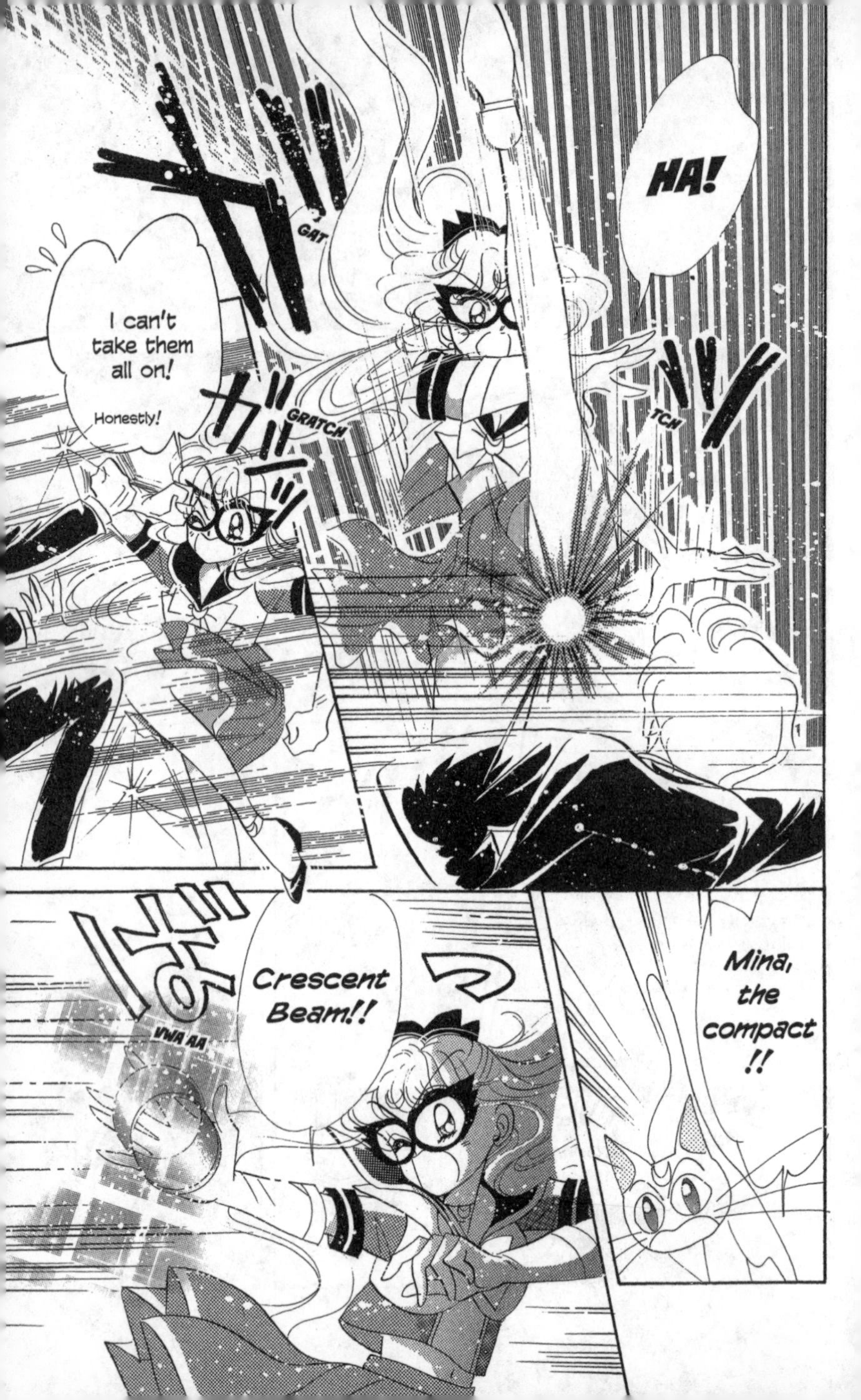
HA!
TCH
GAT
GRATCH
I can't take them all on!
Honestly!
Mina, the compact!!
Crescent Beam!!
VWA AA

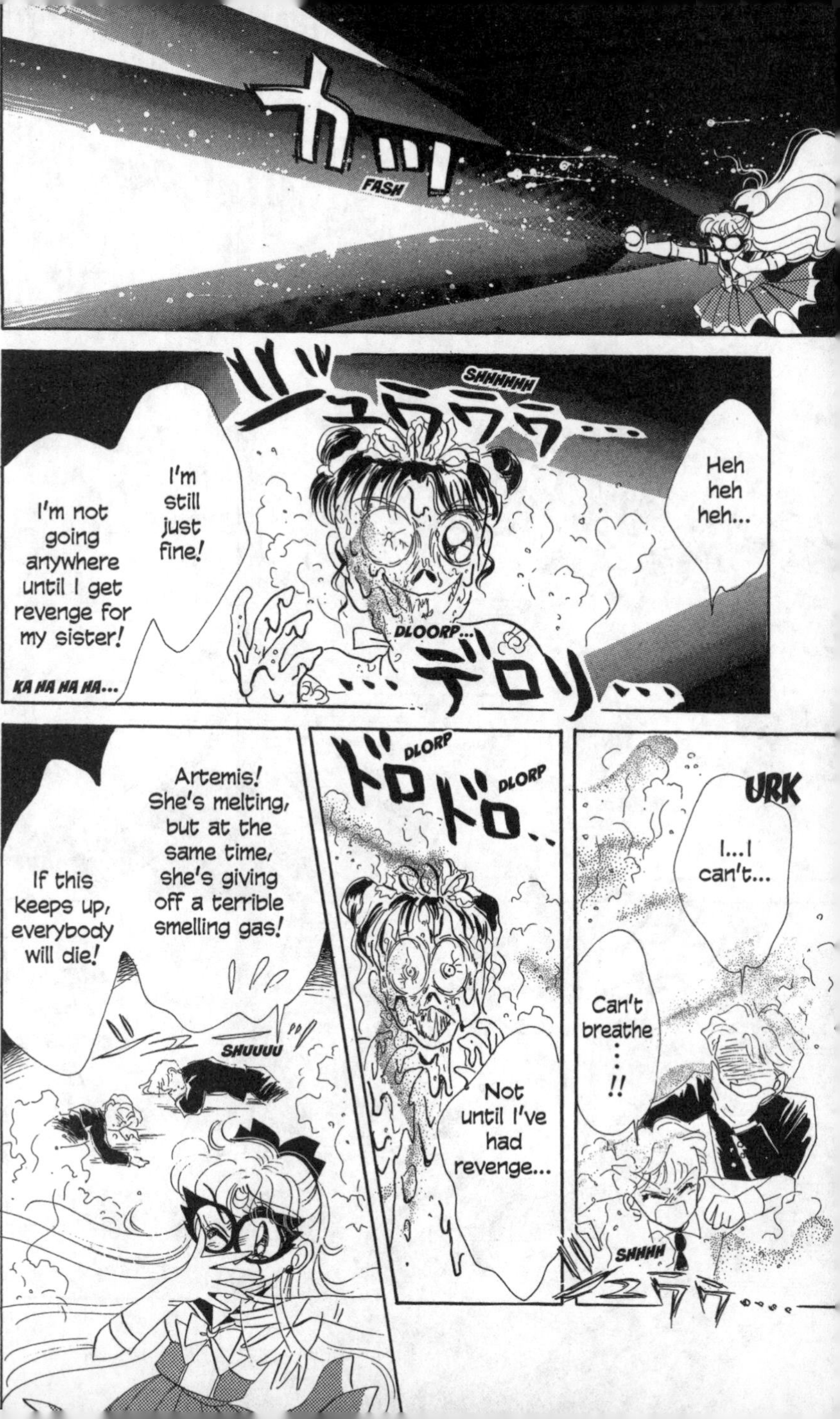
カッ
FASH
ジュラララー...
SHHHHHH
Heh heh heh...
I'm still just fine!
I'm not going anywhere until I get revenge for my sister!
KA HA HA HA...
...デロリ...
DLOORP...
URK
I...I can't...
Can't breathe...!!
SHHHH
シュラララ...
ドロドロ...
DLORP
DLORP
Not until I've had revenge...
Artemis! She's melting, but at the same time, she's giving off a terrible smelling gas!
If this keeps up, everybody will die!
SHUUUU

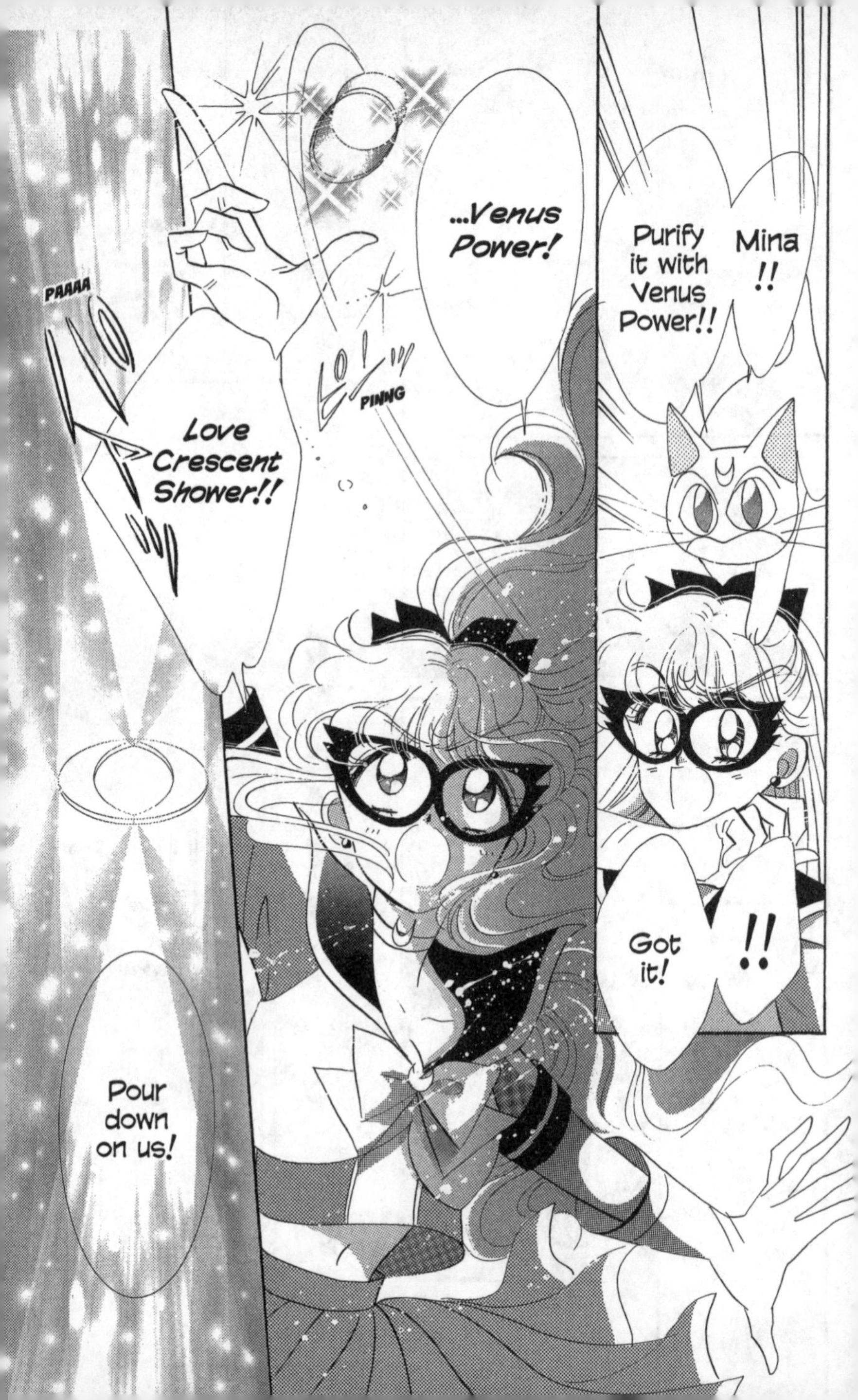

Mina!!
Purify it with Venus Power!!
!!
Got it!
...Venus Power!
PINNG
Love Crescent Shower!!
PAAAA
Pour down on us!

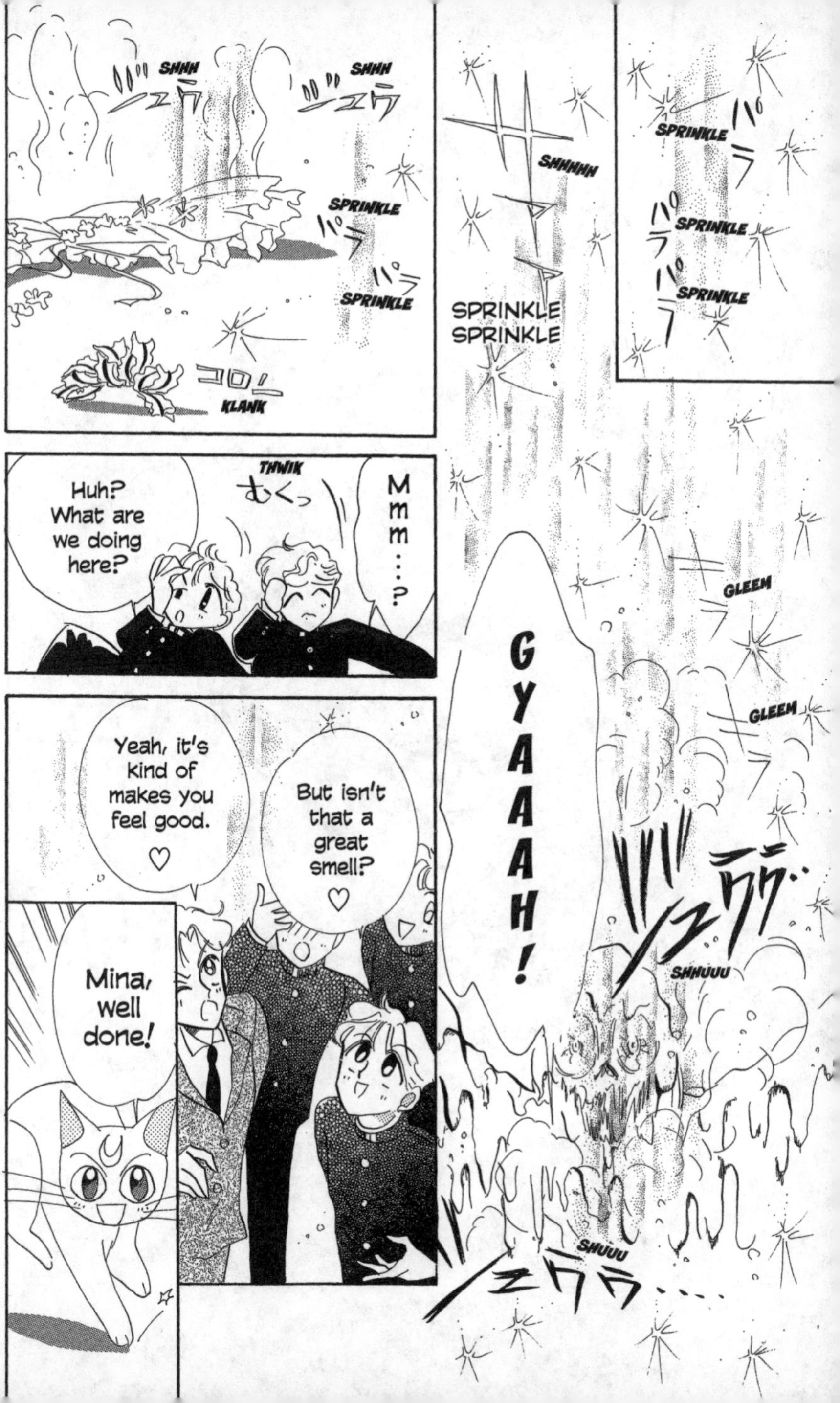
SPRINKLE
SPRINKLE
SPRINKLE
SHHHHH
SPRINKLE SPRINKLE
GYAAAAH!
GLEEM
GLEEM
SHHUUU
SHUUU
SHHH
SHHH
SPRINKLE
SPRINKLE
KLANK
Mmm...?
THWIK
Huh? What are we doing here?
But isn't that a great smell? ♡
Yeah, it's kind of makes you feel good. ♡
Mina, well done!

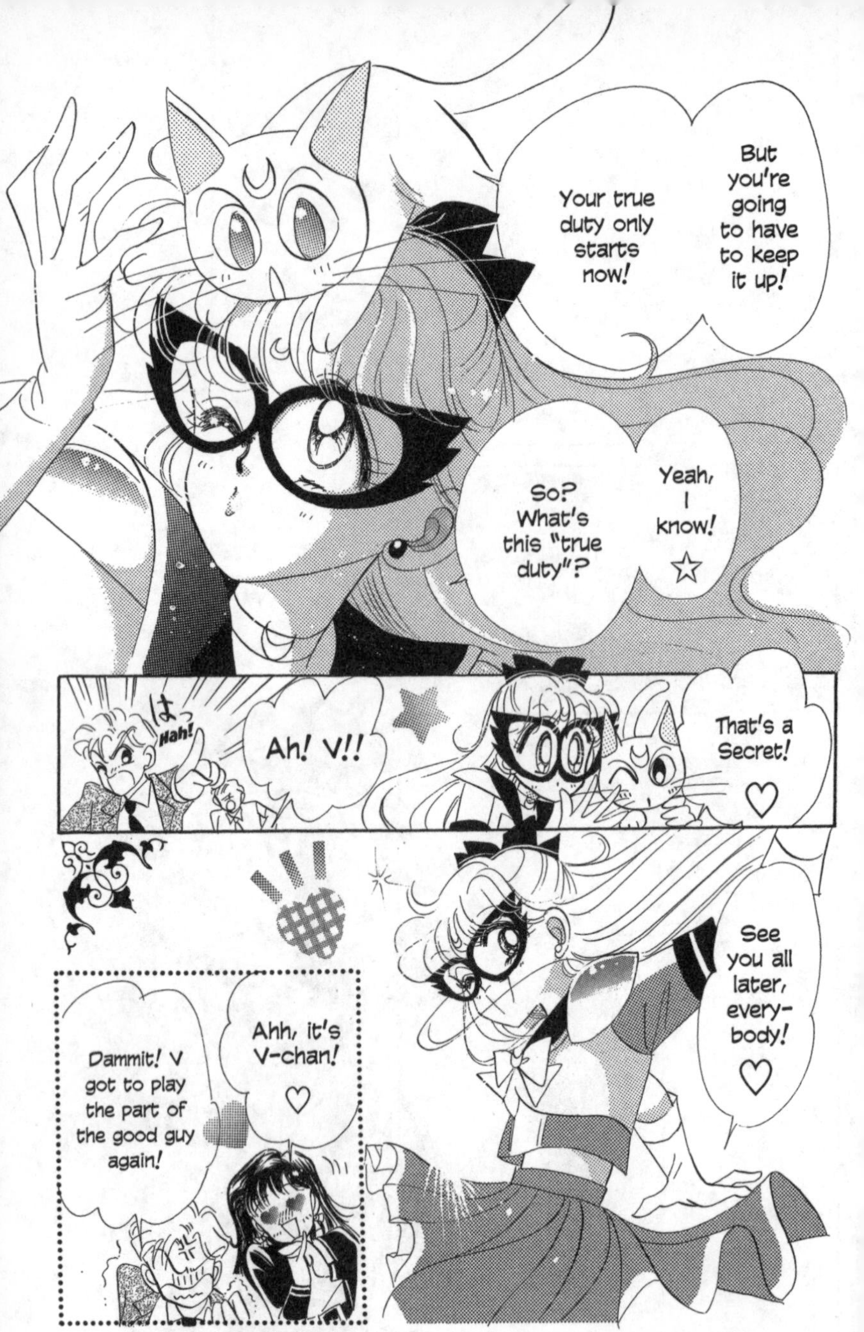
But you're going to have to keep it up!
Your true duty only starts now!
Yeah, I know! ☆
So? What's this "true duty"?
That's a Secret! ♡
Ah! V!!
はっ
Hah!
See you all later, everybody! ♡
Ahh, it's V-chan! ♡
Dammit! V got to play the part of the good guy again!

• The End •

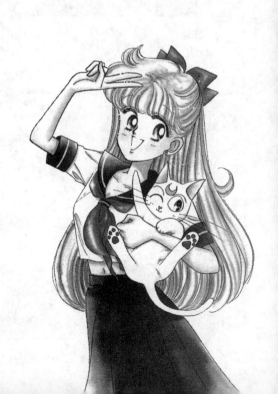

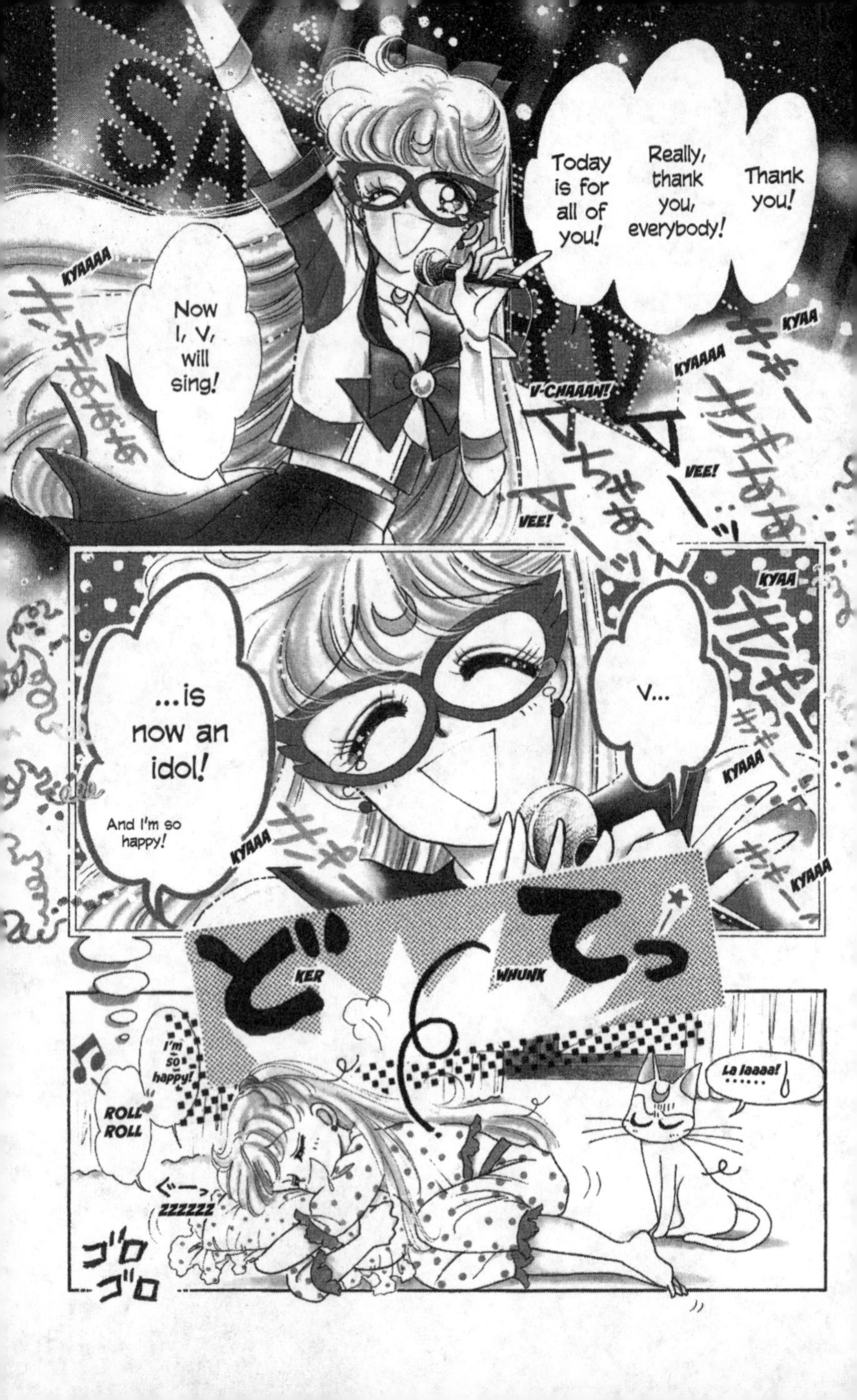
Thank you!
Really, thank you, everybody!
Today is for all of you!
KYAA
KYAAAA
V-CHAAAN!
VEE!
VEE!
Now I, V, will sing!
KYAAAA
KYAA
V...
KYAAA
KYAAA
...is now an idol!
And I'm so happy!
KYAAA
どてっ
KER WHUNK
La laaaa! ......
I'm so happy!
ROLL ROLL
ZZZZZZ

Vol. 5 The Machinations of the Dark Agency

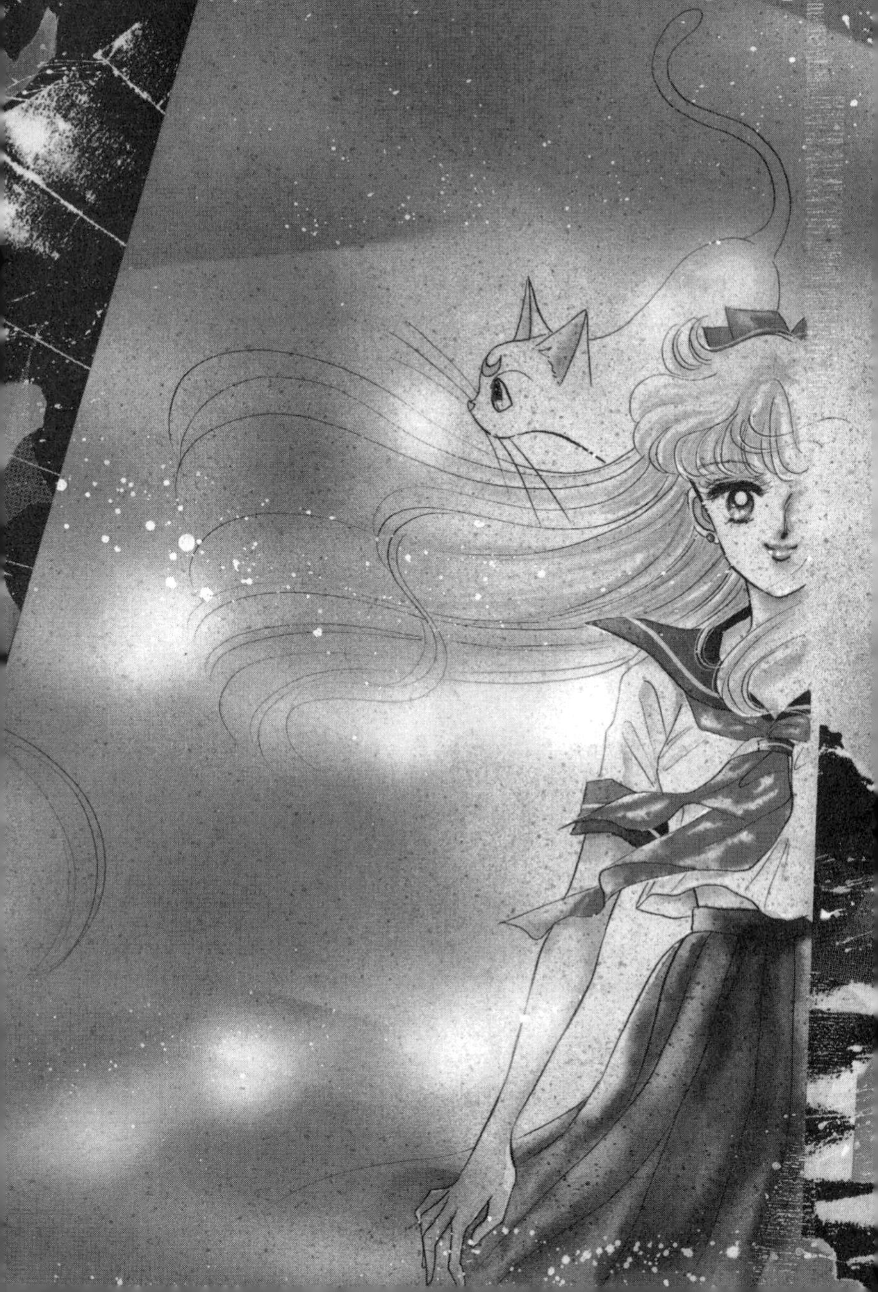

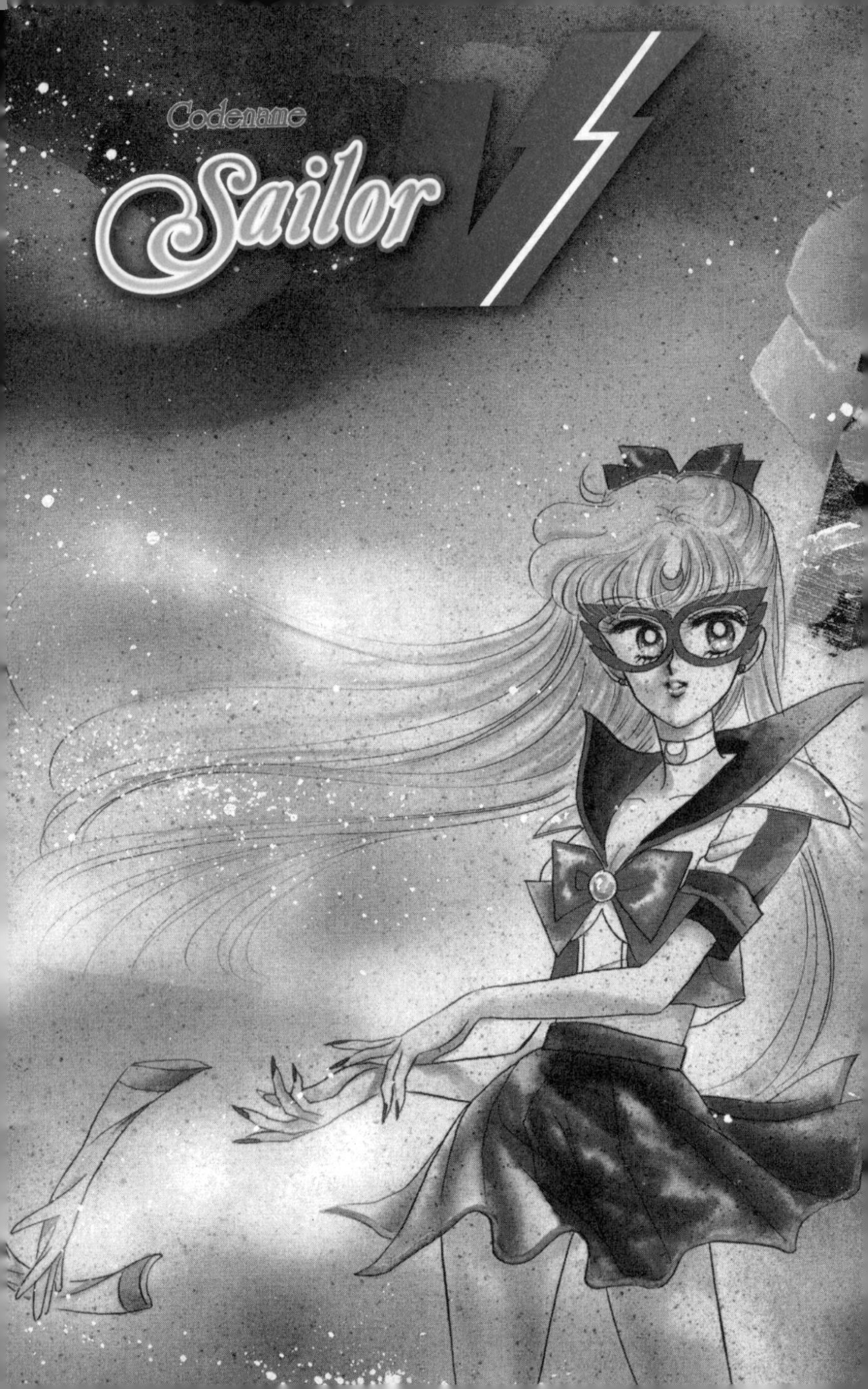
Codename
Sailor V

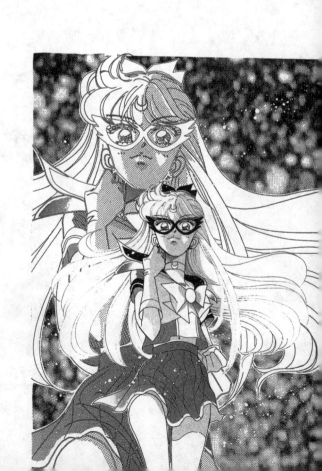

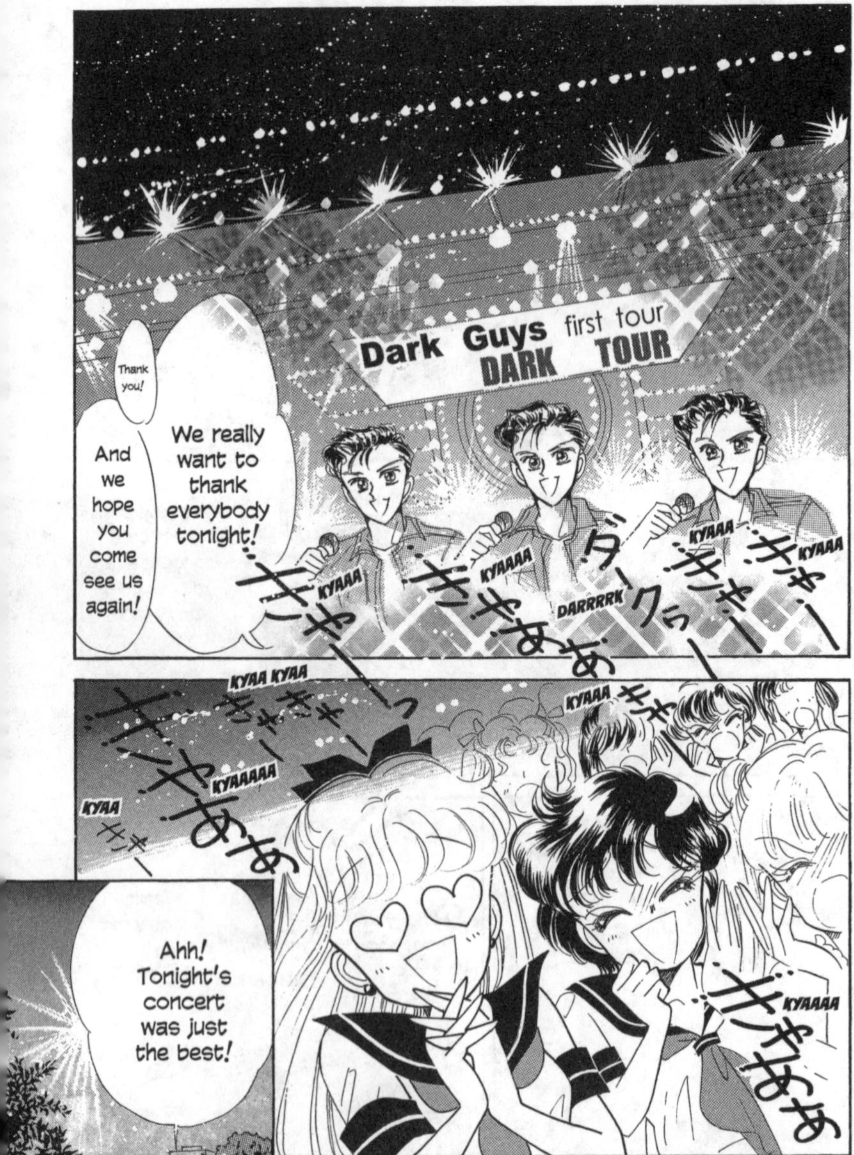
Dark Guys first tour
DARK TOUR
We really want to thank everybody tonight!
Thank you!
And we hope you come see us again!
KYAAA
KYAAA
KYAAA
DARRRRK
KYAAAA
KYAAA
KYAAA
KYAAA KYAA
KYAAAAA
KYAA
KYAAAA
Ahh! Tonight's concert was just the best!

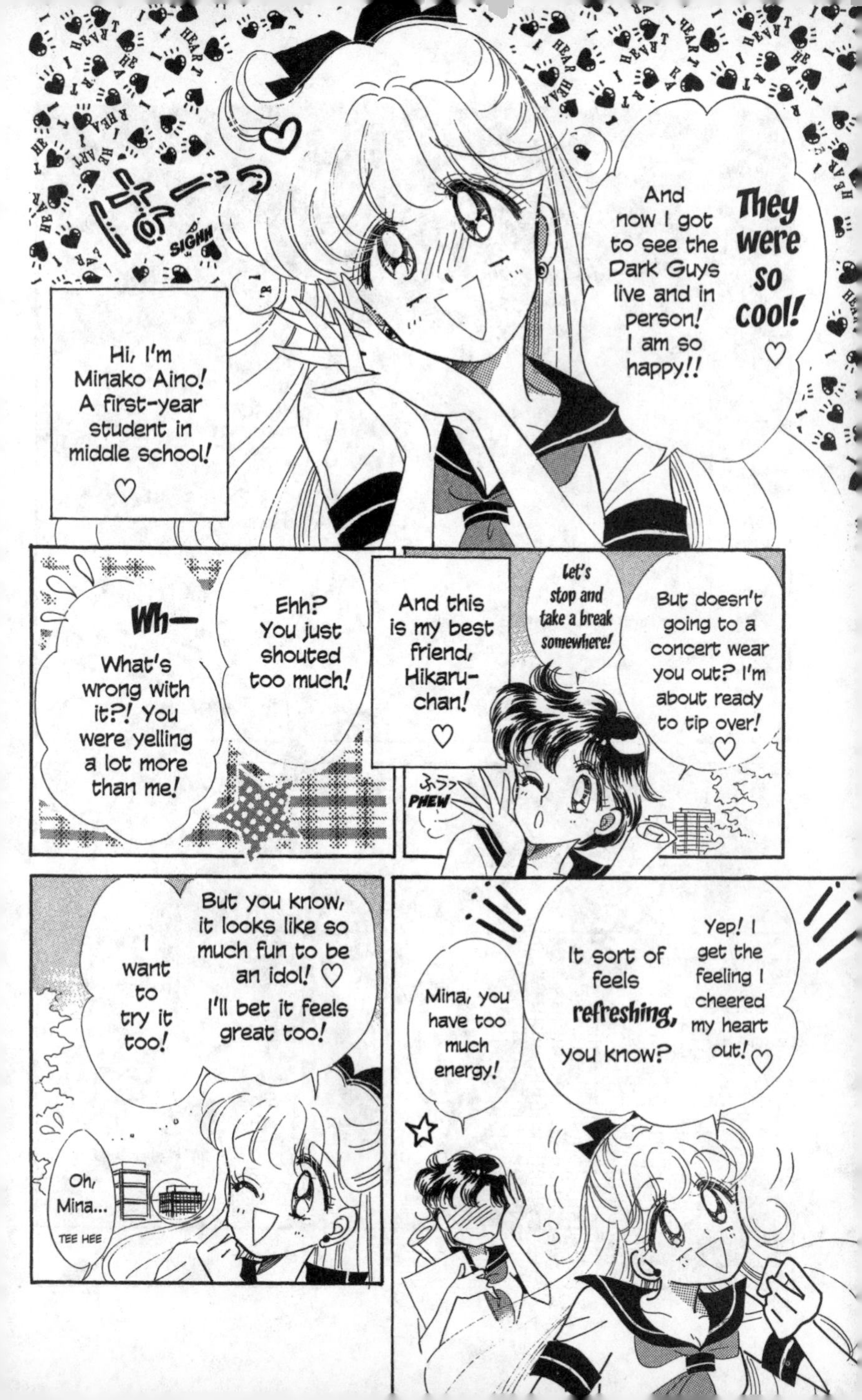
I HEART
They were so cool! ♡
And now I got to see the Dark Guys live and in person! I am so happy!!
SIGHH
Hi, I'm Minako Aino! A first-year student in middle school! ♡
But doesn't going to a concert wear you out? I'm about ready to tip over! ♡
Let's stop and take a break somewhere!
PHEW
And this is my best friend, Hikaru-chan! ♡
Ehh? You just shouted too much!
Wh—
What's wrong with it?! You were yelling a lot more than me!
Yep! I get the feeling I cheered my heart out! ♡
It sort of feels refreshing, you know?
Mina, you have too much energy!
But you know, it looks like so much fun to be an idol! ♡ I'll bet it feels great too!
I want to try it too!
Oh, Mina...
TEE HEE

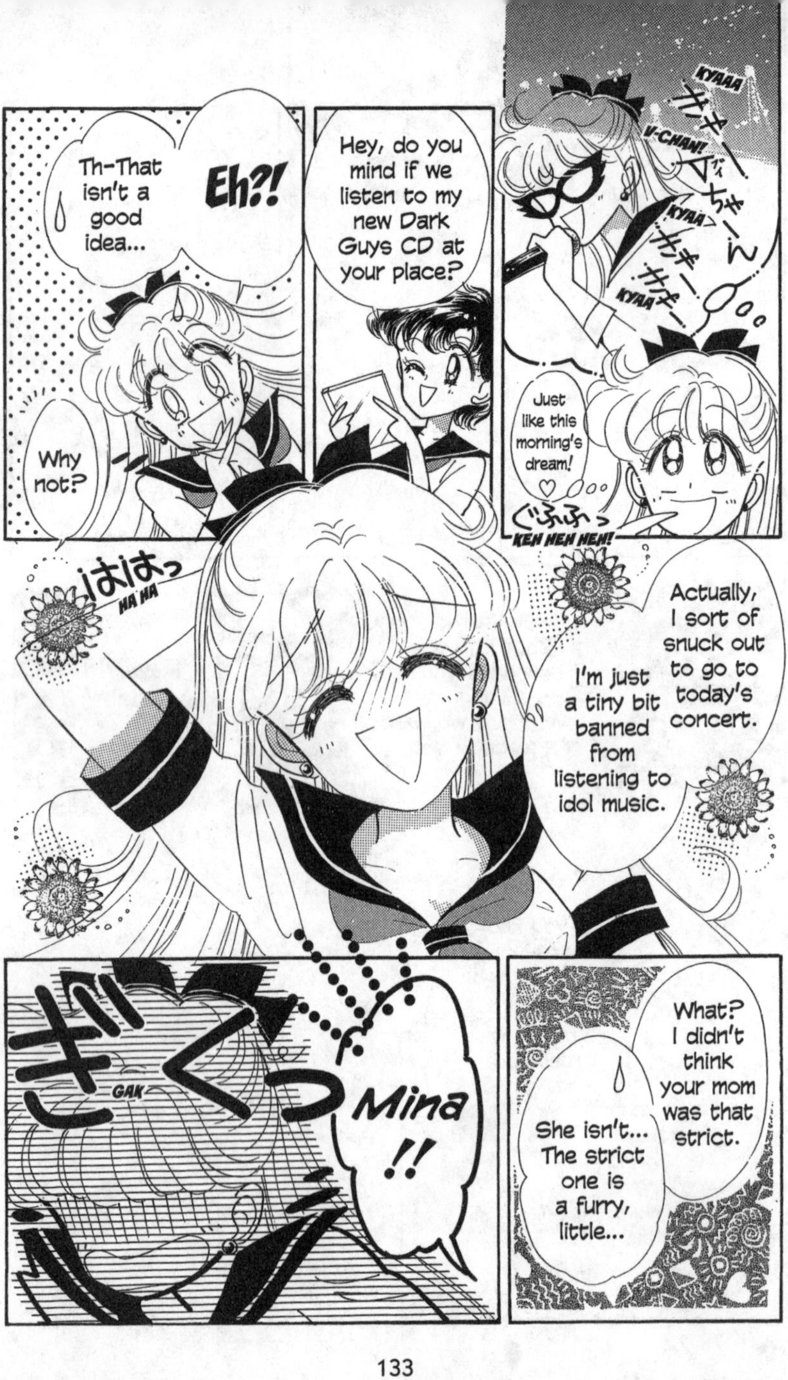
KYAAA
キャー
V-CHAN!
ヴィちゃーん
KYAA
キャー
KYAA
キャー
Just like this morning's dream! ♡
ぐふふっ
KEH HEH HEH!
Hey, do you mind if we listen to my new Dark Guys CD at your place?
Th-That isn't a good idea...
Eh?!
Why not?
ははっ
HA HA
Actually, I sort of snuck out to go to today's concert.
I'm just a tiny bit banned from listening to idol music.
What? I didn't think your mom was that strict.
She isn't... The strict one is a furry, little...
Mina!!
ぎくっ
GAK

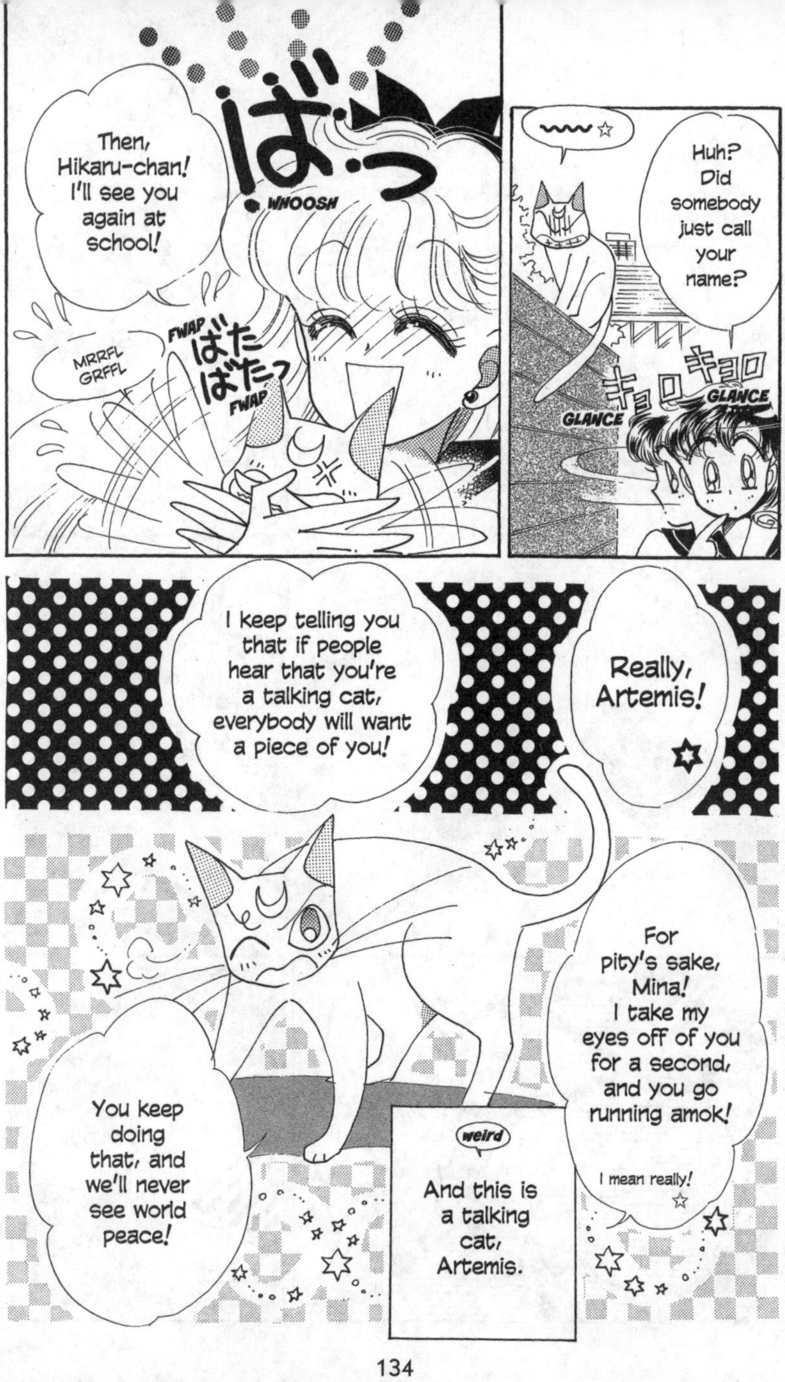

Huh? Did somebody just call your name?
キョロキョロ
GLANCE
GLANCE
Then, Hikaru-chan! I'll see you again at school!
ばっ
WHOOSH
ばたばたっ
FWAP
FWAP
MRRFL GRFFL
Really, Artemis!
I keep telling you that if people hear that you're a talking cat, everybody will want a piece of you!
For pity's sake, Mina! I take my eyes off of you for a second, and you go running amok!
I mean really!
weird
And this is a talking cat, Artemis.
You keep doing that, and we'll never see world peace!

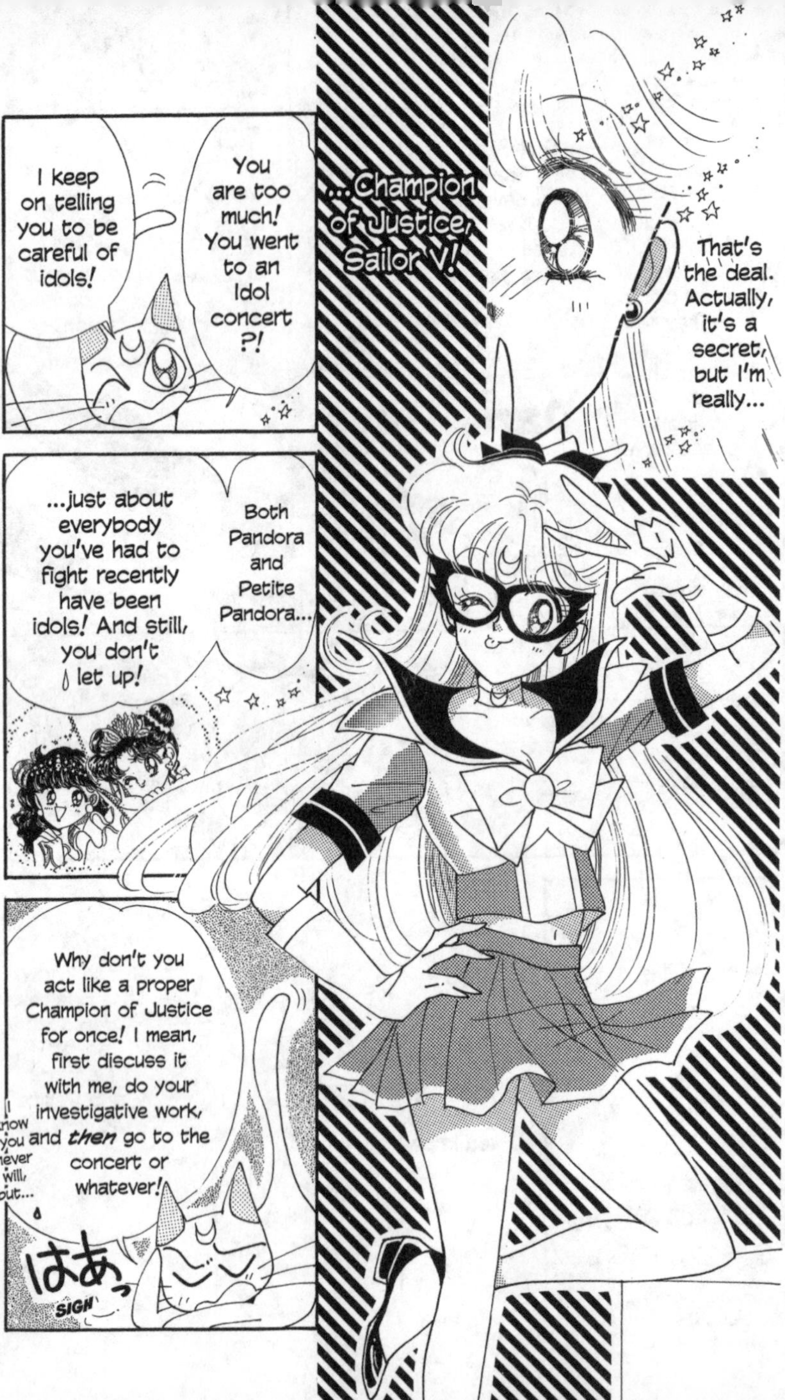
That's the deal. Actually, it's a secret, but I'm really...
...Champion of Justice, Sailor V!
You are too much! You went to an Idol concert ?!
I keep on telling you to be careful of idols!
Both Pandora and Petite Pandora...
...just about everybody you've had to fight recently have been idols! And still, you don't let up!
Why don't you act like a proper Champion of Justice for once! I mean, first discuss it with me, do your investigative work, and *then* go to the concert or whatever!
I know you never will, but...
はあっ
SIGH

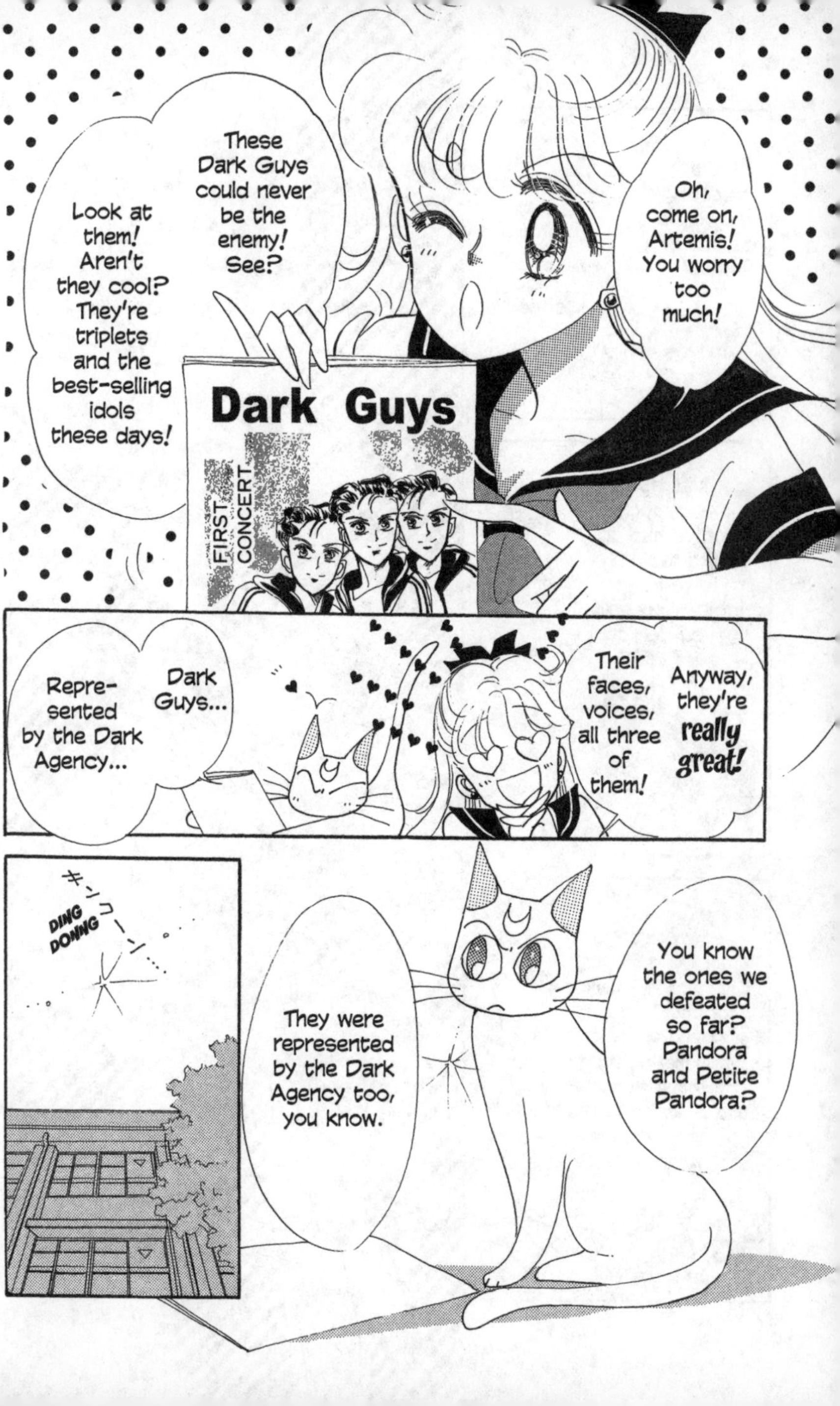
Oh, come on, Artemis! You worry too much!
These Dark Guys could never be the enemy! See?
Look at them! Aren't they cool? They're triplets and the best-selling idols these days!
Dark Guys
FIRST CONCERT
Anyway, they're really great!
Their faces, voices, all three of them!
Dark Guys...
Represented by the Dark Agency...
You know the ones we defeated so far? Pandora and Petite Pandora?
They were represented by the Dark Agency too, you know.
DING DONNG

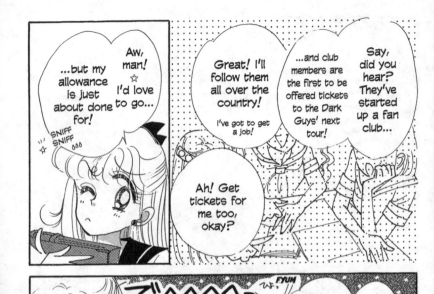

Say, did you hear? They've started up a fan club...
...and club members are the first to be offered tickets to the Dark Guys' next tour!
Great! I'll follow them all over the country!
I've got to get a job!
Ah! Get tickets for me too, okay?
Aw, man! ☆ I'd love to go...
...but my allowance is just about done for!
SNIFF SNIFF
Mina-san...
...at times like this...
FYUM
でへへへへっ
DEH HEH HEH HEH HEH
I know that voice!
Let's go watch a concert *together!*
I've already researched the frequency they use! 470 MHz!
Amano! Why, are you a Dark Guys fan?
You aren't, are you?
Non, non.
Frenchman Amano-kun.
ちっちっ
TSK TSK

Concert Watch = using equipment to pick up wireless mic broadcasts during a concert. It's illegal though.

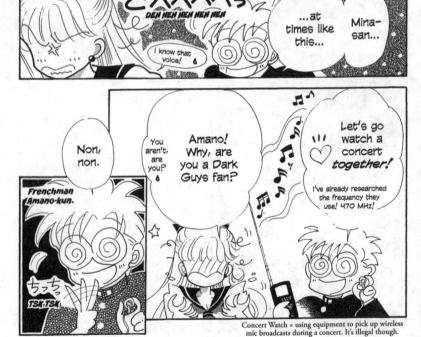

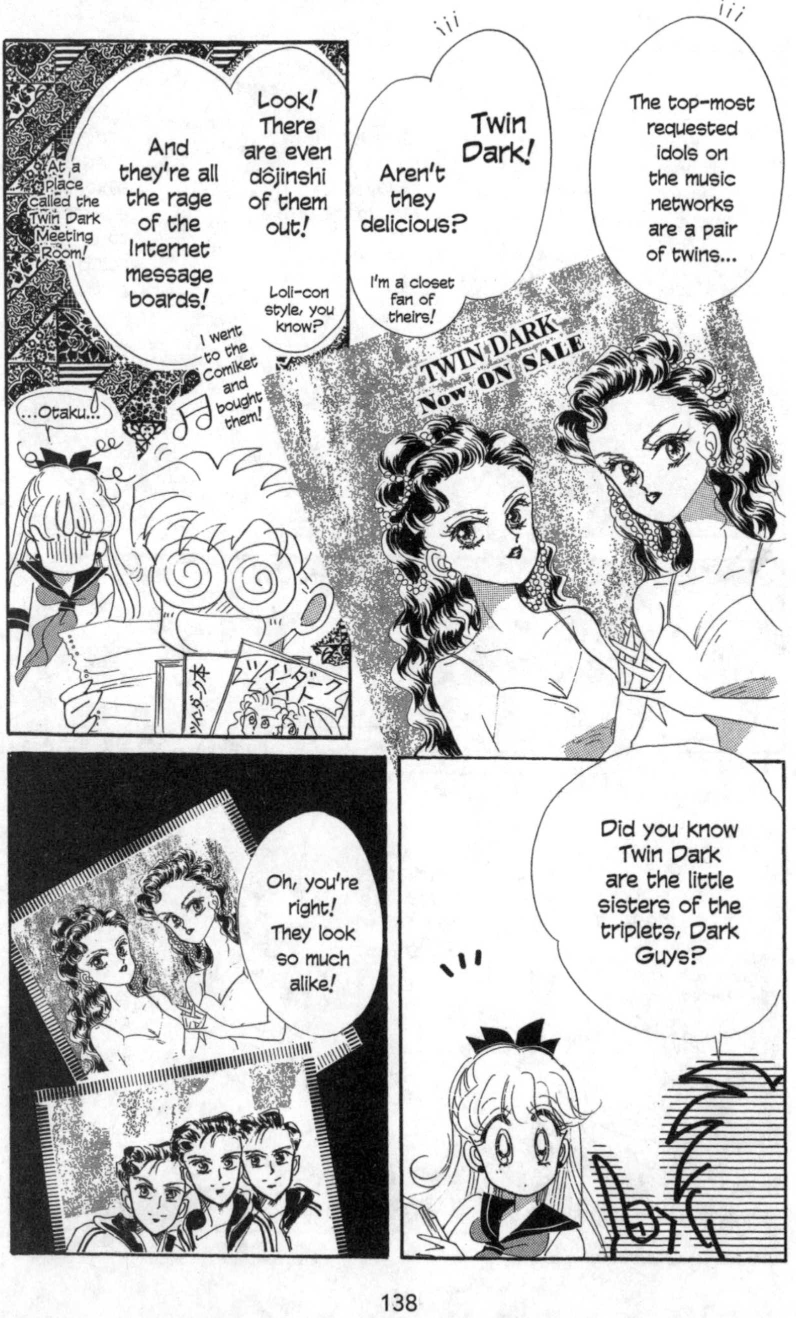

The top-most requested idols on the music networks are a pair of twins...
TWIN DARK Now ON SALE
Twin Dark! Aren't they delicious?
I'm a closet fan of theirs!
Look! There are even dôjinshi of them out!
Loli-con style, you know?
And they're all the rage of the Internet message boards!
At a place called the Twin Dark Meeting Room!
I went to the Comiket and bought them!
...Otaku...
Did you know Twin Dark are the little sisters of the triplets, Dark Guys?
Oh, you're right! They look so much alike!

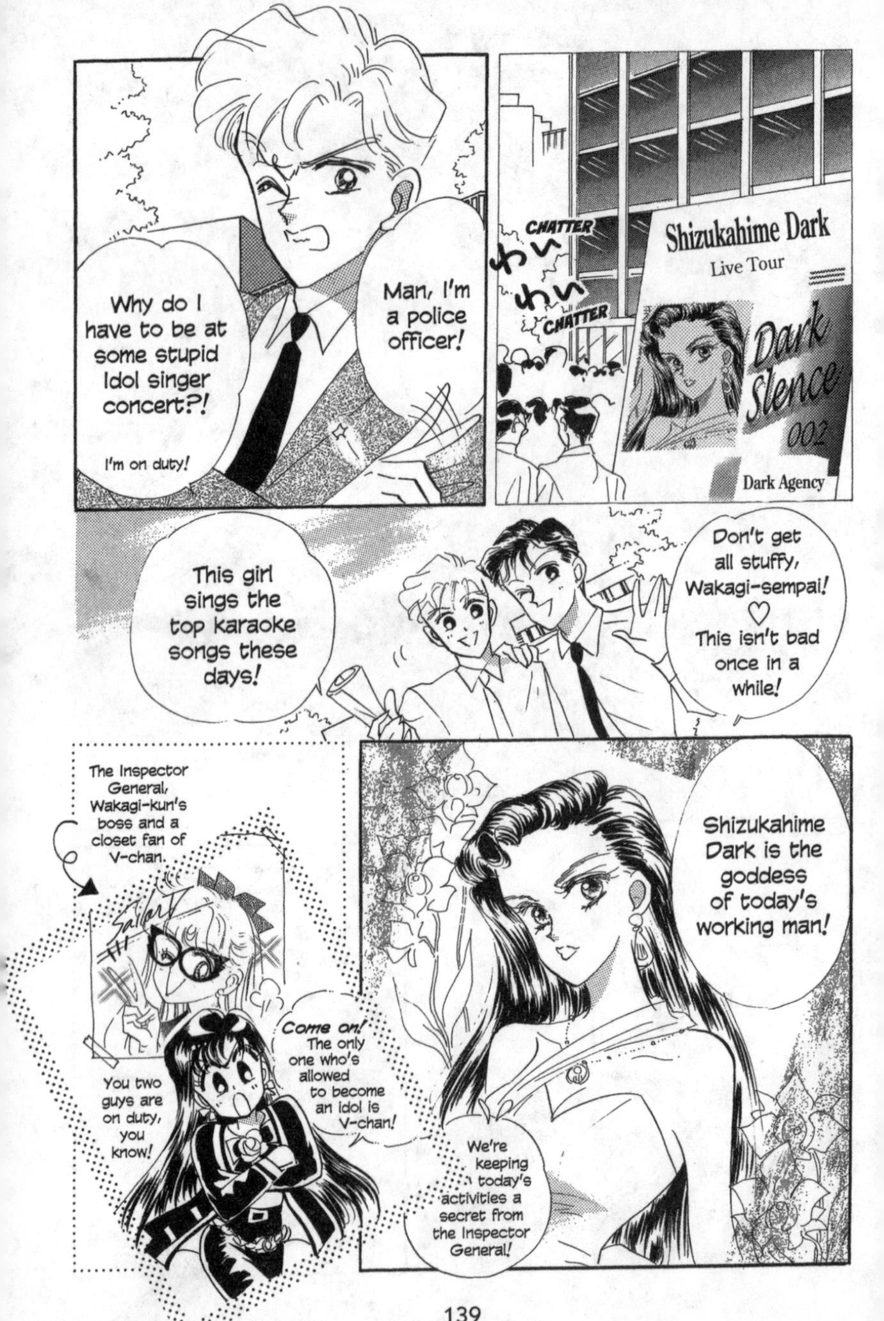
CHATTER
CHATTER
Shizukahime Dark
Live Tour
Dark Slence
002
Dark Agency
Man, I'm a police officer!
Why do I have to be at some stupid Idol singer concert?!
I'm on duty!
Don't get all stuffy, Wakagi-sempai! ♡
This isn't bad once in a while!
This girl sings the top karaoke songs these days!
Shizukahime Dark is the goddess of today's working man!
We're keeping today's activities a secret from the Inspector General!
The Inspector General, Wakagi-kun's boss and a closet fan of V-chan.
Sailor V
Come on! The only one who's allowed to become an idol is V-chan!
You two guys are on duty, you know!

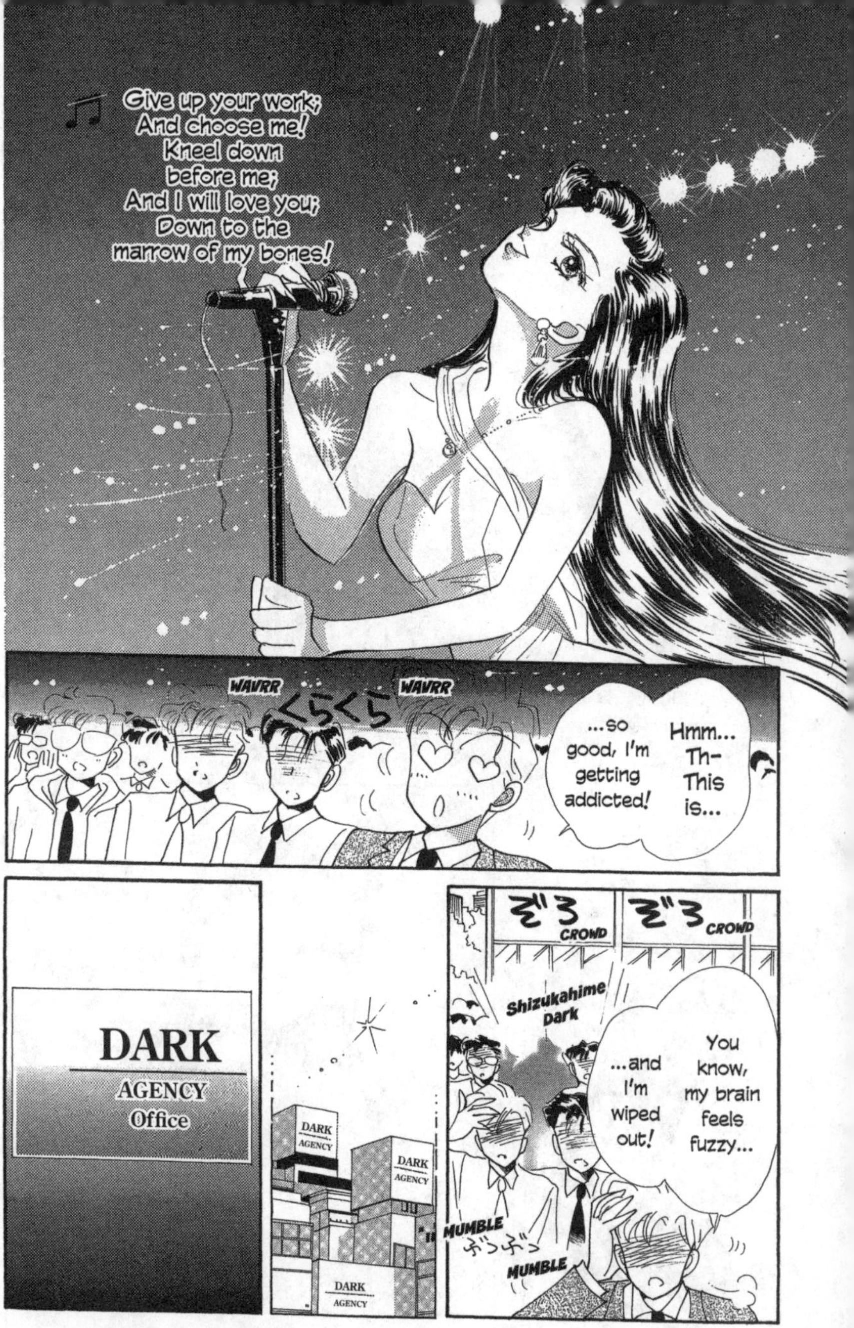
♫ Give up your work;
And choose me!
Kneel down
before me;
And I will love you;
Down to the
marrow of my bones!
WAVRR
くらくら
WAVRR
Hmm... Th- This is...
...so good, I'm getting addicted!
ぞろ CROWD
ぞろ CROWD
Shizukahime Dark
You know, my brain feels fuzzy...
...and I'm wiped out!
MUMBLE
ぶつぶつ
MUMBLE
DARK AGENCY
DARK AGENCY
DARK AGENCY
DARK
AGENCY
Office

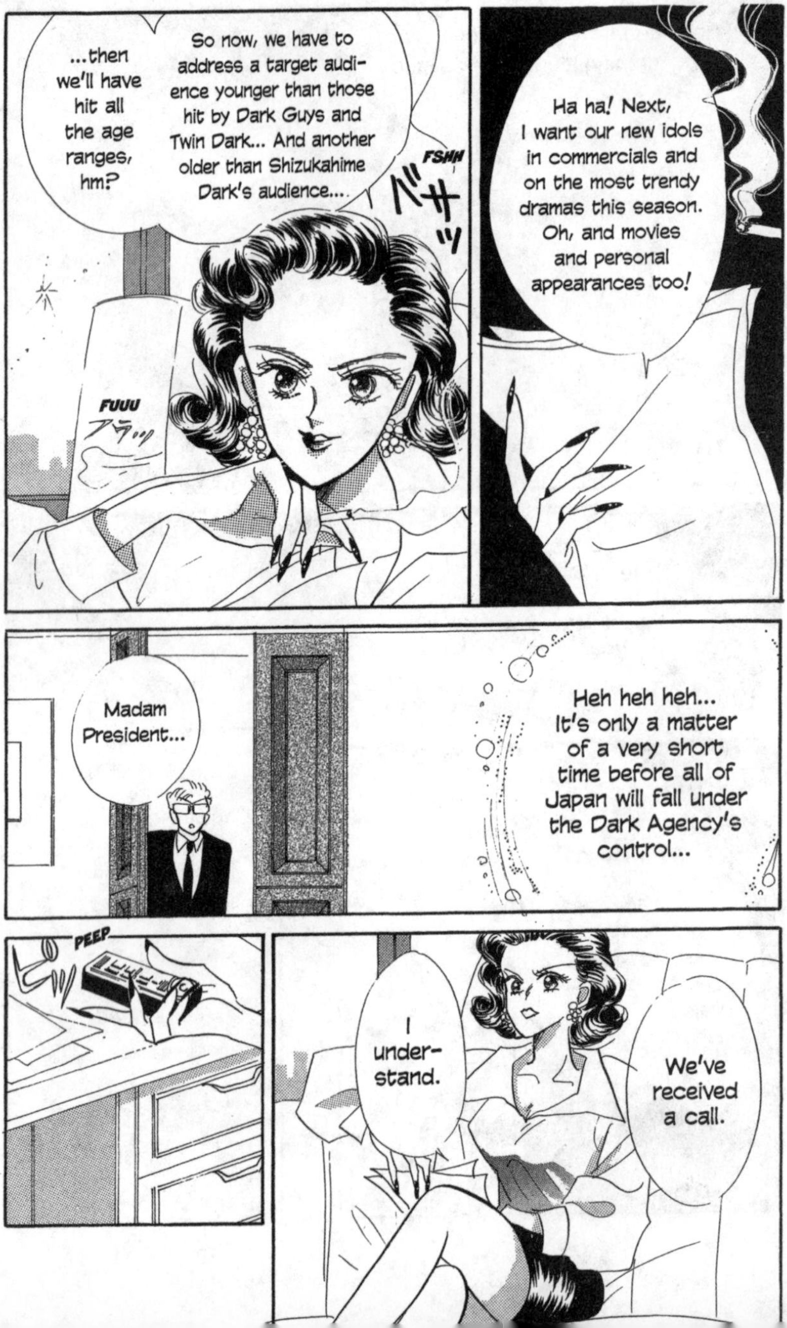
Ha ha! Next, I want our new idols in commercials and on the most trendy dramas this season. Oh, and movies and personal appearances too!
FSHH
ベキッ
So now, we have to address a target audi-ence younger than those hit by Dark Guys and Twin Dark... And another older than Shizukahime Dark's audience....
...then we'll have hit all the age ranges, hm?
FUUU
フラッ
Heh heh heh... It's only a matter of a very short time before all of Japan will fall under the Dark Agency's control...
Madam President...
We've received a call.
I under-stand.
PEEP

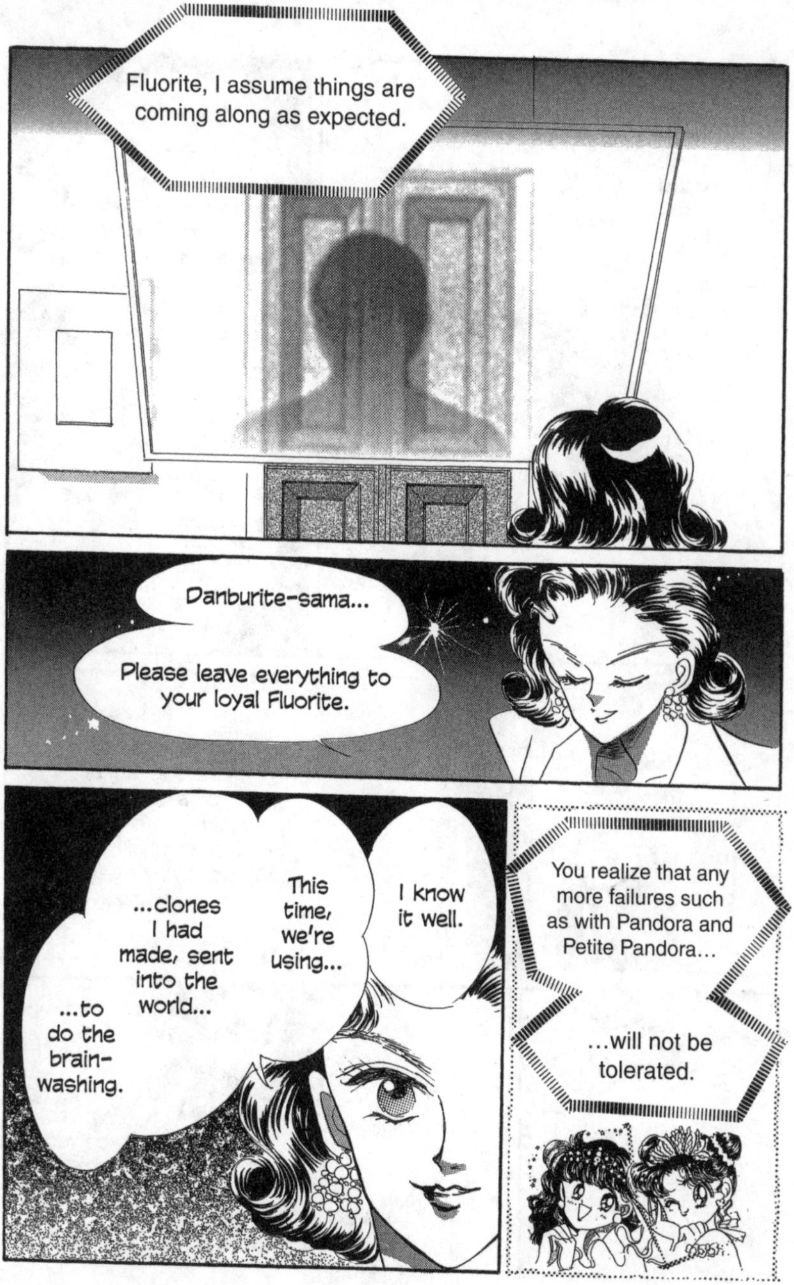
Fluorite, I assume things are coming along as expected.
Danburite-sama...
Please leave everything to your loyal Fluorite.
You realize that any more failures such as with Pandora and Petite Pandora...
...will not be tolerated.
I know it well.
This time, we're using...
...clones I had made, sent into the world...
...to do the brain-washing.

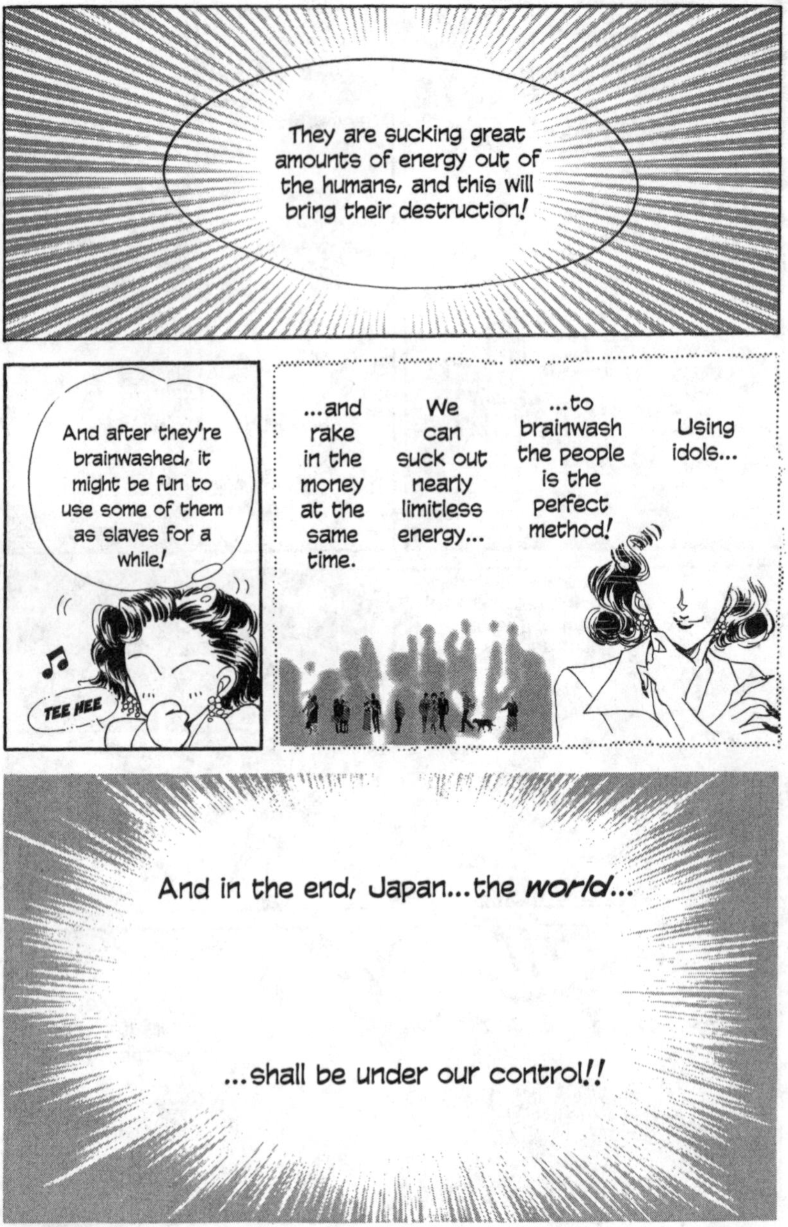
They are sucking great amounts of energy out of the humans, and this will bring their destruction!
Using idols...
...to brainwash the people is the perfect method!
We can suck out nearly limitless energy...
...and rake in the money at the same time.
And after they're brainwashed, it might be fun to use some of them as slaves for a while!
TEE HEE
And in the end, Japan...the *world*...
...shall be under our control!!

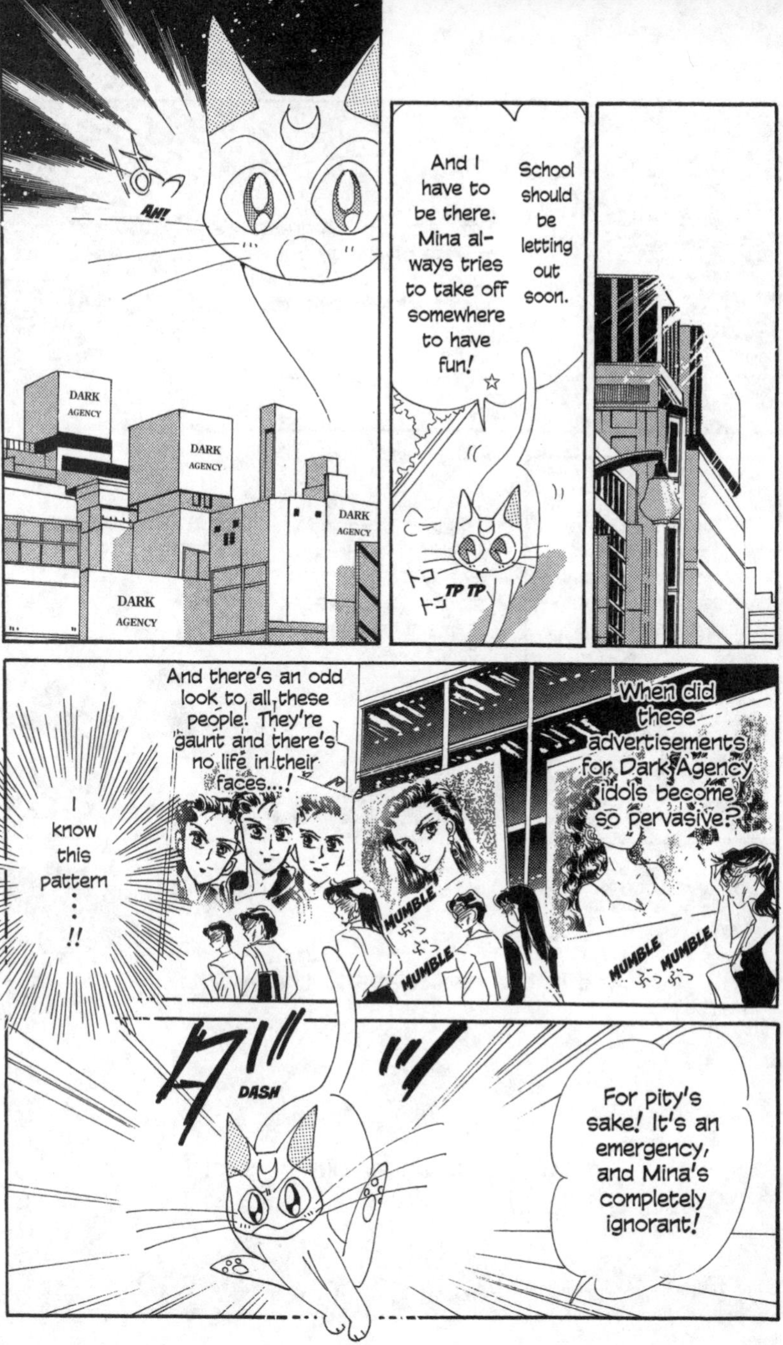
School should be letting out soon.
And I have to be there. Mina al-ways tries to take off somewhere to have fun!
TP TP
AH!
DARK AGENCY
DARK AGENCY
DARK AGENCY
DARK AGENCY
When did these advertisements for Dark Agency idols become so pervasive?
And there's an odd look to all these people! They're gaunt and there's no life in their faces...!
I know this pattern...!!
MUMBLE MUMBLE
MUMBLE MUMBLE
DASH
For pity's sake! It's an emergency, and Mina's completely ignorant!

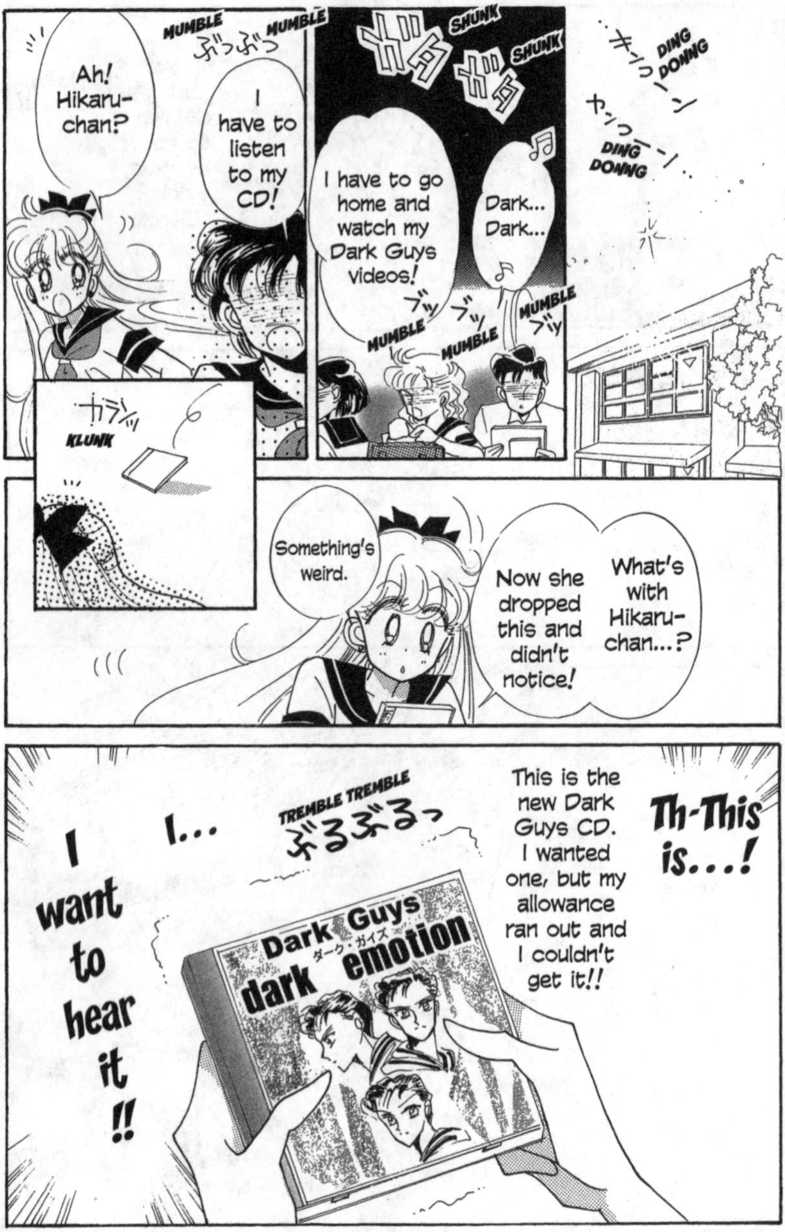
キンコーン
DING DONG
カンコーン
DING DONG
ガタ
SHUNK
ガタ
SHUNK
Dark... Dark...
I have to go home and watch my Dark Guys videos!
ブツ
MUMBLE
ブツ
MUMBLE
ブツ
MUMBLE
MUMBLE
ぶつぶつ
MUMBLE
I have to listen to my CD!
Ah! Hikaru-chan?
カラン
KLUNK
What's with Hikaru-chan...?
Now she dropped this and didn't notice!
Something's weird.
Th-This is...!
This is the new Dark Guys CD. I wanted one, but my allowance ran out and I couldn't get it!!
TREMBLE TREMBLE
ぶるぶるっ
I...
I want to hear it!!
Dark Guys
ダーク・ガイズ
dark emotion

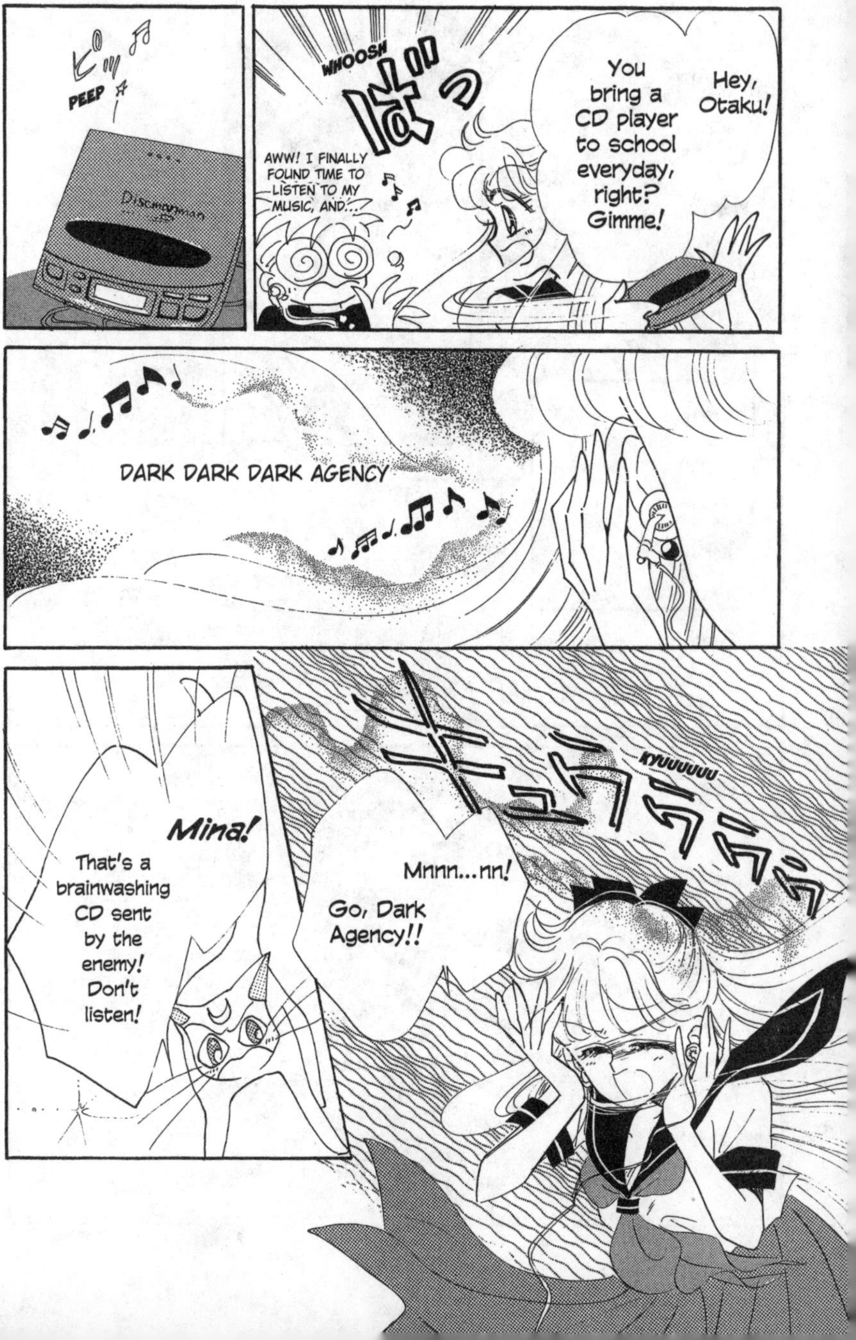
Hey, Otaku!
You bring a CD player to school everyday, right? Gimme!
WHOOSH
ぱっ
AWW! I FINALLY FOUND TIME TO LISTEN TO MY MUSIC, AND...
ピッ
PEEP
DARK DARK DARK AGENCY
KYUUUUUU
Mnnn...nn!
Go, Dark Agency!!
Mina!
That's a brainwashing CD sent by the enemy! Don't listen!

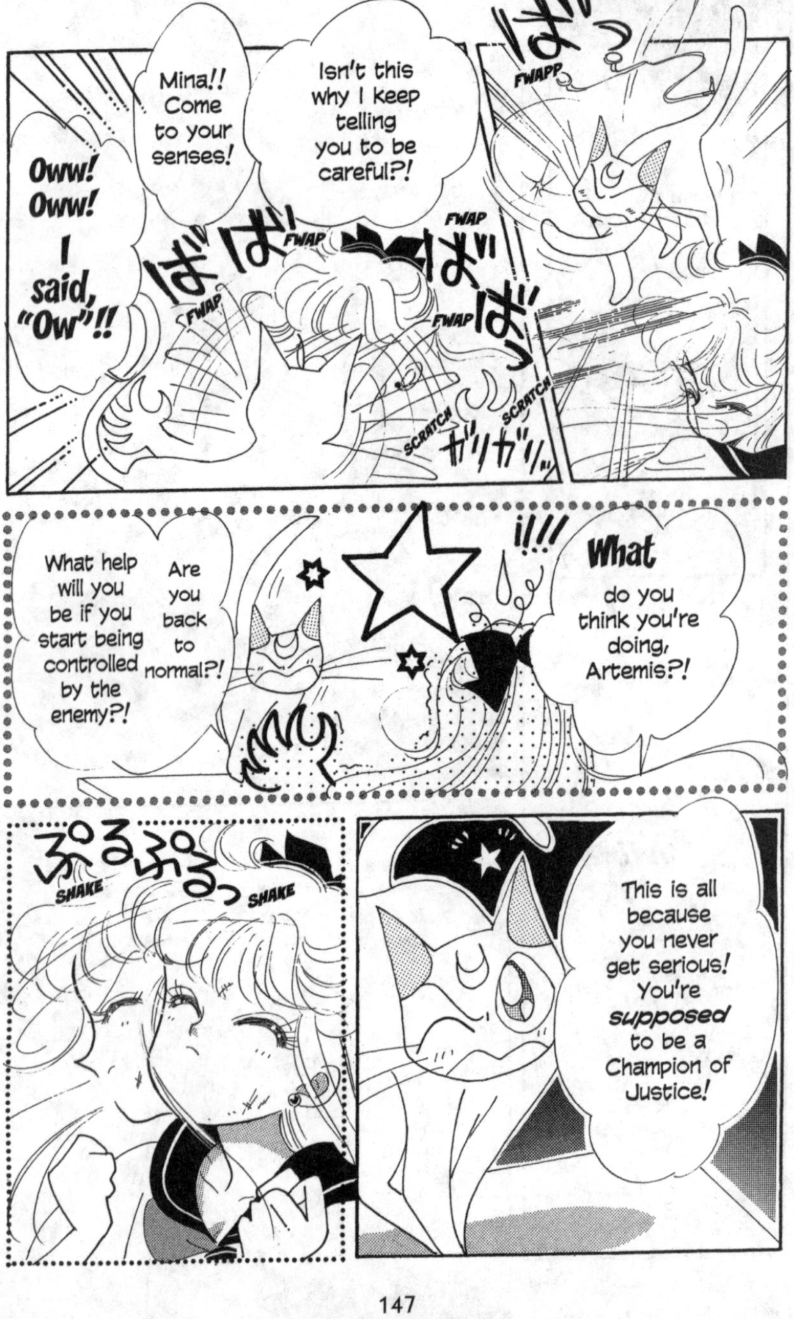

ばっ
FWAPP
Isn't this why I keep telling you to be careful?!
Mina!! Come to your senses!
Oww! Oww! I said, "Ow"!!
ばばばばっ
FWAP
FWAP
FWAP
FWAP
ガリガリッ
SCRATCH
SCRATCH
What do you think you're doing, Artemis?!
!!!
Are you back to normal?!
What help will you be if you start being controlled by the enemy?!
This is all because you never get serious! You're *supposed* to be a Champion of Justice!
ぷるぷるっ
SHAKE
SHAKE

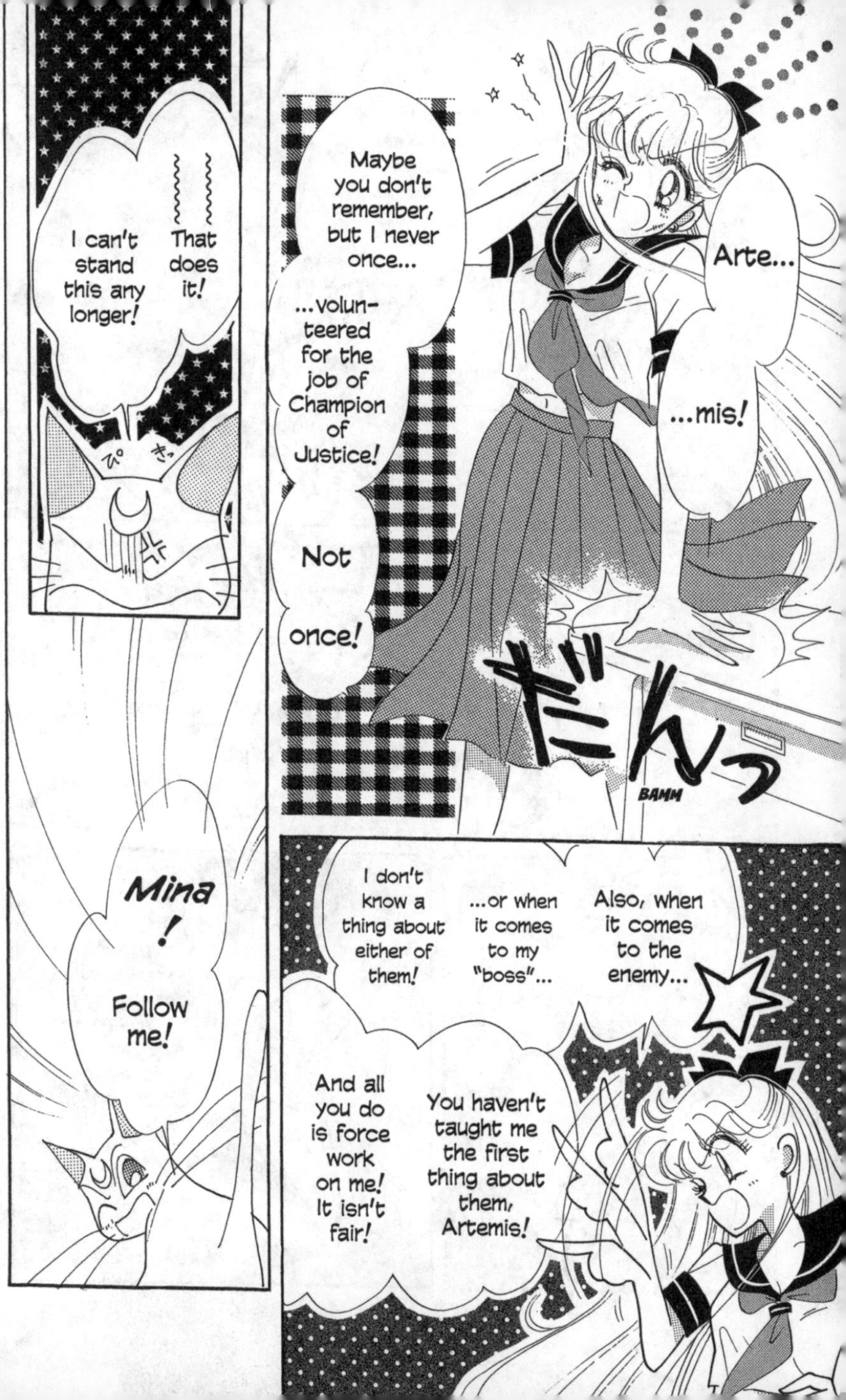
Arte...
...mis!
Maybe you don't remember, but I never once...
...volunteered for the job of Champion of Justice!
Not once!
BAMM
Also, when it comes to the enemy...
...or when it comes to my "boss"...
I don't know a thing about either of them!
You haven't taught me the first thing about them, Artemis!
And all you do is force work on me! It isn't fair!
That does it!
I can't stand this any longer!
ぴきっ
Mina!
Follow me!

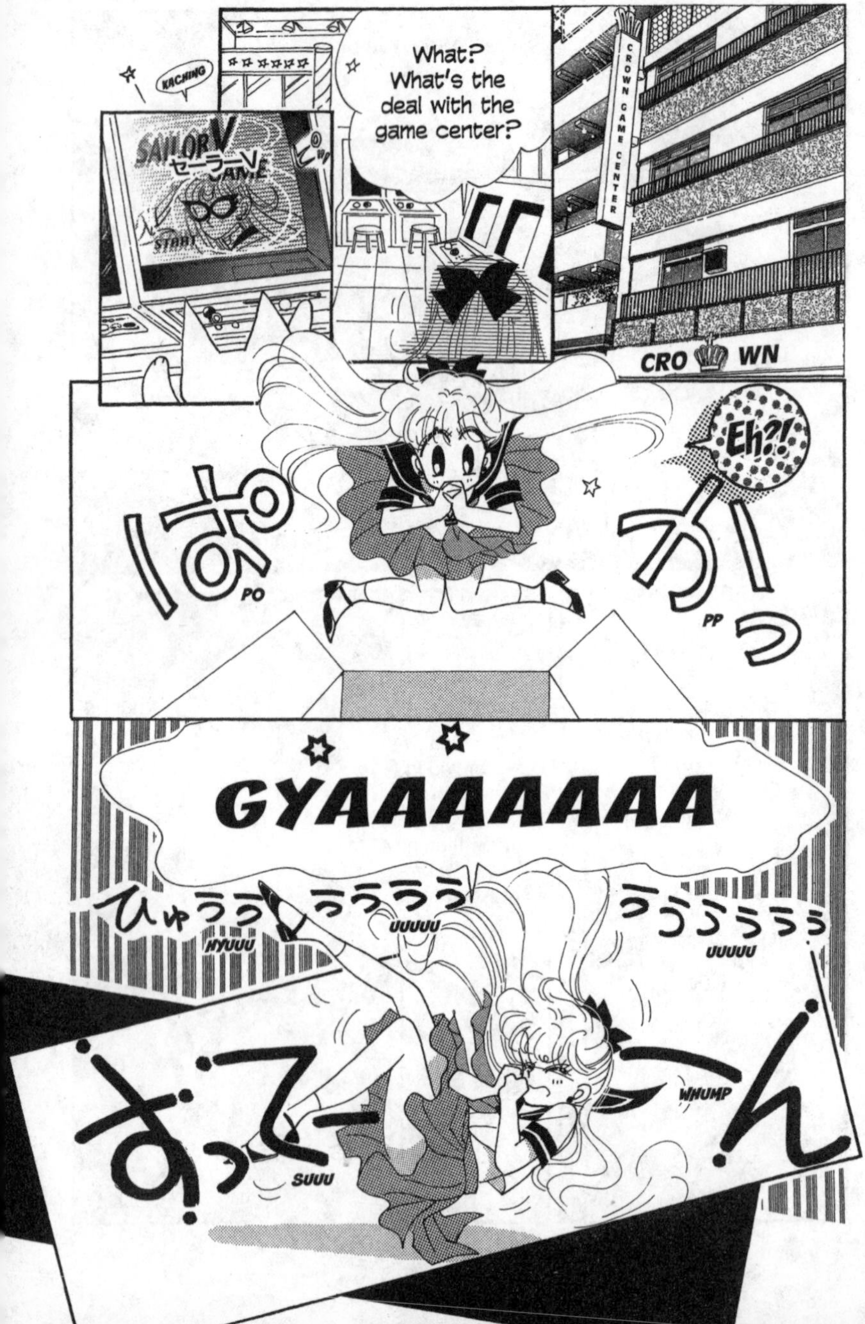
CROWN GAME CENTER
CRO WN
What? What's the deal with the game center?
SAILOR V
セーラーV
GAME
START
KACHING
っ
PP
か
Eh?!
ぱ
PO
GYAAAAAAA
うううううう
UUUUU
うううう
UUUUU
ひゅうう
HYUUU
ん
WHUMP
すってー
SUUU

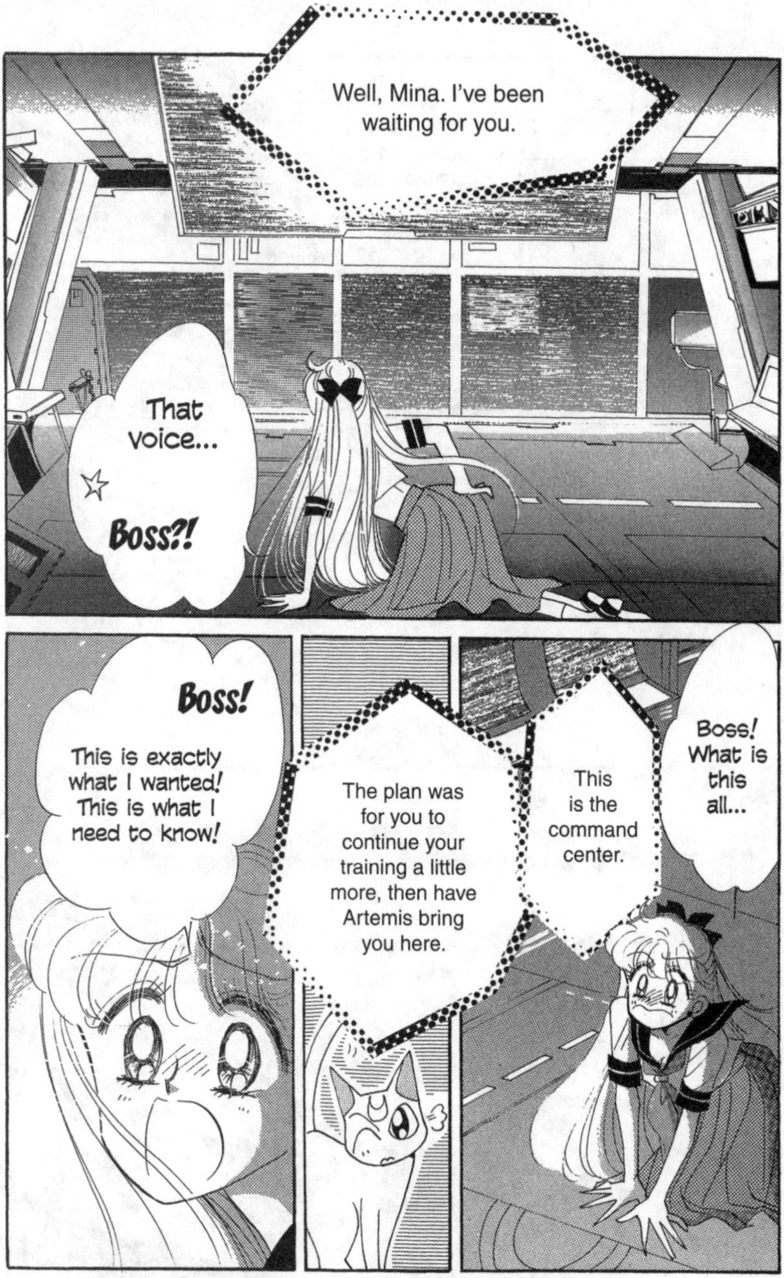

Well, Mina. I've been waiting for you.
That voice...
Boss?!
Boss! What is this all...
This is the command center.
The plan was for you to continue your training a little more, then have Artemis bring you here.
Boss!
This is exactly what I wanted! This is what I need to know!

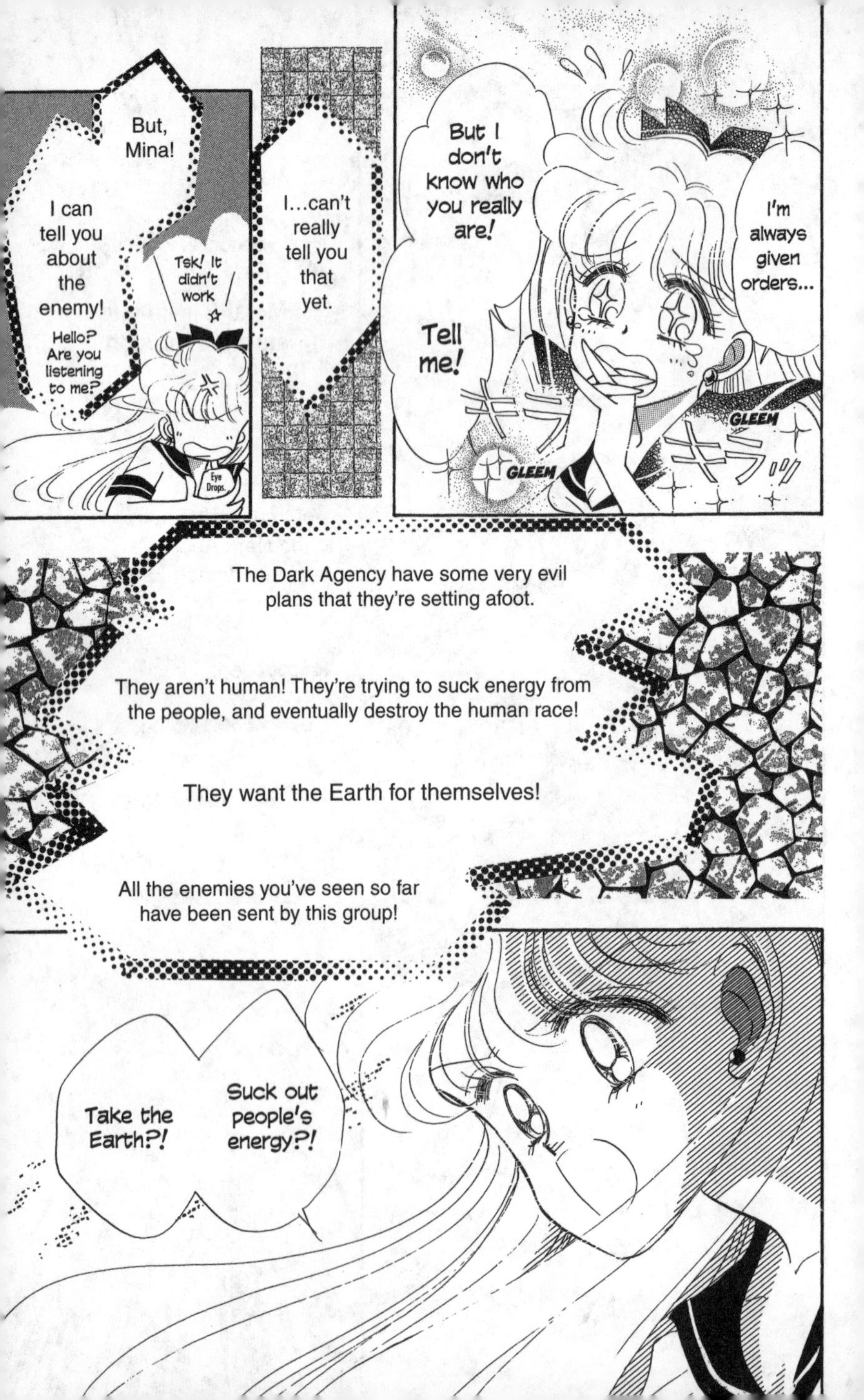
I'm always given orders...
But I don't know who you really are!
Tell me!
GLEEM
キラッ
GLEEM
キラ
I...can't really tell you that yet.
But, Mina!
I can tell you about the enemy!
Tsk! It didn't work ☆
Hello? Are you listening to me?
Eye Drops.
The Dark Agency have some very evil plans that they're setting afoot.
They aren't human! They're trying to suck energy from the people, and eventually destroy the human race!
They want the Earth for themselves!
All the enemies you've seen so far have been sent by this group!
Suck out people's energy?!
Take the Earth?!

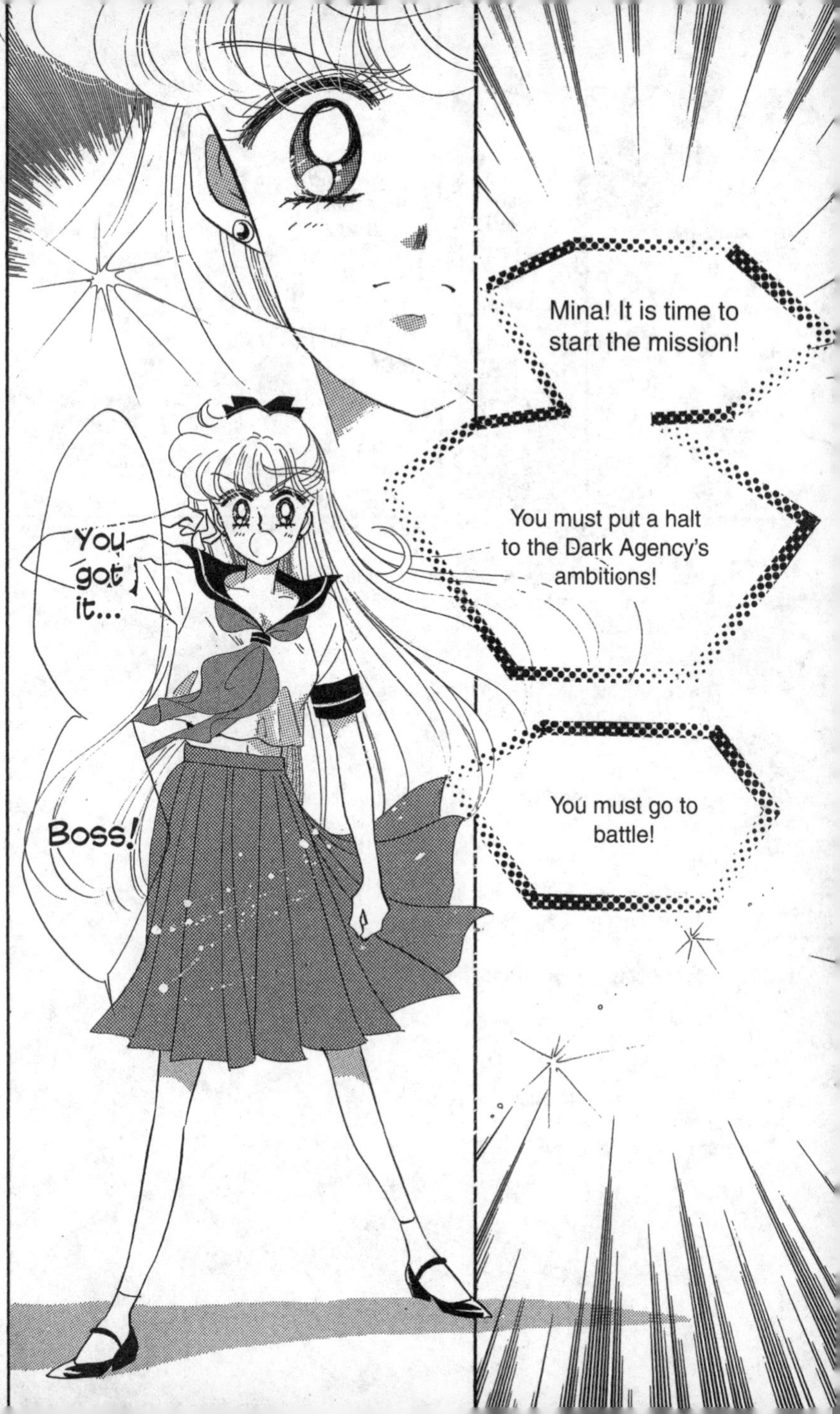
Mina! It is time to start the mission!
You must put a halt to the Dark Agency's ambitions!
You must go to battle!
You got it...
Boss!

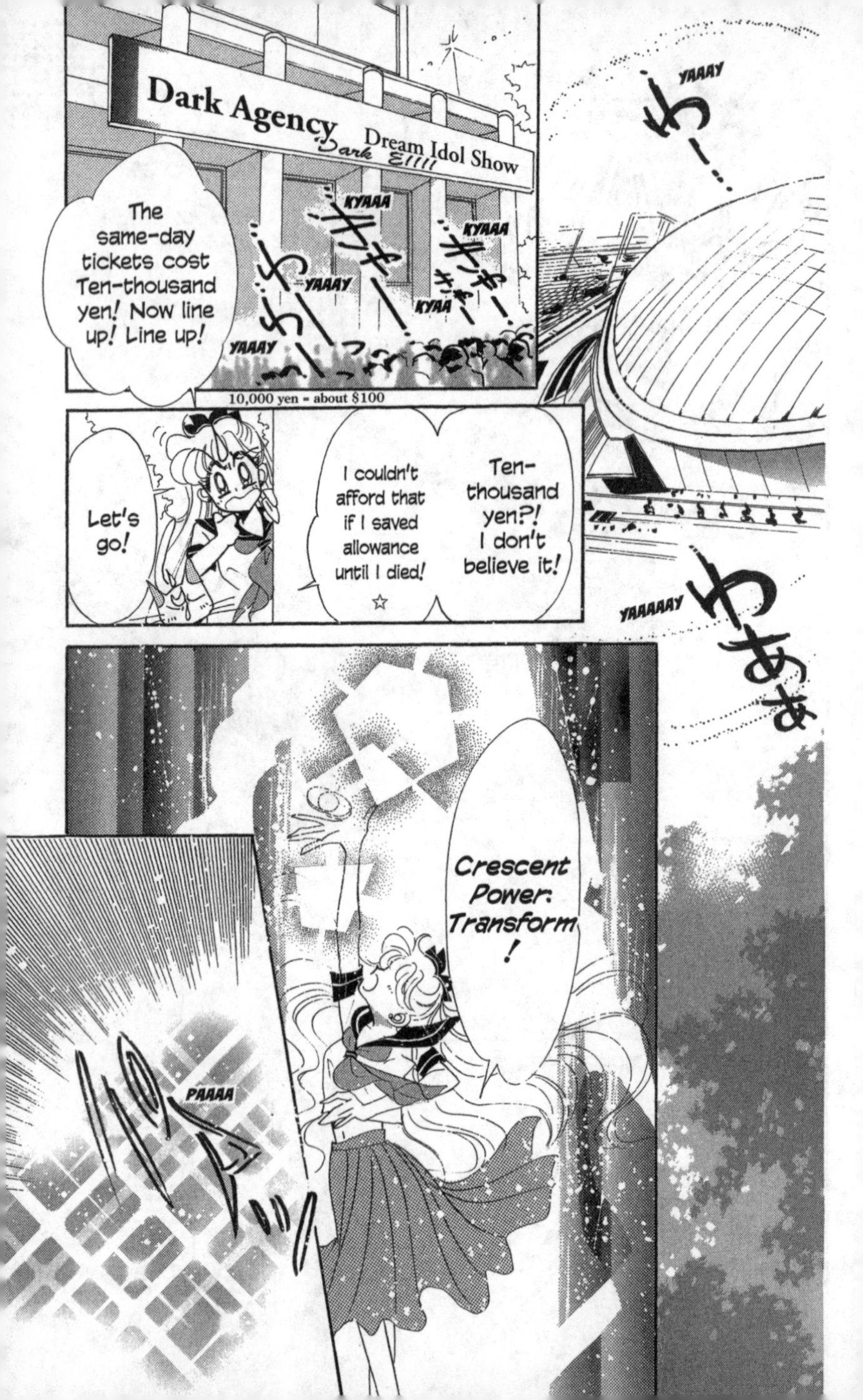
YAAAY
YAAAAAY
Dark Agency Dream Idol Show
Dark E!!!!
KYAAA
KYAAA
YAAAY
KYAA
YAAAY
The same-day tickets cost Ten-thousand yen! Now line up! Line up!
10,000 yen = about $100
Ten-thousand yen?! I don't believe it!
I couldn't afford that if I saved allowance until I died! ☆
Let's go!
Crescent Power: Transform!
PAAAA

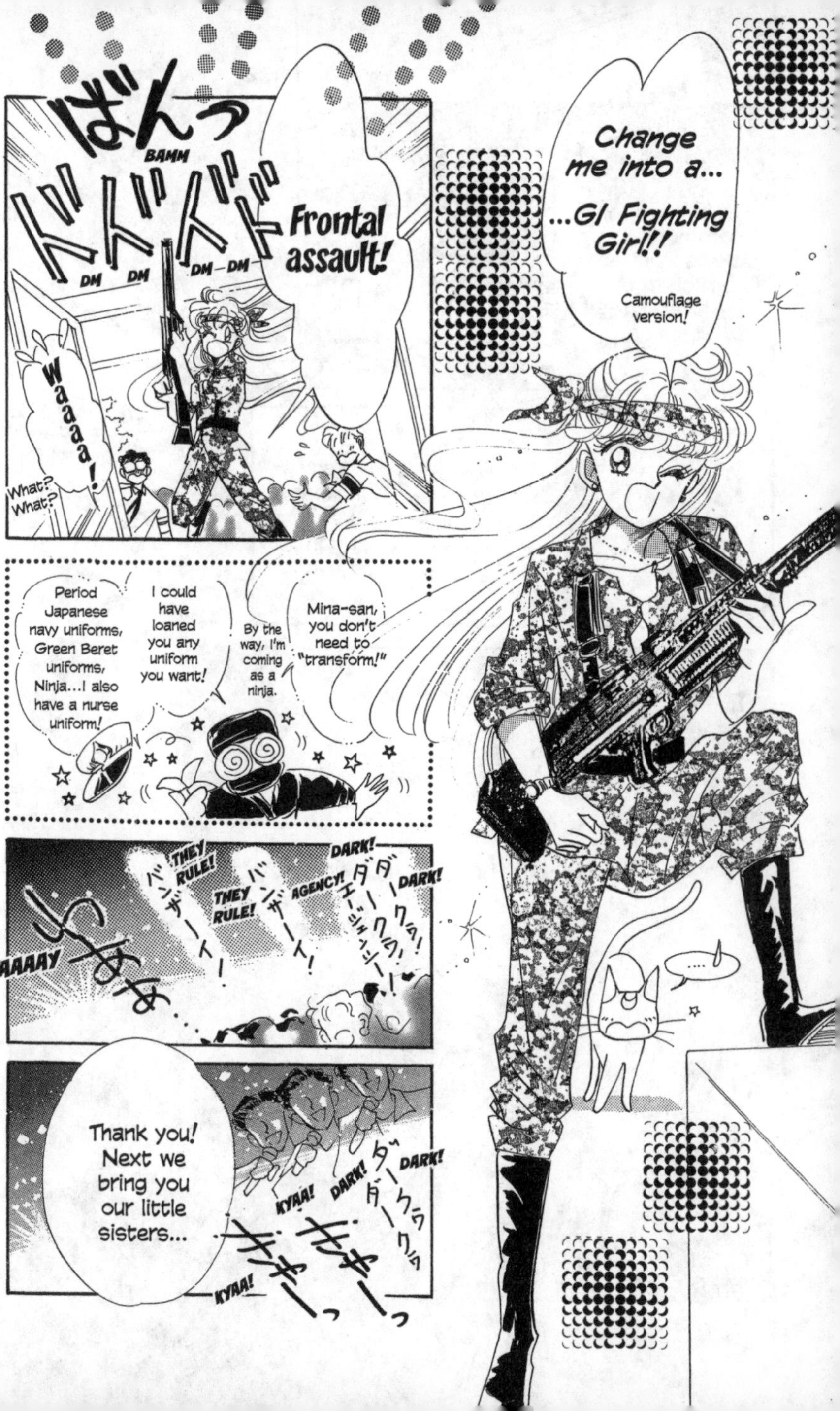

Change me into a... ...GI Fighting Girl!!
Camouflage version!
....
ばんっ
BAMM
ドドドドド
DM DM DM—DM
Frontal assault!
Waaaaa!
What? What?
Mina-san, you don't need to "transform!"
By the way, I'm coming as a ninja.
I could have loaned you any uniform you want!
Period Japanese navy uniforms, Green Beret uniforms, Ninja...I also have a nurse uniform!
ダークダーク!
DARK! DARK!
エージェンシー!
AGENCY!
バンザーイ!
THEY RULE!
バンザーイ!
THEY RULE!
わぁぁ…
YAAAAY
ダークダーク
DARK! DARK!
キャーっ
KYAA!
キャーっ
KYAA!
Thank you! Next we bring you our little sisters...

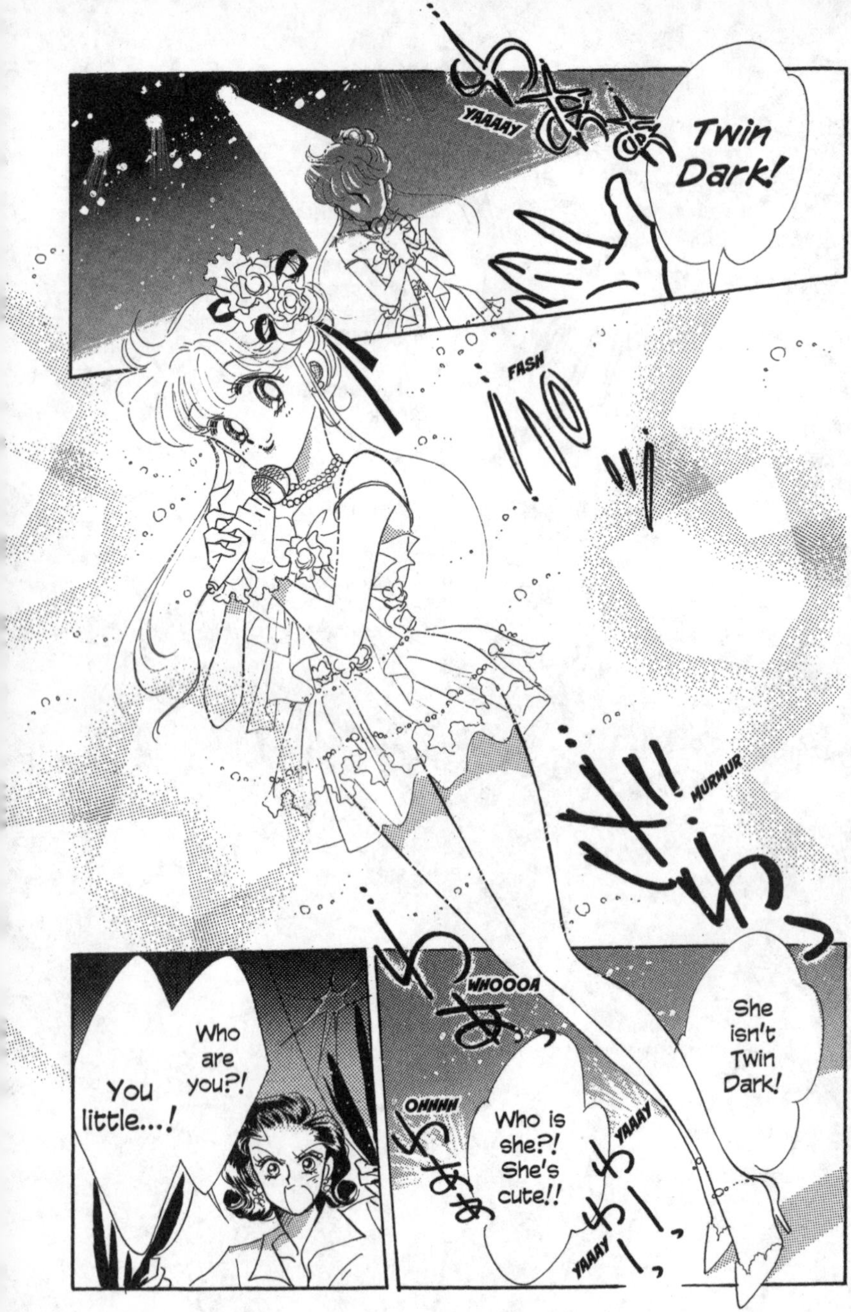

Twin Dark!
YAAAAY
FASH
MURMUR
She isn't Twin Dark!
WHOOOA
Who is she?! She's cute!!
OHNNN
YAAAY
YAAAY
Who are you?!
You little...!

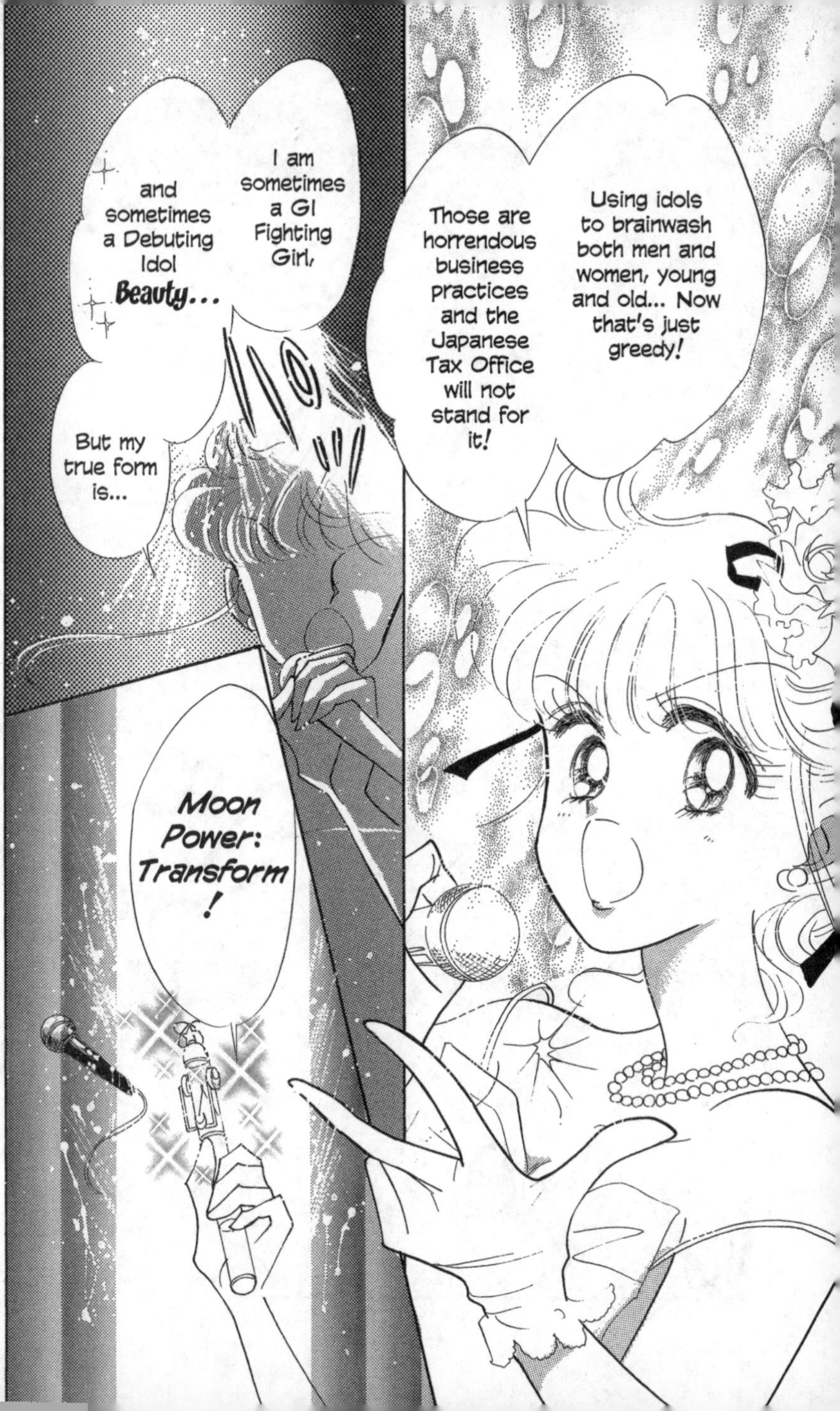
Using idols to brainwash both men and women, young and old... Now that's just greedy!
Those are horrendous business practices and the Japanese Tax Office will not stand for it!
I am sometimes a GI Fighting Girl,
and sometimes a Debuting Idol Beauty...
But my true form is...
Moon Power: Transform!

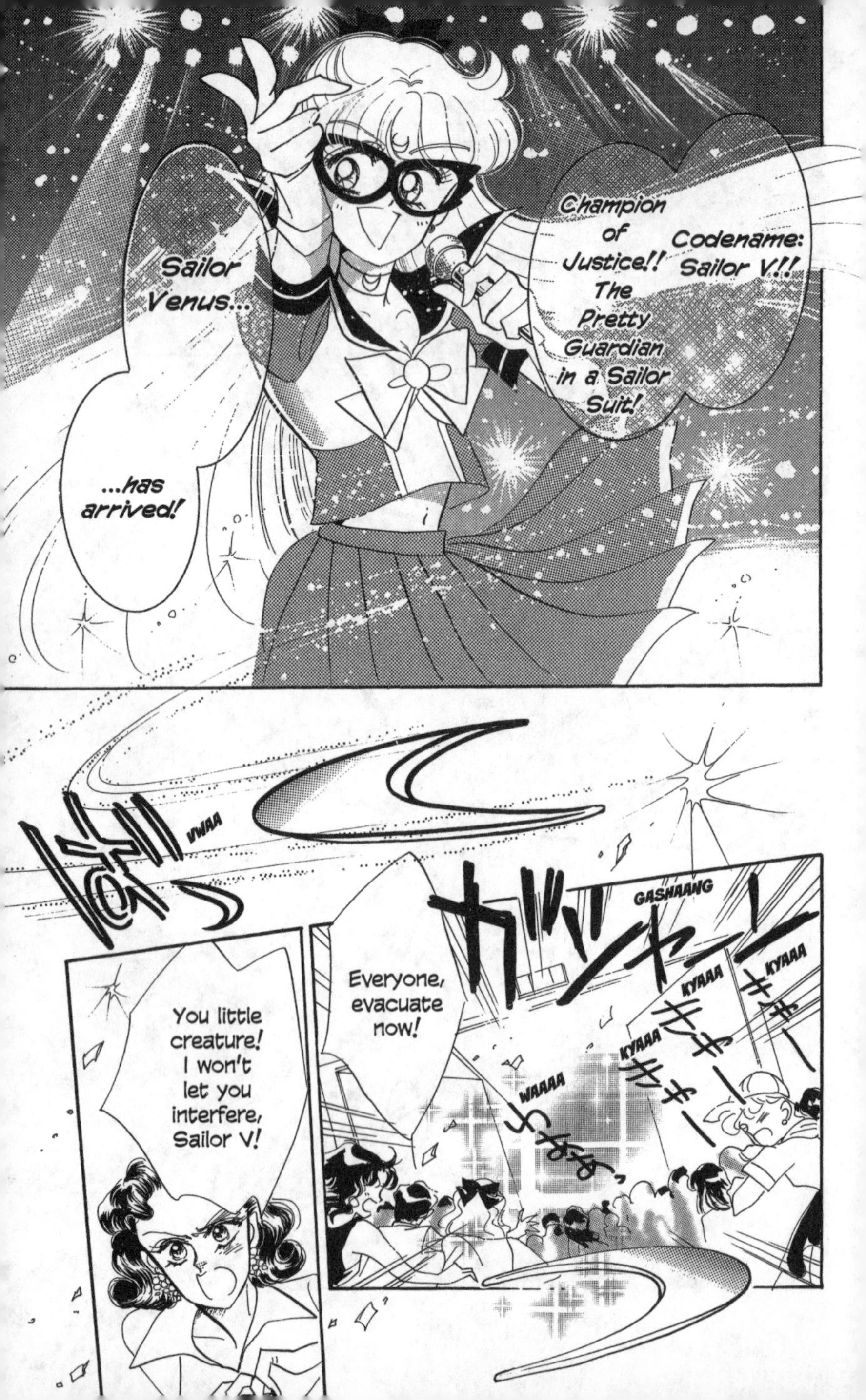
Codename: Sailor V!!
Champion of Justice!! The Pretty Guardian in a Sailor Suit!
Sailor Venus...
...has arrived!
VWAA
GASHAANG
KYAAA
KYAAA
KYAAA
WAAAA
Everyone, evacuate now!
You little creature! I won't let you interfere, Sailor V!

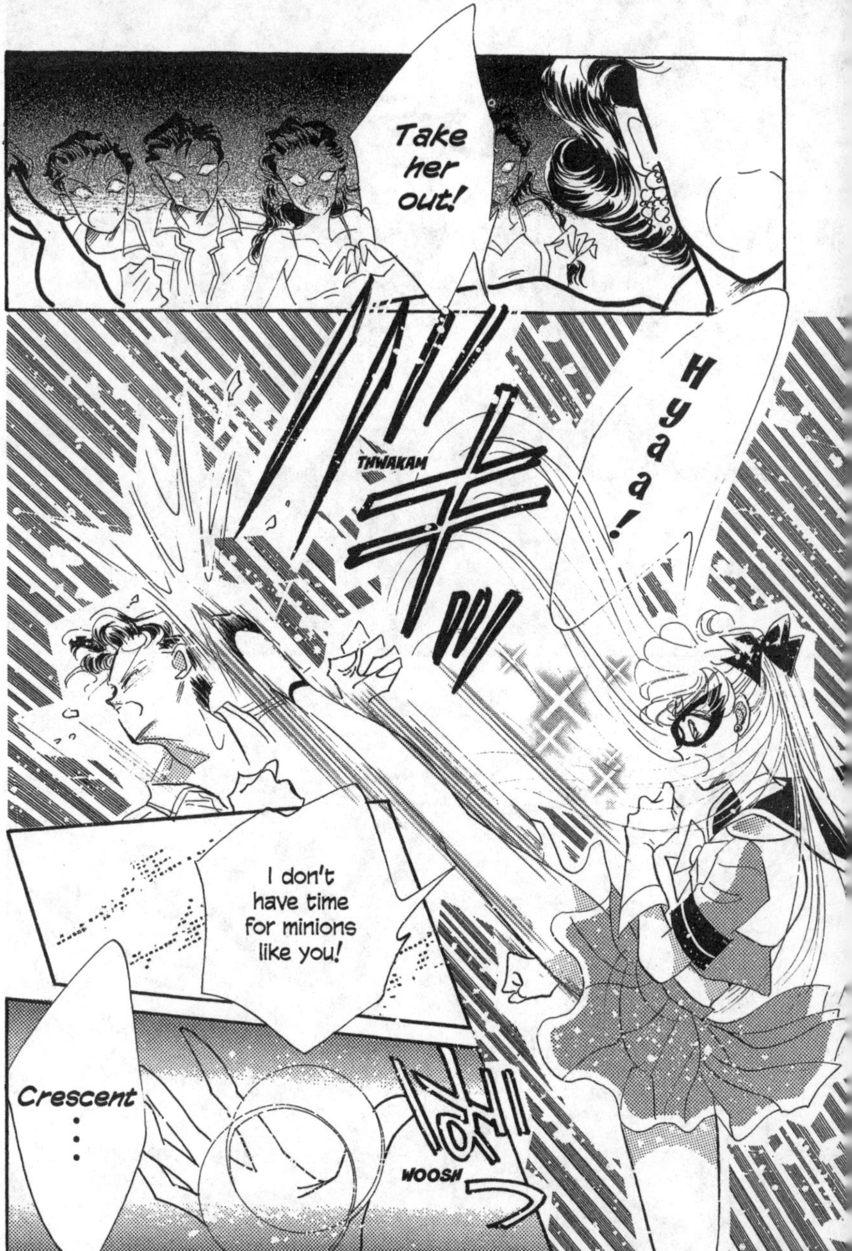
Take her out!
Hyaaa!
THWAKAM
I don't have time for minions like you!
WOOSH
Crescent...

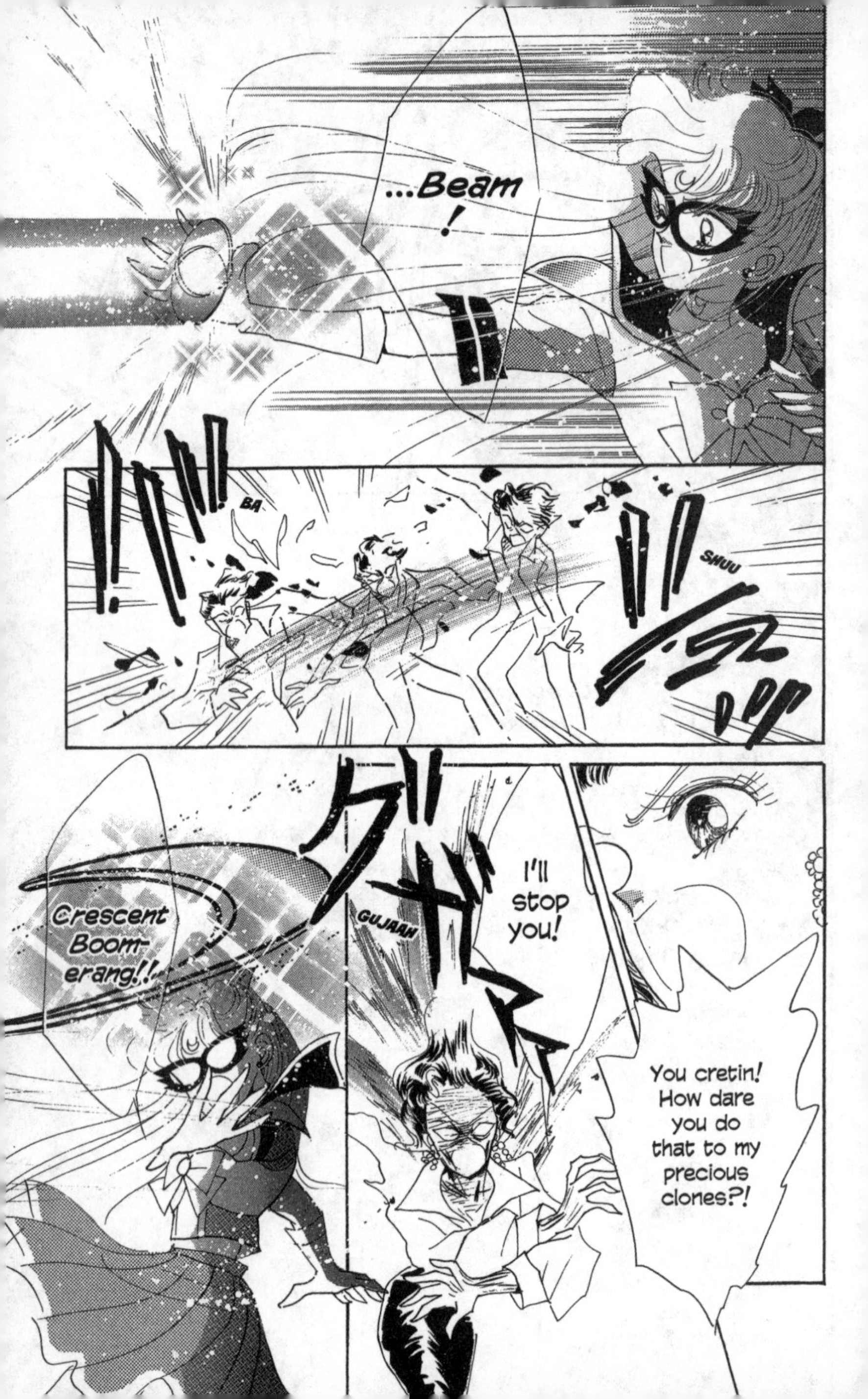
...Beam
!
BA
SHUU
I'll stop you!
GUJAAN
Crescent Boom-erang!!
You cretin! How dare you do that to my precious clones?!

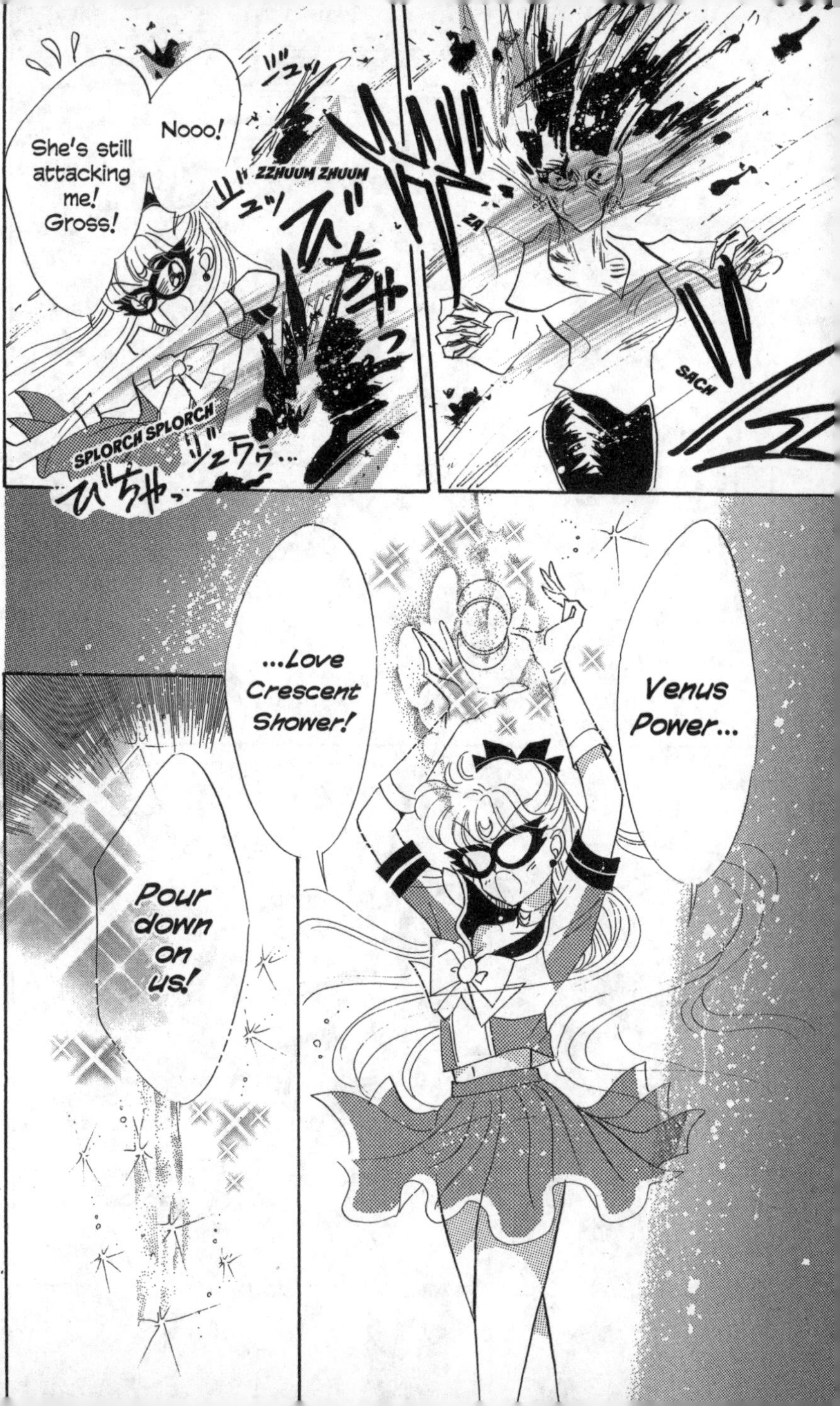
ZA
SACH
Nooo!
She's still attacking me! Gross!
ZZHUUM ZHUUM
SPLORCH SPLORCH
Venus Power...
...Love Crescent Shower!
Pour down on us!

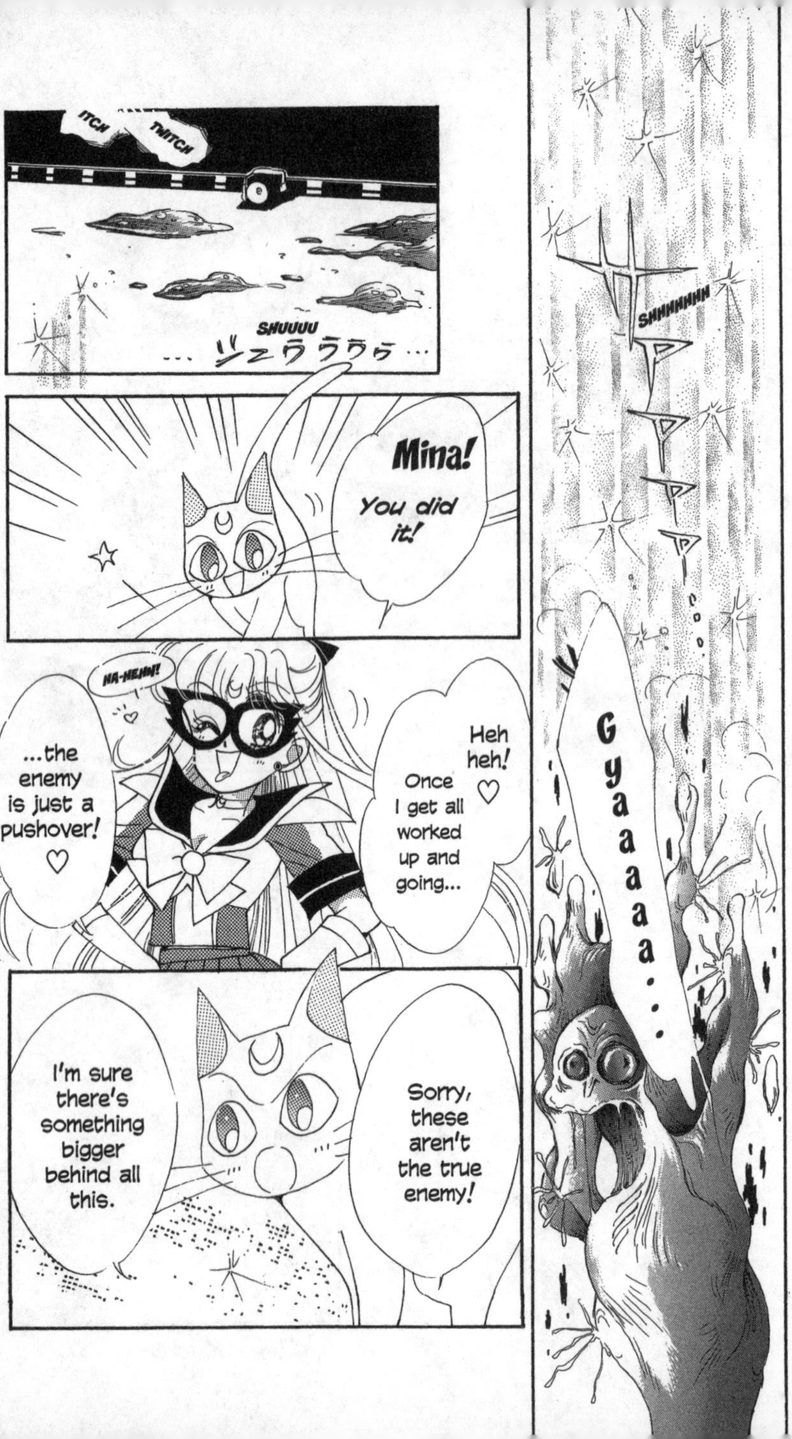
SHHHHHHH
Gyaaaaa...
ITCH
TWITCH
SHUUUU
Mina!
You did it!
Heh heh! ♡
Once I get all worked up and going...
HA-HEHN!
...the enemy is just a pushover! ♡
Sorry, these aren't the true enemy!
I'm sure there's something bigger behind all this.

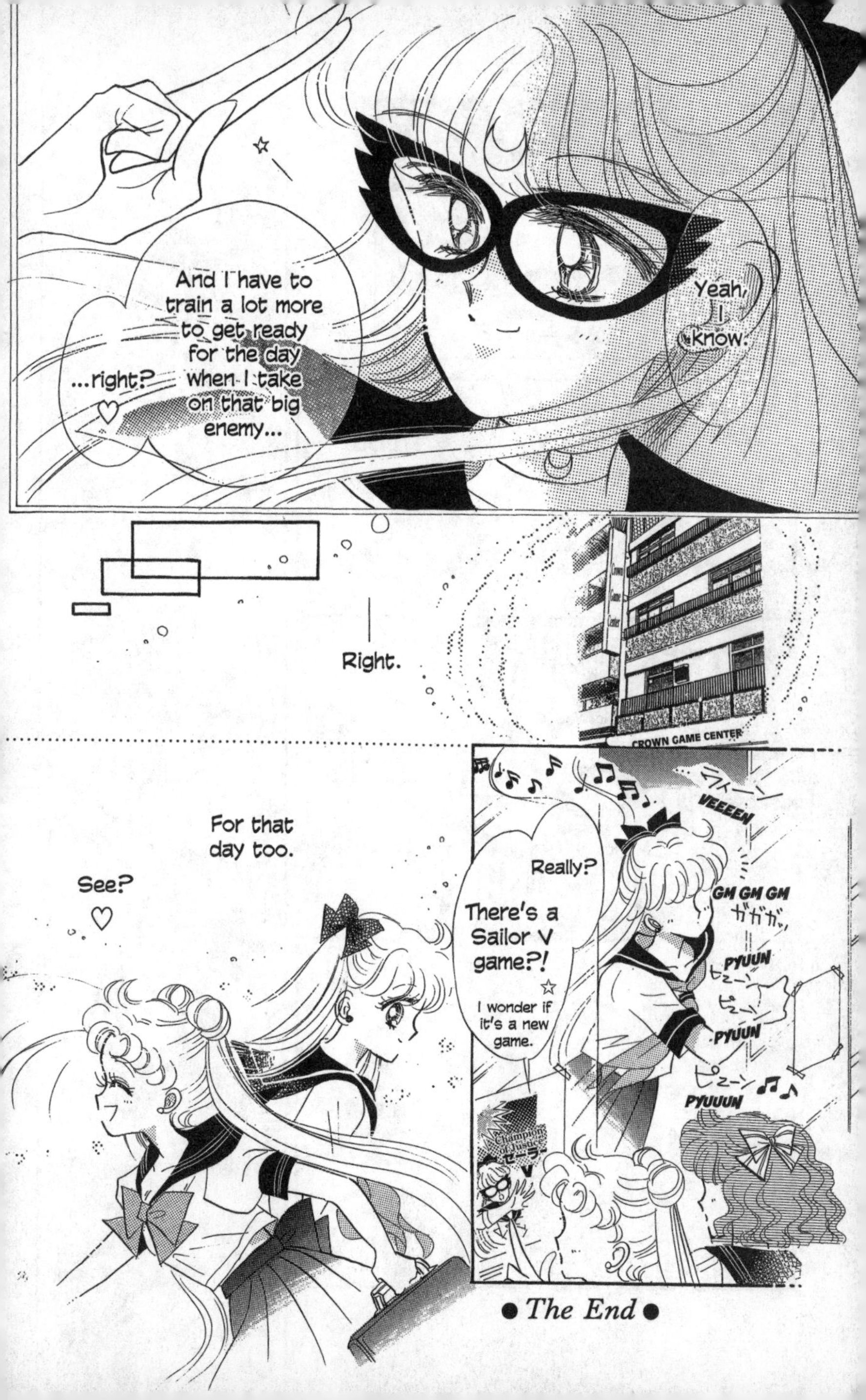
Yeah, I know.
And I have to train a lot more to get ready for the day when I take on that big enemy...
...right? ♡
CROWN GAME CENTER
Right.
VEEEEN
Really?
There's a Sailor V game?!
I wonder if it's a new game.
GM GM GM
PYUUN
PYUUN
PYUUUN
Champion of Justice セーラー V
For that day too.
See? ♡

• The End •

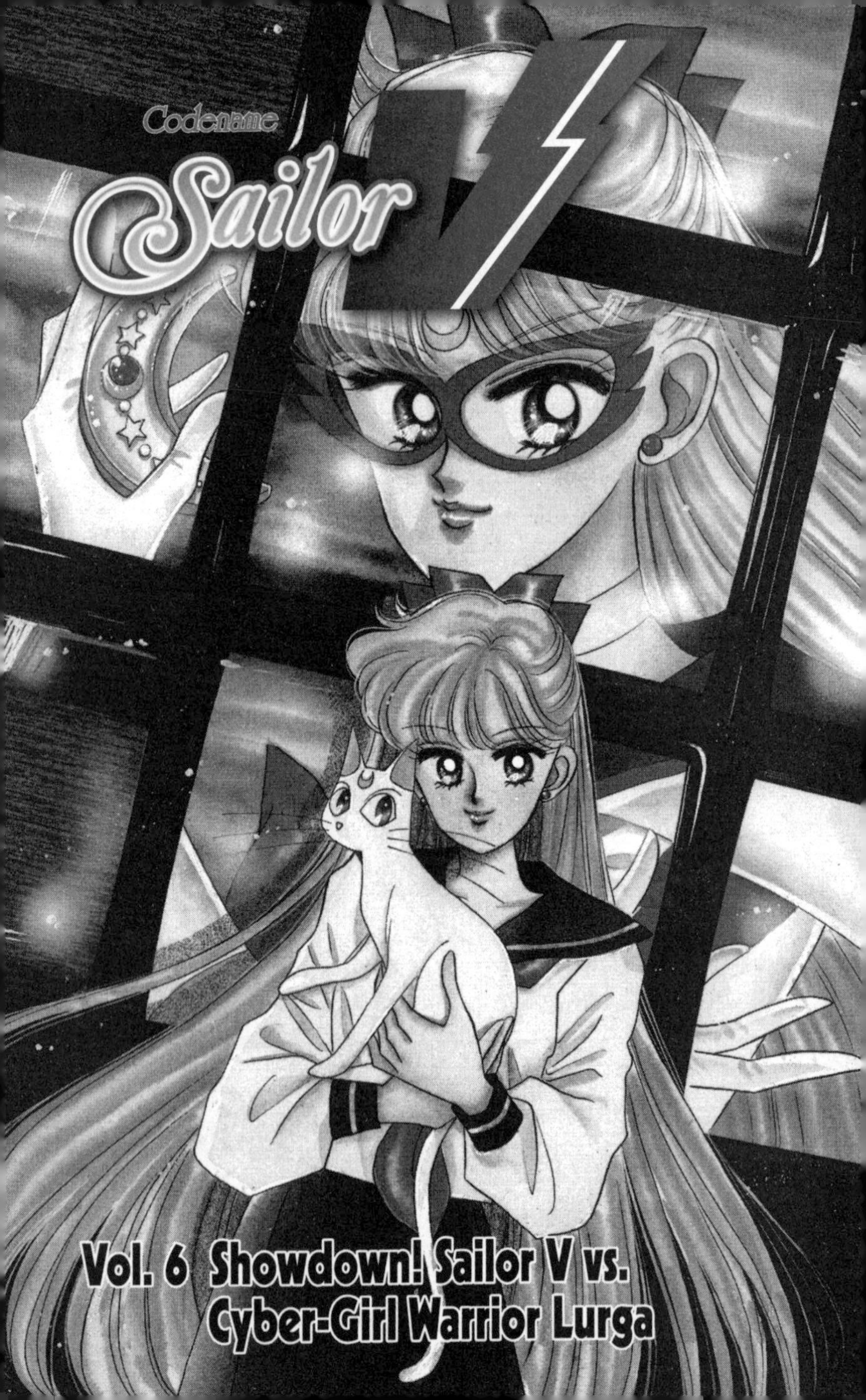
Codename
Sailor V
Vol. 6 Showdown! Sailor V vs.
Cyber-Girl Warrior Lurga

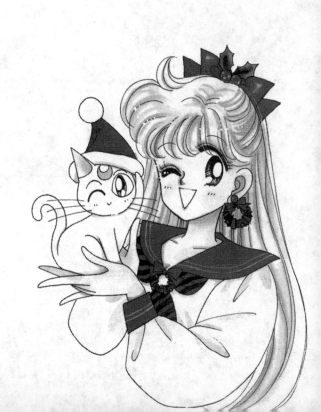

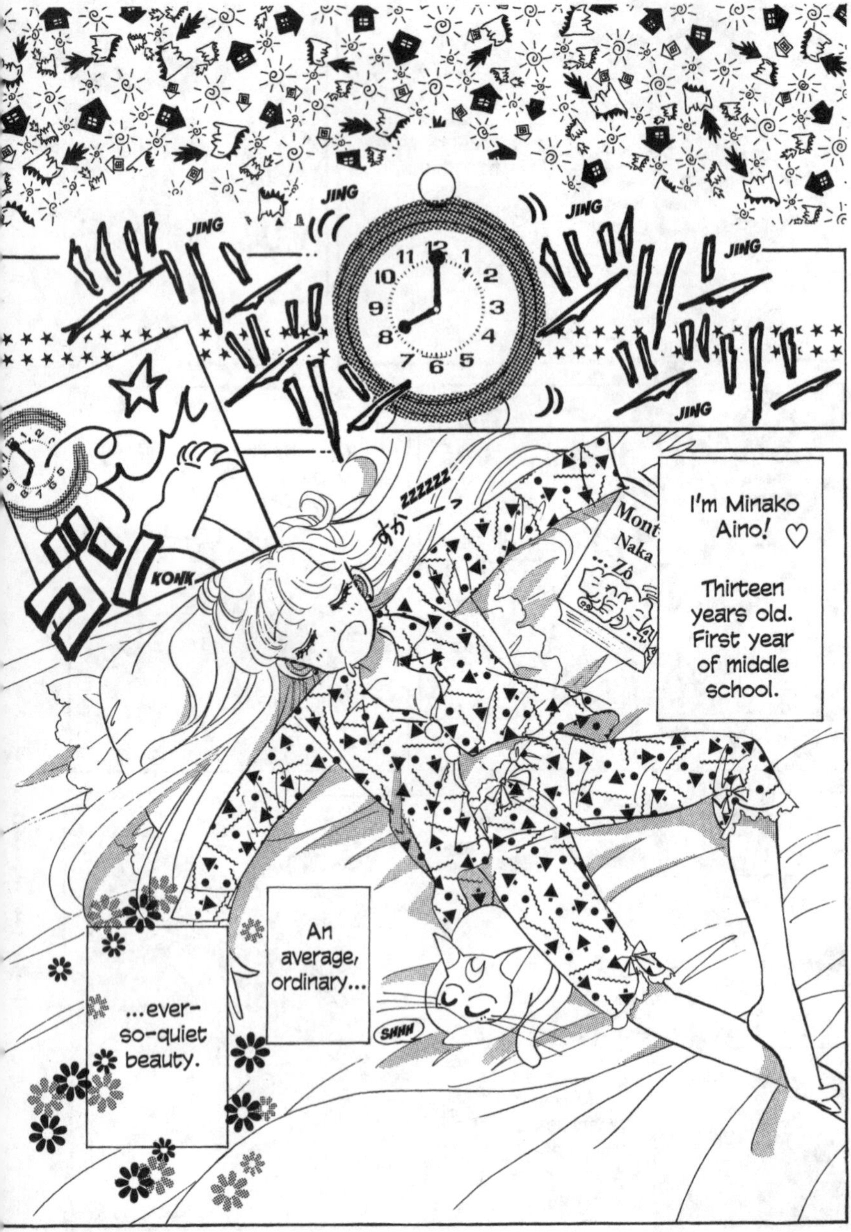
JING
JING
JING
JING
JING
KONK
ZZZZZZ
I'm Minako Aino! ♡
Thirteen years old. First year of middle school.
An average, ordinary...
...ever-so-quiet beauty.
SHHH

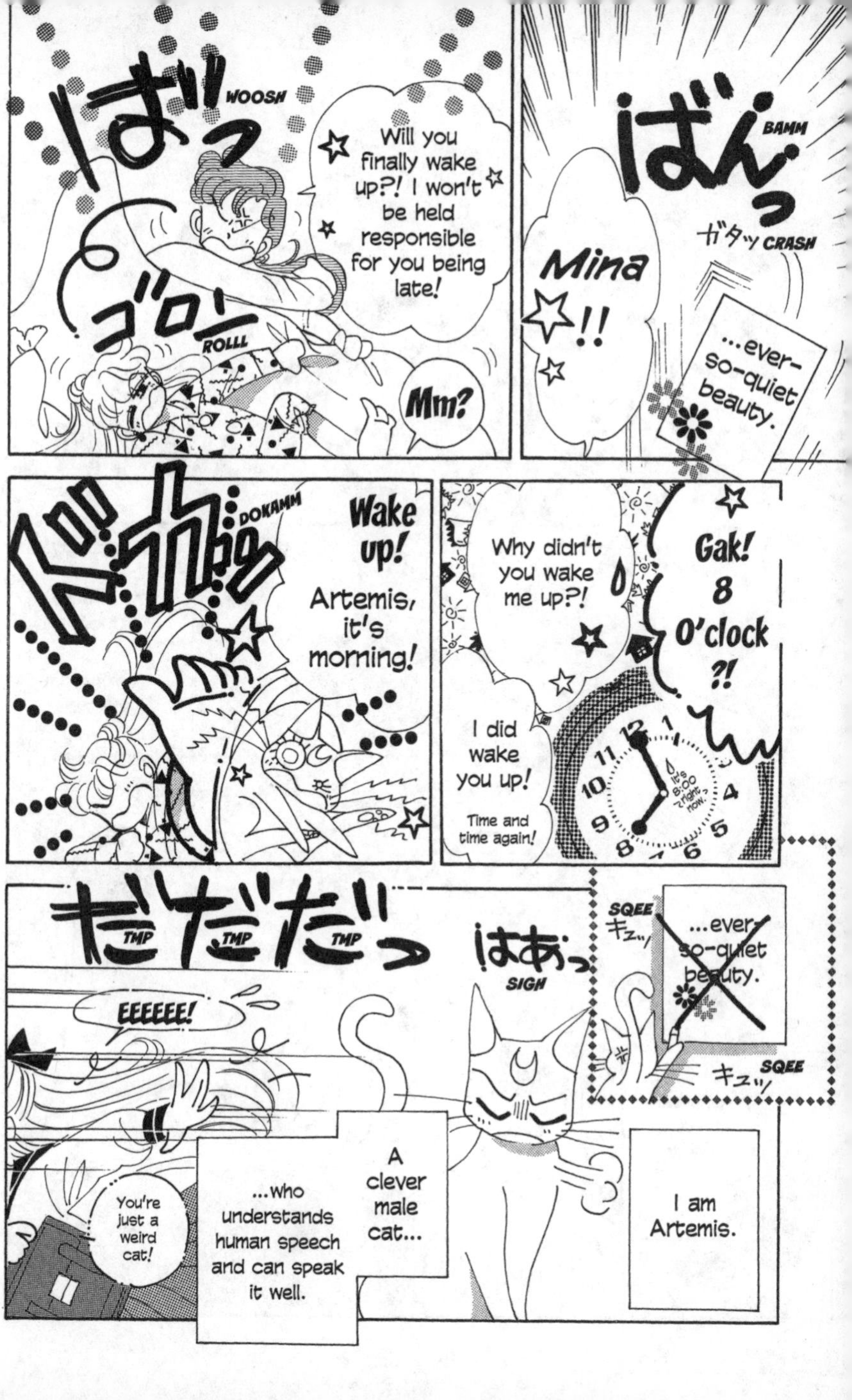
ばんっ
BAMM
ガタッ CRASH
Mina!!
...ever-so-quiet beauty.
Will you finally wake up?! I won't be held responsible for you being late!
ばっ
WOOSH
ゴロン
ROLLL
Mm?
Gak! 8 O'clock?!
Why didn't you wake me up?!
It's 8:00 right now.
I did wake you up!
Time and time again!
Wake up!
Artemis, it's morning!
DOKAMM
SQEE
キュッ
...ever-so-quiet beauty.
キュッ
SQEE
はあっ
SIGH
TMP TMP TMP
EEEEEE!
I am Artemis.
A clever male cat...
...who understands human speech and can speak it well.
You're just a weird cat!

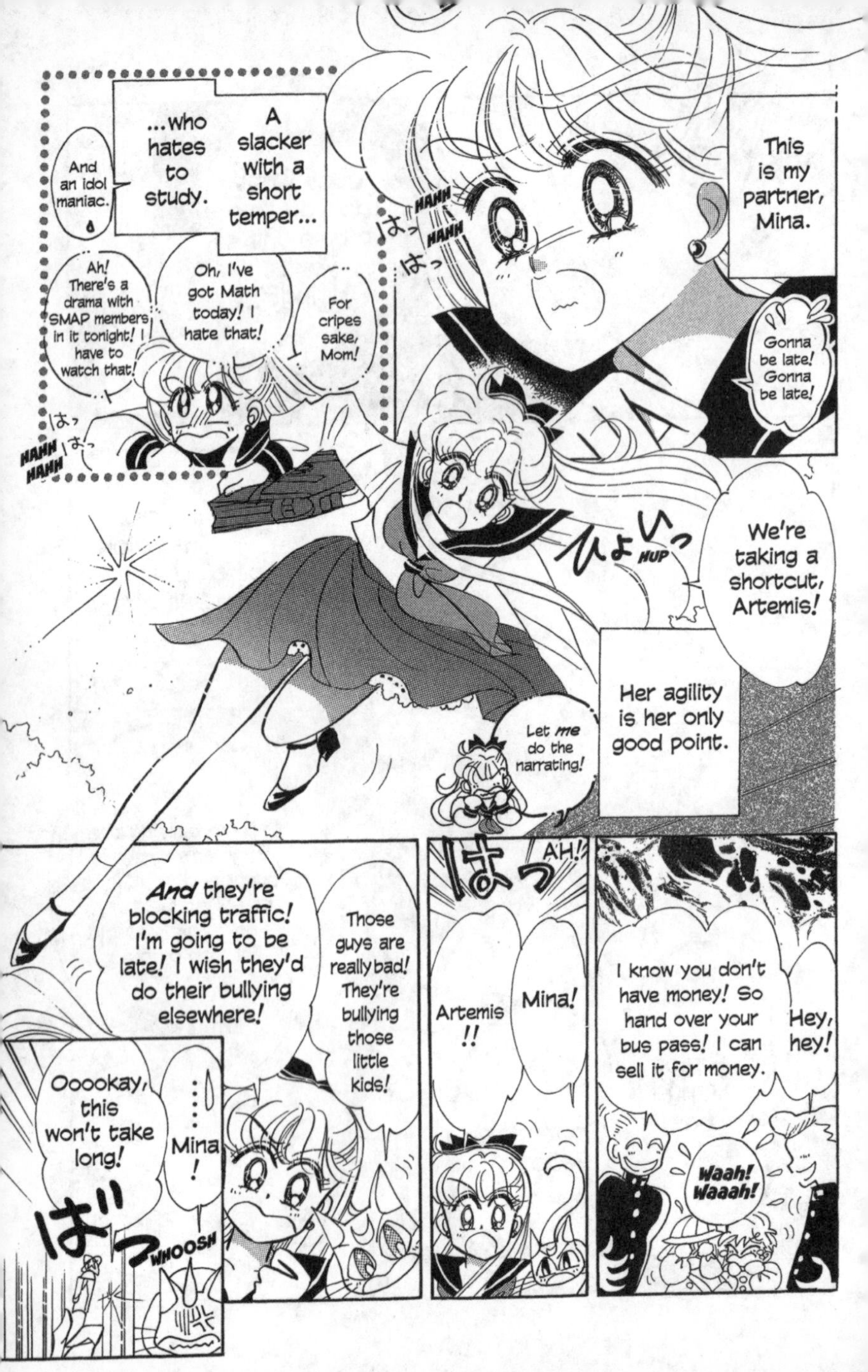
This is my partner, Mina.
はっ HAHH はっ HAHH
Gonna be late! Gonna be late!
A slacker with a short temper...
...who hates to study.
And an idol maniac.
For cripes sake, Mom!
Oh, I've got Math today! I hate that!
Ah! There's a drama with SMAP members in it tonight! I have to watch that!
はっ HAHH はっ HAHH
We're taking a shortcut, Artemis!
ひょいっ HUP
Her agility is her only good point.
Let *me* do the narrating!
Hey, hey!
I know you don't have money! So hand over your bus pass! I can sell it for money.
Waah! Waaah!
はっ AH!
Mina!
Artemis!!
Those guys are really bad! They're bullying those little kids!
And they're blocking traffic! I'm going to be late! I wish they'd do their bullying elsewhere!
...... Mina!
Ooookay, this won't take long!
ばっ WHOOSH

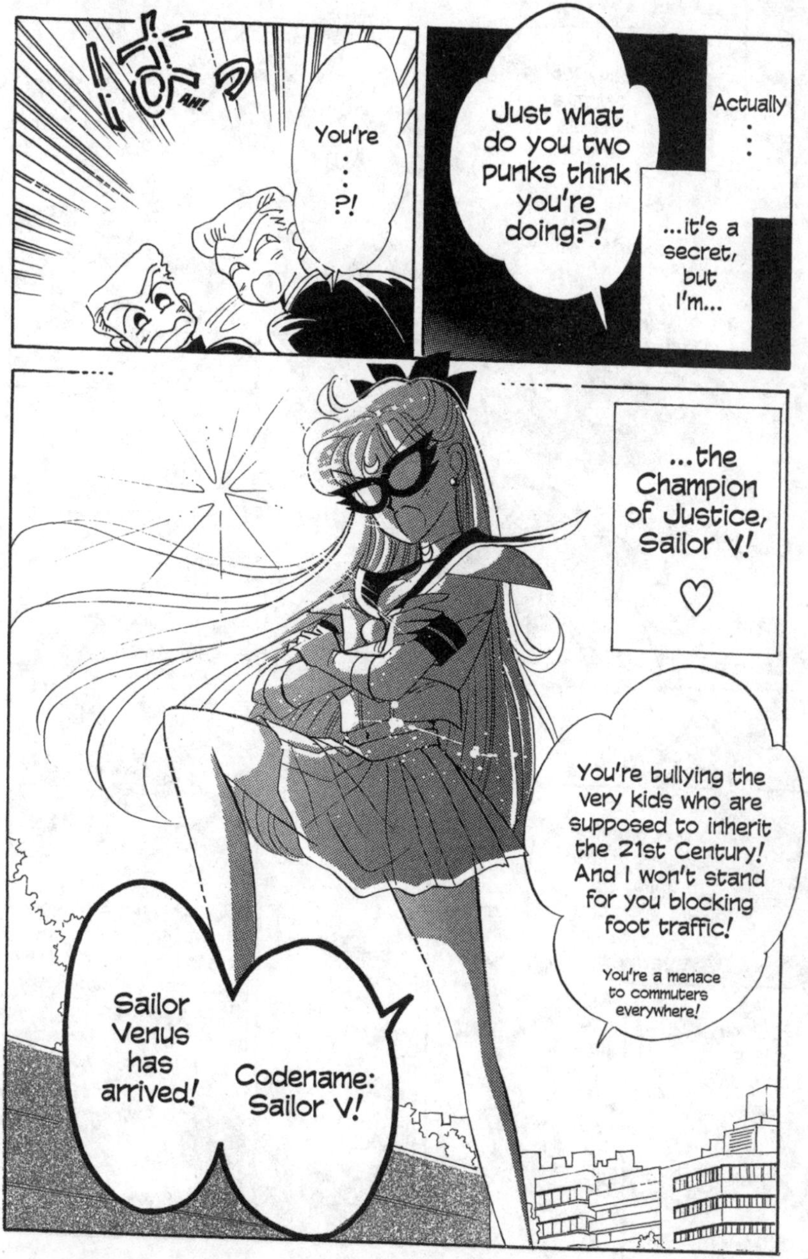
Just what do you two punks think you're doing?!
Actually...
...it's a secret, but I'm...
AH!
You're...?!
...the Champion of Justice, Sailor V! ♡
You're bullying the very kids who are supposed to inherit the 21st Century! And I won't stand for you blocking foot traffic!
You're a menace to commuters everywhere!
Sailor Venus has arrived!
Codename: Sailor V!

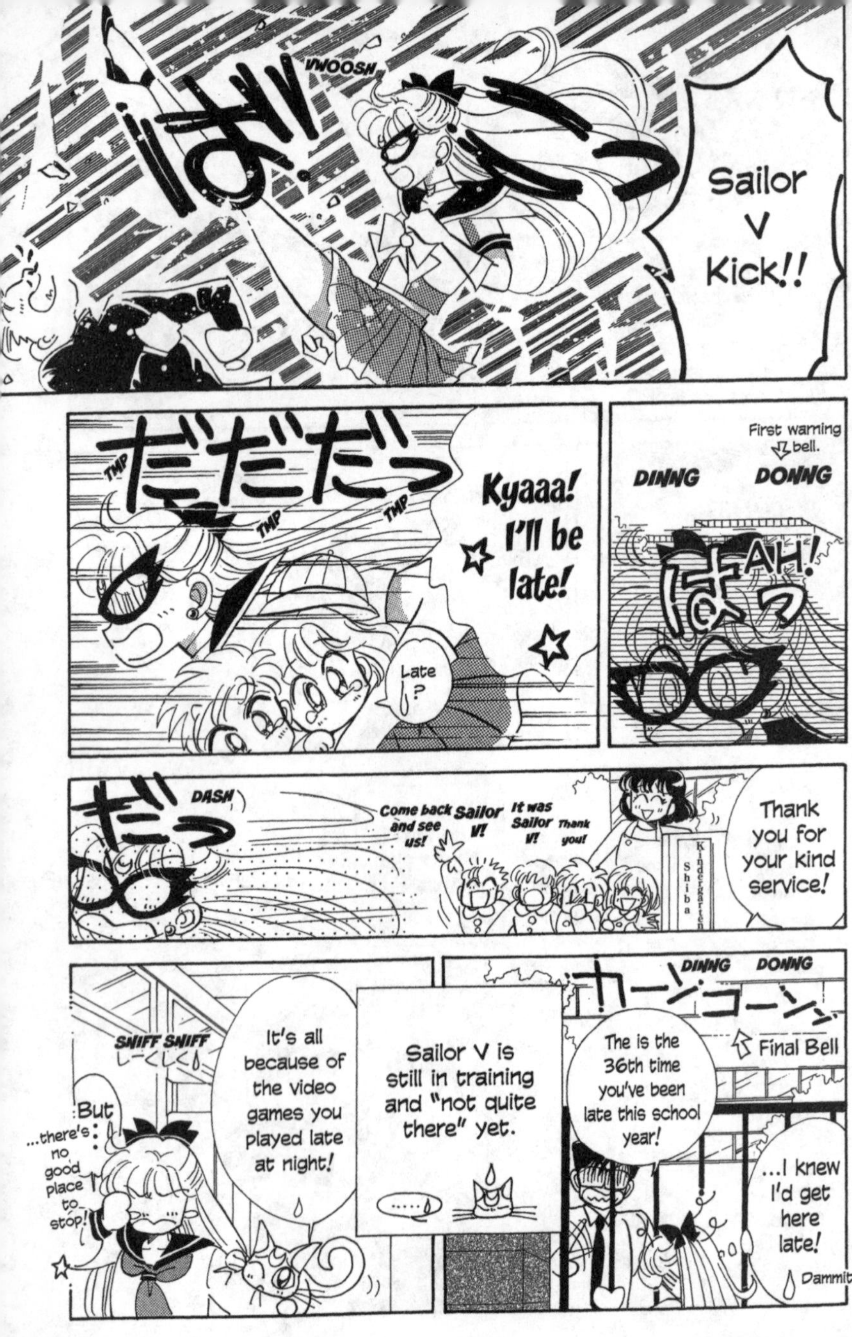

Sailor V Kick!!
ばっ
VWOOSH
First warning bell.
DINNG DONNG
はっ
AH!
Kyaaa! I'll be late!
だだだっ
TMP TMP TMP
Late ?
Thank you for your kind service!
Shiba Kindergarten
Thank you!
It was Sailor V!
Sailor V!
Come back and see us!
だっ
DASH
カーンコーン
DINNG DONNG
Final Bell
The is the 36th time you've been late this school year!
...I knew I'd get here late!
Dammit!
Sailor V is still in training and "not quite there" yet.
......
It's all because of the video games you played late at night!
SNIFF SNIFF
しくしく
But ...there's no good place to stop!

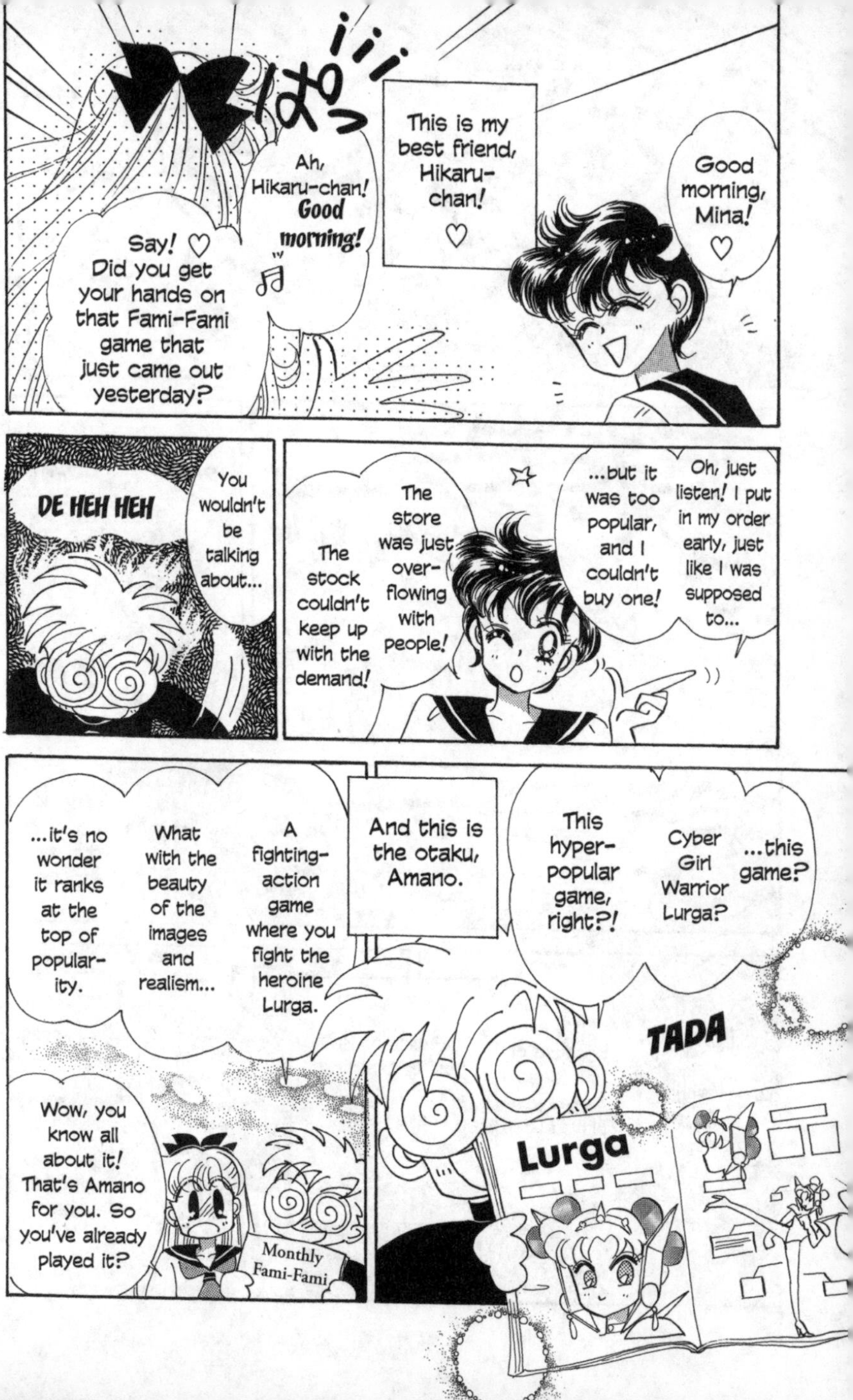

Good morning, Mina! ♡
This is my best friend, Hikaru-chan! ♡
ぱっ!!!
Ah, Hikaru-chan! **Good morning!** ♫
Say! ♡ Did you get your hands on that Fami-Fami game that just came out yesterday?
Oh, just listen! I put in my order early, just like I was supposed to...
...but it was too popular, and I couldn't buy one!
The store was just over-flowing with people!
The stock couldn't keep up with the demand!
You wouldn't be talking about...
DE HEH HEH
...this game?
Cyber Girl Warrior Lurga?
This hyper-popular game, right?!
And this is the otaku, Amano.
TADA
Lurga
A fighting-action game where you fight the heroine Lurga.
What with the beauty of the images and realism...
...it's no wonder it ranks at the top of popular-ity.
Wow, you know all about it! That's Amano for you. So you've already played it?
Monthly Fami-Fami

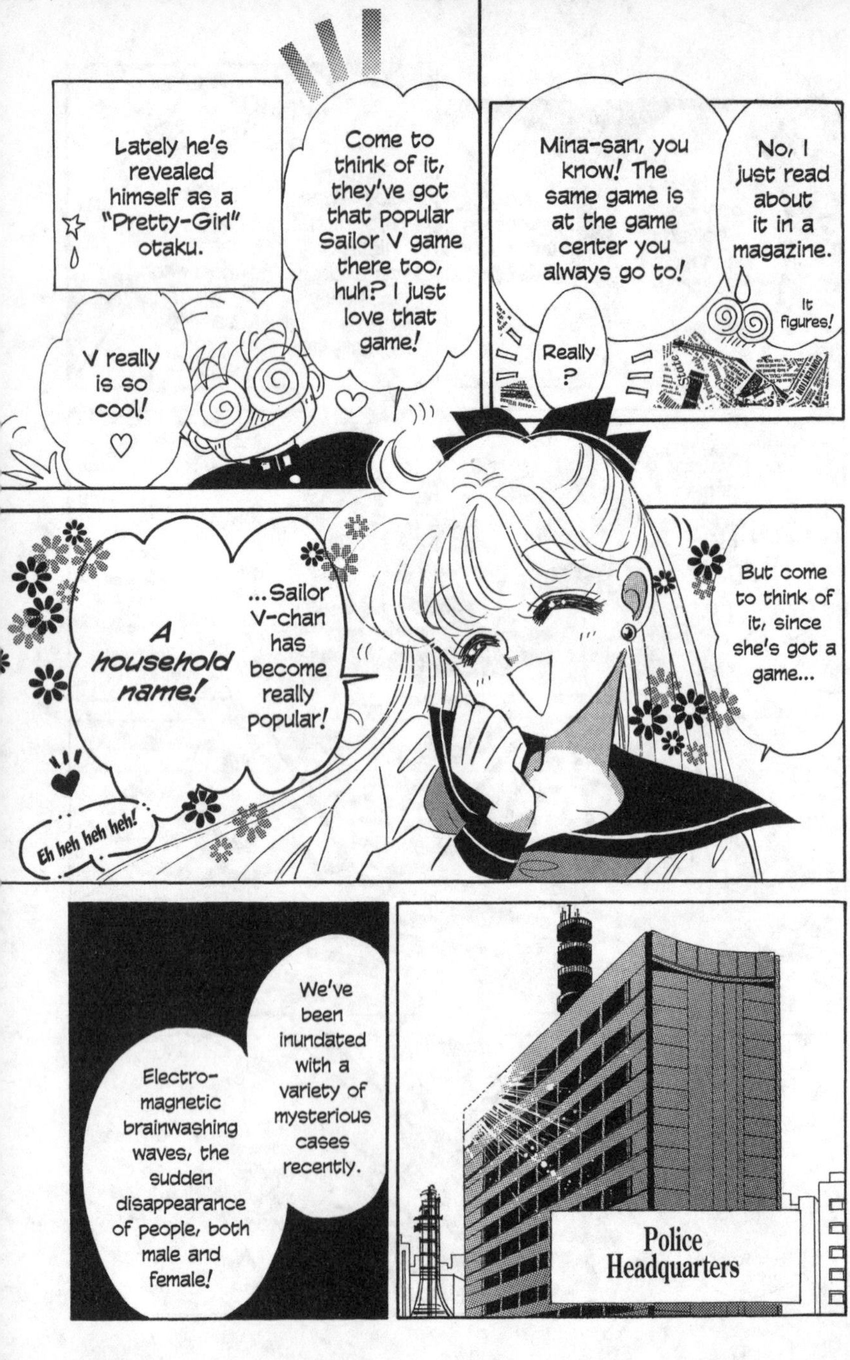

No, I just read about it in a magazine.
Mina-san, you know! The same game is at the game center you always go to!
It figures!
Really?
Come to think of it, they've got that popular Sailor V game there too, huh? I just love that game!
Lately he's revealed himself as a "Pretty-Girl" otaku.
V really is so cool!
But come to think of it, since she's got a game...
...Sailor V-chan has become really popular!
A household name!
Eh heh heh heh!
Police Headquarters
We've been inundated with a variety of mysterious cases recently.
Electro-magnetic brainwashing waves, the sudden disappearance of people, both male and female!

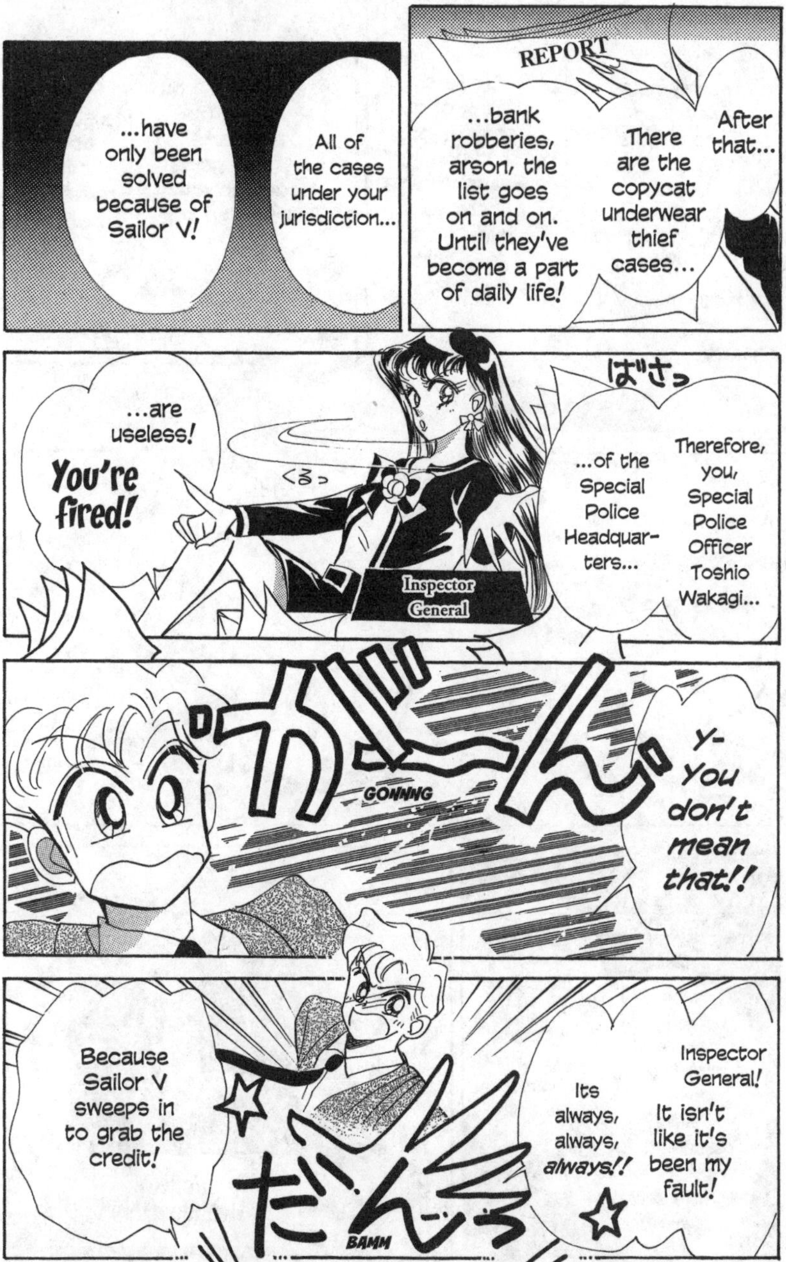
REPORT
After that...
There are the copycat underwear thief cases...
...bank robberies, arson, the list goes on and on. Until they've become a part of daily life!
All of the cases under your jurisdiction...
...have only been solved because of Sailor V!
ばさっ
Therefore, you, Special Police Officer Toshio Wakagi...
...of the Special Police Headquarters...
Inspector General
くるっ
...are useless!
You're fired!
Y-You don't mean that!!
がーん
GONNNG
Inspector General!
It isn't like it's been my fault!
Its always, always, always!!
だんっ
BAMM
Because Sailor V sweeps in to grab the credit!

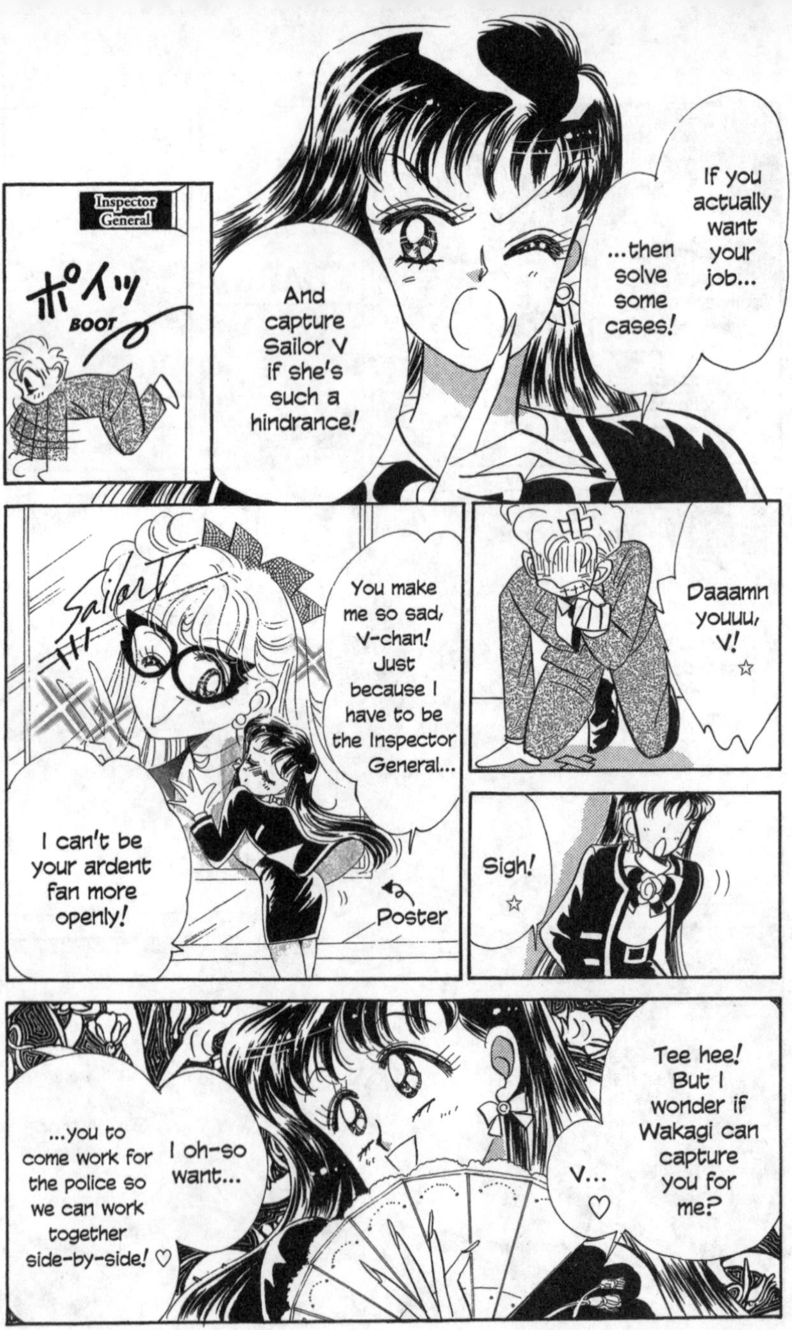

If you actually want your job...
...then solve some cases!
And capture Sailor V if she's such a hindrance!
Inspector General
ポイッ
BOOT
Daaamn youuu, V! ☆
Sigh! ☆
You make me so sad, V-chan! Just because I have to be the Inspector General...
I can't be your ardent fan more openly!
Sailor V
Poster
Tee hee! But I wonder if Wakagi can capture you for me?
V... ♡
I oh-so want...
...you to come work for the police so we can work together side-by-side! ♡

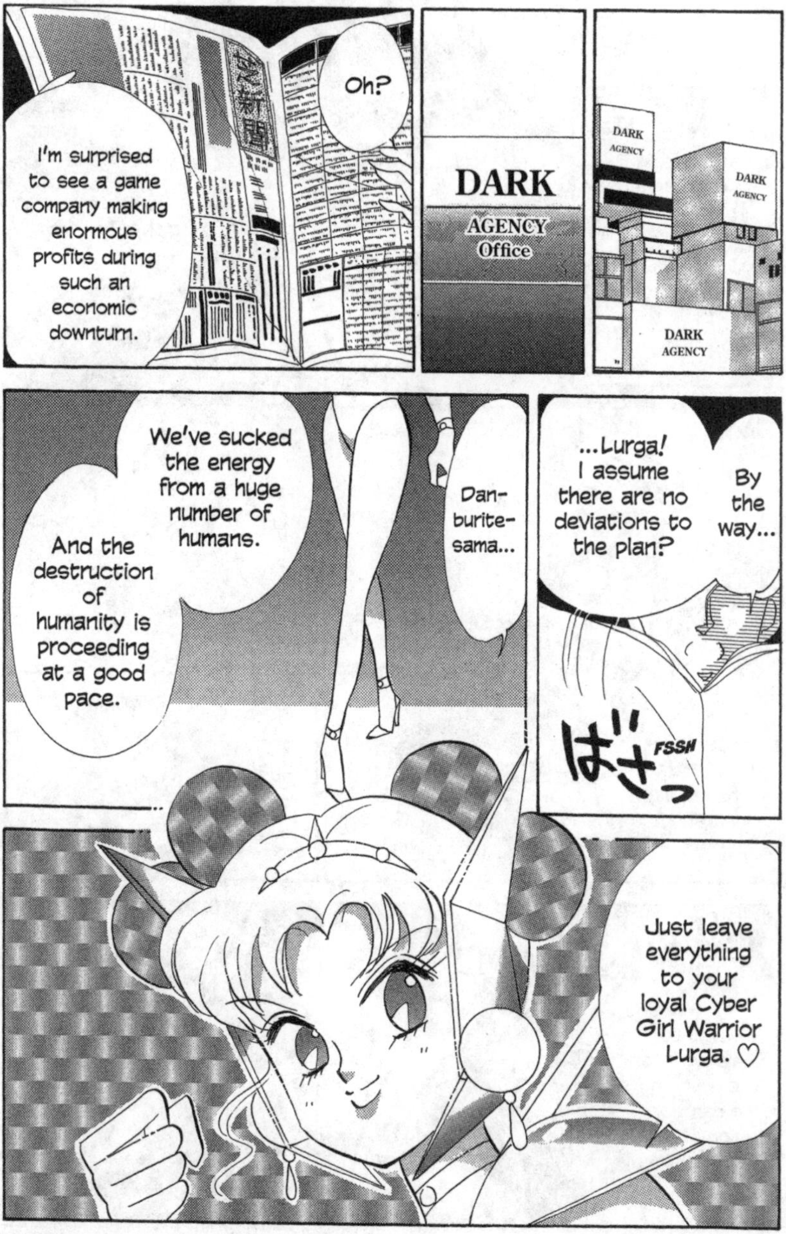
DARK AGENCY
DARK AGENCY
DARK AGENCY
DARK AGENCY Office
Oh?
I'm surprised to see a game company making enormous profits during such an economic downturn.
By the way...
...Lurga! I assume there are no deviations to the plan?
ばさっ FSSH
Dan-burite-sama...
We've sucked the energy from a huge number of humans.
And the destruction of humanity is proceeding at a good pace.
Just leave everything to your loyal Cyber Girl Warrior Lurga. ♡

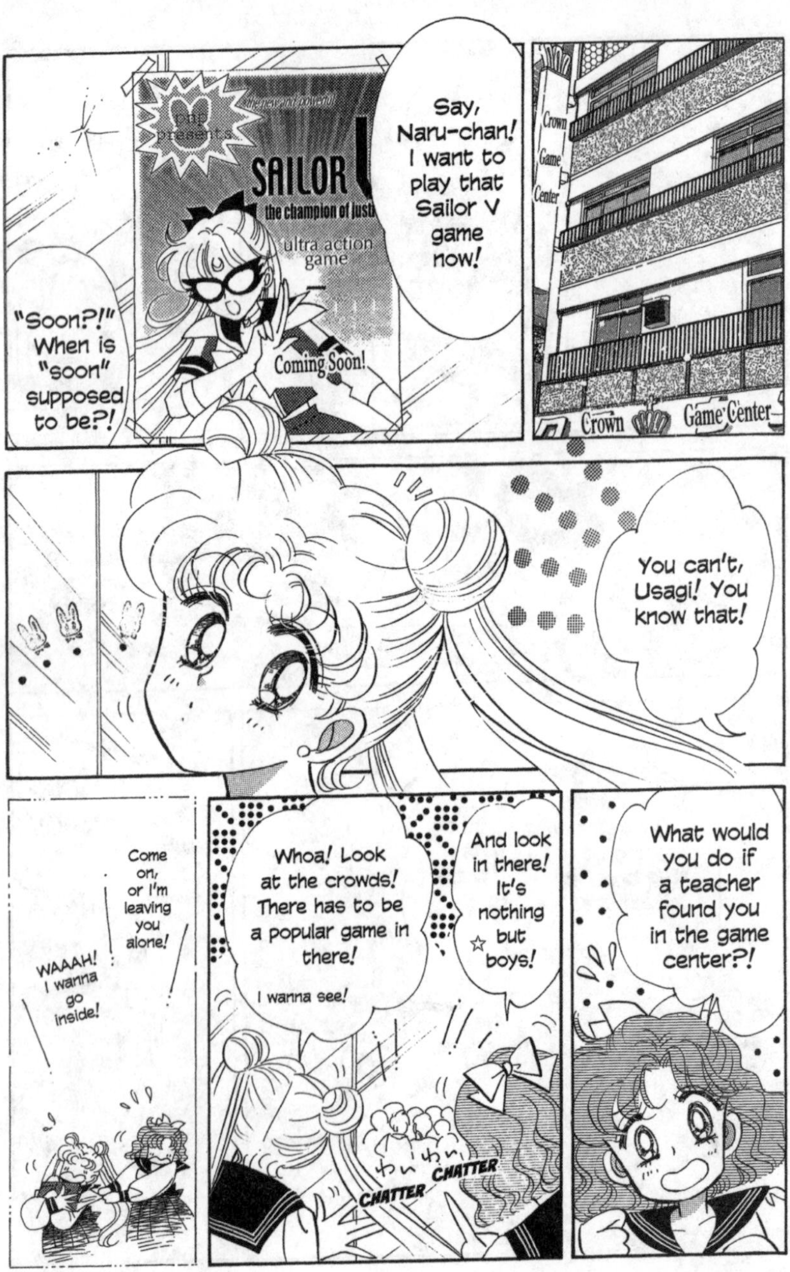
Crown
Game
Center
Crown
Game Center
Say, Naru-chan! I want to play that Sailor V game now!
presents
SAILOR
the champion of justi
ultra action game
Coming Soon!
"Soon?!" When is "soon" supposed to be?!
You can't, Usagi! You know that!
What would you do if a teacher found you in the game center?!
And look in there! It's nothing but ☆ boys!
Whoa! Look at the crowds! There has to be a popular game in there!
I wanna see!
わいわい
CHATTER CHATTER
Come on, or I'm leaving you alone!
WAAAH! I wanna go inside!

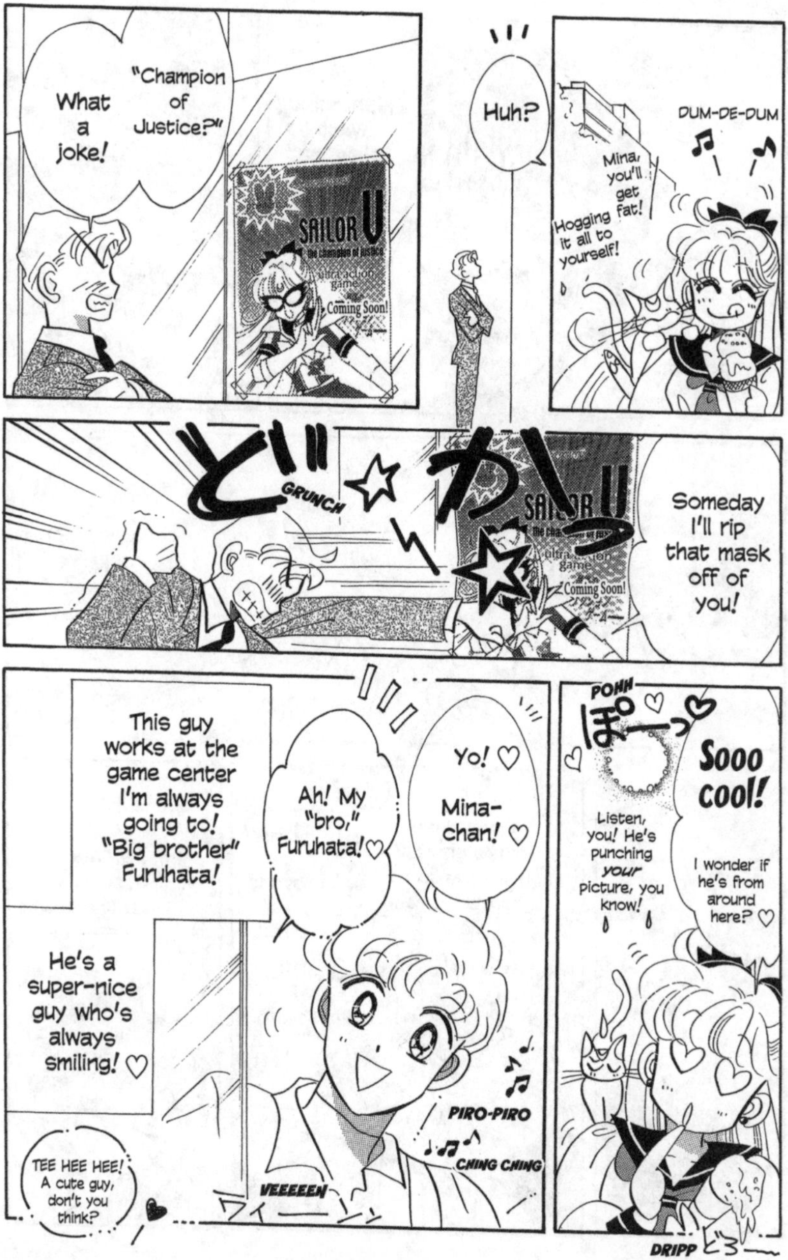
DUM-DE-DUM
Mina, you'll get fat! Hogging it all to yourself!
Huh?
"Champion of Justice?"
What a joke!
Someday I'll rip that mask off of you!
どが っ
GRUNCH
POHH ぽーっ
Sooo cool!
I wonder if he's from around here?
Listen, you! He's punching *your* picture, you know!
DRIPP どろー
Yo! Mina-chan!
Ah! My "bro," Furuhata!
This guy works at the game center I'm always going to! "Big brother" Furuhata!
He's a super-nice guy who's always smiling!
PIRO-PIRO
CHING CHING
VEEEEEN ワイーン
TEE HEE HEE! A cute guy, don't you think?

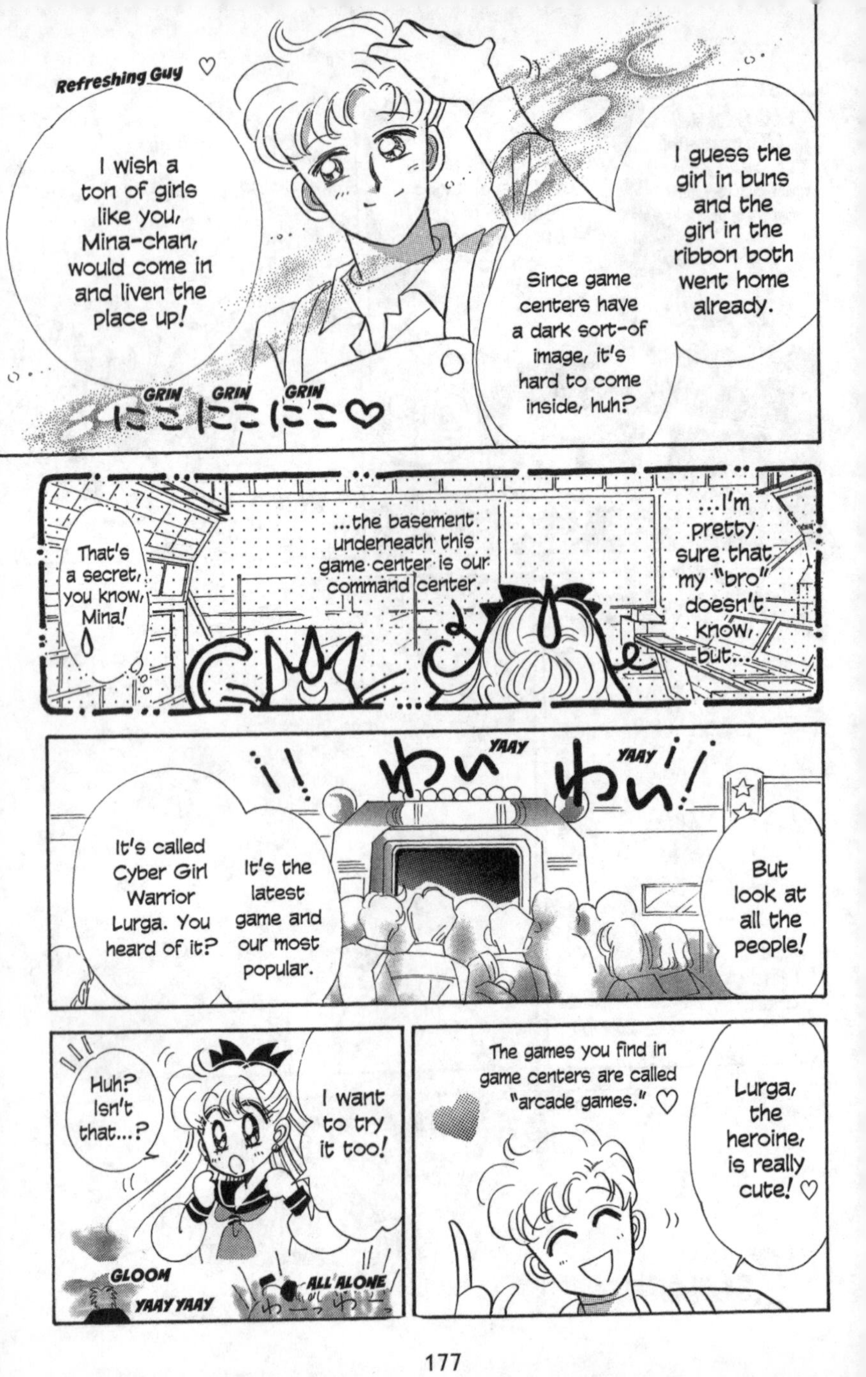

I guess the girl in buns and the girl in the ribbon both went home already.
Since game centers have a dark sort-of image, it's hard to come inside, huh?
Refreshing Guy ♡
I wish a ton of girls like you, Mina-chan, would come in and liven the place up!
GRIN GRIN GRIN
にこにこにこ♡
...I'm pretty sure that my "bro" doesn't know, but...
...the basement underneath this game center is our command center.
That's a secret, you know, Mina!
わいわい
YAAY YAAY
But look at all the people!
It's the latest game and our most popular.
It's called Cyber Girl Warrior Lurga. You heard of it?
Lurga, the heroine, is really cute! ♡
The games you find in game centers are called "arcade games." ♡
I want to try it too!
Huh? Isn't that...?
ALL ALONE
GLOOM
YAAY YAAY
わーっわー

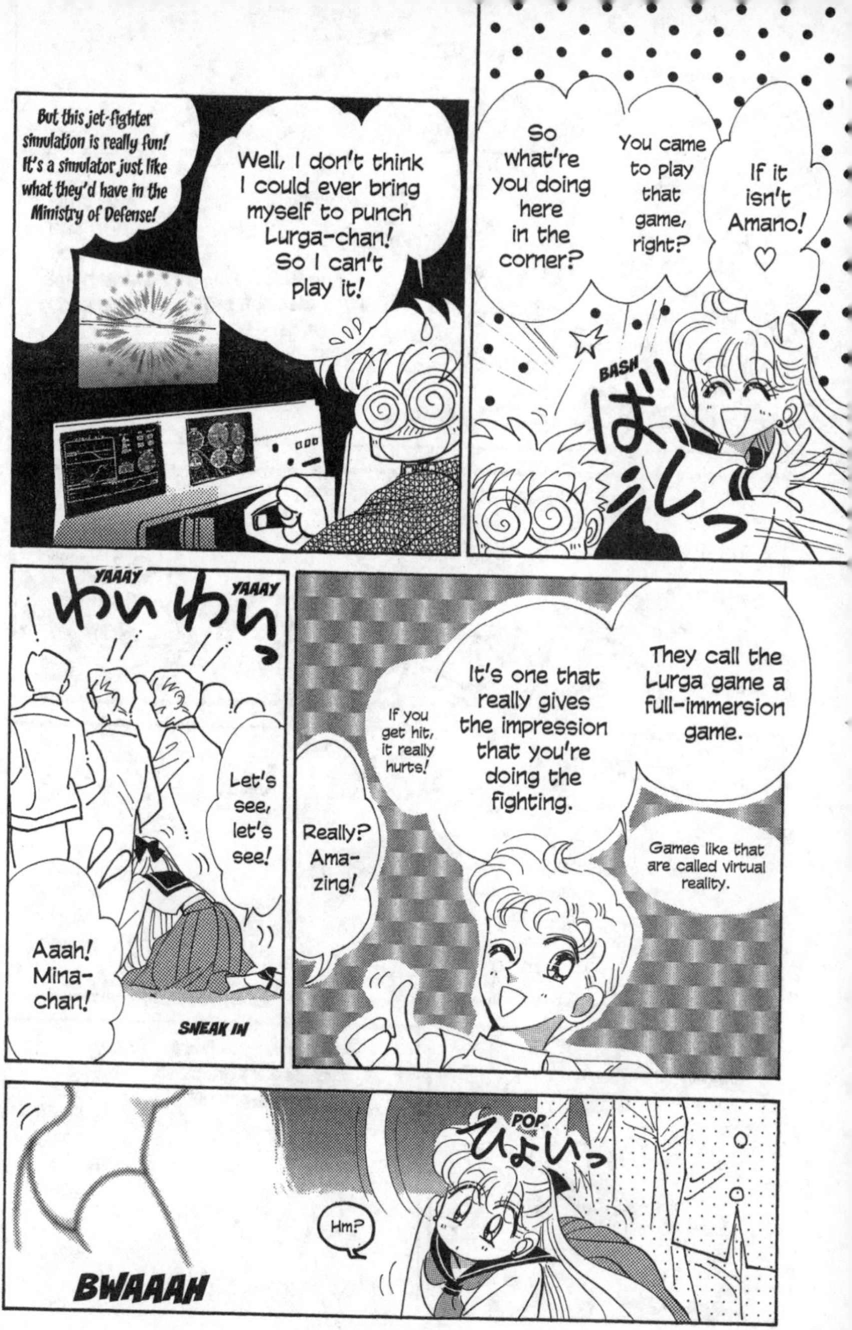
If it isn't Amano! ♡
You came to play that game, right?
So what're you doing here in the corner?
BASH
ばしっ
Well, I don't think I could ever bring myself to punch Lurga-chan! So I can't play it!
But this jet-fighter simulation is really fun! It's a simulator just like what they'd have in the Ministry of Defense!
They call the Lurga game a full-immersion game.
It's one that really gives the impression that you're doing the fighting.
If you get hit, it really hurts!
Games like that are called virtual reality.
Really? Amazing!
YAAAY
YAAAY
わいわい
Let's see, let's see!
Aaah! Mina-chan!
SNEAK IN
POP
ひょいっ
Hm?
BWAAAH

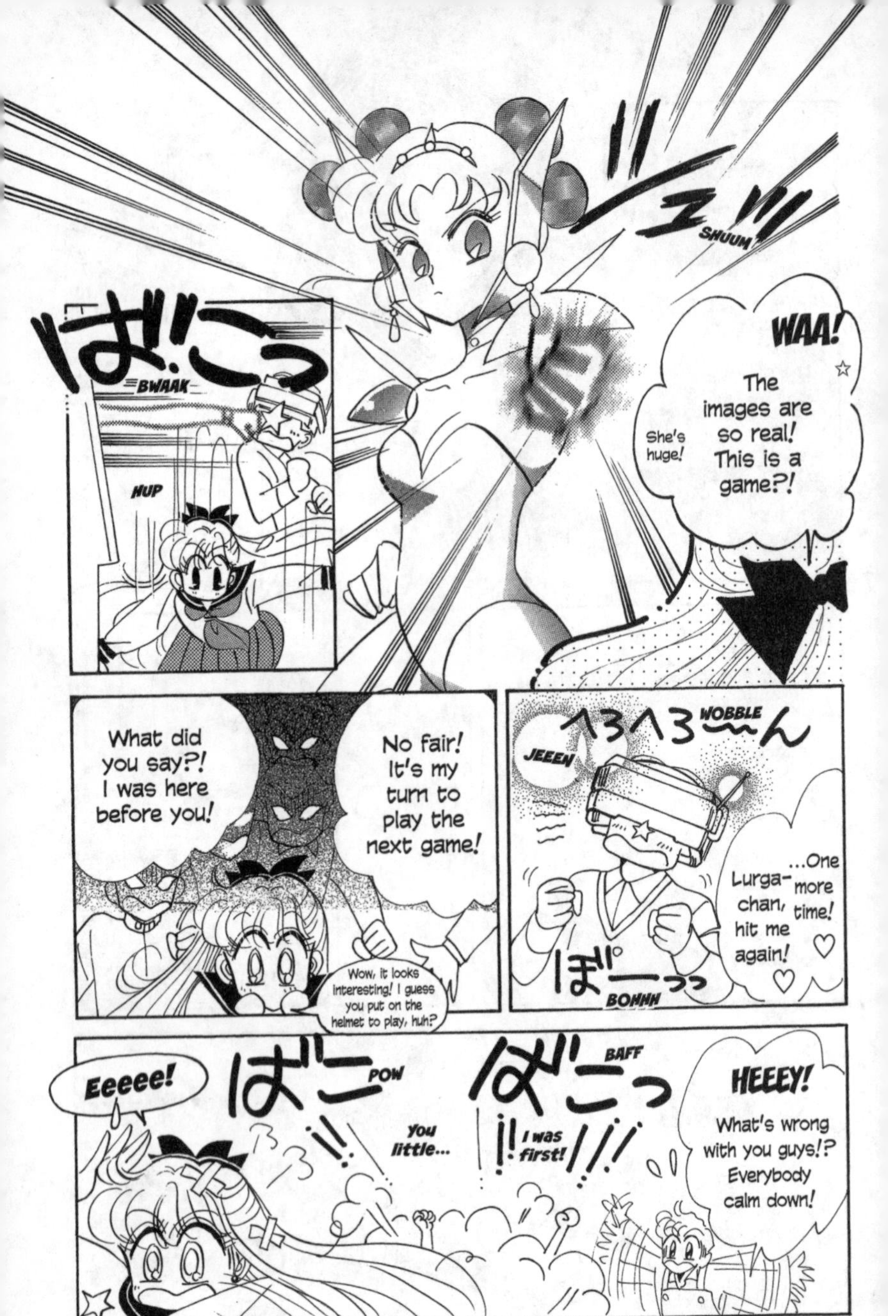

SHUUM
WAA!
The images are so real! This is a game?!
She's huge!
ばこっ
BWAAK
HUP
へろへろ～ん
WOBBLE
JEEEN
...One more time!
Lurga-chan, hit me again!
ぼーっっ
BOHHN
No fair! It's my turn to play the next game!
What did you say?! I was here before you!
Wow, it looks interesting! I guess you put on the helmet to play, huh?
HEEEY!
What's wrong with you guys!? Everybody calm down!
ばごっ
BAFF
I was first!
You little...
ばこ
POW
Eeeee!

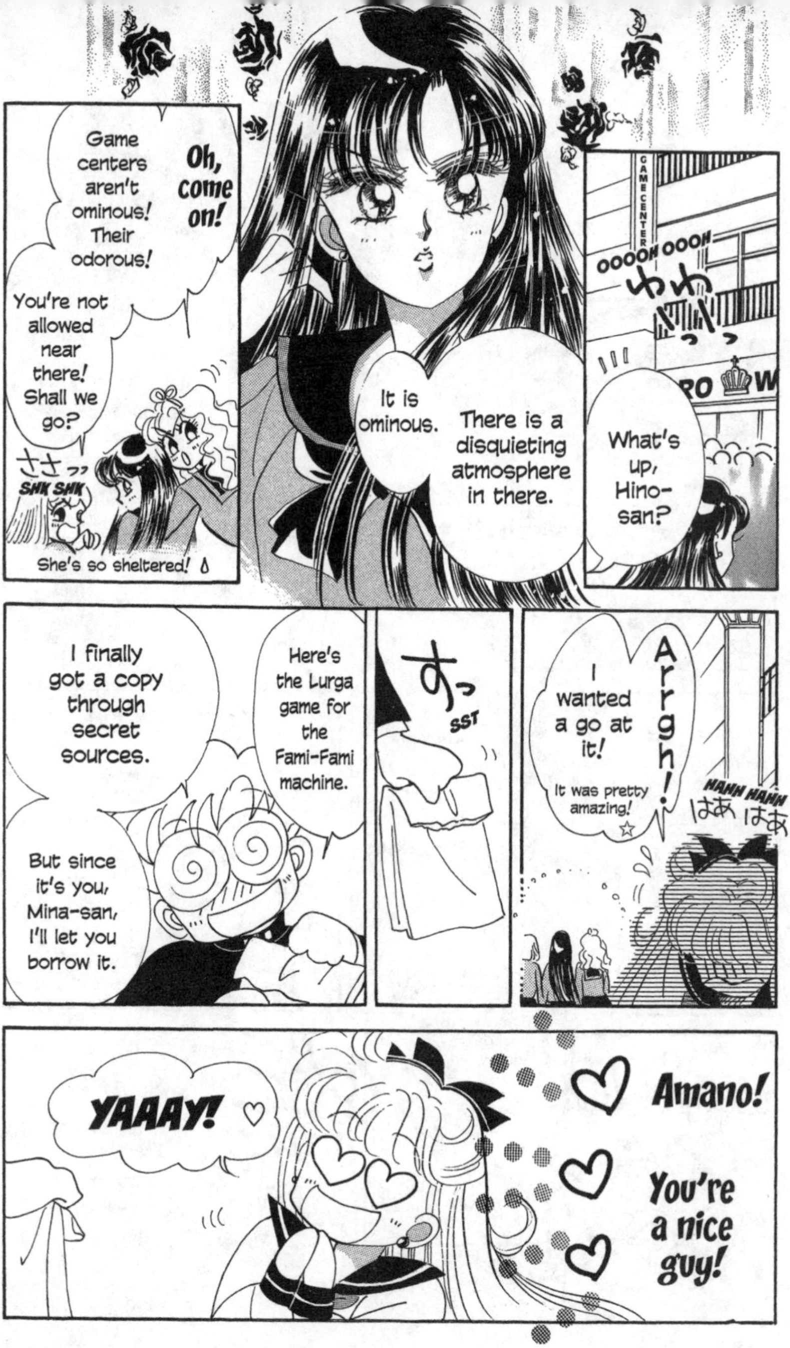
GAME CENTER
OOOOH OOOH
ゆゆ
What's up, Hino-san?
It is ominous.
There is a disquieting atmosphere in there.
Oh, come on!
Game centers aren't ominous! Their odorous!
You're not allowed near there! Shall we go?
ささっ
SHK SHK
She's so sheltered!
Arrgh!
I wanted a go at it!
It was pretty amazing! ☆
HAHH HAHH
はあ はあ
すっ
SST
Here's the Lurga game for the Fami-Fami machine.
I finally got a copy through secret sources.
But since it's you, Mina-san, I'll let you borrow it.
Amano!
You're a nice guy!
YAAAY! ♡

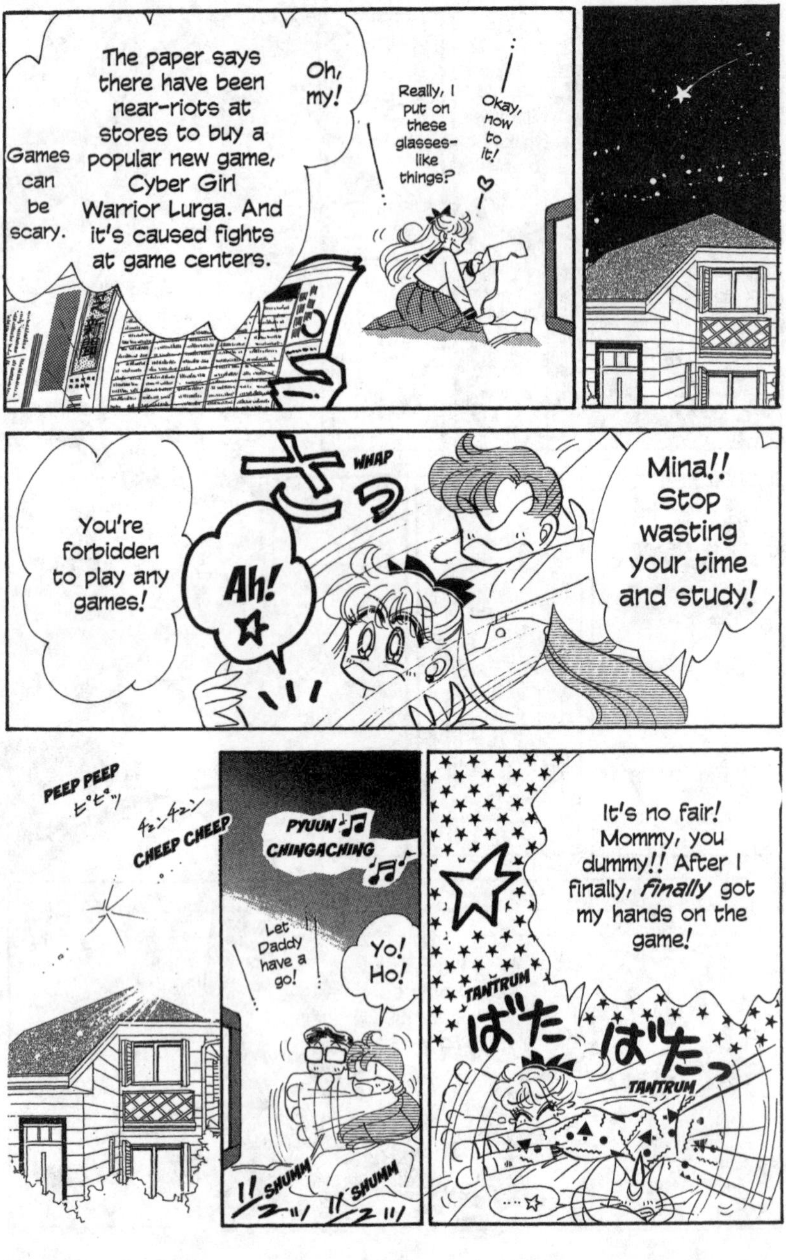
Okay, now to it! ♡
Really, I put on these glasses-like things?
Oh, my!
The paper says there have been near-riots at stores to buy a popular new game, Cyber Girl Warrior Lurga. And it's caused fights at game centers.
Games can be scary.
Mina!! Stop wasting your time and study!
WHAP
Ah! ☆
You're forbidden to play any games!
It's no fair! Mommy, you dummy!! After I finally, *finally* got my hands on the game!
TANTRUM
ばた ばたっ
TANTRUM
…☆
PYUUN CHINGACHING
Yo! Ho!
Let Daddy have a go!
SHUMM
SHUMM
PEEP PEEP
ピピッ
チュンチュン
CHEEP CHEEP

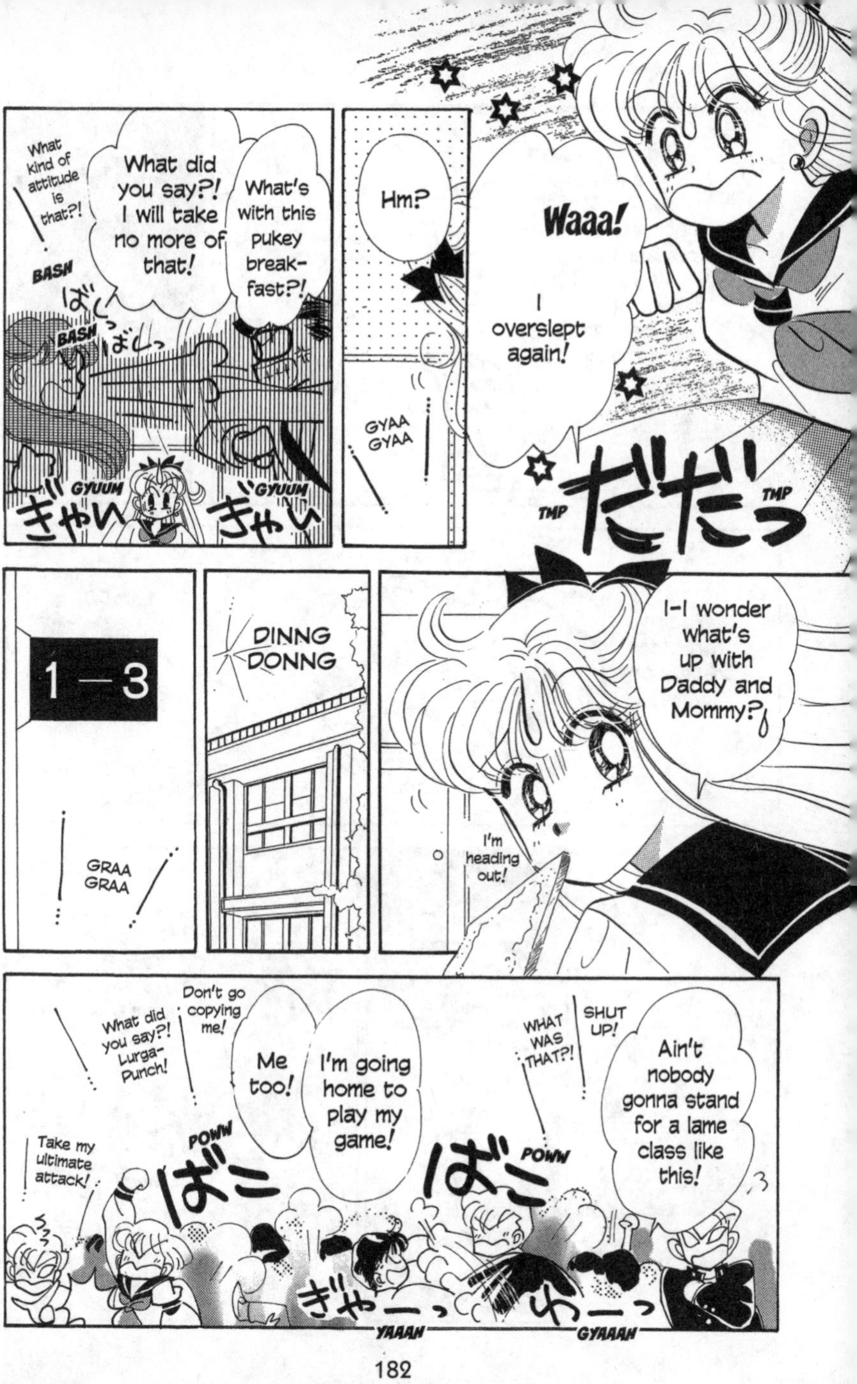
Waaa!
I overslept again!
TMP
だだっ
TMP
Hm?
GYAA GYAA
What's with this pukey breakfast?!
What did you say?! I will take no more of that!
What kind of attitude is that?!
BASH
BASH
GYUUM
GYUUM
I-I wonder what's up with Daddy and Mommy?
I'm heading out!
DINNG DONNG
1—3
GRAA GRAA
SHUT UP!
Ain't nobody gonna stand for a lame class like this!
WHAT WAS THAT?!
POWW
ばこ
I'm going home to play my game!
Me too!
Don't go copying me!
What did you say?! Lurga-Punch!
POWW
ばこ
Take my ultimate attack!
ぎゃーっ
YAAAH
GYAAAH

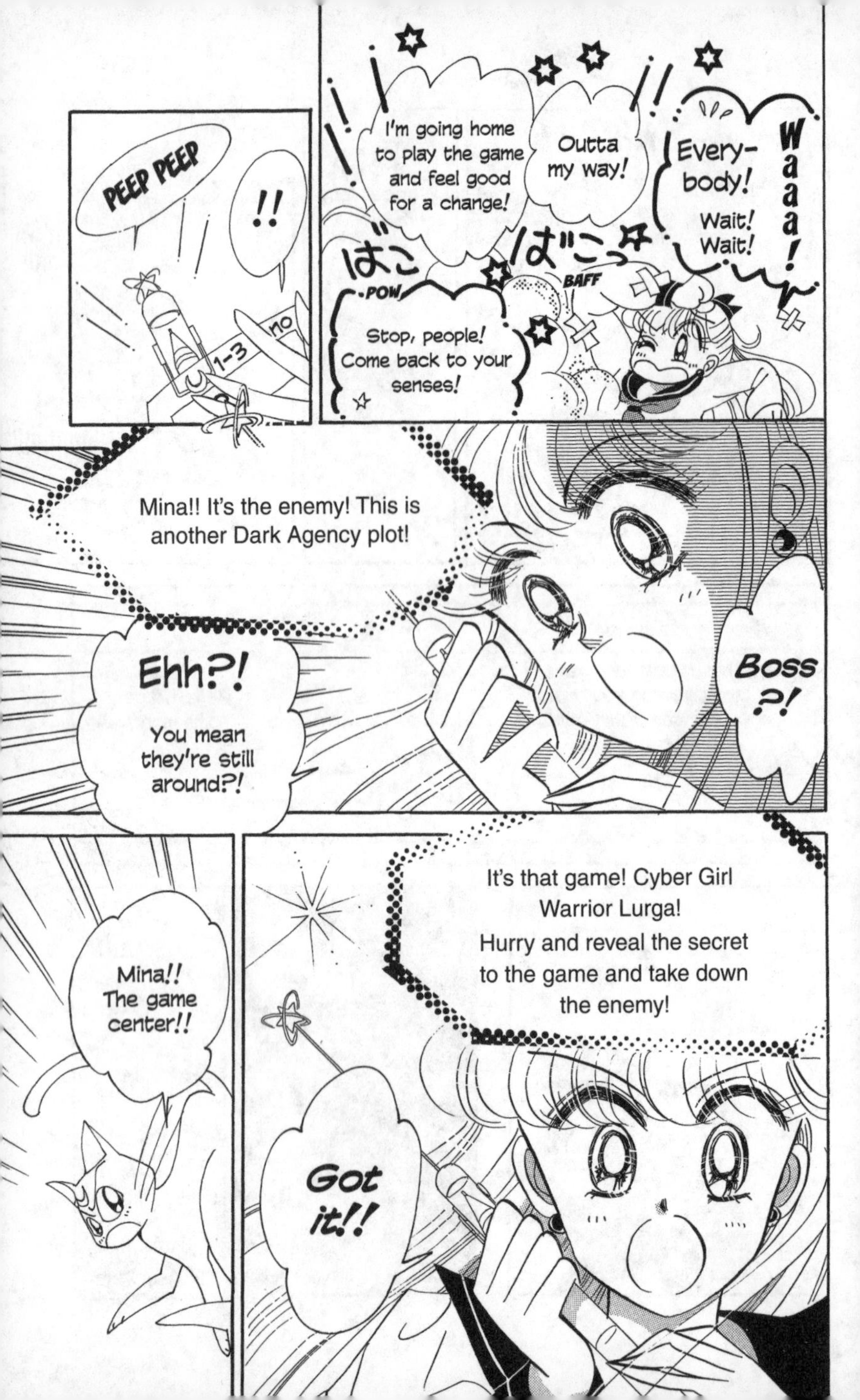
Waaa!
Every-body! Wait! Wait!
Outta my way!
I'm going home to play the game and feel good for a change!
ばこっ
BAFF
ばこ
POW
Stop, people! Come back to your senses!
PEEP PEEP
!!
Boss?!
Mina!! It's the enemy! This is another Dark Agency plot!
Ehh?! You mean they're still around?!
It's that game! Cyber Girl Warrior Lurga! Hurry and reveal the secret to the game and take down the enemy!
Got it!!
Mina!! The game center!!

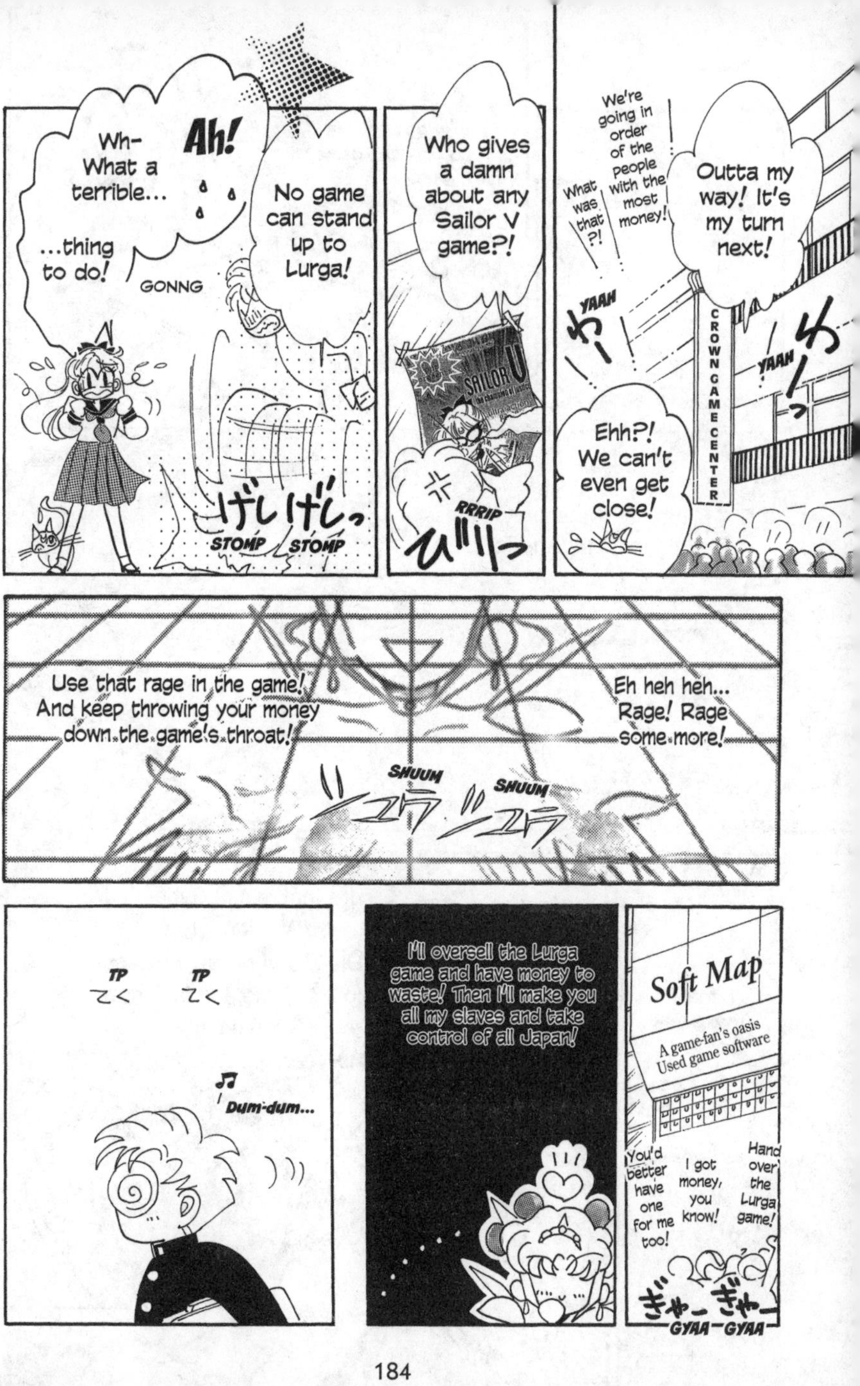

Outta my way! It's my turn next!
We're going in order of the people with the most money!
What was that?!
YAAH
YAAH
CROWN GAME CENTER
Ehh?! We can't even get close!
Who gives a damn about any Sailor V game?!
SAILOR V
RRRIP
No game can stand up to Lurga!
Ah!
Wh- What a terrible...
...thing to do!
GONNG
STOMP STOMP
Eh heh heh... Rage! Rage some more!
Use that rage in the game! And keep throwing your money down the game's throat!
SHUUM SHUUM
Soft Map
A game-fan's oasis
Used game software
Hand over the Lurga game!
I got money, you know!
You'd better have one for me too!
GYAA GYAA
I'll oversell the Lurga game and have money to waste! Then I'll make you all my slaves and take control of all Japan!
TP TP
Dum-dum...

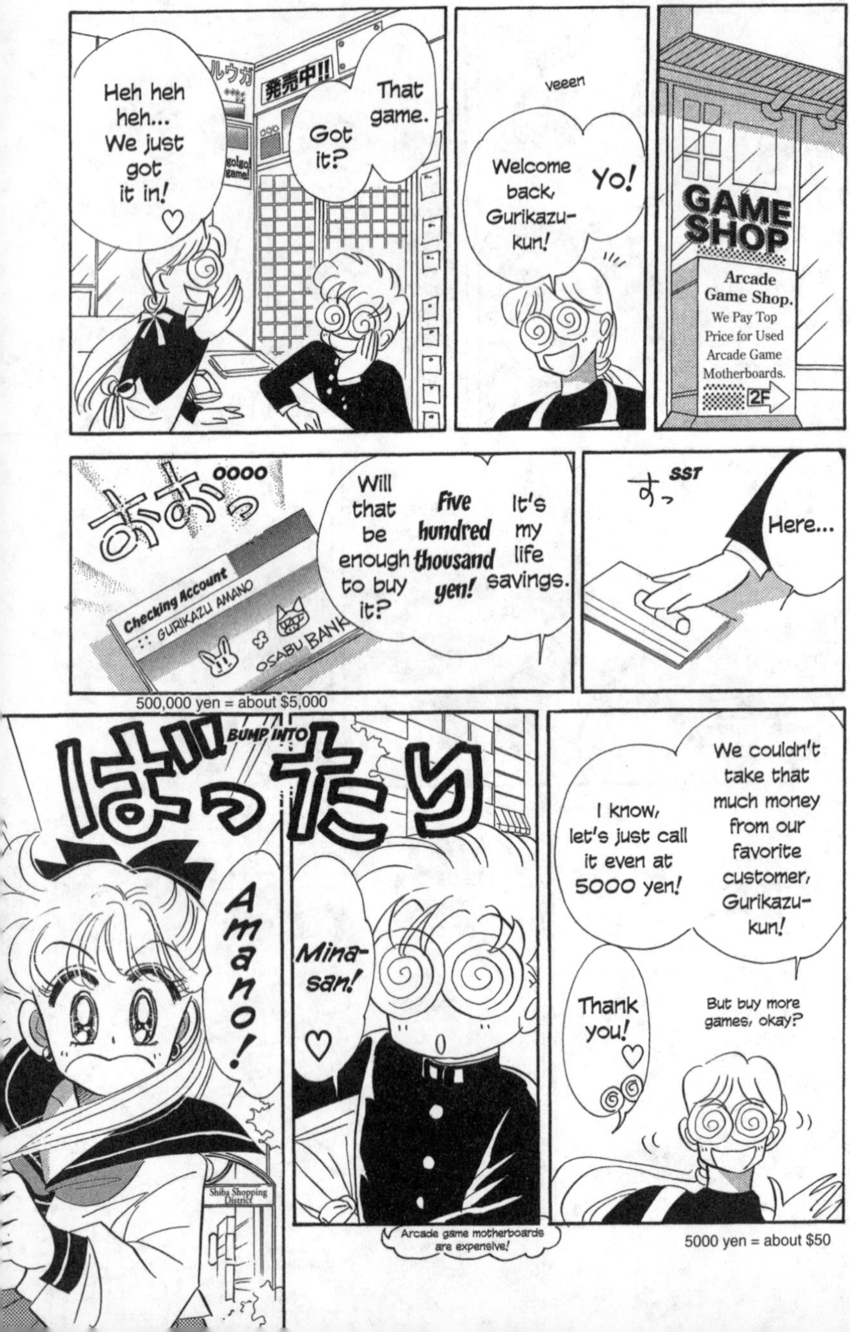
GAME SHOP
Arcade Game Shop. We Pay Top Price for Used Arcade Game Motherboards.
2F
veeen
Yo!
Welcome back, Gurikazu-kun!
That game.
Got it?
発売中!!
go!go! game!
Heh heh heh... We just got it in! ♡
SST
すっ
Here...
It's my life savings.
Five hundred thousand yen!
Will that be enough to buy it?
OOOO
おおっ
Checking Account
GURIKAZU AMANO
OSABU BANK
We couldn't take that much money from our favorite customer, Gurikazu-kun!
I know, let's just call it even at 5000 yen!
But buy more games, okay?
Thank you! ♡
BUMP INTO
ばったり
Mina-san! ♡
Amano!
Shiba Shopping District
Arcade game motherboards are expensive!
500,000 yen = about $5,000
5000 yen = about $50

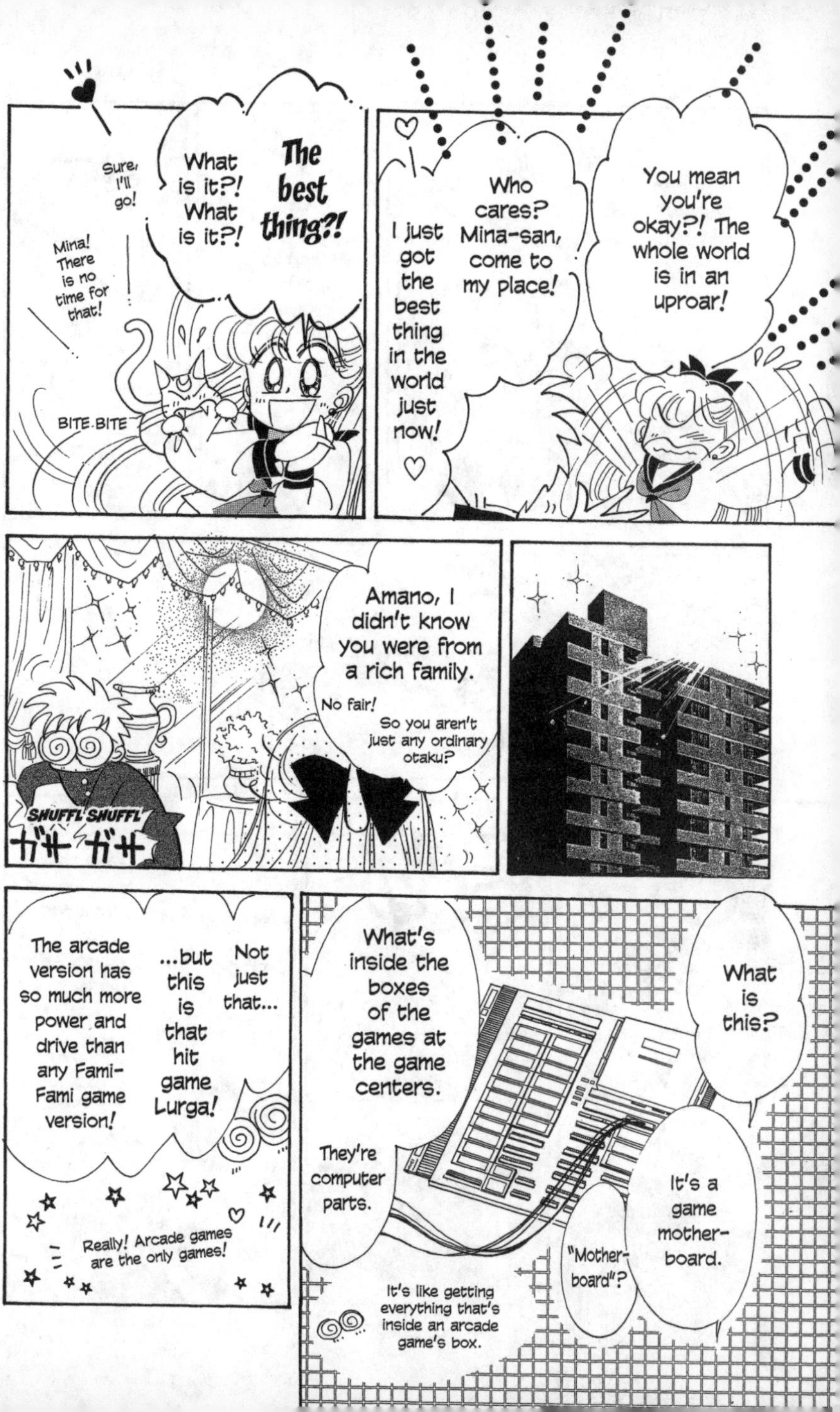

You mean you're okay?! The whole world is in an uproar!
Who cares? Mina-san, come to my place!
I just got the best thing in the world just now!
The best thing?!
What is it?! What is it?!
Sure, I'll go!
Mina! There is no time for that!
BITE BITE
Amano, I didn't know you were from a rich family.
No fair!
So you aren't just any ordinary otaku?
SHUFFL SHUFFL
ガサ ガサ
What is this?
What's inside the boxes of the games at the game centers.
They're computer parts.
It's a game motherboard.
"Motherboard"?
It's like getting everything that's inside an arcade game's box.
Not just that...
...but this is that hit game Lurga!
The arcade version has so much more power and drive than any Fami-Fami game version!
Really! Arcade games are the only games!

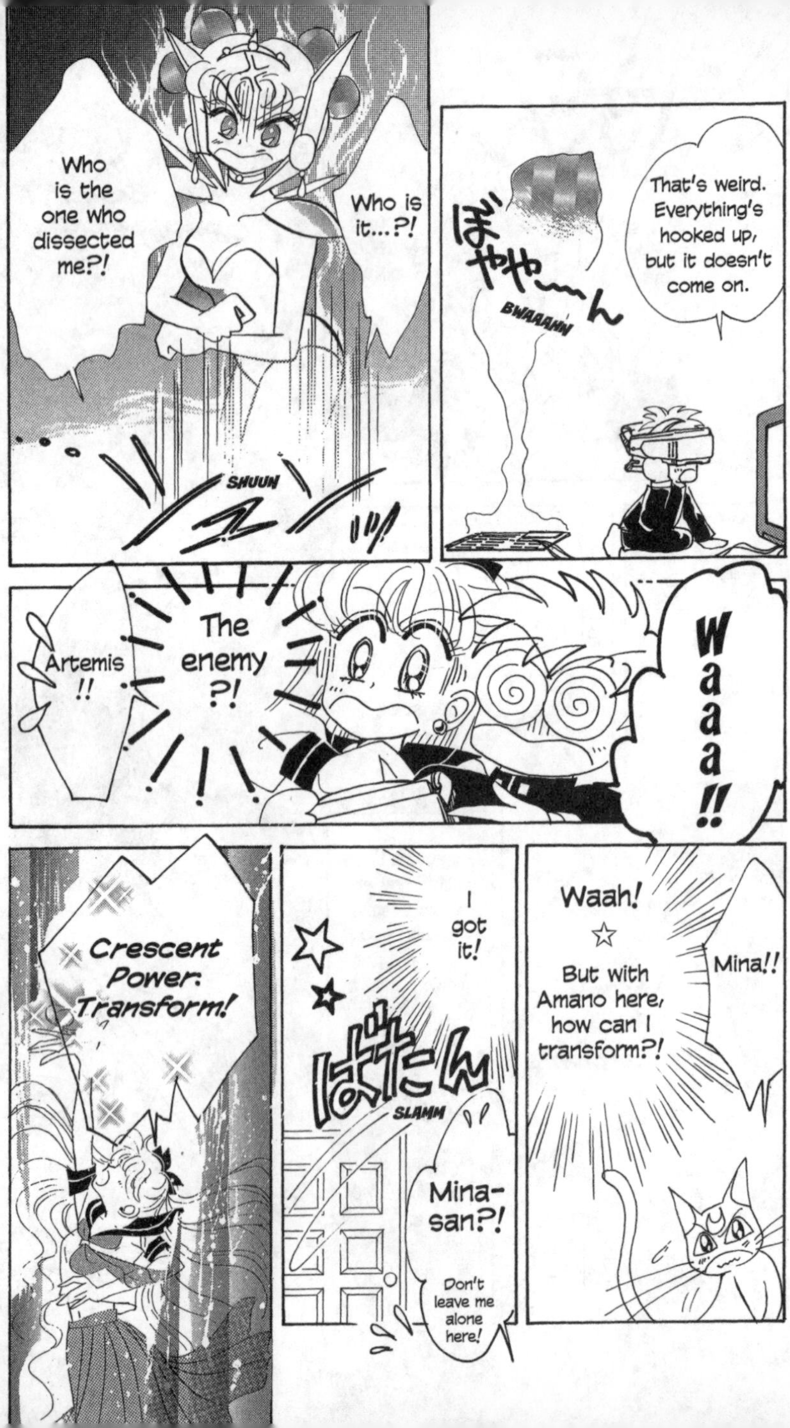
That's weird. Everything's hooked up, but it doesn't come on.
ぼややーん
BWAAANN
Who is the one who dissected me?!
Who is it...?!
...
SHUUN
Waaaa!!
The enemy?!
Artemis!!
Mina!!
Waah! ☆ But with Amano here, how can I transform?!
I got it!
ばたん
SLAMM
Mina-san?!
Don't leave me alone here!
Crescent Power: Transform!

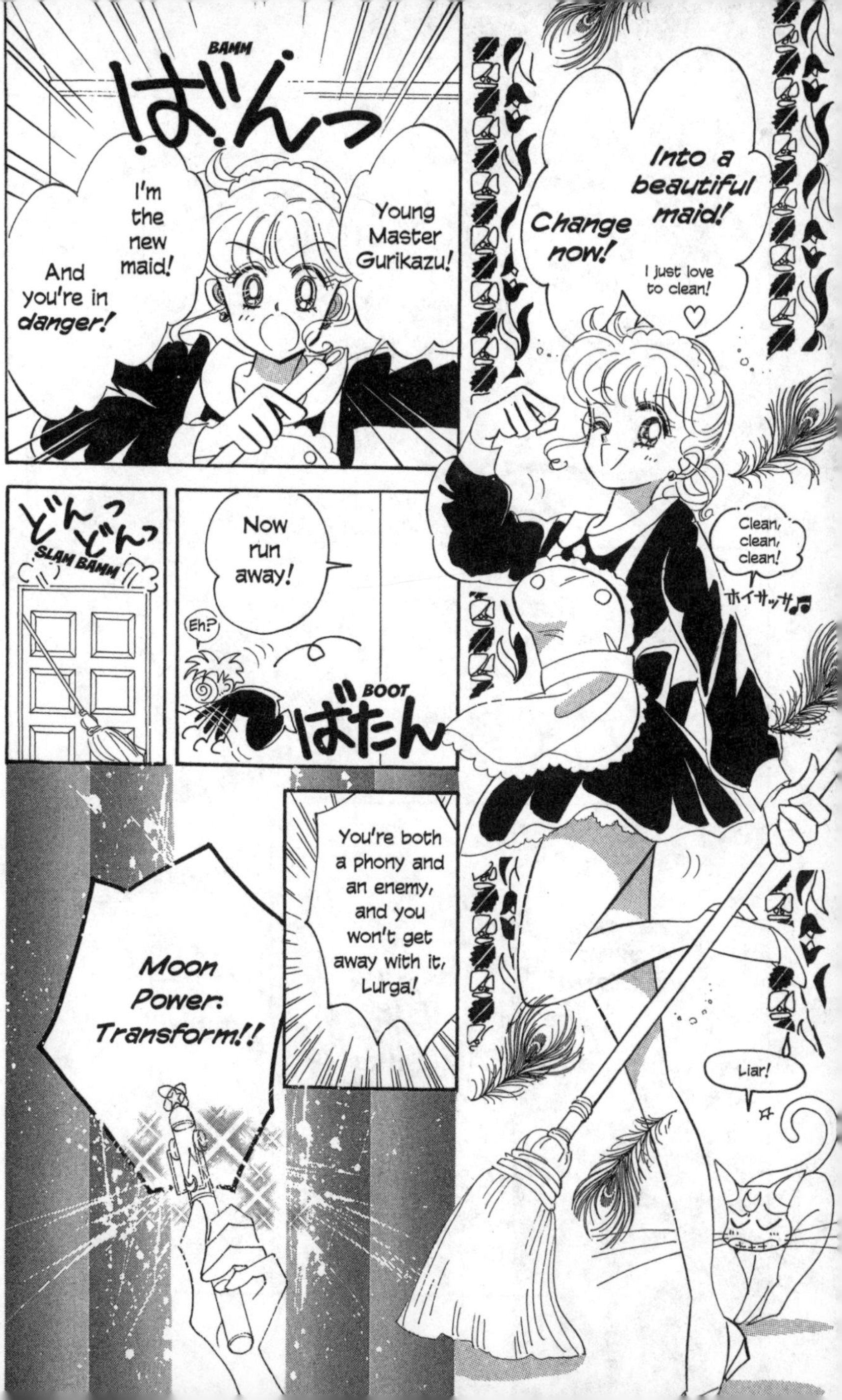

Change now! Into a beautiful maid!
I just love to clean! ♥
Clean, clean, clean!
ホイサッサ♫
Liar!
ばんっ
BAMM
Young Master Gurikazu!
I'm the new maid!
And you're in danger!
Now run away!
Eh?
ばたん
BOOT
どんっどんっ
SLAM BAMM
You're both a phony and an enemy, and you won't get away with it, Lurga!
Moon Power: Transform!!

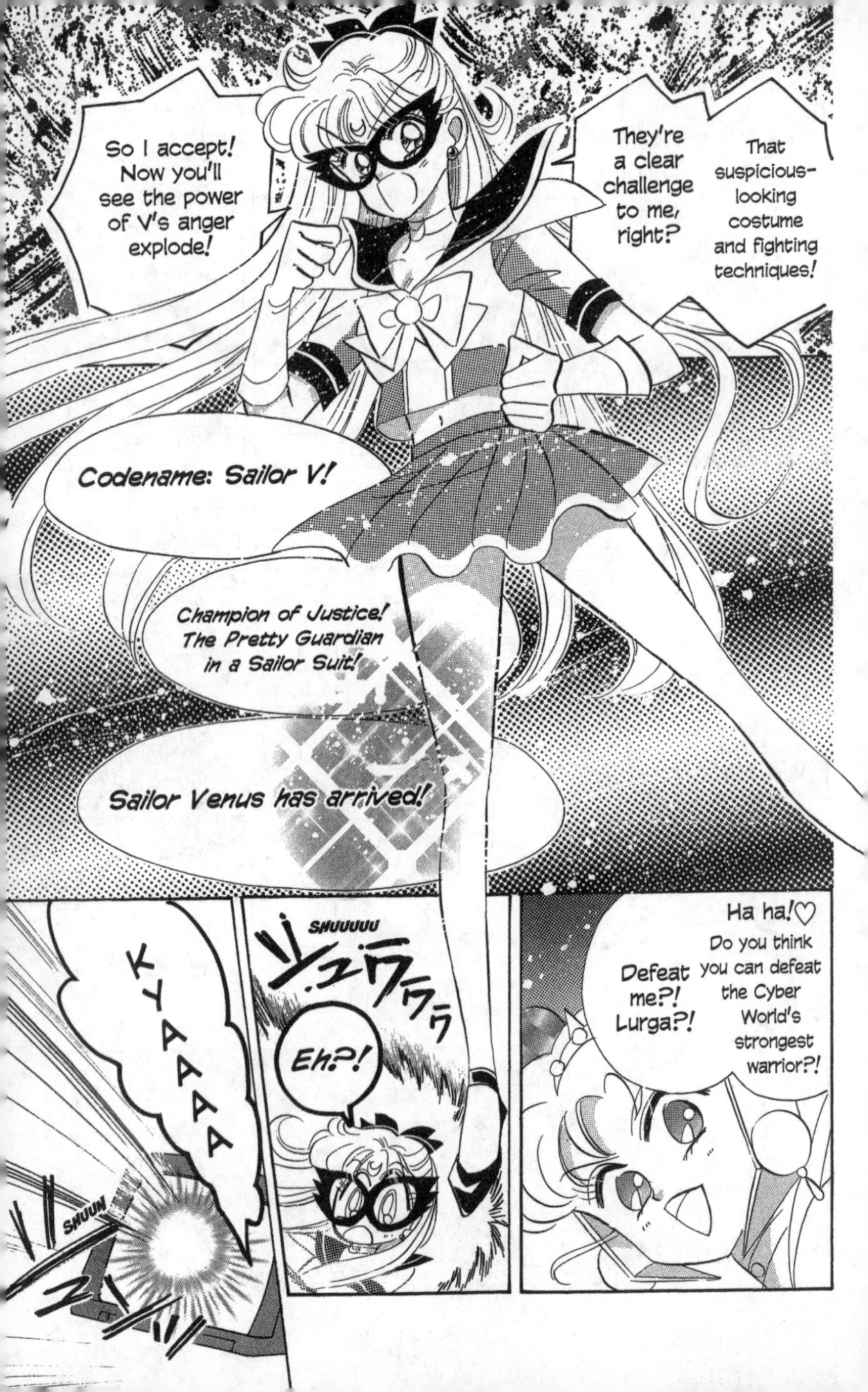
That suspicious-looking costume and fighting techniques!
They're a clear challenge to me, right?
So I accept! Now you'll see the power of V's anger explode!
Codename: Sailor V!
Champion of Justice! The Pretty Guardian in a Sailor Suit!
Sailor Venus has arrived!
Ha ha!♡ Do you think you can defeat the Cyber World's strongest warrior?!
Defeat me?! Lurga?!
SHUUUUU
Eh?!
KYAAAAA
SHUUN

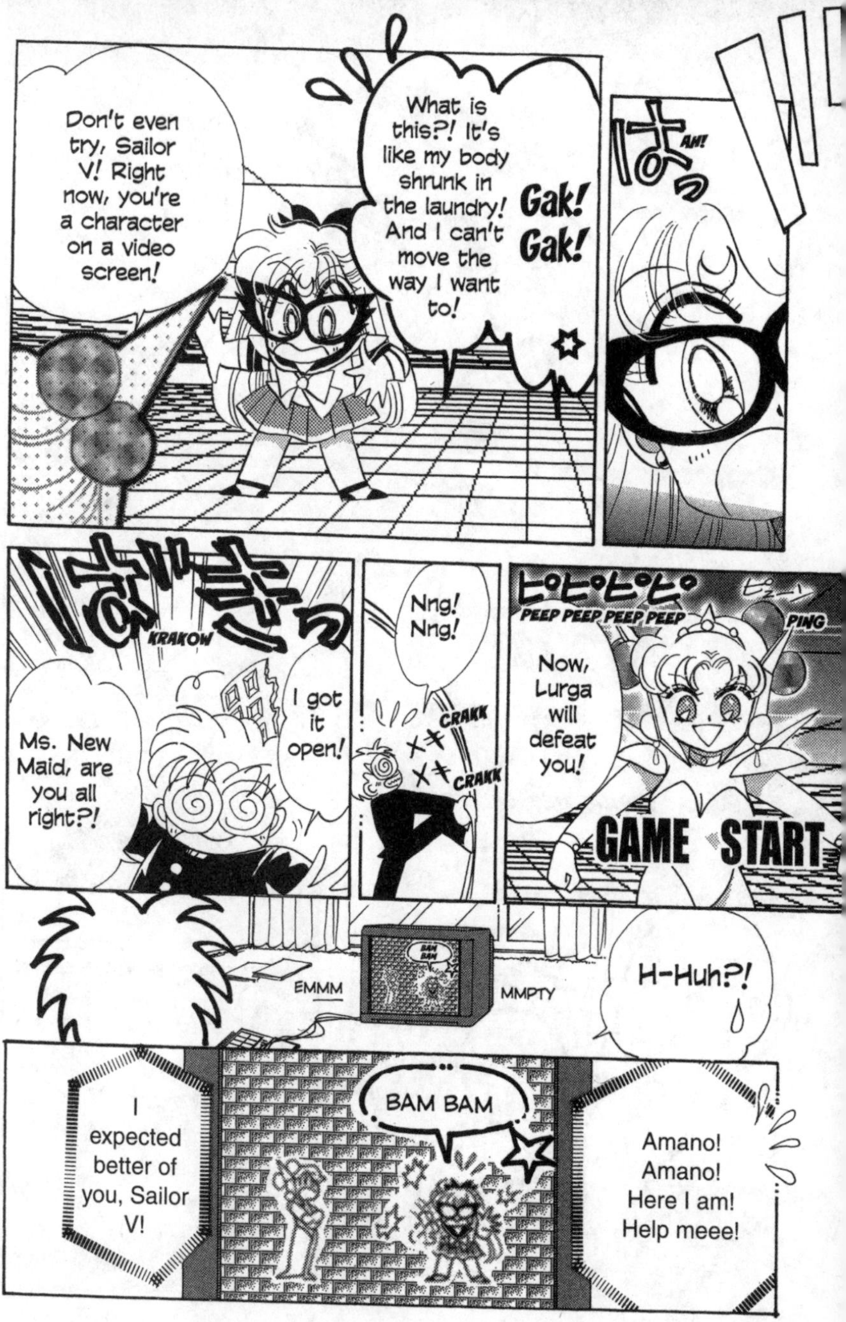
AH!
What is this?! It's like my body shrunk in the laundry! And I can't move the way I want to!
Gak! Gak!
Don't even try, Sailor V! Right now, you're a character on a video screen!
PEEP PEEP PEEP PEEP
PING
Now, Lurga will defeat you!
GAME START
Nng! Nng!
CRAKK
CRAKK
KRAKOW
I got it open!
Ms. New Maid, are you all right?!
H-Huh?!
BAM BAM
MMPTY
EMMMM
Amano! Amano! Here I am! Help meee!
BAM BAM
I expected better of you, Sailor V!

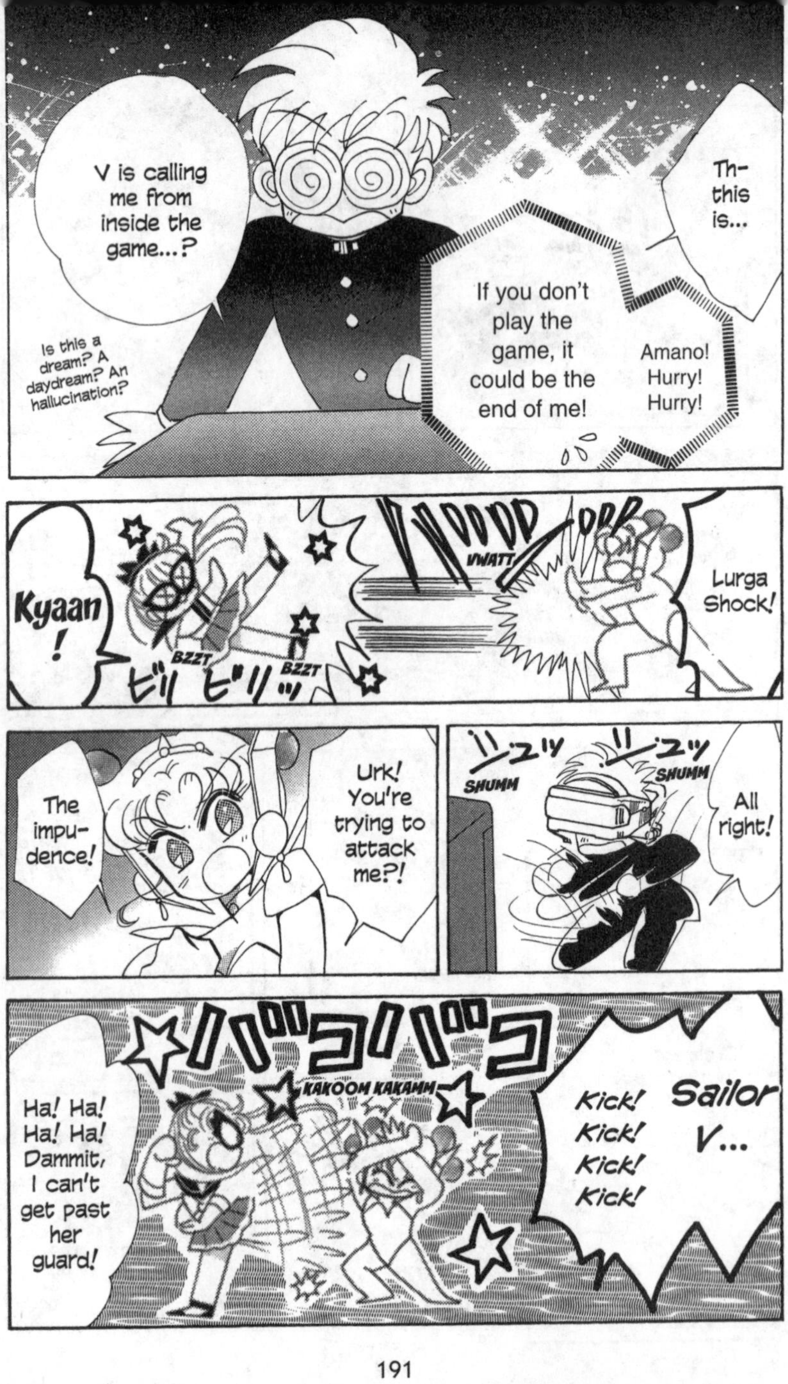
Th- this is...
Amano! Hurry! Hurry!
If you don't play the game, it could be the end of me!
V is calling me from inside the game...?
Is this a dream? A daydream? An hallucination?
Lurga Shock!
VWATT
BZZT
BZZT
Kyaan!
All right!
SHUMM
SHUMM
Urk! You're trying to attack me?!
The impudence!
Sailor V...
Kick! Kick! Kick! Kick!
KAKOOM KAKAMM
Ha! Ha! Ha! Ha! Dammit, I can't get past her guard!

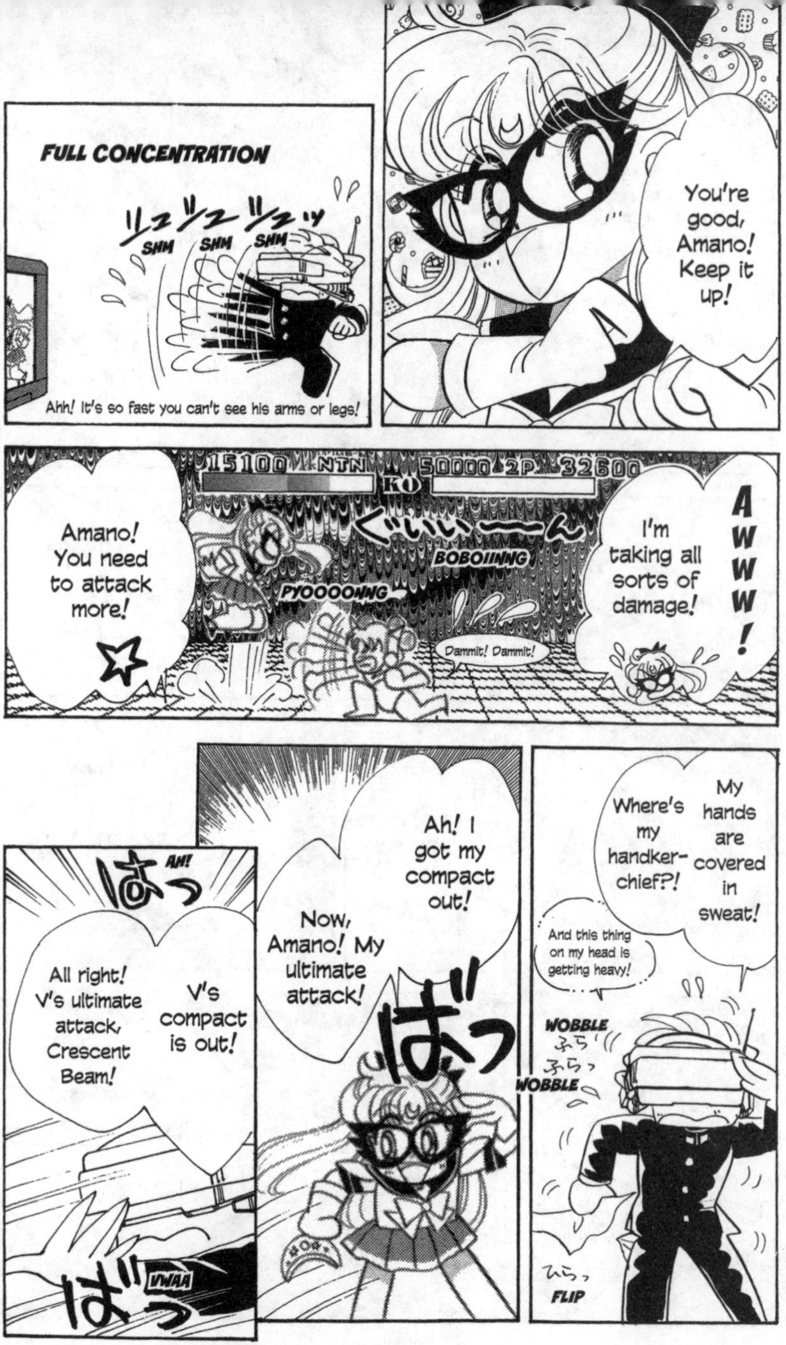

You're good, Amano! Keep it up!
FULL CONCENTRATION
SHM SHM SHM
Ahh! It's so fast you can't see his arms or legs!
15100 NTN 50000 2P 32600
KO
AWWW!
I'm taking all sorts of damage!
BOBOIINNG
Dammit! Dammit!
PYOOOOONNG
Amano! You need to attack more!
My hands are covered in sweat!
Where's my handker-chief?!
And this thing on my head is getting heavy!
WOBBLE
WOBBLE
FLIP
Ah! I got my compact out!
Now, Amano! My ultimate attack!
AH!
V's compact is out!
All right! V's ultimate attack, Crescent Beam!
VWAA

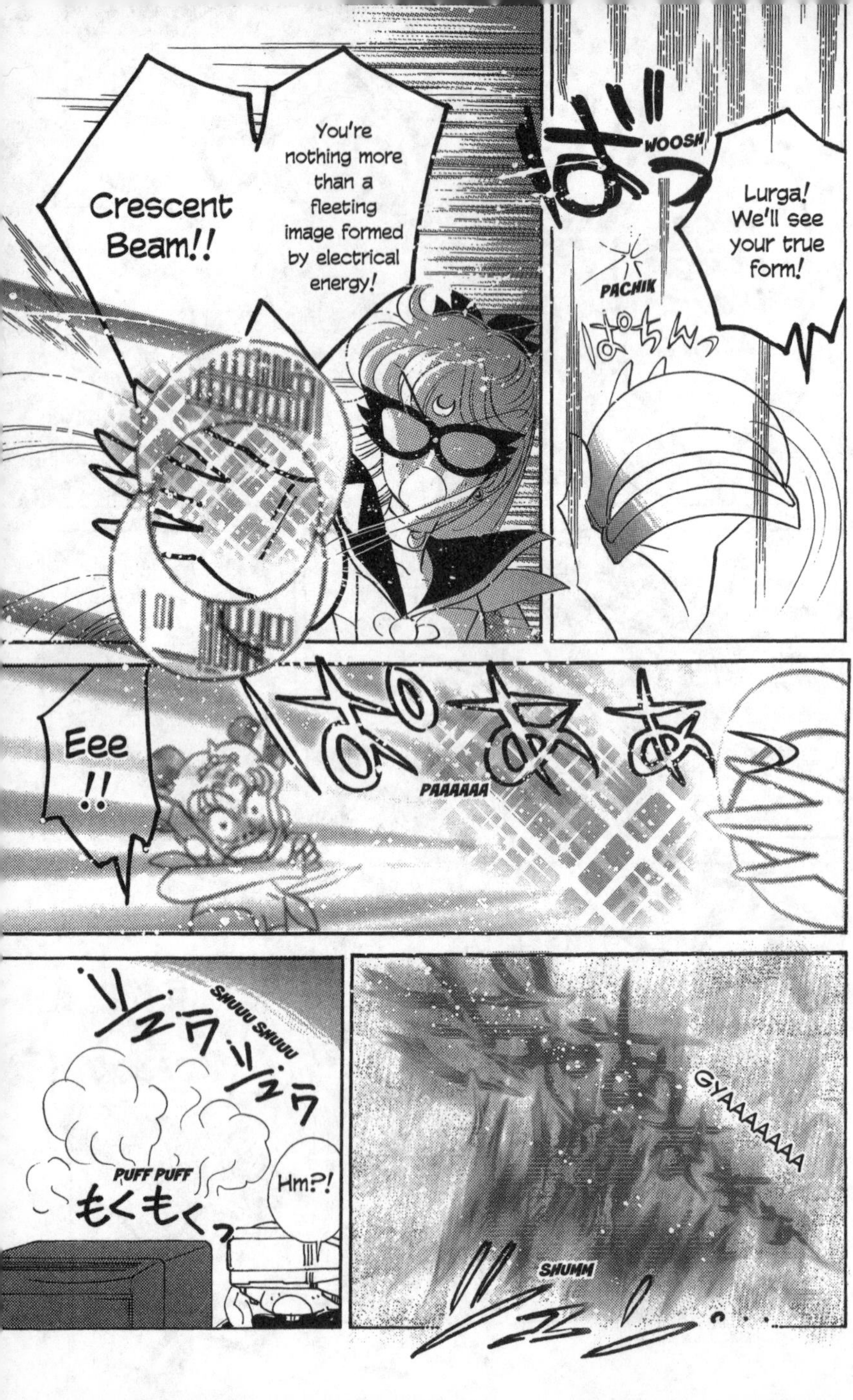
ばっ
WOOSH
Lurga! We'll see your true form!
PACHIK
ぱちんっ
You're nothing more than a fleeting image formed by electrical energy!
Crescent Beam!!
ぱああっ
PAAAAAA
Eee!!
GYAAAAAAA
SHUMM
シュワシュワ
SHUUU SHUUU
Hm?!
PUFF PUFF
もくもくっ

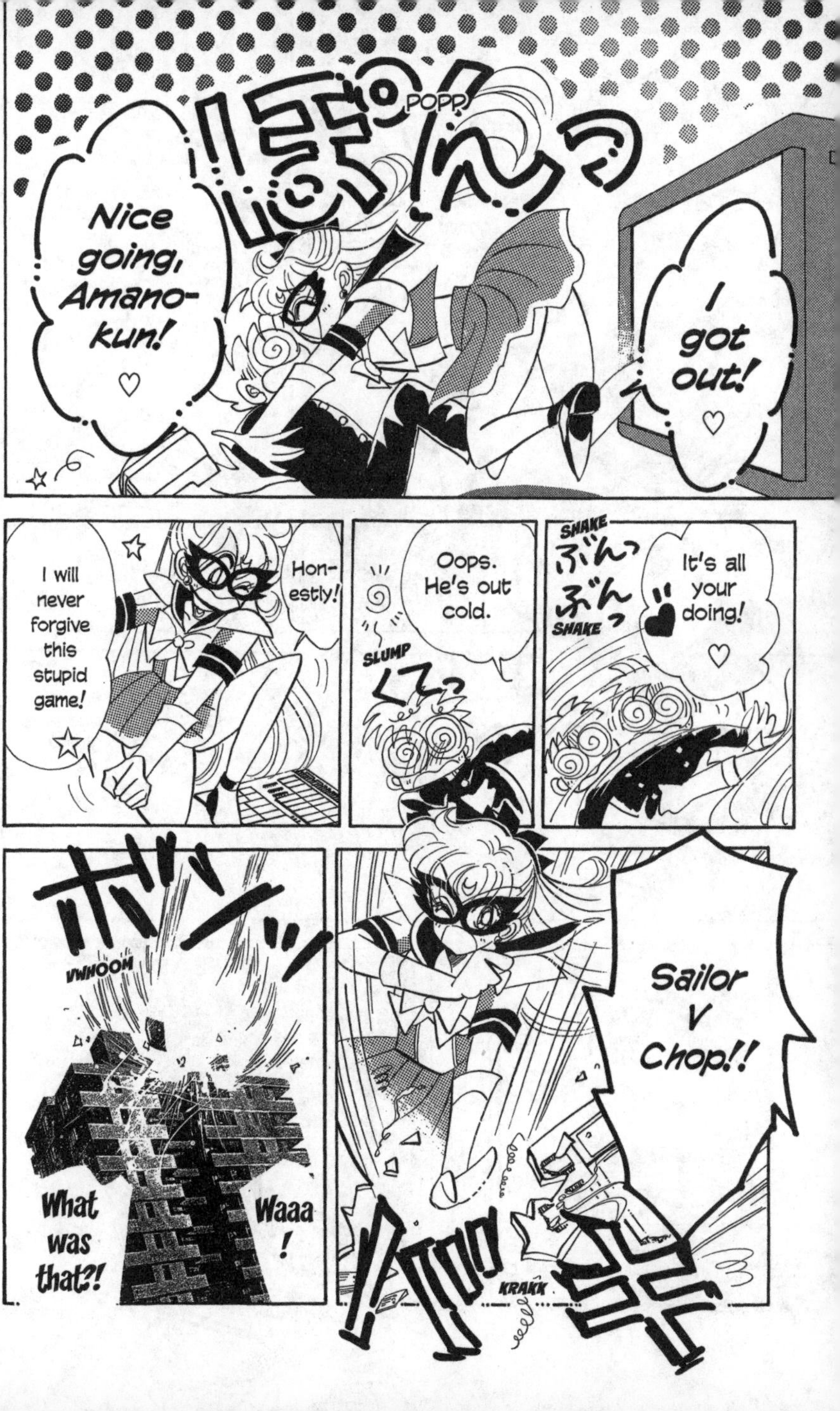

ぽんっ
POPP
I got out! ♡
Nice going, Amano-kun! ♡
SHAKE
ぶんっ
ぶんっ
SHAKE
It's all your doing! ♡
Oops. He's out cold.
SLUMP
くてっ
Hon-estly!
I will never forgive this stupid game!
Sailor V Chop!!
KRAKK
ボンッ
VWHOOM
Waaa!
What was that?!

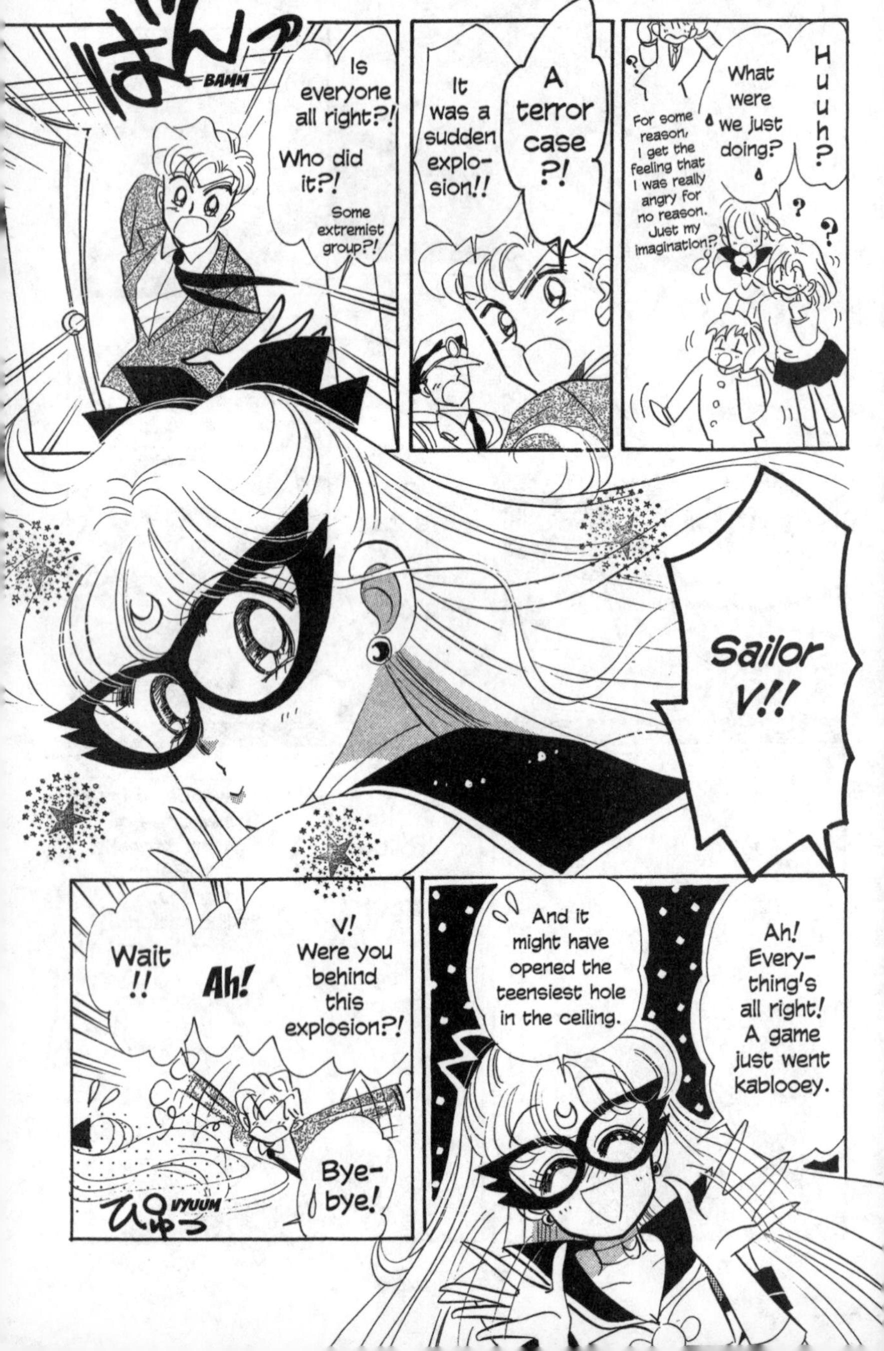
Huuh?
What were we just doing?
For some reason, I get the feeling that I was really angry for no reason. Just my imagination?
A terror case?!
It was a sudden explosion!!
ばんっ
BAMM
Is everyone all right?!
Who did it?!
Some extremist group?!
Sailor V!!
Ah! Every-thing's all right! A game just went kablooey.
And it might have opened the teensiest hole in the ceiling.
V! Were you behind this explosion?!
Ah!
Wait!!
Bye-bye!
ひゅっ
HYUUM

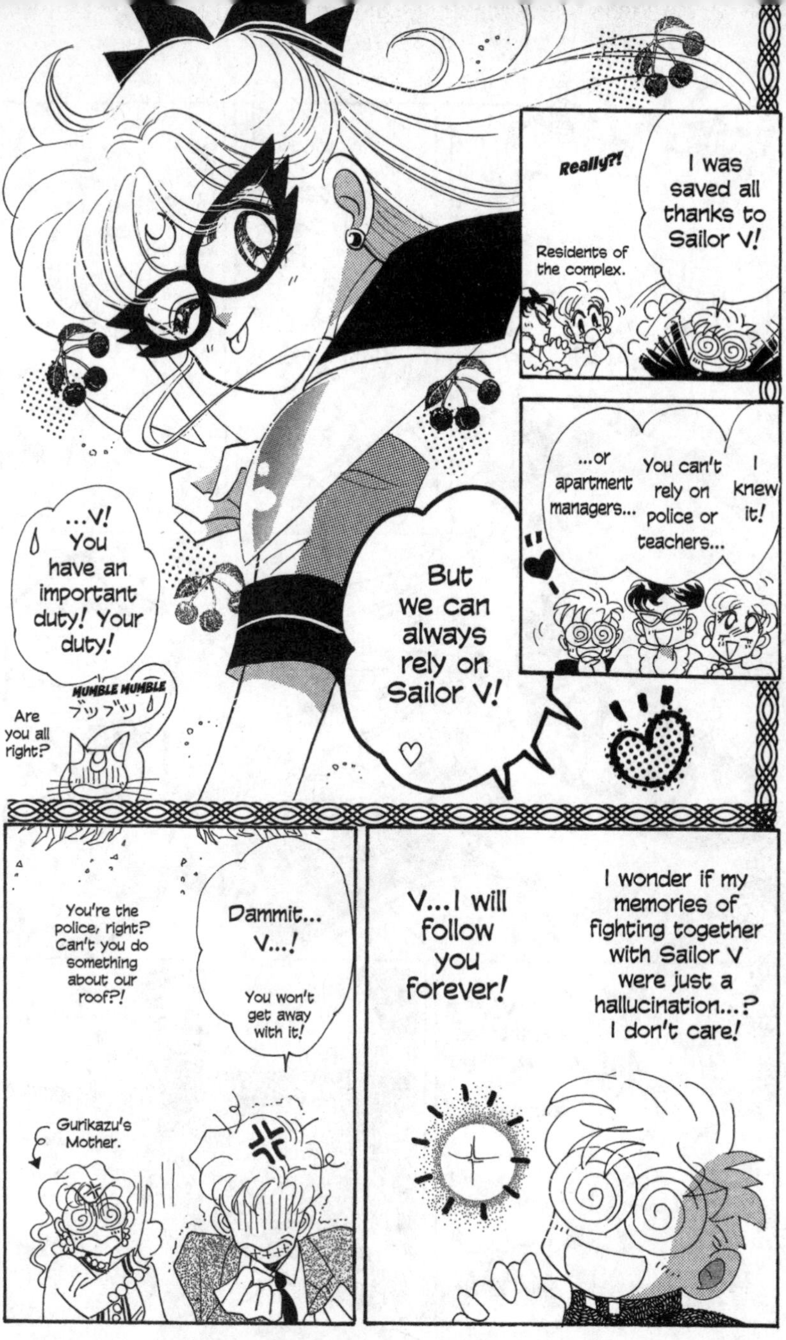
I was saved all thanks to Sailor V!
Really?!
Residents of the complex.
I knew it!
You can't rely on police or teachers...
...or apartment managers...
But we can always rely on Sailor V!
...V! You have an important duty! Your duty!
MUMBLE MUMBLE
ブツブツ
Are you all right?
I wonder if my memories of fighting together with Sailor V were just a hallucination...? I don't care!
V...I will follow you forever!
Dammit... V...!
You won't get away with it!
You're the police, right? Can't you do something about our roof?!
Gurikazu's Mother.

•*The End*•

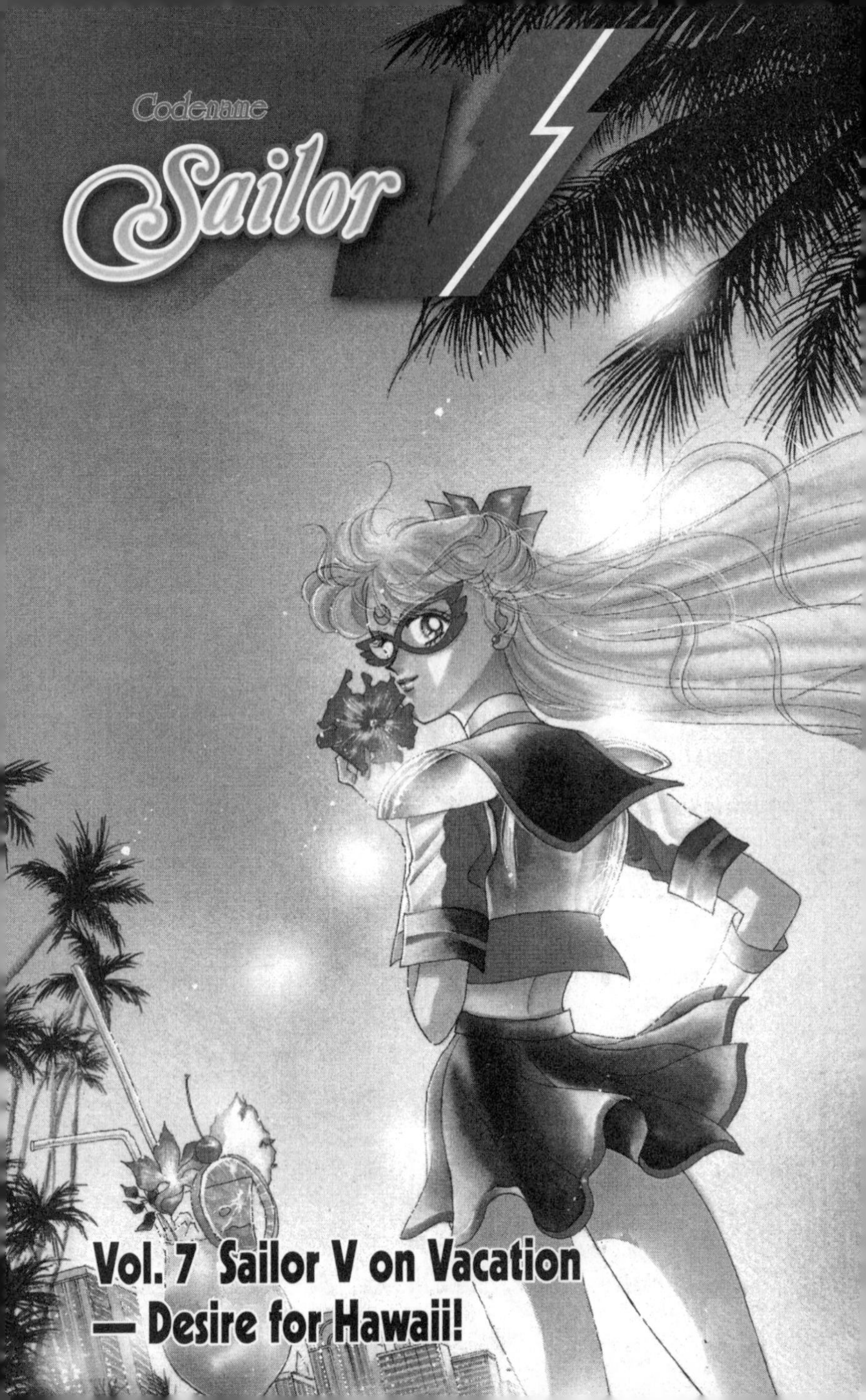
Codename Sailor V
Vol. 7 Sailor V on Vacation
— Desire for Hawaii!

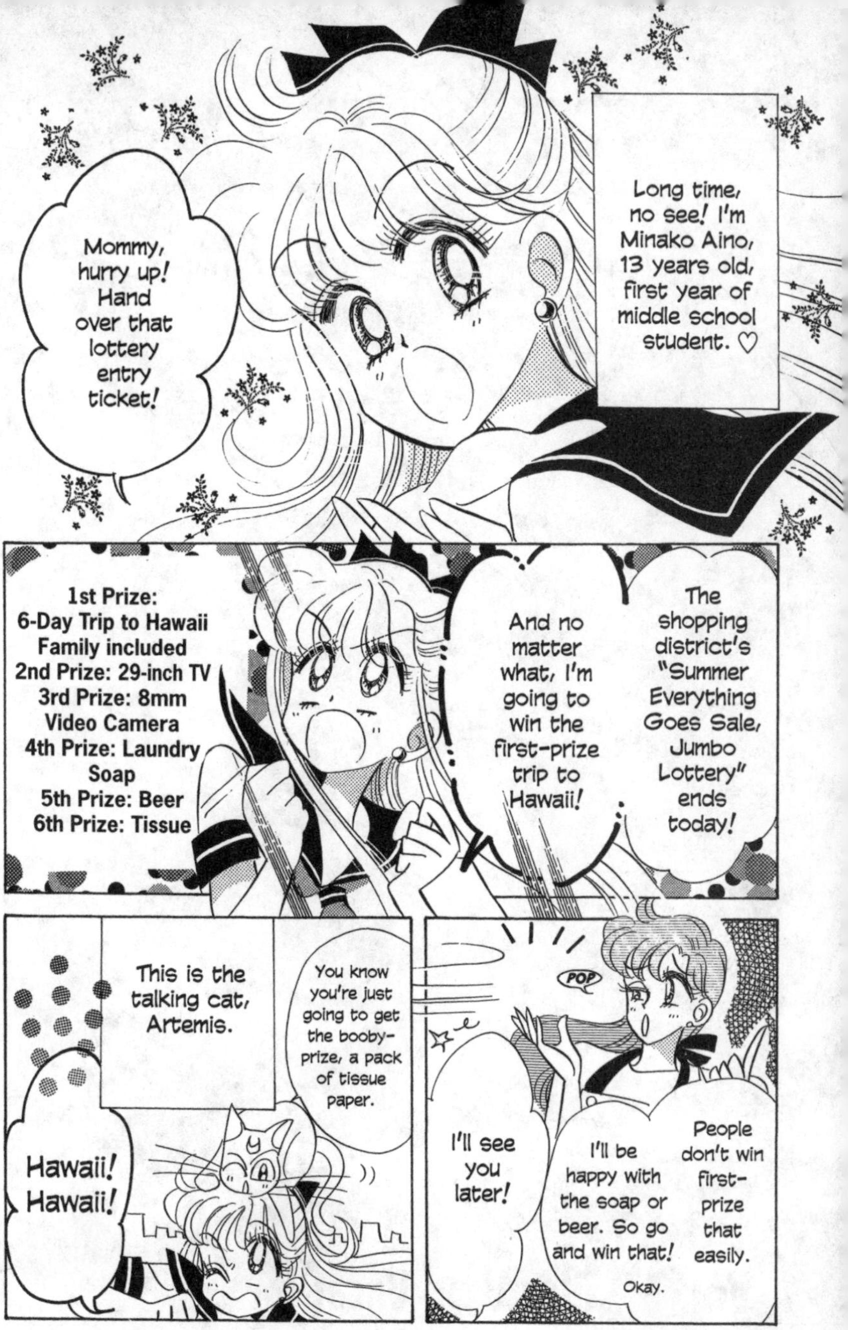
Long time, no see! I'm Minako Aino, 13 years old, first year of middle school student. ♡
Mommy, hurry up! Hand over that lottery entry ticket!
The shopping district's "Summer Everything Goes Sale, Jumbo Lottery" ends today!
And no matter what, I'm going to win the first-prize trip to Hawaii!
1st Prize: 6-Day Trip to Hawaii Family included
2nd Prize: 29-inch TV
3rd Prize: 8mm Video Camera
4th Prize: Laundry Soap
5th Prize: Beer
6th Prize: Tissue
POP
People don't win first-prize that easily.
I'll be happy with the soap or beer. So go and win that!
Okay.
I'll see you later!
You know you're just going to get the booby-prize, a pack of tissue paper.
This is the talking cat, Artemis.
Hawaii! Hawaii!

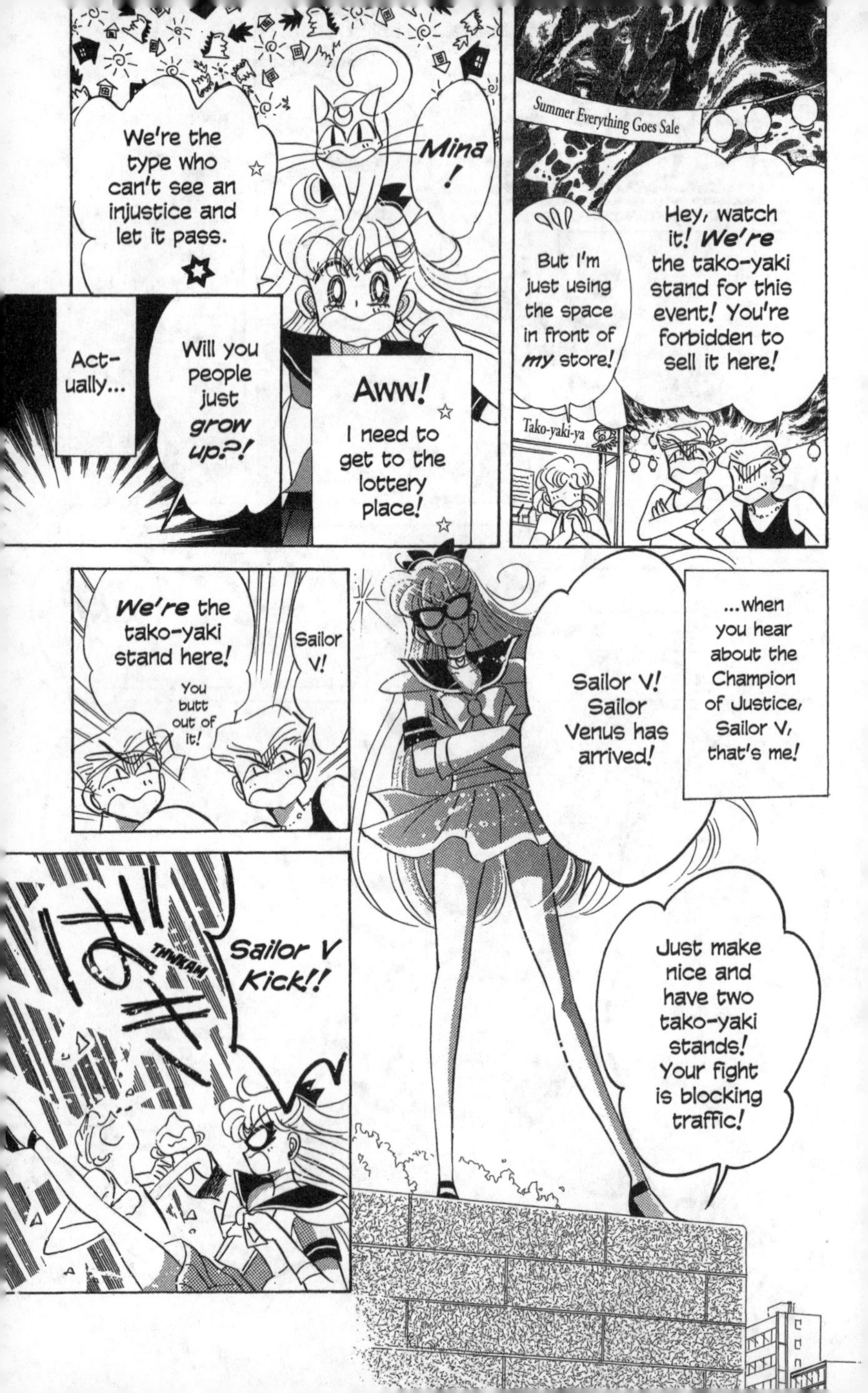
Summer Everything Goes Sale
Hey, watch it! *We're* the tako-yaki stand for this event! You're forbidden to sell it here!
But I'm just using the space in front of *my* store!
Tako-yaki-ya
Mina!
We're the type who can't see an injustice and let it pass.
Aww! I need to get to the lottery place!
Will you people just *grow up?!*
Act-ually...
...when you hear about the Champion of Justice, Sailor V, that's me!
Sailor V! Sailor Venus has arrived!
Just make nice and have two tako-yaki stands! Your fight is blocking traffic!
We're the tako-yaki stand here!
Sailor V!
You butt out of it!
Sailor V Kick!!
THWKAM

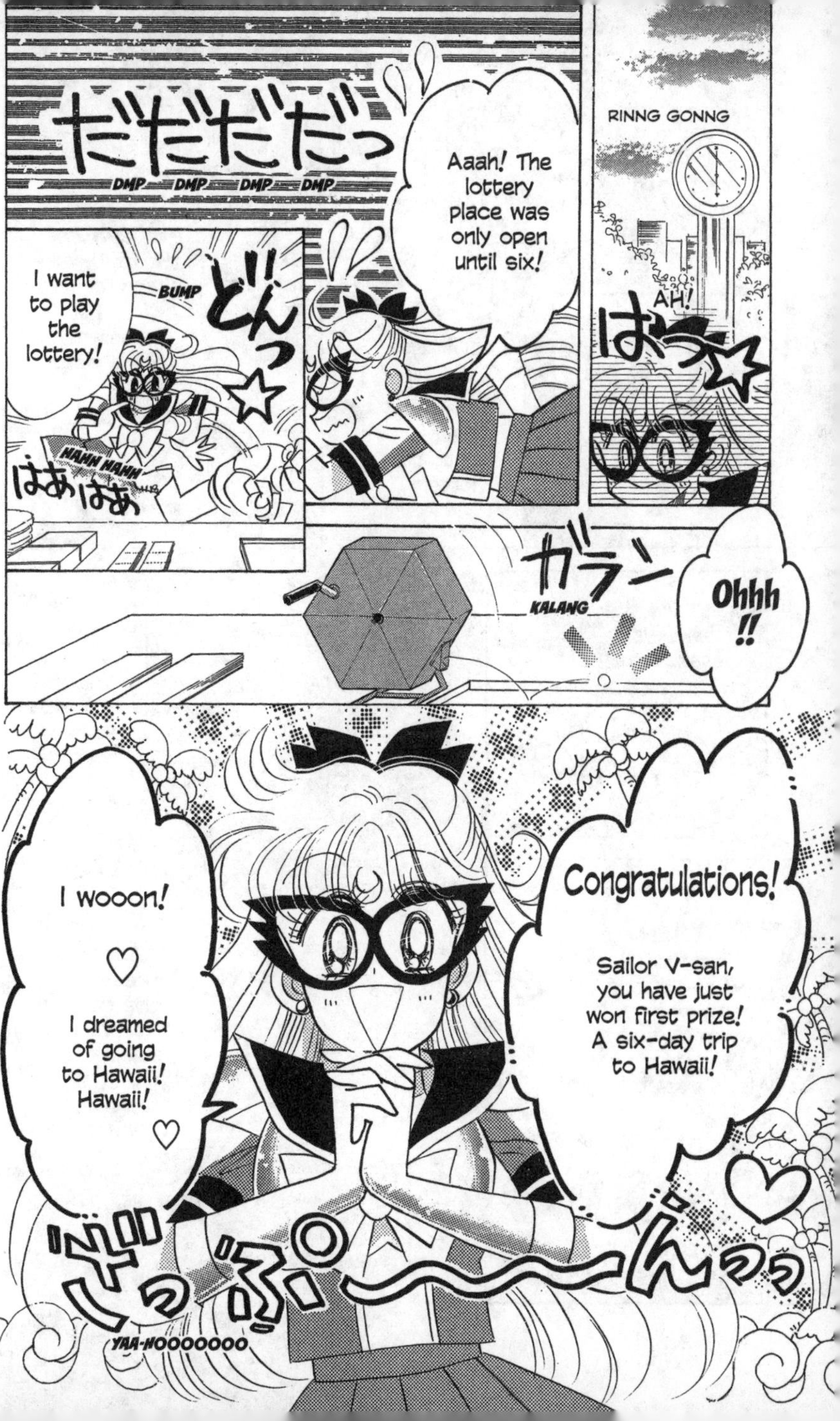

RINNG GONNG
AH!
はっ
だだだだっ
DMP DMP DMP DMP
Aaah! The lottery place was only open until six!
どんっ
BUMP
I want to play the lottery!
はあはあ
HAHH HAHH
ガラン
KALANG
Ohhh!!
Congratulations!
Sailor V-san, you have just won first prize! A six-day trip to Hawaii!
I wooon! ♡
I dreamed of going to Hawaii! Hawaii! ♡
ざっぷーーんっっ
YAA-NOOOOOOO

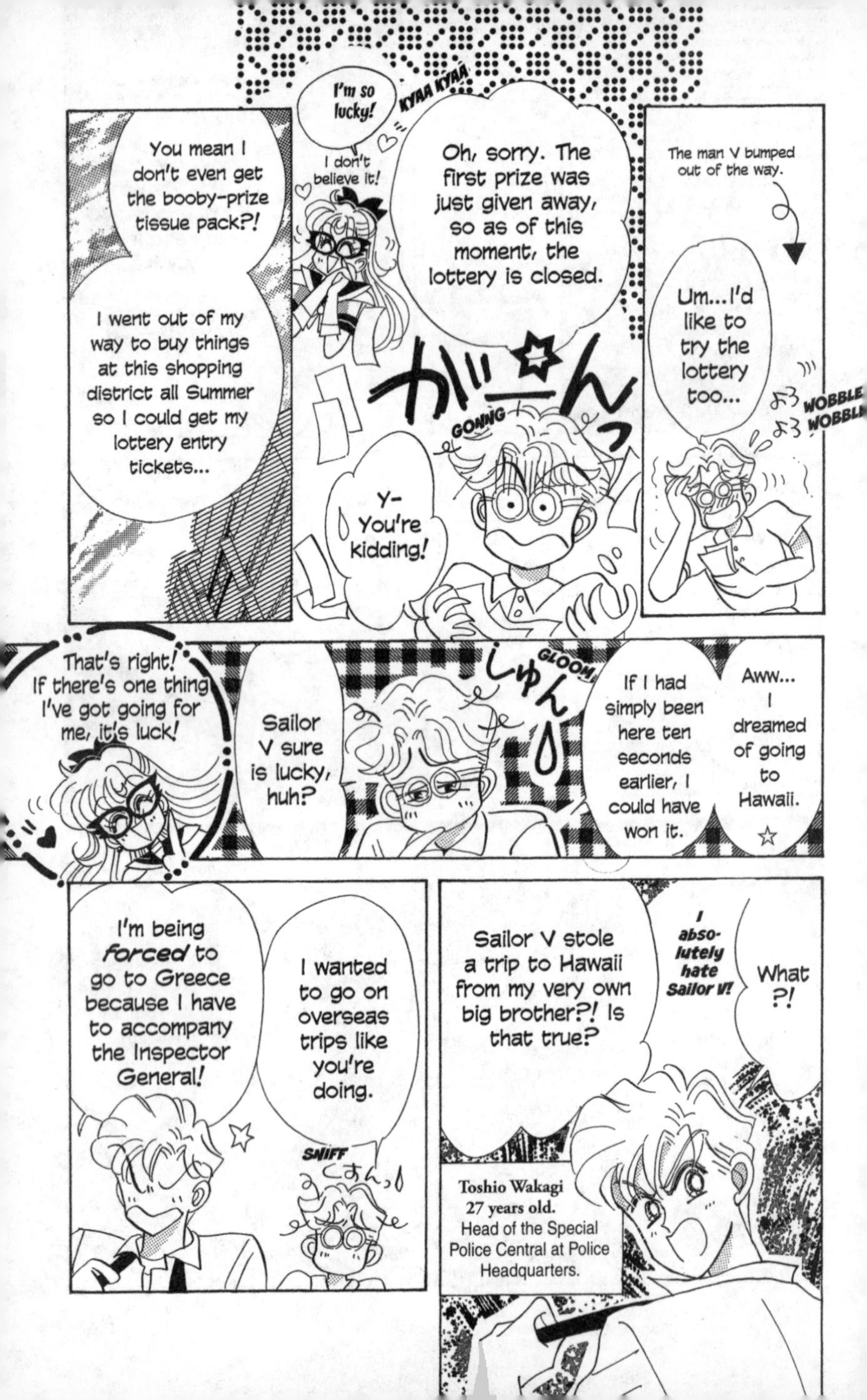

The man V bumped out of the way.
Um...I'd like to try the lottery too...
よろよろ
WOBBLE WOBBLE
Oh, sorry. The first prize was just given away, so as of this moment, the lottery is closed.
I'm so lucky!
KYAA KYAA
I don't believe it!
がーん
GONNG
Y- You're kidding!
You mean I don't even get the booby-prize tissue pack?!
I went out of my way to buy things at this shopping district all Summer so I could get my lottery entry tickets...
Aww... I dreamed of going to Hawaii.
If I had simply been here ten seconds earlier, I could have won it.
しゅん
GLOOM
Sailor V sure is lucky, huh?
That's right! If there's one thing I've got going for me, it's luck!
What?!
I absolutely hate Sailor V!
Sailor V stole a trip to Hawaii from my very own big brother?! Is that true?
Toshio Wakagi
27 years old.
Head of the Special Police Central at Police Headquarters.
I wanted to go on overseas trips like you're doing.
SNIFF
くすん
I'm being forced to go to Greece because I have to accompany the Inspector General!

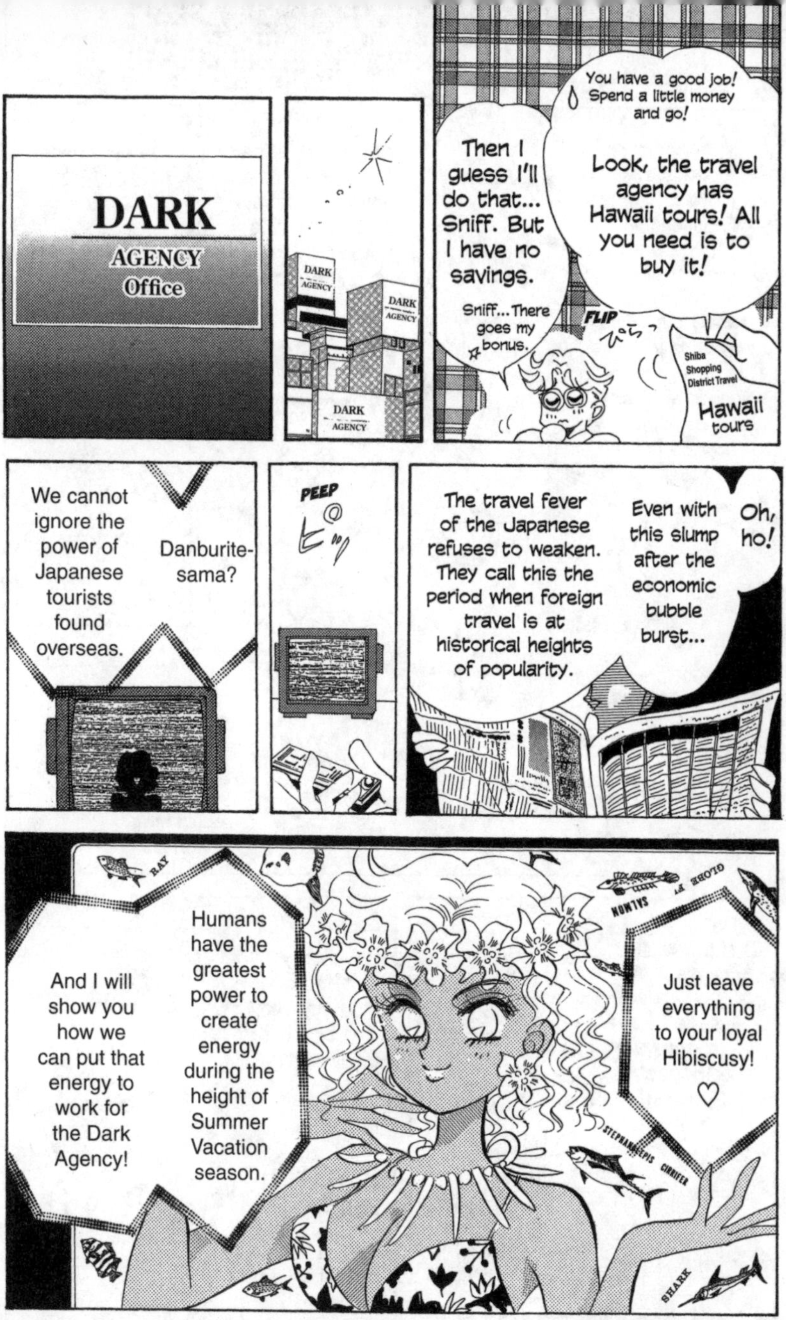
You have a good job! Spend a little money and go!
Look, the travel agency has Hawaii tours! All you need is to buy it!
Then I guess I'll do that... Sniff. But I have no savings.
Sniff... There goes my bonus.
FLIP
Shiba Shopping District Travel
Hawaii tours
DARK AGENCY
DARK AGENCY
DARK AGENCY
DARK AGENCY Office
Oh, ho!
Even with this slump after the economic bubble burst...
The travel fever of the Japanese refuses to weaken. They call this the period when foreign travel is at historical heights of popularity.
PEEP
Danburite-sama?
We cannot ignore the power of Japanese tourists found overseas.
Just leave everything to your loyal Hibiscusy! ♡
Humans have the greatest power to create energy during the height of Summer Vacation season.
And I will show you how we can put that energy to work for the Dark Agency!
RAY
SALMON
SHARK

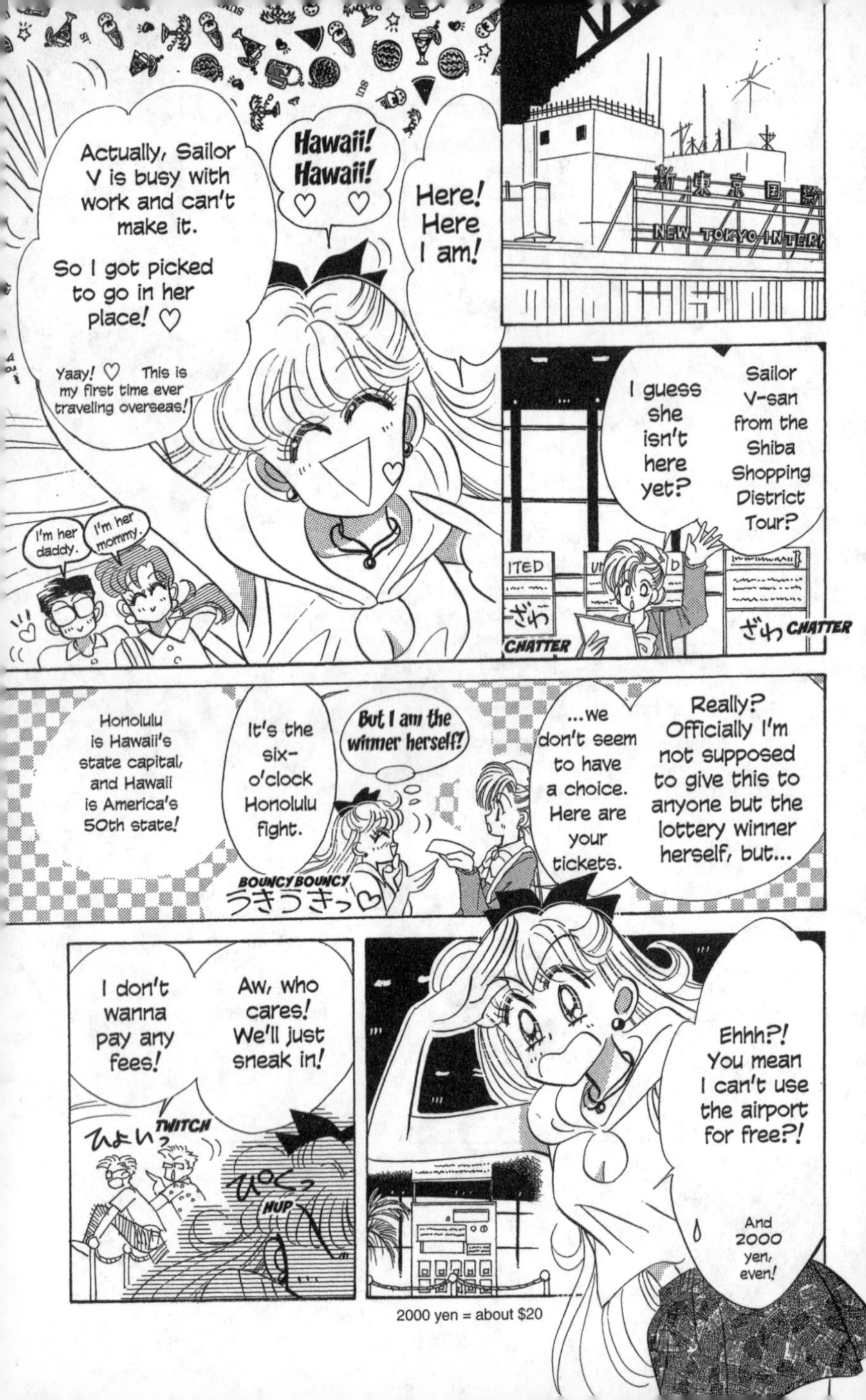

新東京国際
NEW TOKYO INTER
Sailor V-san from the Shiba Shopping District Tour?
I guess she isn't here yet?
ITED
ざわ CHATTER
ざわ CHATTER
Here! Here I am!
Hawaii! Hawaii! ♡ ♡
Actually, Sailor V is busy with work and can't make it.
So I got picked to go in her place! ♡
Yaay! ♡ This is my first time ever traveling overseas!
I'm her mommy.
I'm her daddy.
Really? Officially I'm not supposed to give this to anyone but the lottery winner herself, but...
...we don't seem to have a choice. Here are your tickets.
But I am the winner herself!
BOUNCY BOUNCY うきうきっ♡
It's the six-o'clock Honolulu fight.
Honolulu is Hawaii's state capital, and Hawaii is America's 50th state!
Ehhh?! You mean I can't use the airport for free?!
And 2000 yen, even!
Aw, who cares! We'll just sneak in!
I don't wanna pay any fees!
ひょいっ TWITCH
ぴくっ HUP

2000 yen = about $20

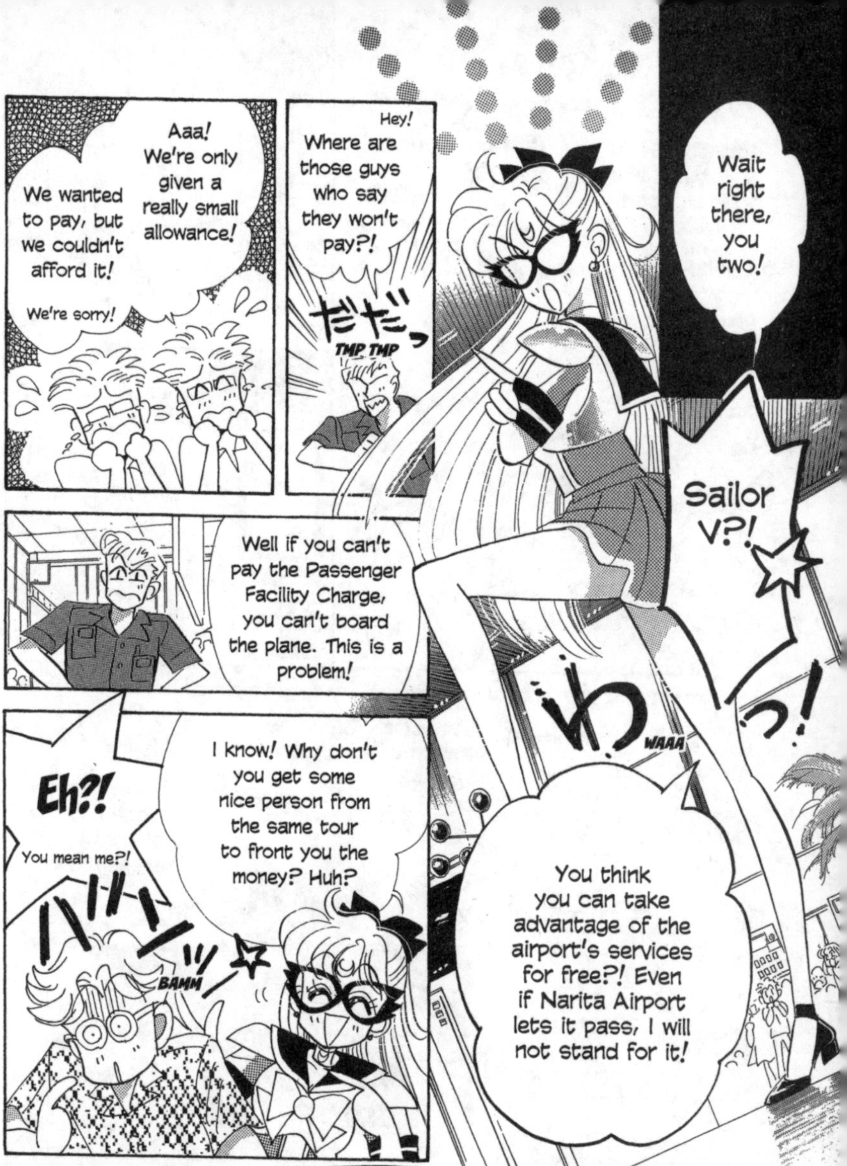
Wait right there, you two!
Sailor V?!
わっ!
WAAA
You think you can take advantage of the airport's services for free?! Even if Narita Airport lets it pass, I will not stand for it!
Hey!
Where are those guys who say they won't pay?!
だだっ
TMP TMP
Aaa! We're only given a really small allowance!
We wanted to pay, but we couldn't afford it!
We're sorry!
Well if you can't pay the Passenger Facility Charge, you can't board the plane. This is a problem!
I know! Why don't you get some nice person from the same tour to front you the money? Huh?
Eh?!
You mean me?!
BAMM
..
..
Waah! But why me...? My own allowance...

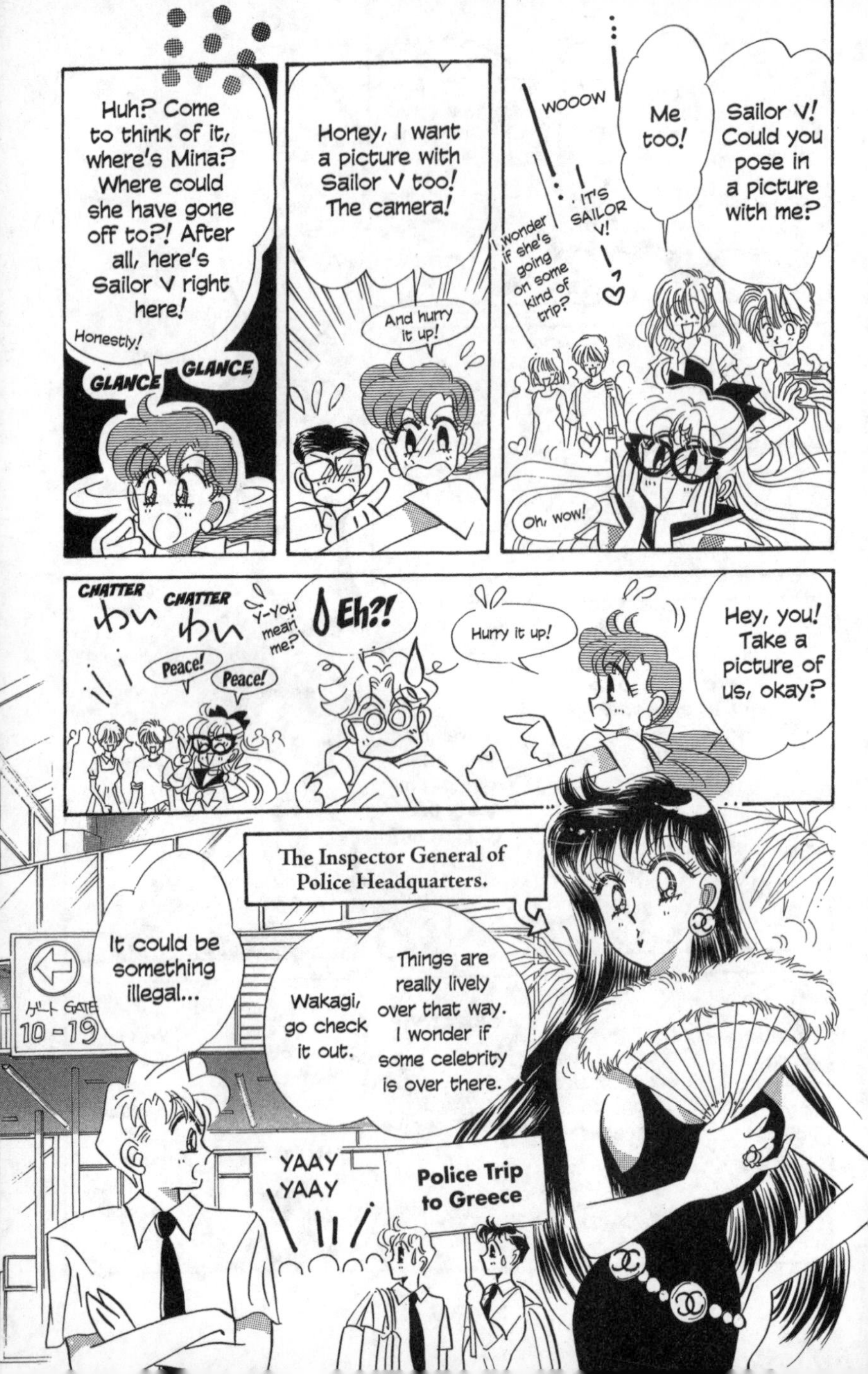
Sailor V! Could you pose in a picture with me?
Me too!
WOOOW
IT'S SAILOR V!
I wonder if she's going on some kind of trip?
Oh, wow!
Honey, I want a picture with Sailor V too! The camera!
And hurry it up!
Huh? Come to think of it, where's Mina? Where could she have gone off to?! After all, here's Sailor V right here!
Honestly!
GLANCE
GLANCE
Hey, you! Take a picture of us, okay?
Hurry it up!
Eh?!
Y-You mean me?
Peace!
Peace!
CHATTER わい
CHATTER わい
The Inspector General of Police Headquarters.
Things are really lively over that way. I wonder if some celebrity is over there.
Wakagi, go check it out.
It could be something illegal...
ゲート GATE
10-19
YAAY YAAY
Police Trip to Greece

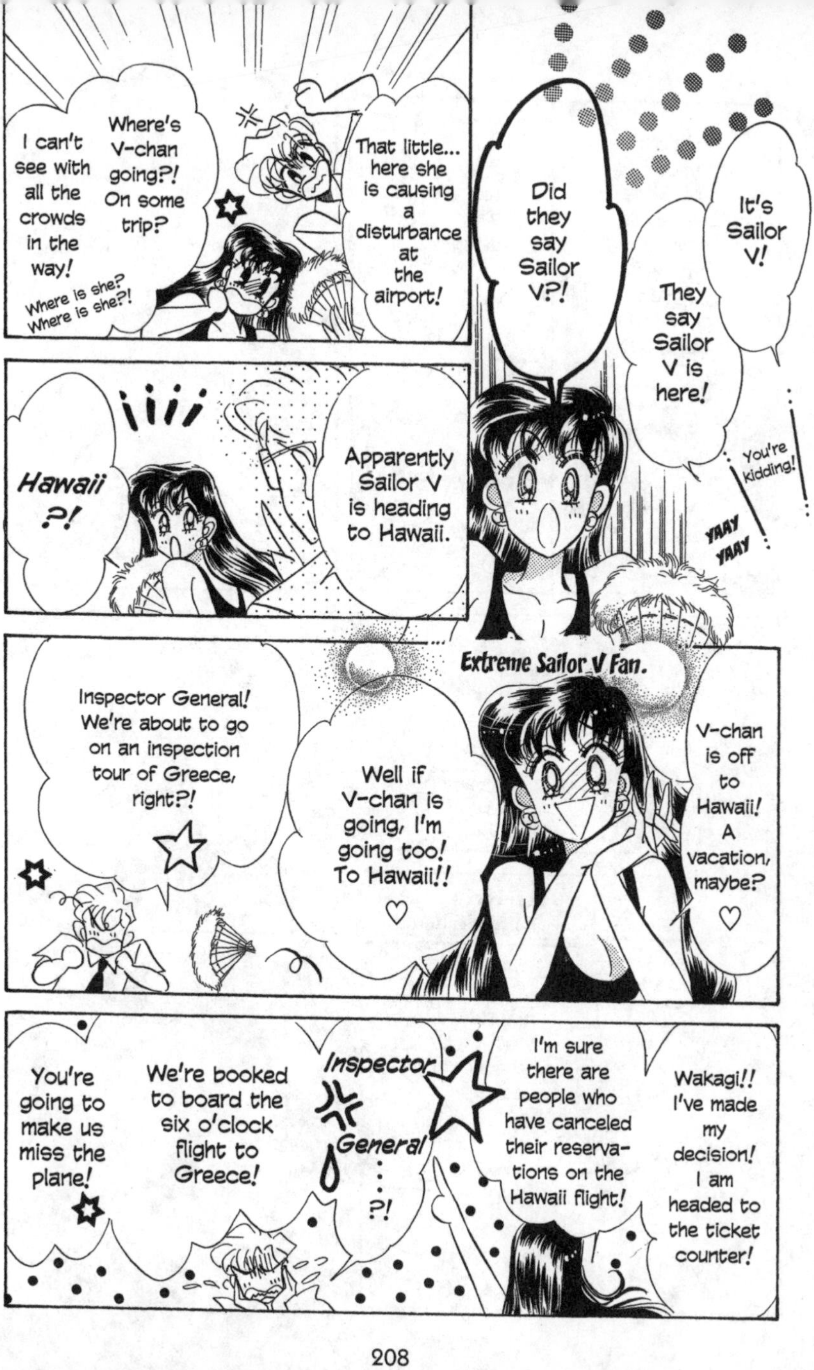

It's Sailor V!
They say Sailor V is here!
You're kidding!
YAAY YAAY
Did they say Sailor V?!
That little... here she is causing a disturbance at the airport!
Where's V-chan going?! On some trip?
I can't see with all the crowds in the way!
Where is she? Where is she?!
Apparently Sailor V is heading to Hawaii.
Hawaii ?!
Extreme Sailor V Fan.
V-chan is off to Hawaii! A vacation, maybe? ♡
Well if V-chan is going, I'm going too! To Hawaii!! ♡
Inspector General! We're about to go on an inspection tour of Greece, right?!
Wakagi!! I've made my decision! I am headed to the ticket counter!
I'm sure there are people who have canceled their reserva-tions on the Hawaii flight!
Inspector General . . . ?!
We're booked to board the six o'clock flight to Greece!
You're going to make us miss the plane!

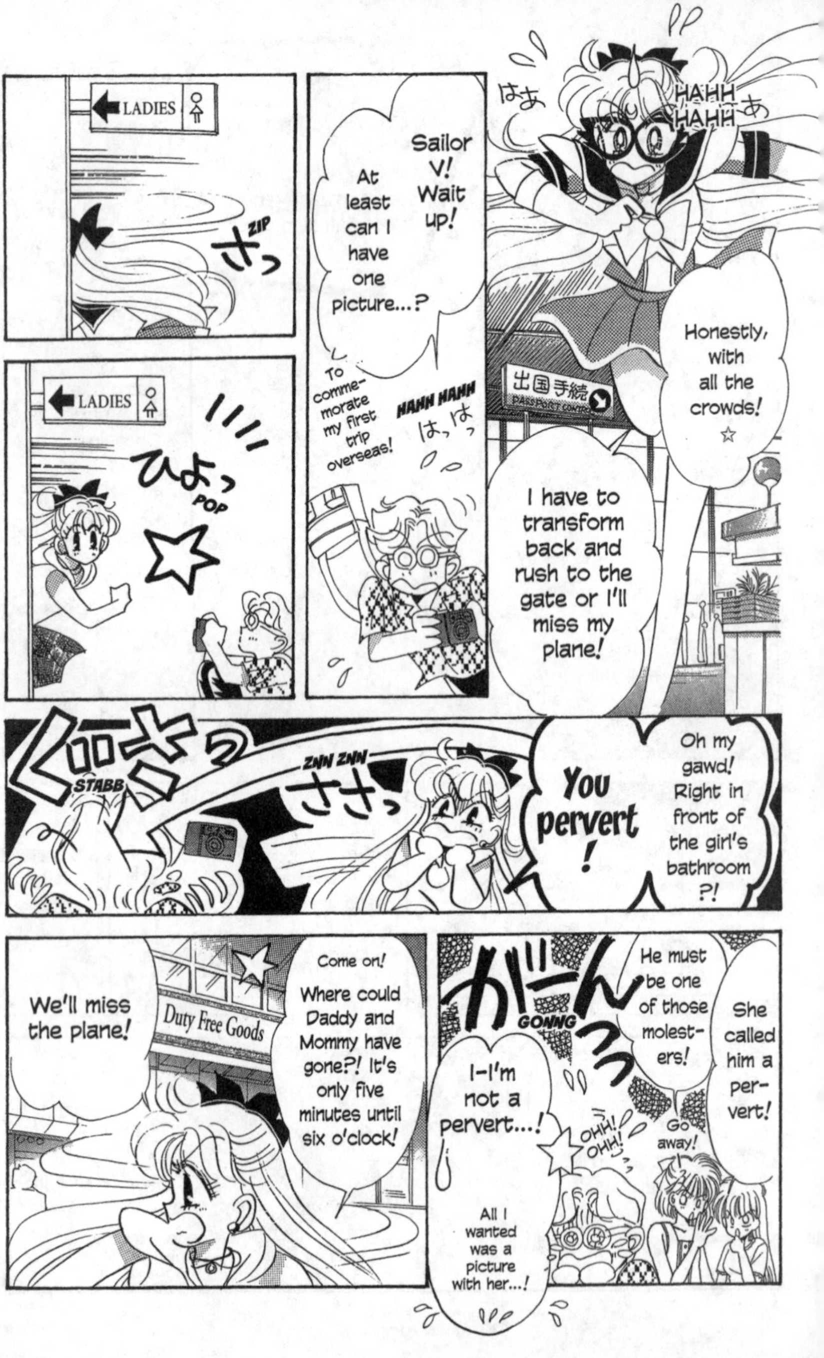
はあ
HAHH HAHH
あ
出国手続
Honestly, with all the crowds! ☆
I have to transform back and rush to the gate or I'll miss my plane!
Sailor V! Wait up!
At least can I have one picture...?
To commemorate my first trip overseas!
HAHH HAHH
はっはっ
LADIES
さっ
ZIP
LADIES
ひょっ
POP
Oh my gawd! Right in front of the girl's bathroom?!
You pervert!
ZNN ZNN
ささっ
STABB
She called him a pervert!
He must be one of those molesters!
Go away!
がーんっ
GONNG
OHH! OHH!
I-I'm not a pervert...!
All I wanted was a picture with her...!
Come on! Where could Daddy and Mommy have gone?! It's only five minutes until six o'clock!
Duty Free Goods
We'll miss the plane!

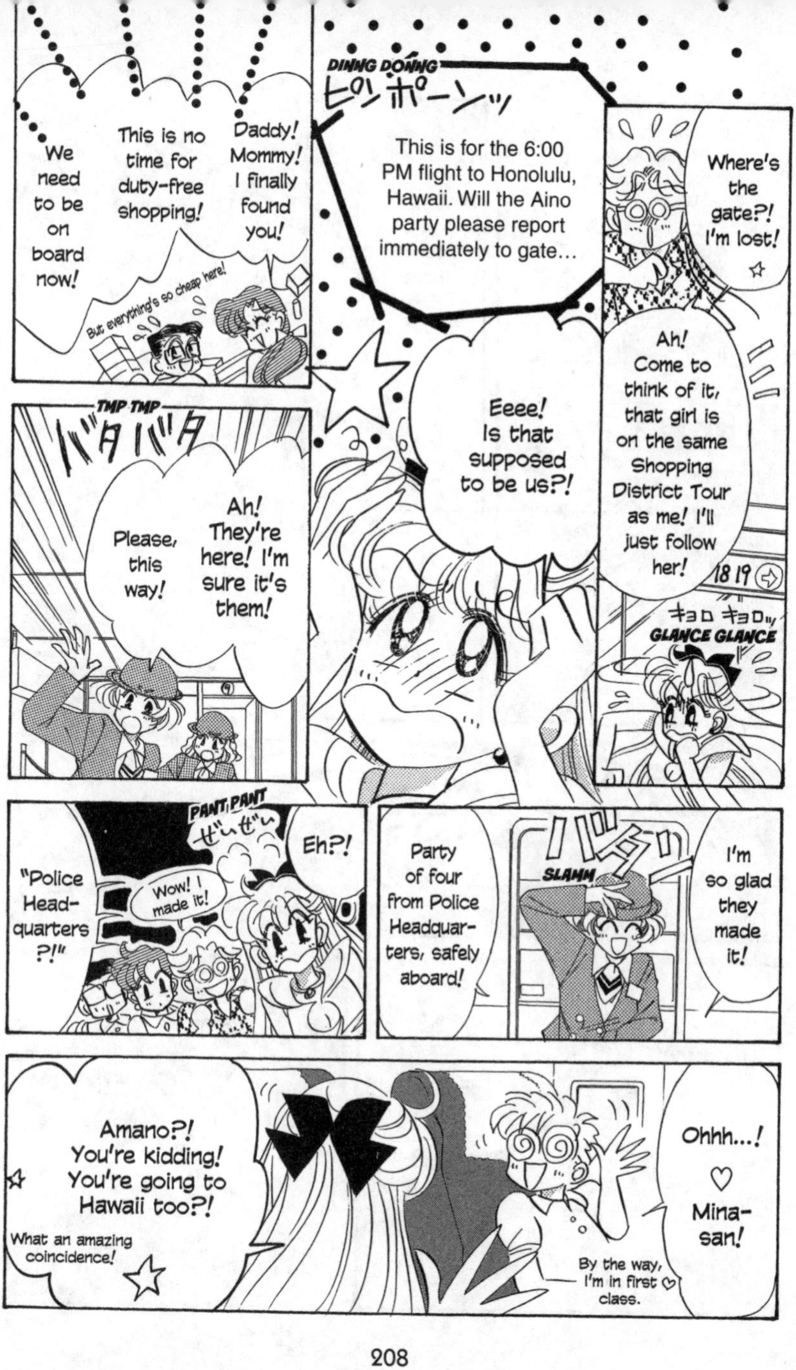
DING DONG
ピンポーンッ
This is for the 6:00 PM flight to Honolulu, Hawaii. Will the Aino party please report immediately to gate…
Where's the gate?! I'm lost!
Ah! Come to think of it, that girl is on the same Shopping District Tour as me! I'll just follow her!
18 19
キョロ キョロッ
GLANCE GLANCE
Eeee! Is that supposed to be us?!
Daddy! Mommy! I finally found you!
This is no time for duty-free shopping!
We need to be on board now!
But everything's so cheap here!
TMP TMP
バタバタ
Ah! They're here! I'm sure it's them!
Please, this way!
I'm so glad they made it!
SLAMM
バタンッ
Party of four from Police Headquarters, safely aboard!
Eh?!
PANT PANT
ぜいぜい
Wow! I made it!
"Police Head-quarters?!"
Ohhh...! ♡ Mina-san!
By the way, I'm in first ♡ class.
Amano?! You're kidding! You're going to Hawaii too?!
What an amazing coincidence!

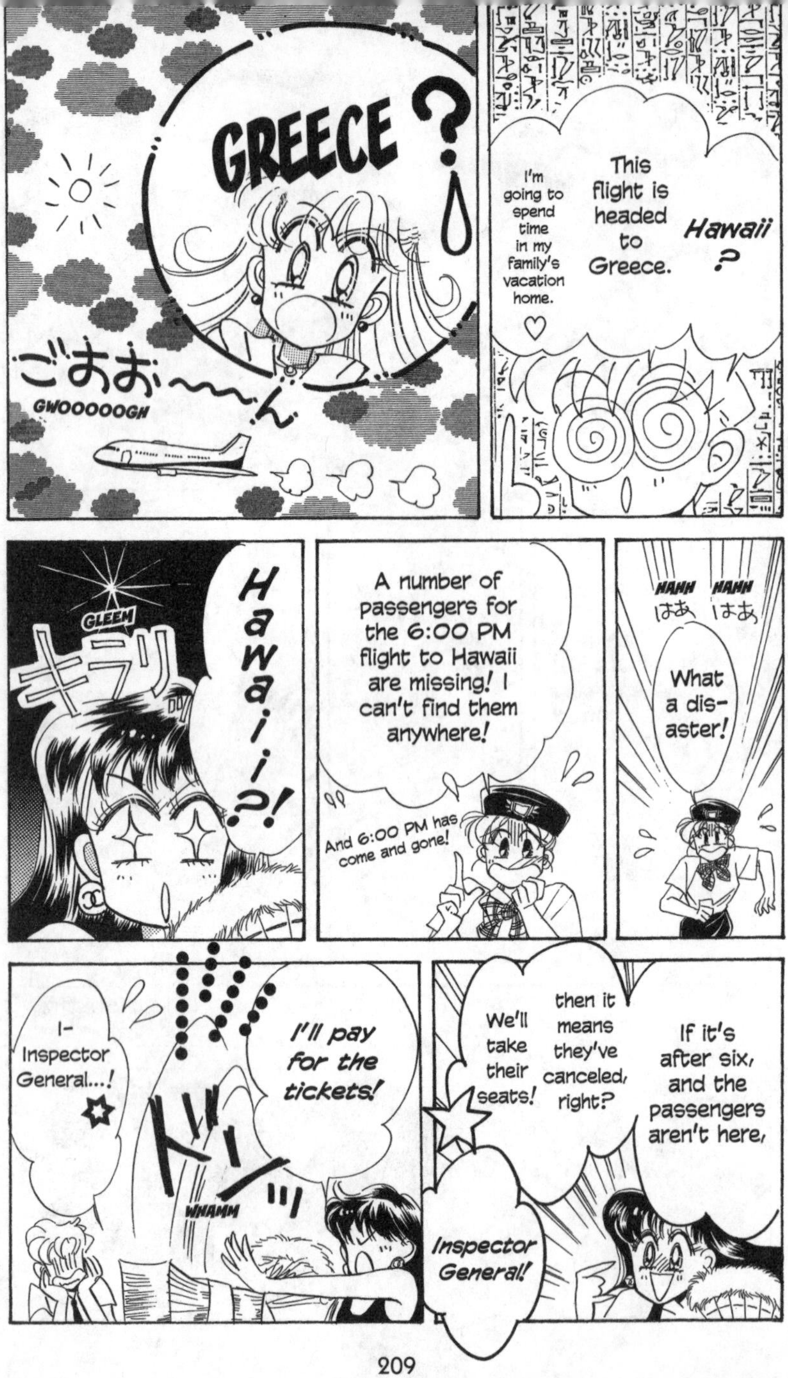
Hawaii?
This flight is headed to Greece.
I'm going to spend time in my family's vacation home. ♡
GREECE?
ごおお〜〜ん
GWOOOOOGH
はあ はあ
HAHH HAHH
What a disaster!
A number of passengers for the 6:00 PM flight to Hawaii are missing! I can't find them anywhere!
And 6:00 PM has come and gone!
Hawaii?!
キラリ
GLEEM
If it's after six, and the passengers aren't here,
then it means they've canceled, right?
We'll take their seats!
Inspector General!
I'll pay for the tickets!
ドン
WHAMM
I- Inspector General...!

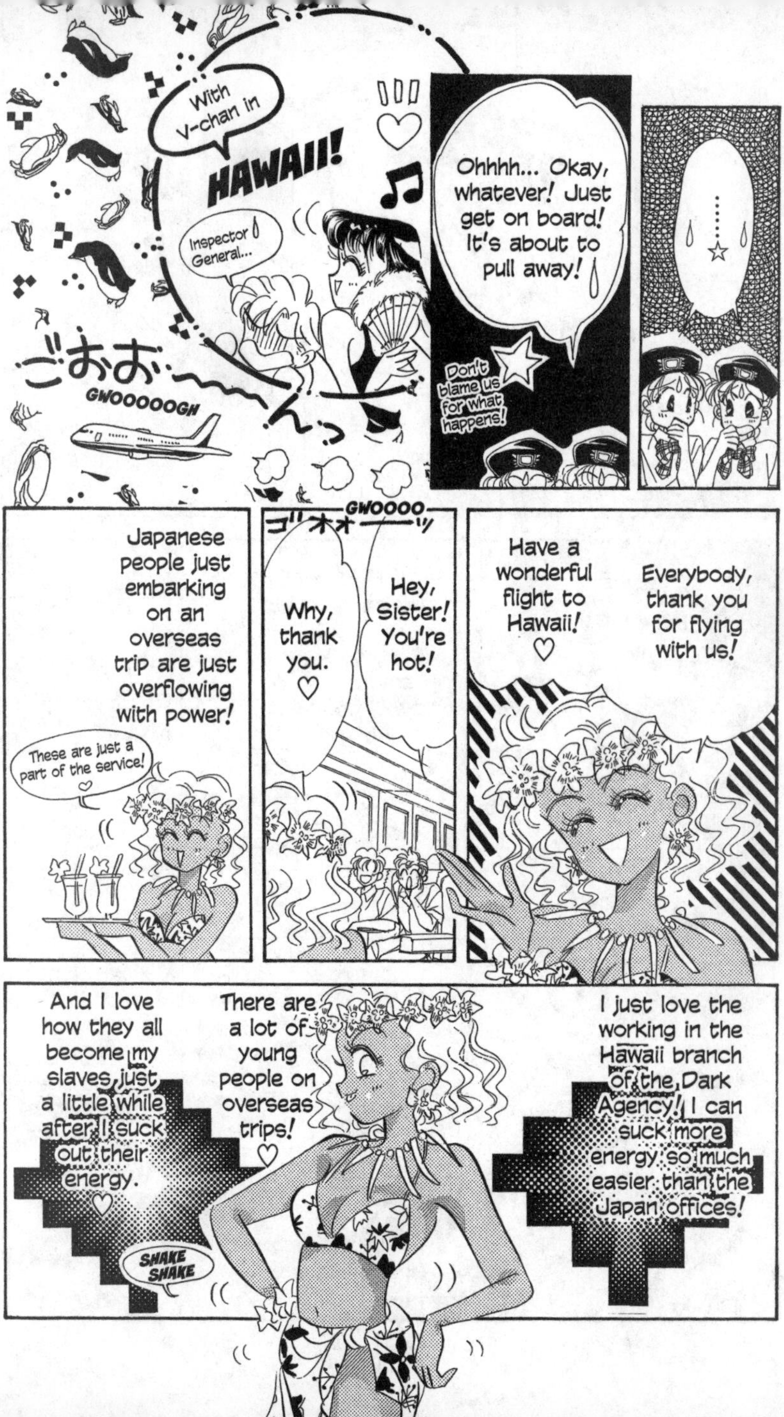

Ohhhh... Okay, whatever! Just get on board! It's about to pull away!
Don't blame us for what happens!
With V-chan in HAWAII!
Inspector General...
ごおお〜んっ
GWOOOOOGH
Everybody, thank you for flying with us!
Have a wonderful flight to Hawaii! ♡
ゴオオーーッ
GWOOOO
Hey, Sister! You're hot!
Why, thank you. ♡
Japanese people just embarking on an overseas trip are just overflowing with power!
These are just a part of the service! ♡
I just love the working in the Hawaii branch of the Dark Agency! I can suck more energy so much easier than the Japan offices!
There are a lot of young people on overseas trips! ♡
And I love how they all become my slaves just a little while after I suck out their energy. ♡
SHAKE SHAKE

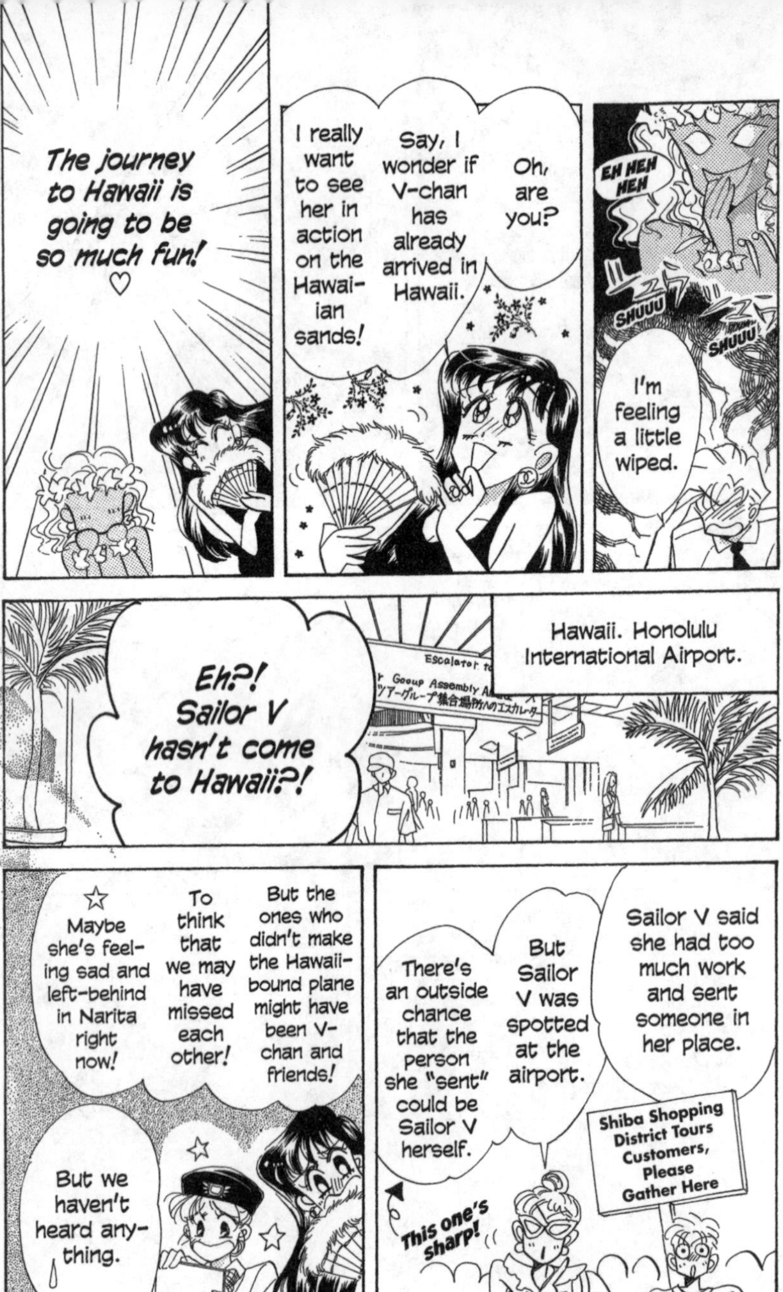
EH HEH HEH
SHUUU
SHUUU
I'm feeling a little wiped.
Oh, are you?
Say, I wonder if V-chan has already arrived in Hawaii.
I really want to see her in action on the Hawaiian sands!
The journey to Hawaii is going to be so much fun! ♡
Hawaii. Honolulu International Airport.
ツアーグループ集合場所へのエスカレータ
Eh?! Sailor V hasn't come to Hawaii?!
Sailor V said she had too much work and sent someone in her place.
But Sailor V was spotted at the airport.
There's an outside chance that the person she "sent" could be Sailor V herself.
This one's sharp!
Shiba Shopping District Tours Customers, Please Gather Here
But the ones who didn't make the Hawaii-bound plane might have been V-chan and friends!
To think that we may have missed each other!
☆ Maybe she's feeling sad and left-behind in Narita right now!
But we haven't heard anything.

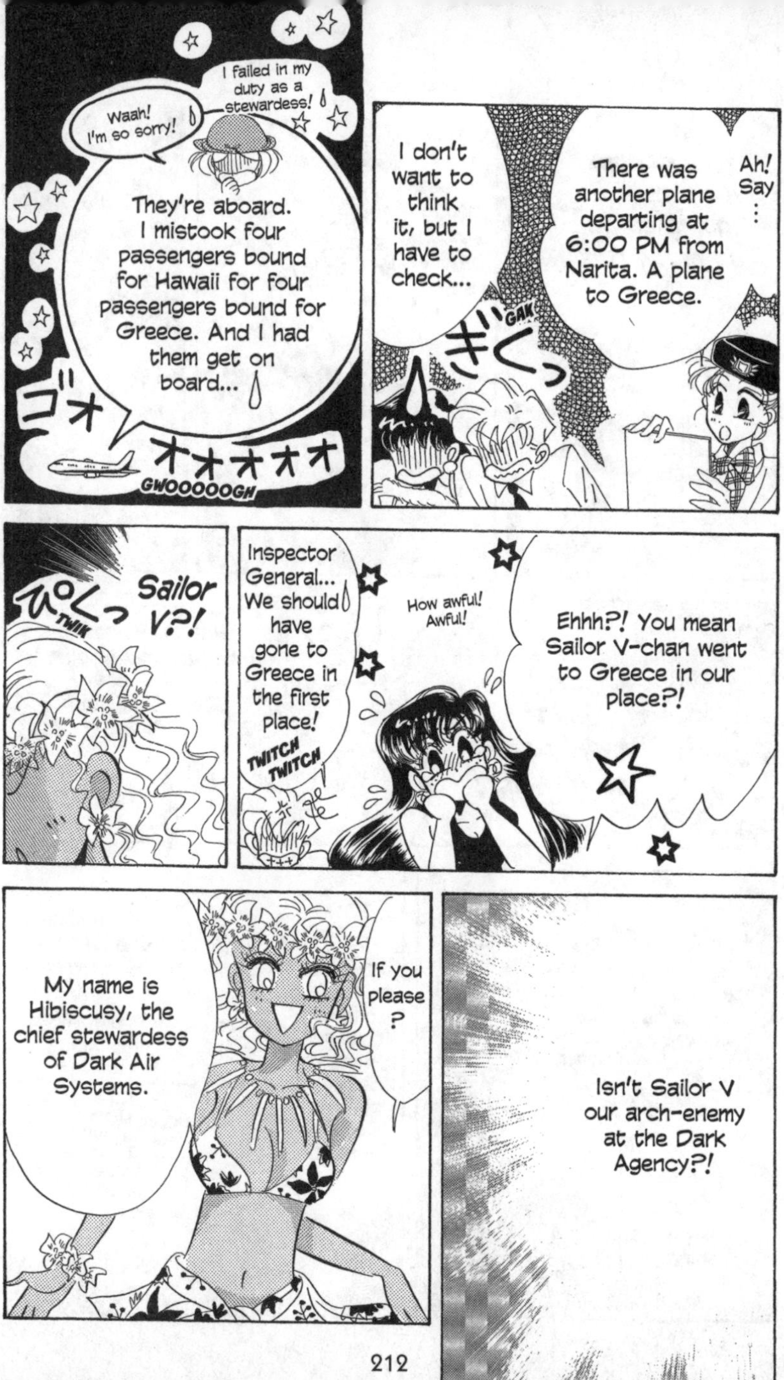
Ah! Say ...
There was another plane departing at 6:00 PM from Narita. A plane to Greece.
I don't want to think it, but I have to check...
ぎくっ
GAK
I failed in my duty as a stewardess!
Waah! I'm so sorry!
They're aboard. I mistook four passengers bound for Hawaii for four passengers bound for Greece. And I had them get on board...
ゴオオオオオオ
GWOOOOOGH
Ehhh?! You mean Sailor V-chan went to Greece in our place?!
How awful! Awful!
Inspector General... We should have gone to Greece in the first place!
TWITCH TWITCH
Sailor V?!
ぴくっ
TWIK
Isn't Sailor V our arch-enemy at the Dark Agency?!
If you please ?
My name is Hibiscusy, the chief stewardess of Dark Air Systems.

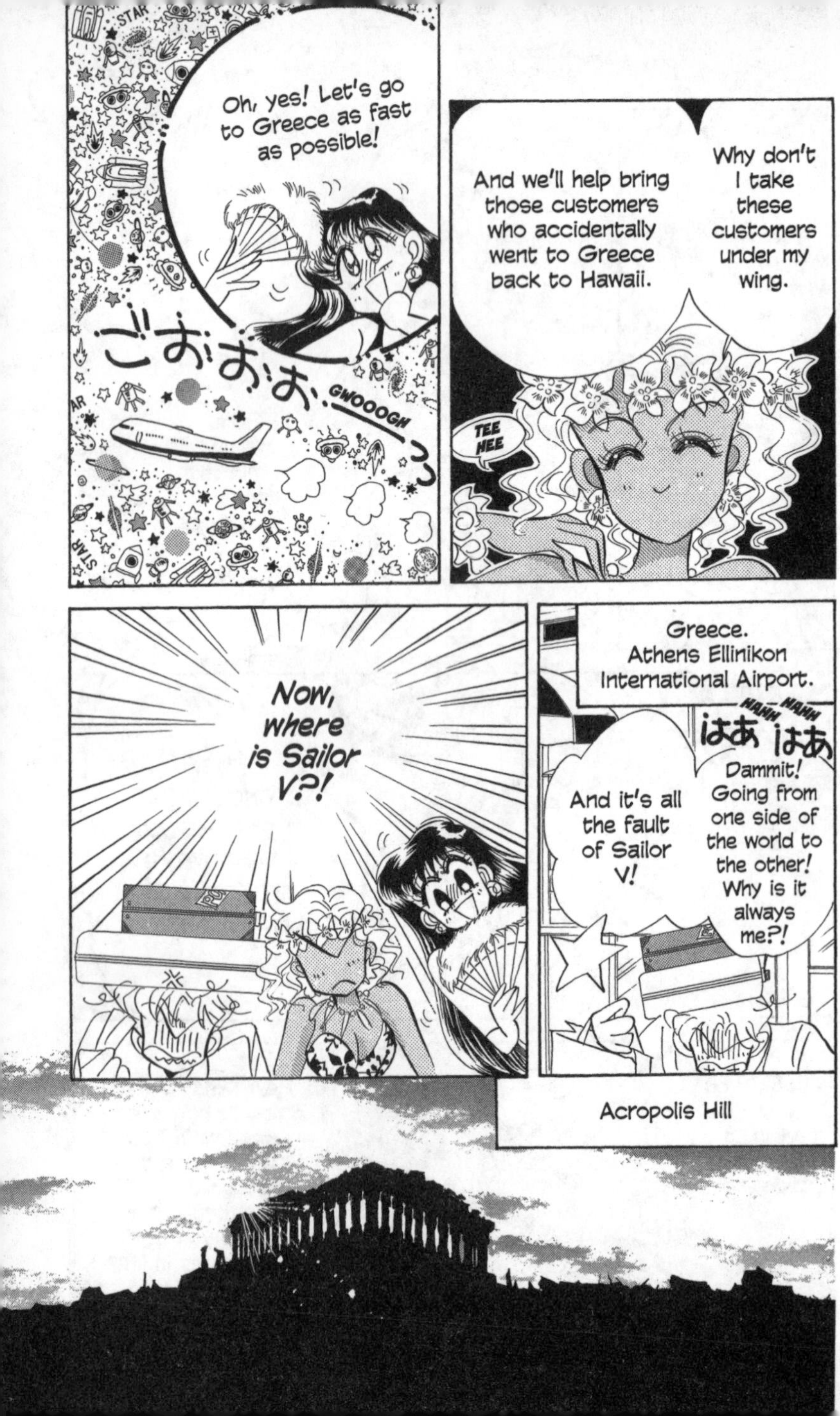
Why don't I take these customers under my wing.
And we'll help bring those customers who accidentally went to Greece back to Hawaii.
TEE HEE
Oh, yes! Let's go to Greece as fast as possible!
ごおおお
GWOOOGH
Greece. Athens Ellinikon International Airport.
はあ はあ
HAHH HAHH
Dammit! Going from one side of the world to the other! Why is it always me?!
And it's all the fault of Sailor V!
Now, where is Sailor V?!
Acropolis Hill

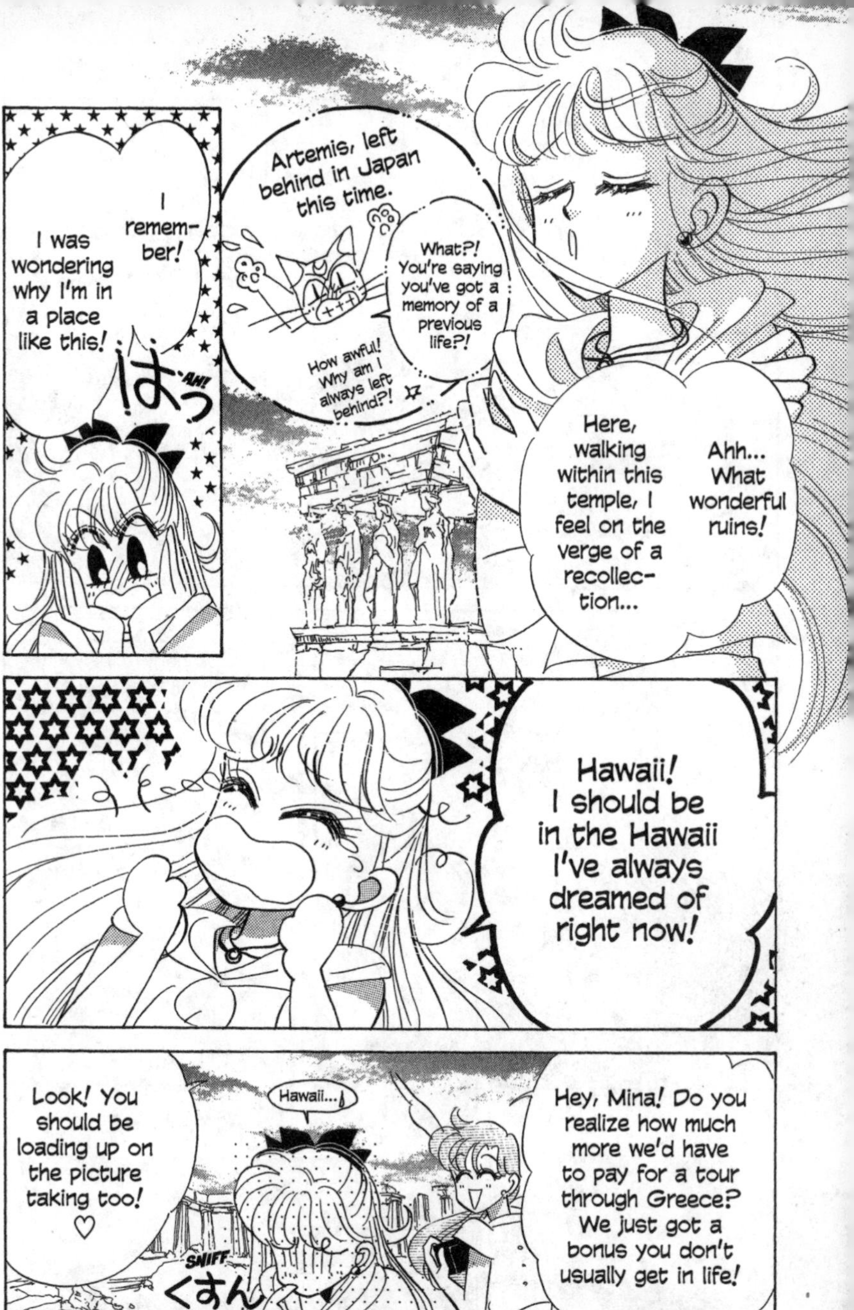
Ahh... What wonderful ruins!
Here, walking within this temple, I feel on the verge of a recollection...
Artemis, left behind in Japan this time.
What?! You're saying you've got a memory of a previous life?!
How awful! Why am I always left behind?!
I remember!
I was wondering why I'm in a place like this!
はっ
AH!
Hawaii! I should be in the Hawaii I've always dreamed of right now!
Hey, Mina! Do you realize how much more we'd have to pay for a tour through Greece? We just got a bonus you don't usually get in life!
Hawaii...
SNIFF
くすん
Look! You should be loading up on the picture taking too! ♡

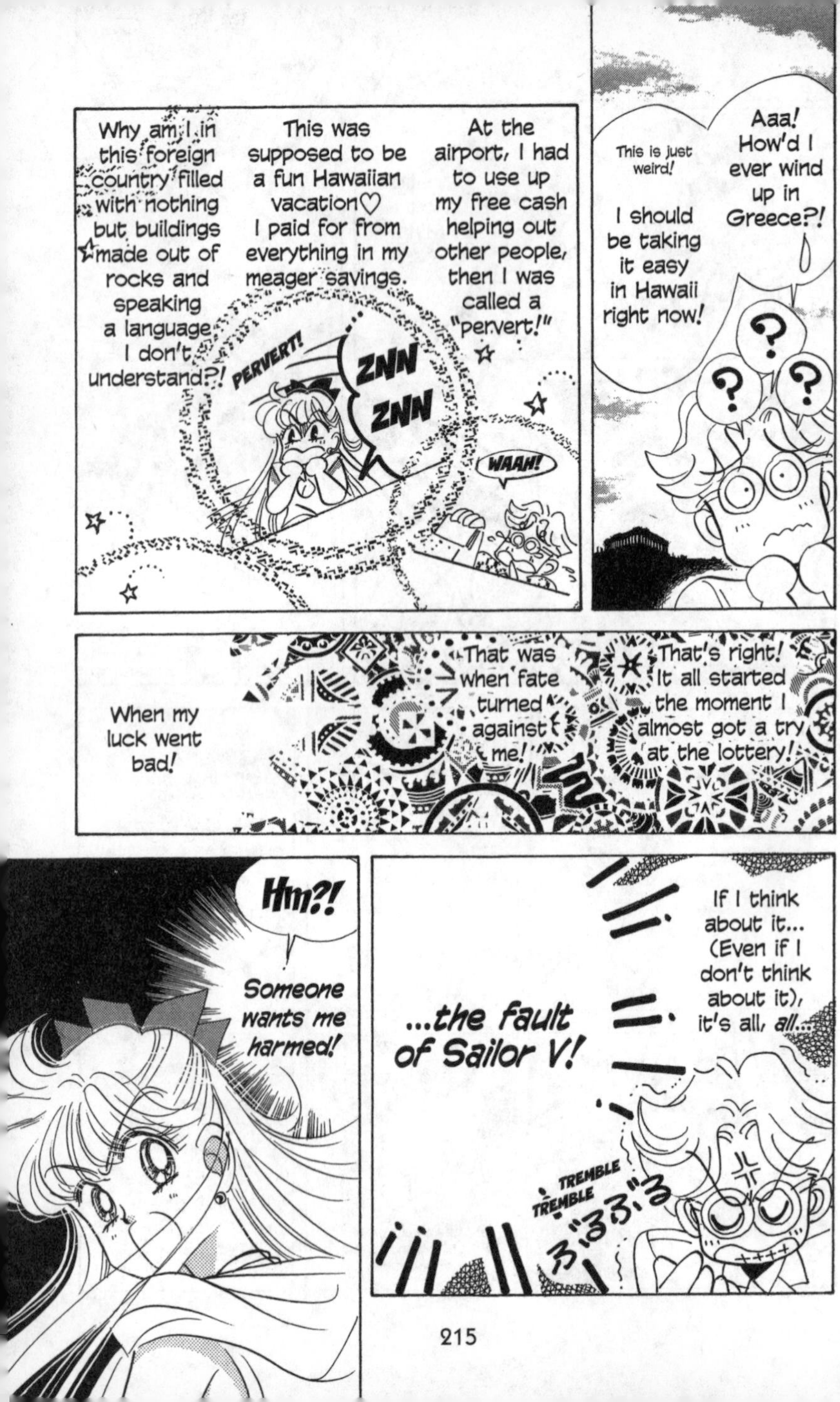
Aaa! How'd I ever wind up in Greece?!
This is just weird!
I should be taking it easy in Hawaii right now!
At the airport, I had to use up my free cash helping out other people, then I was called a "pervert!"
This was supposed to be a fun Hawaiian vacation♡ I paid for from everything in my meager savings.
Why am I in this foreign country filled with nothing but buildings made out of rocks and speaking a language I don't understand?!
PERVERT!
ZNN
ZNN
WAAH!
That's right! It all started the moment I almost got a try at the lottery!
That was when fate turned against me!
When my luck went bad!
If I think about it... (Even if I don't think about it), it's all, *all*...
...the fault of Sailor V!
TREMBLE
TREMBLE
ぶるぶる
Hm?!
Someone wants me harmed!

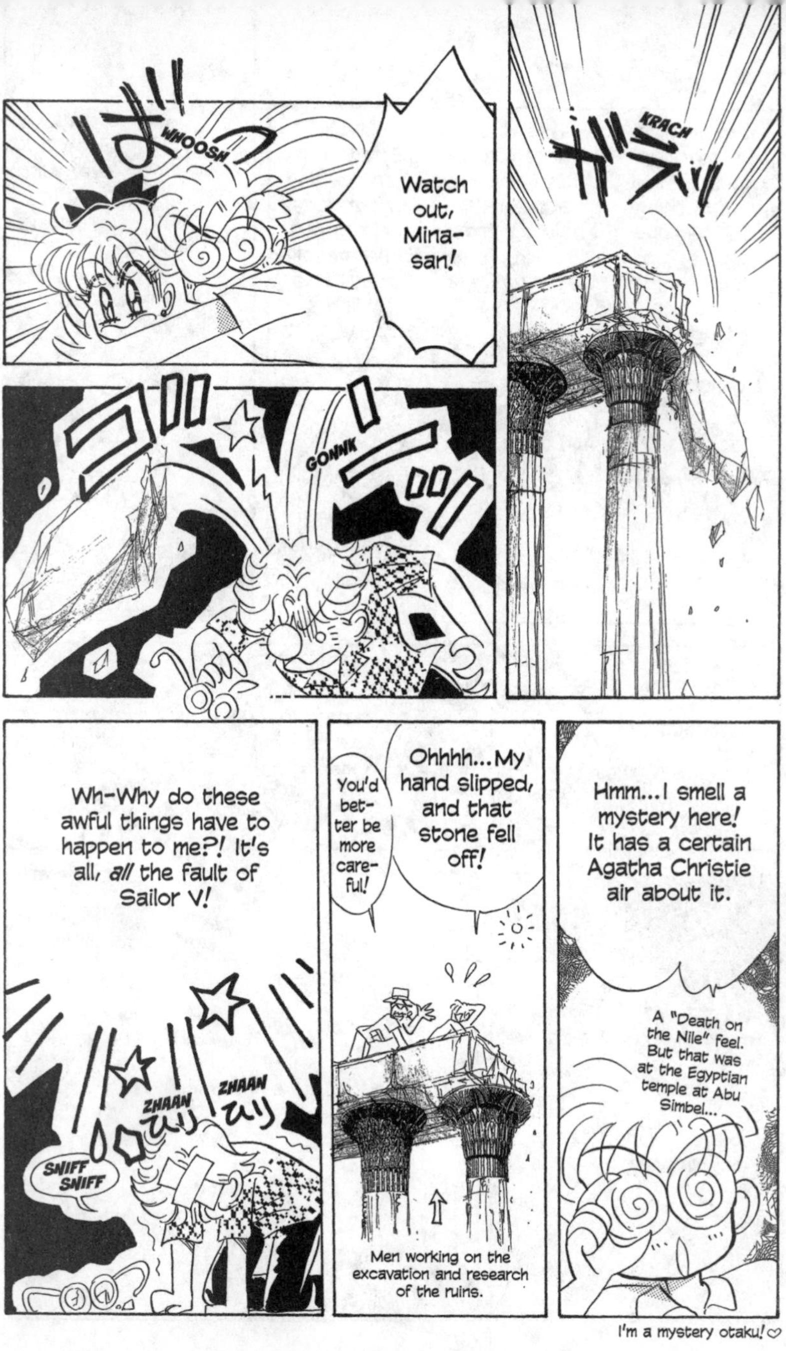
KRACH
WHOOSH
Watch out, Mina-san!
GONNK
Hmm...I smell a mystery here! It has a certain Agatha Christie air about it.
A "Death on the Nile" feel. But that was at the Egyptian temple at Abu Simbel...
Ohhhh...My hand slipped, and that stone fell off!
You'd better be more careful!
Men working on the excavation and research of the ruins.
Wh-Why do these awful things have to happen to me?! It's all, *all* the fault of Sailor V!
ZHAAN
ZHAAN
SNIFF SNIFF
I'm a mystery otaku!♡

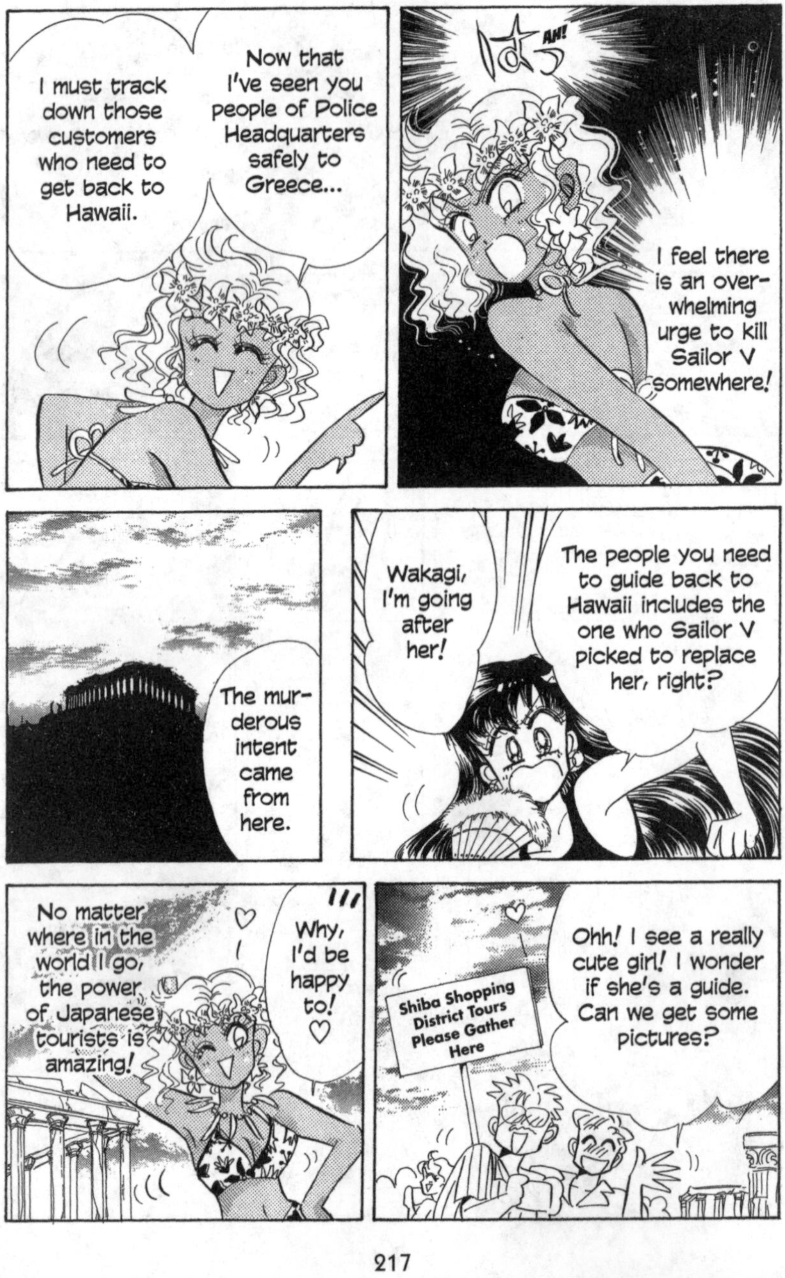
はっ
AH!
I feel there is an over-whelming urge to kill Sailor V somewhere!
Now that I've seen you people of Police Headquarters safely to Greece...
I must track down those customers who need to get back to Hawaii.
The people you need to guide back to Hawaii includes the one who Sailor V picked to replace her, right?
Wakagi, I'm going after her!
The mur-derous intent came from here.
Ohh! I see a really cute girl! I wonder if she's a guide. Can we get some pictures?
Shiba Shopping District Tours Please Gather Here
Why, I'd be happy to! ♡
No matter where in the world I go, the power of Japanese tourists is amazing!

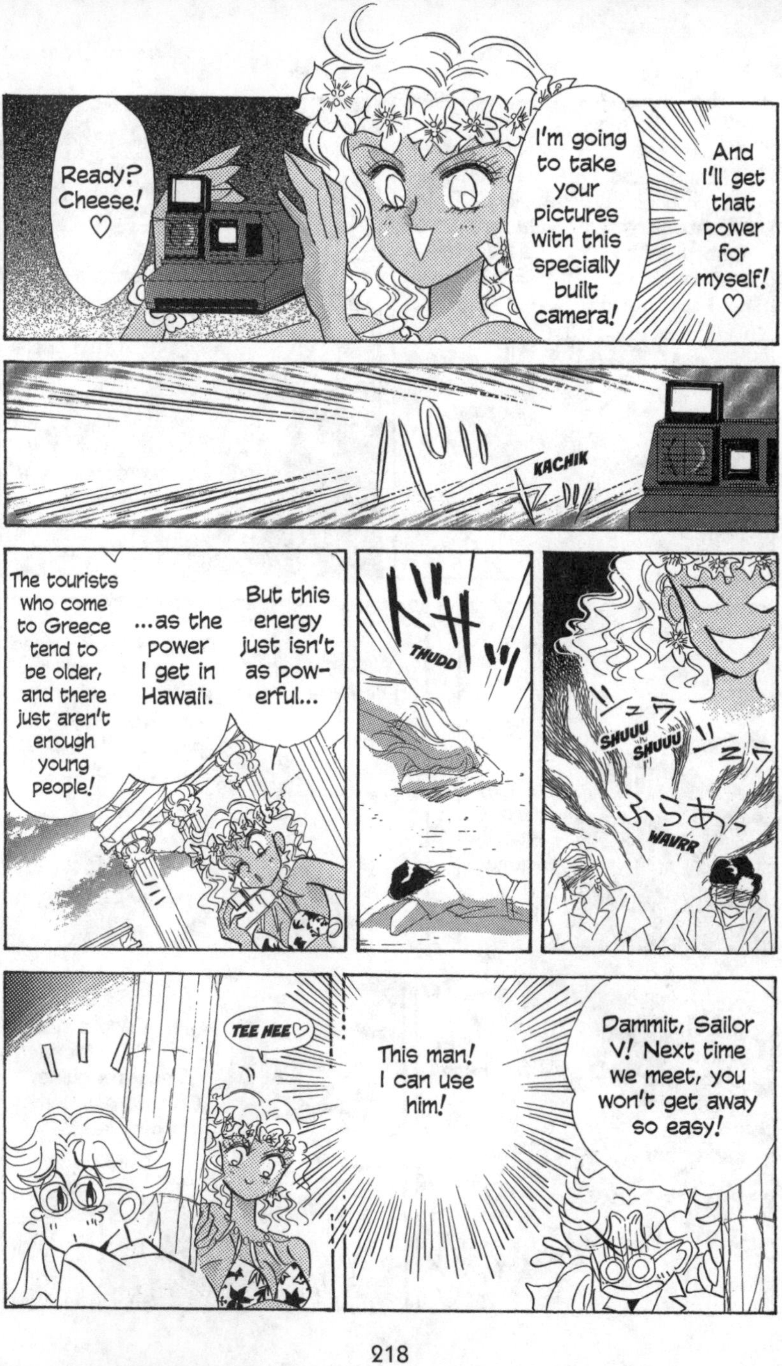
I'm going to take your pictures with this specially built camera!
And I'll get that power for myself! ♡
Ready? Cheese! ♡
KACHIK
SHUUU SHUUU
WAVRR
THUDD
But this energy just isn't as powerful...
...as the power I get in Hawaii.
The tourists who come to Greece tend to be older, and there just aren't enough young people!
Dammit, Sailor V! Next time we meet, you won't get away so easy!
This man! I can use him!
TEE HEE♡

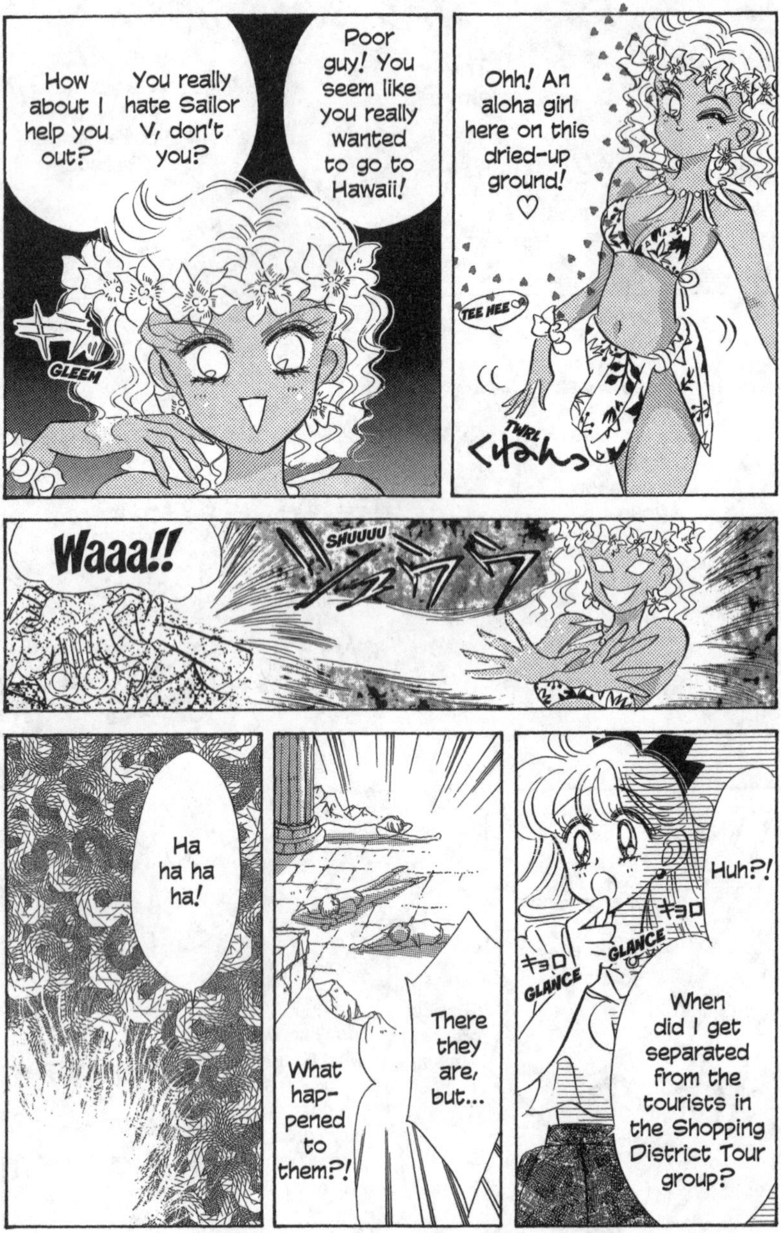
Ohh! An aloha girl here on this dried-up ground! ♡
TEE HEE
TWRL
くりんっ
Poor guy! You seem like you really wanted to go to Hawaii!
You really hate Sailor V, don't you?
How about I help you out?
GLEEM
SHUUUU
Waaa!!
Huh?!
キョロ
GLANCE
キョロ
GLANCE
When did I get separated from the tourists in the Shopping District Tour group?
There they are, but...
What hap-pened to them?!
Ha ha ha ha!

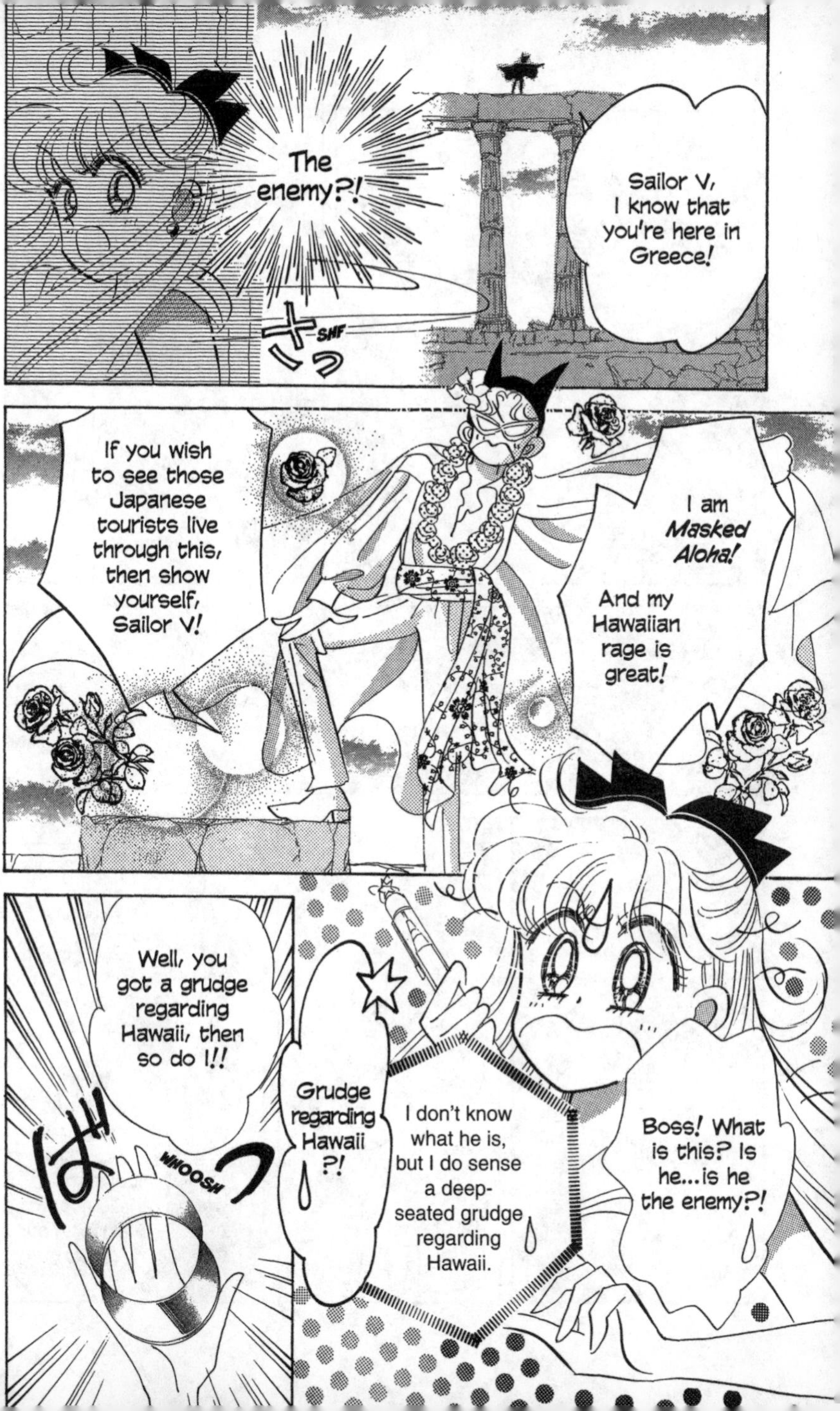
Sailor V, I know that you're here in Greece!
The enemy?!
さっ SHF
I am *Masked Aloha!*
And my Hawaiian rage is great!
If you wish to see those Japanese tourists live through this, then show yourself, Sailor V!
Boss! What is this? Is he...is he the enemy?!
I don't know what he is, but I do sense a deep-seated grudge regarding Hawaii.
Grudge regarding Hawaii ?!
Well, you got a grudge regarding Hawaii, then so do I!!
はっ WHOOSH

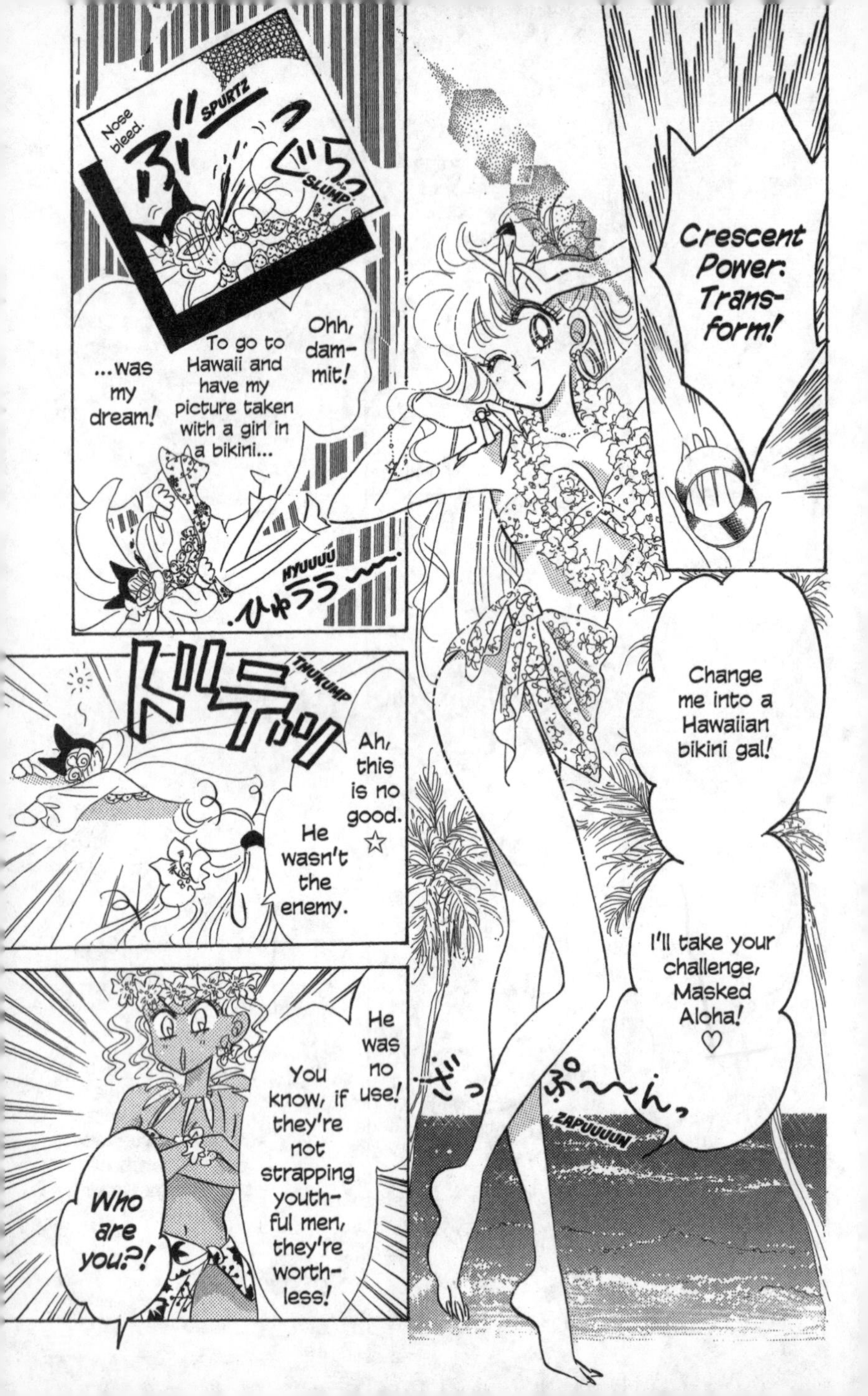
ぶーっ
SPURTZ
Nose bleed.
ぐらっ
SLUMP
Ohh, dam-mit!
To go to Hawaii and have my picture taken with a girl in a bikini...
...was my dream!
ひゅるる〜
HYUUUU
THUKUMP
Ah, this is no good. ☆
He wasn't the enemy.
He was no use!
You know, if they're not strapping youth-ful men, they're worth-less!
Who are you?!
Crescent Power: Trans-form!
Change me into a Hawaiian bikini gal!
I'll take your challenge, Masked Aloha! ♡
ざっぷ〜ん
ZAPUUUUN

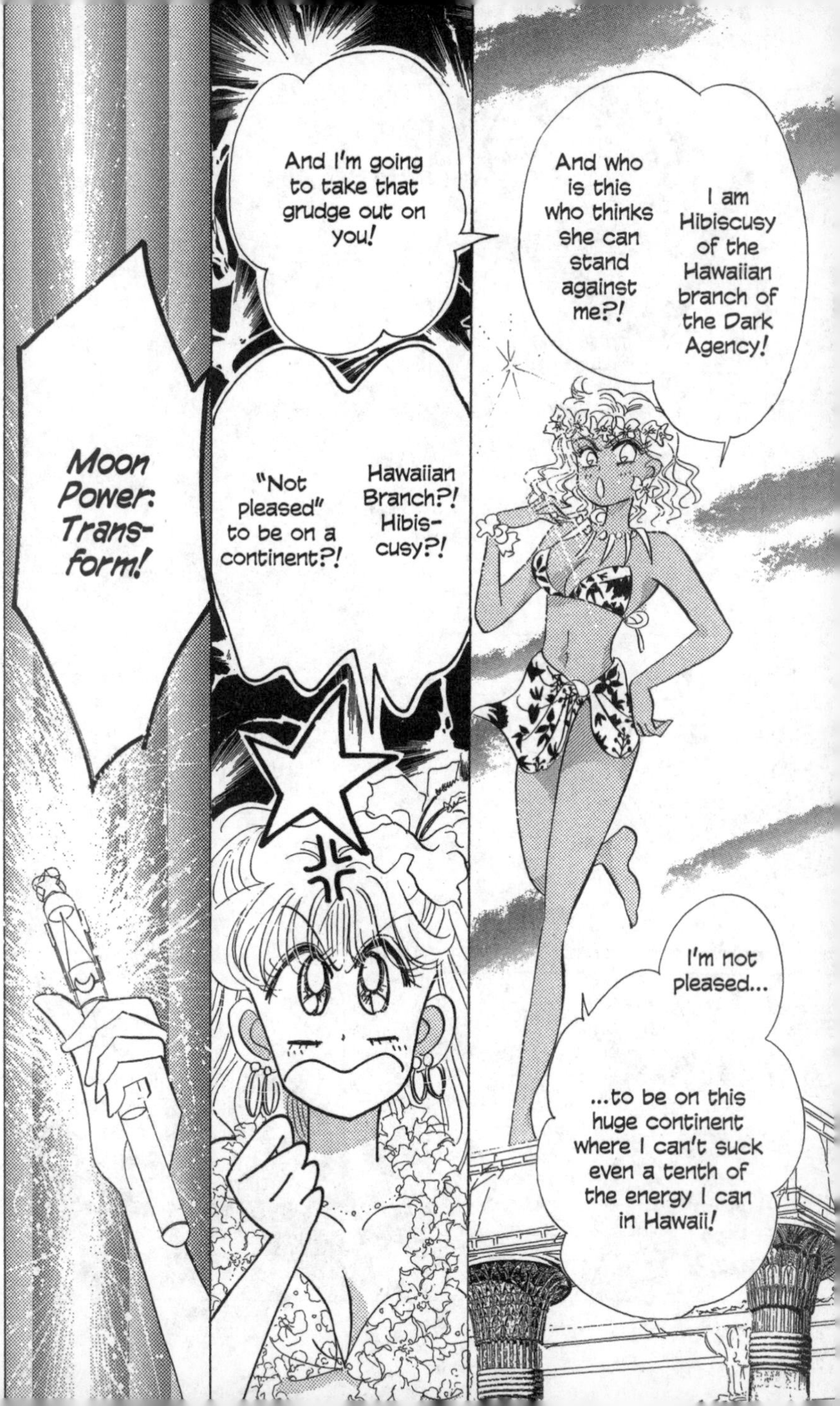
And who is this who thinks she can stand against me?!
I am Hibiscusy of the Hawaiian branch of the Dark Agency!
I'm not pleased...
...to be on this huge continent where I can't suck even a tenth of the energy I can in Hawaii!
And I'm going to take that grudge out on you!
Hawaiian Branch?! Hibiscusy?!
"Not pleased" to be on a continent?!
Moon Power: Trans-form!

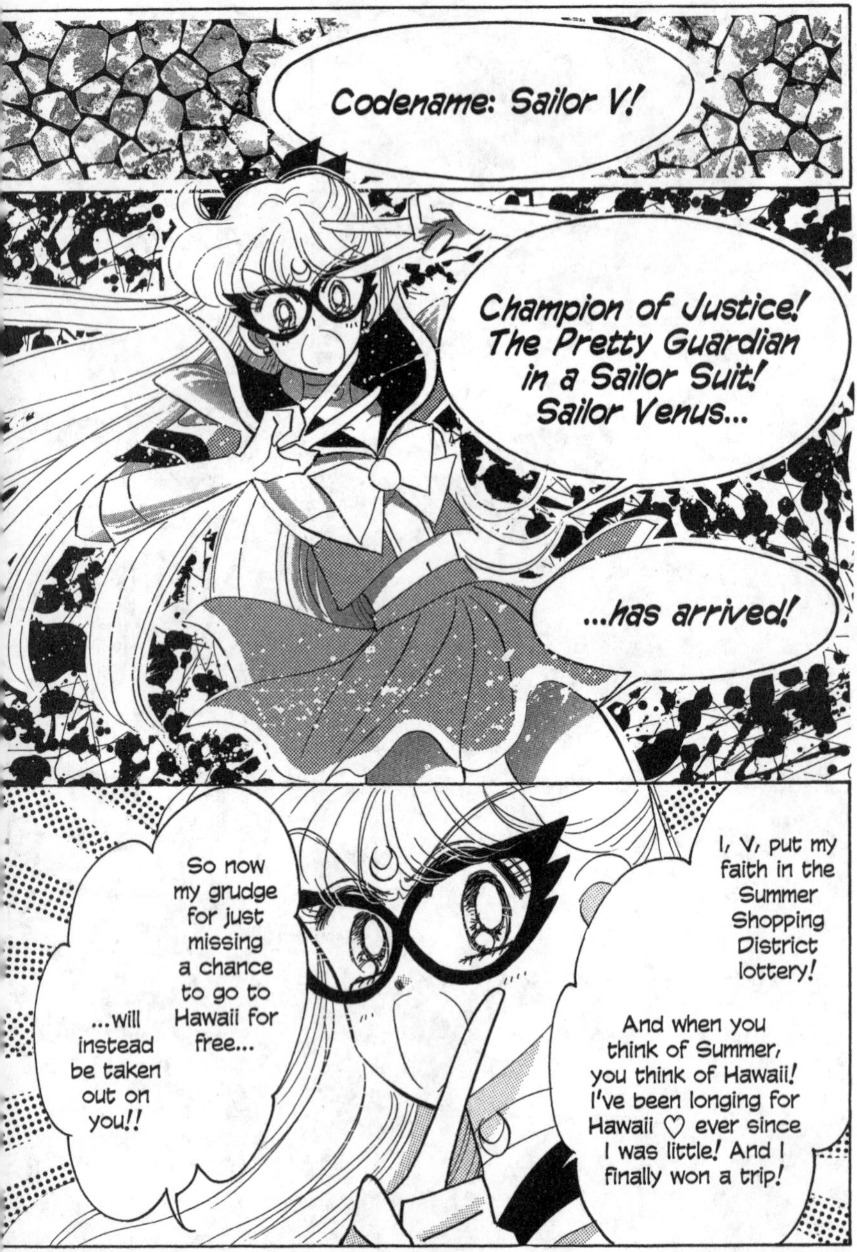
Codename: Sailor V!
Champion of Justice! The Pretty Guardian in a Sailor Suit! Sailor Venus...
...has arrived!
I, V, put my faith in the Summer Shopping District lottery!
And when you think of Summer, you think of Hawaii! I've been longing for Hawaii ♡ ever since I was little! And I finally won a trip!
So now my grudge for just missing a chance to go to Hawaii for free...
...will instead be taken out on you!!

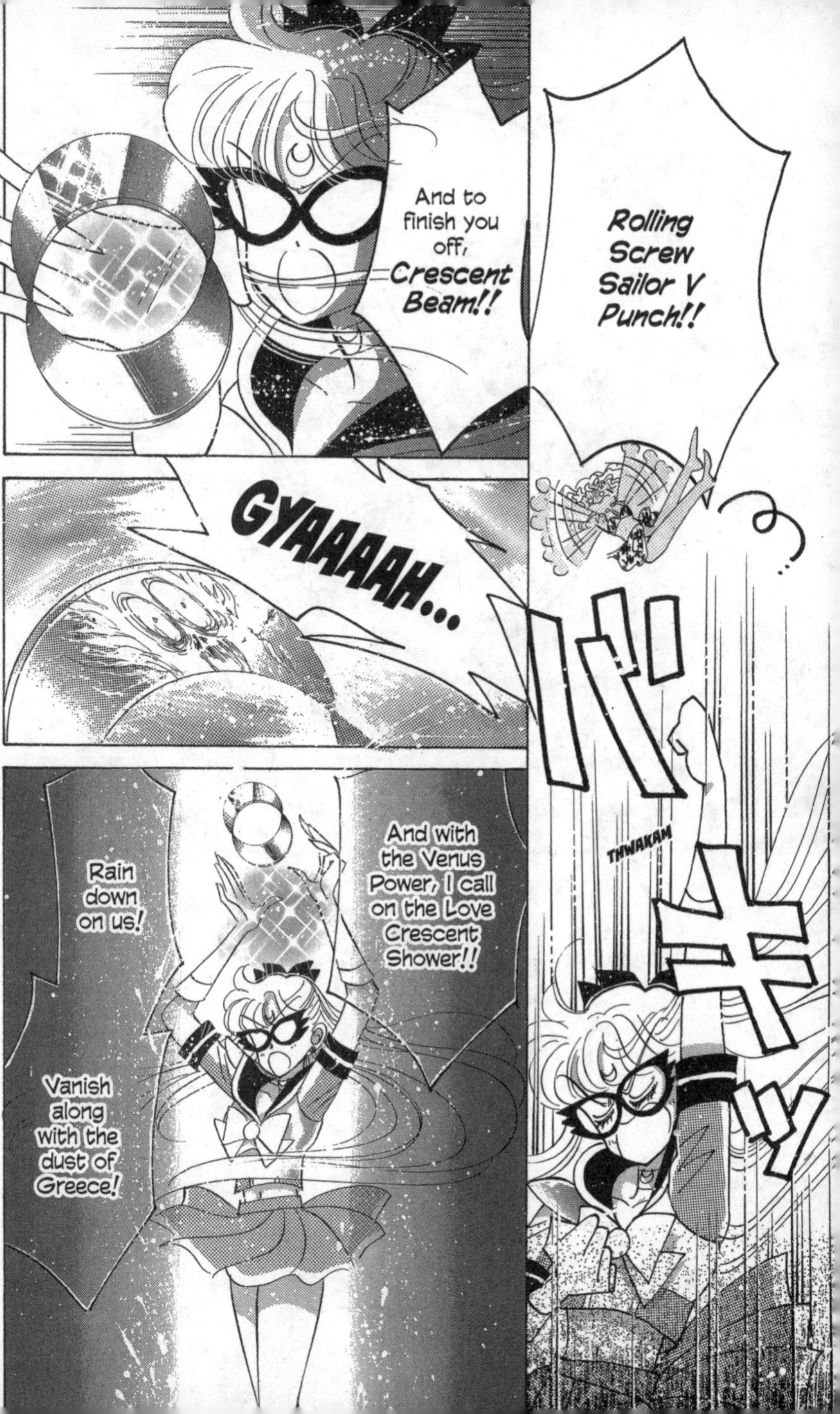
Rolling Screw Sailor V Punch!!
THWAKAM
And to finish you off, Crescent Beam!!
GYAAAAH...
And with the Venus Power, I call on the Love Crescent Shower!!
Rain down on us!
Vanish along with the dust of Greece!

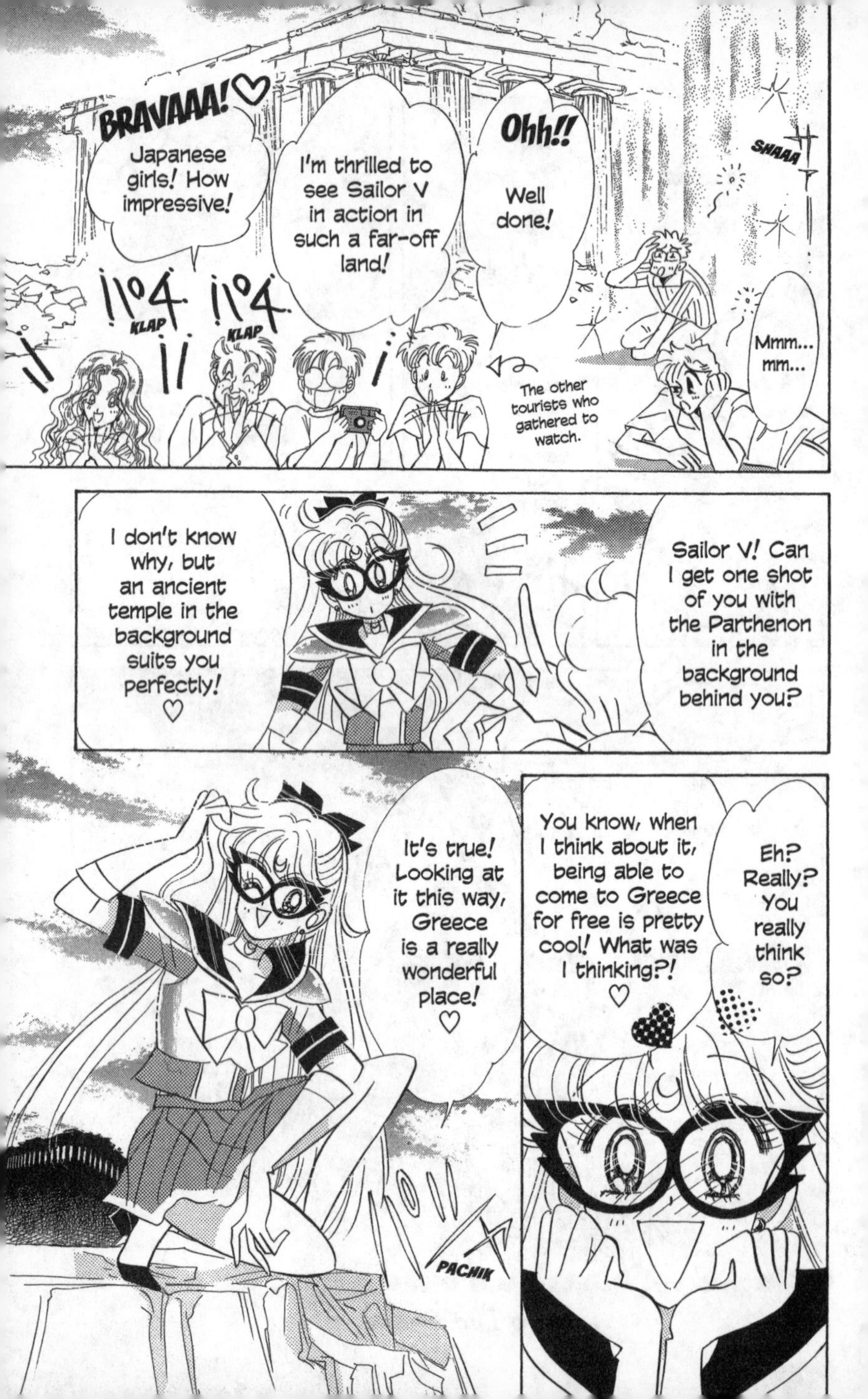
Mmm... mm...
SHAAA
The other tourists who gathered to watch.
Ohh!!
Well done!
I'm thrilled to see Sailor V in action in such a far-off land!
BRAVAAA!♡
Japanese girls! How impressive!
KLAP
KLAP
Sailor V! Can I get one shot of you with the Parthenon in the background behind you?
I don't know why, but an ancient temple in the background suits you perfectly! ♡
Eh? Really? You really think so?
You know, when I think about it, being able to come to Greece for free is pretty cool! What was I thinking?! ♡
It's true! Looking at it this way, Greece is a really wonderful place! ♡
PACHIK

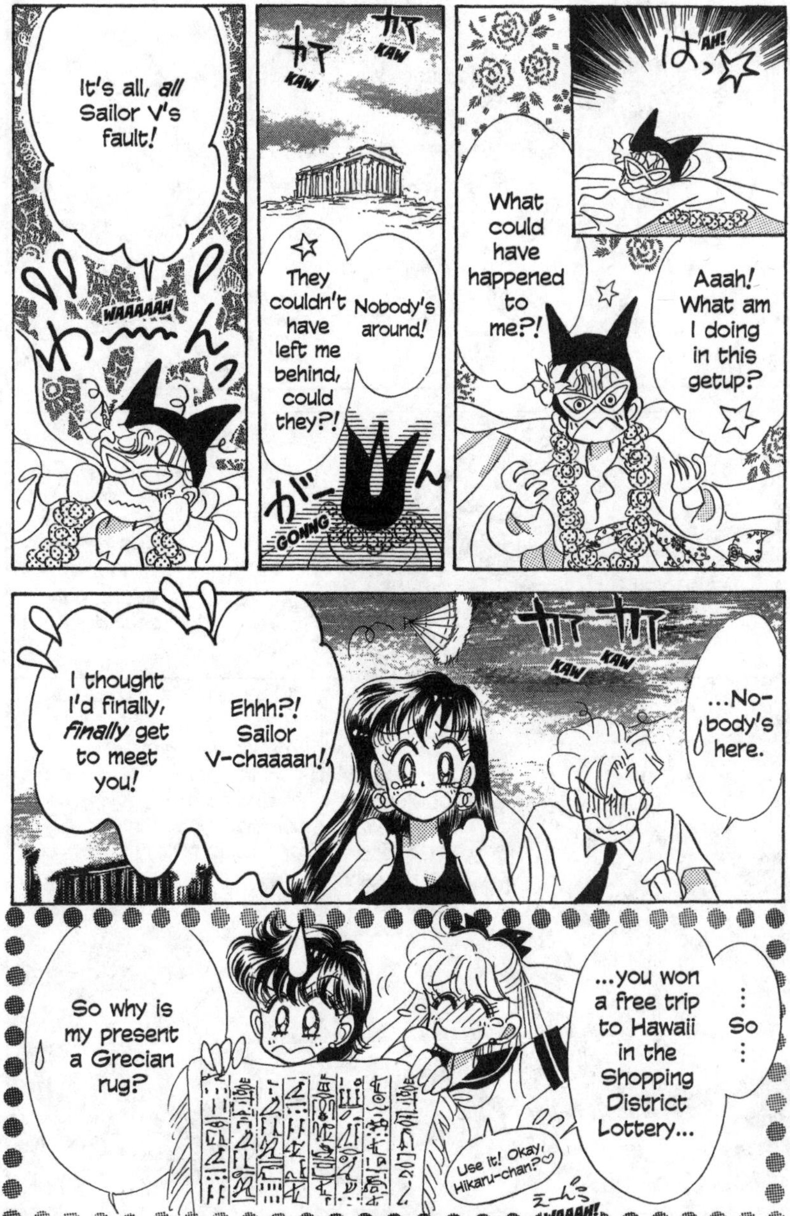
は、
AH!
Aaah! What am I doing in this getup?
What could have happened to me?!
カア
KAW
カア
KAW
Nobody's around!
They couldn't have left me behind, could they?!
がーん
GONNG
It's all, *all* Sailor V's fault!
わ〜〜んっ
WAAAAAH
カア カア
KAW KAW
...No-body's here.
Ehhh?! Sailor V-chaaaan!
I thought I'd finally, *finally* get to meet you!
...So...
...you won a free trip to Hawaii in the Shopping District Lottery...
Use it! Okay, Hikaru-chan?♡
えーんっ
WAAAH!
So why is my present a Grecian rug?

● *The End* ●

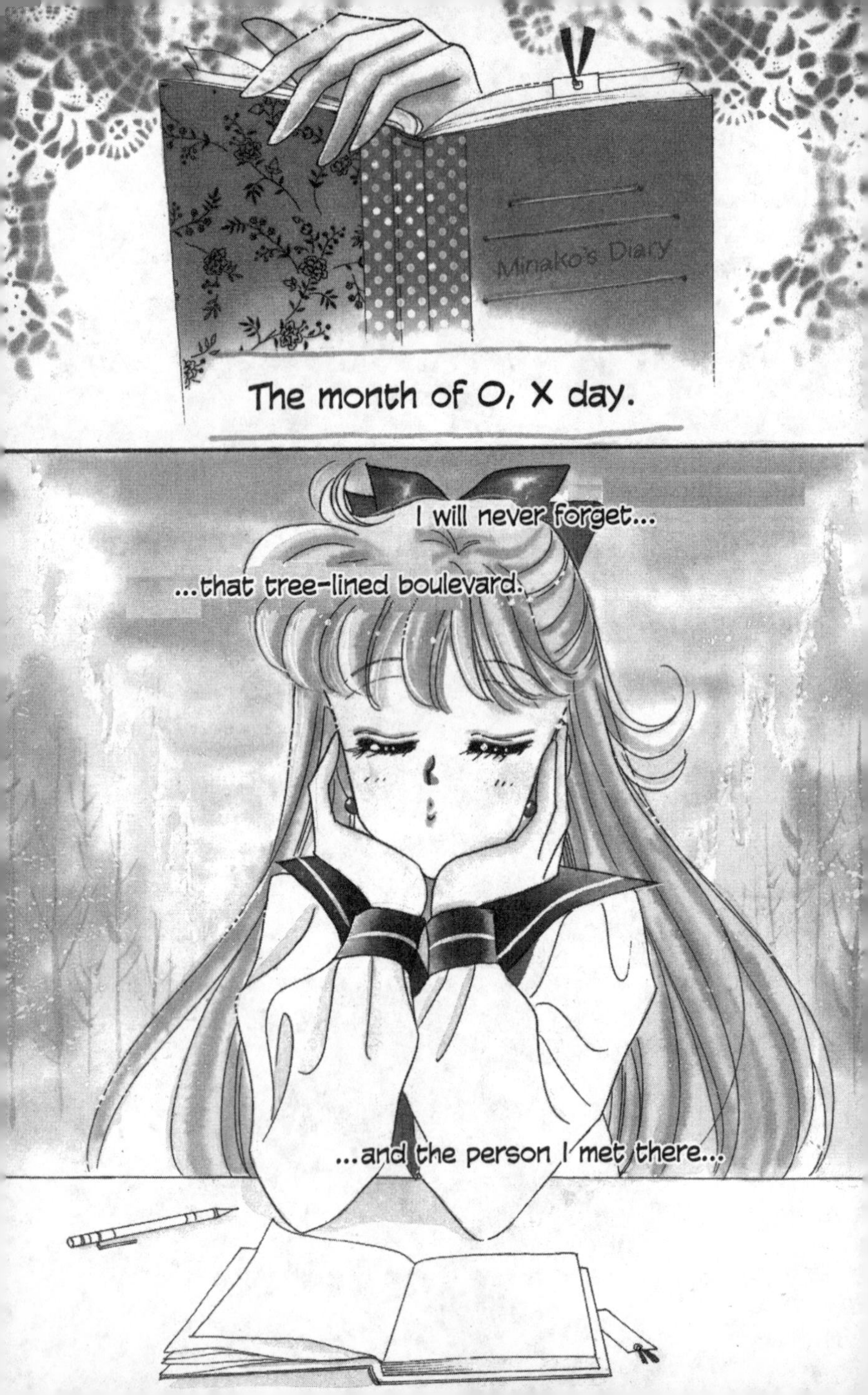
Minako's Diary
The month of O, X day.
I will never forget...
...that tree-lined boulevard.
...and the person I met there...

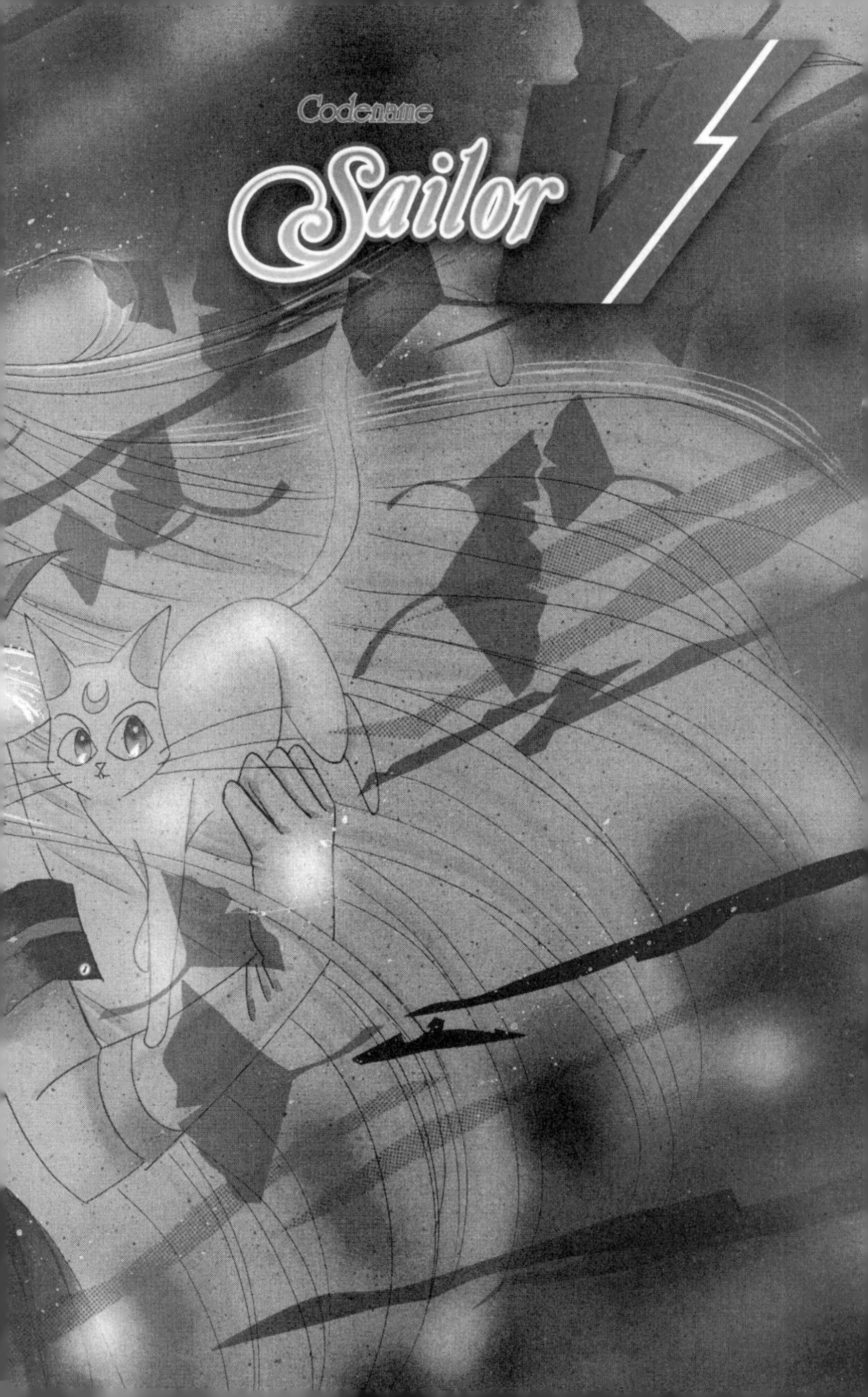
Codename
Sailor V

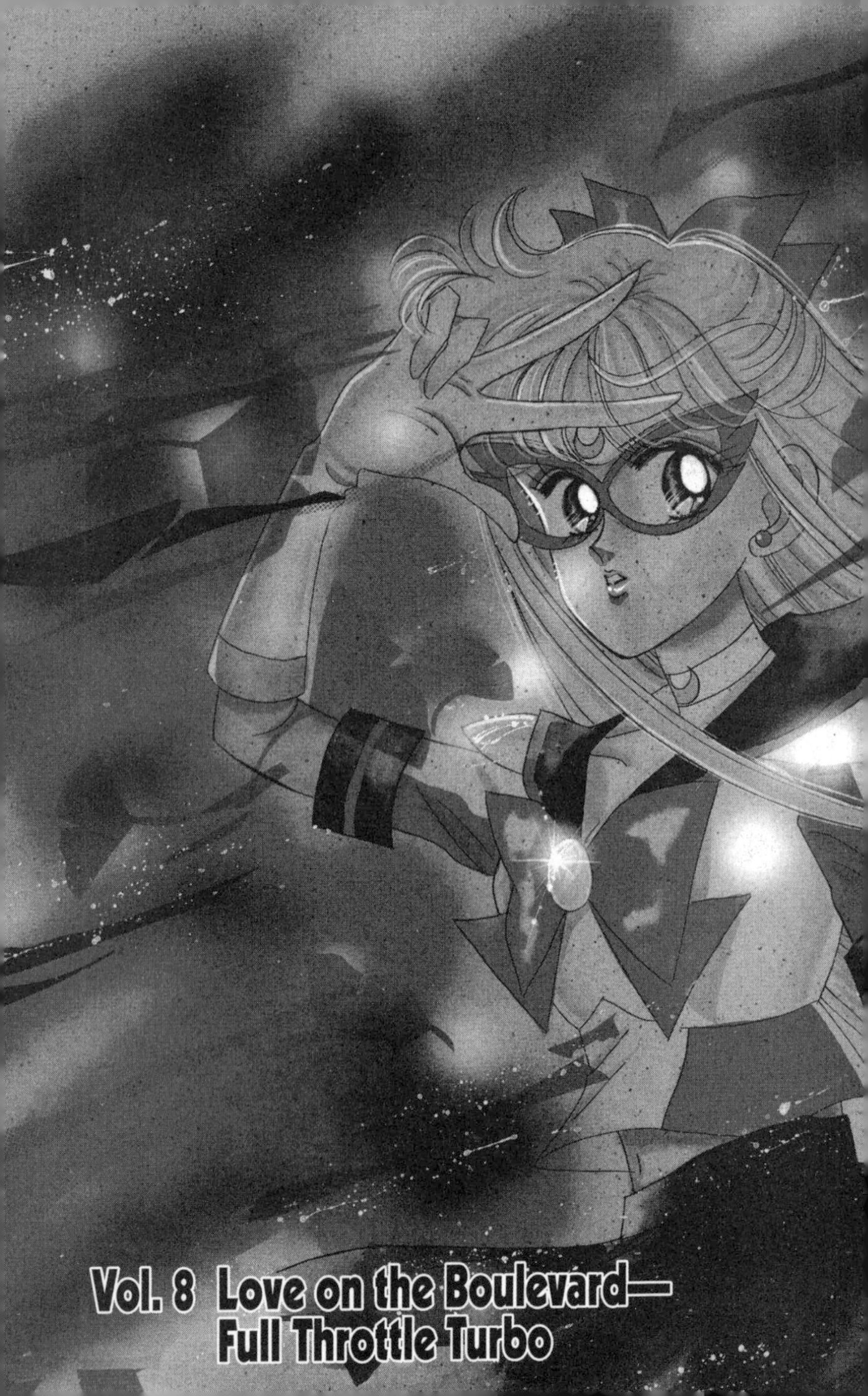

Vol. 8 Love on the Boulevard— Full Throttle Turbo

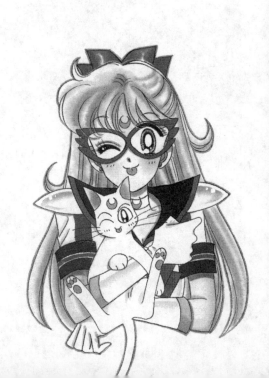

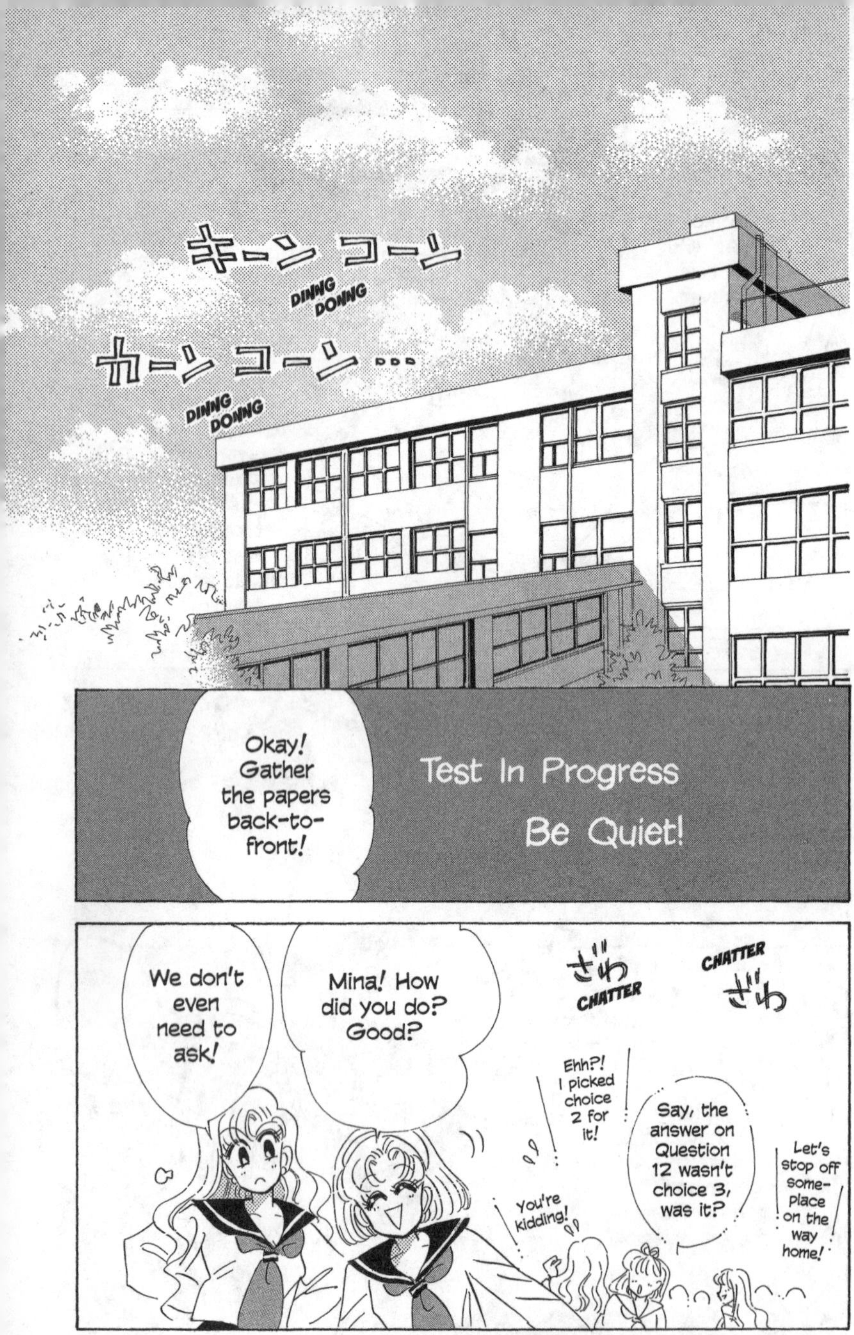
キーン コーン
DINNG DONNG
カーン コーン…
DINNG DONNG
Test In Progress
Be Quiet!
Okay! Gather the papers back-to-front!
ざわ CHATTER
CHATTER ざわ
Let's stop off someplace on the way home!
Say, the answer on Question 12 wasn't choice 3, was it?
Ehh?! I picked choice 2 for it!
You're kidding!
Mina! How did you do? Good?
We don't even need to ask!

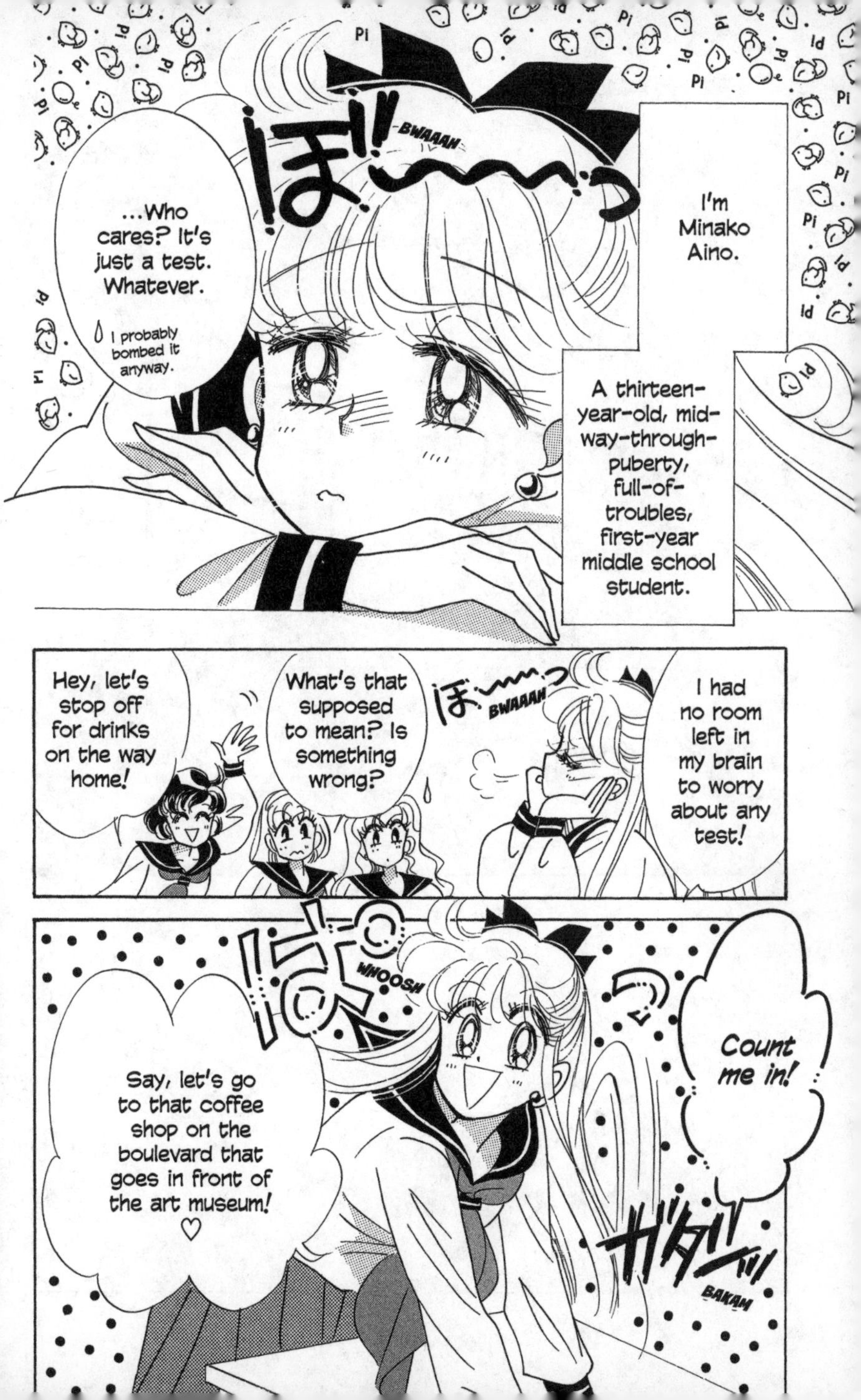
I'm Minako Aino.
A thirteen-year-old, mid-way-through-puberty, full-of-troubles, first-year middle school student.
BWAAAN
...Who cares? It's just a test. Whatever.
I probably bombed it anyway.
I had no room left in my brain to worry about any test!
BWAAAN
What's that supposed to mean? Is something wrong?
Hey, let's stop off for drinks on the way home!
Count me in!
BAKAM
WHOOSH
Say, let's go to that coffee shop on the boulevard that goes in front of the art museum! ♡

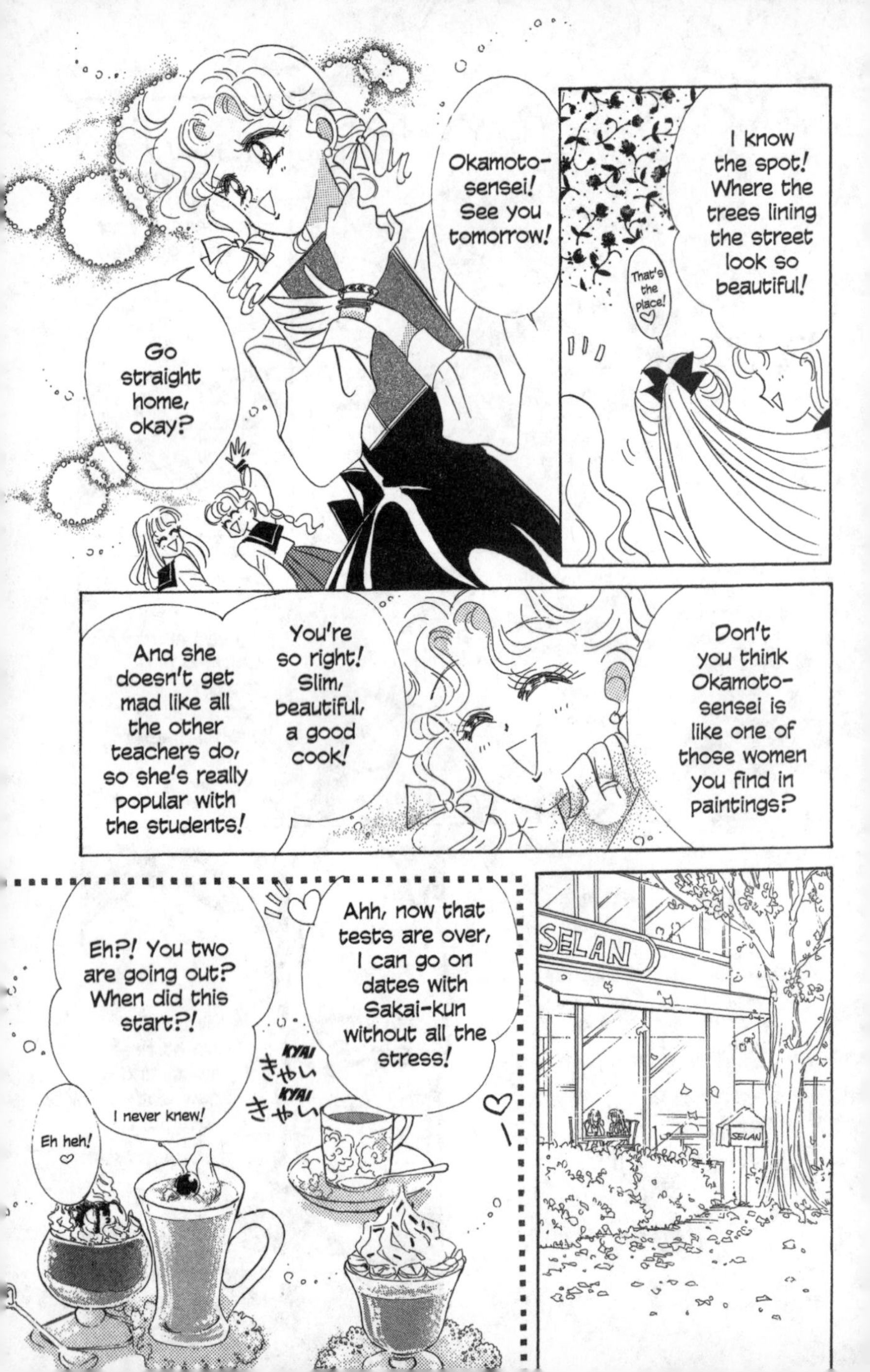
I know the spot! Where the trees lining the street look so beautiful!
That's the place! ♡
Okamoto-sensei! See you tomorrow!
Go straight home, okay?
Don't you think Okamoto-sensei is like one of those women you find in paintings?
You're so right! Slim, beautiful, a good cook!
And she doesn't get mad like all the other teachers do, so she's really popular with the students!
SELAN
SELAN
Ahh, now that tests are over, I can go on dates with Sakai-kun without all the stress!
KYAI きゃい KYAI きゃい
Eh?! You two are going out? When did this start?!
I never knew!
Eh heh! ♡

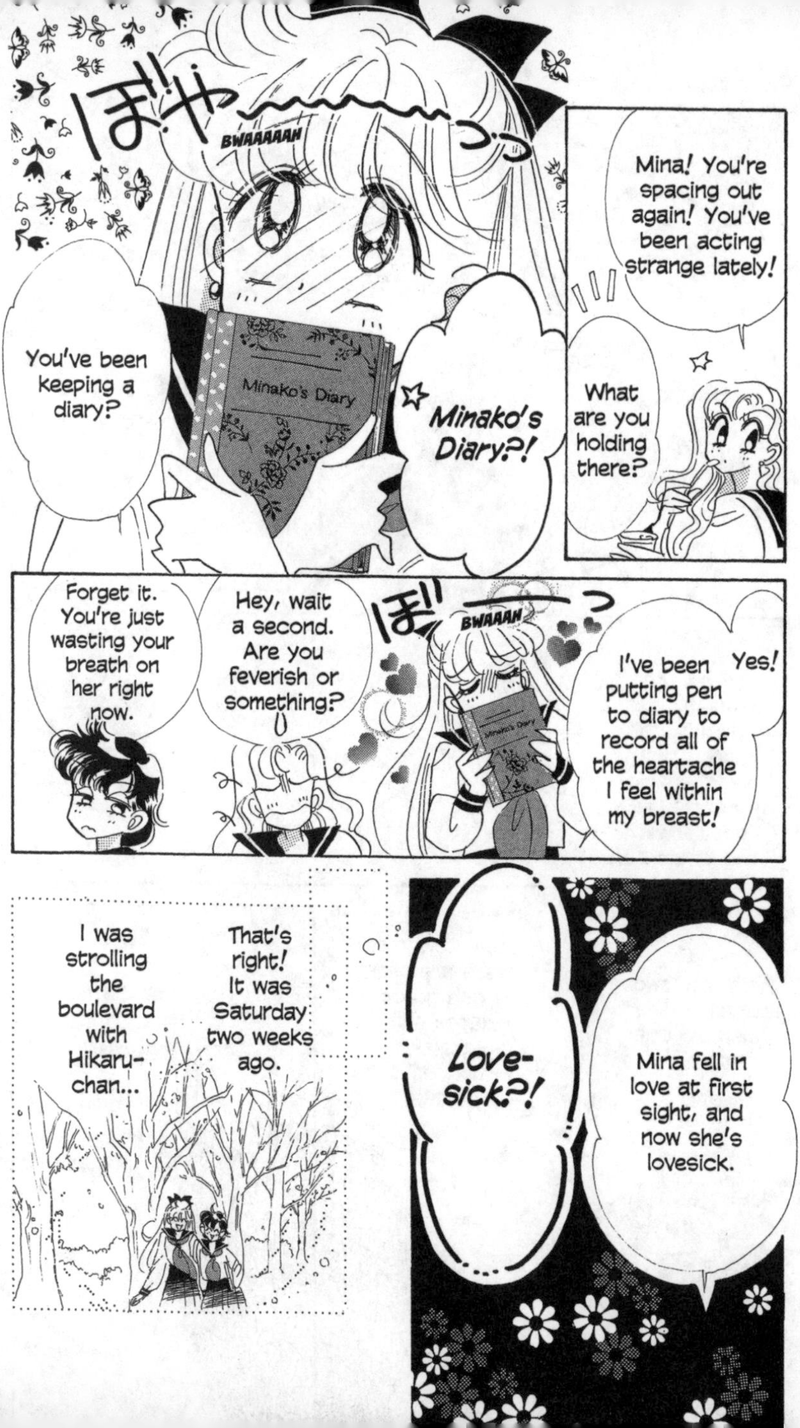
Mina! You're spacing out again! You've been acting strange lately!
What are you holding there?
ぼやーっ
BWAAAAAH
Minako's Diary
Minako's Diary?!
You've been keeping a diary?
Yes!
I've been putting pen to diary to record all of the heartache I feel within my breast!
ぼーっ
BWAAAH
Hey, wait a second. Are you feverish or something?
Forget it. You're just wasting your breath on her right now.
Mina fell in love at first sight, and now she's lovesick.
...Love-sick?!...
That's right! It was Saturday two weeks ago.
I was strolling the boulevard with Hikaru-chan...

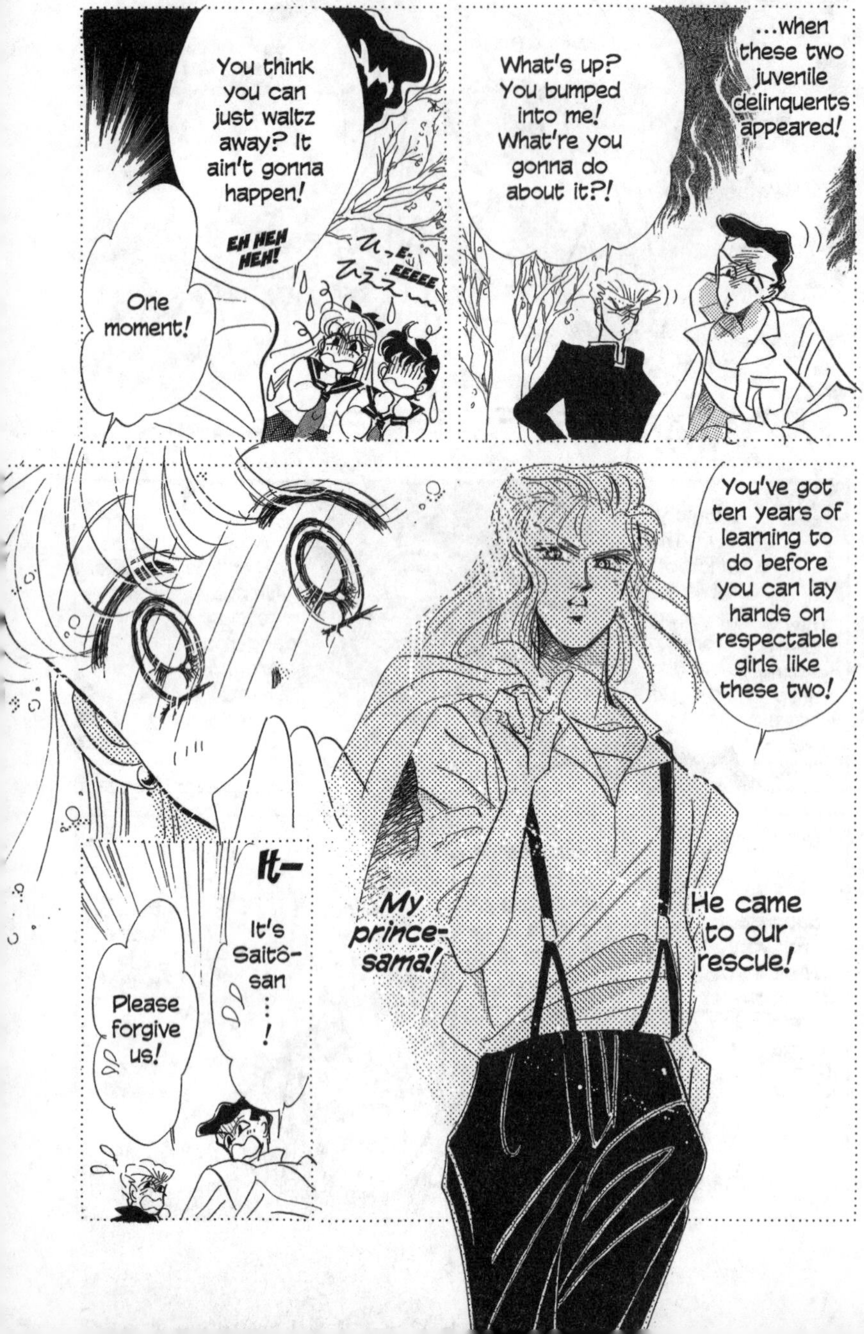
...when these two juvenile delinquents appeared!
What's up? You bumped into me! What're you gonna do about it?!
You think you can just waltz away? It ain't gonna happen!
EH HEH HEH!
One moment!
You've got ten years of learning to do before you can lay hands on respectable girls like these two!
He came to our rescue!
My prince-sama!
It—
It's Saitô-san...!
Please forgive us!

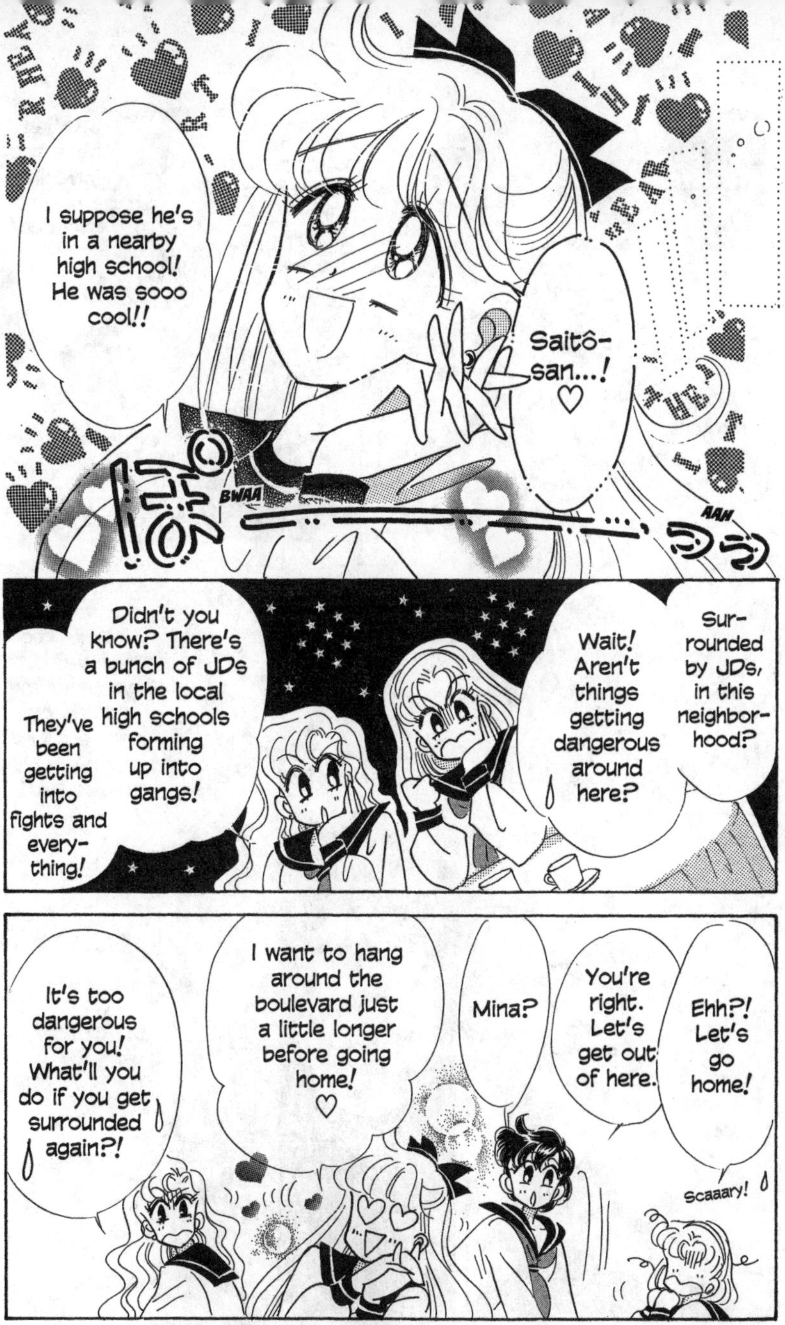
Saitô-san...! ♡
I suppose he's in a nearby high school! He was sooo cool!!
BWAA
AAH
Sur-rounded by JDs, in this neighbor-hood?
Wait! Aren't things getting dangerous around here?
Didn't you know? There's a bunch of JDs in the local high schools forming up into gangs!
They've been getting into fights and every-thing!
Ehh?! Let's go home!
Scaaary!
You're right. Let's get out of here.
Mina?
I want to hang around the boulevard just a little longer before going home! ♡
It's too dangerous for you! What'll you do if you get surrounded again?!

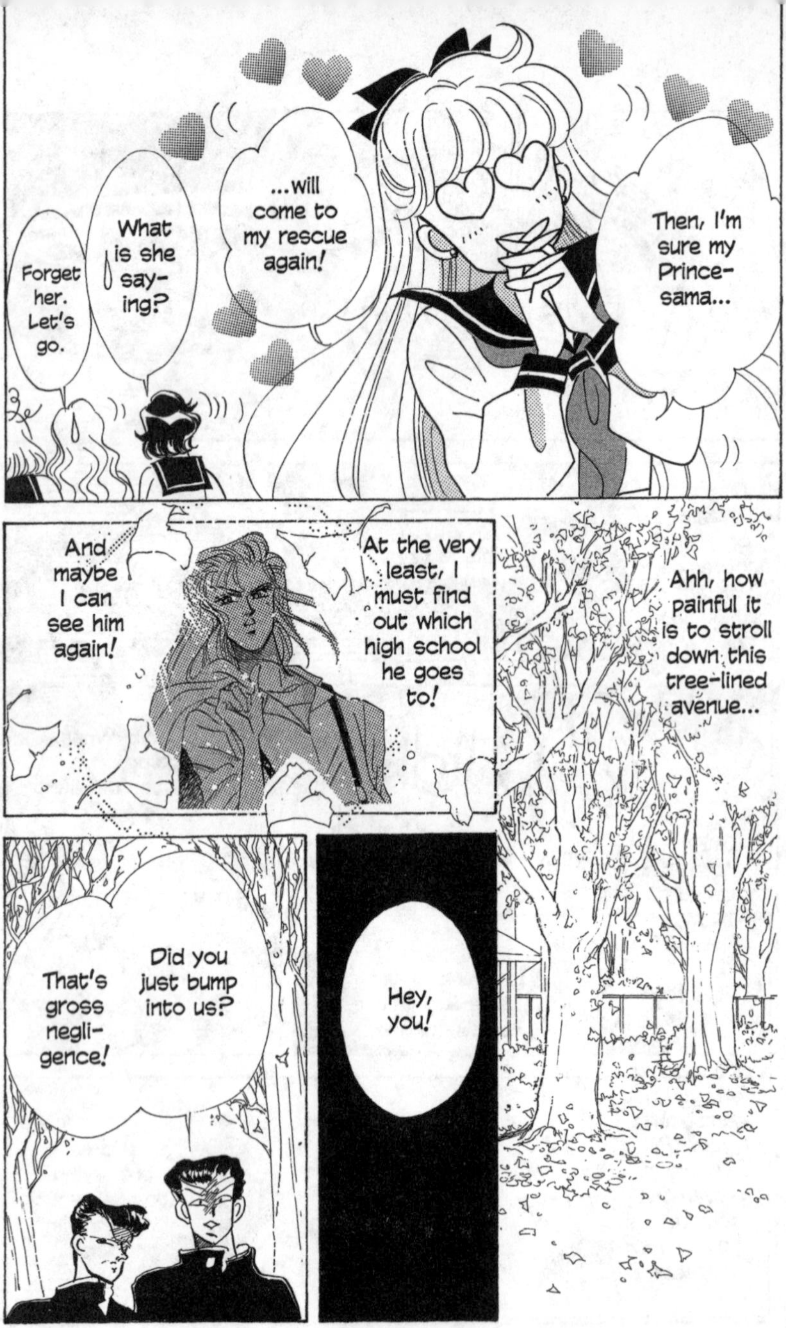
Then, I'm sure my Prince-sama...
...will come to my rescue again!
What is she saying?
Forget her. Let's go.
Ahh, how painful it is to stroll down this tree-lined avenue...
At the very least, I must find out which high school he goes to!
And maybe I can see him again!
Hey, you!
Did you just bump into us?
That's gross negligence!

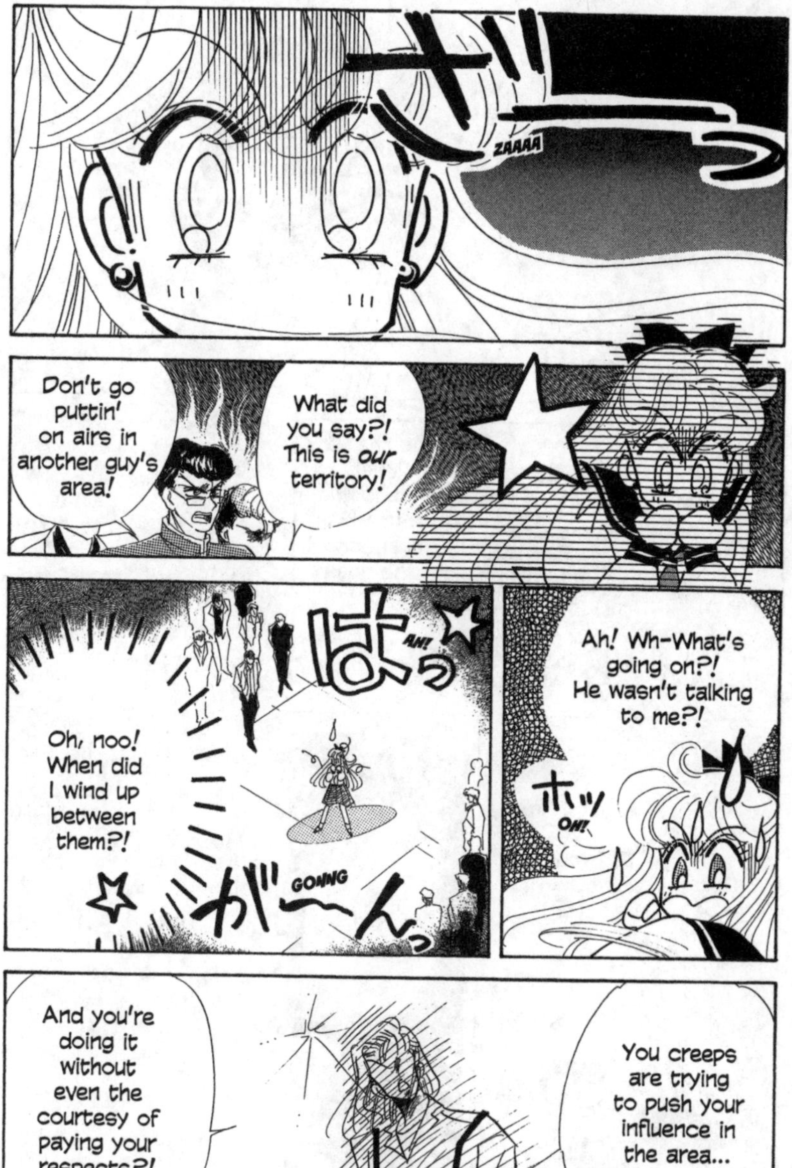
ギーっ
ZAAAA
What did you say?! This is *our* territory!
Don't go puttin' on airs in another guy's area!
Ah! Wh-What's going on?! He wasn't talking to me?!
ホッ
OH!
はっ
AH!
Oh, noo! When did I wind up between them?!
がーんっ
GONNG
You creeps are trying to push your influence in the area...
And you're doing it without even the courtesy of paying your respects?!

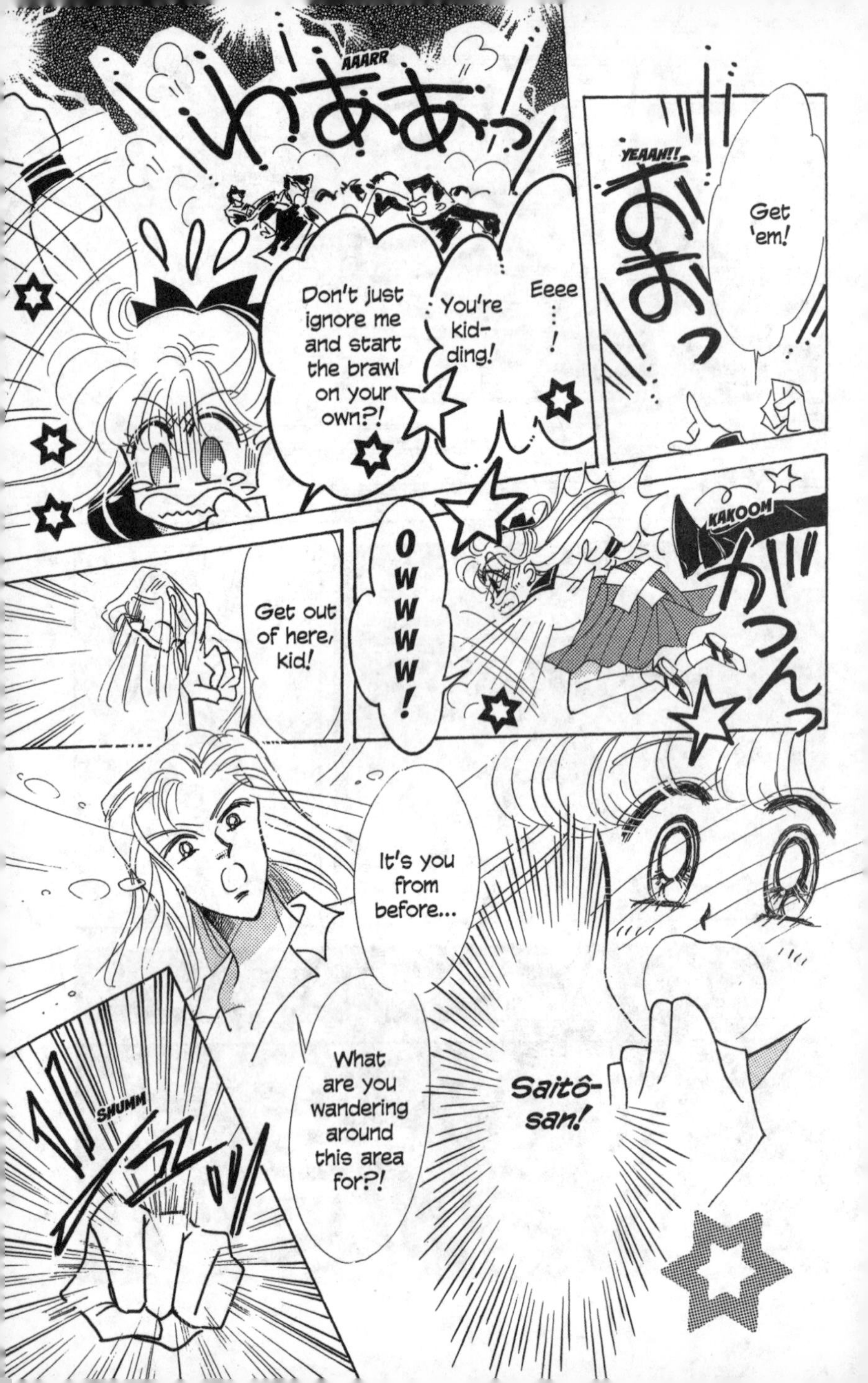
YEAAH!!
おおっ
Get 'em!
AAARR
わあああっ
Eeee...!
You're kid-ding!
Don't just ignore me and start the brawl on your own?!
KAKOOM
がつんっ
OWWWW!
Get out of here, kid!
Saitô-san!
It's you from before...
What are you wandering around this area for?!
SHUMM

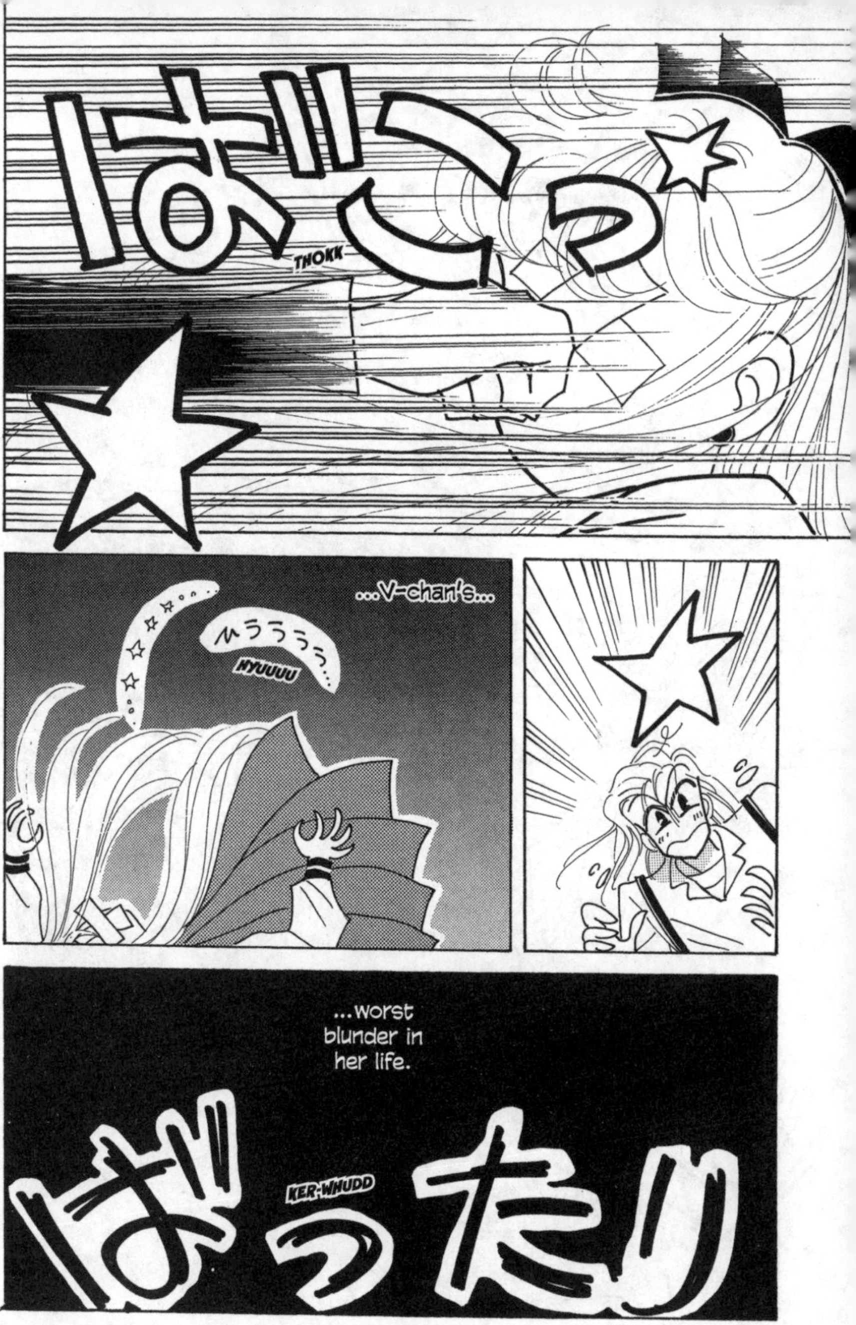
ばこっ
THOKK
...V-chan's...
ひううううう...
NYUUUU
...worst blunder in her life.
ばったり
KER-WHUDD

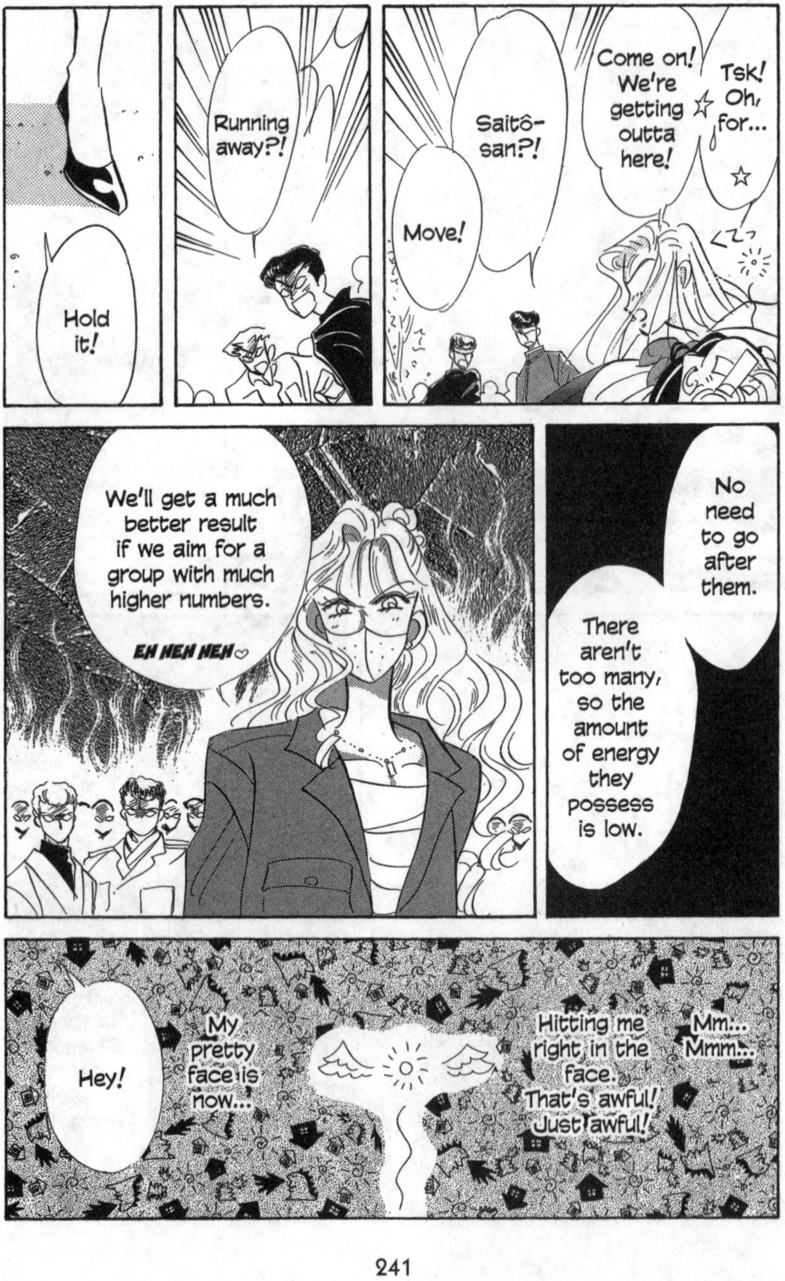
Tsk! Oh, for...
Come on! We're getting outta here!
Saitô-san?!
Move!
Running away?!
Hold it!
No need to go after them.
There aren't too many, so the amount of energy they possess is low.
We'll get a much better result if we aim for a group with much higher numbers.
EH HEH HEH
Mm... Mmm...
Hitting me right in the face. That's awful! Just awful!
My pretty face is now...
Hey!

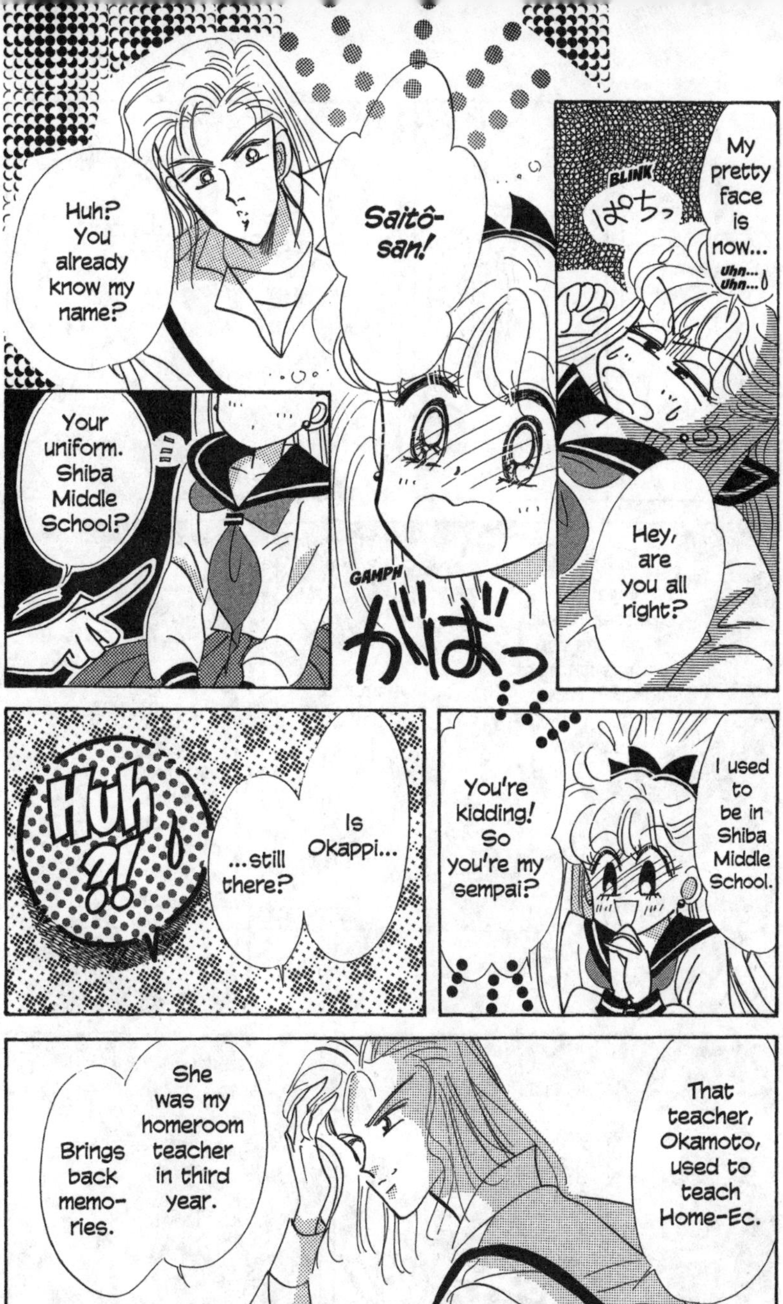
My pretty face is now...
BLINK
ぱちっ
Uhn... Uhn...
Hey, are you all right?
Saitô-san!
GAMPH
がばっ
Huh? You already know my name?
Your uniform. Shiba Middle School?
I used to be in Shiba Middle School.
You're kidding! So you're my sempai?
Is Okappi...
...still there?
Huh?!
That teacher, Okamoto, used to teach Home-Ec.
She was my homeroom teacher in third year.
Brings back memories.

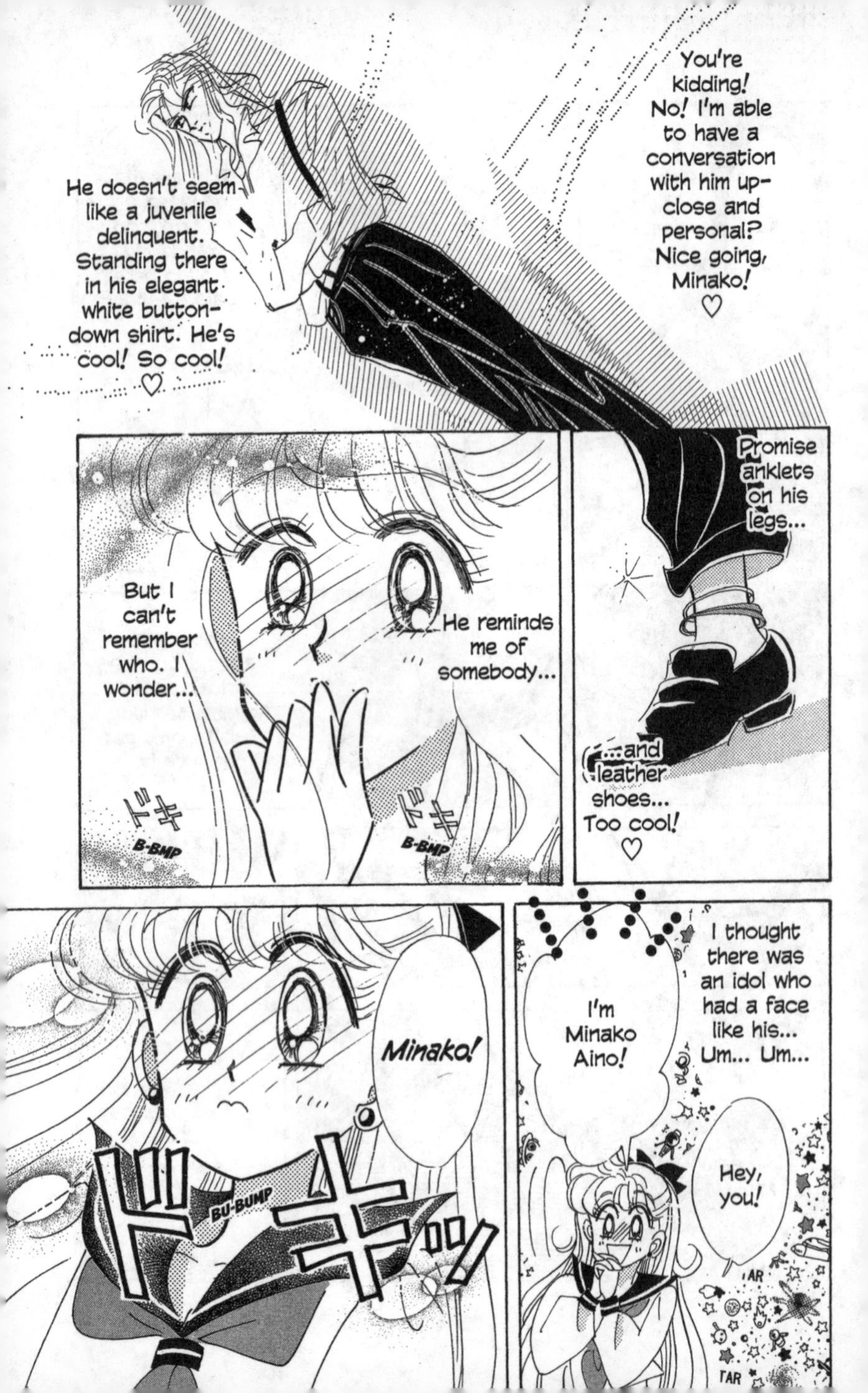
You're kidding! No! I'm able to have a conversation with him up-close and personal? Nice going, Minako! ♡
He doesn't seem like a juvenile delinquent. Standing there in his elegant white button-down shirt. He's cool! So cool! ♡
Promise anklets on his legs...
...and leather shoes... Too cool! ♡
He reminds me of somebody...
But I can't remember who. I wonder...
ドキ
B-BMP
ドキ
B-BMP
I thought there was an idol who had a face like his... Um... Um...
I'm Minako Aino!
Hey, you!
Minako!
ドキッ
BU-BUMP

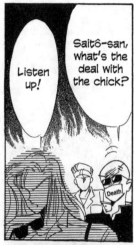

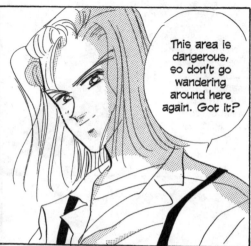

This area is dangerous, so don't go wandering around here again. Got it?
Saitô-san, what's the deal with the chick?
Listen up!
Death
If anybody lays a hand on this girl within the Aoyama territory, Saitô won't put up with it.
Got it, Sir!
Death
Nice to meet you, Minako-san!
OOSH
FWO

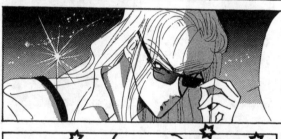

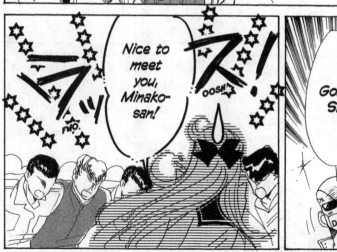

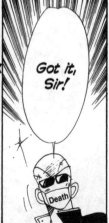

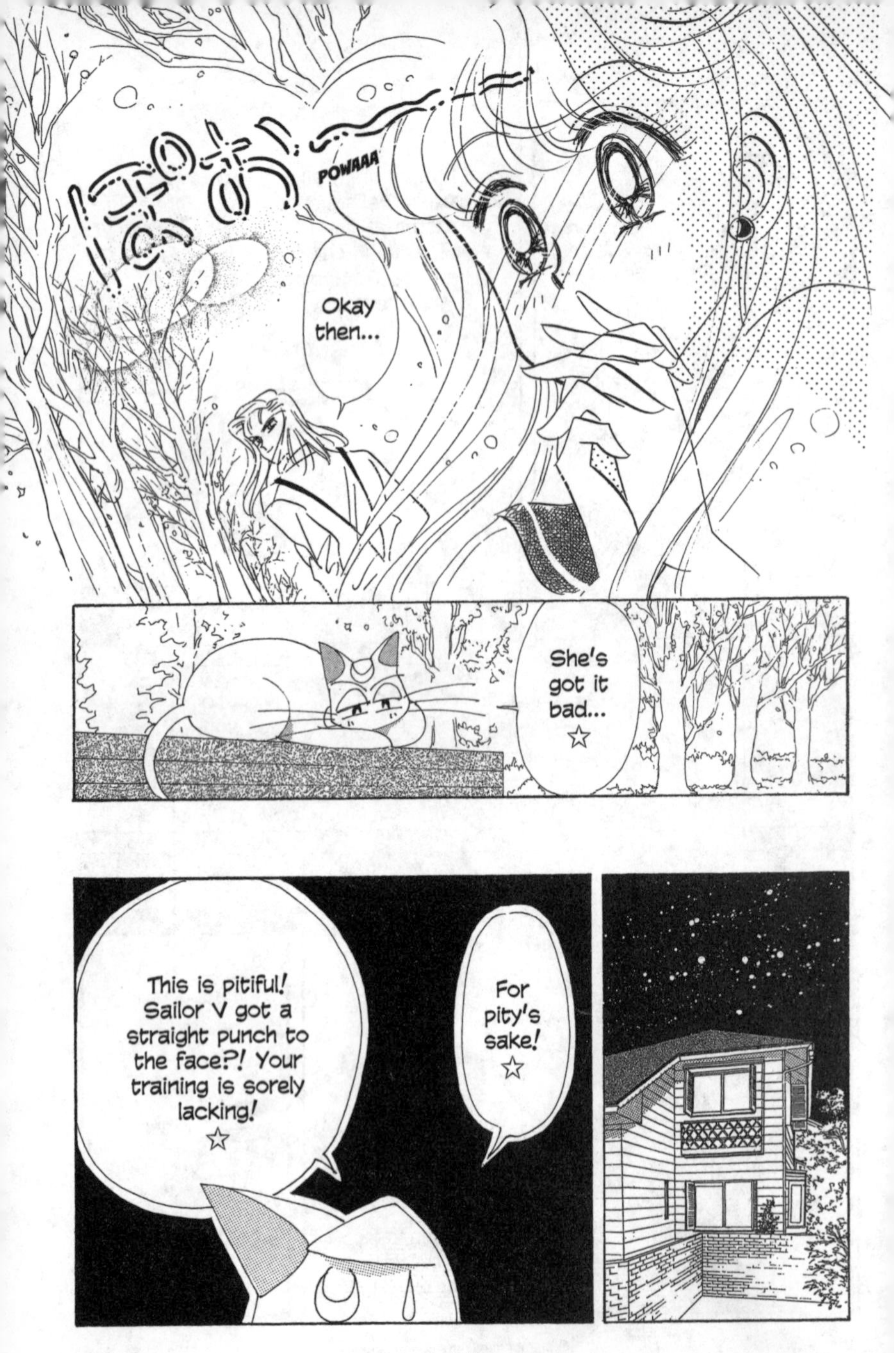
POWAAA
Okay then...
She's got it bad... ☆
For pity's sake! ☆
This is pitiful! Sailor V got a straight punch to the face?! Your training is sorely lacking! ☆

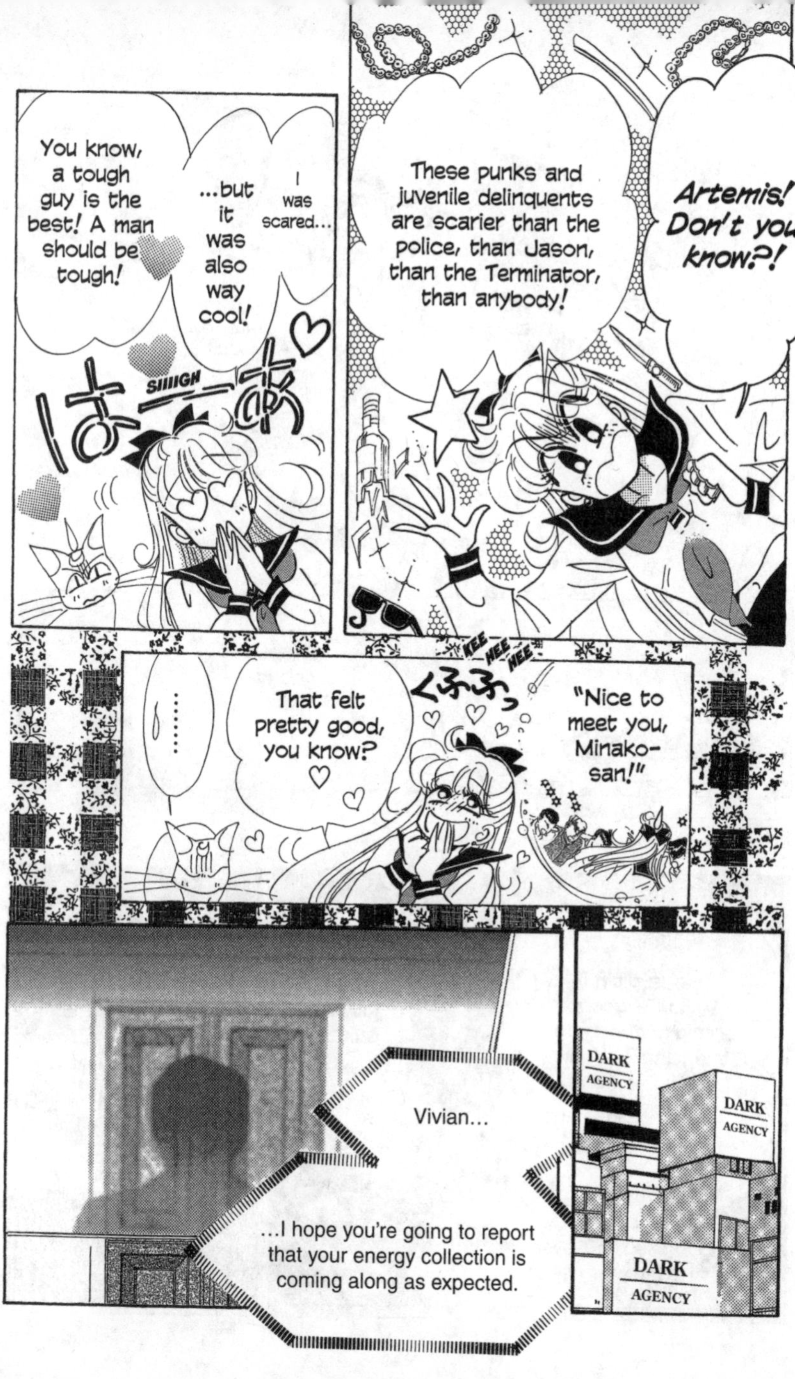
Artemis! Don't you know?!
These punks and juvenile delinquents are scarier than the police, than Jason, than the Terminator, than anybody!
I was scared...
...but it was also way cool!
You know, a tough guy is the best! A man should be tough!
SIIIGH
KEE HEE HEE
くふふっ
"Nice to meet you, Minako-san!"
That felt pretty good, you know?
......
DARK AGENCY
DARK AGENCY
DARK AGENCY
Vivian...
...I hope you're going to report that your energy collection is coming along as expected.

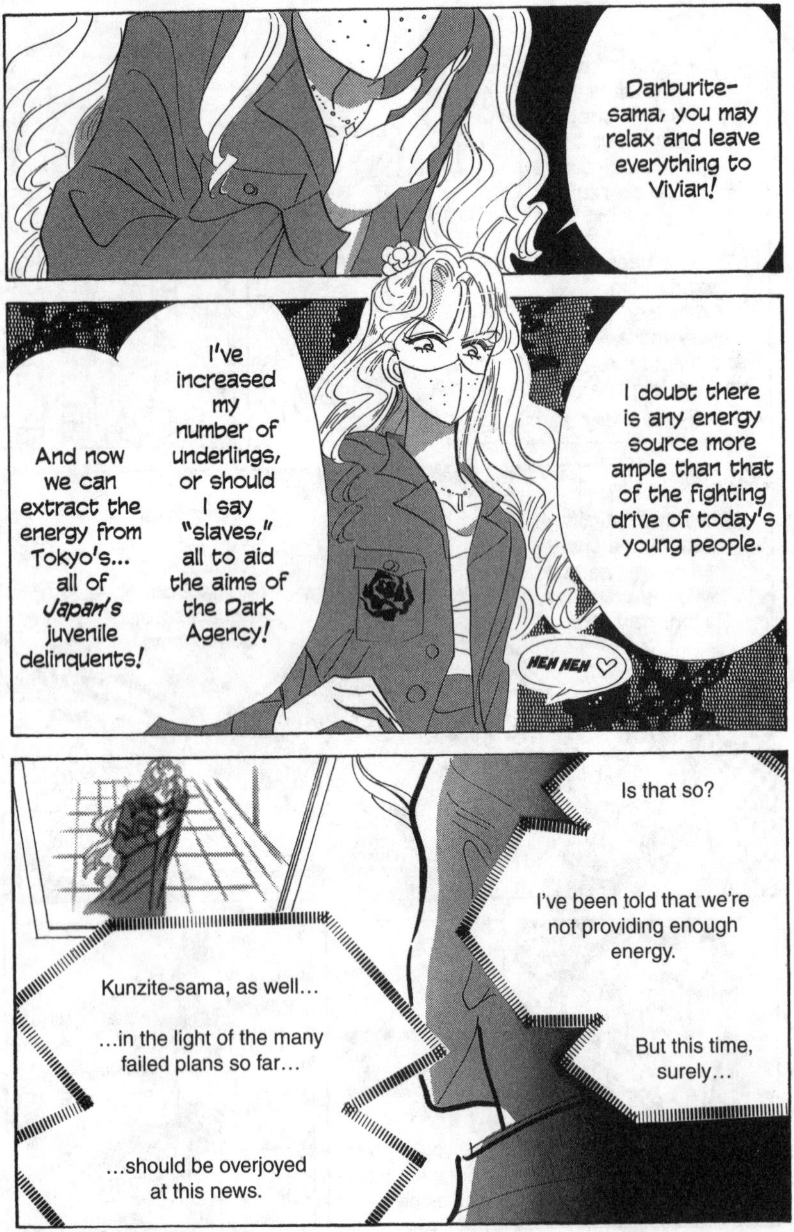

Danburite-sama, you may relax and leave everything to Vivian!
I doubt there is any energy source more ample than that of the fighting drive of today's young people.
HEH HEH ♡
I've increased my number of underlings, or should I say "slaves," all to aid the aims of the Dark Agency!
And now we can extract the energy from Tokyo's... all of *Japan's* juvenile delinquents!
Is that so?
I've been told that we're not providing enough energy.
But this time, surely…
Kunzite-sama, as well…
…in the light of the many failed plans so far…
…should be overjoyed at this news.

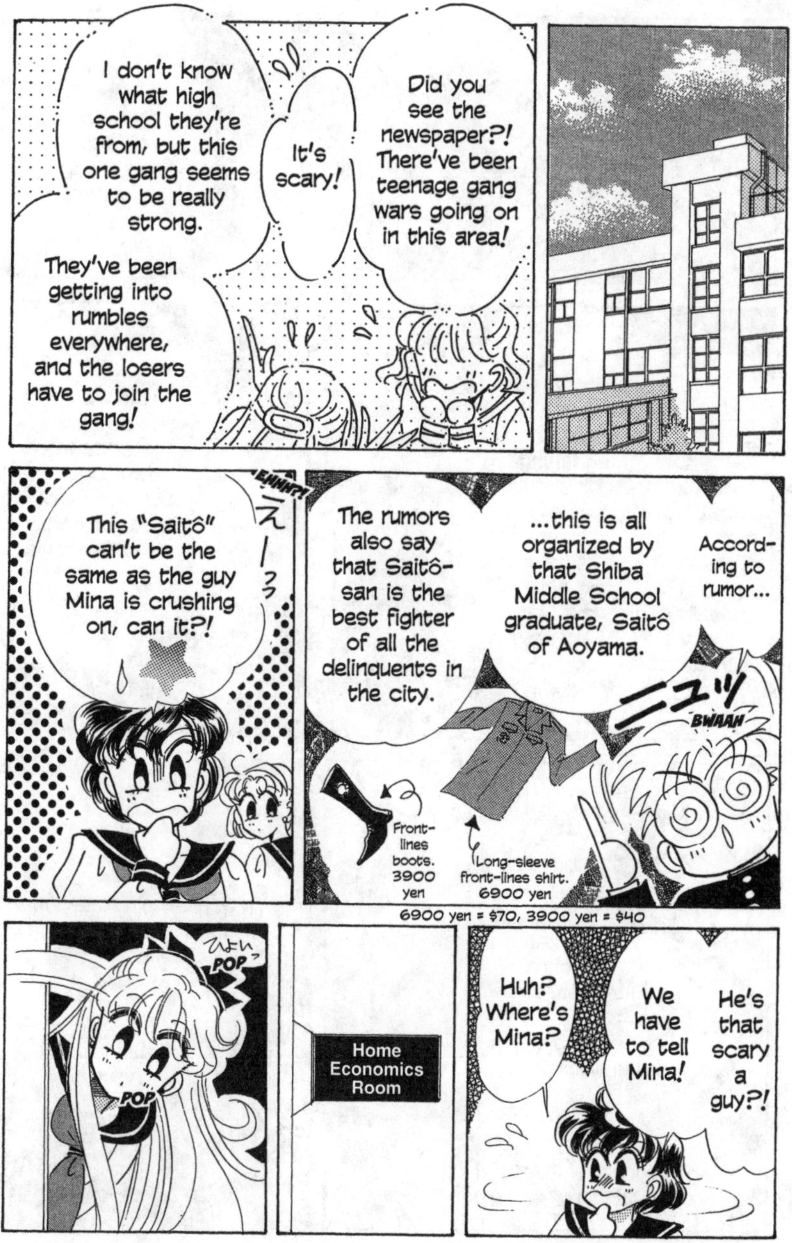
Did you see the newspaper?! There've been teenage gang wars going on in this area!
It's scary!
I don't know what high school they're from, but this one gang seems to be really strong.
They've been getting into rumbles everywhere, and the losers have to join the gang!
According to rumor...
...this is all organized by that Shiba Middle School graduate, Saitô of Aoyama.
The rumors also say that Saitô-san is the best fighter of all the delinquents in the city.
BWAAH
Long-sleeve front-lines shirt. 6900 yen
Front-lines boots. 3900 yen
EHHH?!
This "Saitô" can't be the same as the guy Mina is crushing on, can it?!
6900 yen = $70, 3900 yen = $40
He's that scary a guy?!
We have to tell Mina!
Huh? Where's Mina?
Home Economics Room
POP
POP

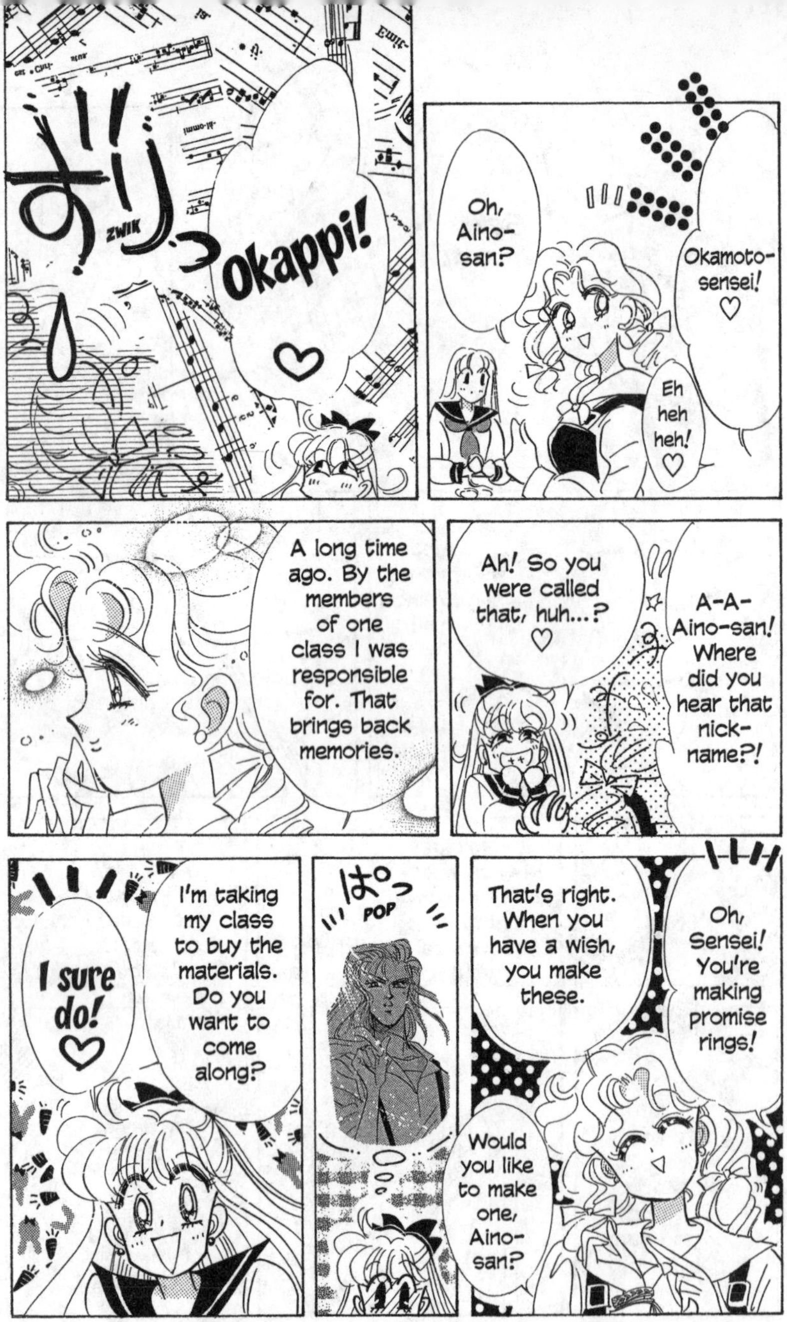
Okamoto-sensei! ♡
Oh, Aino-san?
Eh heh heh! ♡
ずりっ
ZWIK
Okappi! ♡
A-A-Aino-san! Where did you hear that nickname?!
Ah! So you were called that, huh...? ♡
A long time ago. By the members of one class I was responsible for. That brings back memories.
Oh, Sensei! You're making promise rings!
That's right. When you have a wish, you make these.
Would you like to make one, Aino-san?
ぱっ
POP
I'm taking my class to buy the materials. Do you want to come along?
I sure do! ♡

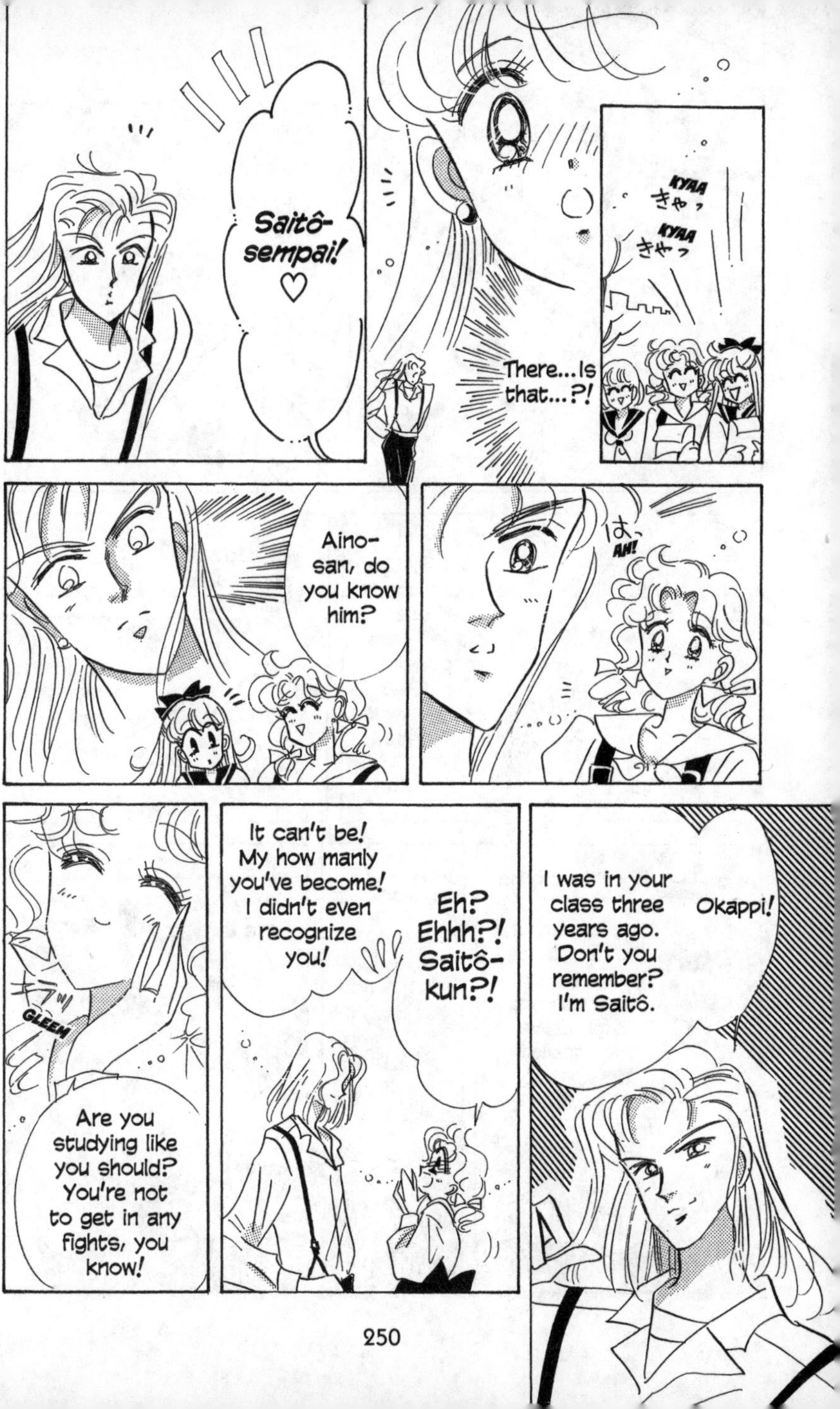
KYAA きゃっ
KYAA きゃっ
There...Is that...?!
Saitô-sempai! ♡
は、 AH!
Aino-san, do you know him?
Okappi!
I was in your class three years ago. Don't you remember? I'm Saitô.
Eh? Ehhh?! Saitô-kun?!
It can't be! My how manly you've become! I didn't even recognize you!
GLEEM
Are you studying like you should? You're not to get in any fights, you know!

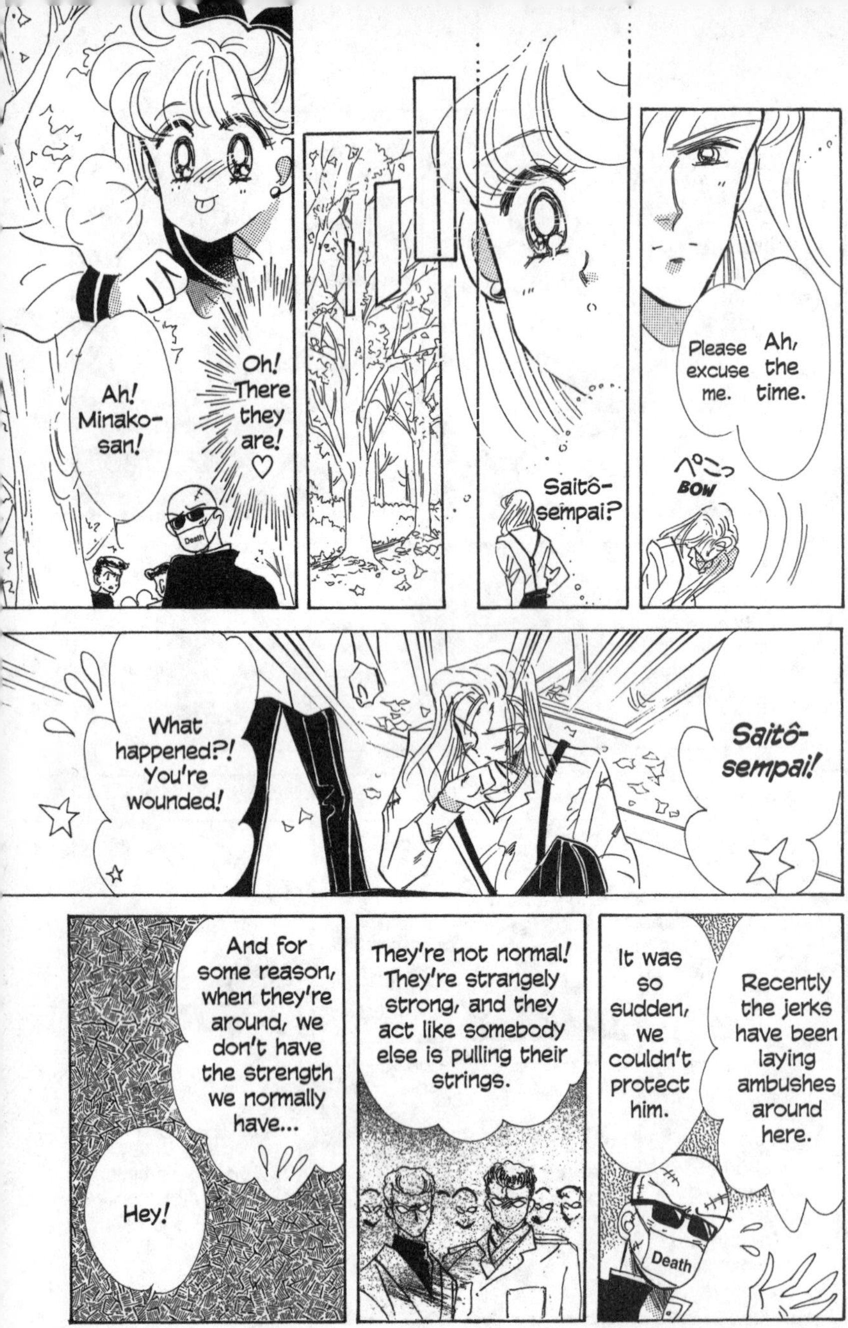
Ah, the time.
Please excuse me.
ぺこっ
BOW
Saitô-sempai?
Oh! There they are! ♡
Ah! Minako-san!
Death
Saitô-sempai!
What happened?! You're wounded!
Recently the jerks have been laying ambushes around here.
It was so sudden, we couldn't protect him.
Death
They're not normal! They're strangely strong, and they act like somebody else is pulling their strings.
And for some reason, when they're around, we don't have the strength we normally have...
Hey!

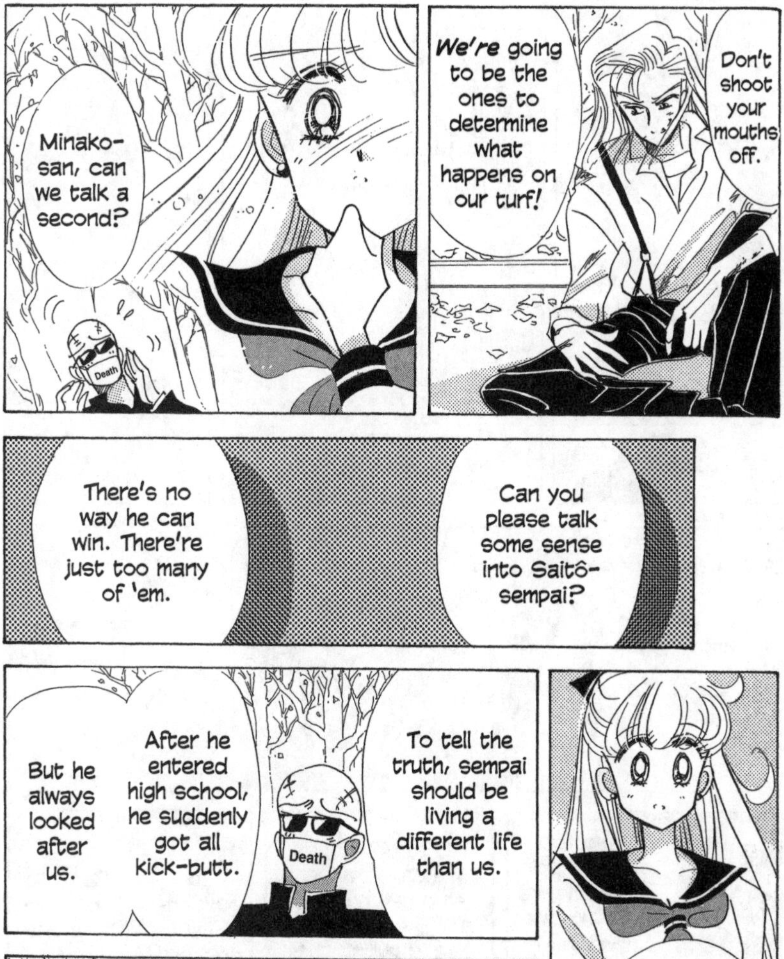
Don't shoot your mouths off.
We're going to be the ones to determine what happens on our turf!
Minako-san, can we talk a second?
Death
Can you please talk some sense into Saitô-sempai?
There's no way he can win. There're just too many of 'em.
If sempai gets caught just one more time, they'll throw him out of school.
To tell the truth, sempai should be living a different life than us.
Death
After he entered high school, he suddenly got all kick-butt.
But he always looked after us.
We'd like to see sempai graduate with a clean record.

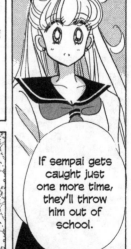

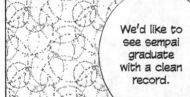

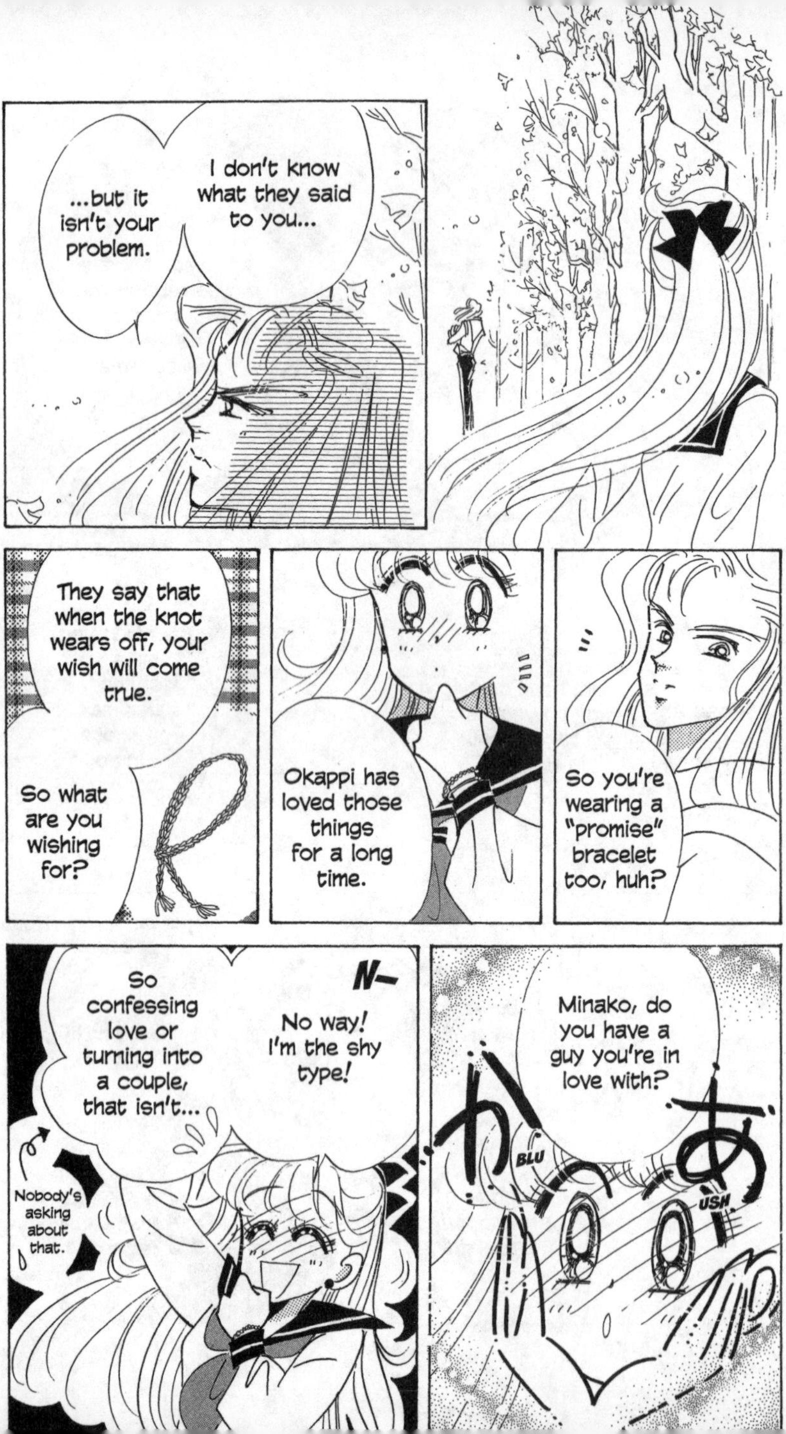
I don't know what they said to you...
...but it isn't your problem.
So you're wearing a "promise" bracelet too, huh?
Okappi has loved those things for a long time.
They say that when the knot wears off, your wish will come true.
So what are you wishing for?
Minako, do you have a guy you're in love with?
BLU
USH
N—
No way! I'm the shy type!
So confessing love or turning into a couple, that isn't...
Nobody's asking about that.

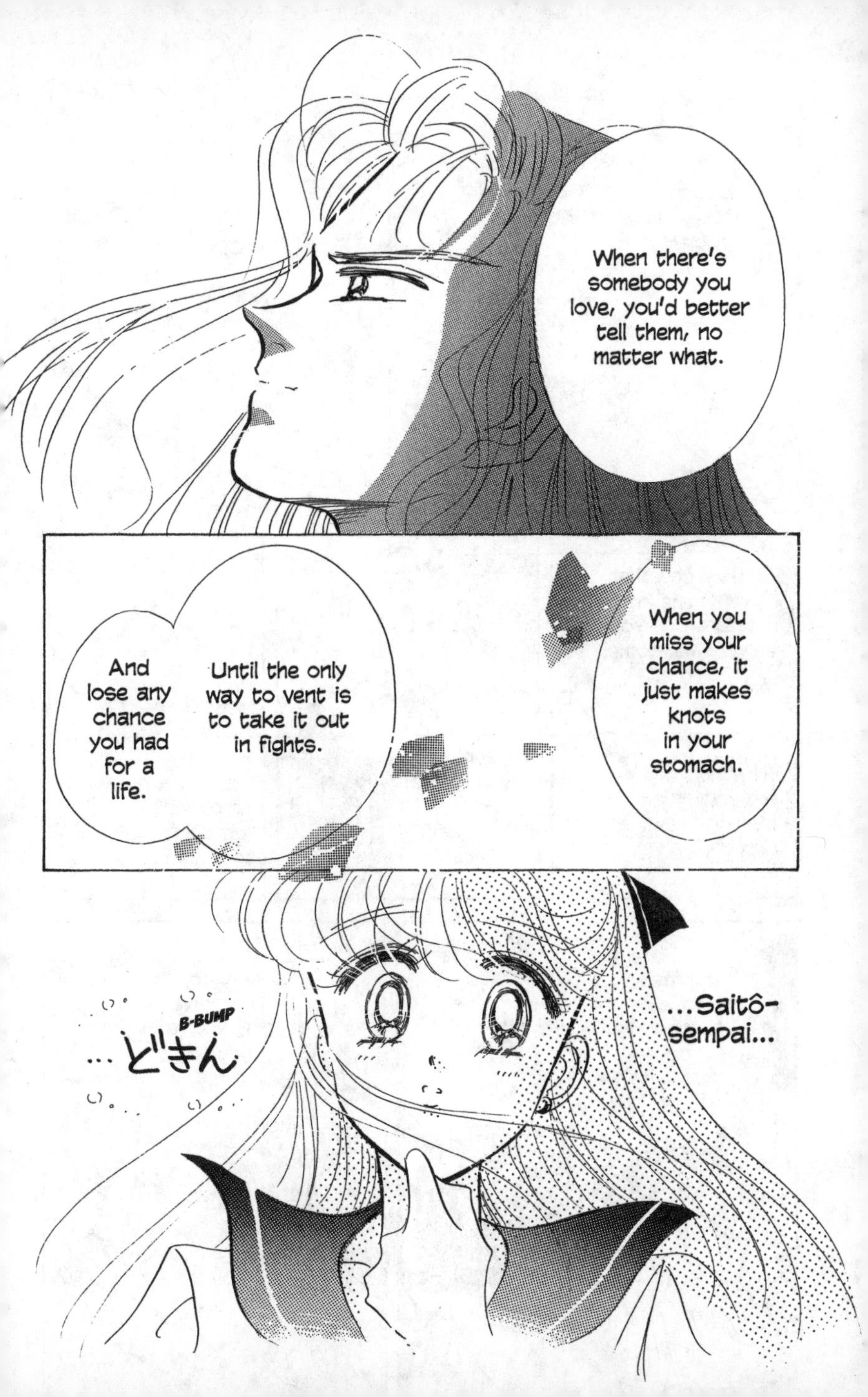
When there's somebody you love, you'd better tell them, no matter what.
When you miss your chance, it just makes knots in your stomach.
Until the only way to vent is to take it out in fights.
And lose any chance you had for a life.
...Saitô-sempai...
B-BUMP
...どきん

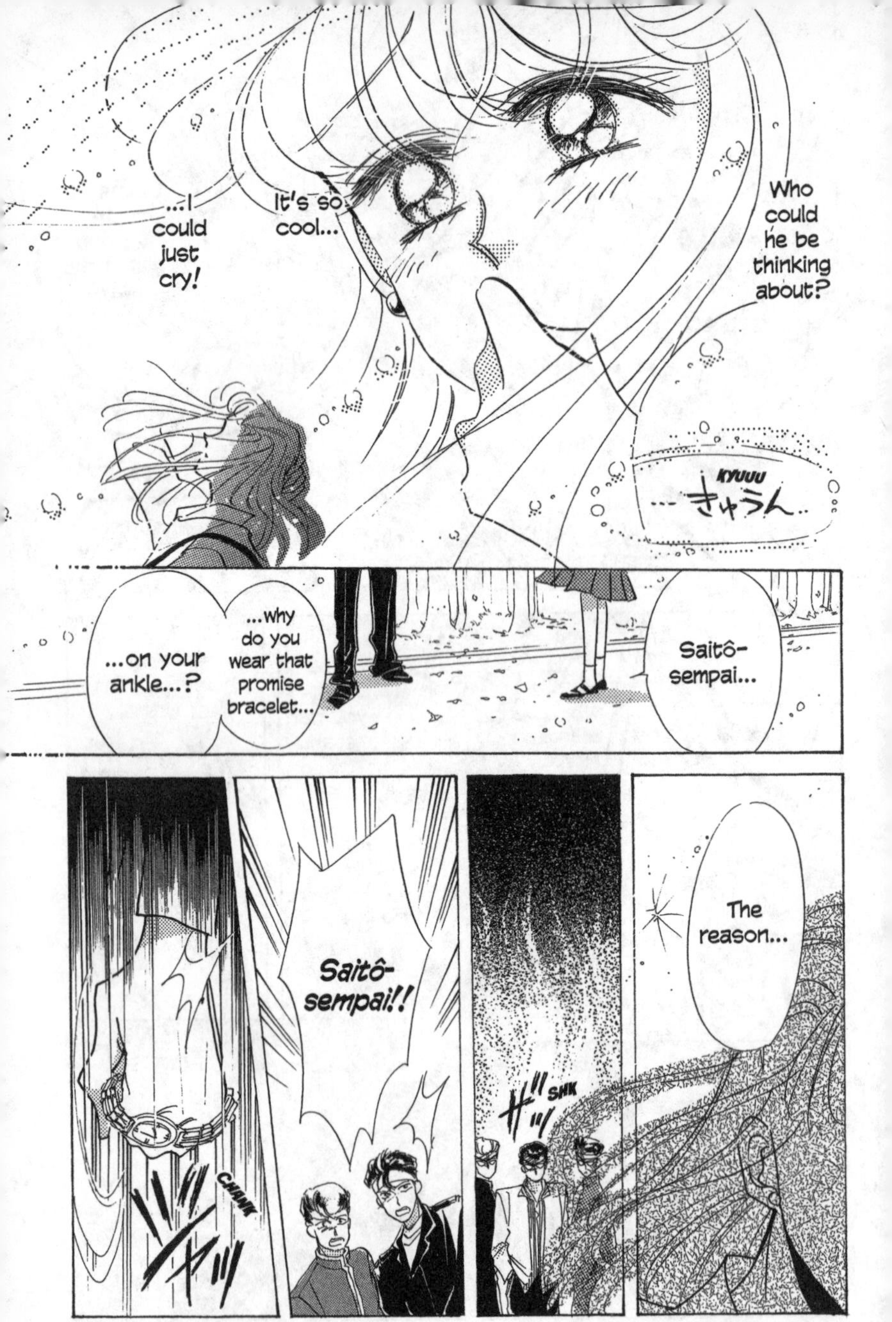

Who could he be thinking about?
It's so cool...
...I could just cry!
KYUUU
…きゃうん…
Saitô-sempai...
...why do you wear that promise bracelet...
...on your ankle...?
The reason...
SHK
Saitô-sempai!!
CHANK

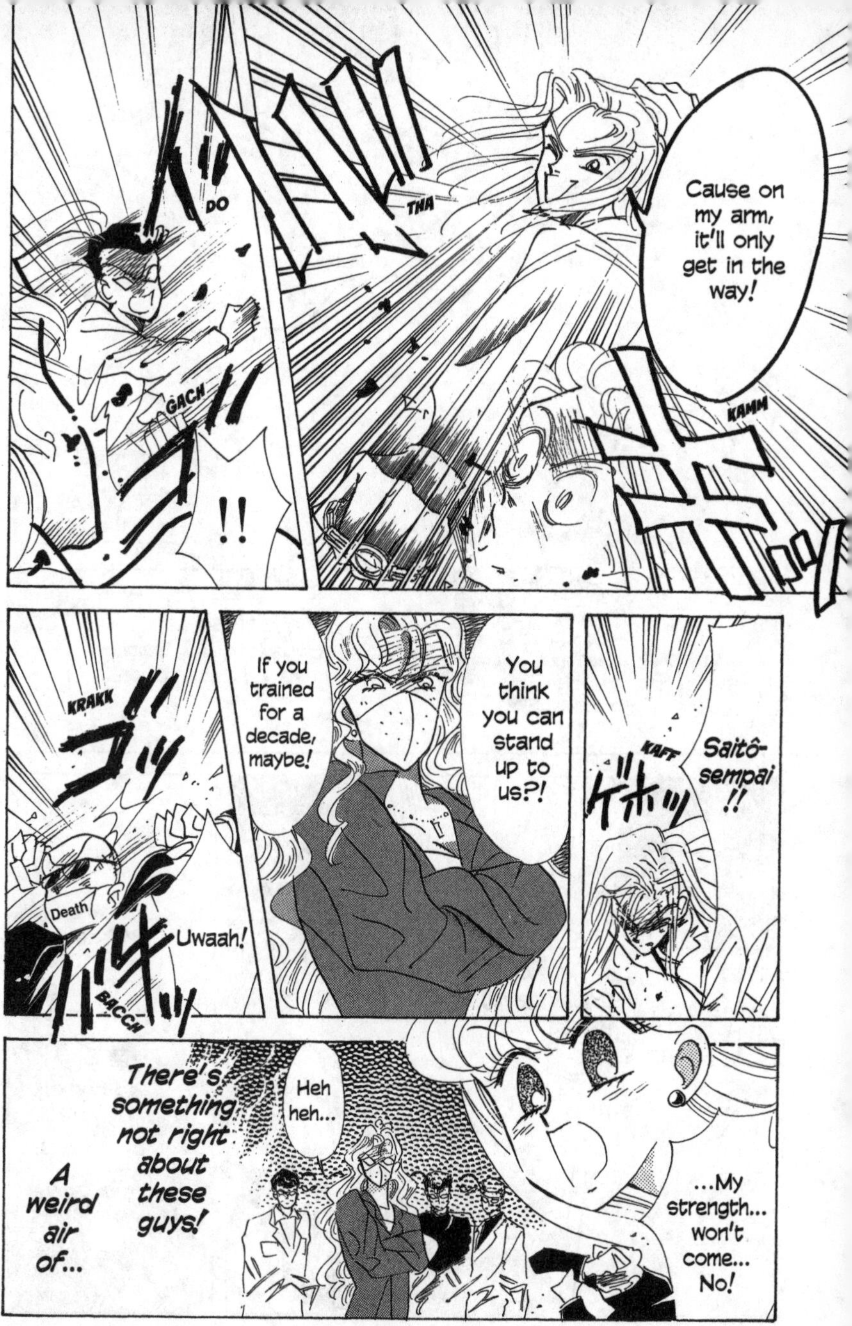
Cause on my arm, it'll only get in the way!
KAMM
THA
DO
GACH
!!
Saitô-sempai!!
KAFF
You think you can stand up to us?!
If you trained for a decade, maybe!
KRAKK
Death
Uwaah!
BACCH
...My strength... won't come... No!
Heh heh...
There's something not right about these guys!
A weird air of...

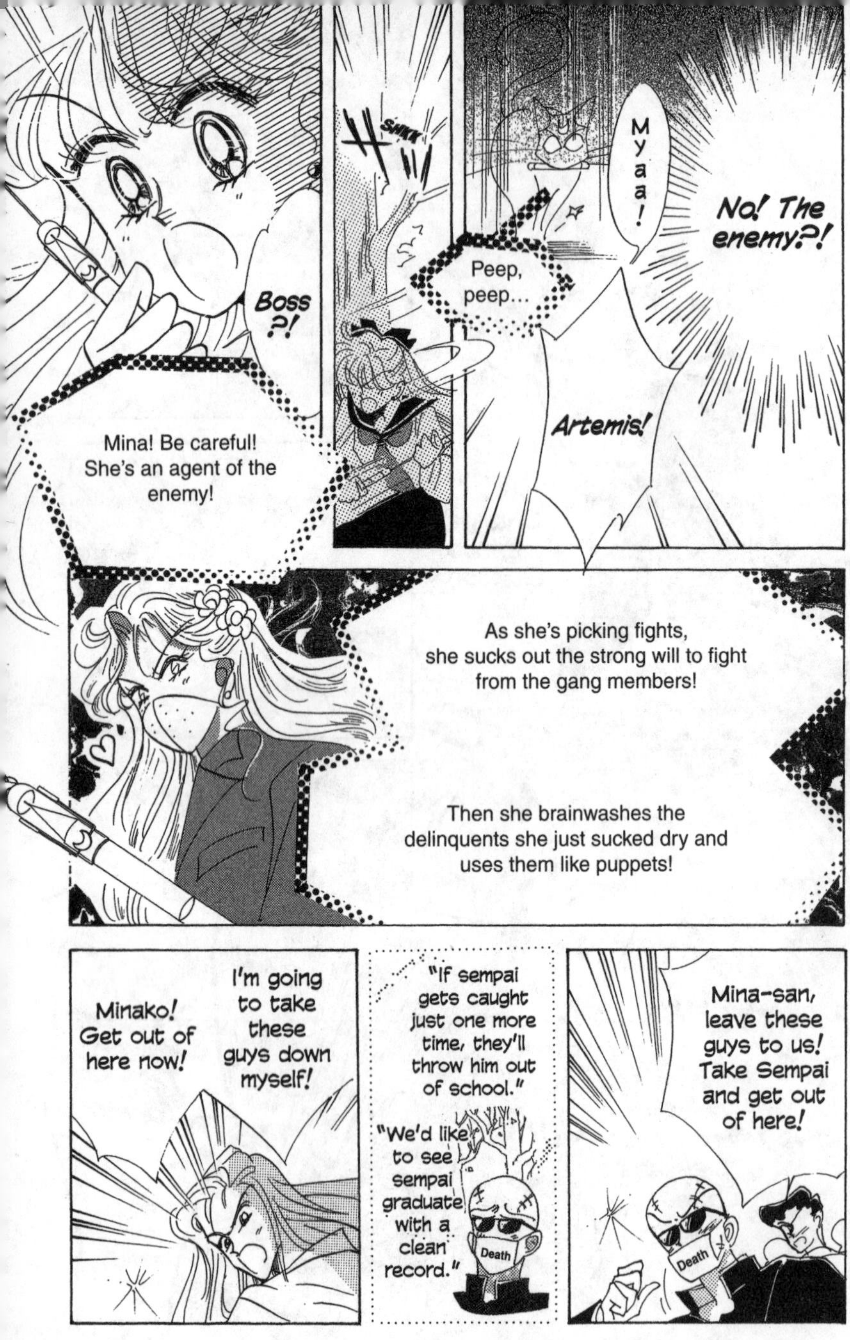
Myaa!
No! The enemy?!
Peep, peep...
Artemis!
SHKK
Boss?!
Mina! Be careful! She's an agent of the enemy!
As she's picking fights, she sucks out the strong will to fight from the gang members!
Then she brainwashes the delinquents she just sucked dry and uses them like puppets!
Mina-san, leave these guys to us! Take Sempai and get out of here!
Death
"If sempai gets caught just one more time, they'll throw him out of school."
"We'd like to see sempai graduate with a clean record."
Death
I'm going to take these guys down myself!
Minako! Get out of here now!

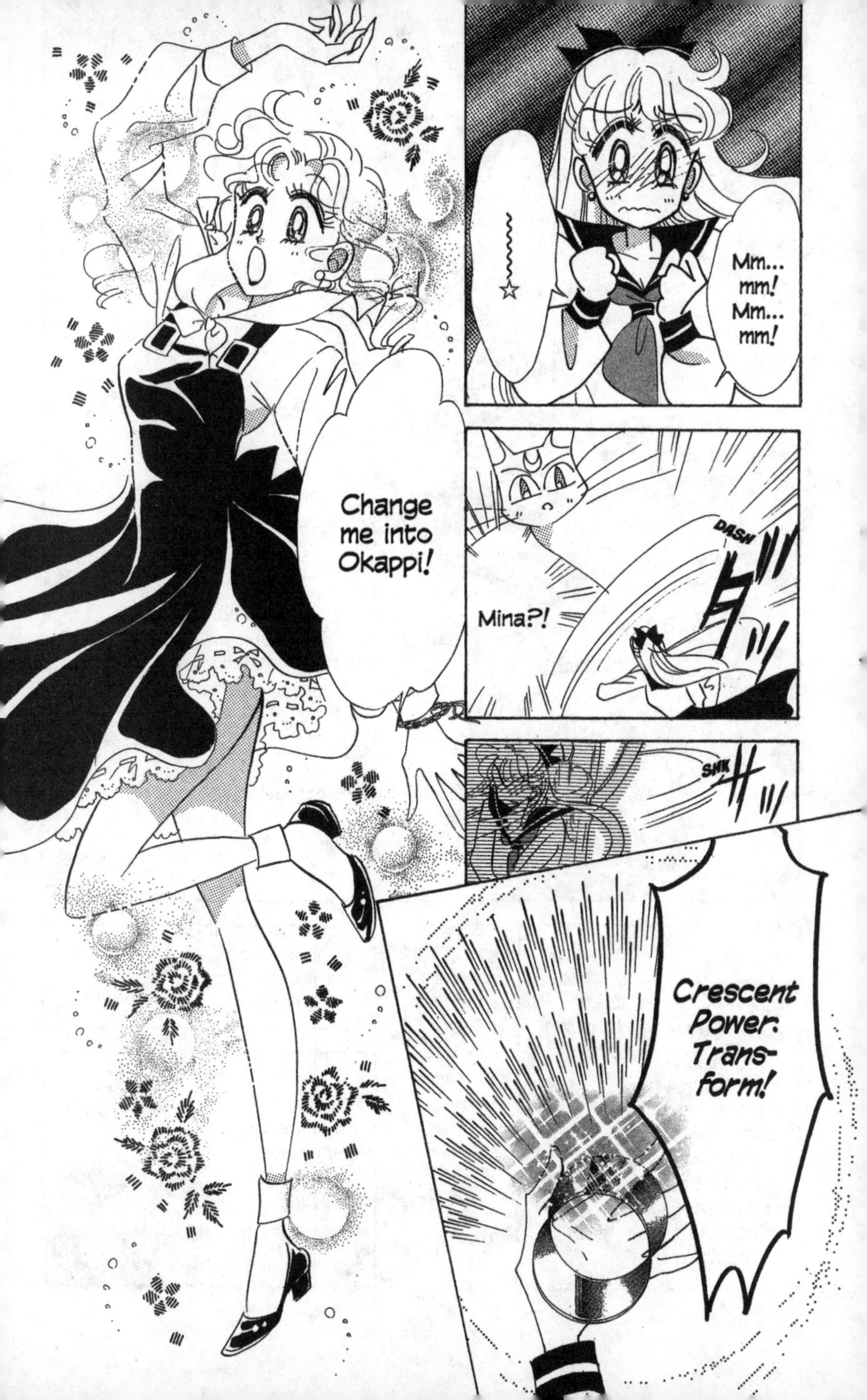
Mm... mm! Mm... mm!
DASH
Mina?!
SHK
Crescent Power: Transform!
Change me into Okappi!

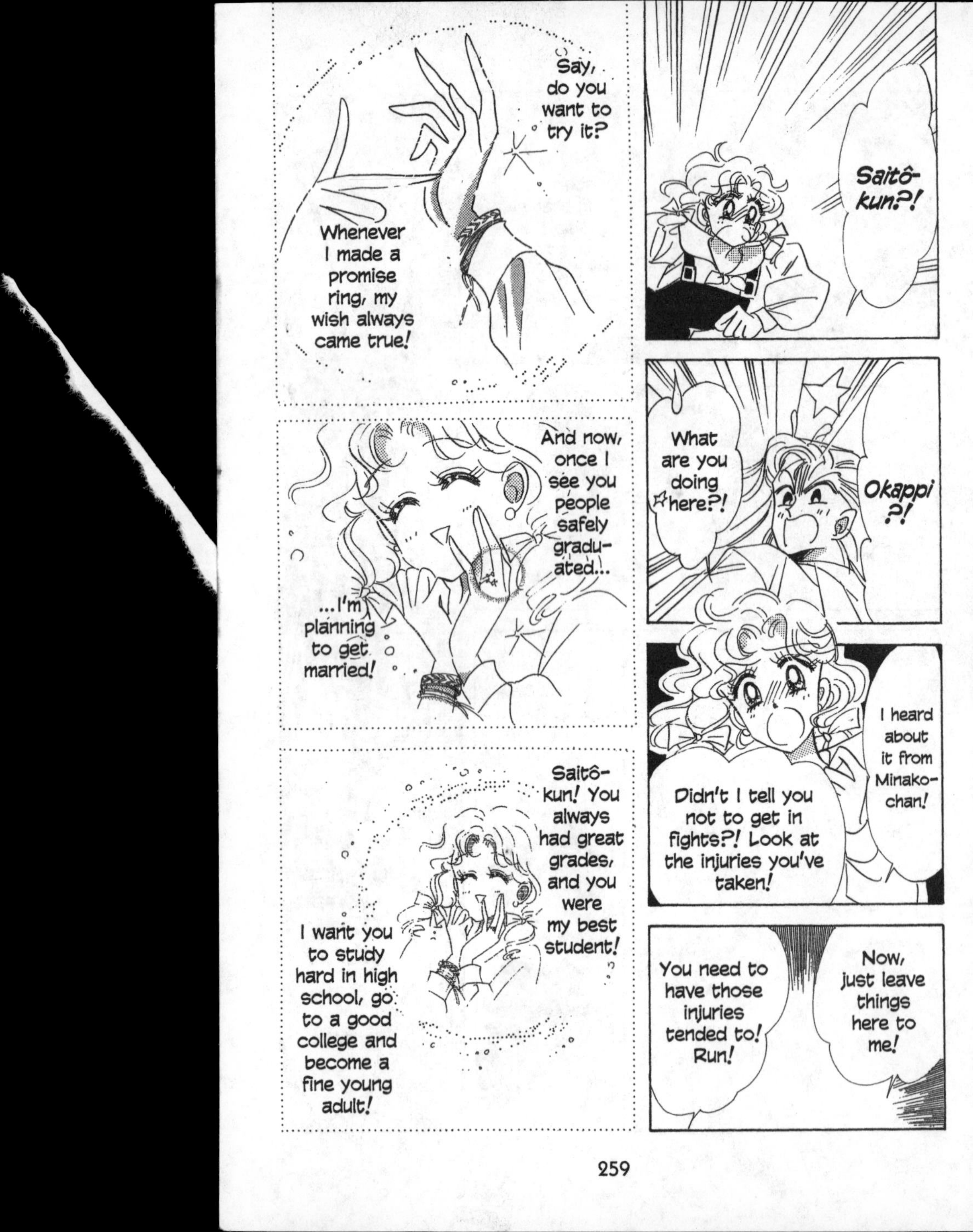
Saitô-kun?!
Okappi?!
What are you doing here?!
I heard about it from Minako-chan!
Didn't I tell you not to get in fights?! Look at the injuries you've taken!
Now, just leave things here to me!
You need to have those injuries tended to! Run!
Say, do you want to try it?
Whenever I made a promise ring, my wish always came true!
And now, once I see you people safely graduated...
...I'm planning to get married!
Saitô-kun! You always had great grades, and you were my best student!
I want you to study hard in high school, go to a good college and become a fine young adult!

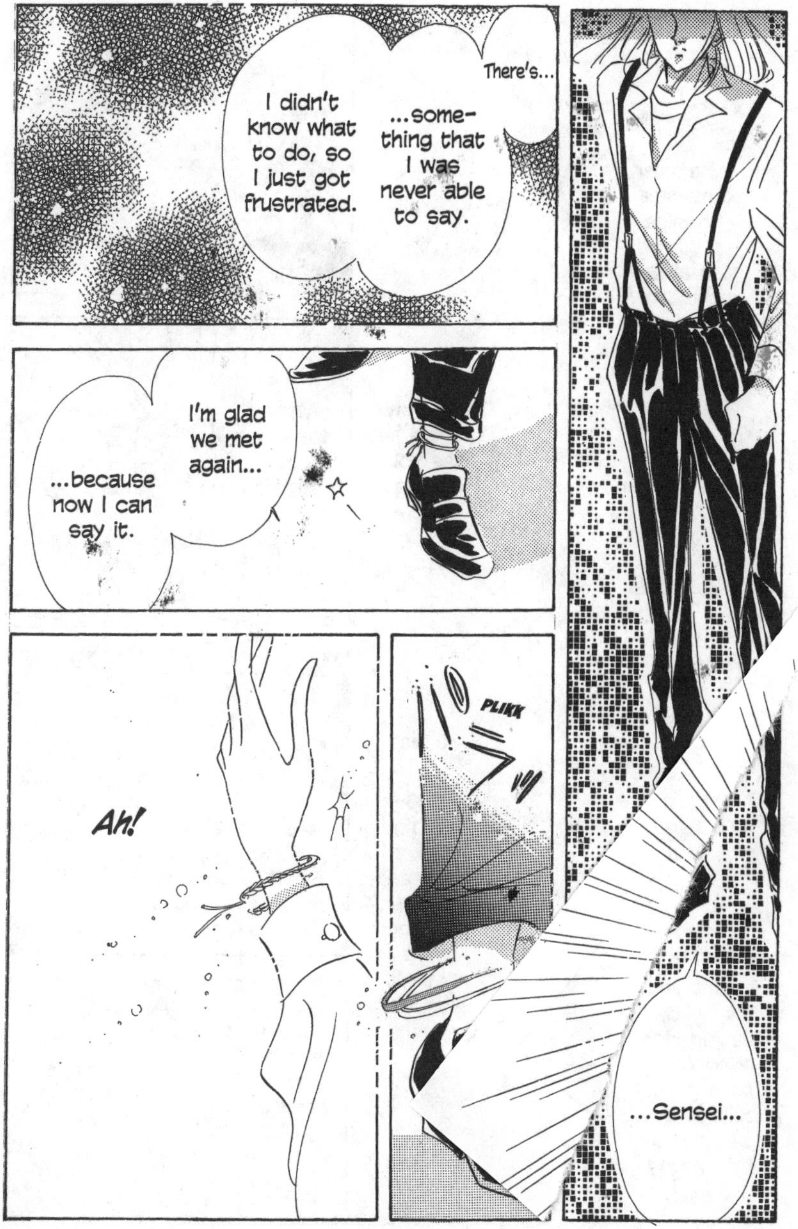

...Sensei...
There's...
...some-thing that I was never able to say.
I didn't know what to do, so I just got frustrated.
I'm glad we met again...
...because now I can say it.
PLIKK
Ah!

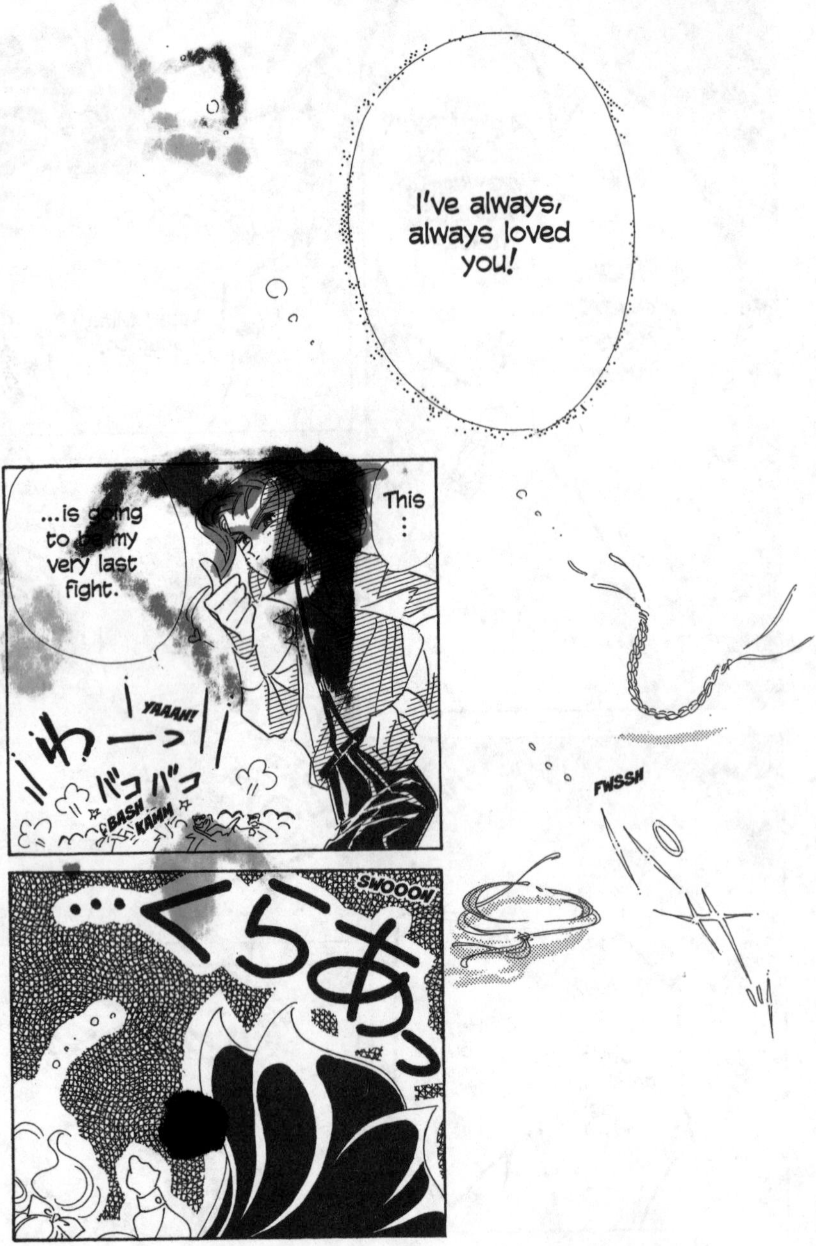
I've always, always loved you!
FWSSH
This...
...is going to be my very last fight.
YAAAN!
BASH
KAMM
SWOOON

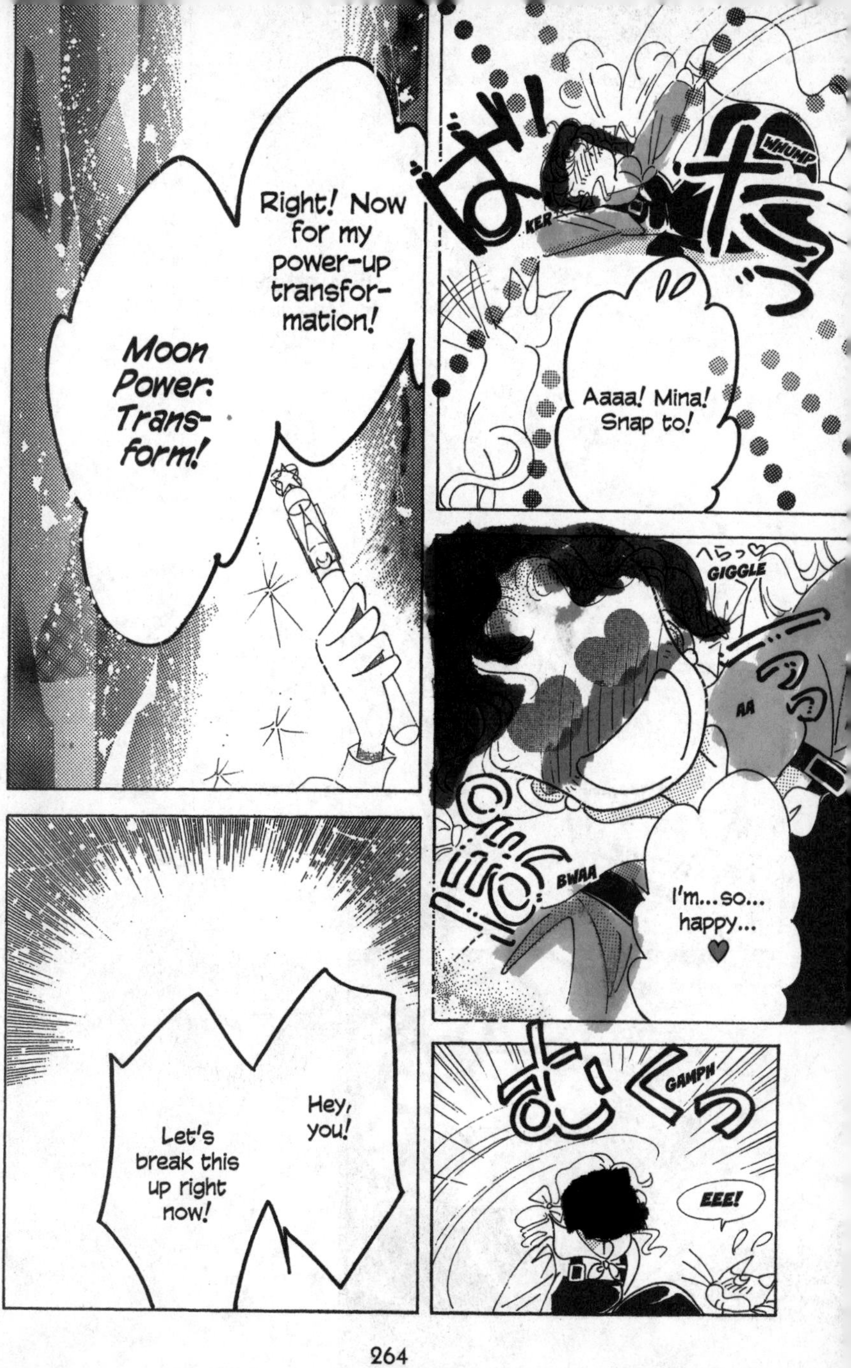
WHUMP
KER
Aaaa! Mina! Snap to!
Right! Now for my power-up transfor-mation!
Moon Power: Trans-form!
へらっ♡
GIGGLE
AA
BWAA
I'm...so... happy...♥
GAMPH
EEE!
Hey, you!
Let's break this up right now!

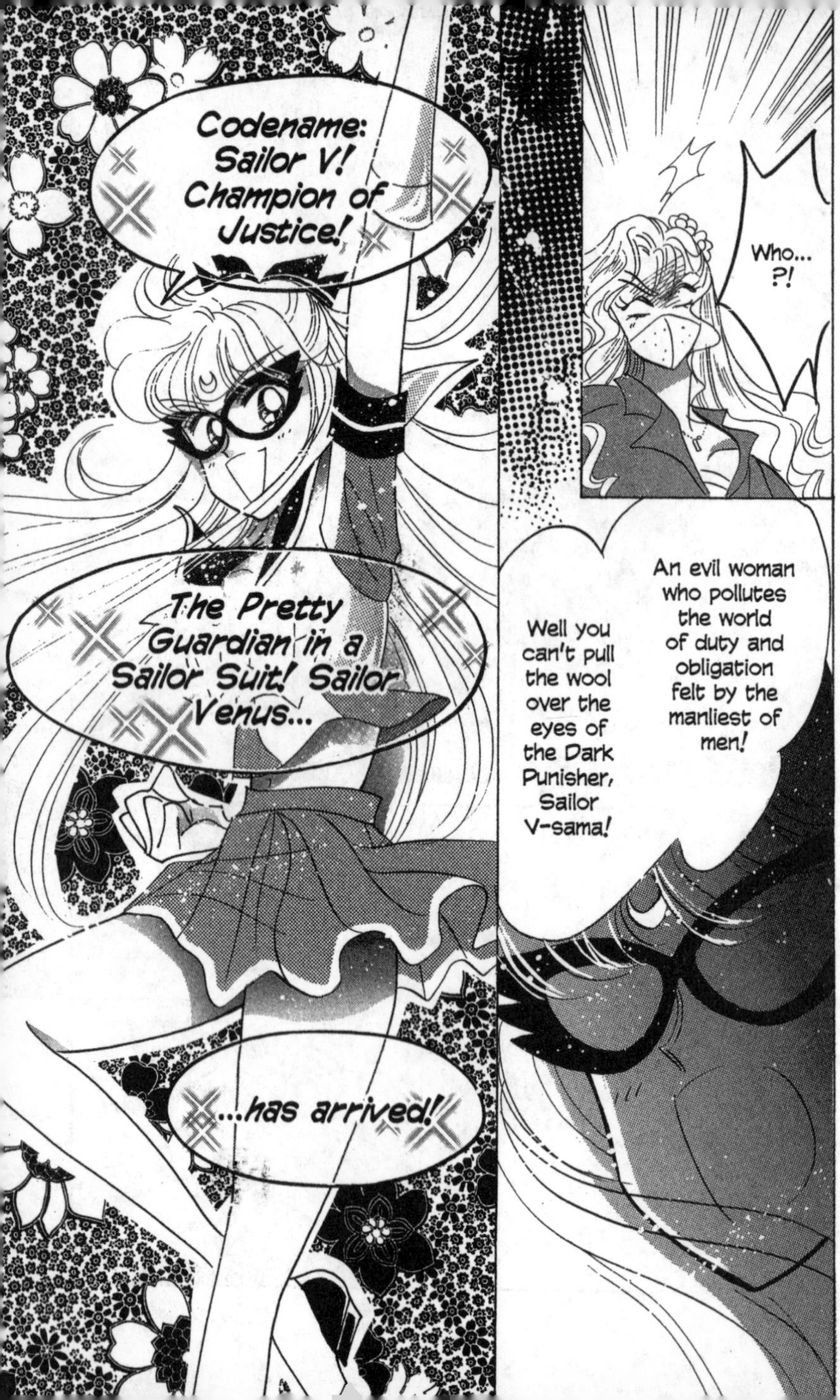
Who... ?!
An evil woman who pollutes the world of duty and obligation felt by the manliest of men!
Well you can't pull the wool over the eyes of the Dark Punisher, Sailor V-sama!
Codename: Sailor V! Champion of Justice!
The Pretty Guardian in a Sailor Suit! Sailor Venus...
...has arrived!

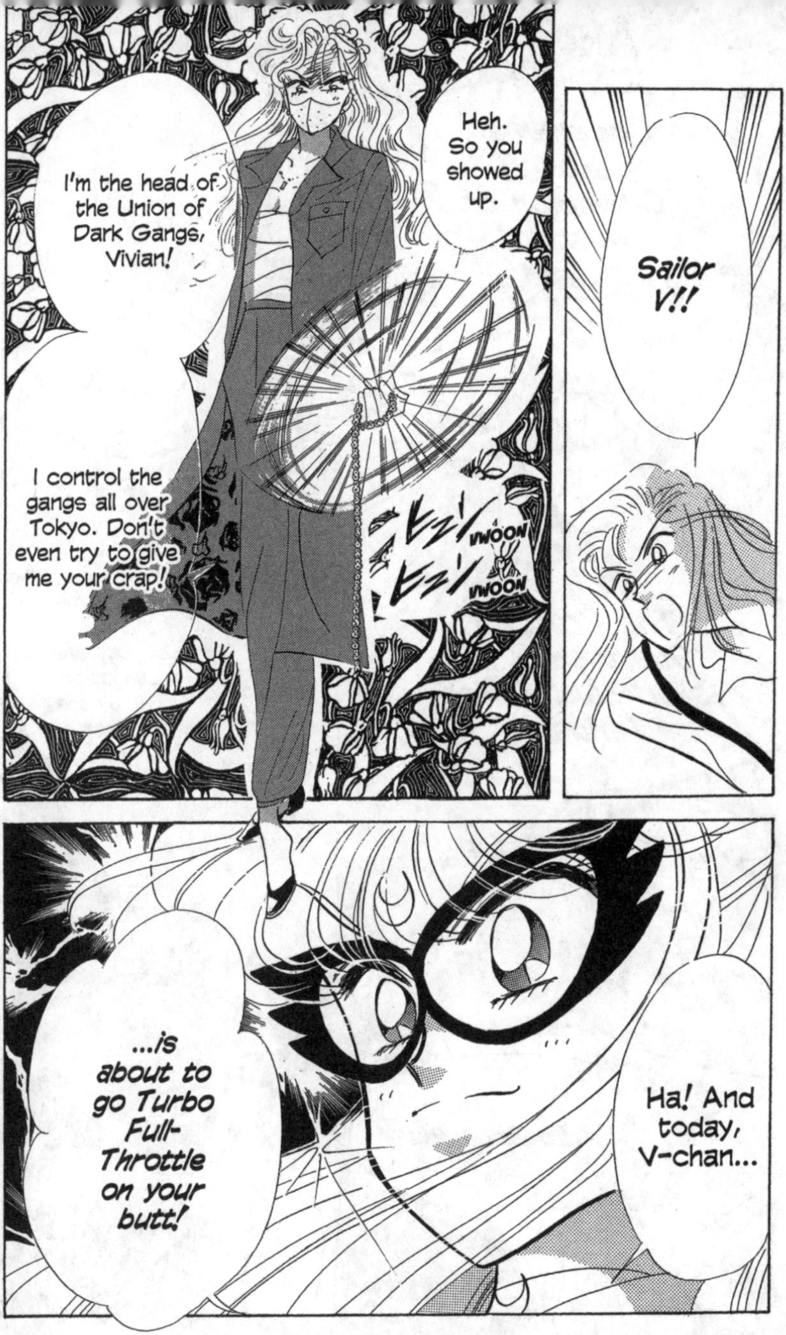

Sailor V!!
Heh. So you showed up.
I'm the head of the Union of Dark Gangs, Vivian!
I control the gangs all over Tokyo. Don't even try to give me your crap!
VWOON
VWOON
Ha! And today, V-chan...
...is about to go Turbo Full-Throttle on your butt!

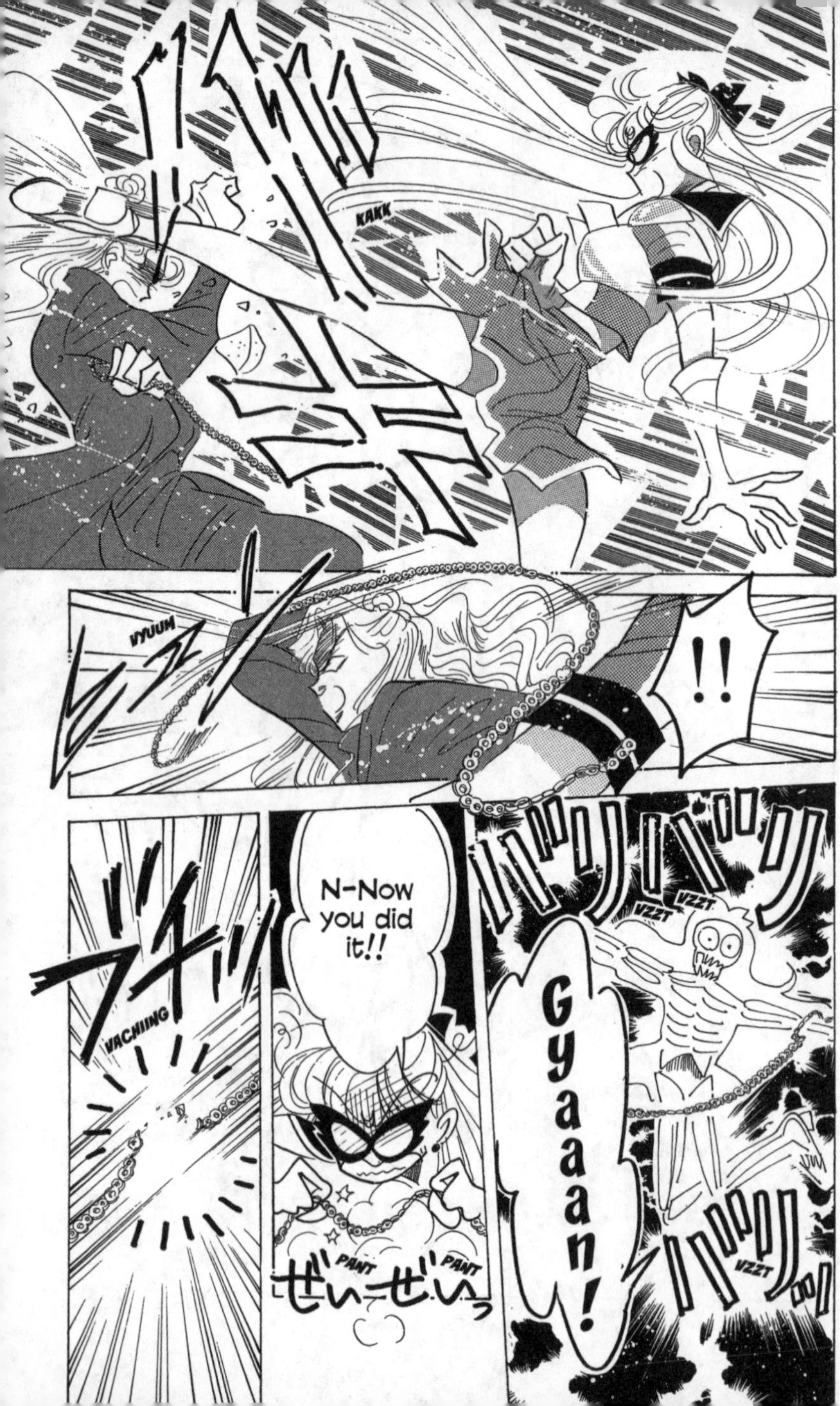
KAKK
!!
VYUUM
VZZT
VZZT
Gyaaan!
VZZT
N-Now you did it!!
PANT
PANT
VACHIING

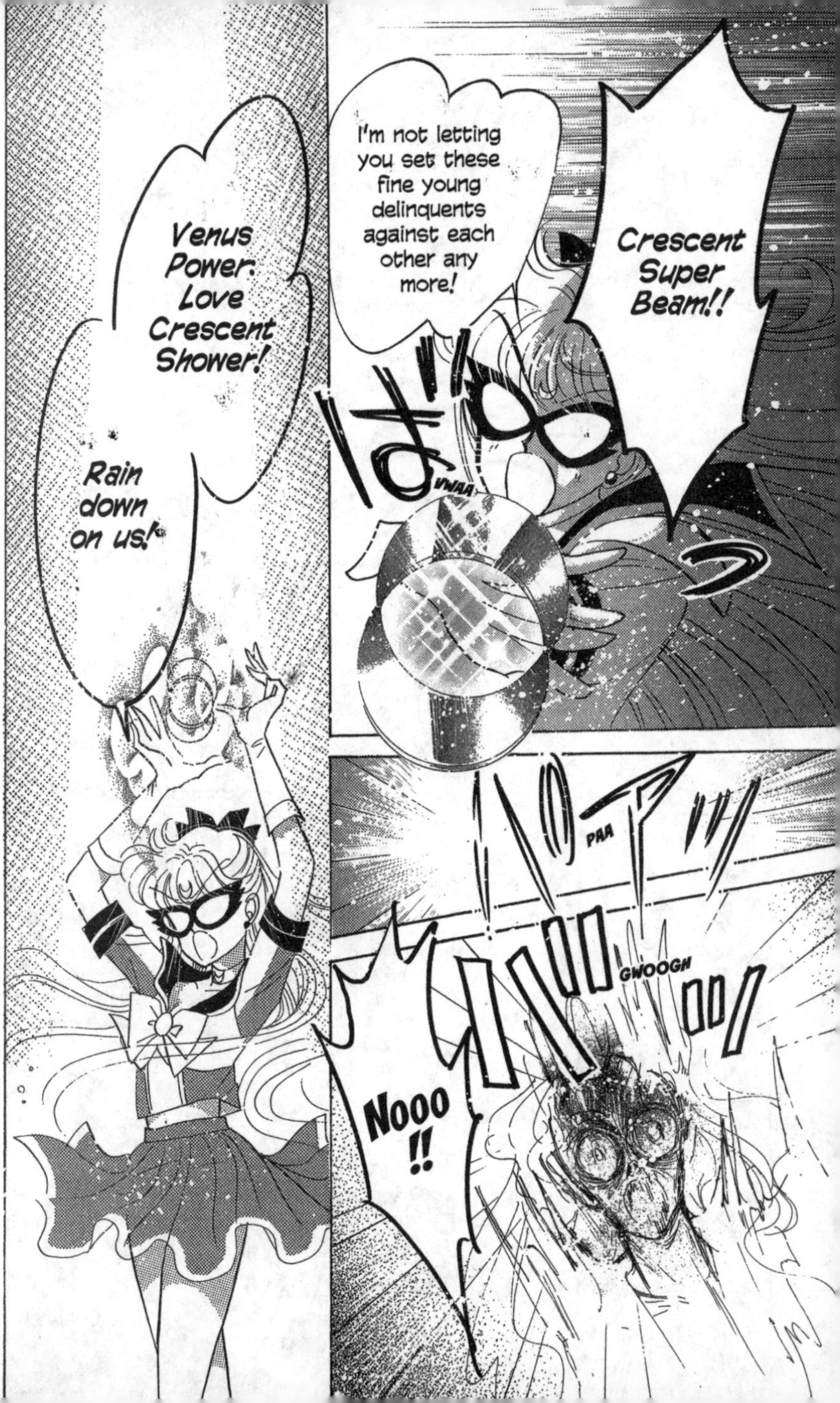
I'm not letting you set these fine young delinquents against each other any more!
Crescent Super Beam!!
VWAA
PAA
GWOOGH
Nooo!!
Venus Power: Love Crescent Shower!
Rain down on us!

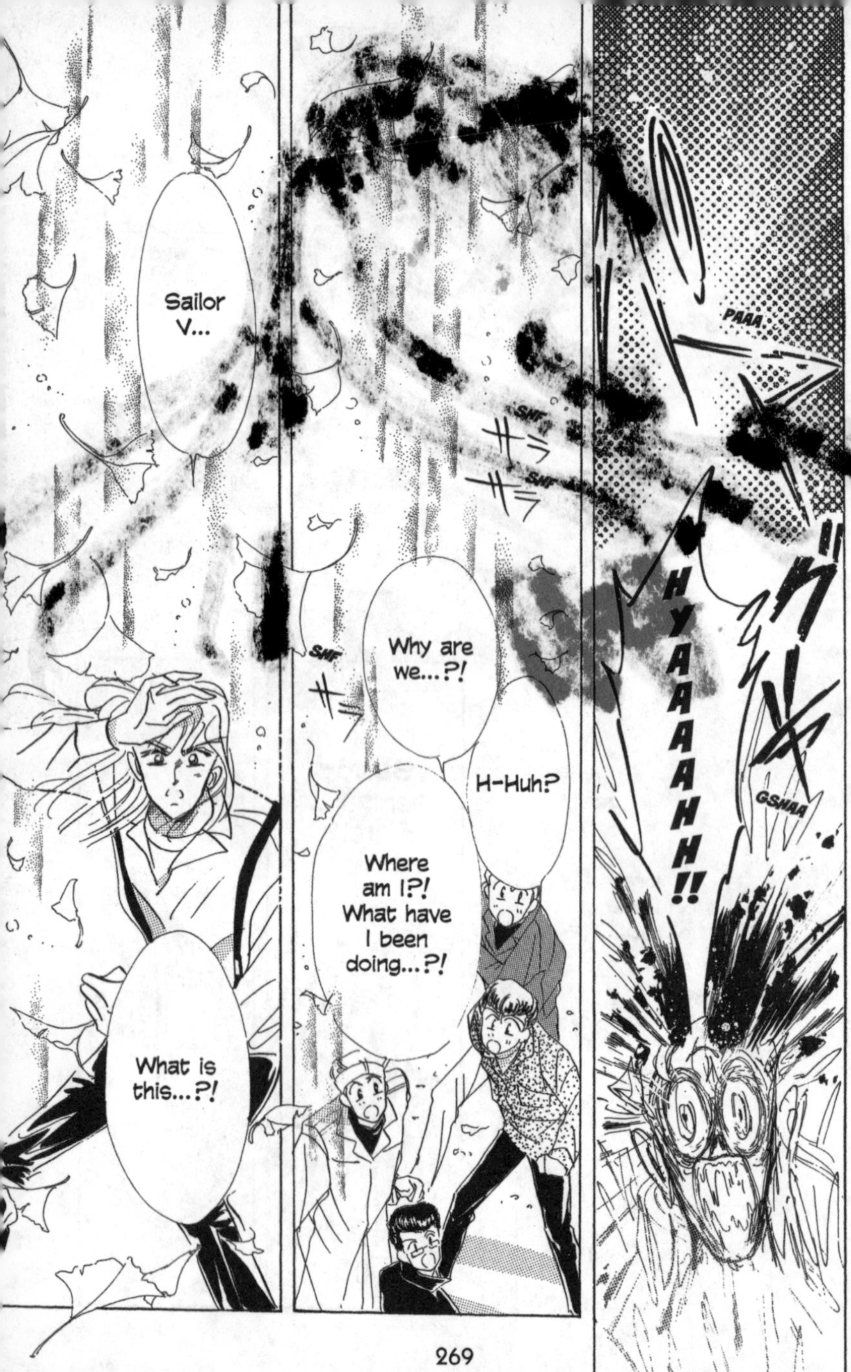
PAAA
HYAAAAAHH!!
GSHAA
SHF
SHF
Why are we...?!
H-Huh?
SHF
Where am I?! What have I been doing...?!
Sailor V...
What is this...?!

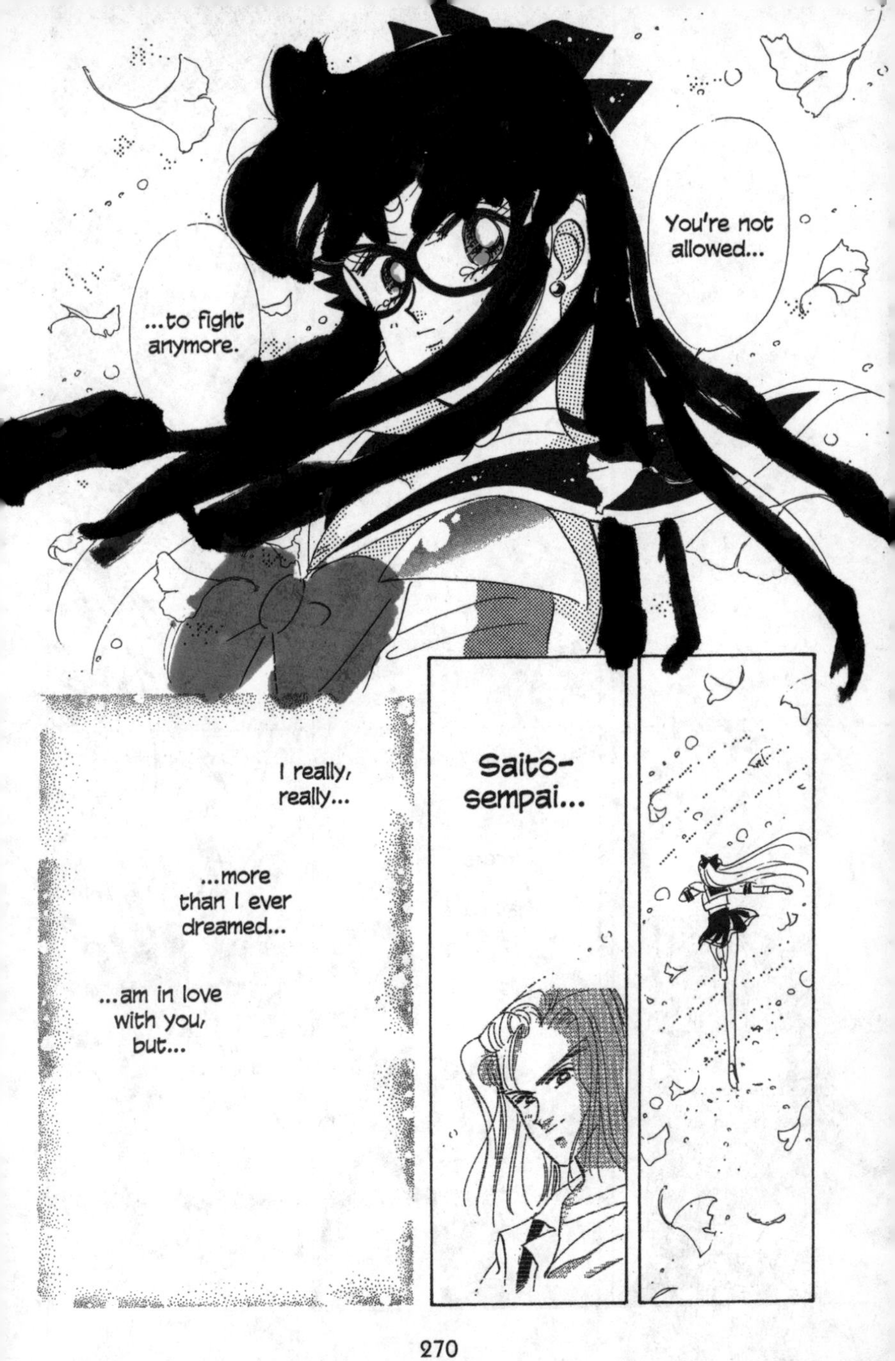
You're not allowed...
...to fight anymore.
Saitô-sempai...
I really, really...
...more than I ever dreamed...
...am in love with you, but...

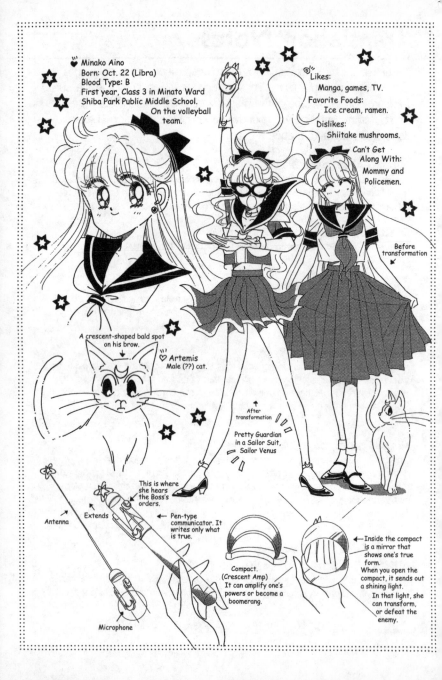

♥ Minako Aino
Born: Oct. 22 (Libra)
Blood Type: B
First year, Class 3 in Minato Ward
Shiba Park Public Middle School.
On the volleyball team.

Likes:
Manga, games, TV.
Favorite Foods:
Ice cream, ramen.
Dislikes:
Shiitake mushrooms.
Can't Get Along With:
Mommy and Policemen.

Before transformation ↘

A crescent-shaped bald spot on his brow.

♥ Artemis
Male (??) cat.

↑ After transformation

Pretty Guardian in a Sailor Suit, Sailor Venus

This is where she hears the Boss's orders.

Antenna

Extends

← Pen-type communicator. It writes only what is true.

Microphone

Compact. (Crescent Amp) It can amplify one's powers or become a boomerang.

←Inside the compact is a mirror that shows one's true form.
When you open the compact, it sends out a shining light.
In that light, she can transform, or defeat the enemy.

Translation Notes

Japanese is a tricky language for most Westerners, and translation is often more art than science. For your edification and reading pleasure, here are notes on some of the places where we could have gone in a different direction with our translation of the work, or where a Japanese cultural reference is used.

Minako Aino, page 3
Minako's last name is "Aino," made up of two *kanji* characters that meaning "love" and "field." But said aloud (disregarding spelling), the last name can mean "of love." It makes sense for the guardian of the goddess of love to be named Aino.

Difficultly Level D, page 7
There are lettered levels in gymnastics that rank difficulty from easiest, "A" to extremely difficult, "F."

Forward Upward Circles, page 8
Also called "Skinning a Cat" in some dialects, this is a simple summersault over a high bar using leg kicks and your own momentum. It's a classic Japanese gymnastics challenge for young students.

Class Structure, page 9
Japan's schools from elementary school through high school split the years into a 6-3-3 system. Six years of elementary school, three years of middle school, followed by three years of high school. Rather than using names like Freshmen, Sophomore, Juniors and Seniors, they use the number of years at that level, for example, first year of middle school.

Night School, page 12
Since one enters a new school, not by simply graduating the previous level, but by passing entrance exams to get into the new school, there is an industry of supplemental schools where students study specifically to pass these entrance exams. The most popular are the evening or night-time schools meant to help prepare for college entrance exams, but since most people who get into elite colleges come from elite high schools, there are such schools that prepare for middle school and high school entrance exams as well.

A Bath after School, page 20
The traditional time for baths in Japan is not in the morning, but in the evening either before or after dinner. A Japanese person feels a little "unclean" going to bed without bathing first.

Magellan, page 24

In the early 1990s, the Magellan space craft spent four years sending back radar-based images of Venus in an attempt to map the planet. It for the most part, did its job, mapping 98 percent of the planet before communication was lost in 1994. Aside from this spacecraft (which was named after the Portuguese explorer who first circumnavigated the Earth), there is very little connection between the name Magellan and the planet Venus. The continent, Aphrodite Terra, is an actual landmass on the surface of Venus, however.

Yakûken, page 46

This is a joke. Shôryûken and Hadôken are two famous moves from the *Street Fighter* series. Yakyûken is one of the names for the Paper-scissors-rock game.

Sentai, page 56

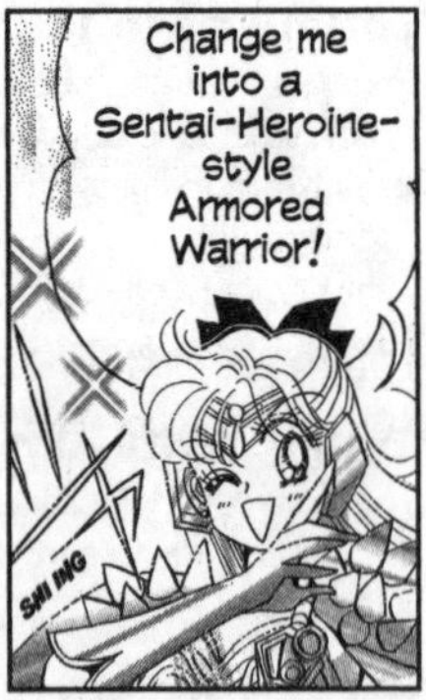
Change me into a Sentai-Heroine-style Armored Warrior!
SHI ING

Sentai could be translated as "Warrior Squad," but it refers to a genre of Japanese entertainment featuring a team of futuristic heroes who battle evil in an attempt to protect the way of life of the people in their charge (usually protecting Japan, the Earth and the human race). Although the anime Science Ninja Team Gotchaman is considered the first "sentai show," Live-action *tokusatsu* (special effects) television shows, such as the shows the Power Rangers series are based upon, have carried on the idea of *sentai* even more than manga or animation. Usually *sentai* members have outlandish weapons and armor.

Airing out futons, page 96

Futons, thin bedding meant to be folded and placed in the closet when not in use, are a staple of Japan even when one has a western style bed. The custom is to air out the futon by placing it on a balcony railing, the roof, on a laundry clothes rod, or other place where the sun can hit the futon on a sunny day. This has a tendency to release musty smells and kill mites and other unwanted pests that might infest the bedding. The stereotype of a slovenly character is one who does not air out his futon regularly.

Nakazo, page 165

The magazine in which Codename: Sailor V was serialized, Run-Run, has a more-popular sister magazine named Nakayoshi. Sailor Moon was serialized in Nakayoshi. Nakazo is a play on that name (zô means elephant).

SMAP drama, page 167

Perhaps the most successful idol band in Japan for the past twenty years is the five-man group, SMAP. Their singles regularly debut in the top ten (if not no. 1), they are much sought-after for product endorsements and television show hosting duties, and the dramas they star in almost guarantees high ratings. During the nineties and early 2000s, the dramas starring the SMAP member, Takuya Kimura, were not only the most-watched shows of the year, but his drama, Beautiful Life, had the highest ratings of any Japanese drama in history.

Fami-Fami, page 170

"Fami-Fami" is the Sailor V world's version of what the Japanese called the Famicom, also called the Nintendo or the NES in the west. Although the Famicom was introduced almost a decade earlier in 1983, it was still going strong in the early '90s, and continued production until 2003.

Bank Books and Hanko, page 185

Although security is getting tighter, even now in most cases, if one has a person's bank book and the custom-made name stamp (*hanko*) that goes with it, one can withdraw as much money as exists in the account from it. So a typical way of showing generosity or a willingness to pay any price in Japanese entertainment is to simply hand one's bank book and *hanko* over to another person.

Lottery, page 198

Shopping districts hold a certain type of lottery to build up anticipation to the day of an event. When one buys a certain amount of goods at the shopping district, one receives one chance to enter into a lottery. On the day of the event, one hands over the ticket at a special booth, and for each ticket the hexagonal box (see illustration on p. 202) is spun until a colored ball emerges. The color that comes out determines the prize received. Everyone walks away with something, even if it's just a pack of tissue paper.

Even if Narita Airport allows it, page 204

The most common nickname for Tokyo's large international airport is, "Narita," for the Chiba prefecture town that is closest. However the official name is New Tokyo International Airport.

Peace & Peace sign, page 205

It is common for Japanese people to hold up a peace sign when posing for picture on vacation or in other fun spots. The origin of this custom has not been pinpointed. It could have come from the American "V for Victory" sign during America's occupation of Japan in the '40s, or from the figure skater and peace activist Janet Lynn, or from actor and singer Jun Inoue who posed that way in a camera commercial, and there are other theories as well. No matter where it came from, the peace sign in photos has been a staple of recreational posed pictures since at least the early '70s.

Jason and Terminator, page 246

Yes, these were Jason (the serial killer from the Friday the 13th movie series) and the Terminator (from the Terminator movie series) in the Japanese original. Those movie series were both very popular in Japan.

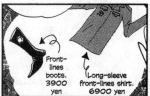

Front-lines boots. 3900 yen

Long-sleeve front-lines shirt. 6900 yen

Front lines shirt and boots, page 248

These kinds of clothes are extremely popular with the yakuza, street gangs, and the organized right-wing fanatic groups in Japan. They are fashionable (with certain people) and don't restrict movement.

Codename: Sailor V volume 1 is a work of fiction. Names, characters, places, and incidents are the products of the author's imagination or are used fictitiously. Any resemblance to actual events, locales, or persons, living or dead, is entirely coincidental.

A Kodansha Comics Trade Paperback Original.

Published in the United States by Kodansha Comics, an imprint of Kodansha USA Publishing, LLC, New York.

Publication rights for this English edition arranged through Kodansha Ltd, Tokyo.

First published in Japan in 2004 by Kodansha Ltd., Tokyo, as *Codename wa Sailor V*, volume 1.

ISBN 978-1-935-42977-7

Printed in Canada.

www.kodansha.us

9 8 7 6 5

Translator/Adapter: William Flanagan
Lettering: North Market Street Graphics

TOMARE!

You're going the wrong way!

Manga is a completely different type of reading experience.

To start at the beginning, Go to the end!

That's right! Authentic manga is read the traditional Japanese way—from right to left, exactly the opposite of how American books are read. It's easy to follow: Just go to the other end of the book and read each page—and each panel—from right side to left side, starting at the top right. Now you're experiencing manga as it was meant to be!